EDUCATIONAL
ADMINISTRATION

Merrill's

International Education Series

Under the Editorship of

Kimball Wiles

Dean of the College of Education
University of Florida

EDUCATIONAL ADMINISTRATION

Robert E. Wilson

Kent State University

CHARLES E. MERRILL BOOKS, INC., Columbus, Ohio

Library of Congress Catalog Card Number: 66-14392

Printed in the United States of America

PREFACE

There are two major methods for achieving skillful administrative performance. The direct experience method plunges a person immediately into the action. In such a manner were early school administrators initiated, and a few still are. As abrupt, sobering, and practical as this method is, it is the slow and expensive way of attaining skillful performance. The trial-and-error approach evades the knowledge which is yielded by the experiences of thousands of pioneers as recorded in professional publications.

The other method—a planned program of preparation—capitalizes upon accumulated knowledge. The vicarious experience of reading, discussing, analyzing, and reflecting, followed by a period of practice, moves a candidate faster toward skillful administrative performance and with less expense to those persons most affected by his actions: students, teachers, taxpayers, and often even the administrator.

This volume is a vicarious introduction to the field of educational administration, not an original approach in itself. It does go one step further. It explores more widely those authorities and goals of the modern school administrator. In addition, the author includes narration that supplements and ties together the varied aspects and viewpoints of educational administration.

Many of the accepted principles for administering schools have been formulated in other disciplines. There is a viewpoint which holds that administration is not a separate discipline, that even the totality of professional education is derived from other disciplines. This judgment invites a complex discussion of definitions and semantics. Nevertheless, this book includes numerous readings from other disciplines which have a bearing upon educational administration.

Other criteria used for determining which among the hundreds of treatises on administration, education, and educational administration are pertinent for an introduction to the field are (1) *currency*—recent ideas gleaned mostly from the professional journals as publicized by practitioners and professors of educational administration; (2) *survival* —those ideas and practices which have stood the time test; and (3) *evaluation*—those practices which have been subjected to appropriate research measurement.

As an introduction for educational administration, the "spray approach" is used to present the entire design for administering schools. Tested how-to-do-it experiences are reported in the readings. Some selections were chosen because of the writer's capacity to motivate reflection well beyond basic administration.

This book strives to be a modern, descriptive anthology of educational administration, validly prescriptive for the generalist in administration. Suggestions are provided in each chapter for stimulating further exploration.

This volume is intended to serve both the educational administration student and the practicing professional. The student receives a complete introduction to all facets of educational administration. Both the student and practicing professional benefit from the inclusion of the writings of more than 200 specialists in the field. The volume provides a compact but comprehensive library which treats the origins, current practices, and future trends of educational administration organization and operation at every level. Part One deals with the nature of administration and of education administration, the principles of administering schools, and the organizational structure for conducting education in the United States. Part Two treats individually the principal functions of educational administration.

REW

1966

CONTENTS

Part One

Nature and Principles of Educational Administration: Organization for Administering Schools in the United States, 1

Chapter 2

Principles of Administration and Organization, 79

Chapter 3

Organization for Administering Public Schools at the Community Level, 149

Chapter 4

Organization for State Administration of Education, 198

STATE BOARD OF EDUCATION . . .

STATE DEPARTMENT OF EDUCATION . . .

Chapter 5

Administration of Education at the Federal Level, 230

FEDERAL PARTICIPATION IN EDUCATION . . .

Chapter 6

Administration of Non-Public Schools, 276

Part Two

Functional Administration in Education

Chapter 9

Administration of School Personnel, 432

THE PERSONNEL FUNCTION . . .

Chapter 11

Administration of Pupil Personnel Services, 589

Chapter 12

Administration of School Finance, 615

Chapter 13

Administration of School Business Affairs, 663

THE SCHOOL MANAGER . . .

SCHOOL ACCOUNTING . . .

INSURING SCHOOL PROPERTY . . .

SCHOOL CONSTRUCTION . . .

PLANT OPERATIONS . . .

THE MAINTENANCE FUNCTION . . .

THE PURCHASING FUNCTION . . .

Chapter 15

Administering a School System — the Superintendent, 779

Chapter 16

To Point the Direction for Educational Administrators, 813

EDUCATIONAL ADMINISTRATION

Part One

Nature and Principles of Educational Administration; Organization for Administering Schools in the United States

Chapter 1

The Meaning of Administration and Educational Administration

The first logical step a student should take as he commences the study of any subject field is to understand the meaning of that subject. The student of administration, however, is immediately confronted with its covert nature. Despite the centuries of administrative practice, there is little agreement among either the practitioners or the scholars as to its precise meaning. Depending upon one's experience, the term produces several images when it is used. It may connote authority to one person, control to another, an image of a boss or an office, an act of managing, respect or disrespect, decision-making, something pleasant or unpleasant, or perhaps an image of affluence.

There are two characteristics of administration which would seem to appear in all the images. Administration implies the presence of several people within a unit; secondly, the existence of some sort of hierarchal relationship among the people should also be evident.

But even these apparent certainties do not persist upon analysis. A person operating in isolation must perform administrative acts. A hermit must plan, make decisions, and accomplish many of the chores normally associated with administration: housing, procurement of supplies, budgeting. Furthermore, there are those who would reject even the stratified relationship implied in administration, especially in the operation of a university or a hospital. There, they say, the administrator should be on the same plane as or even "under" the employees.

What, then, is administration? There is ample literature on the subject; the books and journals even tell how to do it, but it is rarely defined categorically. There have developed several prominent understandings and definitions of the term which we shall discuss.

ADMINISTRATION AS MANAGEMENT

Earliest views of administration equated it with management. In explaining the meaning of management, the dictionaries use expressions such as command, govern, conduct, render and keep one submissive, bring about by contriving, judicious use of means to accomplish an end, and wield with address. Management originally meant conduct of business or household affairs.

These interpretations of administration explain why the management concept fell into disrepute. They are incompatible with a democratizing society, with respect for human beings, and with joint decision-making. The definitions imply a super-being with godly vision but with ungodly powers over serfs. They even suggest an activity less than moral— the attainment of objectives through manipulation.

And yet elements of the managerial attitude are essential to administration. Certainly there must be governing authority vested in administration; there must be some directing of the affairs of others although the mellower terms "guiding" and "stimulating" are more acceptable today. In fact, there are signs which indicate that some aspects of the management concept are regaining respectability in the administration of schools. As school systems have grown large and their administrators have been entrusted with huge sums of tax money, citizens are demanding that school officers be business-like, efficient, and accountable in the conduct of their responsibilities.

ADMINISTRATION AS ORGANIZATION

Administration has been defined as organization, the fitting of many pieces together into a workable pattern in order to accomplish a mission. Organization is the channel through which work flows toward completion. An organization is a unit with jurisdictional boundaries which circumscribe the total scope of operation. There is an arrangement of people in layers from top to bottom, each with carefully prescribed tasks, a flow of vertical control, and provisions for lateral communication and interrelation.

The organizing mind is thought of as a mechanical organ, capable of seeing the numerous parts as individual entities and relating them toward a purpose, but probably incapable of divining a new purpose. An "organizer" is popularly regarded as one who can put things together and can be counted on to get a job done. Today he is sometimes labeled a "systems man."

In order to be an effective administrator under this interpretation, a person needs to learn the purposes of the entity and the processes involved in production. Armed with these knowledges, he is ready to begin. This concept seems in part to describe a school administrator. Yet, it lacks an ingredient which educators would like to see in their leaders — the ability to envision new purposes.

ADMINISTRATION AS A TAXONOMY

Many efforts to define administration have ended in lists of classified activities which purport to describe what an administrator does. One of the earliest known lists which served as a pattern for subsequent taxonomies came from the French industrial scholar, Henri Fayol.[1]

> To Administer is to foresee (plan ahead), organize, order, coordinate and control;
>
> To foresee, that is to say, to look closely into the future and to draw up the program for action;
>
> To organize, that is to say, to incorporate the materiel and social organism of the undertaking (enterprise);
>
> To command or direct, i.e., make the personnel function;
>
> Coordinate, i.e., tie together, unite, to bring into harmony all actions and all efforts;
>
> To control, i.e., to see to it that everything is done in accordance with established rules and given orders.

Another taxonomy which grew out of Fayol's classification and almost into a popular indoor memory sport for administration students appears under the abbreviation of POSDCoRB. The word served for years as a handy device for recalling the elements of administration on the final examination, and stands for planning, organizing, staffing, directing, coordinating, reporting, and budgeting.

One taxonomy led to a slightly different concept of administration. That listing sought to define the job in terms of a person — the administrator. Some lists denote the *desirable* traits of an administrator; others merely the common traits of administrators. Attention was sometimes given to the behavioral characteristics of administrators; sometimes to only those observable characteristics of an administrator in a social setting.

ADMINISTRATION AS DECISION-MAKING

Another understanding of administration envisions it as the singular activity of making decisions. It pictures the administrator as an omniscient figure seated at a mahogany desk to which all information is

---

[1]Henri Fayol, *Administration, Industrielle et Générale,* trans., Paris: Dunod, Editeur, 1920, p. 11.

delivered. After due analysis of data, the truth emerges, commands issue forth, and the wheels roll. This is an unfair over-simplification. It has led to intensive study of how decisions are made, with the goal of determining how their accuracy can be improved.

Although the administrator unquestionably makes desicions, he devotes to them a comparatively small amount of his time today, unless one includes all of those trifling and frequent routine decisions: do I answer the phone or will the secretary? Do I choose the businessman's special or a hamburger? Were administration distinguished on these grounds, everyone would be an administrator. Even the extended problem-solving decisions do not consume the major portion of an administrator's day. The magic of electronics has reduced his allocation of time for this purpose. As further refinements are made, the major factor of making decisions may become merely that of collecting facts — a chore suitable for subordinates, researchers, and leg men — and then merely feeding data into the machine. The mentality of the executive will be needed only for the important and difficult decisions on facts to collect and for interpretation of machine-shuffled data. A second development is the trend toward involving more people in the action. Democratized administration relieves the administrators of nearly all steps in making decisions except the responsibility for seeing that they are made.

ADMINISTRATION AS LEADERSHIP

A more recent definition of administration portrays the administrator-leader as a stalwart knight on a white horse leading his command to the summit. He is inspiring to his followers, dedicated to their cause, faultless in judgment, fearful of no dragon, virtuous beyond reproach, and always victorious.

This concept, with various modifications, led researchers of the 1940's and 1950's to inquire into the nature of leadership. They diagnosed and tabulated the traits of successful administrators hoping that, once discovered, these qualities could be transferred to aspiring administrators. Universities taught courses in leadership. Almost countless publications — books and periodicals — have appeared. Leadership may be the most overworked and misunderstood word in the contemporary literature of administration.

While observers could find many leaders with similar traits, it was difficult to establish cause and effect relationships between the possession of characteristics and success. The influence of situational factors became apparent, not only in the emergence of leaders but in their progress. Distressingly too, one must admit Hitler, Mussolini, Castro, or

Al Capone as successful leaders. In assessing leadership objectively, one is forced to ignore morality, values, and purposes.

The application of personal values and purposes to the expectations of a school administrator confounds the effort to find a single, workable meaning for educational leadership. It is a noble phrase, and no one, except the board of education member who does not understand his intended role, or the misanthropic employee who dreams that all superiors will someday vanish from the working world, denies that the administrator of a school should be a leader. He should be one of those sought-after movers and shakers of society who capably lead people to better things. The confounding aspect appears when one raises these questions: leader of whom, of what, and toward what? There are so many possibilities!

Most recent literature calls for the educational administrator to lead curriculum improvement. But what curriculum? If he elects to lead his flock toward a unification of subject matter, fundamentalists will regard him as anything but a leader. If his curriculum leadership emphasizes vocational preparation of youth, professors of general education, who inherit his "unprepared" products in the undergraduate college, will accuse him of dragging his feet. Teachers may expect the superintendent to lead toward better salaries, while the board of education may respect his leadership ability only when he leads toward a stabilized budget. One community group may hope he will expend his leadership zeal for kindergartens, another, for a winning football season. The classroom teacher may wish that the principal would press his leadership advantage for cleaner floors, but the custodian may hope he will lead toward a shorter work day. Some teachers may expect the supervisor to change grouping procedures; others respect the supervisor for just leaving them alone.

There may even be occasions when the school system is served best as the administrator allows the organization to be dragged or pushed rather than led into a certain direction.

Until that improbable day when people agree on the objectives toward which they wish their leaders to take them, the leadership connotation of educational administration leaves some awkward gaps.

THEORY OF ADMINISTRATION

For many years executives have been trained under these prevailing understandings of administration. An examination of a university's preparatory curriculum, whether for business, government, hospitals, or schools, will reveal the influence of the various viewpoints on the program planners. Most programs incorporate elements of all concepts. But despite the excellence of the curricula from which have emerged some able administrators, conscientious program planners are disturbed by what they see in their graduates.

Some graduates who have completed the full program to a doctoral degree, who have been declared ready for successful performance by the standards of the institution, perform unsatisfactorily on the job. Others, without formal preparation or with no more than a minimum of training, turn out to be successful administrators. Some succeed in one situation but fail in another; an administrator may handle some tasks of executive work admirably, but others, dismally.

These annoying observations have led administrator educators to the obvious conclusion — there must be an unknown element in administration, which is not encompassed in its major conceptual understandings. The curiosity about the existence of unknown quantities has stimulated researchers into an exciting venture which could lead to a new approach to the study of administration. Literature of the last decade speaks often of the administrative theory. The interest is evident in the writings of scholars in business, government, education, and behavioral science. Men search for a theory of administration which could be used successfully by any executive in any situation.

Despite occasional semantic difficulties, theory has become clearer. Theory is not as binding as law, as moral as philosophy, or as uncertain as conjecture. It is currently regarded as a unifying set of assumptions from which testable hypotheses may be derived, and which will serve as a basis for consistently useful action as well as for acquisition of further knowledge. A theory of administration would hopefully insure more scientifically proper decisions and acts in the conduct of school management.

Lately professors of educational administration have been most zealous in their concern with theory. From the work of national groups, the National Conference of Professors of Educational Administration and the University Council for Educational Administration, stimulated by several grants from the W. K. Kellogg Foundation, have come some new insights into the nature of administration and concomitant ideas for training future administrators.

Although the development of theory is not yet ready for application, a fringe benefit came out of the Southern States Cooperative Program in Educational Administration when it produced a lucid definition of administration as merely the "process of getting things done."

EDUCATIONAL ADMINISTRATION DEFINED

Adapting this simple definition of general administration to schools, one can say that educational administration is merely getting a job done in a school or school system. Using a dictionary implication one may say that educational administration is the performance of executive duties in an educational institution. But today the semanticist faces even more difficulty in clearly distinguishing school administration from that of other organizations. The most perplexing question of all is — Who is an administrator? Because of the confusion of titles and functions, tabulators of the number of school administrators find it difficult to issue accurate reports.

That all full-time superintendents and principals could be classified as administrators would seem obvious, but more of their working day is teaching than executing, as they instruct others in the performance of duties. Hundreds of chief school administrators actually carry classroom teaching assignments. Still more complicating, every teacher has administrative tasks: record keeping, public relations, supervision and evaluation, maintenance of facilities. They manage, execute, make decisions, direct, organize, motivate, and lead. Thus any properly trained and motivated teacher who can perform these tasks well should make a good administrator; yet this syllogism is untrue. Likewise, there have even been some mediocre teachers who, when "moved up" to administrative posts have become excellent administrators. These observations suggest that there must be something in administration which distinguishes it from teaching.

One difference is in scope of operations. Both the teacher and the administrator will use similar processes and techniques in accomplishing their respective missions, but the administrator must apply his processes to a wider field — the entire building, system, or community. The effectiveness of similar techniques in the classroom may not carry over in the wider field. Another difference is in the type of person upon whom the techniques are applied. An able teacher who can organize, motivate, supervise, and lead a classroom of children may find that his skills dissipate when applied with adults.

Neither is it simple to distinguish educational administration from business administration, or governmental administration, or military administration. The quick conclusion that the purposes of the enterprise determine the methods of administration will not suffice. That a business exists solely for making a profit does not necessarily change the way its administrators behave. School administrators, too, should be concerned with economic operations; they, too, produce a profit, though its quality or degree may not be so easily measured. Business administrators deal with the same basic tools as do school administrators: people, ideas, things. They, too, organize, direct, motivate, supervise, plan, and make decisions. It is sometimes argued that adminstration is administration regardless of the organization and that if one masters the skills involved in the "administrative process" he can practice his skills successfully in many occupations. Supporters of this view point to the business executives who have been called into governmental administrative assignments in recent years, and to the pirating of executives among industrial organizations. They further say that proliferation of university preparatory programs for administrators could be reduced by creating a single department which would train administrators for all enterprises: schools, hospitals, businesses, or government.

Holders of this mindset look to the common but overlook the unique in administration. One dominant characteristic of administration is its job-centeredness, i.e., the influence of the organizational environment on the administrator's day-by-day activities. The procurement officers for a school and a steel mill, for example, will both be concerned with such activities as product testing, bidding procedures, requisitions and allied records, delivery costs, warehousing, inventory and quality control. Both will be involved in scheduling, planning, decision-making, human relations, budgeting, and evaluation. But neither officer could perform his common functions satisfactorily without a knowledge of the organization's goals and operations. Both officers would, at one time or another, purchase furniture, but the steel plant purchasing agent could not perform the function adequately in a school without a knowledge of the learning purposes which seating serves in an educational institution, the uses to which a teacher puts desk and chairs, the relationships between proper seating and posture of children at their various stages of growth, or the effect of seating upon pupil attention.

The number of successful business executives who find government administration to be almost a foreign activity, offer further evidence for the incompatibility of administration in different occupations.

In an effort to clarify the student's understanding of educational administration, this definition is offered. *Educational administration is the coordination of forces necessary for the good instruction of all children within a school organization into an orderly plan for accomplishing the unit's objectives, and the assuring of their proper accomplishment.*

Administration is primarily a coordinating activity. Literally, coordination equalizes, harmonizes, or synthesizes. When a person performs an administrative act he is chiefly concerned that the various elements under his jurisdiction harmonize into a workable goal-directed unit. Thus some elements he prods, some he steadies, others he retards. He schedules events and persons. To coordinate successfully, the administrator must plan, envision, make decisions, regulate, and communicate. The coordinator does fewer specific tasks and oversees more task performers.

The definition deliberately avoids naming forces necessary for the good instruction so that it can embrace all kinds of administrators in a school system. The essential forces — people, ideas, things — will be determined by the job assignment. An administrator will select only those specific forces which contribute to the achievement of his delineated assignment. His selection of specifics, different from that of the classroom teacher, illustrates a distinction between administration and teaching. In order to make wise choices of elements, however, the administrator must have a thorough knowledge of the useful forces — personnel, supplies and equipment, learning techniques, and goals. This, the job-centeredness of the school administrator's mission, shows why there is little transfer of administrative skill from other organizations to educational institutions, why a distinct preparatory program must be provided to the aspiring school administrator, why administration is not administration regardless of the enterprise.

The definition of educational administration is incomplete without the final phrase, "assuring of the accomplishment." The coordinating activity is largely a readying process although it carries overseeing responsibilities to the task's completion. There is one more important aspect — the evaluation of task performance to guide future undertakings. The educational administrator must not only evaluate the final product but the process and the forces involved. The military administrator in war time might well achieve the unit's objective, lose half of his command and materiel, and receive a favorable evaluation. The school administrator operates in no comparable emergency. The forces which he directs must not only survive but also hopefully improve the attainment of the objective. Hence, his evaluation must concern itself with the condition of personnel, employees and pupils, at the consummation of the objective as well as with the quality of the product.

"Assuring of the proper accomplishment" suggests the authority and responsibility built into an administrator's position.

Elements of all previous understandings of administration may be filtered out of the author's definition. In order to coordinate a unit toward any goal, an administrator must have organizational know-how for arranging events and people. He must be able to envision the relation of the pieces so that they can be "led" and "managed" toward the major objective with an efficient deployment of talents and energies. More than that, he needs philosophical and theoretical understandings in order to assess the quality of performance and accomplishment. Any number of taxonomies could be extracted from the definition: classifying the specific tasks, the qualities needed for executive performance, or a sequence of mental steps an administrator goes through in doing an administrative act. Of course, individual decision-making as well as the directing of decision-making by others occurs throughout the administrator's work week, as he selects appropriate forces for coordinating, and schedules their progress.

WHEN IS AN ADMINISTRATOR ADMINISTERING?

The scholar's eternal difficulty of delimiting the act of administration becomes evident in this discussion. Several observations may be made to spotlight the complexity and, hopefully, may lead to a clearer understanding of administration.

Certain acts which an administrator performs become administrative in nature only because of assignment. Designation of an individual as an administrator makes his acts administrative although another individual not so named may perform the same act. When an administrator plans, makes decisions, gives directions, or stimulates others he is said to perform administrative tasks; when the classroom teacher performs identical operations with students he is not considered to be administering. One must conclude that position and title help to distinguish administration from other actions.

Certain acts become administrative by location. When the business manager signs a check to pay a school obligation he is performing an administrative act as authorized in his charge from the board of education. When he signs a personal check for payment of a family obligation he is not performing an administrative act. When the building principal censures a teacher for failure to prepare lesson plans he is performing an administrative act for which he is held responsible; but if he admonishes his wife for failure to have dinner ready he is not acting as an administrator. When the superintendent speaks before the Kiwanis Club on a proposed bond issue he is acting in an administrative capacity because he has been charged with a duty; when he narrates the color slides of his Lake Louise vacation at the Garden Club he is not performing an administrative act. The distinction between an administrative act and a non-administrative act becomes still finer when it is recognized that in a single telephone call an administrator may perform several roles. The director of curriculum, for example, may call a book salesman whom he has known for many years to order a sample copy of a new history text. While making the request he is performing an administrative task. As he inquires about the salesman's fishing trip he is performing as a friend. As they discuss how the text in question handles the civil rights legislation he is meeting the salesman as a fellow-student and professional colleague.

Although an administrator cannot be identified solely on the grounds of authority and responsibility, every administrative position has power over others. All administrators do not practice the assigned authority in the same manner; some choose not to exercise it at all. However, even when an administrator uses to the extreme the non-directive approach he cannot evade the responsibility for the power which has been designated in his bill of duties. A teacher carries authority and responsibility over students in the classroom but is not regarded as an administrator in the exercise of that power. Therefore, the administrator must be identified by the fact that he has authority over other employed personnel in the organization.

This characteristic of administration introduces the final difference between an administrator and others: scope of influence and imminency of purpose. By virtue of having jurisdiction over other employees of the unit, the influence of his acts is spread more widely. It is inconsequential to argue the importance or longevity of the influence for the sake of a definition; suffice it to say that one is inescapably broader than another. The long-range purpose of all personnel in the school system should be identical — providing the best possible learning for children. However, the teacher works immediately with the recipient in achieving the objective; the administrator is in a service position for the front-line worker. The administrator's imminent objective is to get supplies to the production line, or to procure money to build a room where learning can take place, or to find more workers for the line, or to collect and disseminate new ideas for the way a production problem may be tackled, or to remove roadblocks to better attitudes and production.

There are tangible differences between an administrator and another employee of the organization: salary, length of working year, risk in holding the position, and responsibility. In summary, a given act may be identified as an administrative act by who performs it and who authorizes it; one should also note whether the act utilizes authority over other employed personnel, and determine whether the act is performed directly with the institution's basic product or in supporting others.

Those differences also provide clues for the unique talents required for administrative work. To perform the supporting role one must have technical knowledge of both administrative and teaching procedures. To carry authority over adults and coordinate their efforts he must be skilled in human relations and motivation. To be entrusted with power in an educational institution he needs a deep understanding of the organization's rationale. To deserve the designation of an administrator he needs to stand taller emotionally, physically, and mentally.

DEVELOPMENT OF THE ADMINISTRATIVE FUNCTION IN SCHOOLS

The administrative function has existed in educational organizations from their inception. At the creation of the first school, there were administrative tasks affecting personnel, buildings, finances, supervision, decision-making. The introduction of administrators to look after these functions, however, arose merely from growth and necessity. The few public schools which were started under Massachusetts legislation in 1642 — the first state legal action for that purpose — presented problems of organization, finance, instruction, and many other modern administrative concerns. The responsibilities for performance were shared, however, by the School Committee and the teacher. The arrangement worked satisfactorily as long as schools remained small. Volunteer or elected citizens borrowed time from personal occupations for not only policy making — the major responsibility of boards of education — but also the executive responsibilities. As soon as growth required the use of two, three, or four teachers, the responsibility for overseeing their work, and other administrative chores, it became necessary to appoint a headmaster or principal, usually the teacher with most seniority.

Building administrators could have handled school administration adequately until the growth of cities forced the opening of several buildings within a community. Eventually it became necessary to engage someone to coordinate the work of several principals. The first superintendencies appeared in the early part of the 19th century. Further growth in city districts necessitated the appointment of assistants to assume portions of the central staff administration; thus appeared assistant superintendents, directors, supervisors, and coordinators. At the beginning of the 20th century, larger districts fully accepted the phenomenon of a division of labor in the management of the growing enterprise. The trend toward dividing the total administrative load among specialists in curriculum, business, personnel, has continued to the present time.

The increasing specialization of education and educational administration accounts for the "necessity" reason which induced early school committees to seek administrative help. Even today most individuals regard themselves as authorities on education, at least to a degree. At the same time, nearly all citizens and teachers recognize that there is something unique about administering an educational institution. The acknowledgement of the technical phases which are involved persuaded citizen committees as early as 1800 that neither they nor teachers could handle administration without help.

Another kind of recent growth has expanded the administrative duties and personnel in school systems — that of additional services provided for pupils. Compliant with the demands of citizens for ever-improving education, the modern school system must have specialized officers who look after the services of transportation, food services, pupil attendance, nurses, physicians and dentists, custodians, psychologists, public relations, accounting, and services for the various kinds of handicapped students. Because of a complex of titles and assignments, statistics are unavailable for reporting the number of administrative positions in American schools; the estimated 200,000 reflects the tremendous rise since the day when a teacher and his governing board could handle it alone.

Professionalization of School Administration

For nearly two hundred years, school administrators performed their roles without any formalized preparation. Their administrative skill and knowledge was gained from observation, trial and error, and conference. Not until this century did universities organize programs to ready administrators for schools. Today, approximately 300 universities have graduate curriculums designed for this purpose.

Also in this century, states enacted provisions for certificating college graduates who aspire to the respective positions. From a simple requirement that administrators must have earned a Bachelor's degree, most states have already moved past the specification of a Master's degree in order to be licensed as a superintendent. When the American Association of School Administrators voted in 1959 that members to be admitted to the professional organization after 1963 must "submit evidence of successful completion of two years of graduate study in university programs designed to prepare school administrators and approved by an accreditation body endorsed by the Executive Committee of the AASA," a milestone in self-improvement was reached. Immediately states moved toward demanding that much preparation for certification of the superintendent; by 1964 nearly half of the states had established those certification requirements. The professional organizations for principals and supervisors are currently contemplating similar action for their members. Some states have also created new certificates for the specialized administrators of the central office: business managers, staff personnel and pupil personnel officers, public relations experts, research directors, and school psychologists.

As suggested in the previous paragraph, much of the professionalization of school administration has come from the administrators themselves. Such is one important mark — self-impelled improvement — distinguishing professions from occupations. These national organizations for administrators are dedicated to enhancing their members' performance and contribution to the education of youth:

> American Association of School Administrators
> Association of School Business Officials, International
> Association for Supervisors and Curriculum Development
> Council of Chief State School Officers
> Department of Elementary Principals
> National School Public Relations Associations
> National Secondary School Principals Association

THE SETTING FOR EDUCATIONAL ADMINISTRATION . . . .

PUBLIC EDUCATION IN THE UNITED STATES*

American education today represents one of the most unique systems in existence. Within its relatively short history the United States has developed and extended, perhaps more than any other nation, the egalitarian principle of universal education. In doing so it has developed a concept of public education which is without parallel.

Though American education today is both unique and singular in character, its unpretentious beginnings were both traditional in form and diversified in nature. Attitudes, ideas, practices, and institutions were of European origin. Informal education within the family and an

---

*George V. Guy, "Public Education in the United States." Reprinted from the October, 1963, issue of *Education,* Copyright, 1963, by the Bobbs-Merrill Co., Inc., Indianapolis, Indiana, 95-98.

apprenticeship-type system (based upon the European guild system) formed the lot of the common man. Formal educational institutions and tutorial instruction, however, were available to those of greater means.

Two separate and functionally unrelated factors were fundamental to the development of American education. On the [one] hand, the historic association of an aristocratic and leisure class with humanistic studies provided the basis for the establishment of educational institutions and the transplanting of varied curricula and practices.

On the other hand, a major thesis of the Protestant Reformation — that each man determine his own faith based upon his own understanding of the Scriptures — provided a strong basis for the extension of education and, ultimately, the initial rationale for universal education. This close association of religion and education is evidenced by the fact that education was established earliest and most extensively in colonies where religious motivations were strongest.

Though preparatory (Latin) schools were well established and two colleges (Harvard and William and Mary) were founded prior to 1700, formal education was restricted to a very small segment of the total population. There was little at that time to suggest the major proportions to be achieved later.

EVOLUTION OF PUBLIC EDUCATION

The concept of public education developed by the United States contains three distinct elements, each of which has evolved at a different period of history. Yet they have combined to contribute to the comprehensive nature of public education in this century.

Public Sponsorship

Education first became public in the sense that it was required to exist by law. This first aspect of public education had its beginnings in the theocratic New England colonies in general and in that of Massachusetts in particular. By requiring local civil officials to oversee instruction in reading by parents and masters, the Law of 1642 attempted to utilize the informal educational institutions of the family and of apprenticeship.

In 1647, the Massachusetts Assembly required townships of 50 families to appoint a schoolmaster to teach reading, and townships of 100 families to maintain a grammar school. Thus public education began with colonial governments requiring local communities to see that educational opportunities were made available.

Though this concept of public sponsorship was greatly limited, it served the purpose of establishing precedent and of involving state and local governments in educational matters.

Public Support

The second sense in which education became public was with the provision of public tax money for its fiscal support. This extension of the concept of public education followed by almost two centuries the initial developments in Massachusetts. It was an achievement in principle primarily of the early 19th century.

Beginning essentially with public collection from parents of tuition charges, public sponsorship of education quickly shifted to levying a general tax on real property for school support. With local governments carrying the principal burden, however, state governments recently, more and more, have been providing from their own revenues for the support of schools within their borders.

The role of the Federal Government in education has a long history, and its involvement in educational matters predates the United States Constitution. By its initial grants of land for the support of common schools, the Federal Government did much to materially encourage their establishment and maintenance.

The provision of substantial aid to the states for educational purposes has long been a continuing program of the Federal Government. The Morrill Acts establishing the land grant colleges, the Smith-Hughes Act and subsequent legislation for vocational education, and the recent National Defense Education Act are milestones of a long and active concern. Present legislation before Congress represents a further extension of federal aid to education.

Public Clientele

The third sense in which education has become public is that educational programs have become more and more available to the public at large and, as a consequence, have become more receptive to public and social needs.

The real basis for the scope of public education today emanates from compulsory attendance laws. The first compulsory attendance laws were enacted in the 1830's, but they did not become generally effective until the abolition of child labor and the rising pressure of organized labor in the 1930's. Thus, the achievement of public education in its fullest sense has been a development chiefly of the present twentieth century.

CONTROL OF PUBLIC EDUCATION

Unlike most nations of the world, the control of American education rests directly and primarily with local communities. Though primary control legally resides with states, historically control developed and has largely remained at the local level. Only a few of the 50 states exercise a real degree of centralized authority.

This apparent anomaly undoubtedly is due to the historic concentration of tax support for schools at the local level and thus follows the general rule that control is vested in whoever controls the purse strings. Thus, public education is primarily locally controlled, and state and federal controls are peripheral.

As states have assumed more and more responsibility for tax support, however, they have tended to exercise more and more direct control in educational matters. Though this trend can be expected to continue, further centralization toward federal authority is very unlikely. Though federal control is tangential to points where federal aid is provided (except where Constitutional restraints upon states are involved), it is extremely doubtful that direct federal controls could win legislative approval and/or public support in this country.

UNIQUE FEATURES

Certainly the most unique characteristic of American education is its concept of public education. As this concept has evolved, it has developed its implementation broadly enough to include the common essentials regarded as requisite for social integration and at the same time to provide for the diversities of individual and group choices in an increasingly specializing and technological society.

The comprehensive high school as an institution is a singular example, and its maintenance of a single track system is in marked contrast to multiple track systems in use in other nations. Yet, there is much pressure to modify its character. The insistent demands for more and earlier specialization, for better academic preparation, and for more effective instruction have produced many experimental innovations and posed serious threats to traditional programs.

It remains to be seen whether or not the common educational institutions of the United States can continue to meet the varied demands placed upon them in an increasingly diversified society and can do so without serious modifications.

A second unique feature is the preservation and maintenance of state and local control accompanied by state and local tax support for public schools. Such a proliferation of distinct administrative units is unparalleled. The paradox, however, lies in the fact that a high degree of uniformity among the state systems of public education has been achieved.

That these systems have developed independently to achieve the many common elements they possess is a more significant factor than the many diversities they exhibit. Nor is there little doubt that an increasingly mobile population will further accentuate this trend.

Finally, free public education through twelve years of formal schooling and higher education available at somewhat nominal costs — all at public expense — are unique both in the breadth of their extent and in the education levels at which they are available. Even the severest critics of American mass education marvel at the magnitude of the undertaking.

Yet, the fact that public education is not free is painfully evident. Studies of hidden tuition costs in the 1930's and early 1940's documented the costs of our free public schools, and further studies during the 1960's show little decline in these respects. Economically marginal students of great potential are unable to take advantage of the opportunities that are theirs and human resources are hereby wasted.

National merit scholarship programs and student loan funds have been provided to help retain able students at the collegiate level. Admittedly, they are inadequate to meet current needs, and the drop-out of able high school students has become a serious problem.

The United States must yet remove the economic barriers to full participation in its public high schools, if it is to give full extension to the egalitarian principle of universal education.

EDUCATION IS LAWFUL*

1. *Basis In Divine Law*
   A. *Old Testament,* "Genesis": Man is made in the image of God, (I,26)
      BASIS OF DEMOCRATIC BELIEF IN INDIVIDUAL DIGNITY. An heir to heaven is no hireling or slave to state. "Am I my brother's keeper?" (IV, 9) OBLIGATION.

---

*Richard L. Laughlin, "Education Is Lawful." Reprinted by permission from the *Bulletin of National Association of Secondary-School Principals,* XLIV, 254 (March, 1960), copyright: Washington, D.C., 97-99.

B. "Exodus": Honour thy father and mother. (XX, 12) BASIS OF
   RESPECT FOR TEACHER *(in loco parentis)*

C. *New Testament* adds to A & B Christ's teachings, including "The
   Sermon on the Mount," and "Suffer the little children to come
   unto Me, for of such is the Kingdom of Heaven." EVERY
   CHILD IS IMPORTANT, IMMENSELY IMPORTANT.

2. *Basis in Natural Law*
   As procreators, parents have primary rights and responsibilities.

3. *Basis in English Common Law*
   "The last duty of parents to their children is that of giving them an
   education suitable to their station in life: a duty pointed out by reason,
   and of far the greatest importance of any. . . . Yet the municipal laws of
   most countries seem to be defective in this point, by not constraining the
   parent to bestow a proper education upon his children. Perhaps they
   thought it punishment enough to leave the parent, who neglects the
   instruction of his family, to labour under those griefs and inconveniences
   which his family, so uninstructed, will be sure to bring upon him." — Sir
   Wm. Blackstone — JUVENILE DELINQUENCY PROPHECY?

4. *Basis of State Systems in the United States*
   (A chronological arrangement of pivotal legislative enactments, constitutional provisions, and judicial decisions)

   1642 & 1647—*Massachusetts Bay Colony* laws requiring each *town*
        to teach reading, writing, religion, and colonial laws.

   1784—*New York State* lays foundation for present public school
        system.

   1785—*Ordinance:* "There shall be reserved . . . the lot No. 16 of
        every township for the maintenance of public schools."—
        FIRST FEDERAL GRANT FOR PUBLIC EDUCATION.

   1787—*Ordinance "Northwest":* "Religion, morality, and knowledge,
        being necessary to good government and the happiness of
        mankind, schools and the means of education shall forever
        be encouraged." — Article 3 — CHARTER OF PUBLIC AND
        PRIVATE EDUCATION.

   1788—*U.S. Constitution:* ". . . promote the general Welfare." —*Pre-
        amble:* "The Congress shall have power to . . . provide for the
        common defense and *general welfare* of the United States
        . . ." — Section Eight, No. 1.

   1791—*Bill of Rights:* "Congress shall make no law respecting an
        establishment of religion, or prohibiting the free exercise
        thereof . . ." — Amendment One — No FAVORED RELIGION
        N.B. Released Time in New York upheld by the Supreme
        Court in the recent Zorach case: "The First Amend-
        ment, however, does not say that in every and all
        respects there shall be a separation of Church and State.

Rather, it studiously defines the manner, the specific ways, in which there shall be no concert or union or dependency one on the other."

"The powers not delegated to the United States by the Constitution, nor prohibited by it to the states, are reserved to the states respectively, or to the people." — Amendment Ten — STATE CONTROL OF EDUCATION

1819—*Dartmouth College Case.* Rights of private institutions sustained in this and subsequent U.S. Supreme Court decisions. (Girard College, 1831; Nebraska, 1923; Oregon, 1926)

1836—*Michigan Land Ordinance.* The sixteenth section of each township is granted "to the State for the use of schools." — EDUCATION A STATE FUNCTION

1862—*Morrill* [l] *Act.* FEDERAL AID TO STATE COLLEGES OF AGRICULTURE AND MECHANIC ARTS THROUGH LAND GRANTS

1868—*Fourteenth Amendment:* ". . . nor shall any state deprive any person of life, liberty, or property without *due process* of law . . ." — Section One. — U.S. SUPREME COURT FINAL AUTHORITY IN SOME MATTERS

1876—*Congress compels* new states to give NON-SECTARIAN, PUBLIC EDUCATION.

1889—*Louisiana Case:* Bequests to school districts are valid.

1900—*Virginia Case:* STATE HAS AUTHORITY TO DETERMINE ADMINISTRATIVE STRUCTURE *BUT* MUST OFFER EQUALITY OF OPPORTUNITY.

—*Indiana Case:* "As the power over schools is a *legislative* one, it is not exhausted by exercise. The legislature having tried one plan is not precluded from trying another." — *State v. Harworth* 122 Indiana 462,23N.E.946

1905—*Michigan Case.* RIGHT OF STATE LEGISLATURE TO CREATE OR ALTER SCHOOL DISTRICTS

1906—*Holmes and Bull Furniture Company v. John B. Hedges,* County Treasurer, 13 Washington 698: Responsibility for the creation and organization of school districts is *legislative.*

1914—*Smith-Lever Act.* STATES MATCH FEDERAL FUNDS FOR TRAINING.

1917—*Smith-Hughes Act:* Federal funds provided to assist states in stimulating VOCATIONAL EDUCATION. (Supplemented by later acts sponsored by George *et al.*)

1920—*National Defense Act.* FIRST FED. AID DIRECTLY TO LOCALITIES

1923—*Nebraska Case.* COMPULSORY ATTENDANCE, reasonable regulations, instruction in English, but foreign language lessons O.K.'d.

1926—*Oregon Case:* "The child is not the mere creature of the state. Those who nurture him and direct his destiny have the right coupled with the high duty to recognize and prepare him for additional duties." PRIVATE EDUCATION REAFFIRMED

1927—*Mississippi Case.* Maintenance of school system approved

1928—*Louisiana Textbook Decision.* CHILD BENEFIT THEORY UPHELD. Books, not sectarian, furnished free to private and public schools. AMENDED TO INCLUDE EDUCATIONAL SUPPLIES — 1935

1933-1940 *Emergency Measures:* DEPRESSION (CCC, NYA, CWA, PWA, WPA, FERA, *etc.*); W.W. I (Lanham Act '41, Public Laws, *e.g.,* No. 346-*"G.I. Bill;"* Korean War Public Law No. 550-1952)

1946—*National School Lunch Act*
—*New Jersey Bus Decision.* TRANSPORTATION FOR ALL CHILDREN

1948—*Illinois ex rel McCollum v. Board of Education,* 333 U.S. 203. NO RELIGIOUS INSTRUCTION ON TAX-SUPPORTED PROPERTY

1954—*Brown v. B. of Ed.,* 347 U.S. 483, Sup. Ct. 686. NO SEGREGATION IN PUBLIC SCHOOLS. "EQUAL PROTECTION OF LAWS GUARANTEED BY THE FOURTEENTH AMENDMENT."

1958—*National Defense Education Act.* Funds available for loans to college students. *Teacher Recruitment Inducement:* 50% of debt will be forgiven for five years of teaching.
State School Codes usually determine the minimum program of education. Permissive laws grant local school districts reasonable freedom.

THE TASK FOR EDUCATIONAL LEADERSHIP*

Although faith in the democratic ideal is still common, it is threatened by actions and proposals for action that are of almost daily occurrence. These vary from prescribing how people shall think and censorship of materials to identification and specialization of training for useful segments of the population to serve specific societal needs. Education, as

---

*Reprinted with permission of The Macmillan Company from *The Public Administration of American School Systems,* by Van Miller, 1965, 21-22.

the historic tradition of America, is to be geared to treating people not as things to be directed and controlled and used but rather as clients to be served so that they become responsible human individuals who are useful to each other and concerned about each other.

In speaking of the agencies that influence the development of the young, many persons use the church, the family, and the school as if they were of equal influence in perpetuating democracy. This is, of course, not true. Although the home in which the child grows to maturity has a deep and enduring influence on him as an individual, the nature and direction of the influence result from the caprice of individual parents. There is no degree of uniformity among homes, nor any ready way of getting any degree of uniformity even if it were considered desirable.

Nor does the church exist in this nation as a single agency. There are Methodist churches, Roman Catholic churches, Lutheran churches, Jewish synagogues, B'hai temples, Buddhist temples, and hundreds of others. Each has considerable influence upon the growth and development of the young. All of them collectively do not reach the total population. The respective influences are as diverse as the sectarian doctrines out of which they grow. There is little uniformity among them, and no desirable way of getting ultimate uniformity.

Public education, however, is one means of relating all of the people to each other and to the common life. It can help each understand the value of the differences in homes and sects and all the other social agencies of specialization and difference. It can help each understand that the tolerance of such diversity provides the rich soil for individuality and the stir for progress and development if compatibility and communication are attained. Where families are many and different, it brings all children into communication and to a common way of valuing individuality and using intelligence. Where private and sectarian schools exist, it is the public school that [affects] all of the people. For, as the public school becomes better, as it becomes a vigorous force of good in the local community, it also becomes the model by which other education is judged. Only through its leadership can come the common approach so sorely needed in these times.

Public education can develop a generation of people who will understand the evolutionary reconstruction of our culture, who will seek to expand the area of common agreement about the common good, who will have a secure faith in the democratic ideal, and who will judge alternative proposals for action by this ideal. Public education can do all of this. Whether it will do it in time to resolve present conflicts and to reduce the tensions that come from them will depend in large measure upon the quality of its leadership. Educational administrators must not fail in discharging to their fullest capacity their responsibility to develop such leadership. If they see that needed leadership is provided, the public schools of the United States of America will become the most effective agent for improvement in our society.

EDUCATIONAL INSTITUTIONS CANNOT BE STATIC*

[The institutions of men are never static; be it state, corporation, newspaper, social club, or school, the very nature of the institution and the people collectively identified with it is such as to establish the truism that no man or association of men is precisely the same today as yesterday.

Furthermore, should a gyroscopic device be developed to insure consistency through the years, the organism would soon get out of step with the human milieu in which it operates. New needs emerge; old needs are satisfied or disappear. New tools are forged; new inventions are made; new vistas of knowledge are uncovered by the passage of events.

Since an institution of man cannot remain forever unchanging in an unchanging world, the alternative to growth is decay.

Schools are no exception to this generalization. They must comply with the law of dynamic survival. The social setting of schools evolves; therefore, so must the schools. The "sabre-toothed curriculum" is no answer in this world of H-bombs, socialization, wonder drugs, and automatic household equipment. New knowledge of the process of learning, the conditioners of behavior, the tools of teaching, and the powers of education cannot be neglected, if we claim even honest craftsmanship in our schools.

It is not the theory of those who have contributed to this study of change that all change is *per se* good. We may wisely cling to certain practices in our schools. But, it's just good sense to stop doing things that no longer have a purpose and start doing things that do. Similarly, it is obviously foolish to do things the hard way when a better way for doing them has been found.

The time pattern of change can be found in the historical study of events. The forces favoring or retarding invention and diffusion of new

*Donald H. Ross, ed. *Administration for Adaptability,* Rev. Ed. New York: Teachers College, Columbia University (A Summary of research on adaptability by the Metropolitan School Study Council), 1958, 3, 7-8, (by permission).

ways of doing things can be clinically isolated and, once identified, treated as the powers that they are. Good schoolmen can see beyond the job of administering for immediate survival; they can see the more worthwhile task of administering for dynamic, long-range survival, in other words, *administration for adaptability*.] . . . Ed.

THREE FORCES FOR CHANGE

[The reasoning to this point has been that since all institutions of men are essentially dynamic, the schools cannot and should not be an exception. This line of thought implies one of three forces that compels any school, no matter how good it may be at a particular point in time, to become obsolete if it remains unchanging. This force is the *social setting* education is to serve. To take Harold Benjamin's fantasy, if the curriculum is the best in the world to teach people how to scare off sabre-toothed tigers, but there are no longer any sabre-toothed tigers, it is no longer a curriculum worth teaching. If the educational program is one to train an elite to operate an empire, but there no longer is an empire, the program is obsolete. Arising from the social setting of education are dictates of purpose, of appropriate content, of accuracy of content, of kinds and quantities of persons to be taught, and of depth and breadth and nature of tasks delegated to educational institutions to handle for society.

This statement should not be interpreted to mean that every purpose and every content item of our schools must be held up to and pass the test of contemporary utility. There are continuing purposes and bodies of constant subject matter that are timeless and appropriate for all students of all generations. To say that education must respond to the world in which it finds itself is neither an appeal to frenzied modishness nor a denial of the value of all things older than a fresh egg.

A companion force that compels educational institutions to adapt or to be obsolete is *the growing body of knowledge* of what happens in the processes of teaching and learning, of child development, and of mental and emotional maturing. The findings of psychological research in the period since the turn of the twentieth century have grown in quantity, sureness, and pertinence for educators.

A third force that dictates adapting or becoming obsolete is *the growing body of educational inventions*. It is easy to think of these in terms of newer construction materials, audio-visual aids, and other tangibles for schools to use. But the body of educational inventions includes the whole range of better administrative and classroom practices that is being added to day by day. The teacher who discovers a better way to teach spelling is an educational inventor. The administrator who reorganizes the teacher selection processes of his system is an inventor. This body of know-how demands evaluation and selection of appropriately transferable items.

Thus, conditioned by socio-economic change, by psychological advance, and by a larger reservoir of educational practices from which to select appropriate acts and policies, the best 1950 school, if it remains completely static, cannot be the best 1960 school.]

SCOPE OF AMERICAN PUBLIC SCHOOLS*

HIGH LIGHTS: 1964-65 AND 1963-64
Statistics of public elementary and secondary schools in the United States

	1964-65	1963-64	Change Amount	Percent
Basic administrative units:				
Total school districts	28,814	31,016	−2,202	−7.1%
Operating school districts	25,656	27,174	−1,518	−5.6
Nonoperating school districts	3,158	3,842	−686	−17.8
Pupil enrollment:				
Total	42,784,717	41,536,886	+1,247,831	+3.0
Elementary school	27,077,114	26,375,458	+701,656	+2.7
Secondary school	15,707,603	15,161,428	+546,175	+3.6
Average daily membership..	40,897,345	39,656,082	+1,241,263	+3.1
Average daily attendance	38,475,577	37,281,704	+1,193,873	+3.2
Number of high-school graduates	2,295,599	2,012,226	+283,373	+14.1
Instructional staff	1,788,805	1,721,467	+67,338	+3.9
Classroom teachers:				
Total	1,636,818	1,575,477	+61,341	+3.9
Elementary school	937,854	907,457	+30,397	+3.3
Secondary school	698,964	668,020	+30,944	+4.6
Men teachers	513,101	491,789	+21,312	+4.3
Women teachers	1,123,717	1,083,688	+40,029	+3.7
Average annual salaries:				
Instructional staff	$6,449	$6,203	+$246	+4.0
All classroom teachers	6,235	5,995	+ 240	+4.0
Elementary-school teachers	6,035	5,805	+ 230	+4.0
Secondary-school teachers	6,503	6,266	+ 237	+3.8
Receipts:				
Total revenue and nonrevenue receipts	$24,510,276,000	$22,852,537,000	+$1,657,739,000	+7.3
Revenue receipts by source:				
Total	21,783,543,000	20,150,966,000	+ 1,632,577,000	+8.1
Federal	829,254,000	756,083,000	+ 73,171,000	+9.7

Statistics of public elementary and secondary schools in the United States

	1964-65	1963-64	Change Amount	Percent
State	8,723,162,000	8,059,438,000 +	663,724,000	+8.2
Local, intermediate, and other	12,231,127,000	11,335,445,000 +	895,682,000	+7.9
Nonrevenue receipts	2,726,733,000	2,701,571,000 +	25,162,000	+0.9
Expenditures:				
Total expenditures	$23,040,125,000	$21,359,290,000	+$1,680,835,000	+7.9
Current expenditures for elementary and secondary day schools	18,577,123,000	17,138,751,000 +	1,438,372,000	+8.4
Current expenditures for other programs (community services, community colleges, adult education etc.) when operated by the local school districts	491,826,000	459,135,000 +	32,691,000	+7.1
Capital outlay	3,242,564,000	3,080,967,000 +	161,597,000	+5.2
Interest on school debt....	728,612,000	680,437,000 +	48,175,000	+7.1
Current expenditures for elementary and secondary day schools per pupil in ADM	$454	$432	+$22	+5.1
Current expenditures for elementary and secondary day schools per pupil In ADA	$483	$460	+$23	+5.0

*NEA Research Bulletin, XLIII, No. 1 (February, 1965), 7 (by permission).

THE NATURE OF EDUCATIONAL ADMINISTRATION . . .

WHAT IS SCHOOL ADMINISTRATION?*

School administration in the United States — What is it? In the strictest sense of the term, it is the act of administering; it is what school administrators and all who work directly with them do in stimulating, coordinating, and giving direction to the educational enterprise. It is purpose; it is organization; it is a group of people with their leaders at work in a situation where the prevailing social philosophy is democracy and where government is responsive to the will of the people. It is

*Inservice Education for School Administration, Washington, D.C. By permission of American Association of School Administrators, 1963.

leadership striving to help all people who are affected by school administration understand their roles, feel their responsibilities, and work effectively toward meeting them. . . .

In a broader sense, school administration is the people in a state or local community exercising their political powers in a free democratic government to shape the institution of public education, to give it character and substance, and to use this instrument of their own creation to serve a common need.

School administration is individuals feeling a responsibility for their schools and doing something about it. It's our next door neighbor; it's the editor of the county paper; it's the cashier in the bank at the corner of Fourth and Main; it's Mrs. VanAshbloom who lives in the big white house at the top of the hill; it's 180 million people working together through their school boards; their legislatures, and their state departments of education to build schoolhouses, hire teachers, and educate the children and youth of this land.

School administration is 50 state departments of education and 35,000 school districts with all the laws and rules and regulations that guide and direct them. It's 140,000 school board members and what they do in meeting after meeting extending from the late afternoon far into the night; and it's what the school superintendent does in board meetings, in conferences with his staff, and in an address to the downtown Rotary Club at its Wednesday luncheon meeting.

School administration is planning the program of instruction, developing the school budget, levying taxes, and collecting the money needed to operate the schools. It's bonding the property of the school district to build new schoolhouses; it's procuring a school site, designing a school building, and equipping a school library; it's planning courses of study, measuring pupil progress, and establishing standards for graduation; it's finding the best way to teach children to read and to spell and to solve algebraic equations; it's planning evening classes in which adults can become better acquainted with broad social issues about which they must express an opinion at the coming election; and it's discovering safer ways of transporting children to and from school, of handling power-driven equipment in the school shop, and of using chemicals in the laboratory. School administration is what people all over this land do in planning, supporting, and operating the schools.

School administration is leadership that inspires individuals and groups of people to higher purposes and greater efforts and helps them to see their own responsibilities and commitments in broader perspective. Not all the forces that shape the school originate within. The administrator who can lead the staff, the school board, and the people of the community to rise above their daily tasks and see the school with fresh new vision is summoning the energy and marshaling the forces necessary to keep the school vitally alive. School administration is defined by the American Association of School Administrators as "the total of the processes through which appropriate human and material resouces are made available and made effective for accomplishing the purposes of an enterprise. It functions through influencing the behavior of persons."

School administration is close to people. It touches parents in such intimate ways as the grade on their little 10-year-old daughter's report card and the time she gets on the school bus in the morning. Most people think of school administration in terms of what is done and what happens in their own districts. But like neighborhoods and communities towns and cities, and counties and states, no two districts are exactly alike. They differ in size of geographic area and population, in the ethnic and cultural backgrounds of the people, in community customs and traditions, in economic wealth, and in expectations from the schools. And school administration within the districts is as unique as the personality of the superintendent. Anyone who has traveled a bit over the country and studied school administration to any extent can point to an example of almost any kind of school district that can be imagined. . . .

A DEFINITION OF ADMINISTRATION*

Whatever else administration may be, it is at least the activity that concerns itself with the survival and maintenance of an organization and with the direction of the activities of people working within the organization in their reciprocal relations to the end that the organization's purposes may be attained. This somewhat oversimplified definition, then, provides the basis for selecting the functions that may be called administrative; and in it there are several obvious implications for our inquiry. Prerequisite or at least concomitant to administration is organization. Administration is directly responsible, not for performing the work of an organization, but for attending to its performance; administration in business and industry neither produces nor sells goods, nor does educational

---

*John Walton, *Administration and Policy-making in Education*, Baltimore: The Johns Hopkins Press, 1959, 41-43, 63 (by permission).

administration teach geography. Since administration is charged with the responsibility for the attainment of organizational objectives, it follows that the administrator should know what the objectives are. The assumptions are implicit in the lexical definition of administration; they may be instrumental in making the definition even more precise.

It follows from the definition given above that any activity that is performed to maintain an organization or to direct the activities of people working within an organization toward the accomplishments of the organization's objectives may be classified as administrative in nature. Planning, fund-raising, public relations, and leadership may logically be classified as administration when, and only when, they occur under the above conditions. If, for example, a superintendent of schools engages in lobbying for funds to support a program of education that has been legislated, or clearly decided upon by a policy-making body, he is performing an administrative act; but if he attempts to persuade a state legislature to enact laws changing the accepted purposes of the schools, he is not engaging in administration. If any one of the above-named activities is employed to modify the purposes of an organization, it cannot, according to our definition, be regarded as administrative in nature, nor would we expect persons who are referred to as administrators to be successfully engaged in them.

If we pursue this conclusion, we shall encounter such questions as: When the purposes of an organization are changed in order that the organization survive and prosper, is this activity administration? Since this situation is probably not uncommon, we should decide whether it logically belongs to our definition of administration. If we say that administration is the activity that serves to sustain an organization and to direct its internal energies in such a way that the purposes of the organization may be attained, then it is indisputable that changing the purposes of an organization, even in order to prolong organizational life, is not a part of administration. It is conceivable that an organization might exist for the purpose of modifying another organization's objectives, or that changes in purpose are an organization's objectives, as they may well be in education. Then it becomes an administrative responsibility to provide the mechanisms whereby such changes may be effected.

Within our definition there are really two types of activities: (1) those concerned with the direction of the activities of persons working within an organization, which are labeled co-ordinating activities, and which can hardly be described under any circumstances as other than administrative; and (2) activities such as public relations, which are administrative in nature when they are employed for the accomplishment of accepted purposes. This definition reduces immediately the ambiguity in the use of the concept of administration and should permit more clearly formulated hypotheses of relationships. Also, we are assuming that it corresponds in large measure to the activity pursued by persons called administrators.

So wide an acceptance has our definition of administration gained in the common interpretation that when a person occupying a position that is regarded as administrative becomes known for activities other than the ones we have specified, he is remembered primarily not as an administrator but for the other things he did. Horace Mann, for example, is remembered as an educator, a philosopher, or a statesman in the field of education, but rarely does one read or hear of him as an "administrator." Here the common usage of the wayfaring man is more realistic perhaps than some of the theories of the learned. The fact that famous statesmen, philosophers, and scholars have occupied administrative positions has given rise to the idea that haunts the minds of educational administrators today — that they should all be educational statesmen.

In other fields, also, the common usage respects the distinction between the administrative activity and other functions which are sometimes performed by the same person. In ecclesiastical administration a bishop or a moderator may be regarded as a brilliant theologian, an eloquent preacher, and a poor administrator, excellent in all three, or merely a good administrator. An industrialist who decides the purposes of an organization and then attends to their attainment is regarded both as an entrepreneur and as an administrator. A public official holding an administrative position who engages predominantly in pursuits other than those required to carry out legislative policy soon comes to be regarded as a politician. The fact that administrators who have been theologians, scholars, statesmen, or entrepreneurs are remembered as one of the latter may be due to the fact that in the past the administrative function was not so important to society as it is today. Or it may be due to the fact that the records of administrative achievements are more perishable, less tangible, or simply less spectacular. . . .

ACCORDING TO our definition and analysis of educational administration, its three principal functions are: (1) the discernment or apprehension of an organization's purposes; (2) the direction of activities within an educational organization in their reciprocal relations toward the accomplishment of accepted purposes; and (3) the providing of means for an organization's survival. Of these three functions, the discernment of purpose logically comes first, although in practice the temporal relations are often difficult to distinguish.

THE MAJOR CHARACTERISTICS OF
ADMINISTRATION*

Administration is the art of getting things done, of seeing that processes and methods which assure action are employed, and of obtaining
concerted action from different individuals. Whenever division of labor
occurs there arises the need for someone to coordinate the activities of
the different people working together. When this is done, essential jobs
are accomplished; wasted time, effort and materials are held to a minimum; and relationships between and among the individuals is maintained
on a satisfactory level. This is administration as an integral process with
a genuine purpose and place in affairs of man. Some of the major characteristics of administration are outlined below.

Division of labor is essential to the growth and development of society.
It also permits specialization and creates the need for administration.
Planning, coordination, and many other administrative functions become
essential to insure the continuation of services and commodities of many
kinds. Administration must always concern itself with the execution of
policy. However, policy cannot conceivably cover every possible needed
activity, and thus there is justification for administrative discretion, independent judgment.

Administration is job-centered and the nature of the work to be done
makes a difference in the administrative function. One job might deal
primarily with the production of objects; whereas, another would be concerned with the development of people. Thus, administrative functions
are always discharged in reference to policies that have been established
and jobs that have to be done and the effectiveness of administration is
reflected in the quality of job performance.

Organization is the channel through which the work of administration
is accomplished. It is an ordering of the behavior of individuals which
enables the performance of tasks and the accomplishment of purpose.
As a result of an administrative organization, task performance expectancy is defined, a system of communication and influence exists, both
authority and responsibility are established. Organization, therefore, sets
up a stable pattern of working relationships which enables the individual
to coordinate his efforts with those of others and accomplish the purpose
of the total endeavor. There are numerous types of organization, such as

*Better Teaching in School Administration, Nashville: Southern States Coopera-
tive Program in Educational Administration, 1955, 119-124 (by permission).

the line and staff, each of which has rather distinct characteristics which cannot be elaborated at this point. It is vitally important to note, however, the roles of authority and responsibility as an integral part of organization. Although the many distinctions exist which cannot be drawn at this time, authority is an essential ingredient of administration because it contains the right and power to act and to motivate others. Responsibility is possible only in terms of assigned authority. Thus, in any administrative position authority to get the job done must be commensurate with the responsibility assumed by the individual holding the position.

Although there are many further ramifications of authority and responsibility as they figure in administrative organization, still other factors such as unity of command and span of control are also involved. These factors have emerged as comparatively elementary principles of administration. The first merely indicates that a central authority is essential in order to prevent gross operational conflicts and confusion. The latter principle simply recognizes the fact that there are limitations on the administrative capacity of any individual. When this capacity is exceeded there is a break in administrative organization.

Within any structure there exists an informal organization which enables individuals to function still more effectively. Informal organization, therefore, consists of interpersonal relations which are not specified in the actual administrative organization but which are necessary to the individual in order to maintain his feeling of belonging, self-respect, integrity, and security. Through prior organization and administrative practices, the nature of informal organization is determined.

Although administration is based upon and has recourse to authority, it cannot rely exclusively on authority as the best means for motivating people. Administration in the first sense is officialship and the source of authority is from without the group. Thus, skillful leadership is needed and finds its place in administration. When administration exerts leadership, the source of authority is with the group and can be withdrawn without undue elaboration. It becomes immediately apparent that leadership in administration is a necessary condition to the maximum accomplishment of purpose.

Before considering educational administration directly, it is well to look carefully at the service which education has the responsibility for supplying society. Education in American society must perform the important job of introducing the child to the values of his culture and develop in him the skills which will enable him to earn a livelihood and contribute to the welfare of the group. Although the child would become fairly well adapted to his society by association in it, he needs more formalized training in specialized skills and in finer aspects of cultural behavior. The objectives of formalized education are very familiar to most professional educators, and it is the responsibility of the public school to assist children attain them. This distinctive nature of education in a democracy requires that educational administration be somewhat different from the commonly held concept of administration in business and public life. Educational administration is concerned with getting different jobs accomplished and with exercising somewhat different functions.

A school administrator performs his job by applying these functions to specific administrative tasks. Although these tasks are stated and discussed later, it is important to notice that these functions are always applied as a means to obtaining a better curriculum, a more adequate teaching staff, adequate school finances, functional buildings, and many other desirable developments. A Theory of Educational Administration must find expression through the following functions.

Planning: Planning is a method of approaching problems. Essentially it is defining what is to be done and how to do it. It is examining problems or jobs to be done, gathering information on them, determining alternate courses of action, and making decisions about how the problems shall be resolved or about how the job shall be performed. *Planning as a function of educational administration may be defined as the activity of devising and selecting courses of action directed toward the achievement of educational goals and objectives.*

Organizing: The function of organizing can be thought of in several ways. It may be thought of as structuring. As such, it primarily involves placing jobs, materials, and ideas in a structure. Another way of thinking of organizing is that of defining relationships among people. Duties, rights, and responsibilities are shaped into patterns of activities directed toward the achievement of purpose. Organizing can also be thought of solely in terms of purpose, as a means of unifying efforts to get things done. *Thus, a definition of organizing as a function of educational administration is the activity of arranging and structuring relationships in such a way that a unified effort is made in achieving the goals and objectives of education. Initiating: Initiating is the activity of starting actions essential to the achievement of educational purposes.* This function has two distinct aspects. The first is putting decisions into effect and the second is starting the exploration of new ideas and procedures. It is obvious that understanding must be established before initiation can be really effective, a realization which places importance on the functions of planning and communication.

Coordinating: There are several important needs for coordinating as a function of administration. The complexity of the school program indicates a need for coordination. The necessity for concerted action in the school program reveals the importance of coordination. Coordination is needed to overcome the limitations of planning and organization as well as the inherent limitations of personnel. *The function of coordinating may be defined as the activity of bringing people, materials, ideas, and techniques, and purposes into productive relationships.*

Supervising: As administration is held responsible for the effectiveness of the educational program, it must determine whether or not conditions exist which will make the attainment of educational objectives possible. This function is called supervising and is defined as the activity of determining that essential conditions are provided which will insure the achievement of educational goals. There are two important aspects to the function: determining what conditions are needed and then providing them in fact.

Evaluating: Administration is concerned with the efficiency with which the enterprise attempts to achieve its purpose. Although educational institutions are generally not set up to make money they are concerned with preserving and improving those things which society values. In this sense, evaluation of the efficiency of education is even more crucial than determining financial profits or losses, for the success or failure of attaining educational goals must be measured in terms of social gains or losses. Evaluating, as a function of educational administration, is simply determining how well educational purposes have been achieved.

Communicating: Educational administration relies heavily on the function of communicating, the activity of disseminating meanings throughout the organization which are essential for the proper carrying on of other administrative functions. The process of transmitting meanings involves more than the mere exchange of verbal and written symbols. It can be a simple gesture or a complex series of spoken and written symbols. In any of its many forms, communication is the process through which the behavior of individuals in an organization is influenced.

WHY ADMINISTRATION CANNOT BE A SCIENCE*

To the necessity for making a decision and the futility of logical refutation may be added other attributes of the administrative process and

---

*Robert H. Roy, *The Administrative Process*, Baltimore: by permission of The Johns Hopkins Press, 1958, 14-15, 18-20, 26-27.

some of these, it seems to me, can be stated well by contrasting the role of the administrator with that of the scientist in the laboratory.

Part of this contrast already has been made, at least by inference, because the scientist is bound by logic and reason above all else. He may turn his researches in a given direction because intuition suggests the more fruitful of alternate paths (indeed this could be described as an administrative decision) but once embarked upon experiment, logic and reason must be dominant.

Then too, the experimentalist is not beset by the same compulsion to decide as the administrator. Let an experiment fizzle or yield a dubious result and it may be repeated or modified again and again until the rigors of scientific accuracy are satisfied. This does not say that the scientist need never reach a conclusion but simply that his compulsions in this respect are not so pressing. The reasons for this relate to several interdependent factors.

The scientist's situation, one might say by definition, must be reproducible within very close limits; he must be capable of repeating the same carefully controlled experiments as often as need be for sound conclusions and, moreover, others elsewhere must be capable of doing the same thing by way of verification.

The administrator, of course, has no such facility at his command. He, perforce, must deal with people and for them events march in such a way that no moment or situation ever may be reproduced in its entirety. This is true in the laboratory too, if one considers the people there as well as the physical objects under study. They, the scientists and technicians, are not the same during Experiment No. 2 as they were during Experiment No. 1, and sometimes due account must be taken of this, if scientific rigor is to be maintained. But, nonetheless, the objective of their work, the experiment itself, may be reproduced.

There is another facet of this which can be mentioned, although the point may be strained in the making. Let an administrator err, or put his foot in his mouth, or unjustly castigate an employee, and he sometimes cannot recapture the ground lost by his mistake. He may correct himself or he may apologize but the vestiges of the blunder or the harshness will remain. . . .

The requirement of reproducibility in the laboratory carries with it two implications which also are lacking in the administrative process. The scientist is in control of the variables which affect his experiments and he usually can give them quantitative expression. The administrator often is unaware of the significant variables in the problems and situations which confront him and, even when he knows what they are, he often can neither control nor measure them. . . .

These arguments are applicable to results as well. Scientific experiments are "solved" and the results are quantified. Administrative problems in a very real sense have no solutions and there are no absolutes in the measurement of executive performance. Handsome profit can come from poor as well as good administration and loss can be incurred despite the best direction. The church mortgage can be burned despite, as well as because of, good management. Military victory can come to the bungler and defeat to his opponent, who may be tactically and strategically, i.e., administratively, superior. We cannot measure administrative results other than relatively, although we are all prone to accept such measurements as are made as absolute.

Of what moment is it to dwell upon these very obvious things? Most, indeed the vast majority of decisions are easy to make, the course of action clear. It is not often necessary to search for hidden factors, to weigh and assess and weigh again. If this were not so, we should all go mad from the plethora of decisions thrust upon us as individuals and as members of organizations.

This is true, most decisions are easy and most results not critical. But, infrequent as they may be, there *are* difficult decisions to be made and critical results to evaluate, and it is here that the administrator stands or falls.

These considerations are important only because they may contribute to understanding. Administrators behave in countless situations as though indecision were not decision; they seek to be logical and find only rationalization; they quantify and then use the numbers not only beyond the limits of their accuracy but also as though the numbers expressed all the variables; they sometimes proceed recklessly, as though their steps could be retraced; they are overly satisfied when results are good and overly repentant when they are bad. . . .

Administration is as yet an art, refined in the clinic of experience and subject as well to the native aptitudes of its practitioners. The framework of the administrative environment is in part determined by society, which governs the kinds of problems which arise and the kinds of action which may be taken.

However, at any time and in any society, these problems, of whatsoever kind they may be, demand decisions in such a way that deferment often is not possible; no decision at all often is equivalent to militant action.

In seeking to make "correct" decisions, administrators are prone to rely unduly upon logic and this frequently is futile. Problems arising from beliefs, even when the beliefs are quite fallacious, are not to be resolved by logical explanation.

To these characteristics may be added those which have been described by contrast: the non-reproducible nature of administrative situations, coupled with the impossibility of reversing a blunder; the inability of the administrator to control the forces at work, or even to identify all of them; the difficulty — often practical impossibility — of quantification; and the absence of any but relative measures of results. These attributes are common to administrative situations everywhere.

THE DIFFERENCE BETWEEN AN EXECUTIVE AND AN ADMINISTRATOR*

An executive is one who executes, one who carries out at high level, who achieves. The term has different meaning to different people, and is used loosely. It has a somewhat awesome sound. One person considers only the head of a large corporation or a Federal or State Cabinet member to be an executive. Another regards as an executive each person in an organization who assists subsequently in formulating policy.

At times there is only a fine line of distinction between the terms "executive" and "administrator." The head of each of a number of agencies of the Federal government is officially designated as "Administrator," even though he is its chief executive officer. Many of America's public school "administrators" are executives. A number of them should enlarge their executive functioning.

As used in this article, an executive is one who plans a long-range program, within the framework of legislation and policy, and who in turn creates policy in order to carry out the program which he plans. He not only carries out routine operations, but also uses imagination and rises above routine. Thus, he gives new life and new horizons to the organization, department or school, or other unit which he supervises.

An executive keeps an organization in motion. He plans, organizes, and, through others, achieves large goals for the organization. To carry out these functions, especially when in the public service, it is a high requisite that he be widely respected. He is observed closely by the community as well as by his staff.

Judgment and imagination are readily apparent in his make-up and in his functioning. He has the task of selecting an alternate course of

---

*Homer T. Rosenberg, "An Executive Development Program for High School Principals," *Bulletin of the National Association of Secondary-School Principals,* XLIV, No. 254 (March, 1960), 3-19 (by permission).

action and using it with full vigor when conditions which he cannot control prevent him from doing what he believes would have been best.

FOUR DEFINITIONS OF ADMINISTRATION*

The task of defining the school administrator's job has changed considerably during the past fifteen years. A common concern has developed among the most knowledgeable, responsible educators for adequately defining the nature of school administration as a basis for communication and collaboration.

School district reorganization is dramatically changing the proportion of isolated districts served by single or part-time administrators; newcomers are more frequently starting their careers as staff members of other administrators. Conurbanization (predicted to attract ninety percent of the population into urban strips) will bring school administrators into closer relationships. They will be unofficial "team-maters," although each may serve a separate district. . . .

Periodically, some group or individual has attempted to define the school administrator's job. These definitions have taken such forms as the inclusive type, the exclusive or restrictive type, the division of labor or standardized type, the integrative or relational type.

The inclusive definition has been most common. Any or all of the responsibilities or characteristics of school administration are included. The definition grew virtually as school administrators grew. As the small three-R school took on new functions and expanded, so did the administrator's job. Given the wide variety of situations and people in administration, a massive definition had its golden age of small districts when the single administrator was everything to everyone, although he must have wondered how much of anything he was to anyone! He could not be certain which competence or attribute got — or perhaps lost — him the job.

The inclusive definition probably reached its ultimate in a list of personal characteristics and professional responsibilities. . . .

The excluding or restrictive definition attempts to correct a list that has become too general and too all-inclusive. Some of this was a reaction

---

*Van Miller, "Four Definitions of Your Job," *Overview*, Vol. 1 (November, 1960). Reprinted by permission of the *American School and University Magazine*, 50-51.

to progressive education (especially to life adjustment education). Some of it came from tax conservatives who felt there was a limit to what they could support. Some came from fundamentalists who wanted to restrict the school to narrower, traditional tasks in the hope that this would maintain quality in the face of booming enrollments and new responsibilities. Restrictive definitions placed the emphasis on school-keeping, rather than on school-using.

A current version of the restrictive definition separates administration from policy-making. Here the administrator is a managerial chore boy for the public; educational leadership is left undefined, free-floating, or nonexistent.

The division of labor or standardized type represents another approach to correcting errors in the all-inclusive definition. However, it has its own difficulties. It implies that what a school is and what education is must be standardized apart from the community. (Hence, the community must also be standardized as to its size, its people, its purpose, and its cultural-socio-economic activities.)

In order to relate special positions to the field, the definition of each is developed by survey of those who hold it. Given the variety of situations and people in principalships, directorships, and supervisory positions, the result is likely to be a new all-inclusive list. The composite of administrative definitions in a school system could be even more confused and overlapping than in the inclusive definition of school administration. The desirable competencies and characteristics for to-day's various positions seem to be much more similar than different. If the standardized definition is used, more attention must be given to identifying differences and so relating these differences to each other. (Anyone assigning jobs must also relate the jobs to each other.) At present, this particular type of definition has been directed mostly to newcomers in school administration; it tells them how to get started and leaves further development to their own experience.

During the past fifteen years work on the integrative or relational type of definition has begun. Administrators, scholars, and professors of school administration are phrasing it not for novices but for each other. It provides the common basis for theory, experimentation, and research and for selection and preparation of administrative personnel. When properly worked out, it should provide the basis for helping the nation to use — not just keep — educational institutions. . . .

Free interpretation of the work of several current writers leads us to a description of the integrative type of definition as the development, management, and maintenance of decision-making and action-taking. Three classes of decisions and actions have been identified:

Those pertaining to goals and purposes in the policy-making and policy-interpreting realm; called creative or initiative decisions.

Those pertaining to operation; called intermediary decisions, authoritative decisions, the passing along of orders and commands.

Those pertaining to adjustments within the system and adjustments of the system to the community context; called appellate in that they arise most frequently through the complaints of subordinates. The three classes must be integrated through the overview.

Such a definition recognizes that many tasks are done: financial and business management; management of physical facilities and educational material; ordering of relationships through schedule-making, form construction, laying out of routes; program development and appraisal; internal relations with staff or students; and external relations with public, state authorities, the profession at large. These functions operate everywhere and represent different patterns of staff organization (depending upon the situation and the task.) It is entirely possible that they may provide the basis for differentiation in the organization of a team of administrators.

FACTORS AFFECTING EDUCATIONAL ADMINISTRATION*

THE SEQUENCE OF ADMINISTRATIVE ACTION

Some administrators act first and think or justify afterward. We have seen instances in which their intuition has served well. We have noted other instances, however, in which administrators are forever compensating for or rationalizing the consequences of such behavior. There are also administrators who think first but see so many alternatives that they fail to act when they should. The effectiveness of educational administration seems to be enhanced when there is a system established for moving consecutively through the sequence of administrative actions; planning, deciding, managing, and appraising. An administrative act is not complete until all four steps have been taken. The co-ordinating behavior of which we spoke earlier results at least in part from the

*John A. Ramseyer, Lewis E. Harris, Millard Z. Pond, and Howard Wakefield, *Factors Affecting Educational Administration*, School-Community Development Study, Columbus, Ohio: The Ohio State University Press, 1955, 63-64, 74-76, 113-114.

effectiveness with which the four phases of the administrative task are geared together. A brief explanation of each may be in order.

a. *Planning*. Educational administration, like the situation of which it is born, is always on the move. It moves either deliberately or aimlessly. Administration should be constantly looking ahead. In some administrative situations the foresight is prompted by a concern for improvement of the educational program to raise the level of living and is characterized by long-range plans, fact-gathering, predicting, and testing.

One's objectives have some bearing upon what is planned. Administrators may be classified in terms of the kinds of things for which they plan, such as teachers' meetings, board meetings, with parents, curriculum study, studies of child growth and development, studies of community resources, studies of space utilization, and determination of budgetary needs. Differing solutions in problems of what, when, how, and with whom to plan, result in widespread variations in practice.

b. *Deciding*. Making choices in terms of persons, ways of working, ideas, goals, and materials is an administrative responsibility that cannot be avoided. Choices are always limited by the situation — the financial status, the supply, adequacy in terms of functions, etc. The task involves making judgments pertaining to administrative personnel, instructional personnel, non-instructional personnel, instructional and non-instructional materials, and proposed plans and procedures to be used in subsequent activities.

Whether the administrator is to make the choice himself or involve others in making it, the choice must be made. This is the decisive step in taking action. The choices are not often easy alternatives of good and bad. But selections must be made and the criteria that are used become important.

c. *Managing*. Managing in educational administration falls into two classes; namely, that which deals with things and that which deals with people.

In the first group are such matters as: (1) co-ordinating educational activities, (2) preparing and distributing publicity, (3) expediting the communication of administrative details, (4) preparing reports, (5) managing the transportation system, (6) helping to prepare the annual budget, (7) presenting the annual budget, and (8) controlling expenditures within the budget.

The second group includes: (1) developing working relationships with administrative personnel, teachers, non-teaching personnel, the board of education, lay persons and groups, fellow administrators, professional organizations, students, mass media agencies in communication, and consultants; (2) participating in group action for the purpose of leading staff meetings, sharing ideas by discussion, reaching community decisions, and conferring with parents; and (3) maintaining staff morale and providing time for committee work.

This is where the act goes on. No matter how poor or excellent the planning, no matter how appropriate the choices of personnel, plans, or procedures have been, the operation must be guided, managed, executed, controlled. Often this is mistaken to be the extent of administration itself. The factor which differentiates among administrators is the degree to which managing is integrated with the other phases of the administrative act — whether or not it becomes the dominating phase.

d. *Appraising*. Educational administration in action must include appraisal. The public is constantly evaluating, and sometimes on very inadequate bases. Making assessments on systematic and scientific bases seems to be the task that lies immediately ahead. To do so would seem to involve appraisal of: (1) readiness for change, (2) readiness for staff and community participation, (3) child growth — development and achievement. (4) teaching effectiveness, (5) school facilities, (6) controlling the school program, (7) school board procedures, (8) administrative procedures, (9) cost of education, and (10) the effect of education on living in the community. . . .

THE FUNCTION OF ADMINISTRATION

It is widely accepted that the major function of educational administration is to provide the best possible program of instruction for children and youth. All other functions are subordinate, and must be planned and carried out in such a way that they contribute to the achievement of this end. Functions classed under such headings as staff personnel, pupil personnel, plant management, finance, and public relations must, according to this concept, make their appropriate contributions to the educational program. However, experience reveals that certain functions sometimes become ends in themselves, or, in some instances, competitive functions.

The tendency toward specialization of function seems also to produce a certain amount of autonomy of function. Special staffs are built to carry out particular duties or responsibilities. The degree of integration among them in achieving a common purpose varies greatly from one school to another. It would appear that the size of the school may have some effect upon the extent to which integration can take place. One assumption which is made in this connection is that lack of relatedness is an evil of the large school. Our observations lead to the belief, however, that school systems of all sizes are deficient in respect to integration. We have found both small and large systems where functions are well integrated. There are other systems, big and small, where they are poorly unified.

There are two potential causes of lack of integration: (1) a fundamental misunderstanding of the functional relationship, and (2) a tendency to assume that, as school systems grow larger, separation of functions is inevitable.

There is a persistent and widespread belief that the administrator performs his functions largely within the school building. The concept is just beginning to emerge that he is a leader of thinking about education and an organizer of action required to realize the educational ambitions of the people of the community. . . .

SUMMARY

The School-Community Development Study staff has observed that educational administration is undergoing an evolutionary shift in emphasis from *application of learned technique* to *leadership in human behavior*. This evolution is characterized by uncertainty and anxiety on the part of administrators who are frontiersmen in the transition. Unhappiness in some quarters over this change of affairs is due, in part at least, to misunderstandings which develop among individuals and groups affected by the shift in emphasis and to a lack of adequate theory upon which to base the shift.

In its study of administrative behavior, the staff has been mindful of the fact that ever increasing numbers of students, teachers, board members, parents, and other patrons of the school are getting into the administrative act. More frequently now, administration is stimulating these people to act instead of acting for them. Many conditions, both personal and environmental, determine how these people will behave. The discipline for their conduct, and hence the prospect of improving behavior, is dependent upon the creative release of their intelligence and the arousal of a desire to make optimum use of the related conditions.

Administrative behavior as it affects educational development in a community, then, is a specialized branch of human behavior. It is concerned with the manner in which individuals and groups, working singly and collectively under the stimulus of an appointed leader, create and develop the educational opportunities characteristic of their community. The potentialities of the members of the community, the environmental conditions under which they live, the institutional patterns and arrangements created by and for them, and the educational leadership with which they are provided define the limits of their collective efforts.

Thus, the educational administrator must become a student of the *factors affecting administrative behavior*. He must know not only what they are but something about *where and how these factors affect the behavior* of all who participate in the administrative act. In stimulating people to develop and maintain the best educational program of which they are capable, the administrators know that conditions which affect personal and group decisions must be established constructively.

The collective action of multiple groups under stimuli of various kinds is an organic type of behavior. If the administrator is to understand it, he must study it as organisms are studied. *Relationships* and *patterns,* both static and emergent, are important. They form the framework upon which to organize ideas and research. The growth of these relationships and patterns of behavior is significant, particularly if it is found to exist or emerge along with a common set of recognizable conditions.

Behavior is a complex phenomenon and is always found in complex situations. The influences which give it direction are multiple and may be found to exist at once within persons, in the relationship between individuals and groups, and in conditions external to them. Controls over these conditions are extremely difficult to establish, and precision in measurement is practically impossible. However, concepts and principles of action have been used as bases for observation. As a result, dimensions of administrative behavior are emerging, behavioral patterns and relationships are becoming recognizable, and hypotheses are being formulated about them. . . .

ADMINISTRATION AS MANAGEMENT . . .

ADMINISTRATION IS MORE THAN MANAGEMENT*

School administration is more than management. Like any human activity it is too complex to be charted or diagrammed. Neither can it be analyzed with any great precision. But from one view it is a three-cycle process. We plan, we put plans in operation, and we measure our progress. The cycles are planning, management, and evaluation.

Planning looks to the future. It charts the course. It sets programs, policies, and processes that will make the best use of resources to

---

Management Surveys for Schools; Their Uses and Abuses, Washington, D.C. By permission of American Association of School Administrators, 1964, 26.

accommodate the schools to the needs of the children they serve and the society that supports them. Planning sets the direction of growth. It insures adaptability. It determines the vitality of the institution. Planning rests on the experience of the past, the wisdom of the present, and a vision of the future. It is sound when it makes use of all available data and fills gaps in what is available. It is realistic when it is based on skilled and informed evaluation of the data.

Management is concerned with seeing to it that plans get put into operation. It keeps things going. Basically it looks to the present. In our schools it means supervising the educational program, operating and maintaining the plant, keeping the financial affairs in order, administering personnel policies, and all the rest. Good management makes the best use of what is available to accomplish the agreed-on functions. It makes the plans work.

Evaluation is the process of appraisal — of weighing the facts and seeing their relationships and consequences. It is necessary to effective management and crucial to wise planning. It goes on constantly and is a part of each of the other two cycles. It may be conscious and planned or unconscious and incidental. The most useful evaluation is conscious — skillful and selective observation which takes into account everything that is pertinent and weighs it on appropriate value scales.

In any organization all three cycles must be working. A school district must have both personnel and resources to permit administration to function effectively in all three areas. The fact is that in too many cases planning is now sporadic, evaluation is incidental, and management monopolizes the time and energy of the administration and even of the board....

PUBLIC ADMINISTRATION AS PUBLIC MANAGEMENT*

The consideration of organizational issues just reviewed brought with it a new concept of public administration: the concept of management. Here the field of business administration seems to have provided the precedent. In 1937 the President's Committee on Administrative Management applied the concept of management to the work of the President

---

*John Millett, "Perspectives of Public Administration," from *Preparing Administrators: New Perspectives*, Jack A. Culbertson and Stephen P. Hencley, eds. Columbus, Ohio. By permission of University Council for Educational Administration, 1962, 28-29.

of the United States, with far-reaching results in the institutionalization of the executive in the American system of government. The 1937 report was a major development in the theory and practice of public administration.

In time it came to be perceived that the principal management level of public administration is that of the department, agency, or other operating entity of governmental enterprise. The goal of management is the effective performance of government service. Within the limits of legal authorization and under such policy guidance as may be properly provided through the executive, legislative, and judicial branches of government, administrative officials of an operating enterprise seek to carry out their service under certain standards of performance. These standards involve satisfactory service (timely, adequate, equitable, and progressive), ethical service, and politically responsible service. In realizing these standards of service, management in public enterprise encounters certain common problems: problems of work direction (planning, communications, supervision, and public relations); problems of work operation (organizing, budgeting and accounting, personnel, legal procedure, and work improvement); and problems of internal service (plant construction and maintenance, purchasing, transportation, and facilities for communication).

ADMINISTRATION AS LEADERSHIP . . .

LEADERSHIP AND ADMINISTRATION*

Educational administration has undergone a radical change within the past few years. From a narrow, strictly factual approach to this field, attention is being directed to the theory of administration. Administrators are beginning to ask "why" rather than "what." The most recent research shows concentration on such terms as theory, authority, responsibility, communication, etc.

Unfortunately, the leadership concept has received little thought from those advocating the new approach. American opinion today reflects group assent and asserts the superiority of committee thinking. Thus, we see administrative texts stating that administrators should "go

---

*John F. Travers, "Leadership and Administration." Taken from *American School Board Journal*, CXLI, published by the Bruce Publishing Company, (September, 1960), 38, 50.

together with," instead of "going in front of" subordinates. Or, if a stranger walked into a meeting of teachers and principal, he should be unable to determine who is the principal.

This type of thinking is positively dangerous with regard to our schools. Is this the leadership image we wish to pass on to youngsters? But this is exactly what is taking place. A committee of teachers meets and passes certain resolutions. A group of parents protests over the science curriculum. Pupils are grouped into committees to prepare reports, to formalize decisions, to render discipline, etc.

These processes are excellent, *provided* they do not go to extremes. This is the danger in American education today. Initiative and leadership are not being developed in pupils. If anything, these qualities are viewed with suspicion, and society tends to label such individuals as authoritarian. This is the person who has an idea of his own, or who dares to differ on basic policy. . . .

It is commonly accepted that the schools have the duty of training the future citizens, and the future leaders. But it is psychologically sound to state that learning by imitation is a powerful methodological tool. Therefore, if students see that decisions are made only on a group basic, this becomes the basis of their own decision making. . . .

THE LEADERSHIP FUNCTION

In discussions of administrative theory, the time has come for a more extensive treatment of leadership. This leadership concept should flow from the school board and superintendent throughout the system. Members of the school board are individuals possessing the power of choice. This power should be exercised by each and every member.

The leadership function is based upon the authority that such individuals acquire upon assuming positions of responsibility. It is indeed foolish to ask a person to bear responsibility without also delegating the authority necessary to successfully discharge the responsibility.

It is not the purpose of this article to investigate the nature of authority. Whether the reader feels it flows from coordination, from the consent of those governed, or from the nature of the position, is here inconsequential. What is significant is that authority exists.

THE EXERCISE OF LEADERSHIP

While there may be disagreement on these divisions of administration, (planning, organizing, directing, coordinating and controlling) or on the nature of authority, nevertheless, there should be agreement that with authority, there goes leadership. Since both the board and the superintendent exercise authority, is a clash in leadership function to be expected?

Definitely not. The division of labor within the school system has the board performing the legislative function, and the superintendent carrying out the executive function. Although the superintendent discharges board policies, he should not be thought of as a mere consultant, but should also be considered a leader within his own sphere. In the office of superintendent, there resides the authority and knowledge necessary to direct, coordinate, and control. This authority cannot be fully utilized unless the person occupying the position exercises to the greatest extent possible the leadership function. Without digressing, some aspect of authority is derived from the respect and co-operation of those governed. This will not be forthcoming unless the administrator, here the superintendent, commands it by the strength of leadership he manifests.

The legislative duties of the board require joint action. This is all to the good since possible solutions to school problems will be greatly aided by the varied thought of the board. In this manner, all elements of the community are represented. But this collective action of the board should not negate the leadership of each member of the board.

In the determination of goals and the learning activities essential to the attainment of these goals, each member of the board must maintain his capacity for leadership. Only in this way can diverse philosophies and psychologies be thoroughly investigated for possible use in the school system. Finally, of course, the board votes its approval or disapproval of a given matter, and each member is then bound by the decision of the majority.

However, the conclusion of the board is better for each member expressing his own view rather than merely acquiescing in the opinion of another. Once a decision has been reached by the board, it then becomes the duty of all members to join in collective leadership. Each member implements the board's policy as much as possible; i.e., the final consideration with regard to planning, organizing, directing, coordinating, and controlling. Thus, by discharging the leadership function in a dual role, i.e., as an individual shaping policy and then, as the board, the authority of the board is vastly enhanced.

In Conclusion

Webster's dictionary states that the person who leads is the one who directs action, thought, and opinion. Yet the idea of leadership has not been stressed in educational thought to a degree that has kept it abreast of latest research concerning theory. While we may speculate about the nature of authority, channels of communication, the process of decision-making, etc., none of these features becomes alive and vital unless the person or persons involved show the quality of leadership. This is particularly true of school boards and superintendents. Theirs is the duty to accept the advice and council of groups, committees, etc., but in the final analysis, the authority they possess must be utilized by them alone — it cannot be transferred without loss of prestige and effectiveness. This process and this process, alone, is deserving of the designation — leadership.

KEYS TO LEADERSHIP*

. . . In simple terms, a leader is one who best provides for the desires of his group.

But leadership is complicated. It is intellectual; it is emotional; and it is physical. It is inherited, and it is learned. It is the summation of the total man which must square with myriad desires of the group.

The leader cannot be "far-out." He represents the median. Experience shows that the continuing leader is the one who best fits the mean, or average, of group thinking and feeling in the greatest number of instances. The far-out leader is like the German corporal who forgot to look back; he loses his followers. The leader goose who bends toward the hunting blind on the right or the cornfield on the left will feel the sting of Number 4's from a 12-gauge. The Greeks had to beware of Scylla on the one hand and Charybdis on the other; the modern educator must avoid both John Birchers and leftist liberals.

Briefly, then, the leader is most successful when he represents the desires and purposes of his followers. He may help raise the level of these desires and purposes, but must never get so far out front that he loses follower contact. The Greek theory that virtue is the golden mean between two extremes is a good rule for the leader to follow.

The complexity of leadership is like your safety box at the bank — it requires not two but many keys to open. The potential for leadership is inherent, and all persons have a degree of that potential; some have

*Emery Stoops, "Keys to Leadership." By permission of *Phi Delta Kappan* XLV, (October, 1963), 42-3.

more than others to begin with — just as some men are taller than others. As a matter of fact, height does have a positive correlation with leadership ability. But we are chiefly concerned with leadership characteristics that are learned. These we can improve. Here are some of the keys which improve leadership ability. The good leader:

1. Works beyond requirements . . . and does not call upon subordinates for tasks that he is unwilling to undertake himself.

2. Reports to work on time, regularly, and without obvious effort or complaint. The workers may grouse, but the leader is denied the privilege.

3. Keeps his mind focused upon work to be done instead of watching the clock. He would excuse a subordinate for a dental appointment sooner than he would take the privilege for himself.

4. Administers by policy, and remembers that he is subject to the policy which he himself helped to create.

5. Appreciates difficulties involved in puzzling assignments and offers praise when a subordinate solves the problem.

6. Seeks greater inter-personal security. The secure leader has more compassion for the foibles of followers, and is quicker to extend credit for a job well done.

7. Expresses concern through action, not mere verbalization, for the welfare of the staff, as a means of maintaining high morale, e.g., support of good salary schedules and other employee benefits.

8. Maintains faith in his staff. (If he doubts them, they will doubt him.)

9. Involves others in policy decisions. He must wait out the slowness of group problem-solving, for if he pressures too hard, the slow members of the group will lose face, and interest.

10. Improves programs by starting with worker dissatisfactions and helps find an answer, as opposed to belittling their dissatisfactions or giving them ready-made solutions.

11. Represents the majority desires of his group and moves ahead slowly enough to keep harmony within the group.

12. Keeps all members fully informed and looks upon some internal disagreement as the doorway to further growth.

13. Solves a problem rather than sells a solution.

14. Stresses *what* is right rather than *who* is right.

15. Allows time for consensus rather than ramming through a majority vote.

16. Gives credit for success and forgets, as far as possible, the failures.

17. Accepts responsibility for the outcomes of his group's decisions.

18. Agrees with Walter Lippmann that "the final test of a leader is that he leaves behind him in other men the conviction and the will to carry on."

19. Delegates authority, responsibility, and function. The leader is effective only as he works through people.

20. Concentrates on the essentials of the program. Tangents are tempting, but the leader must not only stay on the main track, but keep pulling his followers back to the main track.

The leader must avoid certain behaviors if he is to maintain the "leader goose" position at the head of his flock. He should:

1. Never show favoritism. But he must recognize individual differences in his group and capitalize upon them. Where is the fine line between recognizing ability and showing favoritism? The leader must find and follow it.

2. Avoid intimacy. When pupils call a teacher by his first name, or nickname, or when enlisted men buddy-buddy with sergeants, respect and leadership qualities evaporate. The Oriental philosopher Laotzu has said: "A leader is best when people hardly know he exists."

3. Don't take criticism personally. Keep calm and weigh all criticisms objectively.

4. Accept loneliness. The crowd has company, but the leader stands by himself.

5. Beware the temptation to exert power. As Lord Acton said, "Power tends to corrupt; absolute power corrupts absolutely." Plato saw this danger when he said in *The Republic,* "The people have always some champion whom they set over them and nurse into greatness. . . . This and no other is the root from which a tyrant springs; when he first appears he is a protector." Continuing, "In the early days of his power, he is full of smiles, and he salutes every one whom he meets."

6. Avoid the temptation to feel tall by cutting down enemies, much less fellow workers, and much, much less a subordinate staff member. This kind of person can hold power only through status position, or police methods, and not through the loyalty and respect of a devoted staff.

Leadership is not moral; neither is it immoral. It is amoral. Leaders can be good, or bad. It is the direction and outcomes of leadership that count. Genghis Kahn, Alexander, Napoleon, Tojo, and Hitler were leaders, but to destruction. Moses, Socrates, Jesus, Mohammed, Gandhi, Horace Mann, and Florence Nightingale were leaders, but to a better life. . . .

ADMINISTRATION AS EDUCATIONAL LEADERSHIP*

Educational leadership involves influencing people engaged in training minds: the great teacher influences other teachers by example; the college professor who writes an education text influences the training of minds through his writings; the dean of a school of education and the president of a teachers' college influence their subordinates; and the superintendent of schools, the supervisor, and the principal influence the activities of teachers, children, and parents. . . .

Leadership may be classified according to (1) its manner of operation, (2) its functions, (3) its source of authority, or (4) the philosophy of the organization the leader serves. Since people tend to define words in the light of their interests, everyone will have his own idea of which of these four concepts of leadership is most apt. . . .

In so far as leadership is concerned with influencing people, we may classify leadership according to the manner in which it exerts this influence:

1. Influence by example and by teaching
2. Influence by mediation
3. Influence by coercion. . . .

An organization must employ leaders to get its work done. Among a leader's most important organizational functions are the following:

1. The legislative function
2. The judicial function
3. The executive function
4. The advocate function
5. The expert function. . . .

The sources of leadership power described historically and prevailing in existing organizations are:

1. Natural sources
2. Divine sources
3. Contract
4. Usurpation. . . .

*Reprinted from *Administration as Educational Leadership* by John A. Bartky, with permission of the publishers, Stanford University Press, © 1956, by the Board of Trustees of the Leland Stanford Junior University, 4, 7-8, 14, 46, 58-60, 77.

The authoritarian leader makes all policy decisions for his organization. He directs his followers by dictating one step at a time and seems to take particular satisfaction from keeping them ignorant of what he is doing or where he is going. The leader personally assigns all tasks and his praise and criticism are highy personalized — that is, distinctly his own and not based on general philosophical premises.

The laissez-faire leader allows complete freedom of individual decision. He directs in no way, but simply makes it clear that his advice is available if it is desired. He never praises or offers criticism.

In contrast to the obviously vicious approach of the autocratic leader and the obviously ineffective approach of the laissez-faire leader, we are presented with the golden mean — democratic leadership. In this form of leadership all policies are a matter of group discussion and decision, encouraged and assisted by the leader. When technical advice is called for, the leader suggests several alternatives, which his followers either accept or reject. Members of a democratic group are free to choose their own work partners, and division of the tasks is left to the group. The leader attempts to be objective in his praise, and criticism. He puts on no airs and expects no privileges because he is a leader. . . .

Teachers and administrators must be careful to conform to their conventional roles in their relations with the public. Role deviations are often interpreted by a community as evidences of inefficiency or corruption. One new principal was most anxious to get across to his consitituency that he was a friendly and approachable person. Hence in his first meeting with the parents he addressed them most informally, deliberately slouching over the rostrum and indulging in slang expressions. Unfortunately, however, the community had set a role for principals to which his behavior did not conform, and he found himself labeled not friendly and approachable but uncouth and uneducated. Teachers can give the same misconception to the public if they do not conform to the role set for them. . . .

ADMINISTRATIVE POWER

A decision is of little worth to an organization if its members refuse to accept it. Administration demands some force, some power it can call upon to enforce its decisions. But Americans in general fear force or power in the hands of anyone, even the majority. The aim of the American Revolution was to destroy power, and the Constitution is more concerned with restricting power than with defining its legitimate functions. This fear of power persists, particularly in the schools.

But power, as we have seen, is essential. Just as a machine needs power to make it go, so an organization needs some motivating force to keep it moving toward its goals. Americans tend to stick their heads into the sand to avoid seeing the power that exists all about them in their institutions. Laws are ineffective without the power to enforce them; moreover, they are the result of conflicting powers, and they grant powers to the victors. The doctor, the lawyer, the merchant, the chief, all possess power of some kind to enforce their decisions. This power may be social pressure or psychological influence, but it is power nevertheless.

There are three main ways by which a leader influences his followers to accept his decisions: he may appeal to their emotions, to their minds, or to their needs.

Influencing by appealing to the emotions is called inspiring. . . .

One appeals to the mind by persuasion. In persuasion, there is an implied moral obligation to present the data and the ideals involved in a decision as objectively as possible. . . .

A third source of administrative influence is threats or appeals to the follower's needs. These are called sanctions; and the process of employing sanctions to get agreement on decisions is known as coercion. Sanctions may be threats (to fire a man, reduce his salary, or otherwise jeopardize his security) or promises (of better job, higher wages, and so on). . . .

The success of co-operation is related to the ability of those cooperating to communicate with one another; consequently, the effectiveness, efficiency, and cohesiveness of an organization depend upon its communication system. A leader fails or succeeds in terms of how well he is able to communicate with his followers.

THE DEPRESSIVE STATE OF
EDUCATIONAL LEADERSHIP*

INTRODUCTION

Educational leadership today is developing into a cult with its own standards of success and its own moral code of behavior. Neophyte leaders are initiated into the mysteries of this cult by schools of education, and practicing leaders deviate from its commandments at the risk of being excommunicated from the educational profession. Teachers are inclined to evaluate their leadership in the light of the cult's Holy Scriptures, and teacher organizations charge school administrators with

---

*John A. Bartky, "The Depressive State of Educational Leadership," by permission of *The Clearing House* (November, 1963), 131-135.

unethical conduct if their leadership does not conform to the cult's moral code. Cultism has come to completely dominate the educational leadership scene.

The educational leadership cult is group oriented, and it emphasizes group process in its rituals. Its converts who become leaders shrink from exercising any dominance and hesitate to contribute their ideas lest they be suspected of trying to influence the group they lead. The group must be left free to decide everything for itself by a process of discussion and consensus. Devotees to the cult assume that a teacher group is autonomous and in no way obligated to the social environment, including the public. Hence, teacher decisions may be in opposition to those made democratically by the public. By concluding that the function of leadership is to serve the needs of teachers, the leadership cult tends to reduce the leader to the level of a domestic servant.

As a consequence of his forced conversion to the precepts of the educational leadership cult, the school administrator is rapidly becoming immobilized, and the attainment of educational objectives is being jeopardized. Destructive negative, rather than constructive positive, feelings are being displayed by the teacher, and school morale is low. In general, conditions have so deteriorated that the public is demanding a new, forceful leadership, and theorists are examining leadership activity in the hope of discovering how to make it more functional. Such endeavors might well begin with a consideration of how the teacher and the school organization interact and the role leadership should play in guiding this interaction. . . .

DIRECTIVE LEADERSHIP

Educational leaders, as agents of the formal school organization, are often tempted to react to undesirable organizational behavior on the part of teachers, or try to inhibit it, by becoming more and more directive. They are invited to increase the degree of technically competent leadership by clarifying, redefining, or strengthening the school structure. They set up all kinds of "information," "education," "communication," and "human relations" programs to further this end. These actions, instead of reducing the fundamental cause of conflict and frustration, often augment it and create new causes. However, leadership may continue in its directive ways, hoping that the time will come when the teachers will adapt, and conflict and frustration will disappear.

That this occurs is evidenced by the armed forces, who insist upon maintaining their structure and who are eventually successful in internalizing it as a value in the eyes of their constituents. However, educational leadership does not have the sanction power of the military and cannot survive long periods of teacher conflict and frustration.

Nevertheless, directive leadership makes teachers dependent upon the leader, and it is possible that once they become accustomed to dependence, some of them, if kept in this state, will learn to contribute effectively. This may partially explain those schools where directive leadership is successful. Perhaps they had more than their share of teachers who prefer to be dependent. . . .

Directive leadership is obviously functional in times of urgency or emergency, when immediate organizational action is demanded. Under such circumstances, a little teacher discomfort may be a cheap price for efficiency. Directive leadership is also necessary when a teacher is uncoöperative and refuses to change his ways. In such instances, some conflict and frustration is often quite effective in encouraging him to modify his behavior. Directive leadership under the name of autocratic leadership may be an anathema to the leadership cult, but it often is the only effective leadership.

PERMISSIVE LEADERSHIP

A leadership approach specifically designed to combat teacher conflict and frustration with organizational structure is a permissive approach. This approach widens the tolerance limits of the organizational role. It is more democratic, more involving, more collaborative, and more teacher centered than the directive approach. Lippitt and White's operational definition of the democratic leader best describes the permissive approach. If we relate their definition to the school situation, we find that the democratic school leader:

(1) Permits all teachers to discuss school policy formation. He invites participation in the decision-making proccess.

(2) Encourages teacher discussion about future as well as present educational activity. He does not try to keep teachers in ignorance of future plans.

(3) Permits teachers to define their own job situation as much as possible. For example, teachers are encouraged to determine the way tasks are to be accomplished as well as the manner in which they are to be fragmented and assigned.

(4) Focuses on obtaining objective facts relative to teacher problems. The leader tries to base any necessary praise or censure upon objective facts. He is never subjective.

These admonitions have become the four commandments of the educational leadership cult. They are the ethical principles that form the basis for evaluating leadership. A school administrator is not presumed to be a leader if he does not conform to these ethical principles.

It is assumed, but not readily demonstrated, that permissive leadership ends in (1) increased teacher identification with the school organization, (2) greater group productivity whether the leader is present or not, (3) increased job satisfaction and teacher morale, (4) greater organizational flexibility, (5) fewer teacher complaints, and (6) less hostility, frustration, and aggression.

Permissive leadership is advertised by the leadership cultists as being the leadership favored by teachers as well as the leadership ending in the greatest productivity. Neither contention is universally valid. Permissive leadership is not necessarily universally favored because not all teachers are actively seeking the job satisfaction it promises, because not all teachers are anxious to participate in school decision making, because not all teachers are seeking the psychological rewards promised, and because not all teachers do want to be independent of school administration. Some teachers become just as frustrated with permissive leaders as others do with directive ones. The claim that permissive leadership invariably leads to higher productivity can be challenged and disproved.

REALITY LEADERSHIP

Recent research in fields other than education leads me to question whether there is one best way (as suggested by the educational leadership cultists) to lead teachers. Fiedler accosts the cultists with the statement that effective leaders do not even try to understand their followers. He insists such leaders tend to make value judgments, are critical, and do not accept poor co-workers. Additional research has found that too much emphasis on maintaining a friendly atmosphere can reduce a group's goal of achieving efficiency. Still others find that groups with little cohesiveness can perform as effectively as groups with much cohesiveness. One study, in attempting to evaluate a directive versus a permissive leader, found that women prefer the former and men the latter. Another study implied that a leader need not even conform to the opinions of his followers.

The question might well be asked, why did an educational leadership cult that favors permissive leadership develop when it is obvious that it does not always work? The answer lies in the following facts. Many educators are inclined to apply what are little more than leadership insights to specific problems as universal absolutes rather than foundations for diagnoses. Permissive leadership principles have become absolutes for cultists. Also, because they tend to apply human relations hypotheses, based upon a consideration of one isolated dimension of reality where hundreds intrude themselves, they are more certain of their findings than they have a right to be. Lastly, because the name "democratic" leadership is attractive and "autocratic" leadership is repulsive, what the former represents is accepted, and what the latter represents is rejected. Also, one who is in favor of the first and against the second seems to be in the same strategic position as one who is in favor of virtue and against sin.

Unfortunately for the welfare of education, the field of leadership behavior has developed by evolving extreme positions. Historically, first came the proponents for organizational needs, with their directive leadership approach. When they had exhausted its possibilities in reaction to the teacher conflict and frustration, they caused the emergence of the proponents of teacher needs and permissive leadership. As a consequence, school needs are now being neglected. However, sooner than swing back to directive leadership, an action demanded by the public and some teachers, let us permit the pendulum to rest close to a middle position. Let us adopt a reality leadership which asks only that we diagnose the whole organizational structure and the teachers and that we swing to directive or permissive leadership as the situation demands: directive when the needs of the school are being neglected, permissive when the needs of the teacher are being ignored.

CONCLUSION

We might conclude by presenting the following propositions as hypotheses for a leadership approach:

(1) There tends to be a lack of congruity between teachers' behavior to satisfy their own needs and the behavior demanded of them by the school.

(2) This lack of congruity can cause conflict and frustration which may end in nonfunctional and even destructive teacher action.

(3) School leadership may circumvent and avoid this behavior either by directing conformance or by permitting a restructuring of the school organization.

(4) If directive leadership does not end in more undesirable behavior, then it is the leadership approach to be employed. Otherwise, a permissive leadership is called for.

(5) The balance between satisfying teacher needs and school needs is a delicate one. Hence, leadership can never assume a static posture such as that recommended by the permissive leadership cultists.

ADMINISTRATIVE ORGANIZATION . . .

THE CHARACTERISTICS OF ORGANIZATION AND ORGANIZATIONAL BEHAVIOR

In the past 15 years most discussions of organization have been devoted to the development of a behavioral theory. It is not clear that these efforts have in fact developed a consistent and systematic set of generalizations or principles about organization. There is no doubt that these discussions have advanced our understanding of organization.

In general, an organization brings together at least four different types of persons. First, there are the operators, the front-line workers who man a production plant, sell the products, or provide a service to the public. Secondly, there are the supervisors on the job who direct and check the work done by the operators. Thirdly, many organizations require a variety of specialists who plan the technical aspects of the job and provide various services which make possible the basic work of an organization. Finally there are the managers who bring workers, supervisors, and specialists into a necessary harmonious whole.

In the organized relationships which exist among these various types of persons, three basic situations occur. First, every person regardless of his level of ability and job assignment experiences certain felt needs: a sense of usefulness, recognition of effort, and consideration as an individual. Secondly, formal relationships based upon an assignment of authority will be supplemented by informal relationships based upon group response to a natural leader or group sense of common interest. Thirdly, there is often real or latent conflict between those in authority and others. One of the deep-seated traditions of our society is the dignity and worth of the individual. Hierarchical relationships of authority appear to challenge this tradition.

The recognition of these behaviorial characteristics of individuals brought together in the working relationships of an organization has done much to achieve a more sophisticated kind of performance by managers and supervisors. It has not been easy, however, to build a realization of behavioral factors into a system of organizational prescription. Beyond the admonition that supervisors and managers must be considerate of other persons as individuals, and must provide a sense of participation in the enterprise and a reward of effort, we have not made too much progress toward a behavioral science of organization.

---

*Millett, *Perspectives of Public Administration*, 26-28.

The studies and the discussion which have taken place do give us a number of maxims which illustrate or refine the generalizations just outlined. A few of these may be mentioned. A formalistic structure of authority and carefully prescribed rules of procedure tend to reduce individual initiative and promote a rigidity of action. The greater the personal satisfaction the individual finds in his work, the higher is his morale and his output. The greater the prestige of an organization, the greater the propensity of an individual to seek identification with it. Organizational equilibrium depends upon motivation, and motivation depends upon a balancing of contribution and inducement. Conflict arises in an organization when decisions are unacceptable to large numbers of individuals, because the probable outcome fails to meet standards of satisfaction or because the probable outcome is too uncertain. Conflict may be resolved by problem-solving, persuasion, bargaining, or an appeal to political support. Organization structure is goal-oriented and adaptive. Innovation is necessary when changing circumstances require the introduction of new programs or new standards of performance. Change is most readily acceptable when the criteria of individual and group satisfaction are observed, and when daily routines or programmed activities are altered gradually. The essence of effective organization is communication.

Such maxims as these will readily commend themselves to persons with extensive experience in organizational activity. Most of them have acquired substantial validity from observed fact. These generalizations constitute an advance in organizational knowledge. They do not exhaust the subject as a field of inquiry, and they do not afford us yet with a comprehensive theory of the behavioral characteristics of organization.

THEORY OF ADMINISTRATION . . .

ADMINISTRATION BACKGROUND WHICH LED TO SEARCH FOR THEORY*

HISTORICAL PHASES IN THE DEVELOPMENT OF ADMINISTRATIVE SCIENCE

Let me begin by turning first to a brief review of the historical phases through which scientific administration passed in its development. In this

---

*Egon Guba and James M. Lipham, "Theory of Administration," from *Administration as a Guide to Action*, Roald F. Campbell and James M. Lipham, eds. Chicago: by permission of Midwest Administration Center, The University of Chicago, 1960.

discussion there will be almost nothing that we can say about educational administration specifically. In its earlier days educational administration went largely unrecognized as an essential component of school operation. Many administrative functions were handled by clerks. The emphasis, in any event, was clearly upon the adjective "educational" rather than upon the noun "administration," as is exemplified by the executive titles that came to be used: the title "principal" is of course a shortening of the term "principal teacher," and even the title "superintendent" referred to the superintendence of instruction rather than of the educational enterprise. Such neglect of the administrative function did not, however, characterize business and industrial operations, where administration was often synonymous with ownership. It is in this area that the development of administrative science can be most clearly charted.

In that administration and ownership were so often synonymous, it is perhaps no accident that the administrative function was first viewed largely in terms of providing facilities and materials which other persons would utilize in the actual production of goods — a kind of *enabling* function, as it were. The administrator was not so much concerned with the operation of the enterprise he headed as in making arrangements for its use; buying, selling, hiring, financing — these were the proper administrative behaviors. It is important to note that the actual methods of production, and sometimes even the provision of appropriate tools, were largely left in the hands of the workers themselves who could use almost any method of operation they pleased so long as some minimal production schedule was maintained.

It was inevitable that someone should question the wisdom of leaving the determination of conditions of operation and production in the hands of workers whose level of skill was so highly variable and whose scientific knowledge was so largely fortuitous. Critics began to suggest that the concept of the administrator's function might well be expanded to include defining the conditions of production. Once optimal conditions had been determined through careful study and analysis, employees could be trained to work in these optimal ways at an all-around gain in effectiveness. Benefits would accrue to the company in the form of increased production and to the worker in the form of higher wages. There seemed little basis to suppose that reasonable employees would not operate according to the "company book" rather than according to their own predilections, so long as they stood to share in the returns resulting from their increased productivity.

Administration thus entered the era of "scientific management," time and motion studies, piece-work rates, functional foremen, and the Taylor, Gantt, Halsey, and Gilbreth methods of efficiency in engineering. These were the ideas that would have received careful attention in any address on the topic, "What Do We Know?" that might have been delivered during this period. And these were powerful ideas that gave a new direction to administration and played an important part in the improvement of American technology. But while this new emphasis radically changed the place of the *worker*, administration as an art remained largely what it had been. Thus, administration in this scientific era was still ancillary to the production process; there was simply one more resource, a human one, to be administered.

The basic notion of the scientific study of the methods and procedures of production touched off a series of studies and experiments that resulted in unparalleled advance in production efficiency. But in the end it was one of these very experiments which brought to a close this period of emphasis upon scientific technology. At the Hawthorne Plant of the Western Electric Company, F. J. Roethlisberger, a member of the staff of Harvard University, began in the early twenties a series of studies to determine the relationship of illumination to production. The studies turned out to be, as someone has said, "the light that failed." For it appeared that there was operative at the Hawthorne Plant some mysterious force that eased production upward with every change in experimental conditions, whether for better or for worse. We who are so accustomed to think in terms of human relations find it difficult, in retrospect, to imagine why it required so much time and so many experiments to make it obvious to these researchers that the mysterious force was a human, attitudinal factor, something that had to do with personal motivation, satisfaction, and morale. When this idea finally *was* realized, however, administrative science as it had been known was irrevocably altered. Scientific management had placed its emphasis upon technical production problems and had ignored human factors entirely, or had at best assumed that these factors could be minimized by rational salary schedules and working hours. Now it appeared that this assumption was unwarranted; human factors apparently could not be so easily controlled. Worse, they had an effect upon production which could be as large as or larger than the effect due to technical factors.

The setback suffered as a result of the discovery of the importance of the human element was a brief one, however. The old methods of scientific analysis which had been so useful in controlling technical factors were, after all, still relevant. Could not human factors be subjected to scientific study just as the technical elements had been studied? If human factors could not be ignored, could some way be found to control them, or better yet, to take full advantage of them in achieving even higher effectiveness?

These questions opened a whole new area of inquiry directed toward administrative control of personnel aspects, rather than technical aspects, of organizations. Studies of motivation, attitudes, values, satisfaction, morale, productivity in small groups, and group dynamics served the new focus of interest. The concept of the administrative function was enlarged to include knowledge of human relations and skill in dealing with people. The industrial engineer had to become a human engineer as well.

This phase of human engineering is the phase in the development of administrative science through which we are presently passing, although I feel that we are near the end of this stage.

THE NATURE AND SHORTCOMINGS
OF THEORY*

A *theory* may be defined as an integrated body of definitions, assumptions, and general propositions covering a given subject matter from which a comprehensive and consistent set of specific and testable hypotheses can be deduced logically. The hypotheses must take the form "If *a*, then *b*, holding constant *c, d, e* . . ." or some equivalent of this form, and thus permit of casual explanation and prediction.

A *good* theory is one which (1) has its definitions, assumptions, and general propositions consistent, insofar as possible, with previous research findings and with careful, although perhaps not systematic, observations; (2) has a minimum number of definitions, assumptions, and general propositions; (3) has its deduced hypotheses in readily testable form; and, crucially, (4) gets its deduced hypotheses verified by proper scientific methods.

It is quite possible to be scientific without using theory. If we include in the realm of science anything which permits accurate prediction, some of the most scientific work in the social sciences has been in the nature of actuarial research, which involves no theory whatsoever. The formation of scales by compiling items that elicit significant differences in response from two groups that are known to be respectively high and low on the variable to be predicted also permits accurate prediction and is therefore scientific even though the scales are not based on theory. Simple hypotheses, which spring from casual observation, can be tested

---

*Arnold M. Rose, *Theory and Method in the Social Sciences*, Minneapolis: by permission of The University of Minnesota Press, 1954, 3-5.

scientifically and, if proven accurate, will lead to valuable insights and predictions. These, too, are not based on theory.

There are certain values to theory, however, which have led many investigators in the older disciplines to make extensive use of it. (1) It is a guide to the formation of hypotheses and trains investigators to look for facts which may ordinarily not be readily apparent. (2) It permits research to be cumulative; that is, it allows the conclusions of older studies to gain support from new research and allows older studies to provide some of the data for new research. (3) It indicates what studies are crucial; that is, it provides one guide for the selection of research problems from among the infinitely large number of possible hypotheses. (4) It permits research to proceed systematically and allows conclusions to take a shorthand form so that they are readily communicable.

There are also certain dangers to the use of theory in science. It may be argued that these dangers are not inherent in the utilization of theory but result, rather, from the misuse of theory. As logically accurate as that may be, it is nevertheless apparent that the use of theory as a guide to research seems always to bring in its train some undesirable consequences:

1. Theory channelizes research along certain lines; it does not encourage equally all lines of investigation. If the theory ultimately proves to be wrong, many years of work are wasted and new ideas have not had a fair chance for expression.

2. Theory tends to bias observation; there are certain assumptions and definitions inevitable in theory, and these limit observation sometimes more than is desirable in a young science. Without a theory we might tend to have alternative definitions and assumptions in a given piece of work. Theory usually limits us to one consistent set of definitions and assumptions.

3. The concepts that are necessary in theory tend to get reified. The tendency to reify concepts may be a general characteristic of human behavior, but the use of theoretical definitions seems to stimulate this human weakness.

4. We are faced with the fact in social science, seldom mentioned but readily verifiable, that replications of a study seldom reach an identical conclusion. This may be the result of poor measuring devices, or it may be due to the fact that we have as yet failed to come to grips with the great diversity and complexity of our subject matter. Until we resolve these difficulties and secure consistent replications for simple hypotheses, are we justified in formulating elaborate theories which assume consistency in findings?

5. Until a theory can be completely verified, which is practically never, it tends to lead to overgeneralization of its specific conclusions to areas of behavior outside their scope. In social science we have been faced with the phenomenon that studies of the maze learning of rats have been used to guide the development of children and that conclusions arising from the investigation of neurotic behavior among adults have been suggested as a chief guide for the understanding of politics. The history of social science shows enough natural tendency to overgeneralize without having the stimulation of theory to encourage this unscientific procedure.

6. If there are rival theories of human behavior, and there will inevitably tend to be in a democratic and pluralistic society, the rivalry seems to encourage distortion of simple facts. Quite frequently scientists can agree on statements of fact but have very serious disagreements concerning the significance or explanation of these facts on a theoretical level. Sometimes even the immediate causes of the facts are subject to agreement but the more basic ones suggested by theory are not.

DEFINITION OF THEORY IN
EDUCATIONAL ADMINISTRATION*

Due to the many varying definitions of theory, it is important to state what is meant by theory and how theory is used as an element of the Competency Pattern. Some people have a contempt for theory and regard it as being synonymous with the impractical. This concept of theory is revealed in such comments as: "This isn't a lot of theory; it really works." It is not uncommon to find persons who regard theory and practice as being somewhat antithetical, very different and unrelated things. On the other hand, we find people who put much faith in theory and derive from it considerable direction. Theory when used in reference to the Competency Pattern means a set of postulates which explain particular phenomena and which are rendered more or less plausible by evidence of facts or reasoning. Thus, theory isn't really practice, but theory is very practical. Theory represents a set of closely related ideas or concepts which help us understand educational practice and give us a practical sense of direction. Therefore, theory provides a framework of concepts and postulates which enable value judgments to be made, phenomena to be understood, and directions to be set. Actually, it is

*Better Teaching in School Administration, 46-48.

impossible to act without a theory. Even the person who says he does not believe in theory or who states that theory is grossly impractical, very ironically must call upon some conception of what constitutes right and proper action before he acts.

A theory of educational administration is, broadly speaking, a collection of concepts or principles that define what educational administration is and that give directions to an individual attempting to be an educational administrator. It is conceivable that a theory of educational administration would include concepts relating to the nature of individual and group life, the major tenets of American democracy, the purposes of public education, the nature of the administrative process, and the functions of educational administration.

A theory of educational administration has an important function in the Competency Concept. Basically, it represents a value framework in terms of which critical tasks of administration are defined, methods of task performance are determined, and appropriate know-how is set forth. In this way theory permeates the entire Competency Concept. It is a primary referent that determines what educational administration deals with, how it functions, and what represents acceptable practices in a democratic society.

In view of this role of theory in the Competency Concept, it is obvious that only a single, consistent theory would be usable in the Competency Pattern. It is also important to recognize that theory emerges from two primary sources: the cultural climate in which it operates, and scientific information. In this way, a democratic theory of educational administration promulgates the management of public education in such a manner as to foster and promote the ideas of American democracy.

THE PLACE OF THEORY IN THE PRACTICE OF ADMINISTRATION*

It seems to me that broadly speaking one may take at least three different stances toward the understanding and improvement of administration in the school setting. One stance is that all the administrator need be is a natural born leader. The successful administrator, it is said, is an

---

*Jacob W. Getzels, "Theory and Practice in Educational Administration: An Old Question Revisited," *Administrative Theory as a Guide to Action*, Roald F. Campbell and James M. Lipham, eds., by permission of Midwest Administration Center, University of Chicago, 1960, 39-42.

administrator by innate personality, by instinct, as it were. If only we could somehow find these natural born leaders, all other problems would take care of themselves. Advocates of this point of view go to all sorts of trouble to prove that our great generals, for example, only "growed up" that way. They say, "Oh yes, ideas or theories are a fine thing, but if you want to get something really important done, get a *practical* man." These people like to show that our great industrial leaders, like our great generals, are typically unspoiled by education — that they are sort of modern "natural heroes" or "noble savages" — and as for knowing anything about such things as "span of control" or "role theory," perish the thought. The successful administrator, it is held, may be hard-boiled but he's no egg-head. We may call this point of view the "born leader" or "natural hero" point of view. . . .

The second stance is that administering a school is essentially a practical problem in *engineering* — human engineering, if you will. The engineer, it is said, is concerned with the solution of practical problems and in solving these problems he applies certain "ways of doing things." He starts out with one state of affairs and wants to achieve another state of affairs, or to use a geographical analogy if I may, he wants to get from one place to another, and to do this efficiently he uses a previously tested set of directions — a proved *itinerary* — telling him the steps he must take. The school administrator is also concerned with practical problems, and he too must apply working prescriptions and practical principles. The improvement of administration depends on the contrivance of better prescriptions, on the production of more exact itineraries; and the successful administrator is the one who applies these better prescriptions, follows these more exact itineraries. We may refer to this point of view as the practical, prescription-centered, or itinerary-oriented point of view.

The third stance is that the crucial need is not more applied principles but greater conceptual understanding. The focus of effort must be not on prescriptions but on theories — not on simple directions but on complex relationships. Or, if we may continue with our geographical analogy (which is of course not to be taken too literally) what we must have are not specific *itineraries* but relational *maps*. Advocates of this point of view argue that in the long run we will improve administration not so much by collecting empirical solutions to operational problems as by attempting to understand educational and administrative processes in more fundamental and relational terms. We may refer to this point of view as the theoretical, concept-centered, or map-oriented point of view. . . .

I believe maps and theories are not only indispensable but unavoidable. To be sure, theories without practices like maps without routes may be empty, but practices without theories like routes without maps are *blind*. The prescription-centered approach to the solution of fundamental educational issues (which I hope is the business of the school administrator) seems to me not only delusive but impossible. So-called practical principles cannot be either meaningfully formulated or effectively applied outside a supporting conceptual framework. Indeed, the inevitability of theorizing or "map-making" in *all* human affairs must be clear to anyone who has inquired into the sources of his own behavior or examined carefully the behavior of others. The question of whether we should use theory in our administrative behavior is in a sense as meaningless as the question of whether we should use motivation in our behavior. Our actions are inevitably founded in our motives and steered toward goals by the relevant explicit or implicit theories that we hold. . . .

In short, the basic question is not whether educational administrators should or should not utilize theory in the solution of their problems — even so-called trial-and-error behavior is based on some valuation, some theory, some presumed "map." The question rather is: Shall we permit the backgrounds of our valuations — the theories we apply — to remain implicit or make them explicit?

RELATION OF OPERATION AND THEORY*

In the organization and operation of schools, changes must be made while the machinery is running. We cannot stop the processes and completely retool for a new design. Procedures in use are modified, practices no longer useful are discarded, and new ways of doing things are originated or adopted. This continuous change in a dynamic organization is influenced by the consideration of the demands of the basic operational principles in terms of the changing purposes of the institution. These changes in procedures and purposes may come because of needs within the institution itself or because of those in its cultural setting. Operational practices, then, tend to go beyond operational theory, and, because of this, theory should be periodically re-examined and restated. Such periodic action stimulates the origination of newer and still better practices

---

*Alfred H. Skogsberg, *Administrative Operational Patterns,* New York: Teachers College, Columbia University. By permission of the Metropolitan School Study Council, 1958, 18-19.

in a cycle of progression. The progression is not made simultaneously at all points on a broad front; rather salients are driven forward and small gains consolidated while the general forward movement is awaited. The base for this reanalysis of theory is a better understanding of the interaction of the basic principles in the patterns of operation.

These principles are not of equal importance in operation. Schools could operate, though not as effectively, with little regard for democracy. A complete disregard of prudence, however, would soon shatter the organization. Operation that makes no adaptations to changing needs will render the institution liable to extinction. The importance of this quality of adaptability has not been emphasized enough. It is very valuable to know more about how adaptations occur and are diffused, so that the process may be accelerated. It is of greater import to recognize that the totality of the dynamic balance of the operation must bolster and enhance adaptability if our schools are to continue to contribute to the progression of society. In this sense, administration is more than the sum of operational practices. Each procedure must be considered as affecting the others and as being affected by them. The total effect, determined by all the practices in interrelated action, is the administrative portion of the whole educational climate.

WHY THEORY IS USEFUL IN EDUCATIONAL ADMINISTRATION*

A theory is a rational explanation of how something is put together, of how it works, and of why it works that way. A theory may never really be tested, but a theory provides a basis for generating testable principles or procedures or hypotheses, and the results of such tests yield presumptive evidence as to the validity of the theory. The physical scientists provide a good illustration in the theorizing about what electricity is and how it works. Such theorizing provided the basis for generating new ideas that could be tested in experimentation and from which a variety of practical applications have been developed. From time to time there are modifications in the theory to bring the rational explanation into line with additional new information. The theory is man's attempt to reason and to explain. It is useful as it guides him to more accurate observation and

---

*Reprinted by permission of The Macmillan Company from *The Public Administration of American School Systems*, by Van Miller. © Copyright Van Miller, 1965, 567-568.

perception and to the better application of what can thus be learned. In the scientific sense, theory is concerned with explaining what "is" and avoids concern with what "ought" to be. It is an attempt to grapple with reality. This is an important distinction in the development of educational administration as a field of study. In the earlier and general exchange of administrative experiences and views each hearer likely weighed the value of what he heard in terms of whether it matched his own notion of what ought to be done or of what would fit the way he saw things. In an attempt to generate concepts, taxonomies, and theory there is an effort to value what can be dependably demonstrated, regardless of who conducts the experiment. The effort is upon developing such dependable definitions, classifications, and hypothetical relationships. It is from this store of generalized knowledge that each practitioner can establish his own practices, weighing them against the values he holds and in terms of the situational context within which he works.

The attempt to build theory — to develop communicable explanations — of educational administration has additional benefits beside that of unifying the field, which was mentioned earlier. It tends to bring the field into focus so that not only the concepts and the classifications are seen — but so that some ordering of relationships is also developed. In earlier pages school administration was described as the accumulation of extra-duty chores that needed someone's attention. When a concept of school administration is developed, new questions arise with respect to which tasks are of the most importance, how such tasks can be related to a central notion of the over-all job, and possibly even whether or not some of the tasks should be done at all by the administrator. Such notions must also include consideration of school administration as it is related to education, to schools, to staff members, to pupils, to the general public, to community resources, to other governmental agencies, to organized societal groups, and the like. Thus administration is considered not as an isolated position to be described, but as a functional and interactive role to be explained and understood.

The development of concepts and of theory also extends man's thinking so as to motivate the search for answers to fill in gaps that appear as he reasons about what a complete explanation must be. As theory provided a table of chemical elements and notions on the nature of matter, it also exposed gaps that directed research into areas where new knowledge was needed. As germ theory of disease developed, new possibilities for study and identification of phenomena were opened up of a different order than arising from descriptive statements of the symptoms of various diseases. Theory development provides a structure from which students can seek to grapple with truth. It provides a framework within which scholars in related fields may direct attention to educational administration and within which educational administrators may more appropriately relate the findings from other fields. Thus educational administration finds a closer affiliation with all knowledge and investigation. Concepts and theories are the mental tools with which man seeks to comprehend reality and to communicate about it.

COMPETENCE AS A SPECIFIC, NOT A GENERALITY*

One of the understandings pertinent to the problem of competency patterning is that competence is specific, not a generality. This means that there are too many jobs, too much knowledge, and too many specialized skills contained in a modern society for any one person to aspire to competence in all of them. In part this understanding, of course, reflects the breakdown of the old faculty psychology and its dependence upon the training of universally applicable faculties. It also reflects the realization that a person may be competent in one task and incompetent in another. A logical extension of this idea reveals that the extent of a person's competence cannot be determined by a simple arithmetical averaging of the things he can and cannot do. Would a man who is competent swimmer but incompetent in riding a bicycle average 50 percent competent? Obviously not; by definition he was a competent swimmer and the average indicated him to be only one-half competent.

Thus, in the light of modern knowledge, competence refers to a specific task performance. A person does not act with the same degree of competence in all the things he does. During a day's activities he will be competent, partially competent, and incompetent, several times. . . .

The important fact is to be found in the close interrelatedness of point of view and competence, and in the recognition of philosophical concepts as integral and functioning parts of any consideration of the nature of competence. Without philosophical concepts it is impossible to construct a defensible competency pattern of any kind. It might be possible to describe what the competent man does, but without a philosophical point of view it will be impossible to say how he does these things and, perhaps of more importance, why. Furthermore, differing sets of philo-

*Orin B. Graff and Calvin M. Street, *Improving Competence in Educational Administration,* New York: by permission of Harper & Row, Publishers, 1956, 89-90, 104-105, 121-122, 255, 263-264, 265-266.

sophical concepts will obviously produce radically differing competency patterns. Rigid concepts will serve to make the behavior patterns rigid, autocratic concepts will define autocratic systems, and democratic concepts will describe competence within the democratic social organization.

Since that remote day when man first realized that there were degrees of quality of behavior, competence has been an interest of the first magnitude. Recognition of the fact that some people were more competent than others raised the question as to how they came to possess their special abilities. Why can some individuals shoot an arrow with more accuracy than others? Is competence determined by an accident of birth or is it learned? What part does skill play, and what is the significance or knowledge in determining competence? Also, what about the individual who seems to possess the necessary skills and knowledge but is unable to achieve the desired competence because of a "bad" attitude?

It is immediately seen that these questions devolve upon that area of investigation known as psychology. If psychology lays any claim to recognition as an organized discipline it must substantiate that claim by its findings which concern the unique factors of human personality. That is, it must deal in those elements which are distinctly characteristic of human behavior, and which distinguish such behavior from that observed in other organisms. It is in this connection that psychology has a direct bearing upon competence. As the science of human behavior, psychology should furnish the facts needed to ascertain whether or not a particular human action is in accord with the best that is known about competent living. Further, it should furnish implications as to how people may learn this "better" type of behavior. To put the matter somewhat differently, before it is possible to describe competent human behavior and tell how it is to be achieved, facts must be had regarding the human organism — what motivates it, what its needs are, how it "should" behave, and how it learns. . . .

The development of the appropriate pattern relationships needed for competent educational administration is a task upon which the administrator must constantly work. Relationships seem to occur in three important kinds of situations. First, relationships are in terms of purpose to be achieved; second, they are in terms of a basic point of view — theory; third, they are in terms of an efficient performance resulting in economy in achieving purpose.

All of these relationships appear in what the psychologists refer to as a perceptual field. It was noted that the relationship criteria are restrictive and selective. However, these restrictions and selections are not designed to cripple the competency pattern but rather to bring about a certain degree of quality. Thus they intensify the need for having a great number of alternatives from which to select.

Finally, the criteria for quality pattern relationships tend to cause the individual to refine his competency pattern — pattern of behavior — toward a point of showing more and more quality. Out of the infinite number of relationships which are constantly occurring the administrator needs to be able to select those which are appropriate to his job tasks. It is believed that this skill in visualizing relationships available is one which can be learned. Further, this kind of learning will need to be a major item in the program of education because there is no assurance that it will come about except as a purposefully taught and learned ability. . . .

Since administration is concerned with the management of materials and persons so as to accomplish purposes, each community will require a different administrative competency pattern. There will be common elements in the administrative patterns of all communities but each administrator will need to recognize the unique possibilities in his community and in his job. The administrator in the highly democratic community will not need too great an emphasis upon the democratic factor within his own personal pattern. The administrator in an autocratic community will need to develop strong capabilities with regard to building up a democratic organization as part of his competency pattern. In a community which is closely knit as to value patterns an administrator will not need to do more than work for a careful evaluation and constant bringing up to date of the existing value systems and behavior patterns, whereas in a community where there is little common understanding of the value patterns subscribed to by the individual members of the community he will face a very different situation.

Even though each administrator's job will have unique characteristics it will also have certain characteristics common to all administrators' jobs. Since there is doubtless no single community wherein all members understand clearly the work to be done by each member, it will always be part of the job to gain better understandings as to task responsibility. Since probably no community has a completely worked out system of values, this is an important challenge. There will always be the tasks of getting people together, making decisions, collecting materials and things, and providing for the execution of policies and plans which have been formulated. Throughout all these activities the administrator will need to continually evaluate his position as it affects the educational progress of his community.

THE ADMINISTRATOR'S TASK

The educational administrator will have a number of critical tasks, on different levels of importance. Those on the simple mechanistic or habit level will include the "simple" skills of driving an automobile from place to place, answering the telephone, and so on. Those on a higher level of skill, the technical tasks, will include preparing budget items, using certain testing and survey techniques, and the like. Finally, those at the highest level will involve stimulating people to make decisions regarding the purpose and nature of the school system and to carry out previously formulated plans and decisions. As in all socially significant work, these leadership tasks are of greatest importance to the success of the administrator's work.

This tends to point up the fact that in certain tasks a great deal of compromise will be possible whereas in others compromise cannot be permitted without jeopardizing the integrity of the whole program. It will be at the latter points that the administrator must hold fast to his concepts regarding his role in the community.

Of immediate interest to the administrator will be the competency patterns of the teachers and staff members within his direct managerial responsibility. They provide an excellent place to start improving competency patterns throughout the community — excellent because here his influence will be most easily applied. The administrator can learn to use the constructive sources of influence — respect and affection — and can improve his own competence by learning not to use the unconstructive sources of influence such as fear, bribery, and the like. What better way is there to provide for the in-service growth of teachers than to get each teacher interested in improving his own pattern of competent behavior?

FOR FURTHER REFLECTION OR INVESTIGATION

1. From your observation of the school administrators with whom you serve, identify the concepts of administration under which they seem to operate. Explain your conclusions.

2. Trace the expansion of administrative positions in your school district, reporting the date and the reasons given for each addition.

3. List the behaviorial characteristics of a favorite school administrator. Compare your list with that of other students in the class to confirm the difficulty in finding agreement upon who should be an administrator. Can a preparatory program be designed to train for those qualities of highest desire?

4. Is democratic administration in conflict with the legal powers granted to a board of education or superintendent?

5. How can a school administrator reconcile the need to develop individualism in students with the necessity to have them conform to standards for the entire unit?

6. Should the quality of leadership in school administration be assessed by the product or the process?

7. Contrast Professor Bartky's views on leadership from 1956 (Admin-

istration as Educational Leadership) to 1963 (The Depressive State of Educational Leadership).

8. Distinguish between theory and philosophy, between theory and principles, between principles and law.

9. Explain the practicing administrator's contempt for theory and the scholar's disrespect for practical solutions.

10. Explain the trend toward providing more interdisciplinary education in the preparation of school superintendents.

11. Why has it taken so long for citizens to accept the need for adequate administrative staffing of public schools while they readily accept the need for it in private corporations?

12. If there is such widespread agreement among practicing administrators and professors of educational administration about the value of the internship for the preparation of future school administrators, why do so few administrators have the experience in their programs?

13. Do state certification requirements for administrators aid or handicap the preparation of good administrators?

14. Should there be individual and specialized certificates for the various kinds of school administrators or just one kind of certificate which would cover all administrative positions?

15. Determine and evaluate the differences in the degree requirements for a future administrator of schools, of private business, or of municipal government.

16. Explain the varying understandings of the meaning of leadership.

17. If, as Roy states (Why Administration Cannot Be a Science), administrators often err in relying upon logic for making decisions, upon what bases should they make their decisions?

18. Compare the definitions of school administration as offered by Walton, by the American Association of School Administrators, and by the author.

BIBLIOGRAPHY

Bartky, John A., Administration as Educational Leadership, Stanford: Stanford University Press, 1956.

————, "The Depressive State of Educational Leadership," *The Clearing House,* XXXVIII, November, 1963.

Bellows, Roger, Thomas Q. Gilson and George S. Odiorne, *Executive Skills,* Englewood Cliffs: Prentice-Hall, Inc., 1962.

Better Teaching in School Administration, Nashville: Southern States Cooperative Program in Educational Administration, 1955.

Brameld, Theodore B., *Education as Power,* New York: Holt, Rinehart and Winston, Inc., 1965.

Cocking, Walter D., *"As I See It."* New York: The Macmillan Co., 1955.

Getzels, Jacob W., "Theory and Practice in Educational Administration: An Old Question Revisited," from *Administrative Theory as a Guide to*

Action, Roald F. Campbell and James M. Lipham, eds. Chicago: Midwest Administration Center, The University of Chicago, 1960.

Graff, Orin B., and Calvin M. Street, *Improving Competence in Educational Administration,* New York: Harper & Row, Publishers, 1956.

Griffith, Dan, "New Forces in School Administration," *Overview,* January, 1960.

Guba, Egon, "Theory of Administration," from *Administrative Theory as a Guide to Action.* Roald F. Campbell and James M. Lipham, eds. Chicago: Midwest Administration Center, The University of Chicago, 1960.

Harvey, Virginia, "The Change That Counts," Educational Leadership, Feb., 1962.

Havighurst, Robert J., and Bernice L. Neugarten, *Society and Education,* Boston: Allyn & Bacon, 1962.

Guy, George V., "Public Education in the United States," *Education,* LXXXIV, October, 1963.

Loughlin, Richard L., "Education Is Lawful," *Bulletin of National Association of Secondary-School Principals,* XLIV, March, 1960.

Management Surveys for Schools: Their Uses and Abuses, Washington, D.C.: American Association of School Administrators, 1964.

Miller, Van, *The Public Administration of American School Systems,* New York: The Macmillan Company, 1965.

————, "Four Definitions of Your Job," *Overview,* I, November, 1960, 50-51.

Millett, John, "Perspectives of Public Administration," from *Preparing Administrators; New Perspectives,* Jack A. Culbertson and Stephen P. Hencley, eds. Columbus, Ohio: University Council for Educational Administration, 1962.

Orlich, Donald C., "The Schools, the Public, and Politics," *American School Board Journal,* CXLVIII, August, 1964.

Professional Administrators for America's Schools, Washington, D.C.: American Association of School Administrators, Thirty-eighth Yearbook, 1960.

Ramseyer, John A., Lewis E. Harris, Millard Z. Pond, and Howard Wakefield, *Factors Affecting Educational Administration,* Columbus, Ohio: Cooperative Program in Educational Administration, 1955.

Rose, Arnold M., *Theory and Method in the Social Sciences,* Minneapolis: The University of Minnesota Press, 1954.

Rosenberg, Homer T., "An Executive Development Program for High School Principals," *Bulletin of the National Association of Secondary-School Principals,* XLIV, March, 1960.

Ross, Donald H., *The Administrative Process.* Baltimore: The Johns Hopkins Press, 1958.

Skogsberg, Alfred H., *Administrative Operational Patterns.* New York: Teachers College, Columbia University, Metropolitan School Study Council, 1950.

Staff Relations in School Administration. Washington, D.C.: American Association of School Administrators, 1955.

Stoops, Emery, "Keys to Leadership," *Phi Delta Kappan,* XLV, October, 1963.

Thayer, V. T., *Formative Ideas in American Education* (From the Colonial Period to the Present), New York: Dodd, Mead & Company, Inc., 1964.

The Professional Preparation of Superintendents of Schools, Washington, D.C.: American Association of School Administrators, 1964.

Travers, John F., "Leadership and Administration," *The American School Board Journal,* CXLI, September, 1960.

Walton, John, *Administration and Policy-making in Education.* Baltimore: The Johns Hopkins Press, 1959.

Westby-Gibson, Dorothy, *Social Perspectives On Education,* New York: John Wiley & Sons, Inc., 1965.

Willower, Donald, "Values and Educational Administration," *Peabody Journal of Education,* November, 1961.

Chapter 2

Principles of Administration and Organization

The administration of social organizations is guided mostly by principles which arise from experience and contemplation. Neither science nor absolutes have yet matured to the point of high usefulness in the management of humans; they are not likely to in the near future, if present knowledge is used as a criterion. The current search for theories of administration possibly holds the most hope for uncovering positive guidelines in administration. But because of the uncontrollable factors in human behavior and the changeableness of organizations, especially school organizations, an administrator must put his faith in those principles which trial and error have shown to be most effective.

These are the principles which *most* administrators have found to be the *most* workable in *most* situations.

(1) *The administration of corporate bodies requires a clarification of legislative and executive functions in concept and in operation.*

Authorities of educational administration agree that the primary function of a school district's governing body is the same as that of all other corporate organizations, public or private, viz., the formulation of policies and legislation for the conduct of the institution's responsibilities. Through the laws and policies enacted by a board of education, professional personnel realize the educational desires of citizens. The highest force of policy implementation is the board's executive officer, the superintendent of schools.

This division of authority between the legislative body and the executive force provides the balance of power needed by every organization for persistent successful operations. The third balancing force common to other governmental bodies, the judiciary, is not so pronounced in public school government. A board of education is legally charged with certain judiciary powers such as in the conduct of hearings for an internal dispute or for an external concern such as the annual budget. The board exercises a further form of judicial function in its evaluation of the superintendent's performance. For the most part, however, the judicial function is performed by established courts of law.

As logical as the principle appears for separating the legislative and executive functions, and as essential as it is for the parties involved to respect the division, finding and maintaining the demarcation line is not always easy in school decisions. For example, after a board of education has formulated a policy as to the type of buildings it desires for the district's children, would the members not likely wish to follow through to examining blue prints and specifications, to inspecting the site and the construction process, to interviewing architects, and to examining the related invoices? All of these acts are executive tasks. Moreover, state laws often require the board of education to stamp official action on these matters, a step at which a conscientious board often balks without firsthand knowledge. The legislative and executive functions do not always lend themselves to simple delimination; but with competent persons in both offices, a school system will be more successfully managed, as the two forces continuously seek to find and respect the line of separation.

(2) *Written policies of the governing body are essential for establishing the direction of executive effort.*

A board of education policy may be defined as a brief statement of belief about the purpose of an educational matter. It tells what citizens of the district want insofar as the board members are able to interpret those wants. Philosophically worded, the policy answers why certain actions should be taken in the school system; it seldom discusses the means or executors for the actions. The administration decides these latter concerns and expresses them in the set of administrative rules and regulations compiled by the superintendent and his staff. The policy directs the executive officer, but does not supply a map. Without the policy, however, the superintendent and staff would not even know where to aim their efforts; nor would the board be able to evaluate progress of its professional personnel. The difference between a policy and an administrative rule spotlights the difference between the legislative function and the executive function.

Every board of education has at least unwritten policies in effect. As a board reflects upon a problem and comes to a decision it has made policy. However, not all decisions of a board constitute policy. The majority of decisions made at a typical board of education meeting are routine, official sanctions: the members "decide" to hire a teacher; they "decide" to award a contract to the lowest bidder; they "decide" not to rent the gymnasium for a community dinner. These are official actions influenced by previously determined policies. In these illustrations, the board should have already adopted policies reflecting their beliefs about the type of teachers for the school system, about the competitive bidding system for conducting public business, and about the proper use of publicly owned school facilities. Most monthly decisions which the board must make become much easier as the members merely weigh the current action against their previous philosophical stands.

Policy is often confused with practice. In loose usage, an administrator may say, "We have a policy against employing teachers with less than a bachelor's degree," or "we have a policy of always granting contracts to the lowest bidder," or "we have a policy against allowing food to be served in the gymnasium." Correctly, it should be said that the *practice* of employing less-than-degreed teachers does not measure up to board policy which expresses the belief that well-qualified teachers will be more effective in the classroom, that the *practice* of awarding contracts to the lowest bidder is consistent with the board's belief that the interests of the public are served better when the lowest of competing bids is given primacy in contracting for work to be done in a public school, and that the *practice* of serving food in the gymnasium is not compatible with the policy that gymnasiums are needed in an educational institution for the physical and recreational development of youth.

A policy may be formed suddenly as a board of education faces and decides on a new issue. However, best policies are formulated at a time of deliberative reflection, not imminent pressure. New situations demanding new policies will arise; conditions will change so that revision of existing policies is necessary. The policies should be written into the published handbook to facilitate continuity, progress, and consistency.

(3) *Administrative personnel do not attain effectiveness without delegated decision-making authority.*

As the need for additional administrators increases with the physical growth of the school system, the superintendent can easily define a job and assign its performance to a subordinate administrator. Much more difficult is releasing the power to make and carry out decisions. A conscientious administrator worries that another's performance may be less satisfactory than his own. An insecure administrator fears a loss of prestige if the performance surpasses his own. An unsophisticated administrator believes his executive image will fade. An authoritarian administrator disallows the freedom necessary for another's performance. An egoistic administrator distrusts others' decisions. A suspicious administrator frets about empire building among his subordinates. An untrained administrator may fail to recognize the need for assistants, to visualize the interrelation of working administrative units.

Delegation of duties without authority to decide and perform is an empty gesture which evades the purpose of employing subordinates. A subordinate officer who lacks the authority to carry out his own decisions will never mature into the responsible assistant needed in a growing school system. Every budding administrator requires the growth which comes from rising or falling on his own decisions. The chief administrator is extravagant with taxpayers' money if he overprotects his decision-making authority and thereby fails to perform his expected coordinating and evaluating functions. Furthermore, failure to delegate authority to others destroys human dignity.

(4) *Job descriptions for all administrative and specialist personnel contribute to individual and unit efficiency.*

The first step toward achieving proper delegation is analyzing jobs according to the system's plan for division of labor, writing the analysis, and then disseminating the descriptions among all personnel in the organization. This step alone will not, of course, assure the second step of actual delegation; but the second step cannot be taken until each officer understands fully what is expected of him. Job analysis will also pinpoint the voids and overlaps of duties. These forms permit long-range planning of work schedules, and prevent the daily assignment of chores which are characteristic of an "Assistant To . . ." title, almost approaching the position of General's Aide. Without the job analysis which prescribes both the expectations and limits of one's authority, there is no equitable measure for evaluating performance. Nor can there be accountabilities without written job descriptions. At the same time, the description must avoid restricting an officer to the degree that he cannot use discretion and initiative when the occasion warrants.

Every administrative and specialist position in a school organization lends itself to written analysis, including the superintendent and building principal. Most of the non-teaching jobs — clerks, custodians, food service workers, maintenance employees, and bus drivers — can and should be described; only the classroom teacher's position cannot. What happens between teacher and pupils in the mystical process of learning is too intangible for job definition. Moreover, holding a teacher to a rigid classroom work schedule would be antithetical to good learning. Nonetheless, a list of expected non-teaching duties as found in the typical school handbook is useful in the orientation of a new teacher and as a reminder to experienced teachers.

(5) *The control and efficiency of corporate bodies demands single accountability for all members.*

The plan of single administrative authority with just one officer reporting to the governing body is known as *unit* control as opposed to *dual* or *multiple* control which provides for two or more chief administrators reporting directly to the board of education. The dual control system contains many weaknesses. An arrangement of more than one accountable officer for the organization invites inefficiency, and denies the operation of a crucial administrative principle — single accountability of all personnel. It is especially crippling in those dual-headed school systems in which one administrator is held accountable for the total success of the enterprise; the other handles fiscal affairs. A superintendent of schools cannot logically be held responsible for the educational attainments of the organization if he does not have decision-making authority over the allocation of funds, subject only to the final authority of the governing body. Finally, the dual-administrative control plan tends to direct a disproportionate share of the district's available funds toward non-educational operations. This fact is clear from an analysis of Furno's annual survey of how districts secure and spend their moneys.[1]

No other organizations in society attempt to function under other than unit control except about one-fourth of the nation's public school districts. Statistical reports on the number are misleading in view of the modified multiple control arrangements in many other districts. The confusion arises from the state laws which require the appointment of a fiscal officer for each board of education, accountable directly to the board. In spelling out the functions of this officer, the laws of some states (especially Pennsylvania and New Jersey) virtually mandate dual control by insisting that the secretary discharge the fiscal affairs of the district. In all states the secretary is the "Board's officer," and many boards have not yet required that he function through the superintendent in handling and reporting funds. In other districts, an able secretary has often been assigned certain executive responsibilities regarding fiscal administration. Furthermore, when boards of education have desired unit control and have clarified the roles of superintendent and secretary through job definitions, the superintendent of the past has often lacked adequate preparation for managing fiscal affairs.

The principle of single accountability applies with equal force within the organization. Not only should the superintendent be charged with responsibility for all tasks and personnel within the school district but also the building principal should be held responsible for all tasks and personnel within his unit. This principle offers few problems in small districts; it becomes complicated to enforce in large districts, as the administrative tasks are allocated to specialized officers in the central office. Central staff officers perform a portion of the superintendent's

---

[1]*School Management,* January, 1960-1964.

task, and in his name; their assignments often bring them in direct association with affairs within a principal's building. At this point, unless the jobs are carefully defined, the relationships between central staff officers and building principals may become confused or strained under the principle of single accountability. The most successful job descriptions state that the central staff officer is responsible for a function throughout the school district, but that the building principal is responsible for all functions and personnel within his jurisdiction. The central officer becomes a *staff*, or *advisory*, officer as he works with a principal, who is called a *line* or *authority* officer.

Schools do not always distinguish between an advisory officer and an authority officer. At some time all administrators are in a line position; similarly, each one is sometimes a staff officer. The adjectives are relative, depending upon the task to be performed and the persons involved. Nevertheless, the principle of single accountability promotes the greatest degree of efficiency. It applies to each employee, who needs to know where authority lies. Division of authority and accountability at any level of the organization introduces delays, indecision, and irresponsibility. Single accountability for all members of an institution is crucial for control in large organizations.

(6) *Vertical, or functional, organization permits specialization, and more skilled performance.*

The growth of large organizations, both private and public, necessitates a division of labor in administration. Growing enterprises of the 19th century were inclined toward a horizontal division of labor, *viz,* a vice-president would be assigned the responsibility over all separate tasks for a segment of the corporation. In city schools, as an example, the total administrative job was divided among assistant superintendents, one for elementary and one for secondary schools, each officer having responsibility for all the administrative tasks — instruction, business, and pupil accounting — within his jurisdiction. Scientific management studies at the turn of the century proved that a division of labor by function would permit greater specialization, thus greater effectiveness in performance. As private corporations then divided administrative tasks vertically by function — for production, or sales, or finance — larger school systems adapted the plan to educational organizations. Thus, the trend turned toward functional organization, with vertical responsibility throughout the school system, kindergarten through the twelfth grade, for the specialized tasks of instruction, finance, personnel, pupil personnel, or public relations.

Vertical organization possesses additional strengths for education, especially in the administration of curricular matters. It encourages a greater articulation of learning from kindergarten through to high school graduation, and it reduces the lateral compartmentalization which tends to develop under the American ladder system of education. It also prevents one level of the system from suffering through the neglect of an ineffective leader.

On the other hand, vertical organization increases the need for top level coordination of the various specialized functionaries in order to balance the emphasis in the total program. Otherwise, an over-zealous administrator may distort the worth of his specialized function.

(7) *Since administration accomplishes its mission through intermediaries, its effectiveness depends upon a highly developed system of communication.*

Administration, by definition, is removed from the basic task of the organization — in the instance of a school organization, teaching. A school administrator ceases to be an administrator when he is occasionally assigned to classroom teaching. This separation from the "production line" is the most difficult part of learning for an administrator; it also explains why many good classroom teachers cannot become equally able administrators. A vast difference lies between teaching children well and getting others to teach children equally well. The difference signifies the importance of the administrator's resources for stimulation. Unfortunately, there is no single approach to personnel motivation. In order to accomplish goals through others, the administrator as much as the classroom teacher must recognize the implications of individual differences.

The larger the organization, the more layers of intermediaries necessarily appear, and the more dependent the administrator becomes on secondary sources of information. While the top administrator may visit the front lines occasionally, and sincerely try to meet directly with teachers, he must make most of his decisions from reports of intermediaries. Similarly, intermediaries relay his messages to teachers.

These conditions call for a skill often overlooked in the selection of administrators — the ability to communicate thought via spoken and written media. Unfortunately, prospective administrators rarely receive preparatory training for developing this skill. The kind of abbreviated but pungent messages needed by a top administrator from his subordinates are quite different from the typical writing habits developed in college.

The need for building into the organization a system for deliberate exchange of information is immediately apparent. It is so important that all of Chapter VIII is devoted to this problem. Only summary points are made here to support the principle. Representative committees facilitate communication. Carefully planned and worded communiques to all elements of the district are essential for reducing the rumors and suspicions which arise from inadequate information. Rarely should it be necessary for any employee of the district to have to read about a major board decision first in the community newspaper. Some administrators in city districts make valuable use of closed circuit television and radio for internal communication.

A plan for lateral communication between the various parallel units of the organization is also necessary; between teachers, between non-certificated employees, between principals, and between central staff administrators. Meetings, written communications, in-service programs, and informal gatherings all help toward achieving lateral communication.

Communication with the patrons of the district is still another facet of this crucial task.

Another is committee operation. Most of society's work is accomplished today through groups. The conference method is especially prominent in educational tasks. The school administrator needs to master all that psychology and group dynamics have to offer for group functioning.

(8) *The best plan of administrative organization, as well as the operation of the plan, is consistent with the organizational aims.*

The major responsibility for training youngsters to understand the functioning of our national philosophy of democratic operations has been turned over to educational institutions. Nearly all public schools have accepted this responsibility as stated in their respective aims of education. Classroom teachers carry the burden of this responsibility in all of their relationships with youth, and most teachers recognize that the best learning takes place under the methodology of "learning by doing." Children must learn first-hand the virtues and the responsibilities which accrue from the democratic process. They have a right to experience the strength which emerges from cooperative endeavors as well as the penalties which result from poor individual or group judgments.

Since teachers are expected to provide these experiences by building a climate for democratic operations, it is reasonable that they would expect to work in such an environment. It is illogical, probably impossible, to ask teachers to develop democratic concepts with children if teachers are forced to live in an autocratic organization. The responsibility for developing democratic understandings, therefore, originates at the top administrative level. The structure as well as the daily operations must be attuned to the democratic philosophy.

The attainment of democratic administrative operations lies largely outside of the organizational structuring. It exists in the intangible realms of attitudes and social interactions. An administrator who subscribes to the spirit of the Golden Rule has little trouble in achieving democratic relations with colleagues. He need only respect the ideas and rights of others with a genuine understanding for human frailties. Hence, the small school which permits frequent face-to-face relationships has an advantage over the large school district, if the administrators are inclined toward democratic procedures. Larger school districts may be forced to build compensating elements into their administrative organizations. A good system of internal communication will facilitate the attainment of proper attitudes; but even this is not enough. The greater the distance between the classroom and the highest administrative level, the more likely will develop labor-management tendencies. Decentralization of decision-making authority through proper delegation and structures which permit face-to-face relationships can shorten the distance.

The various types of advisory councils for the superintendent serve well the aims of communication and democratic operation. Some councils include representatives from all segments of the school system; others may be constituted from only one segment at a time, such as classroom teachers, or principals, or the administrative staff, or perhaps levels of teachers in the very largest districts. Every person in the organization needs the satisfaction which comes from knowing that he has a voice heard at the top, that he has the opportunity for influencing the decisions made about his working environment, and his voice will be heard without fear of retribution. This is the guarantee of a democratic form of government; one's working life should offer no less. One would expect that the voice go all the way to the board of education only when it appears that the highest professional officer is misrepresenting employees to the governing body.

The recommendation for democratic operations by school administrators does not imply that an individual's rights as a citizen in a democratic society are identical to his rights as a member of an organization within that society. The legal prescriptions for a public school system cannot be ignored. The superintendent, for example, may be legally bound for his accountability as head of the organization. The board of education will also hold him accountable. The practice of group decision-making and delegation of authority does not relieve the superintendent of his accountability for whatever is decided and done by members of the organization. Therefore, there are occasions when the highest administrator must veto the recommendations of members — when no better decision will be arrived at through mass participation, when consulting with the members will serve no purpose. This does not entail a conflict with democratic functioning; rather, it is a recognition of the responsibility which people of a democratic government bestow upon their chosen officers.

FURTHER GUIDES FOR DECISION-MAKING

Researchers concerned with improving executive action give much attention to the uncertain origins of sound decisions. The current efforts of a research team at Catholic University of America and ACF Electronics to discover why some people make good decisions and others bad decisions would be a most valuable behavioral discovery of civilization. Those eager to learn this secret would include not only executives but also statesmen, marriage counselors, politicians, brokers, and bookies. The answer would remove all risk, and possibly all fun, from living. At the present writing, the research team's main findings reveal that intelligent people make better decisions more often than unintelligent people, but that the intelligent are no more sure they have made the right decision. Flash decisions are correct less often than deliberative decisions. The team also reported that in their sampling of undergraduate students, future scientists were no more successful than future businessmen at making correct decisions. In short, there remains considerable doubt that humans can master the art of making right decisions. And yet, observation reveals that some executives consistently make a higher percent of correct decisions than others. There must be an explanation.

Some of the complexities of school administrative decisions can be reduced when one recognizes that all decisions are not equally intense or urgent; decisions differ. The primary variance among decisions for the present consideration is in the formulation process. Typical decisions which the school administrator must make can be classified into three categories.

Routine decisions are perhaps the most frequent type made by the administrator. They are of low priority and require little thought. Typical of such decisions are the choice of bid from a list of competitive submissions, setting dates for school events, determining the annual calendar, or planning the bus routes. In fact, the administrator makes dozens of routine decisions daily, as he settles upon the priority of tasks to which he will next give his attention. These decisions scarcely deserve study. They require only specific tools of experience and knowledge, and little research or reflection.

Another common kind of decision made by school administrators may be classified as the emergency decision. A teacher telephones to inform the administrator that he is ill and cannot come to school until noon; a bus breaks down; two students start a scuffle in the corridor; a water line to the school bursts; a torrential rain appears just before school closes. The experienced administrator is familiar with the scores of such emergencies which occur during the year and he takes them in stride. Electrifying as they may be at the moment, the decision for action is made quickly, without strenuous thought. The responsible officer soon appraises the situation, sifts the promising alternatives which have been employed previously in similar emergencies, selects the proper solution, and acts. Again, specific experience and knowledge are the only tools necessary for making the decision.

The third kind of decision causes the most anxiety, in practice and in the minds of those who study the process. The problem-solving type of decision deals with the important elements of educational progress. It is unfortunate that research has not carried us beyond the five basic steps of the decision-making process. Fortunately, within those five logical steps lie the means for quality decisions. They are cited here as the most reliable approach:

1. Define the problem. The correct decision may be missed by focusing on the problem's symptoms or efforts.

2. Gather data which concerns the problem. At this point the administrator's knowledge of research techniques pays dividends. Investigate all reasonable sources of information.

3. Formulate hypotheses among the most likely solutions.

4. Test the hypotheses.

5. Select the best probable solution.

Some authorities list two other steps of the process: put the probable solution into action and then evaluate it. These steps are, of course, essential, but the decision has actually been made with step five. It is vital at this juncture, both for the morale of staff and for their future participation in decision-making, that the time lapse between the decision and its activation be minimized.

THE AIM OF LEARNING

The basic aim of an educational institution is, of course, learning. Therefore, the plan of organization should promote optimal learning for all its clientele. This apparently obvious ideal can become difficult to attain in large school organizations. Several objectives tend to nullify each other. In trying to serve teachers quickly and to satisfy the growing demands of citizens, enough administrative assistants must be employed for the challenge. However, the number itself may become cumbersome and inefficient. If the chief school administrator desires to keep the distance between himself and the teachers to a minimum he may build an organization too flat for his supervisory talents. Studies of administrative organization in industry have produced rough gauges which say that an executive can normally have no more than six to eight subordinate officers reporting directly to him. Beyond that point he deprives his subordinates of efficient help and endangers his own physical health. As he reorganizes the staff to maintain a reasonable supervisory span he may build a structure so tall that effective communication between the superintendent and the classroom breaks down.

Since administration exists only for servicing the teachers' needs in the classroom, the pyramidal layering of intermediate officers must be planned to permit communication, efficient response to problems of the classroom, accountability, avoidance of duplication as well as neglect through omission, and the preservation of physical and emotional well-being. The optimal arrangement will be found through a structure which approximates an equilateral triangle, through well defined job descriptions, a deliberate system of communication, and delegation of authority.

(9) *Administration recognizes and utilizes power to achieve unit goals.*

Power is not an ugly word, except when used maliciously, when employed for the wrong goals, and when coveted. Power is merely the impelling force by which goals are reached. It exists in all human endeavors, wherever people associate. It is sometimes obvious, sometimes hidden; in some groups the members are unaware of its presence until an occasion brings it to the surface. In some groups the power is relatively permanent; in others it is transitory according to the current issue. Power may be designated or casual.

We say that work gets done through an organization, and therefore a systematized structure is designed to facilitate the accomplishment of work. This is referred to as the formal organization, portrayed in a corporation's organization chart. Power flows from the top to the lowest echelon shown on the chart, normally. The organization supplies the channels through which people transmit power to lower segments of the unit. The very thought of such a formidable plan repels the sensitivity of some people who are imbued with the morality of a more popular slogan that all men are created equal. Actually, whatever equality is involved in creation has little to do with the organization of a corporate body for pursuing a mission. The stratification of people within the unit need not reflect upon the ability or dignity of a person whose name appears on the bottom row of the organization chart. This is especially so in an educational institution where its *raison d'etre* is accomplished by teachers. In many instances, the power of the unit may flow upwards. A perceptive superintendent will encourage this direction of power flow as often as possible, consistent with his responsibility and control of the enterprise. A clever administrator may at least permit the illusion that power originates at the bottom. Nonetheless, provision must be made in any responsible group for putting power to work to reach goals — the formal organization.

Lately the attention of several writers and researchers has been focused on another phenomenon which develops in nearly any group. It has been labeled the "informal organization." Its members may or may not have any official designation in the formal organization, but it is the natural coalescence of members with a common interest or cause. In a school system it may consist of older teachers, or a number of high school teachers, or those affiliated with a specific subject field, or principals, or possibly a cross-section of the entire system who rally around a cause. The informal organization may be easily identified; it may escape detection until challenged. It is difficult to assess the strength of the informal organization, but studies indicate that its influence must be reckoned with.

It is a concern of the administrator because it is another power. He has several alternative approaches to dealing with it. He can ignore it, perhaps hoping that it will go away or that his aloofness will weaken its power. This approach may work; however, it may produce a silent defiance or a subverting compliance with the official organization's power. A naive denial of its existence may surprise the administrator when he seeks mass cooperation for a goal. The administrator may face the informal organization directly, hoping for a showdown, possibly expecting that a combat will bring the unseen force into the open, and, hopefully defeat it. That strategy may work; however, it may merely drive the power temporarily underground as it flees for anonymity, biding time until its power is revived. The administrator may choose to sanction the informal organization, perhaps moving its leaders into an official position of the formal organization. That, too, may work, until another cause or other leaders rise to "take over" the informal organization. The administrator may try to infiltrate the informal structure, seeking to anticipate its moves and either blockading, diverting, or antedating its objectives.

Any or none of these strategems may be effective. There is only one certainty. The informal organization will not disappear. Its existence is as natural as grouping. The most probable course of action for the leader, therefore, is to recognize its existence and its power, and use them for the unit's total good. An informal organization can be used as an excellent sounding board for new ideas. A trial balloon released in its midst may forecast accurately the likelihood of its acceptance by the entire staff. A deliberate plan of communication built outside the normal organizational channels, as advocated often herein, encourages the unseen powers and unheard voices to come forward without fear of retribution, and thereby minimizes the incentive for a festering "secret" organization. It permits face-to-face communication, which is the most important of all communicating devices. To be sure, the power phenomenon will be evident in these sessions, as it appears in all meetings, but at least the administrator has better than a fifty-fifty chance of "winning the conference" because of the power emanating from his formal position.

The workings of power have been the object of extensive study by scholars of administration and organization in recent years; the administrator will profit from absorbing all that is known about it. The chief executive of a public body has still another, and perhaps more serious, power structure to be reckoned with in the community and state. Studies of the powers of a community — industrial giants or a coalition of a number of lesser business interests, realtors, labor groups, church bodies, women's clubs, sports fans, service clubs — prove revealing to the superintendent inclined to believe that important educational decisions are made by the board of education or by the faculty. If nothing else has persuaded the public school administrator to leave his ivory tower, an analysis of the behind-the-scenes influences on public education will. Some writers are urging that for the benefit of education, educators must become involved even in the power of partisan politics. It is certain that in view of the state's complete authority over public education, the administrator cannot merely hope that legislators will do right by their responsibility. The influence of persons friendly to education at the national level has yet to be investigated.

The important lesson for the administrator in this scanty discussion of a major problem is that if he is serious about doing good things for education he must recognize the existence of such powers in every communal group, identify and assess their strengths, and seek to capitalize upon them for the benefit of youth. The chief school administrator is in a position to be the most influential power of the community, but the mere holding of the position will not do it alone.

(10) *Organization is a means to an end.*

While the administrative structure for a school system, or any organization, should be built with these tested principles in mind, caution should be exerted to avoid worshipping any organization style. Organization is not the goal of administrative effort, merely the tool for accomplishing the goal in an orderly manner. Yet organization will not accomplish the goal; goals are realized only by human beings. It may be necessary to modify principles and organization in terms of the people available for fitting into the scheme, in accordance with differences of time and place. All school districts are alike, but each has its peculiarities. The school administrative organization should bend in deference to the unique problems and demands of its community. No organizational plan should be allowed to become so absolute that it cannot adjust to changing demands.

To be sure, all corporations are learning quickly that their structures should foster change today in face of competition. An educational corporation should undoubtedly be in the forefront of change. Social organizations, including schools, have traditionally remained behind innovations in processes and thinking. There are defensible arguments today that an organization for learning should not only change its methodology and goals with the presentation of valid reasons for change, but, it should also be developing in youth a receptiveness to change. This plan cannot be left to chance; schools need to gear for change. One must witness the late research under the nomenclature of "planned change." The concept pertains here to the scheme of administrative organization of a school unit. There can be "over-organization" which becomes so rigid as to discourage innovation in procedures and objectives. Admittedly, stability and continuity are needed in any enterprise. Organization can provide both; over-organization can freeze its people to the status quo.

An inflexible organization can also stifle that precious quality in a good teacher — creativity. It can also become so formidable as to discourage self-criticism. It can lull professional people into complacency.

Schools are still confronted with an extremely difficult problem with which they have always been plagued. There is no valid and widely accepted method for evaluating their efficiency of production. How can one judge progress in developing creative, constructively critical, thinking, or moral youth? Even if students are followed years after graduation in order to measure their progress it is impossible to show cause and effect relationships. Consequently, educators and citizens are prone to evaluate a school's success in terms of what they can see: recall of factual knowledge as indicated by achievement tests, numbers of failures, dropouts, diplomas granted, or scholarships won, the appearance of buildings and grounds, balanced budgets, or tax rates. When is an administrative organization working efficiently? One cannot be sure in terms of its ends.

This author will venture the opinion, based upon observation and experience, that most large school systems err as frequently on the side of over-organization as they do on under-organization. Despite the urging herein that school systems need to have written policies, job descriptions, published rules and procedures, and adherence to principles of administrative organization, informal arrangements for staff members are probably more conducive to the ends of an educational institution. The small school system where the chief administrator sees teachers, custodians, or bus drivers daily clearly has an advantage in communications, in the potential for good human relations, in control over operations, and in readiness to meet demands for change. Since the future will see fewer and fewer small school districts, however, the challenge to administrators is to find the organizational plan which serves best the various ends of education.

THE NATURE AND USE OF AUTHORITY . . .

FOUR MAJOR CONCEPTS OF AUTHORITY*

"Authority" has not enjoyed the conceptual unanimity, as four distinct emphases in its study illustrate. These emphases may be designated as the traditional, the functional, the behavioral, and the integrative . . .

1. The *traditional* concept of authority is reflected, for example, in Schell's observation that: "If we are to control, we must provide avenues through which it can function easily and directly. These avenues we speak of as paths of authority. They pass from administrators who determine policy, to the executives who are responsible for the performance of the policy, and then to the employees who perform the actual operations." Proponents of this point of view are numerous, although there are serious difficulties with its formulation.

2. The *functional* concept provides a real alternative to the "trickle down" traditional concept of authority by denying that the chief executive of an organization has a legitimate monopoly of authority which he may parcel out to subordinates. Proponents of the functional approach thus find authority only in the particular job to be done. Authority, there-

---

*Robert T. Golembiewski, "Authority as a Problem in Overlays: A Concept for Action and Analysis," *Administrative Science Quarterly,* IX, No. 1, June, 1964, 23, 48-49, by permission of A.S.Q. and Robert T. Golembiewski.

fore, is sharply limited and is certainly not monopolized by anyone. As Follett explained: "I do not think that a president should have any more authority than goes with his function. . . . Authority belongs to the job and stays with the job." More contemporary statements of this point of view are likely to put matters in less personal terms than did Follett. Such a formulation might note that authority increasingly inheres in "the situation," and individuals as commonly respond to its demands as to an order of some formal superior. The various formulations of the functional concept, however, all imply a concept of authority as "bubbling up" from work.

3. The *behavioral* concept of authority stands somewhat apart. It seeks its data in neither legitimacy nor function but only in the actual patterns of the behavior of individuals as they influence others and are being influenced. Simon is perhaps the foremost contemporary commentator of this persuasion, acknowledgedly relying on Barnard's earlier argument that:

> Authority is the character of a communication (order) in a formal organization *by virtue of which it is accepted* by a contributor to or "member" of the organization as governing the action he contributes. . . . Therefore, under this definition the decision as to whether an order has authority or not lies with the persons to whom it is addressed, and does not reside in "persons of authority" or those who issue these orders.

In standing apart as it does, however, the behavioral concept still bears a significant relation to the other concepts. Function often will help determine who influences whom. Moreover, the behavioral concept is basically a strong reaction against the traditional concept.

4. An *integrative* concept, finally, includes all three emphases above under one conceptual tent. Fayol may be taken to represent this approach. He explained that: "Authority is the right to give orders and the power to exact obedience. Distinction must be made between a manager's official authority deriving from office and personal authority, compounded of intelligence, experience, moral worth, ability to lead, past services, and so forth. . . . [personal authority] is the indispensable complement of official authority."

The integrative bias is apparent. For "official authority" has a meaning congenial to the traditional concept; "personal authority" overlaps significantly with the behavioral concept; and a significant measure of one's personal authority will derive from one's function and the style with which it is performed.

HAMILTON'S CONCEPT OF POWER
AND ITS USE*

The nation's first dominating administrator, Hamilton possessed the qualities most needful to his role. His powers of intuition, imagination, and insight were the mental tools indispensable to forecasting policy and planning for execution. His sense of order and logic was the essence of his ability to organize. He could co-ordinate policy with procedure — he understood relationships. The dissection and the construction of ideas were so natural to him as to seem involuntary. His disposition to command, added to his extraordinary energy and intelligence, made him a natural leader among men, and he was said to have regarded himself as "prime minister" of the Washington administration. John Adams, speaking of his own administration, confessed that Hamilton was "commander-in-chief of the House of Representatives, of the Senate, of the heads of department, of General Washington, and last and least if you will, of the President of the United States." Never could such an administrator be confined within a single portfolio; his was ever the directing mind, the pervasive, commanding influence. With these intellectual powers was combined a detachment resulting perhaps from his alien place of birth but certainly reinforced by his executive disposition.

Hamilton possessed the patience, the perseverance, and the persuasiveness necessary to direct the actions of others, yet the art of managing men was the least of his executive talents. Overborne by his feeling for command, the manipulative-conciliatory qualities which he demonstrated on certain notable occasions failed to achieve full growth. The defect was injurious to his political efforts, for he never fully understood the necessity of popular leadership as the focus for the congealing of national feeling which he hoped to bring about. Although he seldom failed to appreciate the degree to which control is bottomed on consent, he never understood that popular consent does not automatically respond to wise and honest administration. He did not see that to convince the most enlightened strata of the population was insufficient. The consent of the uninformed and misinformed had also to be won. The necessity for securing consent in order to control irked his impulse to command, and that the statesman must find his sanctions in the predilections of the uneducated and illiberal mass of the people seemed contrary to nature

---

*Reprinted from *The Administrative Theories of Hamilton and Jefferson*, by Lynton K. Caldwell, Chicago: by permission of The University of Chicago Press, 1944, 6-7, 26-30, 100-101.

and reason. It was this unwillingness to go to the people that afforded substance for the contention that Hamilton was antirepublican. . . .

The Hamiltonian principle of unity may be developed in deductive form: energy, the essence of good administration, implies effective action; action to be effective must have direction; unity of action insures specific direction and provides the outlet for executive energy. But unity of action cannot be obtained without a unity of command. This unity of command is probable only where there is a single commander for plural commanders tend to disunity. However, if a commander is to execute a unified policy, he must have a unified organization through which to operate. Hence, the unity principle calls for a government in which lines of authority and responsibility are well defined and unimpeded. Thus Hamilton tended to favor a centralized as opposed to a decentralized federal state and did not value highly the contributions of the town meeting and the county court to the energy of government. For he felt that the best safeguard to the people's liberty was not in independent local administrations, potentially obstructive but otherwise ineffective as to national purpose, but in the clear and unmistakable responsibility of a unified national government and unitary executive to the whole people. . . .

"It is a general principle of human nature," declared Hamilton, "that a man will be interested in whatever he possesses, in proportion to the firmness or precariousness of tenure by which he holds it." . . .

Adequate duration of tenure was the only method by which an administration could produce desirable results. This, Hamilton declared, "is necessary to give to the officer himself the inclination and the resolution to act his part well, and to the community time and leisure to observe the tendency of his measures, and thence to form an experimental estimate of their merits." With adequate tenure, the principle of re-eligibility for office would become beneficial, for it would permit the people when they approved his conduct to continue the administrator in office, thereby "to prolong the utility of his talents and virtues, and to secure to the government the advantage of permanency in a wise system of administration". . . .

Hamilton's theory of administrative power flows directly from his thesis that the powers of a government must be adequate to the ends for which it was instituted. . . . . Where these can properly be confided, he held that the coincident powers might safely accompany them. He thought it absurd to confer upon government responsibility for the most essential national interests, without daring to intrust it with the authority indispensable to their proper and efficient management. To the administrator charged with the energetic promotion of the public good as defined by the Constitution and the statutes of the Republic, want of adequate powers would condemn him to fail in his responsibility or to exceed his trust. He could only choose whether to be figurehead or usurper. Either alternative Hamilton saw as destructive to constitutional government. Only a powerful executive could be responsible for the promotion of great interests. Those who, fearing despotism, would bind the executive power by rules and regulations designed to limit and retard the responsible exercise of authority, were inviting the disaster which they sought to prevent. For an ambitious executive with popular support would ultimately demand a free hand to act in pursuit of the public good and, overriding the restrictions prescribed on parchment, would establish a personal rule which would complete the destruction of responsible government.

Of importance equal to competent powers was provision for the adequate financial support of executive authority. Hamilton saw that, without a basis for compensation protected from legislative manipulation, the independence of the executive branch would be merely nominal. . . .

The responsibility of administrators Hamilton understood as twofold in character. "Due dependence on the people" implied conformity to the legal requirements of office, including accountability to the people through their representatives. The other and more characteristically Hamiltonian notion of responsibility was that each administrator must be prepared to act according to the public need to accomplish fully and effectively the tasks which lay within the province of his office. This might require an officer to undertake more than his enumerated duties required. It implied that expansive interpretation of the administrative function which Hamilton's Treasury career came to exemplify. But administrators were not, in Hamilton's thinking, empowered themselves to constitute the law. Where administrators exceeded their powers without regard to their responsibilities, the sanctions of censure and punishment awaited. . . .

One method of preventing the evasion of administrative responsibility was by clearly separating the executive branch from the other great divisions of government. Hamilton feared particularly the encroachment of the legislature upon the executive, believing not only that the power and energy of the executive would be thereby weakened but that he would be rendered irresponsible. Controlled by the legislature, the executive would merely be its tool and could not be held personally accountable for administrative policy. Should the executive power over-awe the legislative, an equally pernicious irresponsibility would obtain. . . .

The safest guaranty of responsible conduct, however, was the ultimate dependence of the executive upon the people. . . . Responsibility, he believed, demanded powers adequate to the fulfilment of the tasks imposed upon the executive.

In summary, then, one may distinguish five major principles which Hamilton believed to be the indispensable components of good administration. Briefly they were: energy, unity, duration, power, and responsibility. Derived from his interpretation of social psychology and his theory of constitutional government, they appear singly or in combination in each of his proposals concerning the structure and function of the federal administrative system. . . .

Alexander Hamilton remains the nation's foremost advocate of "responsible" administration. . . . He did not fear the power of government so long as it was "responsible" power. No great purpose, he believed, could be accomplished by a government inflexibly restrained by checks and divided into mutually exclusive branches. Energy, unity, power, and duration, the inescapable requisites of good government, were intrusted only to a government so constituted that its responsibility to the people was clear and undivided, and Hamilton feared that the Constitution of 1789, with its checks, balances, and divided responsibility, would never be able to provide the nation with a responsible government. . . .

But it was the danger of an executive-legislative deadlock that rendered the American government potentially irresponsible, for a break in the reciprocal co-operation of the President and the Congress paralyzed authority and divided responsibility. Partially responsible agents, Hamilton understood to be potentially, if not actually, irresponsible. This weakness of the national government remains, as indicated by Hamilton, a major administrative and constitutional problem. It was Hamilton's great contribution to thought on administration that he forsaw the problem in the Constitutional Convention; that he labored to solve it under the adopted Constitution; and that, in so doing, he defined for future generations the issue of "responsible" government and marked out conditions necessary to its attainment.

JEFFERSON'S CONCEPT OF ADMINISTRATIVE AUTHORITY*

Although harmonious co-operation has ever been an objective of administration, not often has it been raised to a principle governing administrative policy. Harmony more often has been a means by which the ends of administration were to be effected rather than an end in

*Reprinted from *Administrative Theories of Hamilton and Jefferson*, by Lynton K. Caldwell. Chicago: by permission of The University of Chicago Press, 1944, 130, 133-136, 138.

itself. With Jefferson, however, harmony was both end and means; it was a principle by which some of his most significant administrative decisions were guided. . . .

Simplicity in the administration of public affairs was a first principle with Jefferson. Believing that public functionaries readily seized upon the opportunities of public office for aggrandizement of power, prestige, and fortune, he proposed to reduce to the minimum the occasions for public corruption. He did not encourage any but the ablest men to seek public appointment; he favored low wages and short terms and the abolition of offices wherever possible. Civic duty rather than rewards of money or power should be the incentives for a public career. In part, Jefferson's insistence that public administration be reduced to the simplest possible form reflected a belief that the administration of public affairs was in fact a simple matter. There are not mysteries in public administration, he declared. . . .

Jefferson did not believe that permanent political or administrative arrangements could be or ought to be possible. Each generation had, in his opinion, the right to form its political arrangements to its own liking. Thus precedent and tradition were discounted, and fixed statutory, economic, or constitutional arrangements deemed contrary to the natural rights of men. These natural rights alone were permanent — political methods and institutions were merely temporary arrangements which men should be free to alter with time and experience.

Jefferson's insistence upon the adaptation of institutions to circumstances indicated a pragmatic approach to problems of administrative organization. . . .

Of the foregoing principles which governed Jefferson's administrative thought, none could truthfully be said to have fundamentally altered the course of administrative development in American government. Harmony, simplicity, adaptability — all strongly marked Jefferson's thinking on administrative problems, but they represented personal predilections for administrative arrangements rather than a coherent and systematic theory of administration. In effect the principle of decentralization differed sharply from the others. It, indeed, reflected a personal preference for local control of political affairs and evidenced a highly subjective distrust of professionalized administration and complex administrative machinery, but it was a principle capable of being expressed in objective terms, susceptible of concrete application in constitutions and statutes and in the platforms of political parties. . . .

By a decentralization of duties he held that every citizen personally might partake in the administration of public affairs, thus insuring the maximum degree of republicanism in government. Accordingly, he held it an axiom that good administration would provide for the greatest degree of decentralization possible to the successful execution of public policy. To those who asserted that decentralization of authority would weaken the federal Union, Jefferson declared "that government to be the strongest of which every man feels himself a part." To Jefferson only a decentralized government could be free, and "a free government," he declared, "is of all others the most energetic." . . . Jeffersonian responsibility was essentially an effort to insure the accountability of public servants to the public and yet to provide for the exercise of the judgment and initiative of statesmen on behalf of the public welfare. Therefore, in his definition of responsibility, Jefferson qualified the strict accountability of public officers for a literal conformity to the law with a most important exception governing the conduct of high officers of state in times of crises.

Denying that responsibility required that public officers be permitted a flexible exercise of powers under ordinary circumstances, Jefferson asked: "Is confidence or discretion, or is *strict limit,* the principle of our Constitution?" He believed that limitation was the only correct principle of responsible power; a written constitution and supplementary statutes should prescribe certain explicit duties of public officers and provide certain means for accomplishing what the law required. Responsibility, as understood by Jefferson, implied administration closely checked by legal requirements and exactions, whereas Hamilton's theory of responsibility had the opposite result of vesting top administrators with a wide latitude of discretion in ordinary as well as extraordinary circumstances.

FAILURE TO DELEGATE POWER IS INDICATION OF INSECURITY*

Local autonomy and delegation of authority . . . are restricted beyond organization needs and mores, and beyond that degree which would be optimum. The causes of restriction have been stated as untrained personnel, fear of subordinate error, and, most of all, ego involvement on the part of superiors. This thesis has been advanced hesitantly, because of ignorance, yet with conviction derived from observation of executive behavior. From this conviction has come one specification for a good

Robert H. Roy, *The Administrative Process.* Baltimore: by permission of The Johns Hopkins Press, 1958, 58-59.

administrator: possession of that degree of self-confidence and security which does not require self-aggrandizement through the constant exercise of power.

The consequences of insufficient delegation are serious: dependence of the organization upon those who hold too much power; excessive burdens upon executives of this stamp, who often cling tenaciously to routine trivia; the blockage of subordinate development; and the depressing of subordinate morale through dissatisfaction.

These effects, at least insofar as they apply to subordinates, also can derive from excessive rule making and from the punitive treatment of what are deemed to be subordinate errors in decision making. Rules are just as stultifying to local autonomy as direct orders but are more rigid and hence more likely to lead astray and to violate equity. The punitive treatment of errors, applied too often or too severely, leads only to subordinate caution and indecisiveness.

All of this analysis says much the same thing: that very many executives are prone to hang on to too many decision making prerogatives, by day-to-day behavior, by rule making, by punishing subordinates who venture to decide. The cure is to find executives who are inwardly secure, to frame rules broadly and flexibly — and sparingly, and to use subordinates' errors to educate rather than to punish.

This is a good prescription but, like telling an alcoholic not to drink, one that is hard to follow. Still, some alcoholics do stop drinking when they come to understand the source of their compulsion. Perhaps, through this modicum of understanding, some executive may cease drinking at the fount of power.

ORGANIZATION . . .

FORMAL AND INFORMAL
ORGANIZATION*

Administration exists because formal organization exists. Administrators are responsible within organization and also for organization. Understanding the requirements of organization is an appropriate concern for administrators and students of administration. It is worthwhile to consider how to tighten the structure of — or activate the circuits

---

*Van Miller, "The Informal Organization Man," *Overview,* I (May, 1960), 59-60, by permission of the *American School & University Magazine.*

within — organization in order to arrive at a clearer definition of the role of the administrator.

Three general phases can be considered: formal organization; informal organization as separate though related to formal organization; and organization — formal and informal — as a single area of human interaction.

Organization is always related to the accomplishment of a purpose. The most formal organizations accomplish the clearest and most specific purposes. They also relate the accomplishment of their purpose with their systems of control and their means of perpetuating themselves. Those with clear purposes are inclined to be strong organizations that last and increase in power or size. Such organizations are usually defended on grounds of tradition or the wisdom of the people who founded them. The rationale of their existence is in terms of accomplishment of their stated purposes.

Exclusive concern with formal organization, though useful, has never been as successful in education as in, for example, business, industry and the military. In those fields the purpose is clear. However, the breadth of purpose within any educational agency (other than the specialized school) is wide. Schools, colleges, and state departments of education are multipurpose organizations. An even more significant difference lies in the fact that the broad purpose of any educational organization is to promote change and development (in the human beings) rather than to render a service or produce a product.

A major emphasis of formal organization is on settling operation into a pattern of efficient repetition. In education, where the overall purpose is intimately related to the individual purposes of human beings, repetition becomes the enemy of change.

In the variety and number of reorganizations in education, the rationale most often given is that of establishing a final ideal structure of organization. The literature and experience of the school district reorganization movement, for example, is replete with references to the "right" size and structure.

Attention to formal organization has provided educators with much new knowledge; but it has also presented the danger of seeing organization itself as an end.

Informal organization, the second phase, exists within and around every formal organization. It can either subvert or support a formal organization.

Whereas the emphasis in formal organization is on management of material and processes — including the management of people, informal organization focuses on human relations. Since formal organizations are for specific purposes, they tend to impersonalize their staffs and produce psychic strain. Informal interaction provides catharsis or adjustment to the strain; it may also produce demands for readjustment of the formal organization. Such demands may lead to the establishment of grievance procedures or unions — organizations as formal and rigid as the one which spawned them.

Fear that informal interaction is unnecessary, wasteful, or even inimical to an organization finds expression in the regulation of communication of its members with each other and with outsiders. This is seen in extreme form in a totalitarian state. There administration is likely to pre-empt communications media and to restrict private communication and freedom of expression and assembly. By such means interaction is suppressed or driven underground.

Where informal interaction is viewed as supportive to formal organization then attention is turned to its manipulation. This has led to hidden persuasion, whispering campaigns, and advertising jingles. It has also led to administrative support of such friendly activities as college alumni organizations, PTA groups and citizens advisory committees, and reserve officers' units and their women's auxiliaries. In his responsibility for the well-being of formal organization, the administrator cannot ignore informal interaction. . . .

The third phase, unification of formal with informal organization, seems to arise readily from any attempt to clarify the distinction between the two. This is the concept that they are not really different at all, but rather that each is an aspect of human interaction. This interaction is the basic bond of all human association. It is not supplementary, hostile, or supportive to formal organization; it precedes and underlies formal organization. What is described as formal organization is not the whole of organization — it is simply those aspects with enough consistency and dependability to be recognized. Organizational arrangements are short-hand systems condensing a long sequence of prior communication so that the title superintendent of schools or college dean or department head immediately states a relationship and assignment of responsibilities.

Formal organization symbolizes more than meets the eye. It is not the new directive from the boss that gets action — this directive simply touches off a discussion of what each member intends to do about it. The response to the signal is the real organization.

The informal systems within formal organization react to formal structure. The actual operation is not the formal structure but the reaction to it of individuals conditioned by informal group interaction. It has been noted that administrative orders find their real level of effectiveness after reconstruction at the hands of every participant concerned.

Organization may be considered as highly formalized communication. It is developed through communication and uses communication to function. Interaction systems (communication) may range from formless to carefully formed in terms of their pattern and regularity. Presumably this would range from informal association of those who live in the same neighborhood or work in the same establishment to the most rigidly formal organization conceivable.

It is useful and necessary to talk in terms of formal and informal systems. The difference in direction on several dimensions is provided in the 1952 summer issue of the Autonomous Groups Bulletin. In informal systems individuals tend to view one another in interaction as persons in the full sense; in formal systems they are viewed as performers of functions. In informal systems activities tend to be ends in themselves; in formal systems they are means to ends. In informal systems expression is relatively free; in formal systems reason and emotion are channeled. In informal systems cooperation is implicit and activity is spontaneously coordinated; in formal systems cooperation is explicit and there is conscious coordination of activity.

The administrator is administrator within the formal organization — his post is non-existent without it. But when he is concerned not exclusively with formal organization but rather with both formal and informal organization as a unified field of human interaction, he may be less concerned with organization for the sake of control. He will realize that the control lies in the compatibility of the formal and the informal.

The administrative leader in public education had just as well accept and live within the informal interaction systems. He should not seek to organize or control them through his position of headship, though he may well encourage them. He can do this by providing the right space and physical arrangement of facilities, by work and time scheduling, and by his own deportment.

If he discovers the interactive informal system and then tries to reorganize the formal structure to coincide with it he will be chasing a will-o-the-wisp, for a new informal organization will grow up in reaction to the formal. But he can build a formal organization facilitating and compatible to informal interaction.

The formal system provides the frame on which the informal interaction systems can be supported. The informal systems give vitality to the formal, and provide exploration, appraisal, and the basis for change.

THE INFLUENCE OF ORGANIZATIONAL ENVIRONMENT ON TEACHER BEHAVIOR*

The assertion that the profession of school administration is still in a depressed stage of development cannot be materially challenged. The modern school administrator is the unfortunate descendent of the teaching principal, an office historically restricted to second-rate clerical duties. Though the position has matured enough to include the management of substantial financial resources, no image of the public school administrator as a dynamic educational statesman has penetrated the public consciousness. Rather, typical job descriptions for administrative positions stress skills such as proper supervision of the money flows of the school system, keeping the enterprise solvent, and maximizing services by allocating the scarce resources among the different areas which have demand on them. Public relations chores are fastened on as unavoidable appendages; since the community rarely gives a clear policy mandate, the emphasis place on external relationships tends to vary with passing, short term demands. Administrative meddling in the teaching-learning process itself, however, is not easily tolerated; "get good teachers and let them alone" is a shibboleth still held in high repute by the general public.

As a consequence, the subsequent administrative rejection of classroom supervision incites highly individualistic behavior on the part of staff members; the upshot of these independent tactics is person-oriented rather than goal-oriented conduct. For instance, within a system, one teacher may rule his domain with an "iron hand," another might be working on teacher-pupil planning, the next may have his class utterly out of control, while another might be subject-centered in approach.

In such a contingency, who provides the fundamental coordination, integration, and operational strategy? This is a key question. Since the public educational institution is a continuing enterprise and its survival is seldom at stake, isn't it entirely plausible that "keeping school" may become an end in itself? What we may commonly have is a financially

---

*Donald J. McCarty, "Organizational Influences on Teacher Behavior," taken from *American School Board Journal*, CXLIII, published by the Bruce Publishing Company, July, 1961, 13-14.

well managed operation with little attention directed to the accomplishment of its genuine objectives. Almost by default the structural character of the enterprise itself is forced to act as a sort of psychological teacher and to mold individual teacher behavior in the dominant values of the school system.

THE BOARD'S POLICY MAKING

One can argue that the board of education, through its all-absorbing policy making function, provides the energizing stimulus. This will be true to the extent that staff members really think of the overall goals of the organization, and common sense would dictate that this provision is frequently not met. Since school systems are essentially organized as bureaucracies, technical factors are apt to assume a pre-eminent position.

All educational enterprises are structured hierarchically with a system of roles graded by levels of authority which differentiate one person from another. Work is divided along specialized lines and personal discretion is limited through rules and regulations. Status symbols such as size and location of teaching stations dramatize and validate distinctions between roles. The operational consequence is a set of signals provided by the organization for its members which enable people to know where they belong. The total effect is to build rationality, certainty, and dispatch into the organization. Career advancement and psychic stability encourage the teacher to accept the prescriptions and the result is a fairly consistent behavior pattern on the part of individuals within the organization.

Such an organizational climate is likely to be a more salient influence on teacher behavior than the vague educational philosophy of the chief administrator, if known, or the theoretical mandates prescribed by the local teachers college, if understood. Working climates may vary from school to school, but each system structures its own situation so that behavioral expectations are quite clearly evident.

A SCHOOL WITH TRADITION

Consider a few examples. You have just been employed by Osopeachy High, an old venerated school with firmly built up traditions. Having prestige in educational circles, it caters almost exclusively to a college preparatory clientele. Located in a wealthy suburban area, the financial emoluments for teachers are superb. The impact of such an organization on you cannot help to be considerable; you must learn the behavior patterns which go along with your post. Both the formal and informal rules need to be mastered and these range from appropriate dress and deportment to the models established for pupil-teacher relationships. To violate these norms is to endanger your status in the organization.

You find that Brooks Brothers clothing or its reasonable facsimile is the preferred uniform, that you should try to handle your own discipline problems without referral to the administrative offices, and that your success in teaching will be evaluated by the results of your students on college board examinations. Smoking is permitted in the well appointed teacher lounges, and it is quite acceptable to enjoy a cocktail at the better restaurants in the vicinity. You are supposed to criticize education courses as superfluous and you should model your teaching techniques after the university professor. Competition among students for grades is good; social promotion is bad. And from these relatively gross expectations you are to keep a sharp lookout for the barely detectable cues which are constantly being given.

This example may seem slightly exaggerated, but is it? This school obviously has a clear advantage because its mind is made up before the teacher joins the group. In support of this point, research by Kurt Lewin and his associates revealed that an individual's behavior is sharply conditioned by the structure of his work group. Inasmuch as learning is a process of recognizing symbols or stimuli, learning is facilitated when the situation is understood.

CONFLICTING GROUPS

Contrast the previous case with the Sleepy Valley High School, a rural central school which services a culturally and economically deprived territory. The faculty is divided between two groups of approximately equal numbers. One group is made up principally of middle-aged local women who are permanent fixtures in the community; in general, this group tends to be totally disinterested in changing the status quo, and is well satisfied with an inferior salary schedule.

The other group is less cohesive; it is younger, mostly transient, critical of the administration, salaries, facilities, and the like. However, teachers in this group escape with a jaded cynicism toward the organization and the community. Comments reflecting this attitude such as "What the heck, it's their school," or "Oh well, I'm leaving after this year anyway," are commonplace.

In this particular system you have to make a choice between two behavior patterns, and if you wish to remain, you would wisely select the more powerful group or assume a neutral position. To return to the point with which we started, the organization is a social microcosm, an ongoing society in itself, which acts as a socializing instrument. Successful teachers are those who can identify with the organization and accept as given the prevailing system; man is a remarkably adaptive animal and the most functional way of getting rid of anxiety in any situation is to conform to preferred models.

Given these facts, what is the dysfunctional result of the organization's pressure on the individual? One indictment can be made flatly: in developing and polishing men into similar molds, the tendency is to produce overconformity. If the position of teacher as defined by the organization does not adequately satisfy growth needs, the individual may ossify on the job or seek gratification outside school hours in such activities as building boats, raising flowers, and the like.

Since a school's overall success is irrevocably tied to a board of education's skill in forming, stimulating, and evaluating policy decisions, steps must be taken by the board to limit restrictive organizational influences.

CREATIVENESS AND LEADERSHIP

The first requirement is to sustain the truly creative teacher by permitting a certain amount of goal-oriented idiosyncratic behavior. For example, if the development of critical thinking powers in the student becomes a legitimate objective for a school, teachers should be permitted to experiment with techniques designed to achieve this end. A note of caution needs to be inserted here; eccentricity for its own sake and unrelated to the purposes of the school is pointless exhibitionism.

A second method of attack on organizational torpor is to increase the amount of participation by teachers in leadership acts. Job enlargement at all levels in the hierarchy is normally a more efficient way to structure an organization; if it doesn't seem to pay immediate returns in improved administrative services, the unexpected dividend may well be the boost given to a teacher's individual development. Douglas McGregor has argued that an individual's real potential is never discovered unless he is given an opportunity to self-actualize — that is, to participate in leadership activities as a valued colleague.

The most paramount function facing the board of education is the formulation of clear objectives for the school system. Since educational aims involve value choices selected from among a wide range of alternatives, it is mandatory that the public interest be operationalized in specific terms. Admittedly, to define the public interest [is] an exceedingly complex undertaking; however without a statement of principles the teacher has no standard against which to measure his performance. The exigencies of our times demand sound educational policies as guideposts for the professional conduct of our schools; improvisation on a day to day basis is hardly the desired alternative.

Since our final solution may appear on the surface as another impractical textbook remedy, let us examine the implications of the statement in a real situation. Suppose that a board of education were to state categorically that the principal aim of its schools shall be the development of the minds and the acquisition of knowledge by all children. All other aims, however important and desirable they may appear in themselves, shall be subordinated to this primary aim insofar as the functions of the schools are concerned.

Immediately, the administrative implications of this limited educational objective become apparent. With respect to children, this policy suggests ability grouping, heavy use of standardized achievement and ability tests, traditional type report cards, acceleration of gifted children and non-promotion of low achievers, and absolute standards for each grade level. Teacher[s] in such a system will be encouraged to do graduate study in the arts and sciences excluding professional courses in education; teaching success will depend to a considerable extent on the performance of one's students on standardized tests; rigid conformist, authoritarian teacher types will be most successful.

Whether or not one agrees with the aforementioned policy statement, and only the board of education working within its own community context can make this determination, purposiveness is the essential ingredient needed to counteract the negative aspects of organizational inertia. And much more than mere intellectual understanding of educational aims is demanded. Teachers who affiliate with a school must believe in its cause and subscribe to its goals. Through this kind of firm commitment and personal identification with enterprise objectives, we are able to gain the healthy advantages of individual and self-directed effort without destroying organizational intent.

ADMINISTRATIVE ORGANIZATION SHOULD BE DECENTRALIZED IN CITY SCHOOL DISTRICTS*

Where schools face special problems, administrators must deal with special demands on school staff, facilities, and organization. In disadvantaged communities especially, the school should make of itself a neighborhood institution, for its success depends to a considerable degree on

*NEA Journal, LI, No. 4 (April, 1962), 11-12. (Condensed from statement of Educational Policies Commission.)

the parents' attitudes and the staff's knowledge of family circumstances. These depend in turn on the administrator's awareness of the conditions in which his pupils and their parents live, and on his freedom to make adjustments to those conditions.

Large-city school systems should be so organized that staff services are available in the neighborhood of each school, rather than at only one point in the city. In addition, the administrator of each school should be given freedom of action consistent with his responsibilities.

His independence and initiative should be encouraged and rewarded. He should have funds whose disposition he can decide, opportunity to purchase special materials as needed, and the power to assign staff to special duties. He should be free to turn to civic-minded residents of the neighborhood for advice on the day-to-day adaptations that make his school effective.

Administrators must also pay special attention to the morale of pupils and staff. Any school should have about it an atmosphere of dedication to the interests of its children, and the pupils must see in the school a worthwhile and achievable challenge. But the formidable obstacles pupils and teachers must overcome in disadvantaged neighborhoods are constant threats to the morale of both the staff and the student body. Special administrative efforts are therefore required to sustain morale — rewarding good performance and encouraging experimentation.

So complex is the process of promoting the development of human beings that every school, even the best, is in constant need of adjustment and improvement. A school should be a vibrant, changing place. For the flexible, creative administrator there are ample opportunities — indeed challenges — to change.

ADMINISTRATIVE STAFFING . . .

DOES ADMINISTRATIVE STAFF GROW AS FAST AS ORGANIZATION?*

Is it true that the larger the tribe, the greater the ratio of chiefs to Indians? This question of the relationship between the size of an organization and the size of its administrative staff is of some interest to students

---

*Frank Lindenfeld, "Does Administrative Staff Grow as fast as Organization?" *School Life,* XLIII, 8 (May, 1961), 20-23.

of administration. Opinions differ on the subject, and evidence is meager. A few studies have, however, been made of the relationship in educational, industrial, and other organizations. In general, they point to one conclusion: As the size of an organization as a whole increases, the relative size of the administrative component decreases. . . .

As an organization grows, the number of officials usually increases, but this number may be either an increasing or decreasing proportion of the whole. It is therefore the relative, not the absolute, size of administrative components of organizations that I am concerned with here.

With these reservations in mind, let us look at findings of some studies.

Two studies of American industrial organizations over a long period suggest that the administrative staff does not grow as fast as the total organization. One, by Melman, is an analysis of Census data on U.S. manufacturing industries in the first half of the twentieth century. From his study he concludes, "Large increases in average size correspond with relatively small increases in administrative overhead. This result appears regardless of the criterion used to measure size. . . ." [1]

The other, by Haire, is a study of the life histories of four U.S. manufacturing firms. On the basis of his study, he says: "Management grows in size as the total grows, but more slowly than the total, and it is an increasingly smaller part of the whole." [2] . . .

Terrien and Mills, [4] however, from their study of school district organization in California, conclude that the larger the organization, the greater the proportion given over to its administrative component. In the administrative component, they include the superintendent, his assistants and immediate staff, principals, business manager, and the like; in the nonadministrative, teachers, nurses, custodians, cafeteria workers, and the like. . . .

The Terrien and Mills study suggests that there may be a size limit beyond which the relative proportion of administrative employees does not increase, although the districts they studied, which range in size from 10 up to 4,600 employees, do not seem to have reached this limit. . . .

In the hope of shedding further light on the relationship between the size of organizations and size of administrative components in public

---

[1] Seymour Melman, "The Rise of Administrative Overhead in the Manufacturing Industries in the United States, 1899-1947," Oxford *Economic Papers*, 1951, 3: 62-112.

[2] Mason Haire, "Biological Models and Empirical Histories of the Growth of Organizations," in *Modern Organization Theory*, Mason Haire, ed., New York, John Wiley & Sons, Inc., 1959, pp. 296-297.

[4] Frederick W. Terrien and Donald I. Mills, "The Effect of Changing Size Upon the Internal Structure of Organizations," *American Sociological Review*, 1955, 20: 11-14.

schools, I have replicated the Terrien and Mills study in a secondary analysis of personnel data reported in "Statistics of Local School Systems, 1955-56."[6] The biennial survey includes data on about half of the 3,500 city school systems in the country, grouped under five major categories according to city population as reported in the 1950 Census. The survey is based on a nationwide sample (all cities in the largest group and about one out of every two in the other groups), but is not necessarily representative of all school districts in the country.

From the survey I have selected 323 school systems for reanalysis. . . .

Analysis of the 323 school districts suggests that the larger the size of school district, as measured by total administrative and instructional staff, the smaller the proportion assigned to high level administrative work. . . .

For the smaller school districts, moreover, the finding should be interpreted in the light of the fact that it is usual for a school district, no matter how small, to have one superintendent. Although the proportion of principals is about the same in all sizes of school districts, the relative size of the highest level administrative component declines regularly with increasing size, from 3.1 percent of the whole in the smallest districts to 0.7 percent in the largest.

The proportion of the total staff assigned to supervisory work shows an increase with increasing size, from the smallest to the medium large districts with up to 700 employees. In the largest districts, however, the proportion of supervisors goes down slightly, indicating that there may be a limit to the relative expansion of this type of staff as school districts increase in size.

The ratio of teachers to all instructional and administrative employees increases slightly with increasing size of school systems. If staff members who are not teachers — administrators, principals, and supervisors — are considered as part of the administrative staff, the trend still runs in the same direction: the larger the school system, the lower the proportion of administrators, but this trend is not pronounced as when the administrative staff is defined as only those on the top administrative level.

The administrative components of organizations tend to decrease in relative size as organization size increases. The tendency persists among the school districts studied, even when the number of schools within school districts is held constant. . . .

---

[6]Lester B. Herlihy, *Biennial Survey of Education in the United States 1954-56,* Ch. 3, sec. 1, pp. 42-133.

[7]101 systems from cities with population of 100,000 or over; 43 from those with 25,000 to 99,999; 43 from those with 10,000 to 24,999; 54 from those with 5,000 to 9,999; and 82 from those with 2,500 to 4,999.

The four horizontal comparisons of the relative size of the administrative component within school systems having roughly the same number of schools indicate that the larger the system, the smaller the relative size of the administrative component. Of the four vertical comparisons, three indicate that the larger the number of schools operated within school systems of a given size, the larger the relative size of the administrative component. The fourth comparison, among the largest school districts analyzed, is negative, very likely because too diverse a set of systems was included in the last open-end category for both the number of schools and the size of the school systems in the table.

On the whole, the weight of the evidence reviewed here would seem to run counter to the direction suggested by Terrien and Mills. This evidence, admittedly limited, indicates that the larger the school system, the lower the ratio of chiefs to Indians; this relationship holds among districts having many schools as well as among those with few schools.

STAFFING FOR SCHOOL MANAGEMENT — THE LEGAL FACTOR*

To ask a group of educators the question, "What are the factors in the establishment of administrative and specialized service positions in a local school system?" is to immediately evoke a discussion of a long list of variables. The list would surely include size, money, school law, type of district, kind and extent of cooperative services, attitude and quality of the staff, location of the schools, and management policies.

In this list the four dominant factors or variables appear to be size, money, quality of the staff, and school law. Expressed as a unity of State constitutional provisions, statutes, regulations of State educational authorities, the legal factor may shape the action of local boards of education in the administrative positions they will institute, whom they will employ, and how much the administrators will be paid.

The legal factor has several fundamental parts. One of these is found in the provisions of State statutes that either expressly set forth or imply the power of local boards of education to employ school superintendents, business managers, directors, supervisors, principals, school physicians, and others in administrative or special positions. Provisions in the school laws of 48 States confer varying degrees of employment power on local

---

*Winston L. Roesch, "Staffing for School Management— the Legal Factor," *School Life,* XLII, 5 (January, 1960), 14-15.

school boards either directly or by necessary implication. In general, a local school board has a wide range of permissive authority in deciding on the particular positions to be instituted in a school system. State statutes and other legal requirements may, however, have the effect of narrowing a board's freedom of choice. For example, a State law may set up administrative positions and direct local boards of education of one or more classes of school districts to fill them. The rule-making power of the State education authority may also significantly affect the decision of local boards to employ staff members such as a director of pupil personnel, a school psychologist or physician.

The freedom of choice school boards have in establishing administrative and specialized service positions has not been treated extensively in educational research, primarily because of the widespread acceptance of the principle that local boards of education have the power, either by direct grant or by necessary implication, to establish and fill such positions. There now appears to be a need for an examination of this principle as it *functions* in the approximately 43,000 operating school districts in the United States.

In recognition of this need the Office of Education has conducted a study of administrative staffing in local school districts.

This study shows that some administrative and specialized service positions are expressly affirmed by statute as being within the employment power of local boards — for example, the positions of school superintendent and principal. In at least 44 States the position of superintendent of schools or district superintendent is so recognized. In 33 States laws specify that at least some boards of education may or shall employ the school principal.

There is a marked contrast in the statutory provisions on the superintendency and principalship and those on instructional supervisors. Even though a number of States have introduced specific certification requirements for instructional supervisors as well as principals and superintendents, only a few have specified in their statutes that local boards *shall* employ instructional supervisors. In 24 States statutory provisions expressly authorize governing boards of one or more classes of local districts to employ supervisors of instruction; with few exceptions their authority is clearly permissive. When we consider the duty-to-employ provisions of State statutes, the difference in the legal basis for the position of school superintendent or principal and instructional supervisor becomes apparent. The difference is major.

In 1957-58 in each of 33 States the employment of a school superintendent was expressed in the general statutes as a *duty* of at least some local boards, whereas no State had statutory provisions explicitly directing local boards to employ special instructional supervisors in mathematics, science, music, or art.

This difference is narrowed, but very slightly, by the inclusion of general instructional supervisors. In 1957-58 only one State specified by statute that all or nearly all local boards of education shall employ a general instructional supervisor, in this instance a supervising teacher. Statutory provisions applicable to special subject-matter supervisors in areas other than science, mathematics, and art indicate that in a few States some local boards have the duty of employing supervisors of physical education.

The provisions of State finance acts in which instructional supervisory positions are explicitly set forth does affect employment. In eight of the States financial aid laws either designate instructional supervisor or use the term "supervisor" in provisions for specific financial support for administrative and specialized service positions. Again, however, these laws do not specify that special subject-matter supervisors shall be employed. One State aid act requires a school district participating in the minimum foundation fund to employ a supervisor or supervisor of instruction for a full calendar year.

There are marked contrasts in board authority over pupil personnel positions. An analysis of four positions — director of pupil personnel, visiting teacher, school psychologist, and attendance officer — shows that freedom to employ varies significantly within this cluster of positions. Two of them — the position of attendance officer and school psychologist — may be used to illustrate the variation.

Belief in compulsory education for all children regardless of race, creed, or social status is deeply rooted in American democracy. This belief is reflected to some extent in the general statutes of 42 States providing that local boards of education may establish the position of attendance officer, supervisor of attendance, attendance assistant, truant officer, or an equivalent position. A strong tendency to make the position mandatory and thus to narrow the board's freedom of choice is evident: 23 States prescribe the position as an employment duty of some boards.

Local boards have considerably more discretionary authority to employ a school psychologist than an attendance officer. Such authority is implied. Statutes of 48 States disclose no provisions which specifically authorize or empower local boards to employ professional staff members with the title school psychologist, educational psychologist, or psychologist. Statutory provisions of one State have made employment of a psychological examiner a duty of local boards.

When power to employ is considered in the light of a State's general classification system of school districts, a board's freedom of choice takes on new meaning. Excluding special act or charter school districts, States with one class of local district generally provide the same employment power for the relatively small as for the large districts. They may, however, deal with problems of district size by introducing minimum standards.

States with more than one general class of school districts may utilize the classification system to widen employment authority of some boards and to narrow it for others. The State may disregard its classification system completely in providing for some positions or limit its use to one of several positions.

The power of local boards to institute a particular administrative or service position may also vary as a result of school district requirements that are expressed in the statutes. As these are minimum rather than maximum requirements, they usually affect the employment power of boards in small school districts. As mentioned earlier, the requirements may be keyed to the State's general classification of school districts.

The school superintendency is a case in point. In three States the school district classification system has been used to restrict the authority of small school districts to establish a position bearing the title of superintendent of schools. However, in several other States, also with more than one class of school districts, the same objective has been achieved without recourse to the State's general classification system. Generally, this is done by prescribing that any board of education has the power to employ a school superintendent providing that the school has met the minimum standards. When administrative and specialized staffing positions are considered as a group, more statutory use is made of school district classification system to increase or decrease the employment powers of boards than of any other device.

The study shows that the primary statutory restriction expressly applied to the power of local boards to institute positions is size of system. Size may be expressed in number of teachers or pupils, district population, or in the number and kinds of schools. As a result of school district reorganization and the widespread increase in enrollments, minimums specifying that a school district may have, for example, more than eight teachers tend to have little effect on administrative and specialized service staffing in school systems that operate K–12 or 1–12 programs.

Another kind of statutory requirement is found in school health positions. In at least three States the existence of adequate State, county, or city public health services tends to restrict local boards in the independent employment of school nurses or school physicians. In substance, the laws set forth that positions of school physician or school nurse may be established by a local board of education provided that adequate district public health services are not available or cannot be conveniently obtained. Such legislation generally applies to all or nearly all school districts of a State and therefore has a more significant effect on the local board's freedom of choice than current statutory provisions that set low minimum standards of school district or school size.

As was pointed out in the beginning, the legal variable is only one of several that influence administrative and specialized service staffing. The legal variable, in turn, is composed of sections or parts with decidedly complex structures. State constitutional and statutory provisions empowering local school boards, committees, or agencies to employ staff need to be studied in association with the regulations of State education authorities and court decisions. Functionally, the study should consider the interrelation of powers of local boards, district classification systems, requirements for certification of personnel, duties of staff members and State financial aid programs.

THE ELEMENTARY SCHOOL PRINCIPAL CAN'T DELEGATE*

The administrator of an elementary school faces conditions which require unique leadership qualities. At his level, practically every child is found in school. The range of their abilities and interests is correspondingly great. The parents of these children are young, actively directing their children's growth and unabashedly interested in what the school is doing. The elementary-school principal's attendance district is often a distinct neighborhood, with characteristics which distinguish it from other neighborhoods, suburbs or small communities.

The job, itself, is unique. An elementary-school principal is, under existing conditions, a jack-of-all-trades. Whereas modern secondary-school administration is a team operation, the elementary-school principal is the entire administrative team. The following comparison, taken from a large-city system in the state of Ohio, is offered as illustration. A four-year high school in the system having an enrollment of 1,279 students and a staff of 52 teachers, is permitted the release of teachers' time indicated for the following administrative responsibilities:

---

*Robert E. Lucas and Howard Wakefield, eds., *By Their Bootstraps, An Approach to Elementary School Leadership,* Columbus, Ohio: By Permission of the Ohio Education Association, Department of Elementary-School Principals, 1955, 11.

Athletic manager ....10 periods weekly
Attendance 20   "   "
Books 10   "   "
Cafeteria manager 30   "   "
Journalism 5   "   "
Student government 10   "   "
Treasurer 10   "   "
Visual aids 5   "   "

In addition to the above, which are the equivalent of three teachers devoting full time to administration, the high school has:

1 full-time principal
1 full-time vice-principal
2 full-time secretaries.

An elementary school in the same system, embracing grades kindergarten through six, with an enrollment of 1,346 students and a staff of 32 teachers, has the following provisions for administration:

1 full-time principal
1 secretary, two days weekly.

By direct comparison, disregarding salary differences, the high school has seven persons on its administrative team; the elementary school has one and two-fifths. The current differences in the nature of the two principalships call for differences in function. The desirability of such differences is another matter.

RECONCILING SINGLE ACCOUNTABILITY BETWEEN THE BUILDING PRINCIPAL AND CENTRAL STAFF OFFICER*

Single accountability for all persons in any organization is essential, and the larger a unit becomes the more necessary it is to hold every employee accountable to only one superior. Further, it must be made absolutely clear the duties for which each employee is accountable.

The problem of multiple accountability appears constantly in a school organization because the nature of functions is not precisely divisible. Unless accountability can be clearly fixed, the organization risks ineffi-

*Edwin A. Fensch and Robert E. Wilson, *The Superintendency Team,* Columbus, Ohio: by permission of Charles E. Merrill Books, Inc., 1965, 114-116.

ciency from hesitancy, or refusal, to take the initiative to see that tasks are completed. It should be remembered that the assistant superintendent for instruction, for example, is being held responsible according to the job definition for the success of instructional activities in the entire system, while the principal is responsible for instructional activities within his building. How can these two opposing principles be made harmonious?

One of the keys for reconciling the dichotomy lies in the realm of attitudes. If all administrators keep uppermost in their minds the importance of subordinating personal ambitions and sensitivities to the welfare of the total organization, there is likely to be little difficulty.

Significant here is the approach which a central staff officer uses with principals in seeking their cooperation toward the attainment of an objective. Any officer, including the superintendent, should approach the principal with the understanding that the latter is responsible for whatever happens in his building. With the exception of emergency situations, a staff administrator should always proceed through the principal in carrying out any of the defined functions within a building. If it is a matter resulting in a conflict of opinion, the staff executive should attempt to persuade the principal toward the desired viewpoint. If the principal accepts the viewpoint, then he is free to execute the decision in his building. A principal should be the best-informed and best-qualified person for carrying out the decision with his own staff. The psychological power in this approach is gigantic. The principal feels he has made the decision and is likely to lend his personal strength to its successful performance. Moreover, he is not inclined to dodge the responsibility for a misfire if he feels it is his decision. In this approach, the assistant superintendent, or the superintendent, has acted in a staff relationship, a form of consultancy. The principle of accountability is preserved insofar as the principal and the assistant are both concerned.

On the other hand, should the principal reject the desired viewpoint of the superintendent's assistant, the rejection is the principal's decision and he is accountable for the outcome. There can be no shedding of responsibility. If the matter is of sufficient importance to carry to the superintendent, or even to the board of education for final adjudication, the channels are open for either the principal or the assistant superintendent.

Adherence to this attitude does not mean that the assistant superintendent has abrogated his responsibility for achieving the elements of his job description. There will be occasions to justify his insistence that a ruling has been made on a higher level and a principal must carry through as directed. The principal is not a free agent who can ignore superintendency directives. Rather, he operates within the school system's policies and administrative regulations. However, when he follows central administrative directions which are contrary to his judgment, he is relieved of accountability for outcomes within his building. This assumes that he executes regulations to the best of his ability and does not undermine the effort. Decision-making involves risk and responsibility. This partially explains the urging of administrative theorists to keep decision-making as near to the task as possible. There are other reasons to support this principle, but the resourceful central staff administrator will endeavor to have decisions made by principals as often as he can.

The coordinating function is accomplished on two levels. The principal is responsible for coordinating all functions within his building. The assistant superintendent coordinates a specific function in all buildings. He also is in a position for lateral coordination of several functions in a given building by working with his colleagues in the central office.

Stating it another way, the assistant is in an authority position for the achievement of a function in the entire school system. He conducts himself as if he were in an advisory position for the achievement of a function in any one building. He is a specialized authority officer in relation to all principals but an advisory officer in dealing with a single principal.

The consultive nature of a staff position does not mean, as it is so often construed, that the assistant superintendent sits in waiting for a call for help from a principal. He cannot wait, since he is responsible for the success of the function in one building as much as another. He has an obligation to work with a principal toward the improvement of the function when, in either's judgment, there is a need.

DEMOCRATIC ADMINISTRATION . . .

DEMOCRATIC LEADERSHIP: DOES IT ABROGATE EXECUTIVE RESPONSIBILITY?*

During the late twenties through the forties, administrators were trying to operate under a philosophy which denied certain basic truths about

---

*Howard K. Holland, "Democratic Leadership. Does it Abrogate Executive Responsibility?" *The School Executive,* LXXIX (November, 1959), 76-77, by permission of the *American School & University Magazine.*

people. This inadequate philosophy was summed up in the phrase "democratic leadership," and any school executive who refused to subscribe to it was labeled "authoritarian" or "tyrannical." The dying spasm of his loose bundle of ideas is likely to be one cause of poor administration today.

Included under the heading of democratic methods was the theory that the leader was never supposed to take a definitive stand on any educational issue. He was, instead, to serve as a sounding-board for his faculty. He was to encourage free interplay of opinion among his teachers, to summarize from time to time, to guide gently if the discussion became too random.

The sanction for such ideas was respectable enough two decades ago. Bedded on the foundations of functional psychology, it was seriously believed that teamwork, efficiency and, above all, group motivation would be greater if the leader was not "aggressive."

The fact is that when superiors act as gentle guides there is little leadership. The theory has never worked. Teachers knew it immediately and quietly grumbled about it. Successful administrators kept their peace about the educational theory and did their leading in the ways that came naturally to them.

Another side of the outmoded idea was that the good principal or supervisor was not to have his own prearranged purposes and goals for his group. He was to work with the group, allowing its purposes to "emerge" as the true aims. During this era, no conference was to begin without the leader and teachers having planned goals together.

Indeed, the practice so slowed inter-faculty production that many teachers left the profession in disgust, turning instead to more realistic endeavors where time is money and employers protected their workers from having to assume the responsibilities of the executive.

If there is any single requirement more important than another in leadership, it is the unique ability to apply broad knowledge to creative expectations. This is the meaning of good planning. The true leader has the best overall picture of the educational enterprise. Aims and purposes are his to fashion. They are also his to modify in the light of teacher opinion, providing he is convinced that such opinion makes desirable contributions to the aims.

A RIDICULOUS EXTREME

To be certain, there is frequent need to find out what teachers or patrons want. But educators in the past have carried this step to a ridiculous extreme. Most people have fragmentary ideas of what they want, although usually they are happy to have someone who knows his business clarify these ideas in their minds.

This is not undemocratic. On major issues the people are always to be depended upon. To require them to specify the meaning of their opinions is to give to a group the job of the leader. Even in such professional problems as planning for inservice training or in the consideration of certain issues such as reporting or retention or pupil control in corridors, aims and purposes should be first thought out by the administrator. Thereafter they should be presented to the teacher group with the sincere desire to make reasonable changes.

Probably the most unrealistic aspect of "democratic" leadership was its assumption that the leader was not supposed to impose his personality or ideas upon any of his staff. Some school supervisors would never approach a teacher; the teacher had to come to them.

The old theory held that personal growth and improvement on the part of teachers could result only when the desire for such growth came from them. To be sure, a supervisor or director of instruction or principal could set the stage — could obliquely nudge toward professional proficiency. But they were not allowed actively to direct, to praise or blame, to inspire.

I know some school leaders who still refuse to rate the caliber of teaching of those with whom they work. "Who am I to judge?" asked one, implying that evaluation might impair future progress. Also, the thought is voiced that teachers won't work happily for a supervisor who rates their work.

To make progress in administration in our time requires the acceptance of a few fundamentals, all as old as organized society.

The first fundamental is that all those concerned must accept the fact that the gifts of leadership are unequally divided. Most people do, indeed, prefer to be led. This implies the necessity of intelligent followership.

More important, it requires that those who find themselves in positions of authority work actively to do better the things which only they can do. False humility ruins many a leader. After all, who among men isn't a recipient of personal gifts? Much is expected from those to whom much is given.

The second fundamental has to do with broad characteristics peculiar to leadership. We know, of course, that leaders are often above average in health, energy and intelligence. But we find more important facets in the leaders' qualitative characteristics. Courage heads the list. Courage requires convictions, ability and a willingness to suffer both physically and mentally. The virtue of fortitude is only displayed by persons of great integrity who, by an almost mysterious process, possess tremendous moral strength and are able to convey this tacitly to their followers. We see this in the great military geniuses, in some statesmen, in the other great leaders of our own times and times past.

IMPATIENCE WITH FAILURE

Self-confidence seems to be born of fortitude. Lives of fine leaders show that self-reliance (of the Emersonian variety) produces a disregard for the petty pleasures of life. It really produces an impatience with failure, the true leader being resilient and able to start again at his beginnings without complaining about fate or other people.

The inclination of others to turn to him is perhaps the spring of his effectiveness. A good leader often inspires his followers. The characteristic of the trained leader — often found in the military, labor and industry — is that he looks upon motivating his group as a primary responsibility. He recognizes his own abilities in this direction and consciously uses them for the good of all. Sometimes this is called building spirit or *esprit de corps*.

The third fundamental has to do with the leader's capacity to *take* directions. This is one of the worst stumbling blocks, because human nature seems to have a built-in tendency to desire all power, once a little has been gained. In some of our schools you will find many such little tyrants and educational dictators.

LOYALTY UP AND DOWN

Stature is achieved when leaders frankly admit to themselves that obedience and loyalty on their own parts are desirable and necessary. Loyalty up and down the line is taught in our service academies to the men who must lead thousands in war. The experience of over a century of school administration has shown that loyalty to those above is the proving ground for those below. And when the leader gets to the very top, the maximum obedience is required. To obey a board, or commission or constituency is hard. To obey these in the light of one's own highest principles is the mark of greatness.

These, then, are the coming-of-age signs of school leadership. The good supervisors, directors, principals and superintendents have learned the pitfalls of the false psychology which demanded leadership behavior contrary to the wisdom of centuries of human experience.

The fine leader in our schools is the person with unusual talents for working with people. He recognizes these in himself and humbly dedicates them to the good of the group. His inner characteristics include courage, self-confidence and the urge and ability to inspire those with whom he works.

Above all, he is a master in taking orders. His maturity is built upon loyalty. He never progresses so far upward that he loses his ability to obey.

THE COMMITTEE APPROACH
DESTROYS INTELLIGENCE*

. . . One of the paradoxes of an increasingly specialized, bureaucratized society is that the qualities rewarded in the rise to eminence are less and less the qualities required once eminence is reached. Specialization encourages administrative and technical skills, which are not necessarily related to the vision and creativity needed for leadership. The essence of good administration is co-ordination among the specialized functions of a bureaucracy. The task of the executive is to infuse and occasionally to transcend routine with purpose. . . .

Our executives are shaped by a style of life that inhibits reflectiveness. For one of the characteristics of a society based on specialization is the enormous work load of its top personnel. The smooth functioning of the administrative apparatus absorbs more energies than the definition of criteria on which decision is to be based. Issues are reduced to their simplest terms. Decision making is increasingly turned into a group effort. The executive's task is conceived as choosing among administrative proposals in the formulation of which he has no part and with the substance of which he is often unfamiliar. A premium is placed on "presentations" which take the least effort to grasp and which in practice usually mean oral "briefing." (This accounts for the emergence of the specialist in "briefings" who prepares charts, one-page summaries, etc.) In our society the policymaker is dependent to an increasing extent on his subordinates' conception of the essential elements of a problem. . . .

Philosophical conviction and psychological bias thus combine to produce in and out of government a penchant for policymaking by committee. The obvious insurance against the possibility of error is to obtain as many opinions as possible. And unanimity is important, in that its absence is a standing reminder of the tentativeness of the course adopted. The committee approach to decision making is often less an organizational device than a spiritual necessity.

*Henry A. Kissinger, "The Policymaker and the Intellectual," *The Reporter,* XX (March 5, 1959), 30-35. Copyright 1959 by The Reporter Magazine Company, also by permission of Henry A. Kissinger.

In this manner, policy is fragmented into a series of ad hoc decisions which make it difficult to achieve a sense of direction or even to profit from experience. Substantive problems are transformed into administrative ones. Innovation is subjected to "objective" tests which deprive it of spontaneity. "Policy planning" becomes the projection of familiar problems into the future. Momentum is confused with purpose. There is greater concern with how things are than with which things matter. The illusion is created that we can avoid recourse to personal judgment and responsibility as the final determinant of policy. . . .

The committee system not only has a tendency to ask wrong questions, it also puts a premium on the wrong qualities. The committee progress is geared to the pace of conversation. Even where the agenda is composed of memoranda, these are prepared primarily as a background for discussion, and they stand and fall on the skill with which they are presented. Hence quickness of comprehension is more important then reflectiveness, fluency more useful than creativeness. The ideal "committee man" does not make his associates uncomfortable; he does not operate with ideas too far outside of what is generally accepted. Thus the thrust of committees is toward a standard of average performance. Since a complicated idea cannot be easily absorbed by ear — particularly when it is new — committees lean toward what fits in with the most familiar experience of their members. They therefore produce great pressure in favor of the status quo. Committees are consumers and sometimes sterilizers of ideas, rarely creators of them. . . .

The contribution of the intellectual to policy is therefore in terms of criteria that he has played a minor role in establishing. He is rarely given the opportunity to point out that a query delimits a range of possible solutions or that an issue is posed in irrelevant terms. He is asked to solve problems, not to contribute to the definition of goals. Where decisions are arrived at by negotiation, the intellectual — particularly if he is not himself part of the bureaucracy — is a useful weight in the scale. He can serve as a means to filter ideas to the top outside of organization channels or as a legitimizer for the viewpoint of contending factions within and among departments. This is why many organizations build up batteries of outside experts or create semi-independent research groups, and why articles or books become tools in the bureaucratic struggle. In short, all too often what the policymaker wants from the intellectual is not ideas but endorsement. . . .

Our policymakers do not lack advice; they are in many respects overwhelmed by it. They do lack criteria on which to base judgments. In the absence of commonly understood and meaningful standards, all advice tends to become equivalent. In seeking to help the bureaucracy out of this maze, the intellectual too frequently becomes an extension of the administrative machine, accepting its criteria and elaborating its problems. . . .

One reason why intellectuals outside the administrative machines have not made a greater contribution is that for them protest has too often become an end in itself. Whether they have withdrawn by choice or because of the nature of their society, many intellectuals have confused the issues by simplifying them too greatly. They have refused to recognize that policymaking involves not only the clear conception of ideas but also the management of men. In the process analysis has been too often identified with policymaking. . . .

The intellectual must therefore decide not only whether to participate in the administrative process but also in what capacity: whether as an intellectual or as an administrator. If he assumes the former role, it is essential for him to retain the freedom to deal with the policymaker from a position of independence and to reserve the right to assess the policymaker's demands in terms of his own standards. Paradoxically, this may turn out to be also most helpful to the policymaker. For the greater the bureaucratization and the more eminent the policymaker, the more difficult it is to obtain advice in which substantive considerations are not submerged by or at least identified with organizational requirements. . . .

DEMOCRATIC ADMINISTRATION DOES NOT NECESSARILY MEAN EFFECTIVE ADMINISTRATION*

From one point of view the findings in this study may appear to be disappointing. Because of the general exploratory nature of the investigation, a great many of the statistical comparisons did not show significant differences. Whether this is truly disappointing depends, of course, on the questions one asks of the data and the assumptions one makes about the true condition.

For example, it is a fairly common supposition that the more mature and experienced the administrator, the more effective he will be. Or, again, it is often theorized that a woman is better equipped than a man to fill a position such as that of elementary-school principal. Neither of these assumptions is supported by this study; the differences in the data were not significant.

---

*David Jenkins and Charles A. Blackman, *Antecedents and Effects of Administrative Behavior*. Columbus, Ohio: College of Education, The Ohio State University, 1956, 76-77 (a study of the effects of administrative behavior on teacher behavior).

A third assumption often made is that persons who have democratic attitudes will be effective administrators. Frequently, as in this study, the measure of such attitudes is agreement with democratic statements or a personal declaration of democracy. We were able to find almost no significant relationships between verbalization of democratic attitudes and effectiveness among the administrators in the study. The relationships between what one professes, what he actually does, and what effects his actions have, are apparently not simple ones. And the matter is further complicated by human inconsistency.

It is often taken for granted that the more of a good thing, the better. By way of illustration, selflessness would appear to be a quality with which no one could be too generously endowed. Translated into terms of the administrator, this would mean that ideally he would be primarily concerned with the growth of his staff or be totally permissive. Our findings here suggest that this is not necessarily so. The person who has moved to the extreme position on such values may be less effective than one who has established an intermediate status.

The pattern of personal needs of the administrator was found to be important in determining what sort of influence he would have on the school. This relationship was particularly clear in connection with the communication pattern. We know from this study and from other research that the type of communication which exists in a group is one of the more important variables in determining how that group will work.

We also found a relationship between the pattern of the administrator's needs and his performance, as judged by teachers, in carrying out certain administrative practices. These practices themselves were found to be directly associated, to the degree to which they were effectively performed, with the teachers' general morale and satisfaction.

There is, then, a continuing thread of relationships extending from the personal needs of the administrator, as shown by his personality, through the way he plans and carries out administrative practices and through the communication pattern he develops in the school, to the general reactions of his staff. This is the major finding of the study.

BUREAUCRACY AND TEACHERS' SENSE OF POWER*

... In this study the central issue was the teacher's sense of power with respect to the school system at large — his sense of ability or

---

*Gerald Moeller, "Bureaucracy and Teachers' Sense of Power," *The School Review*, LXXII, 2 (Summer, 1964), 137-157. Reprinted by permission of the University of Chicago Press.

inability to influence the organizational forces which so importantly shape his destiny. It was not the teacher's feelings about himself and his position with respect to the classroom, nor to the profession, nor to the larger society in which he lives which engaged this investigation. Rather, it was the teacher's sense of power vis-a-vis his school system, as the system varied with regard to bureaucratization, toward which the study was directed. . . .

The major hypothesis was that bureaucracy in school system organization induces in teachers a sense of powerlessness to affect school system policy . . . To test the hypothesis, twenty school systems employing from 37 to 700 full-time teachers were selected from the St. Louis metropolitan area. . . . Using an eight-item forced-choice instrument, a group of persons with first-hand knowledge of the school systems in the study made judgments which provided the data for ordering the twenty school systems on a bureaucracy scale. . . . Sense of power was conceived of as a continuum upon which teachers may be ordered; at one extreme are those who feel unlimited in the degree to which they can affect school system policy, and, at the other end are those who feel totally powerless to influence its direction in any way. . . .

The major hypothesis was denied. Contrary to the hypothesis, teachers in bureaucratic school systems were significantly higher in sense of power than were those in less fully bureaucratic systems. . . .

A REASSESSMENT OF BUREAUCRACY AND SENSE OF POWER

From the findings reported in this study have emerged a number of postulates regarding bureaucracy in the public school setting. Certainly bureaucracy, as a rational and, hence, predictable form of organization, does not induce in teachers feelings of powerlessness or alienation from the system. The greater predictability seems to stem from the published policy of these systems which assures teachers of specific avenues of communication up the line to the decision-making centers of the administration. Then, too, the rationality of the bureaucracies presses toward effectiveness of operation and efficiency in employment of personnel, insuring teachers the best possible working conditions within the limits of available resources.

By definition the low bureaucratic school systems are less complex organizations with fewer and less explicit policies. Without specified rules to guide them, administrators of these systems must rely on unanticipated decisions or on traditional community norms — either of which are subject to misunderstanding and, hence, are less predictable than a well-defined policy structure would be.

When the focus is shifted from the school system organization to the individual teacher, the dimension of comparative evaluation becomes relevant. Each member of a social system learns his role in that system and, in so doing, assesses his power in relation to others. This knowledge of relative position in the power hierarchy enables teachers with greater service, of higher social-class origins, and the males in elementary schools to score high on sense of power whether they were employed in high or low bureaucratic systems.

In short, sense of power appears to be influenced by many diverse variables lying within the teacher himself, in his past, in his social groups, in his relations with his supervisors, and in the organizational structure of the school in which he is employed. The general level of sense of power seems to be limited by the organizational variable. Bureaucracy provides the teacher with an understandable and predictable ethos in which to pursue his profession. This predictability, far from reducing sense of power, sets a higher level of sense of power than is found in the less bureaucratized school organizations. To the general level of sense of power set by the organization of the school system the teacher brings his own personal characteristics which differentiate him from his colleagues and enable him to make comparisons of his power in relation to that held by others. Thus, the school system sets the general level of sense of power and the teacher varies from this level by his own personal orientation toward power.

DECISION MAKING . . .

A SCIENCE OF DECISION-MAKING*

Accordingly, from the substance of policy, scholars have turned their tools of analysis to the process of decision-making. The administrative process is described as a cycle of action consisting of decisions made by administrators. Just who is to be identified as administrators has not been made clear. Moreover, the exact relationship between decision-making and action deserves some attention. The two are not necessarily always the same, as scholars of administrative behavior have been quick to point out.

---

*John Millet, "Perspective of Public Administration." A paper read before National Conference of University Council for Educational Administration, 1961. From *Preparing Administrators: New Perspectives,* Columbus, Ohio: by permission of the University Council for Educational Administration (edited by Jack Culbertson and Stephen P. Hencley) 1962, 30-33.

Chancellor Litchfield of the University of Pittsburgh has observed that decision-making in its rational, deliberative, discretionary, and purposive form, is characterized by a definite pattern of procedure. An issue must be identified and defined, an existing situation must be analyzed, alternative courses of action to achieve a desired objective must be calculated, the desired results and desired means must be reviewed, and a definite choice of action must be determined. Decisions are a composite of values, facts, and assumptions. Each or all of these may be subject to change from time to time. Decision-making, therefore, is not a one-time activity but rather a continuing enterprise.

Secondly, Chancellor Litchfield points out that decisions involve policies (the definition of objectives), resources (people, money, materials, and authority, and means of execution (integration and synthesis). Insofar as the value content of these types of decision is concerned, he identifies three major values. Policy decisions seek purposive action. Resource decisions seek economy of operation. Execution decisions seek coordination of action.

In the third place, Chancellor Litchfield relates the decision-making process to a larger context. The dimensions of decision-making are described as a social and political environment, the nature and characteristics of the enterprise itself including its technical procedures, and the personality of the administrator. Litchfield observes that an enterprise generally seeks to perpetuate itself, to preserve its internal well-being, to maintain its status in relation to other agencies, and to realize growth in its output.

This outline for the analysis of decision-making is presented by Chancellor Litchfield as a theory of administrative process. In its outline certainly this theory provides a comprehensive model. Whether such a theory represents a substantial advance over the other approaches to the study of public administration mentioned here, no one can say with any degree of certainty. I suspect that much of what Litchfield outlines becomes comprehensible and useful only after a good deal of extensive study utilizing all available knowledge about public administration.

Professor Simon has presented decision-making from a somewhat different and a more restricted perspective. He emphasizes decision-making as a procedure. He divides decisions into two types: programmed and non-programmed. Programmed decisions are those handled on a routine, repetitive basis through specific processes developed within an organization for dealing with continuing or recurring situations. Non-programmed decisions are the unique, one-time, specific actions taken to meet special situations or problems.

For both types of decisions Professor Simon postulates traditional and modern techniques of decision-making. The traditional method of handling programmed decisions is through a well-defined organizational structure with a system of sub-goals, common expectations, and standardized operating procedures, reinforced by routine long established. For the non-programmed decisions the traditional technique has been the careful selection and training of managers, who utilize tradition, personal judgment, and rules of thumb in resolving important problems.

The modern techniques of making programmed decisions entail operations research and electronic data processing. To be sure, situations subject to such modern techniques must be susceptible of expression in terms of mathematical model, with a criterion function and available empirical estimates of the numerical parameters. Any problem situation not subject to statement in terms of a mathematical model cannot be analyzed with the assistance of electronic data processing. Furthermore, Professor Simon suggests that our knowledge of problem-solving may advance to the point where the very process of human thought itself can be simulated by an electronic computer. Thus would a modern technique of nonprogrammed decision-making be added to the arsenal of management.

This outline of decision-making procedures is useful insofar as it goes. Undoubtedly so-called modern techniques of programmed decision-making will become increasingly popular as managerial competence in quantitative analysis advances. Whether simulation of problem-solving processes will prove possible and advantageous, future experience will have to demonstrate.

Yet there appear to be definite limitations to Professor Simon's modern techniques of decision-making. Will it be possible to reduce recurring situations to mathematical models? Will it be possible to simulate social tradition and values, institutional environment, and individual judgment as the framework within which human problem-solving must operate? As a procedure, Professor Simon's outline offers a helpful guide-line to action. But this procedure can scarcely be expected to substitute for content, which remains the heart of the decision-making process.

The discussion of decision-making which is now going on provides further insight about the administrative process in our society. It seems doubtful, at least at this stage, whether a concentration upon decision-making will provide the desired synthesis of administrative knowledge. If it does, it will have to be developed, I believe, along the outlines proposed by Chancellor Litchfield.

THE SCHOOL ADMINISTRATOR COORDINATES DECISION MAKING*

The next point I would like to make is that we need to focus on decision making, not individual superintendent or principal decision making, but coordination of group decision making. This is not an easy job as you well know. To illustrate the point, I would like to refer you to a recent issue of the *Executive Action Letter*. It tells how the President of the United States is so protected that often he can't make good decisions and that most school administrators are the same way. In power situations, and every one of our school systems is a power situation, it is not always necessary for the boss to tell his subordinates what he wants. They find it out for themselves, and they tell him what he wants to hear.

Do you see the danger in this? It makes me scared to be a superintendent. If you or I freeze in our pattern of operations, we run real risks that our whole staff will get used to what we want, that the school system will rest on dead center, and that it will not go anywhere.

A research study which investigated the effects of administrative behavior on teacher effectiveness in fifty school systems substantiates this point of view. Conclusions of the study were that participation in decision making by all of the persons affected pays dividends. This isn't the easiest or most efficient way, but it contributes the most to good learning.

TEACHER INVOLVEMENT IN DECISION MAKING IS CONSISTENT WITH AIMS OF PUBLIC SCHOOLS**

More than a few administrators and school boards deeply and actively involve teachers in the most basic educational decisions. Teachers in

*Robert S. Gilchrist, "The School Administrator as an Instructional Leader," by permission of the *North Central Association Quarterly*, XXXVII, (Fall, 1963), 187.

**Archie R. Dykes, "Democracy, Teachers, and Educational Decision-Making," by permission of *School and Society*, XCII (April 4, 1964), 155-156.

some school districts have a major voice in policy development, person-nel procedures, curriculum formulation, budget development, and other important concerns. Theirs is a responsible share in the decision-making process. However, for the great mass of teachers, participation in im-portant educational decisions, either directly or by representation, is an activity never experienced.

A fundamental ideal of democracy calls for a co-operative approach to decision-making. It requires that every person have some systematic way through which he can participate, either directly or through his representative, in decisions which affect him. The ideal rests on a basic assumption that decisions so made will be of higher quality and more effectively carried out. It argues that lack of involvement produces un-concern and lack of effective responsibility. . . .

To many who have thought deeply about the new movement among teachers, the most compelling consideration relates to the purposes of education in a democratic society. If among the purposes are those of making our democracy increasingly democratic, more dynamic, increas-ingly responsive to the will of the people, and enhancing of the dignity and worth of the individual, then how the educative process is controlled becomes a matter of urgent concern. . . .

To assume that our schools can contribute to the strength and vitality of democracy without themselves being examples of democracy in action is exceedingly naive. It is too much to expect teachers to instill in the young appreciation and understanding of the democratic way when they themselves are denied a voice in decisions of vital importance to them. The delicate and difficult task of developing faith and confidence in democracy as a social system cannot be accomplished in a setting which is itself barren of democratic processes.

As stated at the beginning, the demands of the teachers for a more important role in the decision-making process are a source of anxiety to school boards, administrators, and the lay public. Change is always accompanied by foreboding and uneasiness, especially if there is threat to power and authority. Certainly, the movement by teachers for a greater voice in educational affairs bodes well to alter the traditional pattern of educational decision-making. However, ability to adjust to change has long been recognized as a test of vitality and strength. The question now facing educational leadership is whether the present organ-izational structure and decision-making process can adjust to the change being thrust upon them by a rapidly maturing profession without a long period of fractricidal strife and controversy.

Intimate involvement of teachers in educational decision-making is fraught with difficulties. The road ahead in school administration would appear much less hazardous if the issue had not arisen. School boards and school administrators then could devote their energies to the solution of the usual, more traditional problems. But then the wisdom and the strength that always come from improved functioning of democracy could not be brought to bear in guiding and directing the educational enterprise. Democracy is never easy. We either accept this fact and conduct ourselves accordingly, or we turn from it and place our trust in other systems of government.

A PRACTICAL LAW OF MAKING DECISIONS*

In all the contemporary fuss about decision making and the mountains of paper devoted to the topic there is, alas, as in so much social research, a preoccupation with methodology and a paucity of conclusions. Persons whose lives are dedicated to the cause of never arriving at a conclusion of any kind are producing more and more words on how to study the decision making process but are largely avoiding the question of what decisions are or how to make them.

The works of certain senior thinkers and doers are exceptions to the rule, for they at least arrive at some conclusions about the magic and mystique of decision making. T. V. Smith used to say that the top policy questions of public life cannot be decided and therefore must be resolved by compromise. Louis Brownlow often observed that when a specialist is promoted to a general post he may learn to make good decisions in every field except the one of his previous specialty. John Pfiffner recently told us in these pages that social research needs to become operational. The prevailing school seems to be in favor of decision making by counting things by machinery. This process may give us a better basis for decision making but surely does not replace the need for a conscious choice by human beings after all the returns have been counted.

Before we can readily improve the decision making business by, for instance, seeing to it that important decisions are considered at important levels, we must examine the natural laws of administratics. The time has probably come to share with readers of this review the revelation of the Law of The Specific Gravity of Decisionism. This law evolved out of

*Herbert Emmerich, "The Specific Gravity of Decisionism," by permission of *Public Administration Review*, XXIV (December, 1964), 250-253.

a lifetime of actual participation in the making of decisions, and unusual opportunities for observing others making decisions interspersed with occasional brief periods of thought.

To appreciate the hypothesis it should be pointed out that its discovery resembles more the unscientific procedures of the physical sciences than the super scientific methodology of the social sciences. Physical science discovery and invention rely greatly on wasteful manipulation of things, imagination, hunch, accident, luck, and synthesis of observations. Announcement of broad generalizations and hypotheses before they have been empirically proven is also a characteristic of physical science. My hypothesis is asserted, perhaps prematurely in the eyes of the social scientists, in the full realization that generations of social researchers that follow will occupy themselves with collecting reams of data to confirm or amend my proposition. But it is basically unassailable and I challenge them to refute it.

The beauty of the hypothesis is that it verifies itself by its simple assertion. I have tried it out numerous times on both theoreticians and practitioners in the fields of government, business and education. The instant and invariable reaction is an affirmative shaking of heads, followed by a veritable avalanche of supporting cases volunteered by my listeners. Like all great discoveries, to paraphrase Sir Arthur Conan Doyle, it seems obvious when once annunciated and people wonder why it was never stated before.

Paul H. Appleby used to assert so cogently that an executive should operate at his proper level and his prescience enabled him to forecast the present discovery. But he well knew, being a decisioneer himself as well as a keen observer of other decisioneers, that top executives are rarely permitted to deal with important questions. In fact the whole structure of hierarchies appears to be designed to serve a central purpose of keeping things away from the boss, particularly important things, lest he should decide them. . . .

CAUSES OF ADMINISTRATIVE MISBEHAVIOR

The staff of a chief executive plays a decisive role in seeing to it that major questions are neither decided at their own level nor under any conditions are referred to him. In the interests of behavioral science it may be well at this time to list some of the causes for this type of administrative misbehavior.

Caste Consciousness

Reference upwards, in the unconscious mind of a subordinate, is heavily charged with the implication of impotency or incompetence.

He has a mortal fear that by mentioning the existence of an important problem to the boss, he will be confessing to a shortcoming and his own caste in the hierarchy will be thereby downgraded, and if he finds it too painful to make the decision himself the matter will find itself tucked away in a roller bearing drawer, for even office furniture does important role playing in the process of non-decisionism.

Status Preservation

Many decisions involve questions of jurisdiction and disputes as to roles, missions, and prerogatives. The subordinate, in cases in which such conflicts are implicit, is aware that a decision unfavorable to his bureau, division, or section will denigrate the status of his unit. There is always the awful possibility that the boss will side with the other unit. Accordingly even when these intra-office differences are bitter, there is one thing upon which the contending parties will agree. It is simply that the boss must under no condition be told that there is a difference of opinion below, or that there is an important question awaiting resolution.

Hyper-Empathy

The staff knows that the boss is a very busy man, that he is having lots of trouble just now with his health, or his family, or the committee on the "Hill" or with the press. A condition frequently develops in the staff which is a morbid type of "hyper-empathy." Consideration for the troubles of the harrassed chief become an altruistic kind of rationalization for not adding to his burdens. Besides he is likely, if consulted, to ask some time-consuming questions and to call for additional data, and after all the associate is certain that he knows the answer and can go ahead and act. So the subordinate goes ahead and makes a decision even if he strongly suspects his own competence to understand all its implications. Frequently the associate acts efficiently and the decision in itself meets all the classical tests even if in some cases he is very much chagrined to find later that as a result of his decision the agency has been abolished.

Myopic Functionalism

There is a big gap between the span of the chief and his subordinates in the perimeters of cognizance. Even his deputy (and there is an increasing doubt in the minds of students of administratics whether there should be an inline deputy) will only be able to appreciate a part of a problem. Only the boss sits in a position which enables him to see all sides of a major question, its implications, and alternatives. Of course his own astigmatism may not permit him to avail himself of the full panorama which his vantage point affords. Nevertheless, the technical chiefs below him are particularly vulnerable to a condition which may be called "functional myopia." They may withhold referral of a decision upward for the reason that they do not see how it could possibly concern the chief, let alone other departments or units, or in fact the agency as a whole. . . .

Policy Decisions

A policy decision is one that requires referral to a higher level. Lest this definition be attacked as a tautoligism or a pleonasm, let me ask the the reader what other brief description can there be? In a more prosaic work I have said, *inter alia,* ". . . The minister will delegate authority to subordinate officials precisely to the extent that he can rely on them to take good decisions and to refer back, for clearance, matters involving policy. Policy matters would be those of an unusual or novel nature (some writers in fact define policy as a new problem), or of major political or administrative importance, or involving special problems of relationships with agencies external to the ministry." Appleby made the brilliant point that delegation can only begin below when major policy has been decided above. It is my observation from work in the field of technical assistance that developed countries are over-developed as to delegation and that the danger is that no questions of any moment will come to the top, just as in underdeveloped countries all questions large and small tend eventually to go to the top. In both cases the possibility of proper decision making on matters of high policy is thus effectively negatived. A policy decision can also be described as one which affects more than one particular case or instance and becomes a general rule. This brings us to case decisions.

Case Decisions

Case decisions involve the application of a general policy to a particular instance of set of circumstances, known as a case. Case decisions, even though lighter in weight, are harder to make than policy decisions because they are aimed at a particular person, place or thing. A policy decision may threaten a lot of people and raise a big stir, but it is not nearly as painful to make as a case decision in which the pain usually can be felt in a specific place. In many instances a case decision becomes a policy decision particularly in the absence of an existing policy (a very common circumstance) and it then becomes a precedent for deciding future cases. In countries having the system known as "common law" the theory is that the decision in a case will govern the decision in the next case if the circumstances are the same and the higher courts have not changed their constitutional minds. When an affluent society is blessed with an abundance of lawyers and litigation it becomes extremely difficult to find out what has been decided and whether the circumstances of one case are identical with that in a previous one. Accordingly in such societies, institutes of law must do mountains of research to maintain the ancient doctrine of *stare decisis* and make it operational. But in executive agencies subordinates are more apt to refer case decisions upwards than policy decisions. They are more painful to make and they appear to have less weight even if they later prove to have been loaded.

Coming now to the main theme of this piece, The Specific Gravity of Decision Making, the hypothesis may be stated as follows:

THE SPECIFIC GRAVITY^{SG} OF A DECISION IS DIRECTLY PROPORTIONAL TO ITS WEIGHT^W AS MEASURED BY ITS IMPORTANCE AND INVERSELY PROPORTIONAL TO THE LEVEL^L OR HIERARCHIAL ALTITUDE AT WHICH IT WILL BE CONSIDERED AND DECIDED.

The equation may be stated: $SG = \dfrac{W}{L}$

It must be born in mind that the concept of specific gravity in physics is that of a ratio. The Columbia Encyclopedia defines it as "A pure number representing the ratio between the mass or standard weight of a given volume of a substance and the weight of an equal volume of another substance taken as a unity." I have not undertaken to develop an extended table of weights of various categories of decisions nor have I assigned a measure of altitude to the various grades in an administrative hierarchy. I think it appropriate to bequeath this problem to the metric branch of the research fraternity. Empirical proofs can eventually be adduced that will confirm my hypothesis. I would advise that the research be postponed, however, until the present underdeveloped art of automatic data processing is improved at least to the extent that decimal series can be used instead of the present primitive binary system of numbers to which our crude electronic digital computers are now addicted.

A more graphic way of describing the theory is to say that the way to evaluate the importance of decisions is to weigh them and that the way to determine the level at which problems will be decided is to measure the height of that level. The ratio between the weight and the height will then determine the specific gravity of the decision. A few instances will serve to illustrate the proposition.

A decision involving, let us say, a field trip of a middle level official would be a case decision and would presumably have a low weight. It is almost certain that the lightness of this decision will cause it to rise to a very high altitude in the hierarchy and it will therefore probably be decided at a top level. A decision on the other hand whether to build high or low level dams in a river valley, or to whom a billion dollar research and development contract should be awarded will have a very heavy weight and will probably hover about at relatively low levels of administrative altitude. *Quod erat demonstrandum.*

It would seem to follow that a dynamic top administrator must spend a great deal of time and energy to see that minor questions are decided below and to contrive methods whereby important problems, both policies and cases, are made artificially to rise to the top so that they can be resolved there. If he is aware of the natural law which invariably tends to move in the opposite direction he will have taken the first step in appreciating what needs to be done. This essay is intended to be diagnostic rather than therapeutic and is not a suitable place to present solutions. It will have accomplished its purpose if it has pointed out a natural law of administratics and if it has encouraged further research concerning it.

POLICY MAKING . . .

A SURVEY OF BOARD POLICY MANUALS*

Although the practice of developing written statements of policy is far from being universal, more and more boards are becoming interested in developing them. Perhaps the attention and support given this movement by authorities in school administration account for much of the widespread interest. Many of them have emphasized that written statements of policy greatly influence the operation of school systems. They have pointed out that written policies, among other things: (1) Foster continuity, stability, and consistency of board action; (2) enable the board to provide for many conditions before they arise; (3) save time

---

*Alpheus White, "Local School Board Policy Manuals," *School Life*, XLII (November, 1959), 23-25.

and effort by eliminating the necessity of making a decision each time a recurring situation develops; (4) aid boards in appraising educational services; (5) improve board-superintendent relationships; and (6) help orientate new board and staff members to their jobs.

State school board associations have also been active in this movement. Numerous articles, expressing the desirability of adopting written board policies, have been included in the associations' periodicals and handbooks. Some associations have prepared suggested policy manual outlines; others have made packets of materials dealing with written policies available for loan.

A RECENT STUDY

What have some school systems accomplished in the way of policy development? To learn the answer to this question and to provide information that would assist others in developing comprehensive manuals, the Office of Education recently conducted a study of 60 manuals prepared by various types and sizes of school districts in 17 States.

Attention was focused primarily on the topics treated rather than on the provisions of each policy. The topics included in these 60 manuals, as analyzed and described in the study, furnish school boards with a wide range of areas to consider when developing policy manuals. Some of the highlights of the study are presented in this article.

SIMILAR TOPICS TREATED

The possible influence of school district size (based on pupil enrollment) on policy coverage was considered in a preliminary analysis of the 60 manuals. Although some variations in coverage were found, distinctive patterns of coverage for different-sized districts were not evident. This perhaps indicates that there is a common core of matters for which every school board of an operating district needs to adopt policies and that this was recognized in the smaller school systems represented in the study.

TYPES OF STATEMENTS

Differences were noted in the amount of detail included in the manuals. Some manuals contained broad statements expressing board policy but left the details required to put the policy into effect to administrative officers. Other manuals were more specific; for example, they prescribed detailed directions, leaving little to the discretion of the professional staff. Such detailed statements are labeled by many authorities as administrative rules and regulations.

As an illustration of the two types of statements, consider the following statement included in some manuals on the selections of personnel: "The superintendent shall nominate all employees to the board of education for selection." Other manuals went beyond this broad discretionary type of statement and indicated the specific items of information about prospective employees that the superintendent had to collect and specified the procedures for persons to follow in applying for a position. Such variations point out the lack of agreement on the specific content of a board policy manual.

DISTINGUISHING BETWEEN POLICIES AND RULES AND REGULATIONS

Some manuals distinguished between the types of statements included. That is, the broad discretionary statements were identified as policies and the detailed statements by such terms as "administrative rules and regulations" or "general procedures." However, this was not the usual practice. Such distinctions were not made in many manuals that contained both types of statements. Where titles of manuals, such as "Policies and Regulations" or "Policies and Procedures," indicated the inclusion of a wide range of information, the contents were not generally subdivided on the basis of the titles.

Among the manuals that distinguished between policies and rules and regulations, there was little agreement on what were policies and what were rules and regulations. Statements labeled in some manuals as "policies" were labeled in others as "rules and regulations."

INTERNAL ARRANGEMENT OF TOPICS

No typical pattern was followed in organizing the contents of the manuals. Although there were some similarities, each manual had its own distinctive internal arrangement. In some manuals the first section stated the board's philosophy of education, described the school district, or perhaps briefly described the board's source of authority. In many manuals the first topic dealt with the bylaws of the board of education.

BOARD OF EDUCATION BYLAWS

Nearly all of the 60 manuals had provisions sometimes referred to as *board bylaws*. Since these provisions specified how the internal affairs of school boards were to be conducted, the emphasis on bylaws is readily apparent. Such ground rules governing board organization, meeting procedures, and deliberations assist members in conducting school board affairs efficiently and orderly.

While manuals differed in the specific topics treated, they dealt with many common topics. Bylaws dealing with such matters as the selection of board members, board functions, duties, and meetings, and board committees were mentioned frequently. Less frequently mentioned in the manuals were bylaws dealing with such matters as the orientation, resignation, and dismissal of board members.

PERSONNEL ADMINISTRATION

Statements on personnel administration covering a wide range of topics were included in every manual. And, in some, more space was devoted to personnel administration than to any other area. Reasons for this emphasis are not difficult to see. The increasing size and complexity of school organization, coupled with unprecedented problems of personnel shortages and rapid increases in enrollment, have contributed to the need for written personnel policies. Development of an able staff is of such significance that it cannot be left to mere chance. Spur-of-the-moment decisions, which hinder the development of a well-functioning and capable staff, can be avoided by the adoption and use of personnel policies.

The personnel provisions in the manuals were related to five broad topics: (1) Employment processes, (2) job requirements, (3) salaries and related benefits, (4) professional growth, and (5) personnel placement changes. Analysis of the provisions within each of these topics revealed that most frequently they dealt with the selection of personnel, job qualifications, duties and responsibilities of personnel, salaries, sick leave, inservice education, and retirement. Less frequently dealt with, though essential to efficient personnel administration, were such matters as personnel orientation, professional conduct, supervision and evaluation of personnel, and promotions.

Of special interest was the large number of manuals (9 out of 10) that contained lists of personnel duties and responsibilities. Many of these lists were comprehensive, covering such positions as the superintendent, business manager, director of instruction, teachers, custodians, and cafeteria workers. These lists contained information common to all job descriptions — a description of the activities and tasks associated with a particular position. School systems that have developed such lists should have little difficulty in preparing complete job descriptions. However, some people would hold that extensive lists of staff position duties and responsibilities, except perhaps for the superintendent as executive officer of the board, would be more properly placed in administrative handbooks than in board policy manuals.

THE SCHOOL PROGRAM

Considerable attention was given in the manuals to school management, pupil personnel administration, the educational program, and auxiliary services.

School management — A wide range of provisions dealing with such matters as the scheduling of school activities, records and reports, instructional materials, and money drives were grouped under the term "school management" in the study. A majority of the manuals contained provisions on at least one of these topics. Many of them dealt with several different aspects of school management.

Pupil personnel administration — As perhaps would be expected, many of the manuals contained provisions on pupil personnel administration. A sizable number of the manuals had separated sections on pupil personnel policies. Primary emphasis was given to the admission of pupils to school, attendance, discipline, and pupil safety. However, many manuals had provisions on pupil assignment, classification, and progress.

The educational program — School boards, having been created to administer the affairs of school districts, have as their major purpose the providing of an educational program. To accomplish this task in the most effective manner, board policies are needed to provide guidance to the professional staff in developing and administering the kind of educational program desired by the community. Naturally, school boards would not be expected to deal directly with the technical or professional aspects of the educational program, but they do need to provide favorable conditions for effective teaching and learning.

The inclusion of policies on the educational program in most of the manuals indicates the interest boards have in this area. While variations existed in the topics treated, many manuals contained provisions on different aspects of the program, such as curriculum, supervision and evaluation of the program, student organizations and activities, and specialized instructional services.

Auxiliary services — Auxiliary or supporting school services, consisting of health, school lunch, and transportation programs, are widely recognized as being necessary components of most school programs. Many of the board manuals had policies related to these auxiliary services. For example, over 70 percent of them contained provisions on the health program.

BUSINESS MANAGEMENT

The operation of a school system is a major enterprise involving many different business activities. Money must be secured and budgeted, buildings must be constructed and maintained, supplies and equipment must be purchased and distributed, and public funds and property must be protected. All of these activities, either directly or indirectly, influence the educational program. School systems need business policies which will foster good business practices and assist in providing the kind of schools desired.

Policies related to many business management activities were contained in the 60 board manuals. Most frequently, provisions dealt with financial accounting, maintenance of property, supply and equipment management, and budgetary procedures.

SCHOOL-COMMUNITY RELATIONS

The establishment and maintenance of good school-community relations are important functions of boards of education. While the personal efforts of board members are important in improving school-community relations, there is also a need for school system policies that give direction to a continuous program. Without accurate and reliable information about its schools and opportunities to participate in school affairs, a community could hardly be expected to support its school intelligently and effectively.

Practically all of the manuals had at least one policy pertaining to school-community relations, and many of them contained a number of policies on this topic. These provisions were related to such matters as the use of school property by the public, interpreting school activities, selling and advertising on school property, citizen complaints, and relationships with community agencies.

USING THE STUDY

While policy manuals need to be hand tailored to fit specific situations, the topics treated in the 60 manuals may be of assistance to school boards in developing their manuals. These topics constitute a basic outline of areas that a number of school systems have considered as important aspects of manuals. From this outline, adaptations may be made to meet individual school system requirements.

FOR FURTHER INVESTIGATION OR REFLECTION

1. Analyze your school district's manual of board policies to determine the board's and superintendent's understanding of policy.

2. Compose brief policy statements consistent with the standards advocated herein for pupil discipline, for use of school facilities by out-of-school agencies, for the function of the superintendent, and for supervision of teaching effectiveness.

3. Write a proper job description for a building principal.

4. Analyze the job descriptions written for administrative personnel of your school system to determine if decision-making authority has been delegated with the job.

5. How does the principle of single accountability operate in your school system?

6. Interview principals and central staff officers of a school district to discover their understandings as to their advisory or authority roles.

7. Assuming the role of a principal, write a detailed bulletin to the teachers of the building on a topic (as assigned by the instructor.) Try it out with members of the class to determine if all interpret the directions as you intended.

8. Develop a lucid and workable definition of democratic administration. Can a school administrator be too democratic?

9. Identify the informal organization of your building and school system. Explain why the power resides there.

10. Design a plan of representation and a method of selection for a system-wide advisory council to the superintendent.

11. Analyze your school system's organization chart in terms of the principles advocated in this chapter.

12. Explain the educator's dislike for efficiency.

13. In the school districts of similar size as represented by members of the class, compare the number, titles, and assignments of central staff officers. How are the differences among districts explained?

14. Appraise Kissinger's analysis of decision making by committees. Can group decision making within a school system be reconciled with the accountability of superintendents and principals?

15. Where is the dividing line between strong administrative leadership and autocracy?

BIBLIOGRAPHY

Bennis, Warren G, Kenneth D. Benne, and Robert Chin, *The Planning of Change*, New York: Holt, Rinehart, Winston, 1961.

Brown, Ray E., "Administration is no Place for Perfectionists," *Nation's Schools*, November, 1964.

Caldwell, Lynton K., *The Administrative Theories of Hamilton and Jefferson,* Chicago: University of Chicago Press, 1944.

Campbell, Clyde M. *Practical Applications of Democratic Administration,* New York: Harper & Row, Publishers, 1963.

Cooper, Joseph D., *The Art of Decision Making,* Garden City, New York: Doubleday & Company, Inc., 1961.

Crowley, Francis, and Geraldine Clemenson, "The Role of Authority in Democratic Educational Administration," *American School Board Journal* CXLVI, June, 1963.

Dewey, John, "Democracy in Education," *The Elementary School Teacher,* IV, December, 1903.

Dykes, Archie R., "Democracy, Teachers, and Educational Decision-Making," *School and Society,* XCII, April 4, 1964.

Golembiewski, Robert T., "Authority as a Problem in Overlays: A Concept for Action and Analysis," *Administrative Science Quarterly,* IX, no. 1 June, 1964.

Hansen, R. G., "Specialist: Threat or Challenge," *National Elementary Principal,* XLII, January, 1963.

Hills, R. J., "Theory, Research, and Practice: Three Legs of Administrative Science," *"School Review,* LXXI, Winter, 1963.

Holland, Howard K., "Democratic Leadership. Does it Abrogate Executive Responsibilities?" *The School Executive,* LXXIX, November, 1959.

Jenkins, David, and Charles A. Blackman, *Antecedents and Effects of Administrative Behavior,* Columbus, Ohio: College of Education, The Ohio State University, 1956.

Kissinger, Henry A., "The Policymaker and the Intellectual," *The Reporter,* XX, March, 1959.

Landis, James M., *The Administrative Process,* New Haven, Connecticut: Yale University Press, 1938.

Leavitt, Harold J., "Consequence of Executive Behavior," *National Association of Secondary-School Principals Bulletin,* XLVIII, April, 1964.

Lindenfeld, Frank, "Does Administrative Staff Grow as Fast as Organization?" *School Life,* XLIII, May, 1961.

Lucas, Robert E., and Howard Wakefield, eds., *By Their Bootstraps, An Approach to Elementary School Leadership,* Columbus, Ohio: Ohio Education Association, Department of Elementary School Principals, 1955.

McCarty, Donald J., "Organizational Influences on Teacher Behavior," *The American School Board Journal,* July, 1961.

Merigis, Harry J., "Delegation in School Administration," *American School Board Journal,* CXLIV, March, 1962.

Miller, Van, "The Informal Organization Man," *Overview,* May, 1960.

Millett, John, "Perspectives of Public Administration," *Preparing Administrators: New Perspectives,* Columbus, Ohio. UCEA, The Ohio State University, Jack Culbertson and Stephen P. Hencley, eds., 1962.

Moeller, Gerald, "Bureaucracy and Teachers Sense of Power," *School Review,* LXXII, Summer, 1964.

Pascoe, D. D., "Three Concepts of Democratic District Leadership," *Educational Leadership,* XXI, November, 1963.

Roesch, Winston L., "Staffing for School Management — The Legal Factor," *School Life,* XLII, January, 1960.

Roy, Robert H., *The Administrative Process,* Baltimore: Johns Hopkins Press, 1958.

Rubenstein, Albert H., and Chadwick J. Haberstroh, *Some Theories of Organization,* Homewood, Ill.: The Dorsey Press, Inc., and Richard D. Irwin, Inc., 1960.

Chapter 3

Organization for Administering Public Schools at the Community Level

The responsibility for public education in the United States rests with the state level of government, in contrast with the customs of most foreign nations which assign authority to the central government. In the formulating of our federal constitution, no reference was made to matters of structured educational plans; whether the omission was fortuitous or accidental we cannot now be sure. We can be certain that the void set a precedent which has been the source of both pride and indictment to the present day. The Tenth Amendment to the Constitution, which amounted to the final major clarification in the division of powers between states and the federal government, assigned the responsibility for educating youth to states by default in these words: "The powers not delegated to the United States by the Constitution, nor prohibited by it to the States, are reserved to the States respectively, or to the people."

The power of the state over public education is absolute. The state can even disband its system of public education as it has done temporarily in a few instances. However, states (except Hawaii which functions as a single district) have delegated to communities most of the operational authority for education. Any authority which a local community exercises over education is a delegated power, and what the state delegates it can also withdraw. Every state retains some of its operational authority for financing and controlling schools. In essence, the operation of American public schools is a partnership arrangement between the state and local school districts.

How this partnership agreement operates may be seen in these exemplary divisions of responsibilities. A local board of education has the authority to employ teachers as it sees fit except that it must employ only those professionals who meet preparatory requirements as prescribed by

149

the state. The state establishes minimum curriculum requirements to be offered in all public schools, but the local community may develop additional courses and sequences. A community may decide to erect a building, but it may have to meet certain construction specifications of the state code. A board of education is normally empowered to select its textbooks and other instructional materials, but in some states the boards must choose from a list of books approved by the state. The state distributes its share of the cost of operating schools to the local district, but only upon conditions of participation prescribed by the Legislature.

Because of the distance between the state and many of its small districts, and because the scope and complexities of education have increased over the years, a third level of responsibility has been imposed in most states. The intermediate level of authority, often known as a county district or supervisory union, is primarily a liaison between the state and the smaller communities.

The central government has not remained aloof from educational activities, however. Although most of its interest and direct encouragement is "come lately," it has promoted education in various ways, including financial, and does exercise some responsibility.

Thus, four levels of government are involved in the administering of public education in the United States — local community, the county, the state, and the federal government. Chapter 2 is concerned only with the community level.

THE LOCAL SCHOOL DISTRICT

The earliest schools in this country may be described as private, religious, charitable, selective in admission, college preparatory, and for boys only. With the first precipitation for extending educational opportunities to all children in 1642 (note that the Plymouth settlement occurred only twenty-two years earlier), the Massachusetts legislature authorized local action on a community basis. As other legislatures took similar action, it became necessary to define the community as a legal entity, in order to accomplish local legal action.

A form of local government was already existent in the New England colonies. Settlers brought with them from England the form of local government with which they were familiar. Hence, the *town* became the local organization for sponsoring a system of public education, and still is the basic local administrative unit there. In the southern colonies settlers had established the *county* as the basis for local government because of the sparse farming population and because some of them had been most familiar with county political units in Ireland. Thus, the county became the natural geographic entity for taxing and for conducting a plan of public education, and still is in most southern states.

The westward movement accommodated citizens from both governmental backgrounds, the town and the county. Thus, the central states were surveyed and developed under a mixture of the *township* and county organizations for local government. Local governmental units for conducting public education originally followed township or county boundary lines. However, with the growth of metropolitan areas and the continual re-arrangement of township and county lines, it became practical to ignore political boundaries in the establishment of local areas for administering education. Therefore, the designation "school district" was created; the name carried throughout the settling of the far west and has come to be accepted everywhere to describe the local governmental unit for operating public schools. It is so used throughout this text.

A school district can be defined as a local independent government created by the state for the purpose of conducting a system of public education within a prescribed geographic area. It is a political unit. It has its own governing body chosen by the electorate, and empowered to perform those acts which have been delegated to it by the state. Its boundaries may or may not be conterminous with some other form of local government. Like other systems of local government, it has the power to levy taxes for the purposes prescribed by state law. It is independent of other local governments except for those districts which are known as *fiscally dependent* districts in which the school's governing body must submit its financial decisions to another local governing body, such as a municipal council, for approval. The school district's governing body has the power of legislation, enacting laws or policies which are authorized by state legislation. Such acts of the board are known as *expressed* or *statutory* powers. It may also make other regulations not specifically named in law, powers classified as *implied* or *discretionary*. Most of the regulations adopted by a board of education are made under its discretionary powers, and the courts have held that the body may make any reasonable law for the conduct of education as long as it does not violate any existing statute nor the exercise of prudent discretion. Further, a board of education has ministerial powers, that is, the obligation to perform certain duties by virtue of the members' holding a public administrative position. The board must perform those duties whether or not they are specified in statute or inferred by discretion.

A school district is classified as an *administrative unit* or administrative district, meaning that it is a complete and independent school system with its own governing body, executive head, and taxing power. It should not be confused with an *attendance district,* that geographic area which serves one building, such as an elementary building or senior high school building. Thus, the typical administrative district will encompass many attendance districts. A high school attendance district will have many elementary or junior high attendance districts within its boundaries. A parochial school's attendance district will often embrace several public school administrative districts. In the many small districts of the nation which have only one building in the entire district, the boundaries for the administrative unit and the attendance unit will be coincident.

Problems and Trends of School Districts

The local school district has stirred considerable argument over the years. Consistent with the traditional American faith in man's right to control his own affairs, it is the device by which citizens maintain control over the learning of their own children. A uniquely American concept, the influence of parents and citizens on public school activities is puzzling to foreign visitors who are accustomed to central domination of their schools, including the performance of nearly all the administrative functions.

"Local control" has become a rallying cry among citizens to the point that they fiercely resist any efforts to centralize authority even to the state level. Possessive pride in the local school system is undoubtedly at the root of much of the progress made in public education as the American competitive spirit aroused people to outdo their neighbors in providing good education for their own children. It is still the most potent appeal in persuading citizens to vote more taxes for education. It is the force which has given all districts of the nation almost a standard curriculum even without centralized direction.

At the same time, the local school district has caused many of the problems in administering public education. The principle of local control over public education is being scored on several counts today, most of which express a concern about the quality of education provided by independent districts. Critics point to the undue amount of time school officials devote to pacifying community pressures while sacrificing their educational responsibilities. The public relations function of American schools, for example, is unknown in most foreign school systems. The time spent by our administrators in campaigns for school taxes is likewise unknown abroad, nor do foreign educators "put up with parental meddling in school affairs." But the most serious problem afforded by the local control concept stems from the local responsibility for financing public education. Since state governments generally have expected local districts to pay more than half the cost of building and operating schools, and since eighty-five percent of the local revenue typically must come from taxes on property, the property wealth of a district has played a decisive role in the quantity and quality of education which the district can provide. The sharp inequities in property wealth among districts has made it difficult, often impossible, for all districts to offer their children an adequate education.

Differences in the values held by people who tend to locate within a given district and their interest in providing good education for their children have also prevented some districts from achieving what other districts do where the people happen to be more willing to allocate larger sums of money to educational purposes. Districts also differ markedly in geographic size, topography, shape, and population.

These differences among districts, aided by the advances in the automotive industry and the public desires for better educational opportunities for secondary school pupils, have been responsible for a dynamic change in the districting system. National statistics are not available to report the number of districts when the nostalgic little red school house dotted the countryside, each building representing a single district with its own governing body, but in 1930 when the first national figures were collected there were 127,000 local school districts reported. So many of these small districts have consolidated at such a pace that by 1964-65 there were only 28,814 local districts remaining, and of these 3,158 are classified as non-operating districts, i.e., districts which operate no schools and send their pupils to neighboring districts on a tuition basis.

The march toward fewer and larger school districts will certainly continue in the next few decades. There are still many small districts, too poor and too inefficiently structured geographically to permit adequate education for their high school students at a reasonable per-pupil cost. Through state laws which permit annexation, gerrymandering of district lines, and other inter-district transfers of territory, many districts have inherited areas which cannot be defended from an economical point of view. It is at the secondary school level where the too-small district leaves its worst mark. In order to provide a variegated curriculum for the occupational aims and needs of youth, a district must have enough students to make it economically sound to diversify. Many of the small districts in rural areas can only afford to offer a college-preparatory curriculum, the most economical offering since it does not necessitate expensive shops and laboratories, and yet typically those districts do not have many graduates pursuing higher education. Such districts usually cannot provide many of the other specialized services for pupils which are regarded as essential to a well-rounded education. The small but wealthy district can afford a quality program but it does so at an unreasonable expenditure per pupil, while the surrounding districts which are weak in property wealth must pay an excessively high tax in order to keep up — and still can't.

The aim is to find the optimum size district with a broader system of tax support which will satisfy two objectives: extend good education to all youngsters at a sensible cost to the taxpayers. This is a major challenge to educators and citizens. Unfortunately, research studies have not yet pointed the way to the ideal size of administrative unit. Some authorities maintain that the minimum size should accommodate 10,000 pupils; others argue that a district of 2,500 pupils in grades one to twelve would suffice. There is a trend toward the county becoming the local school district. Residents of the twelve states which now operate with the county as the basic administrative unit claim that citizens can still maintain local interest in, and control over, their public schools. It is certain that this trend will continue.

BOARD OF EDUCATION

A school district assigns its authority for managing a public school system to a governing body known as a board of education or school committee. Since the district has been chartered by the state, the governing body carries the legal status of a quasi-corporation. It needs corporate status in order to gain the same legal rights and responsibilities of an individual to act — the reason for any incorporation. It has corporate powers similar to those of a private corporation insofar as its right to hold and dispose of property for the state, the right to sue and be sued, and the right to enact legislation governing the schools, personnel, and possessions under its jurisdiction. The primary distinctions between a school corporation and an industrial corporation lie in the board of education's power of taxation but its lack of authority to operate for a profit.

In the majority of school districts, citizens choose their board members at a regular election on a non-partisan, at-large basis. Adhering to the belief that educational decisions and personnel should be exempt from partisan politics, all but six states have now passed laws which require candidates for board membership to run for office under no identification with any major political party. Furthermore, acting upon the premise that board members should exercise their decision-making and legislative powers in terms of the best interests of all children within a district rather than a segment thereof, most members are chosen from the district at large without regard for any geographic, ethnic, political, or religious portion thereof.

In a few districts, largely the metropolitan centers and in several southern states, members of the board of education are appointed by some elective body or officer such as the mayor, city council, or court. The practice is sometimes defended on the grounds that it enables a better selection of persons than if just anyone is permitted to run and everyone is permitted to vote. This belief overlooks the basic premise of democracy which holds that people should have a direct voice in affairs public. Moreover, the attitude evades the fact that the appointive force might be politically motivated. It implies that an appointing body or person can exercise more judicious decisions than can people at the polls.

This anonymous characteristic of board members does present problems in larger communities when the time comes to select candidates for election. Who is responsible for nominating and promoting the cause of suitable persons? The quick answer that citizens will take care of it doesn't suffice in all cases, except, for example, in small communities where leading citizens are well known by voters. Members of the present board often settle on a likely candidate and persuade him to become a nominee. The practice seems to work well; however, there is the ever-present danger of perpetuating too long a single clique of the community. The local Parent-Teachers Association is another source of responsible leadership for this purpose, since parents ought to have a vital interest in their children's education; but this practice may rule out of consideration the sizeable number of non-parent taxpayers in the district. Various self-interest power groups of a community frequently nominate candidates. Even political parties have a behind-the-scenes influence in promoting candidates at times. School employees occasionally take an active part in selecting and supporting candidates, but this method is incompatible with the management of a public enterprise by the public rather than by workers in the enterprise. Of course, any qualified citizen may file a petition and campaign. Probably the most promising approach to finding competent candidates is through the establishment of a school-citizens committee which is unrelated to any particular phase of the school system and represents all interested groups of the community on a volunteer basis. The technique has been used successfully in several communities and seems to be growing in popularity.

Practically all small districts throughout the nation have five members on the board of education; some have just three members. Larger districts tend to choose seven or nine members, and a few districts, more. Still fewer districts function with an even number on the board, maintaining that it permits more frequent unanimous decisions.

Those districts which have substantially larger numbers on their boards of education usually hope for wider representation of community thinking on school matters. Large boards may also be found where the laws permit combining districts to include all members of the former independent districts (such as Pennsylvania's high-school jointure districts). Large boards are difficult to justify. If a district wished to have more of its community elements represented on the board there would be no equitable stopping point within the typical community's conglomerations and special-interest groups. Moreover, that kind of representation defeats the merits of the at-large method of selecting members. It would be difficult to prove that large boards make better decisions than small ones; they are likely to make poorer judgments if they suffer the normal unmanageable pains of large groups in trying to arrive at decisions.

A large governing body also invites the abuse of a basic operating principle recommended for a board of education, viz., that it function as committee of the whole. With many members, and with many problems to face such as a board encounters, the president tends to parcel the business among permanent standing committees, thereby denying each member adequate knowledge of all concerns of education as was intended by the representative system. A member becomes an expert on a small segment of the enterprise but remains an uninformed amateur to the total responsibility with which a board of education is charged by the people. This situation often results in legislation by log-rolling. In fact, the courts have declared that a board of education cannot legally delegate to a subcommittee the powers imposed upon it by the legislature. Further, as one becomes an expert on a limited phase of education he is inclined to violate still another accepted principle of public school management, i.e., the citizen representative to a public body should restrict his activity to the legislative function and remain out of the professional technician's skill — the executive function. This is not to say that committee functioning is entirely out of place on a board of education. There are concerns which can be investigated and handled best by a smaller group of the board, at times just one member. But authorities agree that these subcommittees have only recommending powers and that they should always be *ad hoc* committees which disband as soon as the concern expires.

In most districts, board members serve without remuneration although the state may authorize a small travel allowance for attending meetings. The practice of paying a flat sum per year for board service may be found in a few southern districts, larger districts, and, more commonly, among appointive boards. Now and then one hears the recommendation that board members be salaried, since the desirable caliber of person should devote full time to the job. The recommendation seems to auger a board of superintendents rather than a board of lay representatives of the community which is concerned only with policy. Moreover, unless the salaries were intolerably high the plan would probably not attract the prevailing quality of public servant who is motivated by community service to youth rather than by material gain. The profile of the typical board member as revealed in many studies indicates that he is a business or professional man, a college graduate, and generally represents the upper socio-intellectual stratum.

Each state stipulates the qualifications which a potential candidate must possess. With the exception of minor prescriptions in a few states, regarding age, education, payment of taxes, or being a parent of school-age children, the only requirement for candidacy is that the person be a resident of the district. Laws are more restrictive as to who may not be a candidate than as to who may. Certain persons and positions are declared incompatible with membership on a board of education; notable examples are an employee of the district or one who would profit financially from membership. That legal residency be the only requirement is consistent with the democratic plan for electing public officers to represent their fellow citizens in the management of a public enterprise.

The plan leaves something to be desired, however, in today's operations of public schools. Education has become so technical, and a school system so complex, that a novice to the board of education has much to learn before he can be an effective policy-making representative of the community. Board members often attest to the fact that it requires one year, some say two years, before they feel sufficiently knowledgeable about school law, finance, and educational practices to make sound decisions. For this reason, superintendents spend considerable time, and use numerous techniques, to orient a new board member to his duties. A new board member needs to visit all the facilities, meet at least the key personnel, and read the state code, the minutes of previous meetings, policy handbooks, and the numerous professional journals which are available today. Considerable progress has been made toward "professionalizing" board members through their own bootstrap efforts: workshops, institutes, and the national, state, and regional affiliations with the National School Boards Association.

State laws specify how a board of education shall organize and elect officers, usually at the beginning of each fiscal year. Most boards choose their own presidents, vice-presidents, secretaries, and perhaps the treasurers. The offices of secretary and treasurer are often combined into one position. The authorities of each officer are set forth in law. The primary duties of the president are to conduct the meetings and to sign official documents for the board. He may speak for the board when it is not in session if his statements have been previously sanctioned by the entire body. Otherwise, the courts have consistently held that no member's authority extends beyond the official meeting.

It seems to be the common intent of the laws that a board secretary should serve no more than a clerical and record-keeping role. When the law, or local board regulations, cloak him with more authority they invite a two-headed organization. Clearly the secretary is a board officer, accountable to the board rather than the superintendent; if he is granted administrative or decision-making powers, the organization will have two chief executives, identified in the previous chapter as a *dual-control* organization. The condition is even more complicating if the law permits a voting member of the board of education to be appointed as secretary. Where these conditions exist because of law or custom, an amicable arrangement can sometimes be made through job definitions for the secretary and the superintendent.

Meetings of the Local Board of Education

A board is typically required to meet in *regular* session monthly but many boards find that they must convene more often to cope with their mounting responsibilities. Some boards arrange *special* or *adjourned* meetings in which official business may be transpired. Nearly every board finds it necessary on occasion to meet in *informal* or *executive* sessions, which are not open to the public, in order that members might discuss restricted affairs, or for extended discussions which would consume excessive time at a regular meeting. As vital as these caucus meetings are to the successful operation of the unit, no official action should be taken during those gatherings; some state laws forbid it. Official decisions and legislation should be acted upon only at a public meeting. The courts have ruled that the only official voice of a board may be found in the minutes of the board which are recorded by the board's secretary and approved by the board in a regular session.

Failure to use informal sessions for lengthy discursive matters accounts partially for the unnecessarily extended, inefficient, and often boring regular meetings. A well-planned agenda by the superintendent should rarely consume more than two hours, allowing time for completing official business, participation by visitors when desired, and the useful in-service reports from the school family. A board that does not delegate adequately the administrative tasks to its superintendent and staff will also spend an unreasonable amount of time in meetings. All authorities on school administration agree that the three "doing" tasks of a board of education in best practice are those of legislation for the entire district, appraisal of overall performance, and selection of a competent executive.

In performing the legislative assignment, the board should understand that the resulting policy gives direction to the administrator and staff in carrying out the wishes of the citizens in matters of education. The professional staff may offer technical advice in the formulation of the policy, but the policy is the board's belief. After it has been put in writing, the executive and his staff will know what is expected of them and may proceed to develop rules for implementing the policy. The "what" and "why" of educational matters is the citizens' decision speaking through their board of education; the "how" is a professional decision.

THE INTERMEDIATE SCHOOL DISTRICT

In all states but the twelve where the county school district is the basic administrative unit, and excepting Delaware and Nevada which have no intermediate districts, provision has been made for an intermediate administrative level between the small local school districts and the state to render limited functions and services. The larger city districts are generally exempt from any responsibility to the intermediate office, working directly with the state in accountability.

The intermediate office operates under the administration of a superintendent and board of education but it lacks the most important features of a local administrative unit: taxing power and its own schools. Nonetheless, the intermediate unit is discussed in this chapter in view of its proximity to the community. As already suggested, there are indications that the county may soon become the local administrative unit in much of the United States.

Three forms of intermediate districts have appeared in the history of United States public education: the county, the supervisory union (consisting of several towns) in the New England states, and the township which has largely disappeared as an intermediate unit.

The county as an intermediate district is different from the county as a basic administrative district. In the twelve county-unit states — Alabama, Florida, Georgia, Kentucky, Louisiana, Maryland, New Mexico, North Carolina, Tennessee, Utah, Virginia and West Virginia — the county is the local administrative district, the only independent school district existing in most of those counties. The intermediate district concept is not found in Delaware or Hawaii where the state administrators direct most of the school districts. Similarly, in Nevada the state department of education provides the services which a county intermediate office normally handles. The county as the local administrative unit may be found in some sections of other states.

The county as an intermediate unit is primarily a medium of communication between the state and the local districts. The county as an "arm of the state" was the only purpose of the intermediate office at the beginning, and thus it remains in many counties today. Like the local school district, the intermediate district has only those authorities granted it by the state. Some states have directed that the county develop and extend to rural districts educational services which their small size forbids development on their own. County offices which are blessed with professional and aggressive superintendents have pushed ahead to make available to their local districts the services of supervision, psychological consultation, curriculum development, health services, libraries, instructional materials, special and vocational education. A few counties effect certain economies for local districts through county-wide purchasing, and through planning of pupil transportation services.

The patterns of organization and administration of the intermediate units vary more than do any other organizational units in the American school structure. Their respective governing bodies differ from state to state as to number, method of selection, and powers. The chief school administrators of these units serve under different qualifications for the post, authority and activities, tenure, salary, and methods for selection. The most common method throughout the United States for choosing the county superintendent is popular election.

The future of the intermediate administrative unit is less secure than that of the local districts. While some regions are moving to abandon small local districts and combining them into a one county unit — a fact which suggests a general strengthening of the county office — elsewhere there is movement to spread the intermediate level still wider geographically. The Wisconsin Legislature voted to abolish the office of county school superintendent effective July 1, 1965, and created in its place twenty-five state-sponsored service agencies which will provide services comparable to those customarily assigned to the county office. The Ohio Legislature has a proposal before it at the present writing to develop area service centers of 10,000 pupils to supersede several county offices.

CONTROL OVER PUBLIC EDUCATION . . .

COMMUNITY PARTICIPATION IN EDUCATIONAL POLICY-MAKING IS AMERICAN*

Whereas in the United States the home and the community expect to participate in determining the policies, practices, and financial support of

---

*Thomas E. Benner, "Lessons from the Patterns of Education of Other Countries." From a paper appearing in *Government of Public Education for Adequate Policy Making.* Champaign: by permission of Bureau of Educational Research, University of Illinois, 1960, 47-49.

the public schools, in most other countries of the world no such participation is either provided for or customary. Indeed, to ask for it would
be considered inappropriate or even impertinent!

School matters are dealt with in broad administrative and budgetary
outlines by the national parliament and administered in detail by the
bureaucracy of the national ministry of education. At the head of this
national system is the minister of education, who is usually a member of
the parliament and a layman in the field of education. The minister is,
in effect, a one-man, partisanly political, national board of education.

The bureaucracy of the ministry of education, corresponding to the
state department of education in an American state, is made up of men
and women who have come up through the ranks of the schools. Competence, energy, reliability, conformity, and tactful firmness in carrying
out assigned duties as teachers, principals, or regional administrators are
likely to have counted more heavily in their promotions than originality
or zeal for educational reform.

A staff of inspectors from the ministry visit the schools to make sure
that the prescribed pattern is being followed and to judge the local personnel. Their ratings of teachers and administrators go into the personnel
files of the ministry and are used in determining reassignments and
promotions.

Observers of the highly centralized school systems of New Zealand
and Australia have pointed out that an inspector, especially one of lower
seniority, hesitates to rate a teacher or principal markedly better or worse
than he has been rated previously by another inspector. In another
national school system, teacher evaluation of inspectors is typically
expressed by drawing a finger over an imaginary piece of furniture and
inspecting for dust.

There are, of course, many inspectors who rise strikingly above these
patterns and whose visits are looked forward to by the school staff. Her
Majesty's Inspectors of the schools of Great Britain would place near or
at the top of the inspectorial staffs of other countries. Interestingly, they
are outside of the Ministry of Education and their inspection reports,
which determine eligibility to participate in parliamentary funds, are not
filed in the Ministry of Education.

The local community in most countries formulates no school budget
and, as has been pointed out, is not consulted by the officials who do.
Similarly, it has nothing to say about curriculum matters and does not
participate in the selection or assignment or removal of teachers and
principals. The officials of local government may petition the national
ministry of education to establish new schools or to inaugurate new programs which are provided for in the national laws and regulations.

Such requests may also originate with the ministry's regional or local appointees.

Supplementing and reinforcing this centralized control of education by the ministry of education is the influence of the universities. The bureaucracy of the ministry is largely made up, at higher levels, of personnel who were educated as academic specialists in the universities, who taught their specialty in the secondary school, and who subsequently rose through the ranks.

THE LAYMAN'S DECISIONS ABOUT PUBLIC EDUCATION WILL DECREASE*

What is properly a lay decision and what is properly a professional decision in education? A common answer to this question is that policy making is the responsibility of a lay board of education representing the public, and the administration of board policies is the responsibility of professional educational administrators. Another emphasis can be found in the debates of philosophers of education who deal with the problem in terms of what should be the scope of public control of education particularly in the society committed to democratic values.

Neither of these approaches necessarily describes existing conditions nor is it their intention to do so. We all recognize that, on the one hand, strong administrators often make policy for weak boards and, on the other hand, boards of education often involve themselves in administration, frequently through the mechanism of standing committees. Nevertheless, almost all who consider the lay-professional decision question do so in terms of what the relation ought to be. The question stated in those terms is an important one. However, it is also instructive to develop descriptive analyses which provide a somewhat different focus.

An analysis of the directions of changes in society and in education, and their influence on the role in education of the public and professionals furnishes a starting point. It is our contention that such an analysis leads to the prediction that, over time, the scope of professional decisions will be increased and the scope of lay decisions decreased. The grounds for this prediction can be found primarily in the increasing size of school districts and the greater complexity of their task and administrative organization.

---

*Donald J. Willower, "Lay and Professional Decisions in Education." By permission of *Peabody Journal of Education,* XLI (January, 1964), 226-228.

The trend in the United States is clearly toward fewer and larger school districts. In addition, the tasks and activities of the school have been expanded and have become more intricate. Large organizations formed to carry out complex tasks require the services of varied personnel including many specialists. The "expertness" of these specialists becomes a force acting to legitimate decisions which may be crucial to the organization. While the chief administrator is considered to be a generalist, many of his decisions will be based upon a sifting and weighing of the sometimes conflicting recommendations of specialists. Regardless of what recommendations, or combination or modification of them, are decided upon, the point is that major administrative decisions in large organizations are usually based upon some kind of expert grounds. This makes these decisions more difficult to oppose and this is especially true in the case of the lay person who may wish to question or resist them.

Another factor to be considered is the relative complexity of decision-making in large organizations. For example, the effect of decisions on the various organizational sub-units cannot be safely ignored. In the larger organization, problems of coordination, communication, accountability, and inter-unit conflict may be accentuated, and add complexity.

Lay board members neither wear the mantle of the expert nor are they particularly prepared to deal with highly complex organizational problems. Given complexity and faced with advice having expert support, it is reasonable to predict that board members will restrict the scope of their decision-making, becoming more passive and acquiescent. These conditions, characteristic of the large organization, may be contrasted with the situation in the smaller organization of less complex structure. There, relationships will be more personal. Fewer specialists will be available and administrative personnel will probably be seen to a greater extent as individuals rather than in terms of their specific organizational role. Organizational problems will be simpler and more readily understood. Under those circumstances, there is greater likelihood that board members will see themselves as informed, feel more secure, and be more willing to risk initiation of and commitment to particular decisions. In general then, professional decisions will increase and lay decisions will decrease in scope, as organizational size and complexity increases.

The rationale for this proposition is plausible. However, it seems appropriate to point out that it should be treated as a hypothesis. Additional questions of an empirical nature could also be raised. For example, what part is played by organizational size and complexity of organizational task as separable independent variables leading to the consequences predicted? A number of more philosophical questions can also be raised. To cite one symptomatic of the times, how can the citizenry of a democracy participate intelligently in important educational decisions in the face of increasing size and complexity? This question, which has implications both for administrator-board relations and for the general area of school-community relationships, calls for careful thought and study on the part of all concerned.

FORCES WHICH ARE DESTROYING LOCAL CONTROL OF EDUCATION*

In discussing local control, it might be wise to start with the remarks of Senator Strom Thurmond of South Carolina who has said that "the best way to protect local self-government is to exercise it. If you have a problem, first try to solve it yourself as an individual. . . . If government action is essential, turn first to the lowest level of government. . . . Only as a last resort should solutions be sought through the agency of the State, and above all, don't drop your problem in the lap of the national government, unless your problem falls clearly within one of the specifically delegated powers in the Constitution."

Parenthetically, I might add in relation to this last thought the quotation from the decision of the Supreme Court of the United States in 1942 in the case of *Wickard vs. Filburn,* which included this observation, "It is hardly a lack of due process for government to regulate that which it subsidizes. The moral is that if you get money from Washington, you get control along with it." Concerning the local self-government of our schools, one big difference between American and European education is the centralized responsibility for schools in European nations in contrast to our system of local autonomy. . . .

The Northwest Ordinance of 1787 read in part as follows: "Religion, morality and knowledge, being necessary to good government and the happiness of mankind, schools and the means of education shall be forever encouraged." The ordinance went on to assign lot number sixteen in each township for the maintenance of schools within that township. Thus, in theory, one-sixteenth of the national wealth was assigned to the local communities by the newly organized central government. Nor did that central government retain control over the education to be pro-

---

*Kenneth S. Haussler, "Local Control of Public Schools." Taken from *American School Board Journal,* CXLVII (October, 1963), published by the Bruce Publishing Company.

vided by this grant. Wary of centralized authority, all control of the schools was left to individual states under the reserve powers clause of the Tenth Amendment. In turn, the states decentralized education by passing on to smaller governmental units the control of education. Counties and towns were further split into districts, each with its school supervised by a committee of local citizens. So fierce and sincere was the attachment of citizens to the development of universal, free public education, locally controlled, that in many cases it became the prime program of political parties, the central thesis and effort of individuals and local community groups.

STATE AND LOCAL RESPONSIBILITIES

Expanding demands of education, however, overcame much of this parochial operation of the schools. After 1850, consolidated schools appeared across the country with broader bases of finance and State contributions to local support brought with them minimum requirements of curriculum and expenditure of funds. State laws provided for compulsory attendance, supervision of education, uniformity of textbooks, certification of teachers, and affected practically every facet of school operation. The basic premise of school operation and control as we know it today is for the State to set minimal standards, with no limitation of the local district and with the community going as far beyond these in degree and variety as the local citizenry feel necessary and are willing to support. . . .

There are signs that we may be at a crossroads which will require us to make a choice between this diversity resulting from the measure of local control given to the schools and a uniformity impressed on education by the elimination of local operation and the imposition of further centralized State or National control. Powerful forces are pressing for elimination of variations in educational program and operation as we have seen not only in the name of efficiency, but also in the name of national safety, and of mass instruction.

Few people, if any, disagree with the thesis that the further local control is removed from the people, the less possibility is present that the funds raised for a public purpose will be most effectively spent for that purpose. Now, you have every right to ask the question, — "If there is more or less general agreement on such general principles, why is there any reason for concern?"

The answer, generally, is that many school board members and the great percentage of the public have no realization of the extent to which local control already has been swept away from local boards and placed in centralized authorities. This has been done in such a piecemeal fashion through the years that, unless we pause to study the complete picture, there could be no proper realization. . . .

What are the factors operating to reduce the effectiveness of local control of education? There are, in my opinion, three major factors which must be recognized, and should be frankly discussed by those sincerely interested in the welfare of public education in California, namely:

1. Centralization of Education
2. The Struggle for Power by Various Organizations
3. The Role of Partisan Politics . . .

Let us examine four areas of Centralization of Education as it has unfolded during the recent past.

First of all, the employment of personnel. Originally, the policy of the State in this connection was to limit itself to standards of certification; that is, to provide minimum educational requirements so that the people would be assured that each certificated employee had a qualified educational background. As long as the employee was so certified, the local school board had complete discretion as to whom it should employ. As was stated by the Supreme Court of the State of Washington in the case of *Seattle High School Chapter* vs. *Sharples,* when an injunction was sought to prevent the board of education from refusing to engage teachers who belong to a particular teachers organization, " . . . The employment of teachers is a matter of voluntary contract. Both parties must consent and be mutually satisfied and agreed. On the part of each it is a matter of choice and discretion. However, though qualified, no teacher has the legal right to teach in the schools until the directors willingly enter into a contract for that purpose. . . . Unless limited by statute in some way, the board is entitled to the freedom of a contract, as much so as the teachers are. . . ." However, it is interesting to note that the California statutes are beginning to impose such a limitation upon boards of education.

In 1955 the California Legislature included limitations concerning the recommendations of persons for employment or the refusal or failure to do so for reasons of race, color, creed or national origin. In 1957 they added additional limitations for reasons concerning age or marital status. In 1961 they added restrictions relating to membership in employee organizations or unions and qualifications for teaching positions in such a way as to provide a complete overhaul of hiring practices and teacher education practices. Furthermore, the legislature has, in the last six years, twice introduced legislation which would have required . . . statewide tenure, — that is, counting service with one district when subsequently employed by another district. Such legislation, if successful, would have as its ultimate objective having the teacher-applicant register with the state and then being set to the school district to fill a vacancy, regardless of the district's desire.

The second area in the field of overcentralization of education is in the matter of the authority to dismiss personnel. It is significant to note that the California law has arrived at almost the ultimate in completely removing the authority of the local governing board. Insofar as permanent teachers are concerned, the board has no hearing upon charges which are brought before it; — the dismissal cannot be made without prior court permission in which the board and not the teacher bears the burden of proof. (Unlike any other kind of tenure or civil service law.) In this connection, the California Supreme Court, in the case of *Board of Education* vs. *Ballou,* 21 Cal. App. (2d) 52, criticized the law in this regard in the following language:

"The Legislature has placed upon the judges the duty of determining whether a teacher should be dismissed when charges such as incompetency are filed. A duty essentially administrative has been withdrawn from administrative officials and imposed upon officials exercising judicial functions. It is to be hoped that the legislature will not be prevailed upon to extend this duty so that the courts will be compelled to pass upon all the charges that may be filed against the civil service employees of the state and its various political subdivisions. . . ."

Therefore, it is readily apparent that the powers of governing boards over retention of employees is *practically nil. . . .*

SCHOOL SYSTEM SALARIES

The third area of particular concern in the centralization of the school system is the matter of salaries. Here is a subject which has always been considered the prerogative of the local community as reflected by the governing board of the district. However, even in that area signs are on the horizon indicating a possible change of state policy. Minimum salaries, first placed in the Constitution at $2400 per annum, have been raised by the State Legislature to $4500 per annum. During the 1963 session of the Legislature there was a bill to raise this amount to $5000.

It is, of course, not only the minimum which is affected; the governing board must adjust its entire salary structure to fit the minimum. A bill was even introduced in 1957 to place a maximum salary on certificated employees. With such a trend, one need not stretch his imagination very far to visualize in the future an entirely standardized salary schedule in the state law completely removing the governing boards' discretion in

such matters. Also, in relationship to the salary question, we note that
the legislature has placed rigid restrictions on governing boards in such
matters as compensation for illness, study and travel, and absence
because of bereavement, as well as the method of paying salaries. The
important point is not that these allowances may not be proper, but that
the discretion is removed from the governing boards.

*Now the fourth area of effect is the increasing centralization of our
public school systems.* Now let us explore, for a moment, another field
of legislative trends. After the serious 1933 earthquake, the State of
California adopted the so-called "Field Act" requiring school buildings
to conform to certain building standards. There was, and still is, general
approval of such policy; however, the trend has continued in the direction
of removing all local control over the construction of school plants. For
example, the State Department of Education has set up standards for site
areas which must be met if a district is to qualify for state funds as an
"impoverished district."

The Civic Center Act is a good example of the state requiring the
school district, under certain conditions, to allow the use of its facilities
by various groups free of charge. In many districts this amounts to
thousands of dollars in possible revenue per year. Again — the important point is — that the local boards of education have very little or no
say in this matter. . . .

If I may take you back a few minutes you will recall that besides the
area of Centralization of Education there were two other major factors
which should be discussed. *The second of these is the Struggle for Power
by Various Organizations* and the dolorous effect of this strife on local
control of Education in America.

We are all aware of the number of pupils, employees, budgets, etc.,
and some of the projections for the future. Undoubtedly, as a result of
this situation it has followed that a number of employee organizations
have evolved relating directly to the schools. In addition, there are
numerous other organizations which have a more indirect relationship
to the schools. There are, in fact, over 100 of these almost all of which
maintain a "lobby" in Sacramento and with a national branch maintaining one in Washington. Each organization has its program and its staff
to implement such a program. It is quite natural for each organization to
continue to make its program as attractive as possible for its membership.
Lest there be a misunderstanding, may I emphasize that I firmly believe
in organizations. Among those to which I have belonged are the California School Boards Association and the California Farm Bureau Federation, which are both close knit organizations doing excellent jobs for
their members.

RESPONSIBILITY TO THE PUBLIC

My point is, however, that organizations which are strong and power-ful must, in the public interest and even in their own long range interest, recognize their responsibilities to the public. This responsibility is not met by advocating or opposing legislation merely for the sake of record-ing *victories* at the end of the legislative session. I have noticed with increased concern, a tendency for some educational employee groups to support or oppose legislation merely because a rival group took the opposite position. If there is a sincere endeavor to secure good legislation a much better effort must be made for the various groups to set up a clearing house for proposed legislation. Deadwood should be eliminated; priorities should be agreed upon and set up.

I am afraid that the general public will some day arrive at a conclusion adverse to our interests so the time for some soul searching and self-discipline is *now* while the trend is present but can still be regulated in accordance with the best practices. Let us not be caught in a struggle for power by organizations regardless of their admitted values.

WHEN IS A SCHOOL DISTRICT TOO SMALL?*

There is pretty general agreement among students of school admin-istration that a school district should be large enough to employ at least 40 teachers and enrol 1,200 pupils in Grades I through XII.

California laws make 10,000 pupils the desirable minimum enrollment for newly formed districts, and only in unusual situations permit the formation of new school districts with less than 2,000 pupils. Pennsyl-vania school laws recommend a minimum of 1,600 pupils per district; and the county committees responsible for making school district reorganization plans and proposals in Wisconsin are strongly encouraged to make 800 pupils in Grades I-XII the minimum enrolment for new districts.

A school district with a total enrolment of 800 pupils will have about 200 pupils and from 8 to 10 teachers in the four-year high school. Simple arithmetic and a little plain common sense quickly show that a school

---

*The Point of Beginning: The Local School District, Washington, D. C.: by permission of American Association of School Administrators, 1958, 5-8, 11-12.

of this size can't have a very wide range of course offerings. In a work schedule that provides for instruction in several different subjectmatter fields and four different grade levels, the time of 8 or 10 teachers is about all used up in meeting basic minimum requirements. There is little opportunity left for:

Advanced courses or accelerated programs that challenge gifted pupils and develop their full potential

Remedial work that corrects deficiencies and helps slow learners over difficult places

Course offerings to meet the special interests and to develop the unique abilities that can be expected in a school that serves children from every level and segment of community life.

One needs only to examine casually the enrolment in the public high schools of this country at this time to see that many of them fall far below this minimum standard. Of the 23,746 public high schools in this country now:

13,142 enrol less than 200 pupils
7,117 enrol less than 100 pupils
2,720 enrol less than 50 pupils. . . .

Current reports that high school children are looking for snap courses and are avoiding physics, chemistry, geometry, and trigonometry are frequently based on data from small school districts where these and other equally important courses cannot be offered regularly — in many instances not offered at all. The big trouble isn't spineless kids and soft teachers as some people who are not well informed would have us believe. The real trouble is outmoded school district organization — school district organization that is now called upon to provide services, to perform functions, and to operate programs that were scarcely dreamed of when it was established.

In too many instances children are deprived of educational opportunities they need and want because districts can't employ the teachers and provide laboratory facilities for a good college entrance program. In too many instances children are deprived of good vocational preparation because the school district can't purchase the shop equipment and secure the specialized instructors needed for a high quality program of vocational education.

Meeting minimum requirements, staying on the accredited list, and offering enough courses to meet college entrance requirements are the goals that the school district with inadequate financial resources, meager school plant facilities, and a teaching staff too small to do all that needs to be done, strives so hard to meet. The school board, the superintendent, the principal, the teachers, the parents, and most of all the children themselves may want a high quality program — the best there is in music, art, mathematics, sciences, and vocational education — but it is difficult to weld without a forge or anvil, or to perform chemical experiments without a laboratory. . . .

The school administrator is in a unique position when a group of neighborhoods and communities are seriously considering reorganizing several smaller administrative units into a larger school district. The administrator is generally regarded as the community spokesman on important educational issues. On legal questions of communitywide interest, the judge's opinion is held in high esteem; when religious issues are being considered, particular heed is given to what the minister says: but when it comes to school matters, no other person in the entire community commands the attention that is accorded the school administrator. People may violently disagree with the points of view he expresses, but at least they want to hear what he has to say, and to have the advantage of his thinking in making up their own minds.

The position of the administrator in a school district reorganization program is seldom easy. Not infrequently people get worked up to a high pitch of excitement; emotions bubble near the boiling point; feelings run high and are easily wounded; and tempers are not always kept under perfect control. Unquestionably there is great temptation for the county superintendent who was elected by popular vote, or for the local superintendent who likes to keep everything rolling along nicely on an even keel, to be noncommittal, or to take the position that the people had better let well enough alone, at least for the time being. But an "on the fence" or noncommittal position is impossible for the person who gives the educational interests of children in the community top priority.

The difficult and almost impossible positions in which they are placed at times prevent forward-looking superintendents from taking stands they want to take and giving leadership they want to give to school district reorganization programs. But where reorganization efforts have been successful, the vigorous leadership of both county superintendents and local superintendents has been one of the strongest factors in the whole process. Every community handicapped by weak, inadequate districts should expect such leadership from their school superintendents and should support them in exercising that leadership.

THE LARGE SCHOOL DISTRICT IS BECOMING STANDARD*

Generalizations about school administration are demonstrably more useful than any about today's school districts. There are still far too many relics extant of the earlier, more simple days. According to the Bureau of Census, in 1962 there were more than ten thousand school districts responsible only for elementary schools and for fewer than fifty children. Nearly twenty thousand operated only a single school, although in a few cases it was a large and complex one.

A good many small districts have come under the guidance and administration of an "intermediate district" (often at the county level) which supplements and directs their educational and even their business programs. However, the small district and the district that operates less than the full range of educational programs from kindergarten to grade twelve is anachronistic and slowly vanishing. In 1962 such districts accounted for barely 8 percent of the nation's public school children.

In that same year 12,500 districts enrolled more than three hundred children each and had an average annual budget of more than one million dollars. Seven out of eight public school children went to school in a district that provided both elementary and secondary education. The thousand largest school systems enrolled half of the 37 million public school children and spent half of the nation's 17 billion dollar annual budget for schools in that same period.

The large school district is fast becoming typical. It is a complex organization. Among other things it is a big business. In many a community the school system serves more meals, transports more children, has a more extensive plant, and has a larger payroll than any other business in the community. It touches intimately and directly more homes than any other business. It is supported in part by a property tax laid on all of the property within the district. It is controlled in large part by a locally representative body. The business affairs of most of the citizens in any school district are dwarfed in contrast.

Quite understandably the very size of the operation causes some to demand that it be run strictly by business standards. At the same time many people see that it is so centrally important to the community's children and to the community itself that something more

---

*Management Surveys for Schools: Their Uses and Abuses, Washington, D.C.: by permission of American Association of School Administrators, 1964, 17-18.

than business standards are called for. Almost inevitably there is conflict between views. Although a few people hold tenaciously to the first view and a few to the latter, most people hold both views alternately and even concurrently. Board members, not always consciously, tend to reflect this conflict in their policies and attitude. Superintendents with stamina and courage find this conflict a constant challenge. It is at the point where the two views clash that school administration is seen to require a specialized professional competence, very distinct from that required in any other kind of enterprise.

THE "FATHER OF SCHOOL ADMINISTRATION" SPEAKS AGAINST FISCAL DEPENDENCE FOR SCHOOL DISTRICTS IN 1915*

To protect the schools from being given less than their proper share of funds a number of our States have given to a few or to all of the city school systems in the State the right to determine, usually within certain legal limits, the amount of school funds needed, and to certify the same for levy without interference by any city authority. There has been a marked increase in such authorization within the past fifteen years, as well as several recent attempts on the part of city officials to break down separate authorization. The rather common tendency of city governing authorities is to reduce the school department to a branch of the city government, and then to subordinate the interests of the schools to the interests of the patronage departments — fire, police, streets, water, sewers — of the city. The more political the city government the greater is the danger to the schools. In cities operating under a commission form of government the results are likely to be much better than when a city council has to be dealt with.

The chief argument for city control of the school tax is that it unifies the taxing power, and gives one central representative body control over all expenditures. If the schools are to be free, why not the parks and the health and the police? The answer must be that the schools are too important for the future of our national life to trust them to the whims and trades and log-rolling of a political body, elected with no reference to school administration, and that in but few of our cities has

*E. P. Cubberley, *Public School Administration,* Boston: by permission of Houghton Mifflin Company, 1916, 411-412.

the sense of civic duty been such as to enable the people to place the schools on an equal footing with other city party politics and personal influences are brought to bear. Even when thoroughly honest and actuated by good motives, the members of a city council lack that close touch with educational problems which will enable them to appreciate the large future importance of expenditures for schools, when the school needs come in competition with the pressing and more immediate needs of other city departments. The unity of the city tax-levy is an argument of no importance. No other city department, except possibly the health department, represents any large future interest. Even it is not coordinate with the government, the home, and the church, as is the school.

A POLITICAL SCIENTIST LOOKS AT INDEPENDENCE OF SCHOOL DISTRICTS*

The subject implies that a political scientist may look at independent school government from a different viewpoint than the non-political scientist, and that, I believe, is true. However, as a political scientist who has spent most of his life in education, I think I can approach the subject with a great deal of sympathy for the educators' point of view. That viewpoint, as I understand it, is made up of a number of elements which, when synthesized, lead to the conclusion that independent school government is necessary for the best interests of education. The elements in the picture include the following concepts:

1. Education is the most important function which the community performs.
2. Education is a state function which, when delegated to the local community, should be legally separate from other community functions.
3. Education should be separately financed, and
4. An independent educational system will insulate the schools from politics, will enable the citizen to express his views on educational policy uncomplicated by other community problems, and will achieve greater financial support for education.

---

*Harold Van Dorn, an address delivered at Kent State University, 1960. (Transcribed from tape recording, by permission of Harold Van Dorn.)

There may be other elements in the picture, but these four embody, I believe, most of the concepts which are advanced in support of independent school government. Now I would like to examine these propositions with you.

1. Education is the most important function which the community performs.

I think education is *one* of the most important functions the community performs. In fact, I think it is so important that I am devoting my life to education. At the same time, I find it difficult to think of it as separate from other vital functions which the community undertakes. All these functions are so interrelated, so dependent one upon another, so interactive, that unless there is coordination and integration there cannot be smooth functioning. It seems to me that we must give attention to every aspect of local government if we are to promote a healthy community life. In trying to educate our children we seek well-rounded development. We aim to educate the whole child. We do not pick out one facet of a child's education and say, "This is the most important." Who shall say whether it is more important to train the eyes, or the ears, or the body, or the mind, or the emotional life? The one is dependent upon the other. Of what avail to train the eyes to read if there is no active mind seeking knowledge? And a good mind will function badly under emotional stress. And no training of the mind or the emotions is of much value if the physical body breaks down. And so we say, "Educate the whole child." If this is a sound principle, is it not equally sound to apply it to the body politic? To the community in which we live? Are not community functions equally interrelated? What good to have a fine school, adequately financed, if the building burns down because of an antiquated fire department, or inadequate fire prevention measures? Of what value are well-paid teachers if your child is the victim of a traffic accident because of an undermanned and underpaid police department? How much consolation can you take in your progressive school policies if an epidemic decimates your school population as the result of inadequate methods and understaffing of your city health department? All these aspects of community life are interrelated, a vital part of a functioning whole. You neglect any one at your peril.

To the second proposition — Education is a state function which, when delegated to the local community, should be legally separate from other community functions.

We have already dealt with some aspects of this problem but let us see if the idea that education is a state function is sound and if it alters the picture.

In a legal sense, all local units of government are creatures of the state, and are therefore, as agents, performing state functions. In this sense, an independent school district created by the state is not different from a county or a municipality. All are performing state functions. It has no bearing on the question at issue to say that education is a state function unless it is meant that a state function is one that cannot be performed adequately by a local unit of government. This is obviously not what is meant, for the prevailing system operates through local units. If, on the other hand, it is meant that education, being of concern to the entire state, will require some state supervision, this does not differentiate it from functions performed by other local units of government. City financing is usually supervised by the state. City and county health departments come under state regulations. Since education is only one of a number of state functions being performed by local units of government, this cannot be used as an argument for an independent local unit to perform the function.

Now a look at the third proposition — Education should be separately financed.

There appear to be two reasons why advocates of independent school government want education to be separately financed. First of all they believe, quite correctly, that he who holds the purse strings controls policy. They want independent financing of the school district in order to bolster independence in policy making.

Second, they believe that schools will fare better under a system of independent financing. That is, they believe that the schools will receive a larger share of the total revenue disbursed for all government functions when the schools are separately financed. On the first point, there is no doubt that independent financing will strengthen independent policy making. But the real question is whether educational directors and administrators should be allowed to make policy irrespective of the wishes, needs, and necessities of those administering other branches of local government.

All the functions of government must be carried on. All are designed to serve the same citizenry. All are supported by the same taxpayer. Why should the policies of one service be formulated without regard to the policies of another service?

On the question of whether, under separate financing, the schools fare better than they otherwise would, there is no clear case for the separate system. One of the authorities in this field, A. J. Burke, states, "That there are no significant differences in expenditure levels between fiscally independent and dependent systems." But whatever the facts may reveal in this respect, I believe it can be clearly maintained that it is illogical and irresponsible to plan one part of the community budget without knowing the proposed expenditures for other community services. We once operated our federal government on this irrational basis, but at long last we mended our ways, and by the Budget and Accounting Act of 1921 we provided for a coordinated budget plan to include all items of income and all items of expected expenditures. Proposals are to be submitted by the Chief Executive and approved by the Legislative Branch.

In our personal budgeting we do not plan our expenditures for rent and clothing without taking a look at our mounting food costs, and we certainly total up all the items to see if we're going to be in the red. It seems to me the same principle applies to community budget making. Under coordinated planning we can properly allocate not only current expenditures but also capital outlays. If we're planning to build a new school this year, this is not the time to build a new hospital. If we build a hospital next year, the city hall can wait till the following year. Since school expenditures are often half of the total community outlay, it is extremely hazardous to ignore such a large segment of our spending in our total planning.

Turning now to the fourth proposition — An independent educational system will insulate the schools from politics, will enable the citizen to express his views on educational policy uncomplicated by the other community problems, and will achieve greater financial support for education. We have already dealt with the last idea. But what about insulating the school from politics? To begin with, this may rest on a misconception of politics. Politics is the technique of reconciling the myriad conflicting interests in the community and effectuating the will of the majority. No community service should be immune from this process. Nor should a citizen's views on education be formed in an ivory tower from which the currents of community controversy are excluded. Community life is an indivisible whole. It should not be segmented. It should not be lived piecemeal. It should be an integrated, well-rounded whole.

A TESTIMONIAL FOR FISCAL INDEPENDENCE*

The New York City board of education has been ousted by action of the state legislature and a new board of education is in process of

---

*Taken from *The American School Board Journal* editorial, "The New York Mess," CXLIII (October, 1963), published by the Bruce Publishing Company, 1963, 36.

formation. The action of the State was fully justified and followed a series of scandals growing out of reports of incompetency and fraud in the school construction, maintenance, and repair divisions. The nine member board, made up of men and women chosen on borough, ethnic, religious, and political lines were personally respected individuals, but were unable to cope with the municipal political influences at work in the offices of the business department, particularly the construction and maintenance divisions. The serious hazards in school buildings due to inadequate maintenance and improper repairs were common knowledge for several years. More recently highly placed officials were charged with accepting gifts from contractors and were unable to deny the charges. Their punishment thus far has been little more than dismissal or a slap on the wrist. The ridiculous incident which preceded final action by State Commissioner of Education James E. Allen, was caused by a rat which ran across the path of Mayor Wagner while he was inspecting "rat-and-roach infested" P.S. 119 in Harlem where the teachers had paid for a newspaper advertisement protesting against the leaking roof."

The troubles of the New York City schools have grown almost entirely out of political interference by the city government. The new board of education appointed by Mayor Wagner is made up of individuals recommended by a committee representing outstanding civic, educational, labor organizations, and two local universities. It is expected that the new board will engage in a radical house cleaning of the administrative departments and simplify the almost impossible red tape which has caused the administration and management of the schools to decline steadily in efficiency during several decades. It is also expected that the organizations of parents, citizens, and educators interested in the schools will revitalize neighborhood and city-wide activity and influence so sadly lacking in past years.

In the membership of the new board State Commissioner Allen has asked that the following fundamental conditions be provided:

First, the board of education would have to be a board composed of the best citizens available, selected solely on the basis of competence and qualification for the position.

Second, the board should have sufficient powers and authority to take corrective measures with firmness and speed.

Third, the board should be able to act unhampered by any unnecessary administrative and fiscal controls by the municipal government, and in freedom from the domination of any political party or private group bent on using the school system to promote a special interest or a special conception of public purposes.

Fourth, the principle of local control, so essential to a vigorous and dynamic school system, should be revitalized in its application, so that it can have real meaning in the life of the many and diverse educational communities of the city.

The experience of New York City indicates again that the public schools in every community need the services of a competent board of education which provides nonpolitical and fearless leadership in directing the school system and its professional staff. The weakness of the argument for greater professional independence in the operation of schools is at no time made clearer than in a crisis like that which is afflicting New York City. It is the prompt and sound decisions of the board of education which determine ultimately what the schools do and what the next generation of citizens will be.

BOARDS OF EDUCATION . . .

A VETERAN ADMINISTRATOR PAYS TRIBUTE TO BOARD MEMBERS*

School board members are the forgotten men in American public life. Their work is ordinarily taken for granted. Its importance is not always understood or appreciated. Membership on a board of education is a high public trust. In most cases an unpaid office, it requires unquestioned integrity, unselfish service, and the rigid application of high intelligence.

The work of our thousands of school boards is undobutedly the best American example of democracy in action. Closely tied to the rank and file of the people of their communities whom they represent, school boards are responsible for making and securing adequate provision for educational opportunity in their communities. The tremendous development and growth of the American school system and its generally high state of efficiency are undeniable evidences of the value of their work. Our system of free education for all is generally looked upon by the people of other lands as America's outstanding contribution to world civilization. It is the envy of all people everywhere.

There have been instances and occasions, of course, when certain boards have not lived up to this high public trust. These have been

---

*Walter O. Cocking, "As I See It," *The School Executive Magazine.* By permission of *American School & University,* 1955, 100-101.

the exceptions rather than the rule, and because of that have received attention far beyond what these few unfortunate circumstances just-ified. It should be recognized and widely and frequently proclaimed that on the whole the school boards of the nation have fulfilled and are performing a public duty with outstanding distinction and with great credit to themselves. The history of education in the United States provides the record of a job well done, and to our school boards belongs the lion's share of the credit.

THE LEGAL STATUS OF A BOARD OF EDUCATION*

A school district legally is an agent of the state, responsible for the state function of public school education within a geographical boundary. Thus the district is completely subject to the control of the state. It some-times is referred to as a special function unit, as distinguished from general function units such as counties and cities. Generally it is considered a quasi-municipal corporation, because while it has many of the characteristics of incorporated local government bodies such as cities, its powers are more restricted because its only function is in relation to education. A typical statement on the point is found in the following statement by the Supreme Court of Pennsylvania.

> While a school district is not, of course, an independent sovereignty, it does constitute a body corporate, a quasi-municipal corporation, which is an agency of the Commonwealth for the performance of prescribed governmental functions, being created and maintained for the sole purpose of administering the Commonwealth's system of public education. . . .

It follows from the concept of education as a state function that school board members are state officers, as distinguished from local government officers. This is true regardless of how school board mem-bers are selected and regardless of whether school district boundaries coincide with municipal boundaries. In a leading case involving the right of a state to require that a local government unit levy and collect for the

---

*Robert R. Hamilton and E. Edmund Reutter, Jr., *Legal Aspects of School Board Operations,* New York: Teachers College, Columbia University, Bureau of Pub-lications, 1958, 3-6 (by permission).

support of public schools, the issue was discussed by the Court of Appeals of Kentucky in the following language:

> If the public schools of . . . [a city] were local affairs, over which that municipality had the sole control, it may be doubted if it would be competent for the state to levy a tax on its other citizens to help support them. But they are not municipal institutions at all. . . . The city schools, including high schools, are part of the state's common school system. Their trustees are officers of the state.

GENERAL POWERS AND DUTIES OF LOCAL BOARDS

The powers of local boards have been judicially described in the following language:

> The school board has and can exercise those powers that are granted in express words; those fairly implied in or necessarily incidental to the powers expressly granted, and those essential to the declared objects and purposes of the corporation.

While this definition of the authority of local boards of education is deeply rooted in the law and accepted by courts in all the states, not all courts agree in applications to specific cases. The legal definition of school board authority is essentially a narrow one, but great freedom is granted courts in determining whether a particular power can be classified as "fairly implied" or "necessarily incidental." In concrete situations courts of many states have gone exceedingly far in finding legal justifications for holding that a contested power of local boards was in fact implied when the aim of the local board was deemed clearly worth while educationally. The following chapters contain numerous examples of situations in which local boards, in the absence of express statutory authority, have performed acts of educational significance and have had their actions sustained by courts under broad interpretations of "implied powers." Frequently decisions have been reached after the courts have considered a multiplicity of factors which would have to be evaluated on other than strictly legal bases in circumstances where applicable legal precedents or doctrines were not available.

The history of public education is replete with developments which began with a local board's instituting an innovation carefully predetermined to effect desired change in educational practice where statutes were silent on the matter. When such an innovation was challenged as being beyond the power of the board, the court was faced with the problem of deciding between upholding the innovation as an implied power or striking it down as an action beyond board powers. Public education has been substantially aided by the general disposition of courts to interpret implied powers broadly. It is necessary, of course, to point out that in many instances local school boards have not been judicially supported. . . .

The distinction between actions where a board has abused its discretion and where it has exceeded its powers must be borne in mind. A particular act may be within the express or implied powers of a board and yet be subject to judicial bar if it can be shown that the board acted arbitrarily, capriciously, unreasonably, or in a discriminatory fashion. For example, it is universally true that a local board has the power to establish rules and regulations governing pupil conduct. Yet this undisputed power is subject to judicial interpretations as to whether the board abused its discretion in the exercise of the power in a given situation.

If a board is not already authorized to take certain action, it can acquire authority to perform the act only by statutory enactment. However, a board of education may not refuse to act on a matter where it legally has no discretionary power to decide how or whether to act. Such duties are called ministerial, as differentiated from discretionary. In such a situation the board can be compelled to act either by the state directly or through the courts upon application of one who has a direct interest in the action sought. . . .

While the distinction between ministerial and discretionary duties is often difficult to make, clear examples of the former would include providing courses in state-mandated subjects and following statutory procedures related to pupil transportation. Often a single duty has both ministerial and discretionary aspects. Awarding a contract to the lowest responsible bidder may be a ministerial duty, but discretion would be involved in determination of responsibility of a bidder.

CORPORATE NATURE OF SCHOOL BOARDS

The authority of a local board of education lies in the board as a corporate body. The board legally is the administrative body for the school district, and its power and duties are essentially those of the district. The board exists apart from the individuals composing it. Thus a change in board membership does not change the legal status of the board.

Members of boards of education as individuals cannot exercise the corporate powers of the board. The Supreme Court of Appeals of West Virginia described the legal status of an individual member as follows:

. . . a member of the board individually has no authority of any kind in connection with the schools of his county, except that the president, as such, is required to sign orders, contracts and so forth. The board of education can only act as a board, and when the board is not in session the members, severally or jointly, have no more authority to interfere with schools or school matters than any other citizen of the county.

Actions to be legally binding must be taken by the board as a whole according to statutory and common law procedures. Likewise liabilities of school board members as individuals differ from those of the board as a legal entity.

The powers and duties of a board of education must be exercised by the board as a whole. Boards may not divest themselves of powers delegated to them by the legislature. They cannot give committees of the board, employees of the board, other governmental officials or private persons the authority to perform acts over which the board as a whole has discretionary power. Thus, if the power of employing teachers resides in the board, as it does in almost all jurisdictions, the board as a whole must take action if a teacher is to be legally employed. The basis of the non-delegability doctrine is rooted in public policy. The board is created to perform certain functions for the public. Unless they are performed by the board members as a body, the purpose of having a board is thwarted. This does not mean that individuals or committees of the board cannot be assigned such functions as fact-finding or drawing up recommendations for board action. Such an operational procedure would be desirable at times and would not be contrary to law. The board as a whole, however, must review any recommendations and in an official action accept them before they become effective.

THE LOCAL SCHOOL BOARD MEMBER*

Local school boards are the agencies through which local control of the schools is maintained, but in a legal sense a local school board is a State agency. State law creates and defines its powers; and State law governs its membership.

What the State statutes prescribe for local school board membership, except for boards covered by special legislation, is the subject of a recent

---

*Morrill M. Hall, "The Local School Board Member," *School Life,* XL (January, 1958), 11.

Office of Education study. It finds that these laws vary widely, both within and among the States. But it finds also many similarities — enough to permit a brief sketch here of what may well be called the typical school board member.

HE SERVES ON A BOARD OF 3 TO 7 MEMBERS.

The great majority of school boards in the United States have 3 to 9 members: Most of those in small districts have 3; in large districts, 5 or 7. Only a few have more than 9.

Eight States prescribe a uniform size for all boards, except where special legislation applies. The general statutes in all other States provide for boards of more than one size.

HIS TERM OF OFFICE IS 3, 4, OR 6 YEARS.

Most school board members hold office 3 to 6 years per term. This range takes in all the terms provided by 41 States for all districts covered by the general statutes and by 5 others for a majority of their districts.

Usually, districts select one or more board members every year, though 11 States make all regular changes every other year. Where selections are biennial, the term of office is 2, 4, or 6 years; where they are annual, 3- or 5-year terms are common.

Most commonly, less than half of the members are chosen at one time, but this is not true for some boards in 14 States and all those in 6 others.

HE IS NOMINATED BY PETITION AND
IS ELECTED BY POPULAR VOTE IN A
SEPARATE, NONPARTISAN ELECTION.

More than 95 percent of all school districts select their boards by popular vote: 33 States use this method exclusively except where special legislation applies; 9 others use it for most boards. In only 6 States are board members appointed, and 5 of these have special legislation providing for an elected board in one or more districts.

Where boards are elected by popular vote, candidates are nominated in various ways. The most common method is petition by qualified voters.

Nonpartisan election methods are prescribed for most boards chosen by popular vote. Most boards are chosen in elections held specifically for that purpose on nonpartisan ballots. Others are chosen in partisan elections but on separate nonpartisan ballots. In some States, however, either all or at least some boards are elected on a partisan basis.

HE REPRESENTS THE DISTRICT AT LARGE.

No matter how he is chosen, the board member should represent all the people in the school district: that is a generally accepted principle. Some States divide their districts into areas, such as wards or trustee zones, and require at least one board member to come from each area; or in some other way they limit the number of members from each part of a district. Most school districts choose their board members from the district at large: that is, they may choose any qualified citizen living anywhere in the district.

In all districts where board members are elected from the district at large — and also in many districts that have some type of area representation — all voters are entitled to help elect all board members. In a few States, however, the voters may vote only for the candidates living in their own subdivision; thus, in a 5-zone district with a 5-member board, the voter can help elect only one of the members.

HE IS A QUALIFIED VOTER.

The most common qualification prescribed for board members is that they be qualified voters. However, all or at least some board members in nearly half the States must meet additional requirements; among them are specifications about age, length of residence in district or State, education, character, payment of property tax, and parenthood.

HE RECEIVES NO SALARY.

State laws on salaries for school board members vary. One State may prohibit pay entirely: another may specify a certain amount: a third may specify only a range or a maximum; a fourth may leave all decisions about salary to the districts. Most districts, however, pay no salary at all.

IF HE LEAVES THE BOARD BEFORE HIS TERM IS UP, THE REMAINING MEMBERS NAME SOMEONE TO TAKE HIS PLACE.

When interim vacancies occur on elected boards, usually the remaining members appoint someone to complete the term. On appointed boards — though not on all — the original appointing agency fills the vacancies that occur.

WHAT PROBLEMS DO BOARD MEMBERS BELIEVE THEY HAVE?*

PERCENT OF DISTRICTS REPORTING PROBLEMS OF BOARD ORGANIZATION AND PRACTICE, BY PROBLEM AREA

Problem area	Districts reporting
Total number	1,543

	Percent of total[1]
School board policy	32.6
Selection of board members	21.6
Board-superintendent relationships	21.0
Board meetings	20.7
Orientation and inservice training of board members	14.4
Relation of individual members to the board	9.5
Keeping board members informed	8.0
Relationship of board to other local agencies and organizations	6.9
Board organization	6.0
Board size	2.1
Term of office of board members	1.9
Miscellaneous	9.8

[1]Percents do not add to 100.0 because some respondents listed more than one problem.

*Alpheus L. White, *Local School Boards: Organization and Practices,* Washington, D. C.: United States Office of Education, Bulletin 1962, No. 8, 81. (Above summary from survey of 1,543 reporting districts.)

MODERN BELIEFS ABOUT BOARD MEMBERS ARE NOT NEW*

1938 — EDUCATIONAL POLICIES COMMISSION

"Students of administration have long agreed that the people are best represented and the schools best served when the members of boards of education are selected on a non-partisan ticket, serve for relatively long,

*National Education Association, American Association of School Administrators and Research Division. *Local School Boards: Size and Selection.* Educational Research Service Circular No. 2, 1964. Washington, D.C.: The Association (February, 1964).

overlapping terms, and receive no remuneration for their services. In those cities in which the members of boards of education are appointed by the mayor, it has often been found that they are under pressure to serve the mayor or the party of which he is the leader. This political obligation sometimes results in rewarding members of the party with positions on the professional and other staffs of the school system. Where board members are elected on partisan tickets and feel allegiance to the political organization, a similar situation has been found to exist. The only sound policy is that which frees the members of the board of education from any allegiance except that which they owe to the whole public. Such freedom can best be assured through nomination by petition and election on a non-partisan ballot at a special school election.

"It has seemed wise to expect members of boards of education to serve without pay in order that those who would seek the office for the sake of the remuneration rather than to serve the people may be dissuaded from offering their services to the public. Relatively long and overlapping terms are essential in order that continuity in the program of the schools may be maintained. In those cases in which a majority of the board members are elected at a single election or within a period of two or three years, it not infrequently happens that policies are adopted only to be abandoned before they have been fully tested.

"Good practice requires that the board consist of from five to nine members. This restriction in number makes it possible for the board to act as a committee of the whole. . . .

"Boards of education need to be further strengthened by keeping in close touch with the people. The issues at a single election are often not of the greatest importance and they are sometimes obscured by personalities. Where the people are keenly interested in their schools they should find it possible to present their points of view before the board of education. It is an obligation of the profession to encourage the lay board of education in the practice of inviting the cooperation of organized groups throughout the community. It has been suggested that boards of education would be made more truly representative of all the people if they were elected on the basis of proportional representation. It is essential that even small minorities be given a hearing. The purpose is not that the board shall seek to satisfy every group that comes before it, but rather that it shall act with full knowledge of the constructive thought and criticism provided by the electorate."

(National Education Association and American Association of School Administrators, Educational Policies Commission. *The Structure and Administration of Education in American Democracy.* Washington, D.C.: the Commission, 1938. p. 56-58.)

1941 — UNITED STATES OFFICE OF EDUCATION

"Whether school board members should be elected or appointed is a question upon which there is a difference of opinion, but in general, authorities on school administration are in favor of election by popular vote. The opinion of those favoring the elective method is that the people take more interest in the schools under this method than under the appointive method; that appointment by the mayor or city council places the schools to a great extent in the hands of city officials who are generally elected upon local municipal issues rather than upon school issues which, since education is a State function, are of Statewide concern; that the city officials making the appointments may appoint school board members for local political reasons and that appointment by the city officials offer an opportunity for them to control the board of education. On the other hand it is claimed by those favoring appointments by the mayor that he can be made directly responsible to the people for the kind of board he appoints, and that many men and women well qualified for school board membership will not become candidates for election but will accept appointment by the mayor.

"It is doubtful whether anyone who has made a study of city school administration advocates the election or appointment of school board members by city wards or districts.

SHOULD BOARD OF EDUCATION
MEMBERS BE PAID?*

Some of the reasons given by authorities in school administration for not paying compensation are summarized as follows: (1) the amount offered would not be large enough to attract able men and women but would likely attract officeseekers; (2) payments for services rendered may create the feeling among board members that they must actually operate the schools in order to earn money; (3) it has been proven through experience that capable men and women can be secured without having to induce them with pay; and (4) compensation payments violate the belief that every citizen should assume certain obligations of service to the school district.

---

*Alpheus White, *Local School Boards*, 68-70.

In discussing salary payments, a form of compensation, the AASA stated that:

> The first evil result, then, of paying salaries to board members is that school board membership is placed on the patronage list, and far down on the list at that, because the salaries are small. But inasmuch as salaries are paid for a term of years, those citizens who are willing to work at the salaries offered are likewise willing to spend money and time and to make definite political moves to secure their own election. Therefore, salaries for school board members actually put a school election or appointment on a patronage or political basis. The most important evil result of paying school board members salaries is that they will try to earn the salaries. There is no way in which a board member can feel he is earning a salary except to attempt to do the detailed work that the board pays the trained superintendent and his staff to do . . .

It should be recognized that not everyone agrees with the foregoing statements. Compensation is paid to some board members and is considered by some people to be desirable practice. The following statement expresses this point of view:

> On the other hand, it is well known that the position is one of heavy responsibility, involving much time and work and personal sacrifice, and many persons with equal claim to recognition as authorities in school administration feel that some partial compensation for the member's time and service is not only right and proper but also desirable. Those who hold this opinion cannot see any reason why city councilmen and county supervisors and other similar officials should be paid something for their services and school board members, whose services are equally as exacting and certainly no less important, should be paid nothing. Such a policy tends, they claim, to minimize the importance of the member's duties and to lessen public respect for the office. They point out that the school board member is, or should be, the type of person who serves on the directorates of important business corporations, that directors of private corporations are customarily paid fees for attendance upon meetings, and that the nominal salaries paid School Board Members are in the nature of director's fees and are properly paid. In answer to the claim that such payments attract to Board membership the type of person who is primarily interested in the small financial compensation, they say that director's fees do not work this way in important private business.

LEGAL PROVISIONS GOVERNING COMPENSATION
AND REIMBURSEMENT OF EXPENSES

Specific regulations governing the payment of compensation and reimbursement of expenses are found in the laws of most States. . . .

For example, the laws of Colorado governing this matter specify that board members will not be paid for their services. In 16 other States, it was reported that all board members covered by the general statutes were entitled to compensation, and in 10 other States, board members of certain districts could receive compensation. Such laws often specify the maximum amount that may be received each year. For example, the Utah code specifies the maximum amount that county and city school boards may pay to members as compensation shall not exceed $300 per annum.

The reimbursement of expenses incurred in the performance of board duties is authorized in a number of States. In some States where compensation is prohibited, board members are allowed mileage and actual expense reimbursements. Frequently, States that authorize the payment of compensation also allow board members to be reimbursed for mileage.

THE NEEDS FOR AND DANGERS OF
INFORMAL EXECUTIVE MEETINGS*

The creation of an informed, interested, and articulate public on school problems and school affairs is a goal held by most school administrators and school board members. Few school officials would have the central policy decisions of a school district emanate from hushed deliberations in closed chambers, later to be read to an assembled few in the public square. Rather the goal of school leaders is to encourage open and candid discussions of schools and their needs leading to policy decisions which are indeed reflections of public interest.

Stating the desirable, and reaching its achievement are two quite different matters. To make sound educational decisions, school boards cannot avoid confrontation with the public — many publics in fact. Boards must keep the public informed and at the same time seek to know the public well.

---

*Luvern L. Cunningham, "Executive Sessions and 'Informal' Meetings," taken from *American School Board Journal*, CXLVII (May, 1963), published by The Bruce Publishing Company, 1963, 7-9.

Students of school board operation have long argued that the public interest can most effectively be served when school board deliberations on policy matters are open and in full public view. When boards carry on all discussions and make all decisions in open meetings, then the dual obligations of informing the community and listening to citizens expressions of interest can both be met.

But herein lies an increasingly perplexing problem. Can all policy deliberations really take place in full public view? Even excluding the usual privileges of executive session which permit the discussion of such things as personnel matters or site selection in private, how reasonable is it to expect all other discussions to be open and in full public view? Another way of asking the same question might be: How much of policy deliberation ought to take place behind closed doors? Or what is the proper use of such handmaidens of policy-making as the executive session, committee of the whole, adjourned meeting, or the informal "discussion" meeting?

Because many boards have been soundly criticized for so-called "secret" meetings or other seeming abuses, school boards and school superintendents are now "gun shy." Any practice that smacks of closed-door decision-making is taboo, and in response boards attempt to carry on all deliberations in open meetings. There remains, however, a real question as to whether this practice leads automatically to better decisions.

LEGALITY OF EXECUTIVE SESSIONS

The statutes of many states, in recognition of the necessity to remove some aspects of school board deliberations from public purview, provide for executive sessions or some type of similar privilege. The statutes have not, however, provided specifically for "informal" or "nonaction" board meetings. Quite to the contrary. The courts have taken a dim view of such proceedings and have rescinded board action when it was clear that the discussion related to an issue was held outside a board meeting even though the official action was taken later on in a legitimate board meeting. . . .

Although many policy statements of school boards, large and small, make some mention of executive session and the public nature of their work, citizens often fail to understand why boards sometimes go behind closed doors. More and more situations seem to be arising where public faith and confidence in school board and administrative leadership are shaken because the public believes many board actions are taken in "informal" meetings or that the board is abusing the privileges of executive session. And as is true in so many things the public acts on its perceptions — even though these may be in error.

The problem discussed here in relation to school district policy-making is actually a part of a much larger problem of secrecy vs. public information in all of government. At the national level the terms "privileged" or "classified" are applied to data withheld from the press and the public. The President often appears to hide behind executive privilege as do other prominent officials who refuse to reflect publicly on governmental decision-making which has been based on so-called secret information. Questions of national security and other pervasive public issues are so crucial that discussion of these matters and related actions cannot go forward in complete and open public view.

As a substitute for, or in addition to, executive sessions, some boards hold premeeting briefing sessions. In these meetings the superintendent and his administrative staff present information relative to problems requiring decision in the formal board session to follow. It was this kind of meeting to which the Minneapolis board member objected. Such briefing sessions are held behind closed doors. Similarly some school districts hold luncheons or dinner meetings prior to regular board meetings to accomplish the same objectives. Likewise, there are school boards and administrators who apparently find it necessary to meet in small groups, which do not include all members of the board or the administrative staff, for the purpose of discussing issues confronting the policy-making body. . . .

GUIDES TO ACTION

The course a school district should follow is not clear. The statutes are fuzzy at best, and local practices are probably often at odds with the statutes or even with policies arrived at locally. A few guidelines, however, can be suggested:

1. Accept the fact that not all deliberations can go forward in official business sessions.

2. Discuss the closed-meeting problem in open session and arrive at a local district policy statement, fitting the policy into state law, if such law exists.

3. Strike for a working balance between public and private discussion of school board decisions.

4. Review the policy regularly and keep the community informed on this school district policy.

5. Arrive at a sound working relationship with representatives of the news media on this question.

6. Avoid religiously, reaching the point of decision in any meeting which does not lawfully permit decision-making.

All school board action should be directed toward arriving at the finest decisions of which dedicated men and women are capable. In as much as is possible the setting in which decisions are formulated should contribute to this purpose. Board members are human and as such cannot but be affected by galleries, batteries of reporters, television "play-by-play" announcers, as well as the grinding of cameras and the spinning of tape recorders. Such exposure undoubtedly contributes to the reluctance of some board members to speak their minds, to raise questions, or to seek new information. In other cases, it may inspire grandstand performances.

Although board members are willing to contribute their time and talents to this public service, they are not willing to subject themselves continuously, and oftentimes needlessly, to the vituperations of uninformed critics or to the embarrassment of having to discuss openly questions about which they are not well informed. Public questions cannot be resolved best in a highly formal, stiff, uncomfortable environment.

Local boards and their administrative staffs must face the issue squarely, where it is a problem, and work out a reasonable mechanism for carrying on private deliberations on school issues. They should guard against making decisions in closed sessions of any kind. A high priority should be placed upon receiving and sharing information, extending the background of problems, seeking additional insights which bear upon the issues in question, gaining appreciations for the points of view of individuals who may have values unlike other members of the deliberating group, and holding discussions well in advance of the actual time for decision.

Obviously the ways of the world will not permit a discussion of all questions well in advance of the time for deciding, but for those issues where long-range planning is necessary and possible certainly the background building for decision can begin months and even years ahead. Further, the public or the community served deserves to be informed of board-member practices. Few thoughtful citizens, after examining the need for unfettered inquiry into problems and discourse about them, will find fault with the board that takes its job seriously and conscientiously. Boards should not fear criticism directed at this practice. They should be cautious, obviously, of taking liberties with their privilege and should engage in periodic review of what they are doing.

As stated earlier, secrecy vs. publicity is an increasingly important problem in government. Dewey argued that democracy is dependent upon a vigorous and sustained seeking after the public interest and the translation of public interest into public policy through the legitimate structures of government. School board members are responsible for comprehending public needs and for penetrating into the fabric of public concern, fereting out and tying together the threads of opinion, and translating the feelings of people into public policy. People of intelligence cannot perform this function, even when they have the expert counsel and guidance of carefully trained school leaders, without time for discussion, for perceiving the points of view of others, for pondering the dimensions of the questions, for seeking and analyzing new information, and for engaging in the soul searching that takes place on the threshold of decision.

WHAT DOES A BOARD MEMBER'S VOTE MEAN?*

In guiding board action the superintendent will sooner or later hear a lively and philosophical debate among conscientious members as to what their vote means. RESOLVED: That a board of education member should vote according to what he thinks the majority of citizens desire, rather than in terms of what he thinks is best for the school system in the light of his intimate knowledge on the subject which is not normally available to citizens.

A magnanimous person elected to the board will arrive on the scene with the objective of rendering decisions compatible with what people want. This is morally correct. Eventually, however, he comes to realize that with the exception of items mentioned in his campaign platform, if any, he doesn't know what the majority of citizens desire. All he is likely to hear will come from intimate acquaintances, or from vocal, steamed-up, and immediately perturbed minorities which can be grossly misleading. Moreover, there is no certain way of discovering majority wishes unless the matter is put to public vote. Obviously, this is not practical for the great number of important matters upon which he must make a decision and vote. He also discovers that the mass of citizens, most of whom are apathetic about schools, are not equipped with the facts as he is — even with a good public relations program.

After he has gone through this line of reasoning, he is ready to accept the fact that when a person is elected to public office the people have in

---

*Robert E. Wilson, *The Modern School Superintendent,* New York: Harper & Row, Publishers, 1960, 60. Copyright© by Robert E. Wilson, 1960.

effect said to him, "We have confidence in your ability to make decisions for our welfare. You represent us, but it is up to you to arrive at your own decisions. If we don't like your decisions, we'll let you know about it at the next election." Every board member must come to this conclusion for himself, but the superintendent can hasten the process if he stimulates opportunity for the reasoning to get under way early in the new board member's term of office.

FOR FURTHER REFLECTION OR INVESTIGATION

1. What are the likely outcomes of a plan which permitted members of the educational profession to have the highest decision-making authority in a public school district? From a board of education composed mostly of educators?

2. Discuss the ethics involved in teachers' nominating and actively campaigning for board of education candidates.

3. Evaluate the differing attitudes expressed by the authors in the readings of this chapter pertaining to fiscal independence of school districts.

4. Classify the decisions made at a meeting of your board of education as to being made under statutory or discretionary authority.

5. What are the dangers and the controls of a board's discretionary powers?

6. Identify and analyze the power structures on your board of education. Are they also important powers within the community? How can you be sure?

7. Upon visiting a meeting of your board of education, evaluate the session as to organization and efficiency, climate, agenda, usefulness of the meeting.

8. What problems or issues are proper to justify a board of education's holding an executive session not open to the public?

9. Is a board of education ever justified in holding a meeting without the superintendent's presence?

10. What steps can a superintendent take to keep a board of education in its policy-making role?

11. How many members would be required to assure an adequate representation of all major segments of your community on the board of education?

12. Would partisan appointment or election of board members keep the control of public education in better tune with prevailing thoughts and desires of the community's majority?

13. Justify the existence of the township or county forms of local government today.

14. Evaluate the need for the extent of services provided by the intermediate level of school administration in your region. Could they be handled just as satisfactorily by the state today?

BIBLIOGRAPHY

Angrig, G. R., "Sociological Factors Which Resist School Consolidations," *Clearing House,* XXXVIII, November, 1963.

Benner, Thomas E., "Lessons from the Patterns of Education of Other Countries." Extracted from paper appearing in *Government of Public Education for Adequate Policy Making.* Champaign: Bureau of Educational Research, University of Illinois, 1960.

Burt, Lorin A., "So You're a New Board Member!" *The American School Board Journal,* May, 1962.

Cocking, Walter D., *As I See It.* New York: The Macmillan Company, 1955.

Cooper, Shirley, and Charles O. Fitzwater, *County School Administration,* New York: Harper and Row, Publishers, 1954.

Cubberley, E. P., *Public School Administration,* Boston: Houghton Mifflin Company, 1916.

Cunningham, Luvern L., "Executive Sessions and Informal Meetings," *American School Board Journal,* CXLVI, May, 1963.

DeShane, R., "Effective Intermediate Unit." *Illinois Education,* LII, January, 1964.

Developing Personnel Policies, Washington, D.C.: National Education Association Commission on Professional Rights and Responsibilities, 1963.

Educational Research Service, Circular No. 2, 1964. Washington, D.C.: NEA Research Division.

Feuerstein, Harold, "A System for Nominating Members of Boards of Education," *The American School Board Journal,* May, 1963.

Goldhammer, Keith, *The School Board,* Washington, D.C.: The Center for Applied Research in Education, 1964.

Hall, Morrill M., "The Local School Board Member," *School Life,* XL, January, 1958.

Hamilton, Robert R., and E. Edmund Reutter, Jr., *Legal Aspects of School Board Operations,* New York: Teachers College, Columbia University, 1958.

Haussler, Kenneth S., "Local Control of Public Schools," *The American School Board Journal,* CXLVII, October, 1963.

Holt, Howard B., "Are School Boards Necessary?" *School and Society,* XCI, November, 1963.

Kerr, Norman D., "The School Board as an Agency of Legitimization," *Sociology of Education,* XXXVIII, Fall, 1964.

Krietlow, Burton W., "Organizational Patterns, Local School District," *Review of Educational Research,* October, 1961.

Management Surveys for Schools: Their Uses and Abuses, Washington, D.C.: American Association of School Administrators, 1964.

McPerran, A. L., "State or Local Control: Who is Responsible for Education?" *California Education,* I, October, 1963.

Morphet, Edgar L., and John G. Rose, "Do Small Districts Assure Better Control?" *School Management,* V, June, 1961.

National Educational Association Research Bulletin. Washington, D.C.: National Education Association, No. 2, May, 1961.

Nolte, Chester M., "Powers of Board are Executive, Legislative, and Quasi-judicial in Character," *The American School Board Journal,* CXLIX, December, 1964.

Nugent, Donald, "Are Local Control and Lay Boards Obsolete?" *Educational Leadership,* XXII, November, 1964.

Orlich, Donald C., "What Do Your Minutes Tell You?" *The American School Board Journal,* CXLVI, May, 1963.

Overview, "Nationalism and Local Autonomy," September, 1962.

Packard, John C., "School District Size vs. Local Control," *American School Board Journal,* Vol. 146, February, 1963.

Provisions Governing Membership on Local Boards of Education, Washington, D.C.: United States Office of Education, Bulletin No. 13, 1957.

Radke, F. A., "Local Control: Secret of School's Success," *Nation's Business,* February, 1964.

Schultz, John G., "The Before and After of School District Reorganization," *NEA Journal,* XLVIII November, 1959.

The Structure and Administration of Education in American Democracy, Washington, D.C.: Educational Policies Commission, National Education Association, and American Association of School Administrators, 1938.

Swanson, Chester J., "The School Board and the Superintendent," AASA, Eighty-Second Convention.

The American School Board Journal, "The New York Mess" (an editorial), CXLIII, October, 1963.

The American School Board Journal, "Democratic School Board Leadership," CXLVIII, February, 1964.

The Point of Beginning: The Local School District, Washington, D. C.: American Association of School Administrators, 1958.

Van Dorn, Harold, "A Political Scientist Looks at Fiscal Independence of School Districts." An address delivered at Kent State University, 1960.

Walsh, John E., *Education and Political Power,* Washington, D.C.: The Center for Applied Research in Education, 1964.

White, Alepheus L., *Local School Boards: Organization and Practices.* Washington, D.C.: United States Office of Education, Bulletin 1962, No. 8, 81. (Summary from survey of 1,543 reporting districts.)

————, "Local School Board Policy Manuals," *School Life,* XLII, November, 1959.

Willower, Donald J., "Lay and Professional Decisions in Education," *Peabody Journal of Education* XLI, January, 1964.

Wilson, Robert E., *The Modern School Superintendent,* New York: Harper and Row, Publishers, 1960.

Chapter 4

Organization for State Administration of Education

The people of a state have assigned their authority and control over public education to their legislature. In a real sense, the legislature constitutes a board of education, the governing body, on a state level. Each legislature has passed enabling acts for the establishment of a system of public education, has specified powers for the local boards of education in the conduct of education within districts, has appropriated monies for the support of schools, has passed many laws over the years affecting the management of learning, has relinquished much of its power to local communities, but has still retained its absolute authority over public schools.

Since a legislature must concern itself with many public affairs other than education, all but two states (Illinois and Wisconsin) have created a separate policy-making body just for education — a state board of education. The legislature has delegated its administrative responsibilities insofar as education is concerned to a state superintendent of schools and to a state department of education. Each state makes its own arrangements for these matters and it is confusing to generalize about the functioning of these offices without noting many exceptions.

THE STATE BOARD OF EDUCATION

In 1948 the state superintendents of schools (Council of Chief School Officers) adopted this statement of policy which summarized their judgments about how a state board and superintendent should function:

> In each state there should be a non-partisan lay state board of education of seven to twelve able citizens, broadly representative of the general public and unselfishly interested in public education, elected by the people in the manners prescribed by law. The members of this board should serve for long overlapping terms without

pay. It is desirable that the boards select the chief state school officer on a non-partisan basis and determine his compensation and his term of office. He should serve as the executive officer of the board and head of the state department of education.

At the time of this policy formulation, no state operated exactly in that manner although the boards of eight states could appoint their executive officers. There was no non-partisan elected board which appointed its superintendent. A decade later, eight states had taken action to permit elective boards with authority to appoint the superintendent: Colorado, Iowa, Nebraska, New Mexico, Nevada, Ohio, Texas, and Utah. Today thirteen states elect their board members but only the eight have power to appoint their superintendents. Historically, the election of state boards of education by the people has accompanied the movement to give such boards the authority to appoint the chief state school officer, and it is reasonable to foresee other states moving in the direction of elected boards.

An understanding of state boards of education is confused by the existence of other boards at the state level which have responsibilities for specified educational activities, such as the State Board of Vocational Education, or State Board for Higher Education. The results of these arrangements range in complexity — to sometimes open competition for the taxpayer's educational dollar. The discussion following is concerned only with the state board of education which has primary jurisdiction over the elementary and secondary schools of the state.

The number of members on a state board varies from three in Mississippi to twenty-three in Ohio — one from each Congressional district of that state. The majority of states has a membership of five to nine, approximating the ideal as expressed in the 1948 policy statement. Their terms of office may be anywhere from two years to fourteen years, four or six years being most common, consistent with terms for other public offices. Most frequently they are not members of the educational profession, but may be in some states; elsewhere there is a combination of lay and school personnel. In most states the board is appointed by the governor but in New York the board members are elected by the legislature, and in Washington the local school board members select the state board in convention. The eight-member board in Wyoming is appointed by the State Superintendent of Public Instruction. Although most students of school administration recommend the popular election method of choosing state board members, the other plans are not without merit. The occasional suggestion that a state board be chosen under a combination of popular election and appointment is worthy of thoughtful consideration.

State boards of education may be either powerful or ineffective influences on education, depending upon the charge they receive from the legislatures. A board generously commissioned with authority becomes a policy-making body for all the state's schools. It may formulate and set into motion policies independently of the lawmakers, or it may recommend that the Legislature enact educational laws when the strength of that body is deemed essential for effecting changes in local school operations. The state board will exercise a dynamic leadership in improving the schools as it conceives wise policies. It may also lead as it recommends improvements for legislative action. Such a board may prescribe standards for upgrading the curriculum, for professional certification, buildings, equipment, records, libraries, special pupil services, district organization, administrative procedures, and finances.

Most boards are charged with a general supervisory responsibility for local school operations, acting through the state superintendent and the state department of education. Often they supervise the distribution of state monies as well as those funds received from the federal government.

Some boards have supervisory duties which are peculiar only to an individual state, perhaps over institutions for higher education, private and parochial schools, and various specialized schools such as technical institutions, adult programs, or barber schools. Elsewhere the state board has direct operative authority for schools which admit only handicapped children.

THE STATE SUPERINTENDENT OF PUBLIC INSTRUCTION

Every state provides, usually in its constitution, for a chief state school officer, most commonly entitled Superintendent of Public Instruction, but also known as Commissioner of Education, State Superintendent, or State Director.

States choose their chief state school officers in a variety of ways. In twenty-one states he is elected by popular vote of the people, most frequently on a partisan ballot. The state board of education appoints the superintendent in twenty-four states, while in five states he is appointed by the governor. Each selection method has its supporters.

Where he is an elective officer it is said that he remains more responsive to the will of the people. Moreover, he is able to operate independently from the persuasions of either the governor or the legislature. Probable subsequent membership in the governor's cabinet presumably lends more status to the office. On the other hand, it is argued that a board of education making the appointment can examine more conscientiously the professional qualifications of the person; voters often elect solely on the basis of popularity. An elected superintendent, as any other elective officer, can become preoccupied with politics, it is said:

"The first year is consumed with learning the job; the second year he is ready for action; and the third and fourth year finds him preparing for the next election." His responsiveness to the will of the people, it is claimed, may mean more of a response to partisan or other political forces.

Appointment of the state commissioner by the governor clearly ties him tightly to the influence of the executive branch of state government. Whether this bodes good or evil for the public schools directly relates to the governor's enthusiasm for education. Gubernatorial appointment or popular election yield to the considerable instability of frequent turnover. The term of office, most frequently four years, ranges from one year in Delaware to six years in Minnesota. In twenty states the term of office is not prescribed, the officer frequently serving at the pleasure of the appointing force.

The superintendent is the chief school administrator of the state through which the board executes its decisions. He is often the administrative officer of the state department of education, standing much in the same relationship to that department as a city superintendent does to his central staff. Elsewhere, however, his position as a voting member of the board clouds his executive and policy-making functions. He is generally, although not always in states where he is elected, a certificated and professional educator. In the finest operations he needs the leadership and executive talents of a local district superintendent. There, through his strategic position, he may be the prime mover for good things happening in schools throughout the state. Whether he is such a force depends upon his personal talents as well as the source of his authority. The state's expectations for his stature and productivity are reflected in the salary allocated him, ranging from $9,000 in South Dakota to $40,000 in New York State, the median for all chief state officers approaching $14,000.

STATE DEPARTMENT OF EDUCATION

Radical changes and considerable fumbling have marked the century-and-a-half of the state department of education's efforts to determine its purposes in the uniquely American state-local partnership for public education. When states first began to exercise responsibility for public education, mainly through providing financial support to the local districts, they saw need for only regulatory or enforcing administration at that level. Someone was needed to account for the monies and to verify that the dollars were being used as authorized by law. The function was clerical and inspectorial, and often assigned to an existing state official, commonly the state auditor. It remained for zealous educators such as Henry Barnard in Connecticut and Horace Mann in Massachusetts to demonstrate the state's other responsibilities for education, particularly the leadership function of encouraging communities and legislatures to promote public schools.

The major change in the state office is reflected by the growth of its staff. At the turn of the century the size of state department staffs averaged only three per state, including the chief state officer and clerical staff. While there is still a substantial difference among states as to staff size, all have grown dramatically in this century, particularly New York, which presently employs a corps of over three hundred professional personnel and a greater number of nonprofessional workers.

The size of staff is in almost direct relationship to the aggressiveness of its leaders in designing the department's functions and to the willingness of the legislature to provide funds therefor. The enforcement function continues as a prime *raison d'etre* for staff, and the number of employees has expanded as states provide more money and more regulations. The number of enforcement agents also varies with the state's expectations as to how the function will be carried out. Enforcement through reports from local districts reduces the need for personnel. However, if the state wants on-the-spot inspection to enforce standards a sizeable field staff is essential.

The viewpoint that a state department has a service function to perform has also caused the large growth of staff. A well-staffed department today has both office and field consultants in nearly all the areas of school administration: curriculum, personnel, plant construction and operation, growth projections, pupil personnel, foods services, transportation. The consultancy approach serves the same ends as it does within a local district, creating an attitude of helpfulness rather than of inspection. Some departments aid local districts further in the production of operational guides and audio-visual materials.

The potentials of the research function at the state level are just beginning to be realized in some states. In such departments they go beyond the statistics-gathering-and-disseminating stage, useful as it may be, to initiating developmental projects.

State department employees, fortified by state board members, also fulfill their leadership roles in their relationship with the governor and legislature in obtaining favorable legislation.

The major obstacle to the effectiveness of a state department of education is the persistent confusion as to the proper allocation of authority between the state and local levels. One outgrowth of strong sympathy for local control is the unwillingness of the people, speaking through their legislators, to endow the state department with the necessary money and personnel to perform. In most states the salaries allocated for the department's professional personnel are not comparable to those earned by officers of a city district or of the colleges and universities. This discrepancy, coupled with restrictive Civil Service influence which may offer security and freedom from political interference but may also invite mediocrity of talent and effort, does not make service in the state department attractive to able professionals.

A counteracting force of recent decades is the decided trend toward centralizing more and more functions of education at either the state or national level. In an effort to provide pupils and personnel of the small district with services equivalent to those of the large districts, local boards of education have turned to the state department. This trend is likely to continue as long as small districts exist. The large-district movement may modify the trend, leaving only the difficult task of deciding precisely what functions can best be performed by self-sustaining school systems and which ones by a state department.

There may be in the offing a major upsurge of activity at the state department level as a result of the federal Elementary and Secondary Education Act of 1965. Title V of that act grants money to states for the specific purpose of strengthening their departments of education. Long-needed services may be provided under Title V, including educational planning on a state-wide basis, consultancy personnel for local districts, expanded testing programs, and development of research and demonstration projects. While the title does not envision that the money be used to pay the salaries of additional personnel, more professional employees may be engaged for the state department in order to administer other phases of the Act. Half of the personnel working in state departments prior to the Act were hired for administering the various federally subsidized programs. While the intent of the 1965 Act seems to be supportive of local school districts, they may be weakened inadvertently by increasing the function and authority of both state and national bodies over education.

STATE BOARD OF EDUCATION . . .

SHOULD LEGISLATIVE POWERS OVER EDUCATION BE DIVORCED TO A SEPARATE BOARD OF EDUCATION?*

Most studies of board functions in State government focus upon what existing boards are doing or should do, and not on supporting theory.

---

*Robert F. Will, "Separation of Powers at the Administrative Level," *School Life,* XLIII, January, 1961, 24-27.

Their authors, along with many others, generally assume that sound practice has a theoretical base and that, by some magic, sound practice can be identified without benefit of theoretical constructions. Professional educators, for example, consider it proper and fitting for the control and direction of State educational programs and services to be placed with representative boards. They build upon this assumption by outlining ways and means of best accomplishing this end.

Many professional educators believe so firmly that their position is right that they forget that an objective defense of it is necessary. With the attitude that "anyone can see," they apparently feel no need to justify their position. However, many intelligent men do not "see." The advocates of the strong executive, for example, firmly disagree with educators about the functional role of State boards. (Advocates of the strong executive believe that the Governor should be the chief administrative officer of the State as well as the chief executive officer.) They recognize the need for State boards for certain fixed purposes but maintain that administrative responsibilities of government are almost invariably best directed by a single official.

The breach between these two positions is most clearly manifested when State government is being reorganized. Professional educators generally recommend a State board of education to head the State department of education, while the advocates of the strong executive generally recommend that the Governor appoint a competent administrator, usually called chief State school officer, to head the department.

During our history as a nation, State boards of education have been created to perform a variety of duties and to exercise various powers related to them. A listing of these duties and powers would give some idea of what boards have been established to do, but not why any of the duties and powers were delegated to boards and not to a single officer. Theoretical constructions are needed to support what educators believe to be sound practice.

Agreeing that objective reasons for favoring the board over the single officer do exist, we can surmise that State legislatures are reluctant to delegate certain powers and duties to a single officer. More explicitly, there are undoubtedly certain powers and duties that legislative bodies do not generally entrust to a single officer and certain others that they consider best administered by a deliberative body.

There should be no mystery here. Legislatures usually act with some cognizance of human frailties. A cursory examination of practice, past and present, makes certain deductions possible. In general, State legislatures delegate to boards — other than purely advisory boards, which we are not concerned with here — the functions for which broad discretionary powers are considered as essential to good public administration. In general, legislatures most frequently delegate to single officers ministerial duties, or more specifically, duties that require the use of little or no discretionary power.

There are complications, however, that have taxed the ingenuity of lawmakers. Although representative boards are apparently considered best suited to perform duties concerned with the direction and policy control of programs and services requiring broad discretionary powers, they are generally considered inadequate to cope with the technical duties and responsibilities essential to providing such programs and services. Notwithstanding, professional educators believe that under the law boards can be appointed and organized and duties and powers delegated to them so as to minimize their weakness and at the same time fully utilize their strength. Most professional educators believe that representative boards should be responsible for the direction and policy control of educational activities and for engaging a staff professionally competent to conduct the educational programs and services.

A further complication, much more difficult to resolve, arises: Any board to which the State has delegated such powers and duties as are recommended by professional educators becomes the head of a relatively independent administrative authority in the structure of State government. This violates principles of State government organization advanced by the advocates of the strong executive.

Historically, public administration in State government from 1850 to the early 1900's was characterized by the distribution of executive and administrative powers among a number of State officers and boards. The influence that this practice had on State school administration is evident: All but one of the States admitted to the Union from 1850 to 1957 provided constitutionally for an elected chief State school officer. This official was generally charged with the responsibility of superintending the educational activities of the State. He was usually limited by law to the performance of ministerial duties and his powers were restricted to those necessary in carrying out these duties.

Many of the new States also provided constitutionally for a State board of education, but the majority of these boards were ex officio boards made up of several elected State officers, including the chief State school officer. No matter how the boards were constituted, they were usually responsible for duties that legislatures were reluctant to entrust to a single State school officer, for example, safeguarding educational lands and funds, determining what was to be taught in the common schools — course of study and textbooks — determining who should teach — teacher examination and certification — and governing the operation of one or more educational institutions.

Had time stood still, this arrangement would have been ideal. So long as the duties delegated to State boards of education under such governmental patterns did not require a large staff, State boards could serve as purely administrative agencies. More specifically, the members of the board itself could conduct the board's work. It was inevitable, however, that the ever-increasing demand upon State governments for new educational programs and services should outmode the practice.

Early in the 20th century students of public administration, recognizing the need for changes in State government organization, pressured for reorganizations that would promote greater efficiency and economy. Their arguments were centered on the weaknesses inherent in the diffusion of control and direction of public administration. The growing responsibilities of State government could no longer be met by creating more State officers and boards, for the number of agencies already established made it virtually impossible to coordinate the business of State government intelligently.

Searching for answers, students of public administration proposed that the numerous public administrative agencies be grouped into departments on the basis of related programs and services. Experimentation in a number of States had substantiated the wisdom of this proposal.

At this point the advocates of the strong executive gathered strength. They held that to insure efficiency and economy in public administration, the Governor as the State's chief executive officer should coordinate the business of State government, that he could do this if empowered to appoint a single officer to head each administrative department, such officers to serve at the Governor's pleasure. Thus, the Governor would, in effect, be the chief administrative officer as well as the chief executive officer. The advocates of the strong executive recognized the need for boards to administer duties and responsibilities, or particular phases of duties and responsibilities, that were quasi-legislative, quasi-judicial, or purely advisory, but they relegated these boards to a staff capacity subordinate to the officers heading departments.

Many States utilized departmental patterns in subsequent reorganizations, but with various modifications to minimize the dangers inherent in overcentralization of State administration. Some adopted the basic features of departmental organization under the multiple executive pattern and used boards as functional safety valves. Others prescribed the administrative duties and powers of single officers heading departments in such manner as to make them subordinates of boards for certain department programs. Others named State boards to head particular departments. . . .

Advocates of the strong executive have criticized the employment of boards to head administrative departments of State government largely on the grounds that this practice creates independent administrative authorities in the State government. They hold that practically all public administrative agencies should be functional components of the executive branch of the State government of the sovereign State. Great weight is added to this argument by the fact that the Constitution of the United States apparently sustains this position for the Federal Government. (Article II, Section II, Par. I, uses the term "executive departments.")

Advocates of the strong executive have, however, ignored certain considerations. Foremost, they have constructed theory largely upon the basic assumption that executive and administrative functions of government are inseparable. Alexander Hamilton could well be named as one of the architects of this premise, for as Publius he wrote:

> The administration of government, in its largest sense, comprehends all the operations of the body politic, whether legislative, executive, or judiciary; but in its most usual and perhaps in its most precise signification, it is limited to executive details, and falls peculiarly within the province of the executive department.
> —*The Federalist*, No. 72.

Such concepts did not create theoretical conflicts in public administration so long as the work of government could be regulated explicitly by statute. The weaknesses of theoretical constructions that failed to distinguish between executive functions and administrative functions became apparent when State legislatures found it impossible or impracticable to frame legislation in sufficient detail to direct and control public administration. To solve this problem State legislatures have delegated broad discretionary powers to certain State administrative agencies, permitting them to fill in the details of the law and to adjudicate differences that arise in conducting their business. However, a reconstruction of theory was necessary to preserve some semblance of a separation of powers in State government. Since State administrative agencies were popularly recognized as executive agencies, they could not, without some rational explanation, be delegated what appeared to be lawmaking or judicial powers of the State.

The evolving body of administrative law is the product of theoretical reconstruction. Administrative lawmaking is now firmly established as rulemaking, and administrative adjudication is provided for through structural and procedural arrangements that safeguard the rights of individuals and protect property under the law. Even so, the vestiges of outmoded theory are still evident in the terminology frequently used in rationalizing legislative delegations of broad discretionary powers to public administrative agencies. Rulemaking powers are frequently referred to as quasi-legislative powers, and powers of administrative adjudication are referred to as quasi-judicial powers. Significantly, the term "quasi-executive powers" is rarely, if ever, used in the literature of public administration.

The roundabout approach to the separation of powers in public administration tends to cloud the issues. The atmosphere can be cleared quickly with a simple explanation. Executive functions of State government are determined solely by constitutional law; administrative functions are largely determined under statutory law. Most State constitutions do create several administrative offices in addition to the executive offices, but the State legislature is generally charged with the task of prescribing the duties and responsibilities of these offices. State legislatures in the United States cannot create sovereign executive agencies nor can they delegate sovereign executive powers and duties. State legislatures can and do create State administrative agencies and delegate administrative powers and duties to them.

State legislatures can remove public administration almost entirely from the executive sphere of control, respecting only the constitutional prescription of executive and administrative powers and duties. It is imperative to democratic government, however, that, in doing so, the State maintain a reasonable separation of powers at administrative levels. Here the board becomes an indispensable element in the State governmental structure for public administration.

Theoretical constructions focusing on State government must have the built-in flexibility to support a rational explanation of our republican form of government that provides for relatively independent public administration for a wide variety of public purposes. Examples of independent public administrative authorities are municipal governments, independent districts of State government such as school districts, and self-governing State institutions. Realistically, if all powers and duties were divided conveniently into three departments in each State, the degree of centralization would be alien to our form of government. Decentralized government permits a multitude of relatively independent public administrative authorities to exercise broad governmental powers for particular public purposes.

An independent public administrative authority should logically possess all powers of government at administrative levels essential to accomplishing the purposes for which it exists. In that the powers vested in these organizations — for example, municipal governments — must be extensive, the need for structural and functional separation of powers within the authority is readily apparent. Thus, in every public administrative authority that has broad self-governing powers, structural and organizational provision must be made to facilitate the rule of law.

Each independent public administrative authority — particularly those established for educational purposes — may be likened to a "republic" possessing enumerated powers that have been delegated to it by the State. The separation of administrative powers can thus be accomplished by distributing governmental functions to three departments or divisions similar to those of the State: The legislative, the executive, and the judicial. The legislative department provides for the control and policy direction of the "republic," a responsibility that professional educators believe should be entrusted to a representative body or board. The executive department provides for the technical administration of the "republic," a responsibility that professional educators believe should be entrusted to a technically competent staff employed by the representative body. A chief executive officer would be designated by the board to serve as technical manager.

This arrangement subordinates the technical administration of the "republic" to the civil authority. Provision may be made for a judicial department in the form of administrative courts of tribunals, or through procedural arrangements. The most common procedural arrangement in educational government is made by delegating the responsibility for fact finding and making technical rulings to the technical manager of the "republic," and the civil jurisdiction—when necessary—to the board.

THE CENTRALIZING TREND FOR EDUCATIONAL POLICY MAKING*

. . . At the local level, policy most frequently grows out of the action of the board of education and in some cases the city council. Many boards of education, however, give their superintendents leeway in

*Roald F. Campbell, "Processes of Policy Making Within Structures of Educational Government: As Viewed by the Educator," *Government of Public Education for Adequate Policy Making,* Wm. P. McClure and Van Miller, eds., Urbana: by permission of Bureau of Educational Research, University of Illinois, 1960, 64-65.

formulating administrative regulations which also serve as guides to action and thus constitute policy statements.

Policy formalization for education at the state level is perhaps more complex. In the American scheme of things, the state legislature is clearly the chief policy-making agency in education. Each state has a formidable body of school law which sets the formal limits within which all agencies can act. Literally hundreds of bills affecting education are introduced into each legislative session of most states. These bills reflect the temper of the times and the antecedent movements. When Americanism rides high, there are bills, and some laws, requiring teachers to take oaths of allegiance. When education for the gifted is in fashion, there are bills, and some laws, establishing merit scholarship programs. But formalized policy for education also emanates from state boards of education, special state commissions, state superintendents, state auditing agencies, state building boards, and the state courts.

Even though education is generally thought to be a state function, policy for education is also formed at the national level. The Congress cannot evade such questions as the need for scientists and mathematicians, the lack of research, the shortage of schoolhouses, and state differentials in the capacity to provide financial support for education. Deliberation on some of these questions led to the establishment of the National Science Foundation in 1950 and the passage of the National Defense Education Act in 1958, both major policy enactments.

Educational policy also stems from the executive branch of the national government. The U. S. Office of Education is charged with the administration of the National Defense Education Act. To implement the Act, more than 200 administrators have been added to the Office of Education staff. The administrative regulations formulated by this group far exceed in wordage the Act itself, and in many instances these regulations are policy interpretations. Much of this wordage is the product of the attorneys who in their endeavors to interpret policy actually become policy makers. In the Bureau of the Budget another set of policy makers is at work. What may have seemed to be a simple enactment on the part of the Congress becomes a veritable maze at the hands of administrators, attorneys, and budget controllers, all part of the executive branch of government.

By now it seems abundantly clear that the federal courts also make policy for education. Actually, the U.S. Supreme Court alone has made 45 major decisions, of which the Brown case is but one, on educational issues. These decisions cover such questions as the legality of private schools, public provision of textbooks to parochial pupils, public transportation of parochial pupils, released time for religious education, teachers and subversive organizations, and Negro-white integration.

In summary, may we note that educational policy has its genesis in basic social change, its generation in nation-wide antecedent movements, its deliberation by educators and lay citizens in and out of government, and its formalization in legal expression by local, state, or national government. Basic social changes are usually nation-wide in scope. The antecedent movements are often nation-wide efforts. Inevitably, these forces tend to shift the major policy foci from local, to state, and to federal levels. Only the Congress can provide for education in terms of national survival. Usually states talk of minimum foundation programs. Despite our tradition of localism, local boards of education find themselves more and more working within the frameworks of state and national policy for education. . . .

THE IMPROVING STRUCTURE FOR ADMINISTERING EDUCATION AT THE STATE LEVEL*

There is a discernible trend in State government to a central education agency vested with all powers and duties for administering the State system of education. This trend is now so pronounced that it is possible to describe the agency and provide an objective account of how it functions. The agency consists of a State board of education, a chief State school officer, and a staff. The State board of education constitutes the legislative policymaking component of the agency, and the chief State school officer and the staff under his direction constitute the executive component of the agency.

The State board of education is comprised of representatives of the people and functions as a legislative body. The board enacts rules and regulations pursuant to law and makes educational policy at the administrative level of State government. The chief State school officer is the executive officer of the agency. He directs and controls the staff engaged to do the work of the agency.

There are differences among the States regarding certain characteristics of the board, such as size, method of selecting members, and term of office, but other characteristics are now firmly established as good practice. For example, it is generally accepted that the terms of board members should overlap, that no special interest representation should be permitted, and that no member should be gainfully employed by or

---

*Robert F. Will, *State Education Structure and Organization,* 34.

TABLE 3. — THE STATE BOARD OF EDUCATION (SBE): JANUARY 1963* [IN. = INAPPLICABLE]

States having a SBE for the State system of education[1]	Designation	Chief method of selecting members				Number of members		Term of elected or appointed members, in years	SBE is board for vocational education	SBE is board for vocational rehabilitation
		Elected by the people or representatives of the people	Appointed by governor	Ex officio (By virtue of office or position held)	Appointed by chief State school officer	Total	Ex officio			
		11	31	4	1	434	35	In.	45	42
Total		11	31	4	1	434	35	In.	45	42
Alabama	State board of education	—	X	—	—	11	2	6	Yes	Yes
Alaska	State board of education	—	X	—	—	6	0	3	Yes	Yes
Arizona	State board of education	—	—	X	—	8	5	(2)	Yes	Yes
Arkansas	State board of education	—	X	—	—	9	0	9	Yes	Yes
California	State board of education	—	X	—	—	10	0	4	Yes	Yes
Colorado	State board of education	X	—	—	—	5	0	6	No	No
Connecticut	State board of education	—	X	—	—	9	0	6	Yes	Yes
Delaware	State board of education	—	X	—	—	6	0	3	Yes	Yes
Florida	State board of education	—	—	X	—	5	5	In.	Yes	Yes
Georgia	State board of education	—	X	—	—	10	0	7	Yes	Yes
Hawaii	State board of education	—	X	—	—	11	1	4	Yes	Yes
Idaho	State board of education	—	X	—	—	6	1	5	Yes	Yes
Indiana	State board of education	—	X	—	—	19	1	4	Yes	Yes
Iowa	State board of public instruction	[3]X	—	—	—	9	0	6	Yes	Yes
Kansas	State board of education	—	X	—	—	7	0	3	Yes	Yes
Kentucky	State board of education	—	X	—	—	8	1	4	Yes	Yes
Louisiana	State board of education	X	—	—	—	11	0	[4]6,8	Yes	Yes
Maine	State board of education	—	X	—	—	10	0	5	Yes	Yes
Maryland	State board of education	—	X	—	—	7	0	7	Yes	Yes
Massachusetts	State board of education	—	X	—	—	9	0	9	[5]No	No
Minnesota	State board of education	—	X	—	—	7	0	7	Yes	Yes
Mississippi	State board of education	—	—	X	—	3	3	In.	Yes	Yes
Missouri	State board of education	—	X	—	—	8	0	8	Yes	Yes
Montana	State board of education	—	X	—	—	11	3	8	Yes	Yes
Nebraska	State board of education	X	—	—	—	6	0	6	Yes	Yes
Nevada	State board of education	X	X	—	—	8	0	4	Yes	Yes
New Hampshire	State board of education	—	X	—	—	7	0	5	Yes	Yes

State	Agency				No.		Term		
New Mexico	State board of education	X	—	—	10	0	6	Yes	Yes
New York	Board of regents, university of the State of New York	—	X[6]	—	13	0	13	Yes	Yes
North Carolina	State board of education	—	X	—	13	3	8	Yes	Yes
North Dakota	State board of public school education	—	X	—	5	3	2	Yes	Yes
Ohio	State board of education	X	—	—	23	0	6	Yes	Yes
Oklahoma	State board of education	—	X	—	7	1	6	Yes	Yes
Oregon	State board of education	—	X	—	7	0	7	Yes	Yes
Pennsylvania	State council of education	—	X	—	10	1	6	Yes	No[7]
Rhode Island	State board of education	—	X	—	7	0	7	Yes	No
South Carolina[8]	State board of education	—	X	—	9	2	4	Yes	Yes
South Dakota	State board of education	—	X	—	7	0	5	Yes	Yes
Tennessee	State board of education	—	X	—	11	2	6	Yes	Yes
Texas	State board of education	X	X	—	21	0	6	Yes	Yes
Utah	State board of education	—	X	—	9	0	4	Yes	Yes
Vermont	State board of education	—	X	—	7	0	6	Yes	Yes
Virginia	State board of education	—	X	—	7	0	4	Yes	Yes
Washington[9]	State board of education	—	X[9]	—	14	0	6	Yes	Yes
West Virginia	State board of education	—	X	—	9	0	9	Yes	Yes
Wyoming	State board of education	—	X	—	7	1	6	Yes	Yes

[1] Illinois, Michigan, and Wisconsin do not have a State board of education for the State system of education. The Michigan constitution approved by the people in April 1963 which became effective on January 1, 1964, provides for a State board of education vested with leadership and general supervision over all public education except institutions of higher education granting baccalaureate degrees, and changes the method of selecting the State superintendent of public instruction from election by the people to appointment by the new State board of education. Michigan will be the 48th State to establish a State board of education to head the State system of education and the 24th State to empower such a board to appoint the chief State school officer.

[2] No term specified in law.

[3] Elected by conventions of delegates chosen by local school boards.

[4] Three elected for overlapping 6-year terms and 8 elected for overlapping 8-year terms.

[5] SBE, CSSO, and one person appointed by governor constitute the State board for vocational education.

[6] Elected by the legislature.

[7] SBE and the secretary of labor and industry constitute the State board of vocational rehabilitation.

[8] A constitutional amendment approved November 6, 1962, provides for a new State board of education in South Carolina. The amendment follows: "There should be a State board of education composed of one member from each of the judicial circuits of the State. The members shall be elected by the legislative delegations of the several counties within each circuit for terms and with such powers and duties as may be provided by law, and shall be rotated among the several counties.

Since the power and duties of the new State board of education and the terms of its members has not been provided for by law as of January 1963, this study shows the State organization and structure for public education in South Carolina as it was prior to the constitutional amendment.

[9] Elected by members of boards of directors of local school districts.

*Robert F. Will, *State Education Structure and Organization*, Washington, D.C.: United States Office of Education, Misc. No. 46, 1964, 16.

administratively connected with any school or school system operating in the State. The compensation of board members may become an issue as the legislative policymaking workload of the board increases.

It is now firmly established that the chief State school officer should be a professionally qualified educator with considerable administrative experience. The State board of education has proved to be the best instrument for selecting such a man free from partisan political influence. Although some educators believe that the chief State school officer should serve at the board's pleasure, a fixed term of office is desirable if a separation of powers is to be maintained at the administrative level in the central education agency.

It is generally accepted that the staff engaged to conduct the work of the central education agency should be under the executive direction of the chief State school officer. This staff comprises a service organization commonly identified as the State department of education.

The organization and internal government of the State department of education present problems that cannot be resolved under any one master plan for all States. In this area, each State is dependent upon the administrative competency and skill of the chief State school officer and his principal assistants. Some guidelines for the organization and internal administration of the department of education are provided in this study.

STATE DEPARTMENT OF EDUCATION . . .

THE ADMINISTRATIVE RULEMAKING POWERS OF A STATE AGENCY*

Under our system of government, the State legislative power is vested in the legislative branches of State governments and cannot be delegated to other branches or agencies of State government. Nonetheless, the courts generally agree that public administrative agencies created by law should normally possess the powers and resources essential to conduct the work delegated to or placed with them under the law. The commonsense foundation for this agreement requires little amplification. An automobile without a motor cannot run; one in perfect condition needs fuel to run. Recognizing this, we can view each administrative

---

*Robert F. Will, "State Administrative Rulemaking," *School Life*, XLIV (April, 1962), 19-21.

agency or office to which the legislature has delegated powers and duties as a governmental unit of limited jurisdiction. Each must possess what appear to be legislative, executive, and judicial powers for particular purposes.

The answer to this seemingly irreconcilable conflict of governmental practice and legal theory is not as involved as may first appear. State legislatures cannot delegate their legislative power, but they can delegate legislative functions for particular purposes. These legislative functions are most readily identified collectively as rulemaking, and the power delegated, as the rulemaking power.

DEFINITION

Administrative rulemaking is the process of developing and enacting or adopting administrative legislation. Rulemaking in its proper sphere does not constitute sovereign lawmaking, even though rules may possess the force of a law under legislative sanction. Administrative rules serve to "fill in the details" of particular statutes enacted by State legislatures. They may be grouped under two headings:

Rules of agency management, which identify uniform policies, practices, and procedures that an agency formally enacts or adopts for purposes of internal organization and the control of its property, operating funds, and staff.

Rules of agency conduct, which identify uniform policies, practices, and procedures that an agency formally enacts or adopts to permit the lawful exercise of its delegated powers in doing its work. These rules may be further classified as local and State rules of agency conduct: local rules are adopted by local administrative agencies and apply only in the territory governed by these agencies; State rules are adopted by State administrative agencies and apply generally through the State. . . .

AREA OF CONFLICT

Rules of agency conduct made by State administrative agencies are, in effect, State administrative laws, and as such serve to centralize administrative authority for particular purposes. The people of the United States have always been suspicious of centralized administrative authority, particularly when it is used to regulate specific activities of local administrative agencies and private interests.

Centralizing tendencies in State administration strike at the very roots of laissez faire concepts that have led many persons to believe that the local governments and private entities permitted to function within a State under constitutional and statutory law can do much as they please without interference from State administrative agencies. Those who hold these concepts often challenge the rights of State administrative agencies to apply or enforce their rules. They see central administrative authority as the embodiment of all "isms" that are alien to democratic government.

The fact that centralized administrative authority is necessary in many areas needs little defense. A sovereign government that whittled away its powers to add to the powers of its political subdivisions and private interests would soon cease to exist. Nonetheless, State administrative agencies created to direct and control particular activities of local Administrative agencies and private entities have seemingly insurmountable problems in exercising the rulemaking powers delegated to them.

Most State legislatures now cognizant of these problems have enacted "State administrative procedures acts" to guide State administrative agencies that have been delegated rulemaking and adjudicative powers. State education agencies that have been delegated administrative powers to direct and control particular activities of local school districts and private educational agencies are subject to the provisions of these acts. The phrase "subject to" is used here to accent the fact that State education agencies are required under these acts to file their rules as prescribed and to follow definite procedures in enacting and enforcing them. *If a rule is not properly filed, it is void and unenforceable; if the procedures set forth are not followed, the courts may declare that the enforcement of the rule violated the constitutional rights of individuals.*

COORDINATION AND STRUCTURE

Prior to 1900, States had need for few State administrative agencies to direct and control particular activities of local governments and private interests. Most legislation could be sufficiently detailed to establish what then was accepted as suitable standards of legislative control. State programs and services rarely required large staffs, and many could be administered — or so State legislatures believed — by a single public officer. State legislatures found it expedient, under these conditions, to delegate nearly all State administrative duties and powers to public officials in the executive departments. Even so, certain duties and powers could not be entrusted to one public officer. Thus, State legislatures frequently found it necessary to place these duties and powers with several persons, commonly designated a "board." Many of these boards were composed of a number of elected State officials, a practice that kept the cost of administration down.

As States moved into the 20th century, it became increasingly evident that a more systematic approach was needed to coordinate the work of State government. The growing number of State administrative agencies had so increased the work of State legislatures that it was no longer possible for them to enact legislation in sufficient detail to guide those delegated the responsibility for executing its provisions. Reorganization on departmental lines provided one key to coordination, but departmentalization, in turn, presented separation-of-powers complications that have not yet been fully resolved. Most States had formed administrative departments early in the 1800's, usually under constitutionally designated executive officers. Thus, many States had come to look upon administrative functions as executive functions. In creating new departments for related State programs that did not fit into any of the existing departments, many legislatures chose to place them under single administrative officers who served directly under and at the pleasure of the chief executive officer of the State — the governor.

These practices have created many structural and organizational problems in State government. State legislatures, for example, have been reluctant to place with State administrative departments headed by a single officer rulemaking powers to regulate particular activities of local governments and private interests. Their concern is understandable since rulemaking under executive or one-man control is easily confused with sovereign lawmaking.

Those who have seriously studied these problems are divided as to the best means of solving them. Political scientists, for example, generally favor making the governor of the State the chief administrative officer to solve the problems of administrative coordination. They believe that State legislatures can overcome most separation-of-powers conflicts by providing statutory procedural safeguards. Even so, they do acknowledge the need for departmental boards to exercise quasi-legislative (rulemaking) or quasi-judicial powers for special purposes. Educators generally hold that State education agencies should not be subject to the administrative direction and control of the governor. They believe that State education agencies should possess distinct legislative and executive components or parts to effect a complete separation of these powers at the administrative level. They believe that the legislative components, constituted as boards, should make the administrative rules and determine the policies that direct and control educational activities in the State.

FUNCTIONS AND SERVICES OF STATE DEPARTMENTS OF EDUCATION: GUIDING PRINCIPLES*

In administering the duties delegated to it under law, the state department of education serves a twofold purpose. It is a leadership-regulatory agency for the state system of public education and a governing agency for particular programs that are operated on a state-wide basis.

The manner in which the department functions as a state leadership-regulatory agency differs markedly from the manner in which it functions as a state governing agency. For this reason it is appropriate to examine the role of the department in each capacity. . . .

THE STATE DEPARTMENT OF EDUCATION AS A LEADERSHIP-REGULATORY AGENCY

State departments of education are responsible for enforcing laws and administrative rules and regulations that require local school districts to meet particular standards and comply with specific conditions. In carrying out this responsibility state departments are exercising state-wide regulatory controls. State departments are likewise responsible for providing professional and technical assistance to local school districts to help them meet and exceed the standards prescribed by state law and administrative rules and regulations. In carrying out this responsibility state departments are exercising leadership. The experience of state departments of education has indicated that most educational improvement is a direct consequence of leadership. Leadership activities and services are particularly essential to state educational administration.

Regulatory Responsibilities

(a) *Basis for Regulation.* Regulatory responsibilities are a direct consequence of state authority for education. While states have delegated broad authority to local school districts for the management and operation of the public schools they have also established safeguards to guarantee minimum performance. Standards are established either by the legislature or by a state agency pursuant to a statutory grant of

---

*The State Department of Education, Legal Status, Functions, and Organization. (Rev. Ed.) Washington, D.C.: Council of Chief State School Officers, 1963, 17-28.

authority. Consequently, regulatory responsibilities must be identified expressly by statute or by administrative rules and regulations promulgated to fill in the details of statutes. The establishment of standards and the accompanying power to enforce compliance with them are commonly termed the regulatory function.

(c) *Principles Concerning Regulation.*

1. Procedures for the exercise of regulatory controls by state departments of education should guard against any inroad being made into areas not intended by law. Every precaution should be taken to insure that the responsibility for the operational control of local education programs remains with local school districts.

2. State administrative rules and regulations should be developed through cooperative action among the state department of education, local school districts, and the public. This procedure produces the most desirable administrative standards and encourages voluntary compliance on the part of the agencies obligated to meet them.

3. State administrative rules and regulations establishing standards that are mandatory should clearly indicate minimum requirements. It is important that local school districts be free to develop programs above minimum requirements. The state department of education should endeavor to stimulate initiative in local leaders so that they will strive to exceed the minimum requirements.

4. Where two or more state agencies are concerned with the establishment and enforcement of state administrative rules and regulations, there should be an official cooperative agreement which sets forth the specific responsibilities of each, provides for the point development of standards, and identifies enforcement procedures.

5. Enforcement of a state standard should not go beyond the minimum action required to obtain compliance. Legal procedures to bring about compliance should be used as a last resort. Only when leadership efforts fail to bring about compliance should regularly constituted law enforcement agencies be brought into cases, and then in a diplomatic yet legally proper manner.

6. In order that research and experimentation should not be unduly hampered by laws or administrative rules and regulations, provision should be made to permit the state department of education to waive requirements expressed as minimum standards for particular projects when such action is desirable and necessary.

Leadership Responsibilities

The state department of education should be the leadership center of the state system of education. Effective leadership contributes significantly to the improvement of state and local education programs. Each program conducted by a state department of education should have the resources needed to provide leadership throughout the state. Leadership activities and services may be appropriately identified in five broad categories: Planning, Research, Consultation, Public Relations, and In-service Education.

(a) *Planning* is concerned with identifying needs, determining purposes, and deciding upon the ways and means by which desired outcomes are to be attained. Planning involves the evaluation of alternative courses of action prior to setting the course to be followed. In American society cooperative planning is an appropriate means of determining how resources may be most effectively utilized. It is in the use and development of planning processes that the state department of education should play a decisive role.

Some principles concerning planning are:

1. State educational plans should be developed to meet local, state, and national needs.
2. State educational planning activities should supplement rather than supplant local planning. Local initiative and responsibility should be encouraged and stimulated.
3. Participation of representative groups and individuals should characterize state-wide cooperative planning.
4. Planning should be a continuous and often a long-range process in the development, implementation, appraisal, and revision of state-wide programs.
5. All programs of the state department of education should be coordinated components emerging from and contributing to long-range state-wide planning.
6. Staff participation should be an integral part of the planning process.
7. Appropriate materials and resources should be made available in the planning process.

(b) *Research* is essentially a method of inquiry, concerning the old and the new, the tried and the untried. Its purpose is to find better ways of doing familiar things and of learning how to accomplish other newer objectives that appear to be desirable. It draws its strength from knowledge and establishes its influence through mutual understanding. Some principles concerning research are:

1. Research should help provide the foundation for educational policy. Sound research should contribute to the development of

state education standards in the law and in administrative rules and regulations. Demonstrations and controlled experiments in the field are often important instruments of evaluation.

2. Research in education conducted by the public and private agencies operating within the state should be shared under cooperative arrangements to eliminate duplication of effort and to provide effective channels for the exchange and dissemination of ideas. The department should be a clearinghouse for educational research.

3. Provision should be made under department direction for financing some needed educational research through cooperative arrangements with local school districts, colleges and universities, and private organizations.

4. Positive means should be established to tap the research potential which resides in the professional staff of the department. Research consultants should be available to the professional staff conducting the department's programs to provide assistance and counsel relative to research methods, techniques, and procedures.

5. The department should encourage research and experimentation in local school districts and institutions of higher education.

6. The department should evaluate educational innovations that are being tried out in the state and promote the adoption of those of proven value.

(c) *Consultative services* of a state department of education are characterized by activities directed to the study and solution of problems in education. Newer and better ways of accomplishing particular objectives are constantly being developed. The diffusion of methods, procedures, and practices essential to implement such improvements can be greatly accelerated when staff members of the department are actively engaged in activities directed to the achievement of this purpose. Some principles concerning consultation are:

1. Consultative services should be provided by and through the department to local school districts, state educational agencies, state government officials, and other agencies and organizations subject to the state education laws administered by the department.

2. Responsibility for coordinating interdepartmental and interagency consultative services which are primarily educational in nature and which are directed to state and local educational agencies in the state system of public education should be placed with the state department of education.

3. Consultative services provided by and through the department should be channeled through the duly constituted authorities of

the agency or group served. This increases the effectiveness of the services, minimizes duplication of efforts, and nurtures public confidence.

4. Consultative services provided by the department should be administered by staff members assigned primarily to leadership activities and services. It is recommended that staff consultants be given no authority to invoke regulatory controls.

(d) *Public Relations.* The essentials of public relations are the essentials of good human relations. Good human relations are based upon understanding and mutual confidence, respect for the opinion of others, a desire to render service, a willingness to make and abide by group decisions, and a sensitivity for the concerns of people. . . .

(e) *In-service Education* includes those activities which contribute to growth and improvement on the job. In-service education activities are equally desirable for the staff of the state department of education and for the school personnel served by the staff. . . .

THE STATE DEPARTMENT OF EDUCATION AS A GOVERNING AGENCY

In some states, state departments of education operate certain special schools, colleges, cultural institutions, classes, or programs of direct service to individuals or groups. These direct governing functions are quite different in character from leadership and regulatory functions. When a state department of education exercises the leadership-regulatory function, it deals with another agency which is charged with the operation of a particular institution or program. When exercising the governing function, the state department of education is the agency charged with operating the institution or program. In the one case, there is an agency between the state department of education and the program of operating activities. In the other, there is no such agency. . . .

The state itself is the logical unit for operating certain kinds of educational institutions or programs. It is sometimes necessary to have the state as a single attendance area for special schools for the handicapped and for certain colleges. Smaller attendance areas could not provide essential services efficiently and economically. It may also be desirable to have the state as an operating unit for certain institutions although the attendance unit may be less than the state. There are other programs which some states provide uniformly, such as teacher retirement. Uniformity can best be achieved by having such programs administered on a statewide basis. For these reasons, the responsibility for administering an institution or program may be lodged in the state department of education or in another state agency. . . .

INFLUENCE OF STATE DEPARTMENTS TIED TO FINANCING AND REPORTING*

Prior to 1800, State governments provided relatively few services on a state-wide basis. The belief that central government existed primarily to protect property was common. Such reasoning was easily rationalized by men who had lived under tyrants, for experience had taught them to distrust a concentration of power far removed from individual communities. There was, however, a significant weakness in this point of view. The framers of the Federal and various State constitutions had established a government wherein laws would rule instead of men, and the power to make laws had been vested in legislative bodies. The power that the people needed to govern themselves locally was centered at National and State levels.

The people soon realized that legislative permission was necessary to initiate any corporate activity which was to be financed by public money. The full meaning of this fact was realized when local municipal corporations set out to establish schools for the education of the children of the poor. Paradoxically, many communities wanted to provide free educational facilities, but they could not employ public moneys, even surplus funds, for this purpose without legislative sanction. Local municipal corporations did not possess the authority to raise or spend public money for education. State governments did little more for education during this early period than to delegate limited taxing and spending powers to local governments, and at times to private societies, to enable them to provide common schools; nevertheless, the foundations of the modern State school system may be traced to these modest beginnings.

This activity also marked the origins of what may be called State educational reports. It was recognized at this early date that the State could not authorize the use of public resources without accounting for the manner in which they were used. Public property could not be doled out arbitrarily without eventually destroying the people's faith in government established on the principle of rule by law. State legislatures found it necessary to take measures that would give the people an accounting of public money raised and spent for education. Thus, they provided a means whereby every transaction involving public property would be supervised by a responsible agent or agency. Trustees were appointed

---

*The State Department of Education Report, 1953, "The Origins and Changing Concepts of the State Department of Education Report," Washington, D.C.: United States Office of Education, 1-7.

for all public resources that were used for educational purposes at the local level of government, and these trustees were invariably required by law to furnish statements of accountability to the people they represented and served. The statements that they prepared were the first educational reports required by the State.

Once a precedent had been established to employ public resources for education, the demands for school legislation increased. Local municipal corporations and private societies in ever increasing numbers sought permission to obtain and employ public funds for the operation and maintenance of common schools. Nor were all these requests limited to providing educational experiences for paupers. Many communities began exploring the practicability of operating school for all children and youth. Ambitious plans for cheap universal education were eagerly discussed in the meeting places of the Nation. It was this activity that heralded the era of small State appropriations, permanent school funds, and land grants for education. Obviously, public opinion was in support of providing common school facilities at public expense. By 1825 every existing State was giving aid to local communities for education.

With the increased demands for school legislation and State aid, members of State legislatures soon recognized that a legislative body could not intelligently supervise the educational activity of a State without the help of an administrative agent to do the work involved. They also realized that earlier provisions for establishing financial accountability at the local level were wholly inadequate. Laws, unfortunately, are not self-administered, nor do they always achieve desired results. The inadequacies of the law could be overlooked when only local money was being employed for education, but the use of State money entailed responsibilities which could not be ignored. . . .

To further complicate matters, additional problems growing out of earlier school legislation confronted State legislatures. Most school legislation in the past had been enacted primarily to enable local governments or private societies to maintain schools at public expense. As could be expected, few schools had been organized in the sparsely populated and undeveloped parts of the various States. Insofar as substantial sums of State moneys were being made available for the encouragement of common schools, steps had to be taken to distribute these moneys so that every child in the State might have educational opportunities. The work involved in collecting and verifying the information that was essential to provide a basis for intelligent legislative action could not be done by a committee of the legislature. A responsible agent was needed to superintend State educational programs.

As a general rule, legislative bodies attempt to have the work of government accomplished as economically as possible. The size of every job is determined after an analysis of the duties that it is thought to embrace. Since most State legislature at first viewed the superintending of the State system of common school as a simple matter of perfecting a system of maintaining records and reports and preparing a small State report, few could justify the creation of a separate agency or the employment of a full-time official for this purpose. A majority of the State legislatures assigned the task to a constitutional officer in the executive branch of government who served ex officio as the State superintendent of education. . . .

EARLY STATE DEPARTMENT OF EDUCATION REPORTS

When State legislatures eventually realized that the State school system could not be adequately superintended by an education committee of the legislature, a part-time agent, or an officer of the executive branch of government acting in an ex officio capacity, they created the administrative agencies which are commonly referred to now as State departments of education. In its rudimentary form, the State department of education was composed of one full-time officer and in some States, a governing board. Collecting and processing information remained the principal duty of this officer or the governing board of the department, but they were called upon to work closely with the people. In his first report as Commissioner of Education in New Hampshire, Charles B. Haddock clearly summarized the job that was expected:

> The Commissioner is required, annually, in the month of June, "to make to the General Court a Report upon the Common Schools of the State, which shall comprise the substance of the returns from the several towns, and such information and suggestions as seem to him useful." He is to procure six hundred copies of the report to be printed, and laid before the General Court, to be disposed of at their discretion.
>
> Such are the main features of our system of Common School education — simple, yet comprehensive. Conformed entirely to the democratic spirit of our people, in as much as it gives the immediate management of the Schools to the people themselves, it, at the same time, provides for an intelligent and efficient public legislation; by means of the Annual Returns and Reports required to be made to the Government, through the Commissioner, whose business is not so much to prescribe as to learn and to teach, it maintains a regular communication of the Legislature with the towns and districts, and facilitates the diffusion of useful improvements and new lights, from whatever quarter derived, over the whole State.

Size of professional staffs[1] of State departments of education engaged in programs directly supplementing or supporting programs of local school systems and institutions of higher education, by State and interval: 1962*

Size interval									
1 to 50		51 to 100		101 to 150		151 to 200		201 and over	
State	Staff	State	Staff	State	Staff	State	Staff	State	Staff
Wyoming	16	Kansas	51	Kentucky	113	Georgia	160	California	249
South Dakota	19	Colorado	52	Louisiana	121	Texas	175	New York	271
Arizona	23	Mississippi	52	Virginia	126	Illinois	179		
North Dakota	23	Tennessee	55	North Carolina	[2]143	Pennsylvania	199		
Alaska	23	West Virginia	62						
New Hampshire	26	Washington	63						
Nevada	27	Connecticut	64						
Vermont	29	Michigan	65						
Idaho	32	Iowa	66						
Montana	34	Wisconsin	71						
Rhode Island	35	South Carolina	72						
Utah	38	Missouri	77						
Maine	40	Ohio	84						
Delaware	41	Oregon	84						
New Mexico	41	New Jersey	85						
Alabama	43	Florida	90						
Nebraska	45	Oklahoma	90						
Hawaii	46	Massachusetts	91						
Indiana	48	Minnesota	100						
Maryland	48								
Arkansas	49								

[1]Does not include: (a) Staff engaged in the direct operation of a school, college, university, or intermediate administrative unit, and (b) staff conducting programs that are not considered integral parts of the State system of education in all States, e.g., vocational rehabilitation programs, State museums, State libraries, State archives, and State library extension programs.

[2]Does not include staff under the executive direction of the comptroller or the director of curriculum study and research.

*Robert F. Will, *State Education Structure and Organization*, 33.

THE CHIEF STATE SCHOOL OFFICER . . .

The constitutional chief State school officer: January 1963*
[In. = inapplicable; indef. = indefinite]

States in which CSSO is constitutional officer	Article of constitution, by title, in which office of CSSO is established	Method of selecting CSSO[1]	Date of next election, by month and year	Term of office, in years
Alabama	Executive	EP	Nov. 1966	[2]4
Arizona	Executive	EP	Nov. 1964	2
California	Education	EN	Nov. 1966	4
Colorado	Education	B	In.	Indef.
Florida	Executive Dept.	EP	Nov. 1964	4
Georgia	Education	EP	Nov. 1966	4
Hawaii	Education	B	In.	Indef.
Idaho	Executive Dept.	EP	Nov. 1966	4
Illinois	Executive Dept.	EP	Nov. 1966	4
Indiana	Education	EP	Nov. 1964	2
Kansas	Executive	EP	Nov. 1964	2
Kentucky	The Executive Dept.	EP	Nov. 1963	[2]4
Louisiana	Public Education	EP	Apr. 1964	4
Michigan	Education	EP	Apr. 1963	2
Mississippi	Education	EP	Nov. 1963	4
Missouri	Education	B	In.	Indef.
Montana	Executive Dept.	EP	Nov. 1964	4
Nebraska	Education	B	In.	Indef.
Nevada	Education	B	In.	Indef.
New Mexico	Education	B	In.	Indef.
New York	Officers and Civil Depts.	B	In.	Indef.
North Carolina	Executive Dept.	EP	Nov. 1964	4
North Dakota	Executive Dept.	EN	Nov. 1964	2
Ohio	Education	B	In.	Indef.
Oklahoma	Executive Dept.	EP	Nov. 1965	4
Oregon	Education and School Lands	B	In.	Indef.
South Carolina	Executive Dept.	EP	Nov. 1966	4
South Dakota	Executive Dept.	EN	Nov. 1964	2
Utah	Education	B	In.	Indef.
Virginia	Education and Public Instruction	G	In.	
Washington	The Executive	EN	Nov. 1964	[3]4
West Virginia	Education	B	In.	Indef.
Wisconsin	Education	EN	Apr. 1965	4
Wyoming	Executive	EP	Nov. 1966	4

[1]Key:
    E = Elected popular vote
    P = Partisan ballot
    N = Nonpartisan ballot
    B = Appointed by State board of education
    G = Appointed by governor
[2]The incumbent is ineligible for reelection for the 4 years succeeding the expiration of the term for which he is elected.
[3]Term coincident with that of governor making the appointment.

---

*Table furnished by Robert F. Will, United States Office of Education.

FOR FURTHER REFLECTION OR INVESTIGATION

1. From a listing of the services provided to schools by your state department of education, prescribe what other services might properly be provided. Should the department deal only with small districts since larger ones can provide their own special services?

2. Why are states reluctant to give up the practice of electing the state superintendent of schools?

3. Discuss the advisability of a single state board of education with jurisdiction over all educational institutions, elementary through college, public and private.

4. Since state governments have absolute authority over public education, why haven't educational opportunities been equalized throughout the state? Can they be equalized? Should they be?

5. Justify the common practice of paying a local school superintendent a higher salary than the state superintendent.

6. Is a state board of education subject to more or less political pressure than a local board?

7. With the state's power, why hasn't it enforced proper districting?

8. Discuss the feasibility of the state legislature handling policy making and law making for education through a sub-committee of that body rather than by a separate state board of education.

9. Would it be practical and wise for the state department of education to sponsor a state-wide placement service for teachers and administrators?

10. Should the state have any authority over selection of textbooks for the school of the state?

11. Plan an ideal composition of a state board of education, with prescriptions for the method of selection.

12. What are the probable alternatives to a strong administrative and aggressive legislative leadership for education at the state level?

13. Through interview or questionnaire, tabulate the number and type of reports required of schools by the state and determine what use is made of the information.

BIBLIOGRAPHY

Babcock, Robert S., *State and Local Government and Politics*, New York: Random House, 1957.

Beach, Fred F., and Robert F. Will, *The State and Education: The Structure and Control of Public Education at the State Level*, Washington, D.C.: United States Office of Education, 1955.

————, and Andrew H. Gibbs, *Personnel of State Department of Educa-*

tion, Washington, D.C.: United States Office of Education, Mis. No. 16, 1952.

_____, *The Structure of State Departments of Education.* Washington, D.C.: United States Office of Education, 1949.

Bock, Edwin A., ed., *State and Local Government,* Tuscaloosa: University of Alabama Press, 1963.

Burr, Samuel E., *The Development of Fiscal Relationships of State Departments of Education,* Washington, D.C.: The American University, 1960.

Campbell, Roald F., "Processes of Policy Making Within Structures of Educational Government: As Viewed by the Educator," from *Government of Public Education for Adequate Policy Making,* Urbana: University of Illinois, 1960.

Darrah, Earl L., and Orville F. Poland, *The Fifty State Governments: Compilation of State Executive Organization Charts,* Berkeley: Bureau of Public Administration, University of California, 1961.

Graves, William Brooke, *American Intergovernmental Relations,* New York: Charles Scribner's Sons, 1964.

Masters, Nicholas A., Robert H. Salisbury, and Thomas H. Eliot, *State Politics and the Public Schools,* New York: Alfred A. Knopf, Inc., 1964.

McPherron, A. L., "State or Local Control: Who is Responsible for Education?" *California Education,* I, October, 1963.

Michigan Education Journal, "Status of State Superintendency." XCVI, September, 1963.

Pierce, Truman M., *Federal, State, and Local Government in Education.* Washington, D.C.: The Center of Applied Research in Education, Inc., 1964.

The State Department of Education, Legal Status, Functions, and Organization. Washington, D.C.: Council of Chief State School Officers, 1963.

The State Department of Education Report, 1953, "The Origins and Changing Concepts of the State Department of Education Report," Washington, D.C.: United States Office of Education, 1954.

Thurston, Lee M., and William H. Roe, *State School Administration,* New York: Harper & Row, Publishers, 1957.

Will, Robert F., "State Administrative Rulemaking," *School Life,* XLIV, April, 1962.

Will, Robert F., *State Education Structure and Organization,* Washington, D.C.: United States Office of Education, Misc. No. 46, 1964.

Chapter 5

Administration of Education at the Federal Level

In the history of American centralized government, education arrived very late as a matter of consuming interest for those in authority. It has still not arrived, even after the momentous action of the 1965 congress, if one measures interest in terms of general financial support of the large segment of formal educational endeavors—elementary and secondary schools. Within the first decade of the Nation's existence as a federation, Congress did demonstrate some concern about educating youth when it gave its encouragement for the development of schools in the 1785 Land Ordinance. However, some historians claim that the provisions of the Northwest Ordinance were motivated more to induce settlement of that territory than to foster learning. The fact that Congress recognized its inducement does indicate an admission that it thought education important.

The problems incumbent upon Congress immediately after the Revolutionary War and the imminent challenge of building a new nation enable one to sympathize with our forefathers' low priority given to development of schools. Moreover, colonists were still under the influence of their continental past in which education was regarded as a responsibility of the church rather than government. Some spoke and wrote about the need for more extensive educational plans for more youngsters. American revolutionary leaders were part of the widening liberalizing forces of the times, observable in western man's thinking. Thomas Jefferson is credited with being the most prominent and clairvoyant spokesman for extending educational opportunities. He developed a plan for public schools and called for public libraries and liberalized universities. Other leaders of the Colonial period who raised their voices in behalf of education included Benjamin Franklin, James Madison, Thomas Paine, and George Mason. Evidently, the earliest statesmen reflected deeply upon the matter and reacted to the awakening spirit that education for all, like most affairs of government, was a responsibility which should be handled at levels much closer to parents than the central government could ever be.

Despite its hands-off policy, the federal government has participated in education, defined broadly, in many ways, including financial aid. In fact, more than four billion dollars of the Federal budget in the years just prior to 1965 found its way annually into some channel of educational activity. Through their representatives at the National level, citizens have expressed their interest in education in six general categories: (1) grants of land, (2) grants of money, (3) emergency measures, (4) special interests, (5) court rulings, and (6) establishment of the United States Office of Education. Only acknowledgment, not discussion, will be given in this work to the many voluntary groups that exercise influence on education at the national level but have no legal authority over it: the National Education Association, the Educational Policies Commission, the National Congress of Parents and Teachers, and others.

FEDERAL GRANTS OF LAND FOR EDUCATION

The first federal land grant, appearing in the Northwest Ordinance of 1787, specified that one-thirty-sixth of the land of the Northwest Territory (Ohio, Indiana, Illinois, Michigan, Wisconsin) was to be reserved for the maintenance of public schools. The interpretation of this prescription came to mean under the subsequent surveying of land that one section (a square mile) of each township would be so reserved. Section 16 of each township was arbitrarily chosen to be the school section in the admission to the Union of the first state carved out of the Territory, Ohio, and set a precedence for other states in the Westward Movement. Most of the sections were sold or leased, and the income therefrom was used to finance schools.

Numerous parcels of land were also set aside from the public domain for the development of colleges. Income from salt lands and swamp lands was used to promote public affairs, one of which was schools.

By the time of the Civil War, Congress had taken the first significant move toward the creation of a system of land-grant colleges and universities throughout the United States. In the Morrill Act of 1862, 30,000 acres per each Senator and Representative then in Congress was reserved in each state for the establishment of colleges of agriculture and mechanics. In those older states which did not then have that much land unclaimed within their borders, the equivalent in land script was granted which entitle such states to select land elsewhere in the public domain. In nearly all cases, the income from the sale of these acres was used for the initiation and support of agricultural and mechanical colleges. Eventually, sixty-nine land-grant colleges were established in the states and territories. Several have since become state universities, although they still receive federal support.

In addition to making a major contribution toward reaching the goal of a complete system of public education, from first grade to college, the Morrill Act marked the beginning of practical and professional training at the higher level. The Act represented a growing protest against the classical curriculum of higher education which had been enjoyed previously only by a few. In this act, as in most direct supports from the federal level, can be seen the efforts to overcome the social lag between local progress and the welfare of the people as defined by those in power.

FEDERAL GRANTS OF MONEY FOR EDUCATION

The first Federal grant of money for education came with Ohio's admission as a State in 1803. The authority was expressed in the enabling law which provided that five percent of the proceeds from the sale of public lands would be reserved for internal improvements; part of this went to schools. Other states repeated the pattern. Monies also came to the support of schools from the extraction of natural resources on Federal lands, especially the National Forest Reserve and the 1934 Grazing Act.

The next direct money grants were offered by the Second Morrill Act of 1890 in which $15,000 was appropriated by Congress to each state for the operational support of its land-grant college. The amounts were increased substantially in later appropriations. The Second Morrill Act also provided that no state would receive its appropriation if racial segregation were practiced at its land-grant school although it was not denied if a state provided "same and equal" colleges for Negro students.

Further money grants came during the present century with the encouragement of vocational training in high schools: the Smith-Lever Act of 1914, the Smith Hughes Act in 1917 which initiated direct grants to high schools, the George-Deen Act of 1936 which added distributive education to the list of vocational preparations, and the George-Barden Act of 1946 which superseded the 1936 provisions and increased the amounts. Other recent money grants to schools are delineated elsewhere in this chapter.

The Elementary and Secondary Education Act of 1965

It is difficult to classify the Elementary and Secondary Education Act of 1965 as simply a federal money grant to support education. The act comes close to being the first general support of elementary and secondary schools. Certain portions of the grant may be used as school districts see fit: teachers' salaries, textbooks, school building construction, and curriculum aids; but there are sufficient restrictions to prevent the act from being considered general support. It could be classified as an emergency action of the federal government inasmuch as the espoused rationale for the legislation was to combat the inadequate education being offered to children of low-income families. The emergencies seemed to be poverty, national defense, school dropouts, and unemployment attributable to poor education. And the act could be construed as special interest action on behalf of the national government. The enactment is summarized here under the classification of a money grant to education, since it is clearly the largest sum appropriated by Congress, most of which will go to elementary and secondary schools, and the broadest in purposes. Labeling it as an omnibus bill, however, should be tempered with the recognition that some districts will not benefit at all.

In addition to the amount of money involved ($1.3 billion), this act is noteworthy in other respects. It skirts one of the previous obstacles to massive federal support stemming from the church-state issue by extending moneys to children attending private schools in the same proportion as there are low-income families represented there, but to be managed through the administration of the local public schools. It encourages cooperative efforts on the part of administrators of public and parochial schools in the development of programs to improve education for all educationally deprived children in the joint use of teaching materials, equipment, and buildings. Further combined ventures may rise from the section of the act which encourages school cooperation with those community groups that came into being from the earlier enacted Economic Opportunity Act.

The act itself does not take a stand on the controversial issue of racially segregated schools. However, the amount of money involved will undoubtedly increase integration efforts in view of the 1964 Civil Rights Act which decreed that no federal funds could be distributed to any project operated on a discriminatory basis.

A stated objective of the 1965 act was that of "equalization of educational opportunity" on a national level; its major allocation of money is aimed primarily at improving the programs of schools which accommodate large numbers of low-income families. In view of the tendency for poverty to mottle in the country, the large urban areas and the lands of marginal productivity will benefit substantially more than the more affluent regions.

Among the five titles of the Act, Title I disburses the major amount—over $1 billion. That sum is misleading, however, since it is not all "new money" for education. Title I amended and incorporated the old Public Law 874 which aided the familiar "federally impacted" communities, those school districts crowded by federal activities in the area.

Other titles of the 1965 act provided monies to strengthen state departments of education and to spur educational research and innovation. Title III permits the revolutionary direct negotiation between the federal government and a local school district for developing new programs without going through the state department of education. Perhaps the most precedent-setting facet of the act grows out of its assignment for administration to the United States Office of Education. As discussed later in the chapter, this is far more money than has ever previously been entrusted by legislators to educators. It may forerun a changing attitude on the part of national law-makers and political executives, and a way out of the diffusion of educational interest and financial support at the federal level.

It is too early, at this writing, to assess the impact of the Elementary and Secondary Education Act on school administration or national welfare. Though the effect may escape precise measurement, there can be no doubt that schools and society have been influenced by other federal actions in regard to education: the Morrill acts, provision for vocational education, the National Science Foundation, the National Defense Education acts, and the National School Lunch Act. Whether the 1965 Act has opened the door to general support of education, national policy for education, decreasing local control over education, breaching of the church-state wall in the education of youth, or to a giant federal boondoggle in America's schools — all of which have been claimed for the Act — must bide the observation and evaluation of future generations.

EMERGENCY FEDERAL SUPPORTS
TO EDUCATIONAL INSTITUTIONS

The emergencies of war and economic depression have been the primary rationales for federal measures which encourage education, although most of the legislation persisted long after the emergency waned. The first such measure was enacted following World War I through the Smith-Sears Act of 1918 which established training programs for the rehabilitation of wounded veterans. The program was discontinued in 1927, but in the meantime the opportunities were extended to persons disabled in industrial accidents, and was renewed following World War II; lately the emphasis has been shifted to "physical restoration of individuals."

The national school lunch program was initiated in 1932 as an emergency measure to provide food for needy children. Administration of the program has been shuttled among various Washington offices but finally came to rest in the Department of Agriculture which deals also with disposal of farm surpluses and with farm price supports. Several major precedents in school operations have resulted from the school lunch program. It represented the first national financial aid to non-public schools and to elementary schools. Also, elements of the principle of equalization of educational opportunity on a national basis may be seen in the administration of the measure since the fiscal ability of states is recognized in the amounts distributed.

Other emergency actions of the Depression Years contained economic concerns as their primary motivation, but aided education indirectly. The Civil Conservation Corps, begun in 1933, combined a work and study program in the various CCC camps, and was discontinued with the appearance of another emergency — World War II. The National Youth Administration of 1935 helped needy and worthy youngsters to stay in school by providing jobs at high schools and colleges. Some actual training centers established under NYA were deemed to be in competition with public schools. The Works Progress Administration provided construction jobs for many school buildings and public libraries.

World War II brought on several educational crash programs financed by the federal government to ready men and women for the technical occupations needed in civilian production as well as in military specializations. Many men earned a portion of their undergraduate college degrees under programs of the Army, Navy, or Air Force. The United States Armed Forces Institute, still operating in 1966, enabled thousands of military personnel to enhance their educational attainments through correspondence courses. The largest federal aid to education program ever launched, the "GI Bill," grew out of the emergency. The Lanham Act, enacted in 1940, supported schools in areas impacted by the presence of government installations. The aid continues under what is known as Public Law 815 and Public Law 874 (until 1965,) which have been extended to communities impacted by industries doing business with the federal government and to the construction of college buildings.

The National Defense Education Act of 1958 was the latest major federal legislation motivated under an emergency support for certain programs of public and private schools prior to the new Elementary and Secondary Education Act of 1965.

FEDERAL SPECIAL-INTEREST SUPPORTS OF EDUCATION

The diversified activities of various divisions of the federal government account for the major expenditures by that level for educational purposes. These projects are regarded not as efforts to promote the cause of education but as means to improve the performance of personnel in the respective offices, or for the development of the new through research. Each department of the Executive Branch and several other agencies have educational programs. The impressive scope of programs and expenditures is detailed in the 1959 survey of federal educational projects in the report found later in this chapter. As pointed out, there is no overall federal administration of these activities, not even a policy to guide future actions. This void results in inevitable duplications, wastes, and omissions in the federal government's factious interest in education.

SUPREME COURT RULINGS REFLECTING INTEREST IN EDUCATION

It may appear far-fetched to regard the actions of the United States Supreme Court as a national interest in education inasmuch as the initiative to hear cases does not come from the national level. Notwithstanding, the decisions reached there reflect a sympathy for the cause of education. Only a few disputes arising from the local or state courts have gone as far as the Supreme Court, and then only when the issues affect the federal Constitution or what is considered national policy. Nevertheless, the impact of these decisions upon school practices has been powerful.

One of the first such decisions, the famous Dartmouth College Case in 1819, clarified the right to establish private schools exempt from complete supervision of the state. Further buttressing of this right came shortly thereafter when the Court ruled in the Girard College case that a private college could preclude from admission those whom it wished. The national government, speaking through its Supreme Court, curtailed the state's power over schools in ruling upon the Nebraska Case

(1923) when saying that the state legislature could not prohibit the teaching of a foreign language in private schools. The majority opinion was based on the grounds that such a state law would contradict due process privileges of the Fourteenth Amendment which guarantees a parent limited authority over the instruction of his child.

The historic Oregon Case of 1926 set a precedent which has not since been challenged. The issue arose over an Oregon statute which required all children of school age to attend a public school. In an unanimous decision, the Supreme Court held that parents could elect to educate their children in non-public schools. The decision has been the basis for the right of parents not to send their children to any formalized school if they could prove that the substitute provisions were equivalent to that provided in a public school.

Several cases involving the church-state conflict have landed in the highest court. The first significant ruling, on the Louisiana textbook case in 1930, authorized the practice of furnishing textbooks, and later, other teaching supplies, out of tax monies to pupils in parochial as well as public schools. In 1946 the Court popularized the child-benefit theory in distribution of tax monies as it sanctioned the New Jersey practice of using buses owned by a public board of education to transport youngsters to a parochial school. A year later the Court seemed to separate church and state in the Illinois McCollum Case when it insisted that children could not be compelled to participate in religious instruction provided in the public schools. More recently, the Court has ruled that religious exercises, including prayer, could not be conducted in public schools.

Still more recently the Supreme Court has spoken on the question of racial segregation in public schools. Earlier, in 1954, the Court upset the "separate but equal" doctrine under which some communities maintained racially segregated schools. It said that state-imposed segregation of pupils by color or race violated protection guaranteed by the Fourteenth Amendment. It decreed that lower Federal courts should proceed to enforce desegregation of institutions. In 1963 the Court strengthened its original position by ruling that a board of education could not permit transferring pupils within the district as a means to preserve segregated schools. In the same year the Court eased the opportunities for a complainant against segregated schools to bring his case to the highest court.

Despite the influence which the Supreme Court's decisions have had upon educational developments, it should be pointed out that some state statutes and state supreme court rulings are in conflict with actions of the Federal Court. The distinction between state and federal authority over education is still not clarified.

THE UNITED STATES OFFICE OF EDUCATION

The United States Office of Education was created by an act of Congress nearly one century ago, shortly after the close of the Civil War in 1867. While some viewed the creation as a step toward having a source for national policy formulation on educational issues the office has never been allowed to become such. Congressmen thought of it more as a clearing house for educational information, and thus it has largely remained for a century. It has never exercised any power over schools except for those few instances in which Federal monies were distributed. The Office was a controversial step at the inception, and it remains so today.

The U.S. Office of Education has always been an agency of the Executive Branch in the Federal Government, always a part of some department except for the first year. The enabling legislation included the phrase, "Department of Education," but the name was changed to Office of Education in 1868, re-titled Bureau of Education two years later, and changed back to Office of Education in 1929. Nor has it been exactly clear where the Office belongs in the administrative structure. It was first assigned to the Department of the Interior, remaining there for nearly seventy years. In 1939 it was transferred to the Federal Security Agency. Then in another reorganization move in 1957, the Office was made a part of the newly created Department of Health, Education, and Welfare. That the Office is not a separate department with its chief officer becoming a member of the President's Cabinet as in most foreign countries is a source of regret by those who favor the Federal level having more stature and authority. The fact remains, however, that the mood of American citizens has never brooked the thought that that level would inherit much power over education.

Thus, the United States Office of Education is one of five major agencies which are administered within the Department of Health, Education, and Welfare. It is on the same organizational plane as the Social Security Administration, the Public Health Service, the Pure Food and Drug Administration, and the Vocational Rehabilitation Administration.

The data-collecting function of the Office for disseminating educational information to Congress and other interested persons was the prime justification for its establishment and continues as a primary task.

Many other duties have been delegated to the Office as detailed in Figure 1 and in the job descriptions found among the accompanying readings of this chapter. It has grown into an organization of over

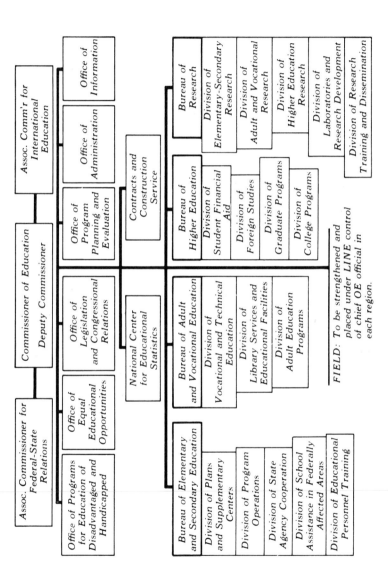

FIGURE 1

ORGANIZATION OF U.S. OFFICE OF EDUCATION — JULY 1965

1,600 professional and non-professional employees, headed by a Commissioner who is appointed by the President of the United States. Departments and functions are re-shuffled often, usually accompanying each new commissioner and each major addition of tasks. The latest organization, as of July, 1965, is shown in Figure 1. It reflects the influence of recent legislation which accents direct financial aid to the nation's elementary and secondary schools, support of institutions of higher education, research, programs for education of disadvantaged youth, and nationwide equalization of educational opportunities. The offices and divisions concerned with internal administration, dissemination of information, relationships with Congress, library services, adult and vocational education, and international education are of long standing. Under the new organization there is one Deputy Commissioner and two Associate Commissioners. The Office maintains regional field headquarters to provide better liaison with schools and to facilitate the performance of the Washington Office's responsibilities. Advisory committees, created either by statute or by request of the Commissioner, operate directly with him. Presently the Office involves over 100 consultants from education in policy formation and special projects.

Nearly all monies distributed by the Office of Education for support of educational projects as authorized by Congress are channeled to school districts through each state's department of education. Some monies may be exchanged directly between the Office and a school district under Title III of the 1965 Education Act. However, the principal use which a local school administrator or teacher has for the Office is in the vast supply of published educational materials. There is scarcely a common problem faced by local districts for which the Office has not already prepared a valuable document. Over a hundred printed publications are issued annually by Office personnel, most of the documents being distributed free to consumers.

Probably the most significant contemporary service of the U. S. Office of Education is its encouragement of research. The Cooperative Research Branch granted 131 new requests for projects in 1963. The Media Research and Dissemination Branch issued seventy more contracts for study projects. Twelve and one-half million dollars were spent by the Division of Educational Research in that year. The $100,000,000 allocated in the 1965 act for research in education has not, at this moment, allowed planners of projects to catch their breath, but there can be expected a burst of research ideas from universities and school districts. Part of that act almost dares educators to be imaginative and innovative.

Other major responsibilities of the Office pertain to land-grant colleges, financial aid to federally affected areas, administration of the various vocational education aid programs, and the National Defense of Education Act. There is reason to believe that the stature and influence of the Office will be greatly enhanced by the amount of money it will administer under the liberalized provisions of the N.D.E.A., and under the new act of 1965.

Notwithstanding the impressive size of this office and of the 1963 budget of approximately $800,000,000, the large proportion of which was distributed for various educational purposes in this country and overseas, nor of the Elementary & Secondary Act of 1965, the Office does not administer the major share of federal monies alloted for education. As examples, the Department of Agriculture manages federal funds for the support of a school's food services; the Veterans' Administration handled the biggest federal support program ever provided for education — the "G. I. Bill;" the Defense Department oversees the various military schools in U. S. and abroad; the Department of State administers most of the overseas investments in foreign education. The National Science Foundation is still a separate agency. The Department of Interior directs schools on federal reservations.

This diffusion of responsibility for federal educational funds was scored in the Hoover Commission Report for Reorganization of Federal Services which urged that educational interests of the national government be streamlined and centralized. However, little action has been taken toward that goal since the release of the report, nor is it hopeful that the departments will soon surrender their prerogatives to control their respective portions of federal appropriations for education.

The future role of the Office of Education is ambiguous. The voices clamoring for a strengthened office are more numerous, more brazen, and more prominent. It is said that now, following the 1965 action, the national government has become a full partner with states and communities in conducting educational efforts, that at long last education is officially recognized as a national interest. There are conditions which seem to presage a centralizing of policy making and financing of education. Should this occur, the opportunities for administrative specialist service in education at the national level will increase. Congress has already authorized a major increase in the number of the positions in the Office of Education for the years just ahead.

On the other hand, it is uncertain whether the perennial voices which speak against nationalizing influence on American education are stilled or merely dormant. It seems a fantasy to expect that the deeply ingrained faith in local and state control of public education has waned, or that conditions have changed enough to warrant abandonment of community interest in the education of children. It is already well known through experience how citizens lose interest in supporting education when a higher government takes a very heavy hand in the financing. Even if extensive financing and power over education should be centered at the national level, it is problematical whether political forces would entrust that power to an educational office much more in the future than they have in the past.

FEDERAL PARTICIPATION IN EDUCATION . . .

THE LONG HISTORY OF FEDERAL SUPPORT OF EDUCATION*

In terms of the life span of our relatively young country, Federal participation in education has a long history. In recent years, however, the areas of cooperation between Federal agencies and local educational authorities have increased considerably. A pattern for such cooperation is beginning to emerge and is likely, in the future, to affect our approach to many of the educational problems facing our people. It will be useful in this report to analyze the nature of this cooperation, discuss some of the programs that have been developed, review the educational tasks with which Americans must cope, and to restate some age-old principles.

The most important of these principles, and one which public opinion has never challenged, is that education in the United States is the responsibility of the States and local communities. This tradition is as old as the Republic itself and the years have proved its wisdom. Whether it reflected their recent unfortunate experience with a remote government or a deeper insight into the relationship between education and a free society, the founding fathers were, according to James Madison's notes of the Constitutional Convention of 1787, consciously agreed that the education of youth should properly be left to local authority. The men whose ideals shaped the future destiny of the Nation were determined to keep our social and political institutions close to the people. They were fearful of any policy which would make it possible

---

*Annual Report of the Federal Security Agency, 1952, Washington, D.C.: United States Office of Education, 1953.

for a central government to dominate the thinking of the people, and thus undermine their individual freedom of thought and action.

LOCAL CONTROL OF EDUCATION
HAS BROUGHT REWARDS

This fundamental policy with regard to education has been richly rewarding. Local control has stimulated popular interest in our schools. Americans have taken pride in the efforts made locally to educate their sons and daughters. They have considered it a right to have a voice in deciding what the schooling of their children should be. Generally they have proved willing to provide the means of maintaining their educational institutions. There have been exceptions. Some citizens and some communities have been, and still are, remiss in providing the necessary minimum of education for their youth. But in this respect they certainly do not represent the general American attitude.

Local responsibility has made education a vital force in American life. More than anywhere else in the world local efforts to make the educative process effective have brought a wide variety of teaching materials and methods into our schools. Out of these local variations in practice has come a body of teaching experience which has eventually proved useful throughout the Nation. True, not all communities have kept pace with educational progress. Some communities have clung to outworn educational ideas and methods. But the net effect of our national policy of local control has been the development of a vital, serviceable, and democratic school system. Contrasted with conditions in other lands where education is placed in a single governmental educational authority, the advantages of our decentralized system of control of education are easily apparent.

To summarize, local control keeps the schools close to the lives of the people; it stimulates and maintains their interest; it makes possible the expansion and growth of our school system along lines related to the needs of the local community; it keeps American schools steadily upon the road of progress; it preserves the freedom and democratic spirit of American education; it safeguards the liberty of our people. Surely there is no need to reemphasize here the soundness of the basic principle of State and community responsibility for education.

The question must then be raised: What responsibility does the Federal Government have for education in the United States? And if it does have any responsibility how can this be met without undermining the principle of local control of education? Abstract discussions of the problem are not likely to be fruitful. The situation must be considered in terms of the facts that exist today, the economic and social conditions which impinge upon education in the United States.

The record will also show that Federal activity in the field of education has slowly but steadily increased over the years. When the Nation was young the National Government came into possession of extensive lands west of the Appalachian Mountains. Eventually when arrangements were made for the sale of these lands, provision was made whereby the sixteenth section of every township was reserved from sale and used for the support of public schools. As new States were formed from the public domain, the section grants for schools were confirmed to them. The Federal Government in those early days was interested in the general education needed by all youth if they were to grow up as intelligent and productive citizens.

Decades later, however, the educational activities of the Federal Government were related to more specific needs of the American people. In the middle of the nineteenth century Senator Justin Smith Morrill of Vermont became convinced that a new type of higher education was needed in this country, especially by the sons and daughters of the working classes, which would lead to employment in the agricultural and mechanical arts. Recognizing that the stimulation of such instruction was a national responsibility, the Congress passed, and President Lincoln signed, the Morrill Act in 1862. Subsequent legislation, over a period of years, has increased Federal support to the land-grant colleges and the agricultural experiment stations in the several States. The institutions benefited by these laws will testify that all this was achieved without imposing Federal control or interference.

More than half a century later another important Federal venture into the field of education occurred. Leaders in business, industry, and labor became aware that the United States was behind other countries in providing vocational training for its working people. They joined with educational groups to urge the extension of opportunities for this type of education in the high schools of the Nation.

The Congress, recognizing that this was a national problem, enacted the Smith-Hughes Act of 1917. This act was followed in later years by several supplementary laws, the latest of which is the Vocational Education Act of 1946 commonly known as the George-Barden Act. This legislation has made millions of dollars available to the States on a matching basis, and it has also provided excellent consultative services. Without Federal aid, vocational education in the United States would certainly not have developed as fully as it has in the past 35 years. As in the case of earlier grants, Federal aid for vocational education has involved no attempt at Federal domination or interference.

Public Laws 815 and 874 of the Eighty-first Congress, signed by the President on September 23, 1950, and September 30, 1950, respectively, were designed to discharge the financial responsibility of the Federal Government to communities affected by Federal activities and to provide funds for a survey of school plant needs throughout the Nation.

The story of this development goes back to World War I. But the problem really became acute during World War II when various branches of the Government, especially the Army, the Navy, and the Air Corps, rapidly acquired large parcels of local property for Government use which then became tax-exempt. In many localities large numbers of school-age children suddenly were brought into schools near military bases, compelling communities to make provision for two or three times their normal school population. The problem created by the Federal activities was clear. The first action to relieve the situation was the passage in 1940 of the Lanham Act which provided for aid to defense-connected areas in order that the war effort would not be impeded. Under the Lanham Act loans and grants were made available only where it was impossible for the school district otherwise to provide facilities and where the shortage of school facilities would clearly impede the war effort.

Federal aid for school construction under the Lanham Act ended shortly after the surrender of Japan. But large numbers of children were still found in the schools within war-affected areas and the problem of educating them remained critical. A temporary program providing Federal financial assistance for operating expenses of these schools was continued year by year. A number of Federal departments and agencies besides the Army, Navy, and Air Corps also gave such assistance to school districts. The variety of agencies and the lack of a single Government plan for dealing with the problem on a Nation-wide basis caused the widest variation in regulations and in the amounts of the payments made to school districts.

EDUCATIONAL PROGRAMS OF THE FEDERAL DEPARTMENTS AND SPECIAL AGENCIES*

Practically all of the departments and other agencies of the Federal Government are carrying out one or more educational programs. Federal educational activities cover all levels of education from elemen-

*Charles A. Quattlebaum, *Federal Education Policies, Programs and Proposals, Part II,* Washington, D.C.: U.S. Government Printing Office, June, 1960, 3601372. (Prepared in the Legislative Reference Service of the Library of Congress.)

tary schooling to graduate training at the Nation's leading colleges and universities. The instruction includes virtually all subject fields known to man. Federal educational activities directly affect a large percentage of the population and indirectly affect the remainder of the population of the United States and its possessions. Most of the Federal educational programs are concerned, however, with higher or adult education or specialized training. The Federal Government contributes relatively little to the support of elementary and secondary education in the United States. [Reorganization of departments and the addition of programs since 1959 have altered some of the following activities.]

DEPARTMENT OF STATE

In seeking to promote a better understanding between the American people and the people of other countries as an implementation of foreign policy of the United States, the Department of State is engaged in extensive activities of educational importance. These activities, carried out in relations between the United States and other countries, involve exchanging students, teachers and other persons, exchanging knowledge and skills, aiding American-sponsored schools abroad, cooperating with other countries in technical training, and related projects.

Other educational activities conducted by the Department of State are for the training of employees in the work and objectives of the Department and training foreign service officers in the field of foreign affairs. In carrying out these activities the Department principally utilizes its Foreign Service Institute.

The technical cooperation program of the International Cooperation Administration includes the bulk of ICA educational activities. The ICA Office of Educational Services performs numerous functions in this field.

DEPARTMENT OF THE TREASURY

The educational activities of the Department of the Treasury include training persons for the performance of duties in the Coast Guard, the Bureau of Customs, and the Internal Revenue Service. In addition all of the bureaus of the Department conduct formal inservice training for technical, managerial, and executive development of certain employees.

Besides operating formal schools such as the U.S. Coast Guard Academy and the U.S. Customs Inservice Training School, the Department utilizes the services of certain colleges and universities for resid(at instruction of selected personnel, and employs other media to obtain its educational objectives.

OFFICE OF THE SECRETARY OF DEFENSE, AND JOINT CHIEFS OF STAFF

The Department of Defense operates three colleges and two institutes which serve all branches of the Armed Forces. These are: (1) the Industrial College of the Armed Forces, (2) the National War College, (3) the Department of Defense Military Assistance Institute, (4) the Armed Forces Institute, and (5) the Armed Forces Staff College.

Arrangements for the administration and fiscal support of these educational institutions vary. The Joint Chiefs of Staff and the Department of the Army bear responsibilities for the Industrial College of the Armed Forces and the National War College, which train selected military and civilian personnel for important assignments. Under the technical direction of the Joint Chiefs of Staff, the Armed Forces Staff College, with fiscal support by the Navy, trains officers for duty in joint operations. The Army is executive agent for the Military Assistance Institute, an educational facility operated under contract, for the training of officers for duty in connection with Military Assistance Advisory Groups. Under the operational control of the Assistant Secretary of Defense (Manpower, Personnel and Reserve) the U.S. Armed Forces Institute offers the Armed Forces correspondence courses at all educational levels.

DEPARTMENT OF THE ARMY

Prominent among the Army's educational programs are those administered by the Office of Deputy Chief of Staff for Military Operations. These programs include the operation of the Military Academy at West Point, the administration of the Army service school system, the operation of the Army extension course program, and the Reserve Officers Training Corps program, the training of military personnel in civilian institutions, and training activities connected with military assistance to other countries.

Other educational activities of the Department of the Army are concerned with the training of civilian employees, research through contract with educational institutions, education of dependents of military and civilian personnel, raising the academic educational level of

Army personnel, foreign area specialist training, and operation of the U.S. Army Information School.

DEPARTMENT OF THE NAVY

The Department of the Navy operates various service schools for naval personnel, and provides for the training of selected naval personnel in civilian schools. It has programs for training both civilian and enlisted naval personnel to become commissioned officers in the Navy and Marine Corps. This activity is carried out at the Naval Academy at Annapolis and other institutions of higher learning. The Department also arranges for its naval personnel to engage in educacational pursuits through correspondence courses, especially through the U.S. Armed Forces Institute and the Marine Corps Institute.

The Department discharges responsibilities for the education of school-age dependents of its personnel residing in certain localities, and operates school buses for the dependents of some of its employees. It provides for the education of the natives on certain Pacific islands. It also provides for scientific studies of naval needs and problems to be carried out at educational institutions.

Besides the Naval Academy and the Marine Corps Institute already mentioned, schools and other educational institutions operated by the Navy include the naval air technical training schools, the U.S. Naval School of Aviation Medicine, the Naval War College, special officer schools, Marine Corps officers schools, and the Industrial Relations Institute.

DEPARTMENT OF THE AIR FORCE

The Air Force Directorate of Personnel Procurement and Training administers nine educational programs. These include technical, specialized, and flying training, and medical education, besides the Air Force Reserve Officers Training Corps program and operation of the Air University, the Air Force Institute of Technology, the Air Force Academy, and an Extension Course Institute.

The Directorate of Civilian Personnel provides apprentice training, specialized scientific and technical courses, graduate study, fellowships and other educational arrangements for selected civilian employees. Other programs of the Air Force include research contracts with educational institutions, an academic and vocational educational services program for military personnel, and provision of primary and secondary education for dependents of military and civilian personnel overseas.

DEPARTMENT OF JUSTICE

The educational program and/or courses of the Department of Justice fall into the main categories of: (a) those for inmates of penal and correctional institutions, (b) those for aliens preparatory to naturalization, (c) those for employees of the department, and (d) those for law-enforcement officers from State, county, and local government organizations. The activities are carried out through established national institutions such as the FBI National Academy, and the Immigration and Naturalization Service Border Patrol Academy, and through field law enforcement schools, formal classes at penal and correctional institutions, the preparation and supplying of citizenship textbooks for use in the public schools, correspondence courses, and other methods.

POST OFFICE DEPARTMENT

The Post Office Department operates several extensive training programs affecting all levels and categories of its employees. It operates the Postal Inspector Training School for student-inspectors employed throughout the United States and its possessions. The Department also provides instruction for authorized international visitors interested in U.S. postal operations.

DEPARTMENT OF THE INTERIOR

The educational activities of the Department of the Interior are of wide variety and scope. Outstanding among them is the elementary and secondary schooling of Indian, Eskimo, and Aleut children living on reservations or where public school facilities are not available. Among the other activities of this Department are the apprenticeship and college cooperative research programs of the Bonneville Power Administration, safety training for employees of the Bureau of Mines and for employees in the mineral industries, visual education of the public in conservation of mineral resources, inservice training of departmental employees, and aid to public education in American Samoa and in the Trust Territory of the Pacific Islands.

DEPARTMENT OF AGRICULTURE

The Cooperative Extension Service of the Department of Agriculture, operating through the land-grant colleges, has become an educational force toward improvement of the economic welfare, health, and community life of rural families. Besides maintaining this nationwide educational service in cooperation wth the States, the Department works closely wth the land-grant colleges and other educational institutions in numerous research projects for the advancement of agricultural knowledge. Useful information developed from this research is disseminated to farmers and to the public through the Extension Service and other agencies of the Department.

Training activities, including demonstrations and consultative services, are also carried out by several other agencies of the Department. The Department administers the national school lunch program providing a midday meal to the students of participating schools throughout the Nation. Among its other educational activities and aids to education are contributions to the agricultural training of certain foreign nationals, and payment to school funds of Arizona and New Mexico a portion of the gross proceeds of national forests in those States.

The Department generally supervises the operation of the U.S. Department of Agriculture Graduate School.

DEPARTMENT OF COMMERCE

A total of 38 educational programs of the Department of Commerce are reported in this survey. These include educational programs directly operated by the Department, and other activities in the field of education directly affecting educational institutions. The first of these categories includes inservice training of employees and of certain foreign nationals, and the operation of specialized training schools. The second includes contractual arrangements with educational institutions for research, the provision of courses at universities for qualified employees, and financial aid to the State maritime academies. In carrying out some of its programs the Department utilizes the services of a number of colleges and universities.

Important educational institutions operated by the Department include the Merchant Marine Academy at Kings Point, N.Y. and the National Bureau of Standards Graduate School.

DEPARTMENT OF LABOR

In performing its statutory function of promoting the welfare of wage earners in the United States, improving their working conditions and advancing their opportunities for profitable employment, the Department of Labor carries out four major educational programs. These are concerned with the promotion of all types of training for workers in industry; staff training and development by the Bureau of Employment Security involving assistance to State employment security agencies; training of State safety inspectors and safety training of representatives of unions and of State agencies and maritime personnel, and inservice training of the Department's own employees. In addition, the Department cooperates with other Federal agencies in affording selected foreign nationals industrial training and opportunities for study of American industrial processes.

The main activity of the Department in the field of education is the promotion of apprenticeship and other training in the skilled trades.

DEPARTMENT OF HEALTH, EDUCATION, AND WELFARE

... The Department of Health, Education, and Welfare is outstanding in the field of education in that it contains the one office in the Federal Government charged by Congress solely with educational responsibilities, namely the Office of Education. Every phase of education in the United States is served to some extent by the Office of Eduation. ...

The many programs of the Public Health Service in the field of education include nurse training; grants for training in cancer control; medical, dental, and dietetic internships; grants for construction of health research facilities at educational institutions; specialized training of officers in the Public Health Service; financing of medical research fellowships; provision of medical traineeships; aid to the States in training State and local health service personnel; and other services.

Besides the Office of Education and the Public Health Service, other constituent agencies of the Department of Health, Education, and Welfare performing educational services are Gallaudet College, the Food and Drug Administration, Howard University, the Office of Vocational Rehabilitation, the American Printing House for the Blind, St. Elizabeths Hospital, and the Social Security Administration. The last-named agency administers programs of aid to the States in training workers to provide child welfare services and health services to mothers and children. The Office of Vocational Rehabilitation cooperates with the States in rehabilitation educational services for individuals having disabilities that handicap employment. St. Elizabeths Hospital operates a number of programs of medical, nursing, and related training.

LIBRARY OF CONGRESS

Contributions by the Library of Congress to education are a result of its functions as a great research library. Like any other library to whose collections there is general access, the Library of Congress may be considered an educational institution. Among its activities which are educational under dictionary definition are its general services, distribution of catalog cards and technical publications, and provision of raised type and "talking" books for the blind.

VETERANS' ADMINISTRATION

The Veterans' Administration administers three large educational programs for veterans and their surviving children. These programs provide (1) vocational rehabilitation for disabled veterans, (2) readjustment training for World War II and Korean veterans, and (3) war orphans educational assistance. In addition, the Veterans' Administration provides training for some of its employees. All of these programs are carried out wholly or partly in established educational institutions.

Vocational rehabilitation training for World War II veterans will be terminated on July 25, 1960. With few exceptions, Korean conflict veterans must complete such training before February 1, 1964.

Except for a small number of persons, "readjustment" training for World War II veterans closed on July 25, 1956. Such training for Korean veterans may continue to January 31, 1965.

Benefits to disabled veterans include allowances for subsistence, tuition, books, supplies, and equipment. Under the "readjustment" training program, veterans receive educational allowances for themselves and allowances for dependents. War orphans' educational assistance is in the form of an allowance for subsistence, tuition, books, and other educational costs.

NATIONAL SCIENCE FOUNDATION

The National Science Foundation gives direct support to graduate students, to advanced scholars and teachers, and to programs and projects, for improvement of science education. It also makes grants, mainly to persons in colleges and universities, for basic research in the sciences.

SMITHSONIAN INSTITUTION

The Smithsonian Institution has a 113-year-old grant of power from Congress to perform services for the "increase and diffusion of knowledge among men." Some of its activities are directly instructional; others basically subserve education. These activities include scientific research and publication of research findings; operation of an international exchange service for the exchange of governmental and other scientific and literary publications; the collection, preservation, display, and interpretation of works of art; the acquisition, exhibition, and dissemination of information concerning wild animals from all over the world, and the exhibition and interpretation of the national collections representing anthropology, botany, geology, zoology, engineering, industry, history, and graphic arts.

HOUSING AND HOME FINANCE AGENCY

The Housing and Home Finance Agency promotes education through loans to educational institutions for student and faculty housing, through advances to State and local governmental agencies for advance planning of school projects, and through providing the Office of Education technical assistance in the administration of a program of Federal aid to school construction in "federally affected" localities. It allows credit for local construction of schools in certain urban renewal project areas. It also operates training programs for personnel of the Agency and provides technical training for foreign visitors.

U.S. INFORMATION AGENCY

Educational aspects appear in the principal oversea programs of the U.S. Information Agency. These programs are concerned with increasing understanding between the people of the United States and the people of other countries, the sale abroad of American books and other communication materials, and support of publication of American textbooks in foreign languages and of American binational cultural centers.

The Agency also operates several types of training programs for its personnel.

ATOMIC ENERGY COMMISSION

Educational programs of the Atomic Energy Commission include contract research carried out at colleges and universities, the provision of fellowships in scientific fields, and education for dependents of employees and contractors at Commission installations. Other programs of the Commission are designed to provide opportunities for employees of Atomic Energy Commission installations to continue their academic study for credit toward scientific degrees, to instruct scientific personnel in the techniques of handling radioisotopes and in uses of radiation instruments, and to accomplish other purposes.

Examples of some other educational activities of the Commission are (1) the provision of aid for nuclear equipment and loan of nuclear materials to colleges; (2) development of special courses, films, and other teaching tools; and (3) sponsorship of summer institutes for faculty members. Altogether, 52 educational programs of the Commission are described in this report.

GENERAL SERVICES ADMINISTRATION

Activities of the General Services Administration promotional to or subserving education are the donation of surplus personal property to States for educational, public health, and civil defense usage; the transfer of real surplus property and loan of certain kinds of equipment to educational institutions; and making available the collections of the National Archives and Presidential libraries for research and study.

In some cases using the facilities of colleges and universities, all of the constituent units of the General Services Administration conduct inservice training programs for their personnel.

TENNESSEE VALLEY AUTHORITY

In carrying out its statutory responsibility for the conservation and development of the natural resources of the area affected by its activities, the Tennessee Valley Authority pursues a number of educational undertakings in cooperation with nearby educational institutions, particularly land-grant colleges and other agencies. Several of these programs are concerned with the use of research, demonstration, and instruction to develop forest, agricultural, and mineral resources and to carry out other purposes.

Other educational activities of the TVA are designed to promote an understanding of the Authority's program of development, to guide TVA officials in relation with State and local educational agencies, and to provide other employee training.

The TVA also conducts farm and school workshops to prepare persons to teach students and farm groups effective usage of electrical equipment.

OTHER FEDERAL AGENCIES

Of 17 independent agencies carrying on educational activities not already described, the majority reported various inservice training programs, aimed at orientating new employees or training other employees for more efficient service. Some of these agencies are also providing training for certain foreign nationals, in cooperation with the Department of State.

Among other educational activities of independent agencies not already mentioned are the following; Federal Aviation Agency — utilization of scientific talent and facilities at academic institutions for research in aeronautics; Civil Service Commission — conduct and coordination of Federal interagency training; Selective Service System — training of military reservists for the operation of an expanded system in case of national emergency; U.S. Government Printing Office — Cataloging, indexing, and distribution of public documents; Canal Zone Government — operation of a public school system in the Canal Zone; and U.S. Botanic Garden — exhibition of botanical specimens and dissemination of related information to scientists, students and other persons throughout the country.

DISTRICT OF COLUMBIA

The Board of Education of the District of Columbia operates the public school system of the District, a Veterans High School Center, a teacher-training college, and the Capitol Page School, and provides supplementary educational opportunities and benefits. Other educational activities are carried out by the Board of Public Welfare; the Department of Corrections; and the Fire, Health, and Metropolitan Police Departments.

The Board of Public Welfare and the Department of Corrections operate programs of academic, vocational, and social education for children placed under their charge. The Fire Department and the Metropolitan Police Department both have inservice training programs. Besides carrying out a broad program of this type, the Health Department provides health education for clinic patients and for the general public, and limited training of certain medical and health personnel of private agencies and institutions.

EDUCATIONAL ACTIVITIES OF INTERNATIONAL ORGANIZATIONS IN WHICH THE UNITED STATES PARTICIPATES

Of 26 international organizations in which the United States participates, 2 are concerned primarily with education. Activities of the others involve education to some extent.

The two organizations in the first category are the International Bureau of Education (IBE) and the United Nations Educational Scientific and Cultural Organization (UNESCO). The IBE serves as an international information center for activities relating to education. UNESCO promotes collaboration among member states in the fields of education, science, and culture.

Following are some examples of educational activities engaged in by other international agencies in which the United States participates: Caribbean Commission — conduct of study and demonstration tours, seminars, and conferences; Food and Agricultural Organization of the United Nations — award of scholarships and fellowships to nationals of underdeveloped countries; International Atomic Energy Agency — grant of fellowships and conduct of seminars; International Bank for Reconstruction and Development — conduct of training courses in economics and finance for nationals of member states; North Atlantic Treaty Organization — sponsorship of fellowships and visiting professorship programs; United Nations — provision of technical assistance through fellowships, experts' services, and seminars; United Nations Relief and Works Agency for Palestine Refugees—provision of elementary, secondary, vocational, and teacher education for Palestine refugees in the Near East.

TOTAL EXPENDITURES FOR FEDERAL EDUCATIONAL ACTIVITIES

This report contains information concerning the expenditures, generally on an obligational basis, for the fiscal year 1959, for the programs reported. The nature of the information necessarily varies considerably. In some cases exact figures were given by the agencies; in others, estimates. In occasional instances no figures on obligations for the programs were obtainable; but in such cases the explanatory information given may be of almost equal interest to the reader.

It has been pointed out in the "Introduction" to this study that, although the programs reported herein are "educational" under dictionary definition, there are wide differences of opinion as to whether the expenditures for the programs should be charged to educational or to other purposes, since frequently the primary or ultimate objectives are noneducational in nature. For this reason *it would be impossible, from data presently available, to arrive at a generally acceptable estimate of the total expenditure for Federal educational activities.*

In this connection it might be pointed out that education *usually* is aimed at some ultimate goal, such as preparation for an occupation, or training for better citizenship. In having noneducational ultimate objectives therefore, Federal educational programs are not markedly different from the educational systems of State and local governments. On the other hand, many of the Federal programs are relatively informal, or are educational mainly in the sense of promoting or subserving education.

In a number of instances, agencies reported that funds expended for an educational activity are not separable from those expended for more general purposes in which that activity is included. Seldom is there an appropriation specifically for the educational program. In many cases certain expenditures specifically for the educational activity are known, but these amounts do not include all costs of the program, and the other costs may be practically indeterminable. For example, extended study

Actual or estimated obligations reported by Federal agencies for educational activities, fiscal year 1959

[Subject to the limitations set forth in the preceding explanation]

Department of State	$171,771,168
Department of the Treasury	26,953,272
Department of Defense—Office of the Secretary	3,240,884
Department of the Army	309,272,000
Department of the Navy	482,208,990
Department of the Air Force	370,208,990
Department of Justice	3,194,442
Post Office Department	5,366,505
Department of the Interior	66,102,315
Department of Agriculture	[1]428,532,246
Department of Commerce	4,802,243
Department of Labor	7,908,135
Department of Health, Education, and Welfare	713,700,127
Library of Congress	14,753,519
Veterans' Administration	627,405,000
National Science Foundation	111,202,739
Smithsonian Institution	4,913,107
Housing and Home Finance Agency	290,600,000
U.S. Information Agency	117,653,015
Atomic Energy Commission	[2]57,000,000
General Services Administration	2,794,582
Tennessee Valley Authority	3,558,174
Other Federal agencies	21,353,445
Total	3,844,494,898
District of Columbia	56,393,670
Grand total	3,900,888,568

[1]Activities considered by the Department to be educational under a narrower definition, $65,490,579.

[2]Costs instead of obligations.

Note — International organizations in which the United States participates: Total U.S. contribution, $99,300,000, expenditure for educational activities not separately identifiable.

would usually be necessary to determine what portion of the cost of construction and maintenance of multiple-purpose buildings should be charged to their educational usage. Likewise it would be difficult in some cases to determine the part of the cost of an educational program represented by the pay of hundreds or thousands of trainees receiving widely varying compensation from the Government while in training, according to their respective ranks or classification levels and the amount of time devoted to the educational process. In general, such costs of the individual programs as could be determined only by extensive study are not included in the fiscal data appearing in this report.

The figures given below were furnished by or computed from data supplied by the agencies concerned. These figures generally represent obligations for the fiscal year 1959 for most or all of the educational programs of each of the departments and other agencies of the Federal Government. The figure given for each separate department or agency is more meaningful if considered in connection with the information given on the activities of that agency elsewhere in this report.

Although representing the most comprehensive data of this kind presently available, the table on page 257 may nevertheless be misleading if quoted without the full preceding explanation. Considered in conjunction with this explanation, the total is significant. It represents the estimated minimum expenditure during the fiscal year 1959 for the programs covered in this survey.

FEDERAL ACTIVITIES FOR EDUCATION
ARE WITHOUT AIM
OR GUIDING POLICY*

The Federal Government has no comprehensive policy or organization for the administration of its educational programs. However, every enacted measure affecting education has contributed to the establishment of some phase of Federal policy. Furthermore, some important legislation, such as Public Laws 815 and 874 of the 81st Congress, 2d session, and the National Defense Education Act of 1958 (85th Cong., 2d sess.) has specically set forth broad elements of Federal policy.

---

*Charles A. Quattlebaum, *Federal Education Policies, Programs and Proposals, Part III,* 1-4.

The question of establishment of a comprehensive policy for Federal action and organization in the field of education involves the question of the responsibilities of the central educational agency and its position in the Federal structure.

The Office of Education in the Department of Health, Education, and Welfare is the only agency charged by the Congress with responsibility for promoting the cause of education throughout the country. However, the administration of Federal educational activities is scattered throughout the Federal structure and is mainly carried out by agencies in furtherance of their own particular functions. While many Federal agencies directly administer large educational programs, the Office of Education carries out its responsibilities principally through educational systems and institutions maintained under State authority. This fact raises the question as to which method of administration of Federal educational programs is preferable. The question of Federal influence or control over education has been a primary consideration in important discussions of proposals concerning what the Federal Government should or should not do in this field. Programs seeking strictly Federal objectives generally entail Federal operation and hence complete or extensive Federal control. On the other hand the amount of Federal control in Federal grants to or in cooperation with the States and institutions for the attainment of mutual objectives may be slight. The extent of Federal control desirable depends largely upon the nature of the Federal objectives sought, and does not necessarily extend to any control over State or local educational policies. . . .

The survey shows that while there is occasional cooperation among several agencies in the administration of a specific educational program there is little or no cooperation among the departments and agencies in the administration of Federal educational activities as a whole. Frequently a large educational undertaking is administered entirely independently by a single Federal agency. No agency has statutory overall responsibility for the coordination of these activities. This situation raises the question of the desirabilty of giving the central educational agency responsibility for the coordination of all Federal activities in education. . . .

In the field of education, as in other fields, the Nation has been not so much concerned with comprehensive organization as with satisfying special needs or interests. Thus Federal agencies desiring to utilize education or educational institutions for special purposes have obtained diverse authorizations for a variety of programs not tied to any general Federal policy. Although there is some interest in the consideration of broader policy, some of the existing separate educational programs are deeply rooted historically and many people are in favor of separately maintaining them.

The question of the desirability of the establishment of a comprehensive Federal policy and organization for education, or at least for broader and more definite policies in this field, raises the question of *feasibility* of consolidating or coordinating Federal educational activities in a single agency. . . .

Not only is there no blanket legislation giving all Federal agencies similar authority to enter into contracts with educational institutions for research, but also there is no overall legislation governing the distribution of such contracts with respect to geographical areas. Some agencies have reported that their contracts have been awarded to institutions adjudged best equipped to perform the desired services. The question of what other considerations may have influenced the awarding of such contracts is open for further study. Many of the largest Federal contracts are given to some of the Nation's largest and most heavily endowed universities. This fact raises the question of the effects of Federal payments to educational institutions upon the stronger and the weaker colleges and universities and upon the geographical distribution of opportunities for higher education in the United States. . . .

In some cases, at least, it is questionable as to whether Federal payments to institutions of higher education selected by Federal agencies may be contributing to making "the rich richer and the poor poorer" among the colleges and universities. It is assumed that this is undesirable, in view of the extent of Federal contracts with colleges and universities, the possibilities here set forth point toward a need for the consideration of overall Federal policy governing the distribution of the contracts. . . .

Another significant finding from this study is that Federal activities in education generally are in the nature of Federal programs of specialized or technical training, provisions for the education of special groups, support of training particularly in agriculture and the mechanic arts, and other activities not aimed at the promotion of basic elementary and secondary education nor higher education in general. . . .

This study shows that the many extensive educational activities directly administered by the Federal Government consist principally of education for the national defense. The vast majority of Federal funds expended for educational purposes are used for defense-connected programs. These include the provisions for the education of veterans, research carried out at institutions of higher education under contract with defense agencies, special provisions for the education of dependents of military personnel, and for other children in defense areas, training of military personnel directly by Federal agencies and at civilian educational institutions, all of the programs authorized by the National Defense

Education Act of 1958, et cetera. This report sets forth the various authorizations for Federal educational programs relating to the national defense. . . .

Another consideration suggested by the findings from this study is the question of whether Federal promotion of education could be more effectively used as a "before" rather than as an "after" measure for the prevention of crime. One of the important educational programs described in this report is that operated by the Department of Justice for inmates of Federal penal and correctional institutions. This activity operates at a cost of well over a million dollars a year, in addition to the far greater cost of conviction of the prisioners and maintenance and operation of the prisons and correctional institutions.

This activity provides general and vocational education to enable prison inmates to acquire such knowledge and occupational skills as will enable them to adjust to society and earn a livelihood upon release. Without questioning the desirability of this activity, some people believe that the provision of adequate educational opportunities and guidance for exceptional children through Federal-State cooperative programs would greatly reduce crime, although others have pointed out that many educated people have become criminals. . . .

THE UNITED STATES OFFICE OF EDUCATION . . .

ORIGIN AND HISTORY OF THE OFFICE OF EDUCATION*

"Pass this bill and you give education a mouthpiece and a rallying point. While it will have no power to enter into the States and interfere with their systems, it will be able to collect facts and report the same to Congress, to be thence spread over the entire country.

"It will throw a flood of light upon the dark places of the land. It will form a public sentiment which will arouse to increased activity the friends of education everywhere, and ignorance will fly before it."

These historic words of Representative Ignatius Donnelly from Minnesota were uttered on June 5, 1866, in the congressional debate on a bill to establish a Department of Education in the Federal Government.

The testimony of Representative Donnelly formed part of the background of events and contributions that led to establishment of an agency

---

*School Life, XXXV, Nos. 8,9 (May, June, 1953).

for education within the Federal Government structure and authorized functions which the Office of Education has carried on for nearly 100 years in the service of education.

Now a part of the new Department of Health, Education, and Welfare, the Office of Education was originally established upon the request of leading educators for assistance that would aid the States and the people to establish and maintain efficient institutions and systems of education. Its creation was a recognition that the Federal Government, without controlling education, could do much to promote the cause of education. . . .

MOVEMENT FOR A FEDERAL OFFICE OF EDUCATION

As early as 1839 Henry Barnard induced those in charge of the 1840 United States Census to collect data concerning illiteracy, schools, academies, and colleges. The data were used by educational leaders in their efforts to promote education. These men also felt a great need for a central agency that would collect and disseminate educational statistics and general information on education, and from time to time, beginning in the 1840's, they made various proposals for the establishment of such an agency. The data obtained through the Census proved very helpful, but educators expressed need for a much greater service than the mere collection of data. Almost every national educational meeting of any importance gave attention to the question and took some action to bring about the creation of a Federal office of education. Among these meetings were a national convention in Philadelphia (1840) of the friends of common schools and the regular conventions of the American Association for the Advancement of Education, the National Teachers' Association, and the National Association of School Superintendents.

Educational leaders who promoted the idea of a Federal educational agency had in mind a number of things such an agency should do. They wanted an official agency for the exchange of educational information among the States, a means of diffusing knowledge of the science and art of education and of the organization and administration of education. They suggested that the head of the agency should attend educational conventions, publish an educational journal, and make an annual report on the progress of education in the United States and foreign nations. These leaders thought that the Federal educational office should maintain an education library containing educational reports and documents from the States and from foreign countries, educational books, plans, and models of schoolhouses and furniture, and school apparatus.

What was contemplated for the office was something more than collecting and reporting educational information, important and necessary as that function was. The educational leaders wanted an office that would make comparative studies of schools and school systems in this country. The Federal office, they said, should be a means through which more efficiency and uniformity would be secured in the educational movements of the country. They asked for the establishment of a bureau of education that would make suggestions for the advancement of education in the States and encourage the adoption of school systems "adapted to our form of government." Such a bureau, it was said, would "prove a potent means for improving and vitalizing existing systems" of education. It was clearly intended that a national office of education should actively stimulate and influence the development of education throughout the Nation. . . .

THE ACT

The text of the organic act creating the department is as follows:

"An Act To Establish a Department of Education (Approved March 2, 1867).

"Be it enacted by the Senate and House of Representatives of the United States of America in Congress assembled. That there shall be established, at the city of Washington, a department of education, for the purpose of collecting such statistics and facts as shall show the condition and progress of education in the several States and Territories, and of diffusing such information respecting the organization and management of schools and school systems, and methods of teaching, as shall aid the people of the United States in the establishment and maintenance of efficient school systems, and otherwise promote the cause of education throughout the country.

"Sec. 2.   And be it further enacted, That there shall be appointed by the President, by and with the advice and consent of the Senate, a Commissioner of Education, who shall be intrusted with the management of the department herein established, and who shall receive a salary of $4,000 per annum, and who shall have authority to appoint 1 chief clerk of his department, who shall receive a salary of $2,000 per annum, 1 clerk who shall receive a salary of $1,800 per annum, and 1 clerk who shall receive a salary of $1,600 per annum, which said clerks shall be subject to the appointing and removing powers of the Commissioner of Education.

"Sec. 3.   And be it further enacted, That it shall be the duty of the Commissioner of Education to present annually to Congress a report embodying the results of his investigations and labors, together with a statement of such facts and recommendations as will, in his judgment, subserve the purpose for which this department is established. In the first report made by the Commissioner of Education under this act, there shall be presented a statement of the several grants of land made by Congress to promote education, and the manner in which these several trusts have been managed, the amount of funds arising therefrom, and the annual proceeds of the same, as far as the same can be determined.

"Sec. 4.   And be it further enacted, That the Commissioner of Public Buildings is hereby authorized and directed to furnish proper offices for the use of the department herein established." . . .

Nine days after the President signed the act creating the Department of Education, he appointed Henry Barnard as Commissioner of Education, an office he held until March 15, 1870. For years Barnard had been engaged in educational work. He was Secretary of the Connecticut Board of Commissioners for Common Schools (1838-42), State Superintendent of Schools in Rhode Island (1848-49), State Superintendent of Education in Connecticut and Principal of the State Normal School (1850-55), Chancellor of the University of Wisconsin (1858-60), and President of St. John's College at Annapolis, Md. (1866-67). He was an educator, administrator, editor, author, and scholar. He had been untiring in his efforts for the creation of the Department of Education....

CHANGE OF NAME

The educational agency created by the Congress in 1867 was known as a "Department of Education." The original draft of the bill presented by Mr. Garfield asked for the establishment of a bureau of education in the Department of the Interior. Apparently the word "department" was adopted to give the Commissioner of Education the power to appoint his subordinates. He was not, of course, a member of the President's Cabinet.

The office did not continue long under the title "department." . . .

The Congressional Globe makes but brief mention of the alteration in the status of the Department of Education. There was no debate on the subject in the House or the Senate; the change from "Department" to "Office of Education," under the direction of the Secretary of the Interior, was effected in committee. It is significant that the act creating the Department of Education in 1867 was not repealed. . . .

In the appropriation act for 1870 the title of the "Office of Education" was changed to "Bureau of Education" without altering the status of the Commissioner as regards salary and duties. In 1929 the title "Office of Education" was adopted. . . .

In the reorganization of Government agencies on July 1, 1939, the Office of Education and its functions and personnel were transferred to the Federal Security Agency. The vocational rehabilitation function was continued in the Office of Education until it was organized in a newly established Office of Vocational Rehabilitation, Federal Security Agency, in 1943. . . .

During World War I the Office of Education received appropriations to carry on certain educational activities related to the war effort. Among these were promoting school gardens, social studies, and the Americanization of immigrants. After 1934 Federal emergency relief funds were allotted to the Office to conduct certain educational investigations and demonstration projects with the use of unemployed persons. The educational program of the Civilian Conservation Corps, which trained more than 3,100,000 enrollees, was carried on under the general supervision of the Commissioner of Education. During World War II the Office carried on several extensive training programs and a student war loans program. More than 14,000,000 persons were enrolled in the training programs, which cost $410,000,000, and 11,000 college students received a total of $3,250,000 in loans.

Soon after the passage of the National Defense Act following the outbreak of hostilities in Korea the Office of Education was designated by the National Security Resources Board as the focal point for the relationship of Federal agencies with the schools and colleges. The Office administers the laws which provide a program of assistance for school construction and operation and maintenance in federally affected areas. To the Office was assigned responsibility as the claimant agency for the allocation of controlled materials for school and college construction. It also has certain responsibilities for the operation of an educational advisory service for the college housing program.

The Office renders a considerable amount of assistance to other Federal agencies and to Senators and Representatives on educational matters.

THE INEFFECTIVE PAST AND UNCERTAIN FUTURE OF THE U. S. COMMISSIONER OF EDUCATION*

During the ninety-five years since Henry Barnard became the first U. S. Commissioner of Education in 1867, fifteen commissioners have served terms ranging from the brief term of Lee Thurston, who died

---

*Donald W. Robinson, "Commissioner of Education: Our (Most, Least) Important Government Post," *Phi Delta Kappan,* XLIV, December 1962, 106-115 (by permission).

two months after his appointment, to the seventeen years of William T. Harris. The staff of one clerk and one messenger available to assist Barnard has become a staff of 1,300 workers ready to welcome their new boss when he assumes his duties as the sixteenth commissioner.

During these ninety-five years the USOE has evolved from a purely fact-gathering and statistics-sorting office to a post of critical importance in reflecting national concerns over the state of our schools. It is today potentially a position of crucial importance in mobilizing educational opinion and exerting national leadership to improve our already creditable performance — without imposing national standards. . . .

Today the office is in a most difficult situation, quite aside from the problems created by the temporary vacancy at the top. Its authority is circumscribed, its salaries limited, its functions divided among many agencies. It is buffeted by gusts of criticism, some deserved, some not. An example of the latter occurred when a prominent critic, on one visit, lambasted the commissioner for running a political office and on the next berated him because he was not down at the Congress lobbying. . . .

The United States Commissioner of Education is responsible for the conduct of this complex office. He presides over a staff of 1,300 employees and administers the spending of three quarters of a billion dollars a year. He heads one of the three divisions of the Department of Health, Education, and Welfare and has frequent access to top leaders in all branches of the government. The commissioner can exert his influence on national legislation affecting the schools and he can speak out to influence the thinking of educators at all levels.

Yet for the second time in little more than a year the search is on for a new commissioner. The number of nationally known educators who are reported to have refused the appointment . . . is making people ask why this is such a spurned position.

Many explanations have been advanced.

One top administrator in the office reflects a popular view when he says that a $20,000 commissionership will not attract a $35,000 superintendent. He adds that every school superintendent in the Washington metropolitan area except one (Washington itself) receives a higher salary than the commissioner. . . .

WHY IS THE OFFICE OF EDUCATION INEFFECTIVE?

One of the principal reasons why the commissioner's chair is vacant and the office relatively impotent is that Congress has persistently hedged its operations with too-precise mandates. For reasons unknown, Congress appears not to trust this agency to exercise intelligent initiative. And without freedom to exercise initiative it is impossible to attract and retain superior leadership in adequate quantity.

Congress, which properly insists that the National Institutes of Health generate new lines of research that have hardly been dreamt of when its appropriations are authorized, and which sensibly allows the National Aeronautics and Space Agency to do such things as establish an unauthorized two-million dollar fellowship program, grows testy when the U. S. Office of Education uses its funds to improve a library exhibit at the Seattle World's Fair, and suddenly grows adamant and inflexible about the expenditure of funds in only the precise ways that were congressionally intended when the money was appropriated.

Another difficulty arises from the way the educational effort is dispersed among many government departments. In 1959 federal support for education amounted to $2.4 billion dollars, of which only 728 million or 31 per cent was administered through the Department of Health, Education, and Welfare. The Agriculture Department operates a graduate school with 6,500 part-time students, offering liberal arts courses and several different degrees. The Department of Interior runs schools for Indian children and for children of National Park Service employees. The Atomic Energy Commission runs the schools at Los Alamos. The armed forces run schools for children of servicemen overseas. Smaller educational programs are conducted by at least twelve other federal agencies. . . .

Another problem that continues to plague the Office of Education is the continuing argument over whether it should continue the tradition of assisting state and local officials to do the jobs the way *they* want them done or whether it should assume more initiative in persuading state and local officials to follow what the office considers the most effective way.

Given freedom and support, the Washington office should be able to maintain a larger stable of superior talent than the fifty states could hope to assemble. Certainly far better than the 30,000 separate local districts could maintain. Such a superior staff as Washington could maintain, and to a degree does even now, would be wasted if it were constrained to offering technical knowhow and forbidden to offer policy advice. The federal office should continue to serve and encourage policy development in the states and localities where basic educational responsibility resides. But local agencies are feeble policy makers if they lack stimulation and provocation, without compulsion, from a competent, respected, national body. . . .

National leadership can contribute to the improvement of educational quality without imposing a standard curriculum or examinations or certi-

fication standards. The desire of the USOE to contribute to the raising
of standards does not imply an intent to set up examinations to measure
that quality or to establish norms to define it. It does imply an urge
for more status and more funds and more operational initiative to enable
the office to inspire local leaders to want to match or excel the best
schooling provided anywhere in the nation — best by their own local
standards. The U. S. Public Health Service has undoubtedly contributed
to raising America's health standards. It is not accused of regimenting
or controlling local health agencies. . . .

One inescapable question is, "Can the United States Office of Education expand its leadership role without instituting pernicious federal
controls?" Obviously it cannot assert effective leadership without being
accused of exerting undesirable controls, for this bogey is an inevitable
accompaniment of all federal action in the area of education. . . .

A SECRETARY OF EDUCATION?

The last four commissioners of education agreed when they appeared
together this year on a television show that the best solution for the
woes of our education office is to elevate it to department level and
the commissioner to secretary with cabinet rank. As Commissioner
McMurrin expressed it, "It is ludicrous for the Post Office, which is
essentially a business operation, to be represented in the cabinet while
education is not. Education should be represented at the cabinet level
by a secretary who is responsible for the bulk of the government's educational involvements, not just a small fraction of them. It should be
represented by a secretary who represents education, not education
along with health and welfare."

One argument advanced in support of the secretaryship is the need
to clothe the national education spokesman with enough authority that
he can confidently speak for American education. Today no one in this
country occupies a position from which he can synthesize the divergent
voices and speak for education. . . .

OTHER PROPOSALS

Not everyone is eager to have the office elevated to department level.
The National Education Association is reported to favor some strengthening of the office, but without major shifting of authority, presumably
on the assumption that national leadership should emanate not from a
government body but from the teaching profession itself, as represented,

let us say, by the NEA. Others reply that the danger of monolithic power structures is just as great in nongovernmental bodies as in government agencies. The source of leadership, they say, can be given the dignity and prestige of official rank and office without clothing it with power to enforce conformity.

James Allen, the New York State commissioner, has recommended that the President create a committee of able citizens to determine the character and scope of our responsibility as a nation for education and to decide upon a federal education structure for carrying out that responsibility. Allen's own proposal would be for the appointment of a national board of education resembling New York State's Board of Regents, which supervises and sets standards for all education in the state. It would be a policy-making body of lay citizens and professionals, and it would appoint a commissioner free to speak on behalf of education without necessarily reflecting the policy of the President or the Secretary of Health, Education, and Welfare. It would be prohibited by law from interfering with local control of education, but it would exercise general control over operations and policies of the USOE. . . .

There is no clear evidence at this writing whether either the secretaryship or the national board will be adopted. Congressional leaders are loath to express themselves. . . .

U. S. COMMISSIONERS OF EDUCATION

Commissioner	President Making Appointment	Years in Office
Henry Barnard	Johnson	1867-1870
John Eaton	Grant	1870-1886
N. H. R. Dawson	Cleveland	1886-1889
William T. Harris	Harrison	1889-1906
Elmer E. Brown	Roosevelt	1906-1911
Philander P. Claxton	Taft	1911-1921
John J. Tigert	Harding	1921-1928
William J. Cooper	Hoover	1929-1933
George F. Zook	Roosevelt	1933-1934
John W. Studebaker	Roosevelt	1934-1949
Earl J. McGrath	Truman	1949-1953
Lee Thurston	Truman	1953 (2 mos.)
Samuel Brownell	Eisenhower	1953-1956
Lawrence G. Derthick	Eisenhower	1956-1961
Sterling McMurrin	Kennedy	1961-1962
Francis Keppel	Kennedy-Johnson	1962-1966
Harold Howe	Johnson	1966-

When this nation's leaders become thoroughly convinced that educational standards are a matter for national concern, they will devise an agency equal to the task of reflecting that concern in positive leadership. Other facets of our society — agriculture, labor, business — are far more prominently represented in our government than is education. . . .

Leadership in education is needed at every level. It is clearly needed at the national level, not to dominate the nation's thinking, but to encourage leadership at all levels. There is much evidence that a department of education could attract and retain the education talent that could provide more of that kind of leadership.

THE U. S. OFFICE MUST TAKE LEADERSHIP IN ATTACKING EDUCATIONAL PROBLEMS*

The record justifies the conviction that other educational problems, national in scope, can be dealt with through cooperative study and effort on the part of the educational agency of the Government and the State and local authorities. Certain problems of that type now exist. Some are already receiving attention; others are not. An examination of the present American educational scene and a look into the future will show that we have now entered a period in our national history when the Office of Education must take the initiative in organizing cooperative attacks on these problems. Indeed, the best interests of the school system of the Nation and of our people as a whole will not be well served if such leadership is not assumed in the days immediately ahead. . . .

The Office of Education is the central point of contact between the Federal Government and all of the diverse and far-flung branches of the American educational system. It is in constant touch with each State department of education and, through them, with the vast metropolitan school systems, the great consolidated rural schools, and each lonely one-room schoolhouse, no matter how isolated it may be. As the principal focal point for the recommendations of such national organizations as the National Education Association, the American

*Annual Report of the Federal Security Agency, 1952, Washington, D.C.: United States Office of Education, 1953.

Council on Education, the National Congress of Parents and Teachers, and the National Citizens' Commission for the Public Schools, the Office is increasingly being recognized as the appropriate channel for the presentation of the points of view of these organizations to the Executive Branch and to the Congress. In the international field, the United States Commissioner of Education is being called upon with increasing frequency to serve as the spokesman for American education abroad.

In accepting this call to service the Office of Education recognizes a profound obligation — an obligation not only to the American educational system as a whole, in which the Office staff deeply believes — but an obligation to all of the American people. Actually it is a double obligation which places upon the Office a double responsibility, neither aspect of which can be ignored except at the Nation's peril.

Simply stated, it is this:

In developing solutions to national educational problems of the sort described earlier in this report, the Office of Education must:

(a) evolve plans for the application of Federal leadership and resources where and as necessary to meet these national problems.

At the same time the Office must:

(b) safeguard assiduously the values and benefits traditionally associated with State and local control of education. . . .

NATION'S SUPERINTENDENTS WANT LIMITED LEADERSHIP FROM U. S. OFFICE*

Supported both by mid-twentieth century needs and by history, the following functions and policies of the U. S. Office of Education are deemed sound:

1. To collect, publish, and distribute statistics on school and college activities throughout the nation.
2. To allocate funds for educational research to responsible educational agencies at state and local levels as Congress directs.

---

*The School Administrator (Statement adopted by Executive Committee of American Association of School Administrators on federal, state, and local relations, especially the role of the U.S. Office, at meeting in Philadelphia, September, 1962) XX, No. 3 (November, 1962).

3. To cooperate with and assist local and state agencies and institutions in promoting education and in identifying emerging needs.

4. To allocate to states federal funds appropriated by the Congress for educational purposes in the states and in manners designated by the Congress.

5. To provide official liaison on educational matters with the authorities of foreign nations and develop appropriate cooperative working relationships between American educators and those from other countries.

6. To promote the cause of public education at all levels and explain the basic needs which educational authorities face at local and state levels.

7. To report to Congress and the public generally on educational matters of general public welfare.

Some principles of operation deemed to be sound and which the AASA Executive Committee believes should be followed by federal officials in both legislative and administrative branches:

1. Federal legislation and activities of federal educational officials, whether in the U. S. Office of Education, the National Science Foundation, or in other branches of the federal government, should be consistent with the deeply embedded American philosophy, previously adhered to, that the administration and control of public education are responsibilities of state and local authorities. Exceptions, such as schools in territories, schools on reservations, schools abroad for American service personnel, and military schools and colleges, should be made.

2. Except in time of war or other dire emergency, no agency of the federal government, nor the Congress itself, should allocate or distribute funds in a manner that weakens or undermines the principle of freedom of choice in the educational pursuits of any individual.

Grants of funds — whether in the form of scholarships in a specifically designated content field or in support of a particular instructional program — that cause students to pursue courses of study that agents of the federal government want them to pursue constitute a federal control of serious consequence. On the other hand, for a student to accept funds for a specific program results in self-denial of another program of possibly equal value to society and which would be more suitable to his interests and aptitudes.

The use of funds to regulate the lives of young people and to direct their educational future into avenues other than those they choose of their own free will can be detrimental to the true spirit of liberty and freedom of choice as political measures of a restrictive and directive nature. America must not inadvertently —by financial support in terms of scholarships in certain fields or subsidy of special programs — become indirectly responsible both for controlling the lives and vocations of youth and for weakening the principle of state and local control of public education.

3. Congress should always be sensitive to the importance of giving support to the principle of state and local control of public education. It should scrutinize each legislative proposal to determine whether or not it has controls, obvious or hidden, which will tend to shape the content of or give direction to the educational program and therefore exercise federal control. It should confirm its faith in the principle of local and state control, at the same time recognizing the federal government's responsibility for helping finance the schools by making substantial appropriations to states to be used according to state plans for the operation of public education.

4. In all of its operations, through all of its activities, and through all allocation of funds, the U. S. Office of Education and other federal agencies should strive to build up local and state education systems, rather than to supersede them by a belief that federal officials or federal agencies can do the job better.

The pre-eminence of the American public school system among the nations of the world is forceful evidence of the values of local and state control. The initiative that has been stimulated and the sense of responsibility for public education that has been developed through local control is the very lifeblood of the public school system. There has been a strength rather than a weakness in diversity of educational programs.

5. In performing their official functions, the U. S. Office of Education, the National Science Foundation, and all other federal agencies and their employees should not attempt to determine the social purposes to be served by the schools; nor should they determine the ends to which the instructional program should be directed or what specific curriculum aspects need strengthening.

Except in time of war, the power of the federal government should not be wielded by the U. S. Office of Education or other federal officials or agencies through the development of special projects or the allocation of public tax money to shape in specific form the content and character of the curriculum in any state or in any school system.

Education is far too intimate a concern to parents and to local neighborhoods and communities to be brought under the control of any agency or any group of people far removed from close acquaintance with the home and community life of children and youth. The national purpose will not be neglected by state and local officials since they, too, have a major stake in the nation's welfare. If there are federally developed data and information which are useful to education authorities, the federal government should make them available.

6. Federal agencies should not incorporate funds in their budget to finance and promote specific programs for curriculum development.

FOR FURTHER REFLECTION OR INVESTIGATION

1. Discuss the advisability of a national board of education.

2. Are political pressures, partisan and otherwise, normally more severe on public governing boards at the local, state, or federal level?

3. Analyze the citizen's concern over "local control" of children's education.

4. What per cent of a school district's budget would have to be provided by the federal government in order for that level to exercise effective control over the school system?

5. Interview local school authorities — superintendent, principal, and appropriate teachers — to determine the extent of control exercised by a higher authority from the district's participation in NDEA benefits, the national school lunch program, or the vocational education subsidies.

6. Could a state or a local school district afford to reject the aid offered in the 1965 Elementary and Secondary Education Act if it wished to do so for the sake of a principle?

7. Discuss the probable impact of the 1965 Elementary and Secondary Education Act in the following respects:

a. How any portion, or the total, of your school system might be affected.

b. Sections of the act which encourage sharing of facilities between public and non-public schools of your community.

c. Section of the act which authorizes direct project negotiations between the U. S. Office of Education and a local school district.

8. Why has there been so little progress made in centralizing and coordinating the various financial ventures of federal agencies in behalf of education? Should they be centralized?

9. Discuss the reasons for and the implications of Federal activities designed to improve educational opportunities outside of established school framework through programs such as Head Start, Job Corps, and the Economic Opportunity Act.

BIBLIOGRAPHY

Alford, Albert L., "The Elementary and Secondary Education Act of 1965 — What to Anticipate," *Phi Delta Kappan,* XLVI, June, 1965.

Annual Report of the Federal Security Agency, 1952. Washington, D. C.: United States Office of Education, 1953.

Blauch, Lloyd, "Review of Historic Background of the Office of Education," *School Life,* XXXV, May, 1953, 117-124, June, 1953.

Campbell, Roald, L. L. Cunningham, and Roderick McPhee, *The Organization and Control of American Schools,* Columbus, Ohio: Charles E. Merrill Books, Inc., 1965.

Conant, James B., *Shaping Educational Policy,* New York: McGraw-Hill Book Company, 1964.

Harris, Seymour, *Education and Public Policy,* Berkeley, California: McCutchan Publishing Corporation, 1965.

Kursh, Harry, *The U. S. Office of Education: A Century of Service,* New York: Chilton Books, 1965.

Organization Manual, Office of Education. Washington, D. C.: Department of Health, Education, and Welfare, September 26, 1963.

Patton, Robert D., "Whither the U. S. Office of Education?" *Journal of Higher Education,* XXXIII, November, 1962.

Pierce, Truman M., *Federal State and Local Government in Education,* Washington, D.C.: The Center for Applied Research in Education, 1964.

Quattlebaum, Charles A., *Federal Education Policies, Programs and Proposals,* Part II, Washington, D.C.: U.S. Government Printing Office, June, 1960.

Robinson, Donald W., "Commissioner of Education: Our (Most, Least) Important Government Post," *Phi Delta Kappan,* XLIV, December, 1962.

The School Administrator, XX, November, 1962. Statement adopted by Executive Committee of American Association of School Administrators on federal, state, and local relations, especially the role of the U.S. Office, at meeting in Philadelphia, September, 1962.

Chapter 6

Administration of
Non-Public Schools

In common usage, a non-public school is thought of as one sponsored either by a church or a private foundation. It is typically identified by these three characteristics: (1) the absence of financial support from public tax funds, (2) the requirement of tuition or fee payment for those who attend, and (3) the lack of free admission privileges for all youngsters residing within its geographic attendance area. However, it is becoming increasingly difficult to distinguish public and non-public schools on the basis of these three characteristics.

Many private and parochial schools receive some support from tax funds. Any elementary or secondary school in the United States may participate in the benefits of the National School Lunch Program, assuming it complies with the requirements of the program. Also, sections of the National Defense Education Act apply to parochial schools as well as to state schools. Private schools may participate in the tax fruits of the 1965 Education Act. Some parochial schools even benefit from the locally raised school tax dollar if agreements are made to share the use of public school facilities — buildings, buses, or personnel. Most of these financial aids may be described as minor, and a non-public school is considered in this chapter as one which does not receive a major portion of its operating costs from public taxation.

A non-public parochial school cannot be distinguished solely on the basis that it charges fees for attendance. Some Catholic schools are supported entirely by subscriptions and donations from the church membership and are free to pupils of their families. Contrariwise, a few public schools levy special-purpose fees for those in attendance.

Nor can the distinction be made entirely on the grounds of free accessibility of admission for all youngsters within the geographic area. Some parochial schools are open to children of non-church members residing within the district. The primary difference in this regard is that

276

children are not legally compelled to attend a non-public school. Moreover, the free-and-open characteristic of public schools is still debated in some communities where attendance is restricted by race.

This chapter discusses non-public schools in their common connotation — those supported and controlled by a religious order or those supported primarily by tuition and private subsidies.

Approximately fifteen per cent of all students enrolled in the nation's elementary and secondary schools attend non-public schools; the total number by state is shown in Table 3. Accepting the assumptions which the United States Office of Education employs in projecting future enrollments, there will be an estimated twelve million pupils enrolled in non-public schools in the 1979-80 school year (Table IV), almost as many children as were enrolled in all of the nation's elementary and secondary public schools at the beginning of the twentieth century. This phenomenal growth augurs well for opportunities in administrative careers in non-public schools except that, as noted later in this chapter, non-public schools typically employ fewer administrators than do the public schools.

DIFFERENCES IN THE ADMINISTRATION OF NON-PUBLIC SCHOOLS AND PUBLIC SCHOOLS

The similarities in the administration of public and non-public schools are readily apparent. To the degree stated earlier, administration is administration, teaching is teaching, learning is learning. The objectives, methodologies, and outcomes of teaching and administration have commonalities in all educational institutions. Only the differences which have implications for administration will be emphasized here.

The manner in which private and parochial schools are financed lies at the root of many of the differences in administrative activities. The mass of state laws pertaining to public schools for budgeting, public hearings and reporting, accounting, purchasing, taxing powers and limitations, operating and capital outlay restrictions are not applicable to a non-public school. General legal provisions affecting financial transactions of all organizations within the state do, of course, apply. However, financial accounting procedures are greatly simplified in non-public schools. That is not to imply that administrators of private and parochial schools are relieved of financial worries; those administrators will attest that their problems in finding sufficient funds are severe. The raising of funds for parochial schools is usually not the responsibility of their respective superintendents or principals; rather, the revenue-seeking is left in the hands of church officials.

Table 3. — *Number of students enrolled in nonpublic secondary schools offering grade 9-12 subjects, by State and by relationship to church, 1961-62*[1]

State	All nonpublic schools		Church-related schools		Non-church related schools	
	Number	Enrollment	Number	Enrollment	Number	Enrollment
United States	3,782	1,092,901	3,062	975,156	720	117,745
Alabama	34	5,895	20	4,397	14	1,498
Alaska	10	471	9	453	1	18
Arizona	26	5,468	18	4,689	8	779
Arkansas	18	2,326	17	2,247	1	79
California	252	73,675	194	65,429	58	8,246
Colorado	39	8,158	31	7,313	8	845
Connecticut	93	25,490	47	15,150	46	10,340
Delaware	16	3,928	12	3,544	4	384
District of Columbia	28	7,553	19	6,260	9	1,293
Florida	81	10,619	51	8,297	30	2,322
Georgia	31	5,897	16	2,614	15	3,283
Hawaii	22	7,553	19	4,727	3	2,826
Idaho	11	1,036	11	1,036	....	....
Illinois	180	92,474	153	87,969	27	4,505
Indiana	54	20,061	51	18,991	3	1,070
Iowa	97	19,205	97	19,205	....	....
Kansas	42	9,064	41	8,977	1	87
Kentucky	76	16,977	70	15,995	6	982
Louisiana	101	22,830	90	21,486	11	1,344
Maine	57	10,511	23	3,930	34	6,581
Maryland	82	21,052	65	18,274	17	2,778
Massachusetts	223	59,546	153	47,360	70	12,186
Michigan	218	64,354	210	63,383	8	971
Minnesota	90	26,524	84	25,693	6	831
		3,591	71	3,452	2	138

M......	90	29,0?5	85	26,??3	13	2,082
Montana	20	4,148	18	4,021	2	127
Nebraska	60	10,280	58	9,621	2	659
Nevada	2	930	2	930		
New Hampshire	38	7,275	29	5,859	9	1,416
New Jersey	143	49,530	105	45,058	38	4,472
New Mexico	28	4,128	26	3,964	2	164
New York	398	144,130	299	128,218	99	15,912
North Carolina	43	3,336	30	2,240	13	1,096
North Dakota	22	2,957	22	2,957		
Ohio	159	66,320	143	64,051	16	2,269
Oklahoma	29	3,445	28	3,350	1	95
Oregon	36	7,264	33	6,835	3	429
Pennsylvania	271	116,683	222	107,490	49	9,193
Rhode Island	27	8,523	24	8,230	3	293
South Carolina	24	3,205	17	2,002	7	1,203
South Dakota	24	2,419	22	2,307	2	112
Tennessee	49	9,724	32	5,613	17	4,111
Texas	108	21,760	96	19,624	12	2,136
Utah	10	1,658	10	1,658		
Vermont	24	5,575	11	3,264	13	2,311
Virginia	70	13,559	45	9,208	25	4,351
Washington	66	11,341	61	10,591	5	750
West Virginia	22	4,561	19	3,964	3	597
Wisconsin	97	36,454	93	35,873	4	581
Wyoming	2	363	2	363		
Outlying parts	65	9,651	57	8,750	8	901
Guam	6	745	6	745		
Puerto Rico	55	8,558	48	7,666	7	892
Virgin Islands	4	348	3	339	1	9

¹Preliminary Report on Offerings and Enrollments in Grades 9-12 of Nonpublic Secondary Schools, 1961-62, Washington, D.C.: United States Office of Education, 1963, 17.

TABLE IV

School-year enrollment in grades K-8 and 9-12 of regular public and nonpublic schools in 50 States and the District of Columbia: 1949-50 to 1979-80[2]

[In thousands]

School year	Total public and nonpublic			Public			Nonpublic		
	K-12	K-8	9-12	K-12	K-8	9-12	K-12	K-8	9-12
				ACTUAL			ESTIMATED		
1949-50	28,632	22,199	6,433	25,216	19,464	5,752	3,416	2,735	681
1951-52	30,520	23,947	6,573	26,678	20,770	5,908	3,842	3,177	665
1953-54	33,333	26,262	7,071	28,964	22,649	6,315	4,369	3,613	756
1955-56	36,052	28,317	7,735	31,314	24,413	6,901	4,738	3,904	834
1957-58	38,953	30,120	8,833	33,696	25,801	7,895	5,257	4,319	938
1959-60	42,372	32,753	9,619	36,147	27,630	8,517	6,225	5,123	1,102
				PROJECTED Series B					
1964-65	48,940	36,109	12,831	41,190	29,959	11,231	7,750	6,150	1,600
1969-70	53,145	38,737	14,408	44,096	31,593	12,503	9,049	7,144	1,905
1974-75	58,215	42,361	15,854	47,710	34,070	13,640	10,505	8,291	2,214
1979-80	65,666	48,497	17,169	53,249	38,587	14,662	12,417	9,910	2,507

[2]Kenneth A. Simon, Enrollment in Public and Nonpublic Elementary and Secondary School, 1950-1980, Washington, D.C.: United States Office of Education, Circular No. 692, 1962, 6.

This fact introduces a major difference in the public relations function. The accountability of a non-public school is to its patrons only, not to the entire population of the area.

Not all private and parochial schools even operate under the authority of a governing body. Teachers and administrators of most Catholic schools are responsible only to the pastor of the parish, or to the bishop, without any intervening body. Where boards of education are created for non-public schools the members are usually appointed by the church officer who is also responsible for the schools. The board is more of an advisory group; it may give general direction to the school's actions through its limited policy-making function but is not subject to state laws which control the behavior of boards for public schools.

The near future may witness a change in this respect, however, accompanying the general liberalizing unrest within the administration of Roman Catholic affairs. A special committee of the National Catholic Educational Association recommended this year that lay boards be created for its parish schools. Under the proposal, members of the parish would vote on candidates nominated by a parish-appointed nominating committee. The seven-member board, with the bishop and diocesan superintendent as exofficio but non-voting members, would have restricted policy-making powers comparable to a public school board of education. Much of its work, under the proposal, would be administrative in nature rather than legislative.

The curriculums of non-public schools are quite similar to those of public schools except in the allowance for religious instruction in parochial schools and the special-purpose nature of prep schools which largely gear their offerings to the classical education. There are few non-public high schools which could be labeled comprehensive schools. Vocational programs, except for business education, are practically non-existent.

Administering the personnel function is substantially different for non-public schools. Denominational schools, especially Catholic, try to use professional workers of the church as much as they can. The recent growth of Catholic schools, however, precludes an adequate supply of sisters or brothers; approximately one-third of the instructional staff in the nation's Catholic schools are lay teachers who are paid for their services. Often these salaries are not competitive with the local public schools and, therefore, the recruitment task is arduous. It is aggravated further by the fact that lay teachers are not eligible for the state's fringe benefits of tenure, retirement, or sick leave. The degree and certification requirements of the state do not always apply with equal force to any of the non-public schools. Even in those states which license non-public schools and stipulate that their teachers meet comparable preparatory requirements of public school teachers, there are usually waiver provisions which relax the requirements for private school teachers.

The most measurable difference in the administration of public and non-public schools is in the extent of administration. Private and parochial schools use substantially fewer administrators than do public schools. One explanation lies in the fact that most private schools are small. As independent entities, they function comparably to the tiny public school district which has just one administrator for the entire system. And, as in the small public school district, many of the administrative chores are performed by teachers. But even in the large metropolitan parochial school systems there are far fewer administrative assistants than in their public school counterparts. The use of only building principals, and perhaps a superintendent, is commonplace. Part of this condition has already been explained by the absence of legal mandates which thrust extensive record keeping upon public schools. Even the amount of money handled by church schools is substantially less for a comparatively sized public school system since the major item of any educational institution's operating budget—salaries—is negligible in the parish which utilizes unpaid teachers.

Further, it can be generalized that private schools do not provide as many services to their pupils, such as transportation to and from school, medical, and psychological services. Guidance counseling and physical education are often lacking in the church school. Enforcement of the state's compulsory attendance laws is assigned to the public board of education. Census taking is performed by the public school for the parochial school. Supervisory services and curriculum consultancy are very limited in private schools, if they are offered at all. Very few special education classes are conducted in non-public schools. It is often argued that even the disciplinary responsibilities are eased for teachers and administrators of non-public schools since wayward-inclined pupils are not compelled to attend those schools.

THE CHALLENGE OF NON-PUBLIC SCHOOLS
TO ADMINISTRATORS

A major challenge facing the administrators of both public and non-public educational institutions in the decades ahead is the need to find ways for compatible operations which serve the best interests of young people. Barring an unforseen national catastrophe, both kinds of institutions will grow quantitatively. No longer are there heard any responsible voices questioning the right of either institution to exist in the United

States, nor the right of parents to educate their children at the institution of their choice. But basic to the existence of all schools is adequate financial support, and the competitive struggle for a share of people's dollars could foretell a clash which might dissipate learning in both public and non-public institutions. The preponderous publications of late, samples of which are included in this chapter, indicate the strong feelings about use of public tax money for support of private schools.

The summarizing points in favor of greater tax support of private and parochial schools are these: (1) private schools serve a public need and relieve the general taxpayer of considerable expense which he would otherwise have to provide, (2) in the process of serving a public need they should not be deprived of adequate resources to provide quality education equivalent to that of the public school, (3) parents who pay the costs of a private school for their children must still pay taxes for the support of public schools from which they do not receive equivalent benefits, (4) parents should be allowed to combine religious learning with general learnings for their children, a privilege being increasingly denied in the public schools, and (5) private schools constitute a wholesome competition which prevents public schools from relaxing under a monopolistic condition.

On the opposite side it is pointed out that (1) taxpayers should not be compelled to support a voluntary educational institution which they have not sanctioned by public vote, (2) private schools are not accountable to any public agency at the community level, (3) extensive general financial support of existing denominational schools would result in other denominations proliferating the educational scene to the general dilution of educational support, a development which would revert the total educational effort of the nation to that of two centuries ago in which public schools were for the indigent and church schools served the economy's elite, (4) aggrandizement of the church school would encourage needless divisiveness in the nation to weaken the major objective of the public school, which is to promote common understandings in a democratic, free society, and (5) substantial public tax support of private schools might lead to public control which would eventually preclude the uniqueness which a private school can offer to a nation that prizes diversity.

Debate on these points inescapably arouses people at two of their most sensitive and vulnerable characteristics: philosophical concepts and income. Therein lies the challenge to educational leaders — to find workable solutions without suffering harm to the education of children. Since citizens depend upon educational leaders to find paths through obstacles to nearly all of their educational problems, another potent

reason appears for the broad intellectual preparation of school administrators in both public and non-public schools. As discussed in the
preceding chapter, the path may have been started by the 1965 Education act which pressures the two sets of administrators into communal
pursuits in a constructive way. With more tax revenue going to non-
public schools and with private schools conducting their affairs similarly
to public schools, the future of both institutions makes for interesting
speculation.

STATUS OF NON-PUBLIC SCHOOLS
IN UNITED STATES . . .

ENROLLMENTS IN NON-PUBLIC HIGH SCHOOLS*

Although nonpublic secondary schools are not large numerically compared with all secondary schools, they continue to play a significant
part in education, particularly in the East. They have a strong appeal
to individual parents who are able and willing to pay for more individualized attention in small classes, for indoctrination in the moral and
religious principles they value, for more ready entree into specific institutions of higher education, and for other claimed advantages. The
reputation for scholastic excellence enjoyed by some nonpublic secondary schools may not be generally applicable to the entire group, but
high standards are maintained by a number of them.

Some denominational schools make no attempt to offer a complete
high school program but are more concerned with giving the high
school student a year or two of the proper religious orientation along
with a minimum academic program before passing him along to public
high schools or other types of schools. The Seventh-Day Adventists and
Missouri-Synod Lutherans operate a number of schools of this type,
as well as their complete high schools and academies. The Roman
Catholic church is increasingly attempting to offer a diversified and complete high school education for all of its constituents, particularly in
areas where there is a high concentration of Catholic families and sufficient financial backing from parents. Where individual parishes are not

---

*Diane B. Gertler, *Statistics of Nonpublic Secondary Schools*, 1960-61, Washington, D.C.: United States Office of Education, Circular No. 707, 1963, 1-2, 9.

Table E.—Church relationship of nonpublic secondary schools, by region, 1960-61

Church relationship of nonpublic schools	Total	Number of schools, by region								
		New England	Mideast	Great Lakes	Plains	Southeast	Southwest	Rocky Mountains	Far West	Outlying parts
All schools	4,053	486	1,001	735	464	657	204	86	420	75
Nonchurch-related	787	187	226	60	24	169	24	11	86	13
Church-related	3,266	299	775	675	440	488	180	75	324	62
Baptist	22	1	1	3	.....	13	2	.....	2	1
Christian Reformed	67	.....	2	38	8	6	2	2	9	.....
Friends	25	3	15	2	2	1	.....	1	1	.....
Jewish	46	3	36	4	.....	1	.....	.....	2	.....
Lutheran	64	1	6	19	21	4	3	3	7	.....
Methodist	22	2	4	1	2	8	4	.....	1	1
Presbyterian	20	.....	2	1	2	9	4	1	1	.....
Protestant Episcopal	107	19	26	6	7	29	6	2	12	1
Roman Catholic	2,523	258	635	551	371	317	130	48	213	57
Seventh-Day Adventist	282	10	31	43	16	72	23	14	73	2
Other church-related	88	2	17	7	11	28	6	4	13	.....

able to maintain complete and comprehensive high schools, schools are sponsored by an entire diocese or archdiosese. This has resulted in a number of large schools, such as those in the Archdiocese of Philadelphia. . . .

RELIGIOUS AFFILIATION

Certain precautions should be observed in interpreting the figures presented on the church affiliation of schools in table E and other tabulations in this presentation. Many research workers ask for data on "independent schools" in an attempt to analyze the exclusive private school characterized by small classes, individualized programing, and advanced or challenging curriculums aimed primarily toward the higher entrance requirements of the most selective institutions of higher education. This type of school is not equivalent to the nonchurch-related category in the current survey. Some of the nonchurch-related schools probably meet the above criteria, but so do a considerable number of church-related schools, particularly among the long-established academies along the eastern seaboard. No valid generalizations with regard to relative scholastic excellence or exclusiveness can be drawn on lines of church affiliation.

An analysis of the church relationship of non-public schools, as shown in table E, indicates that church-related schools outnumber nonchurch-related schools in all regions, especially in the Plain States, where 95 percent (440 schools) of the nonpublic schools are church-related, and in the Great Lakes area, where 92 per cent (675 schools) are church-related. New England has the highest proportion of nonchurch-related schools — almost two-fifths (38.5 percent) of its nonpublic schools.

PROTESTANT SCHOOLS IN THE UNITED STATES*

When Martin Luther announced his conviction that every member of the German nation should be able to read the Holy Scriptures and that Christian princes and public officials might do worse than spend their money on public education, he provided an assignment in edu-

---

*Arthur M. Ahlschwede, "The Protestant Schools: Purposes, Programs, Financing." By permission of *Phi Delta Kappan*, XLV (December, 1963), 136-140.

cation which states and churches ever since have been trying to fulfill. It is not as if education since the sixteenth century has been sharply discontinuous from the remarkable enterprise of the previous age, ventilated and illuminated as it was by the insights of the Renaissance. The new interest in both classical and vernacular languages, fostered by the humanistic stance of the Renaissance, and the embryonic stirrings of scientific concern continued through the Reformation period, perhaps not fed but certainly not quenched by the more distinctly religious activity of the Reformation period.

Nevertheless, the forces inherent in the Reformation movement were both close enough and strong enough to make lasting changes upon the existing philosophy and practice of education. Protestant concern for the printed Word, both as Bible and as exposition thereof, gave strong impetus to the rising feeling that education could no longer be the prerogative of those with status and was actually to provide the working tools for the reception and the study of a saving gospel by all of God's children. The thesis that Bible and catechism were to be placed in the hands of every Hans and Lisa had the inevitable corollary of universal education.

In addition to these considerations, it should be pointed out that the Protestant definition of the pastoral office with its emphasis on preaching and teaching excludes two other definitions of the minister, that of an unlettered charismatic leader or as a similarly untutored sacramental functionary. The Protestant definition makes it clearly necessary for the church to insist upon an "educated" clergy and to provide arrangements for such education.

As if these considerations were not compelling enough, it is additionally true that all of the theological premises in Protestantism that reduced the gap between "sacred" and "secular" similarly reduced, if they did not completely wipe out, the possibility of any clear distinctions between "religious" and "secular" education.

This apparently gratuitous review of religious and educational developments in past centuries has been invoked chiefly to demonstrate Protestantism's historic stance astride both major streams of contemporary educational practice — that is, public and private, tax supported and independent — as well as its willingness to lend dignity to very different types of schools.

The ecclesiastical origin of most American educational institutions, especially before the founding of the land grant colleges, is well known. Considerably less known and more difficult to delineate are the factors responsible for the diversification of educational practice among the various independent church bodies of America. The rather early transformation of certain denominational colleges into so-called "church-related" institutions and thence into large "private" universities stands in continuing contrast to another movement. This is the persistence of elementary religious education at the parish level and secondary education on the inter-parish level, and the continued maintenance of institutions of higher learning as powerful agents of denominational stabilization and thrust. It can scarcely be denied that for the most part education within the Protestant family has taken the status of rather loose relationship to the formal ecclesiastical organizations which have mothered them, keeping their denominational characteristics largely by virtue of the denominational affiliation of board members and the similar affiliation of supporting congregations and societies.

The many directions of this overall development have massively contributed to the chaos in terminology which practically paralyzes much of the communication in this area of nationwide concern. A large institution of higher learning which has long ago lost its close denominational ties, which makes no attempt whatsoever to speak for the church, which furthermore makes no attempt to serve a constituency which can be denominationally identified, and which is increasingly getting its support not from church sources but from student fees, from large foundations, and from public and quasi-public sources, can obviously no longer be called denominational; it is increasingly becoming doubtful whether it can be called "private."

In contrast to this entire flow of the main stream of American educational practice, there has been a continuing, if smaller, trend toward religious education which continues to define itself as not only "religious," in a vague sense, but as distinctly and honestly kerygmatic and doxological. Included within this trend is the growing movement in Christian elementary schools which have been conducted for many years by such groups as The Lutheran Church—Missouri Synod, the Seventh Day Adventists, and the Dutch Reformed. Not only have these schools survived the many prophecies of their impending demise; their number has increased substantially, and parishes of other denominations, such as the Episcopalians, the Presbyterians, and the Baptists, have entered this field. Although the detractor would be able to point with occasional justification to less than wholly sanctified motives here and there (for example: to avoid integration, to avoid bad public school situations, and even as a status-seeking and status-maintaining device), these institutions of learning are generally associated with a strong concern on the part of church people that their children receive a thorough training in the teachings of the Christian faith.

The general practice is that schools of this nature are operated directly by the congregations and parishes, although deviation from this practice is not uncommon. Occasionally these schools are operated by almost independent associations which are affiliated with their respective churches in much the same way that senior institutions relate themselves rather loosely to their denominational parents. Probably the most persistent debate in the area of the administration of these institutions is the one which revolves around tuition payments. The traditional practice is for the entire parish to bear the total financial burden without imposing any additional cost upon the parents who happen to have children in the school, much as the total population of the school district presumably bears the total cost of education for its school population. A significant minority of these schools, however, is supported partially or totally by tuition payments; in certain localities, these schools can without much effort break even financially.

There is a similar diversity at the secondary school level. The most venerable of these institutions are, of course, the preparatory schools of the East. Like their senior counterparts, most of them have, or had, denominational affiliations, however loose. Anyone who is at all acquainted with the sociology of American religion will not be surprised to note that this affiliation is much more likely to be with the Episcopal church than with any other American denomination. But here, too, there is another end to the spectrum. Certain other churches, mostly conservative, and some even fundamentalistic, have taken it upon themselves to establish Christian secondary schools, either on a parish or inter-parish basis. As one would imagine, instruction in religion is heavily emphasized in such schools, although almost invariably there is also a very real attempt toward academic respectability. There is usually a heavy emphasis on participation in denominational programs, and every effort is made to give the school a distinctly denominational flavor. School loyalty becomes practically identified with denominational loyalty.

The administration of such schools is generally by means of an elected board, which in turn employs the school administrators. The support comes from a combination of congregational contributions or assessments and student fees, which generally are kept reasonable.

If the spectrum of variability in administration and support is broad at the elementary and secondary level, it can be said to cover the whole landscape at the college and university level, mostly because of the history which we have briefly sketched.

It would perhaps be helpful to identify four large clusters. The first cluster consists of the private universities to which we have alluded, which were born out of religious concern, but which presently have lost practically every vestige of such denominational affiliation. The administration and support of these schools is so well known that description is unnecessary.

The second cluster consists of smaller liberal arts colleges, which probably maintain a fairly active denominational affiliation, at least in name and government, but which seek eagerly to deny "denominational narrowness" in their teaching or in their appeal. These schools are very likely to have substantial endowments, wealthy patrons, and loyal alumni. They are likely to be extremely proud of a liberal arts tradition, a tradition which is probably as humanistic as it is religious. But they are also likely to be in financial distress.

A third cluster finds itself at the other end of the scale. This group finds itself intensely interested in religious education and to that end commits itself to a program which is predominantly religious (although probably not *theological,* in the traditional sense). Accreditation, tradition, and *liberal* education constitute low values. Here would be found many, but not all, of the Bible schools and institutes as well as the training schools for many of the lay and semi-professional workers of some of the less traditional and more fundamentalistic church bodies. These are usually under strict denominational control, although not necessarily by the denomination as a corporate body. Many of the church bodies involved in this classification operate their activities through almost autonomous boards and commissions.

The fourth cluster is somewhat more difficult to describe and identify. It would consist of those schools which have a real interest in religious education and are explicitly Christian in their outlook and instruction, but with it carry on an educational program which perpetuates the finest traditions of educational practice. To be particularly specific in the identification of these schools or, for that matter, to put any school into any of the four clusters we have identified, would certainly tend to reflect the bias of the author. This is particularly true inasmuch as he has himself been identified with a program of education which seeks desperately to maintain itself well within this final classification.

In this connection it might be helpful if the author illustrates some of the arrangements for administration and support by citing the scheme of organization which obtains in his own church body, The Lutheran Church—Missouri Synod. This church body divides its concern for the education of its constituents into two large categories, one called parish education, the other called higher education (the latter a long established misnomer for "ministerial" or "professional" education). Parish education naturally covers a wide range of church activity, including such traditional features of parish life as Sunday schools, Bible classes, vacation Bible schools, adult education courses and programs, and family life education. However, also included in this category are the 1,372 parochial schools operated by the affiliated churches of North America. These schools have an enrollment of 154,955 students. There are additionally twenty-one community Lutheran high schools, with a total enrollment of 9,939 students and teaching staff of 491.

Inasmuch as these elementary and high schools are all under parish or inter-parish sponsorship, the denominational and district boards of parish education exercise no direct control over them. These boards are, however, extremely influential in the establishment of school policy and practice through the suasion which they exercise upon administrative boards and officers and by their powerful voice in the placement of personnel. This is particularly true in the instance of the placement of graduates of the church's teachers colleges. The first teaching assignment for most graduates is, as a rule, designated by a College of District Presidents, acting largely upon the advice of district superintendents of parish education, with concurrence of college placement officers.

A different situation obtains in the area of higher education. These schools are obviously not operated or governed by individual parishes, but by the denomination itself. In contrast to the practice obtaining in many denominations, the Missouri Synod retains the practice of owning and operating its own schools for the preparation of the clergy and of parochial school teachers. Furthermore, the church maintains for this purpose schools at three levels: high-school, college, and seminary. There are sixteen of these schools in the United States and Canada: eleven are junior colleges (ten of them with high-school departments), one is a two-year senior college for prepastoral students, two are four-year teachers colleges, and two are seminaries.

The administration of these institutions is strangely dual in character, the duality of the administration, however, emphasizing the single point that the school is definitely under ecclesiastical administration. The two branches of the administrative pattern are the local boards of control, elected by the synod and responsible to it, consisting of pastors, teachers, and laymen, and meeting at least bimonthly. On the other hand is the Board for Higher Education of the central church body itself. This board meets monthly and operates through an executive staff, chiefly for the purpose of coordinating the work and curriculum of the schools and of providing proper disbursement and administration of the synodical subsidy, which in the fiscal year 1963-64 will run to $8,275,000 for operating accounts. In addition, a sizeable amount is provided for capital expenditures on existing and new campuses. The board also exercises a substantial staffing function, insisting on its right to approval of staff appointments.

The local boards of control have a very real and important function with respect to the establishment of budgets, disbursement of funds, and the maintenance of the local program of the respective colleges. However, the precise relationship of the local boards and of the Board for Higher Education to each other and to still another board, namely, the Board of Directors of the synod, is constitutionally a somewhat moot point. Theoretically, neither of the boards is specifically and clearly subordinate to the synodical Board of Directors, since both are responsible only to the synod. However, this Board of Directors has a final voice in the allocation of funds, after budget requests are carefully weighed by the several boards and screened through a process of fiscal review.

The degree of outright support of the entire higher education program by the denomination as a corporate entity far exceeds the proportion which is customary in American church circles and is called by many people a genuinely unique operation. The synod accepts as an outright obligation the payment of all professors' salaries, maintenance of all educational buildings, and initial construction costs of all educational and most auxiliary buildings.

In addition to the educational areas described above, in which the synod as an organization is actively involved, many congregations and individuals within the church provide generous support for Valparaiso University in Valparaiso, Indiana. This growing university (approximately 3,000 students) has been extremely successful in maintaining both the image and full function of a Christian university while at the same time building a solid academic reputation.

Returning now to the general Protestant scene and aware of the complexity and variability of Protestant educational practice, we cannot be very surprised that Protestants have had a hard time coming up with any unanimous responses to certain contemporary educational issues. The issue of federal support for education would certainly be such a case in point. Some Protestants would consider any sort of governmental support of religious education to be inherently immoral; others would consider it a violation of traditional American practice; others would consider it a dangerous step for both church and state; and still others would consider it highly desirable and are hopeful of early actualizing of programs of help. Underneath this spectrum of varied responses lie some rather fundamental issues. These issues may be considered as additional to the basic, formal constitutional issue as well as the one which is circulated *sotto voce* among church politicians, namely, "Which denomination stands to gain the most?"

Among these issues are the following:

1. Is there a legitimate distinction between private and church schools? Certainly not all private schools are, or ever were, church schools, and some that were are hardly that any longer. On the other hand, we have heard an administrative officer of a large university operated by one of the historic orders of the Roman Catholic Church argue that his university was a private university and not a church university, because it was not receiving its support from *diocesan* funds. Is this a legitimate point?

2. May an institution accept governmental funds for the support of one program or department and not for another department on the ground that one is entitled to support and the other one not? Is this closing our eyes to the anonymity of funds and the degree to which they can be shifted around? If the government helps to support the program in science, does this not release additional funds which the school can then spend on its religion department? If the government builds a science building, the college will be better able to build a chapel. The arguments involved here are even more elusive than those, of the last decade, involved in the issue of pupil transportation, free milk, and free textbooks.

3. Would a governmental-subsidy program for private schools but not for church schools tend to cause church schools to deny their religious functions, or to hide it? Currently there are still some distinctly religious schools which are fighting against the tide of teaching only such platitudes as "moral and spiritual values" or "Christian literature" or "ethics" instead of teaching the Christian gospel. Certainly, it is already a problem at many schools as to how an instructor bears witness to his own Christian conviction in non-religion courses without violating the institutional expectations, all af this despite highly touted "academic freedom."

At the moment, Lutheran schools would stand strong in their conviction that they would forfeit any and all support rather than give up any of the following prized adjectives: religious, Christian, denominational, or Lutheran. But it is very likely that the pressure would be on. And the diversity of Protestant educational history and practice would make even the philosophical controversy extremely difficult.

The variety in American Protestant educational philosophy and practice is a direct reflection of American religious pluralism. Certain forces in Protestantism have pulled toward maximum accommodation to the common denominators of American culture. Other forces have pulled in the direction of confessionalism with its attendant separateness and distinctiveness.

It seems to be a safe generalization that educational practice has followed a pattern: the more accommodation, the less denominational control and the greater readiness to assume the characteristics of "public-private" schools; the greater the confessionalism, the greater the denominational control and the greater insistence on a distinctively religious character for the school.

This generalization is not without its exceptions. It will be most interesting to note whether the issues now confronting the "church-related" schools will be met in the ways that have become characteristic of their specific types or whether they are really sufficiently crucial to issue in new responses and a consequent new alignment of the pieces of the total Protestant picture.

HISTORY AND CONTROL OF CATHOLIC SCHOOLS*

Before 1820

In addition to the historical developments toward complexity shared with public schools, the history of Catholic education in the United States supplies a chronology of events unique to the administration of Catholic Schools.

Between 1640 and 1820 were a number of firsts in an era in which relatively few Catholics were to be found in the whole area that has become the United States. It was around 1600 that the first schools within what is now the continental United States were founded by the Spanish Franciscans in Florida and New Mexico. Within the thirteen original colonies, the first Catholic school was established in Maryland in 1640, only five years after the Boston Latin School was founded.

The first religious order of women to teach in the schools of what became the United States were the Ursuline Sisters, who opened a school for girls in New Orleans after arriving from France in 1727. The first parochial Catholic school was St. Mary's School in Philadelphia, a school which was in existence in Philadelphia by 1767, but the tuition-free parish school for boys and girls opened in 1810, at St. Joseph's Parish in Emmitsburg, Maryland, by Mother Seton and her American

*From *American School Administration, Public and Catholic*, by Raymond F. McCoy. Copyright 1961 by McGraw-Hill Book Company. Used by permission of McGraw-Hill Book Company, 27, 29-31, 39-40, 48-50, 112-114.

order, the Sisters of Charity, more fully represents the prototype of today's parochial school. The first Catholic college, Georgetown, was founded in 1789, and the first seminary, that of the Sulpicians in Baltimore, opened in 1791.

1820 to 1884

The period between 1820 and 1884, however, really provided the historical background for the Catholic educational system as we know it today. It was in these years that Catholic religious leaders concluded that if Catholic youth were to receive a Catholic education in the United States, previously thought possible within the framework of public education, it would have to be in schools supported without public funds. It was after a bitter controversy on this subject in NewYork City around 1840 that Bishop John Hughes, vigorous proponent of public support for the eight Catholic schools of his diocese, called for parochial schools everywhere; he himself established thirty-eight new schools in his diocese before his death twenty-three years later.

Successive decrees of four councils of Baltimore, one provincial and three plenary councils, reflected the changing attitudes of the hierarchy, that resulted in the present parochial school system. The First Provincial Council of Baltimore (1829) merely judged it "absolutely necessary that schools should be established in which the young may be taught the principles of faith and morality, while being instructed in letters"; but parish schools were not specified. By 1852, the First Plenary Council of Baltimore exhorted the bishops of the United States to establish schools in connection with all the churches of their dioceses and to support them with the revenues of the parish to which the school was attached. The Second Plenary Council of Baltimore (1866) referred to parochial schools as the only remaining remedy in view of the dangers in Catholic children attending public schools. The Third Plenary Council of Baltimore (1884) definitely ordered the erection of a parochial school near each church within two years unless postponement was allowed for grave reasons by the bishop.

After 1884

From 1884 on, Catholic schools moved toward complexity at an accelerated pace. Diocesan school boards, first instituted on a lasting basis in the Fort Wayne diocese in 1879, were instituted in eight other dioceses by 1900. While the Archdiocese of New York appointed an archdiocesan inspector of schools in 1888, the first superintendent of Catholic schools is credited to Philadelphia in 1894.

As the names of Horace Mann, Henry Barnard, and William T. Harris stand out in the general history of American education, those of three Catholics, all bishops, dominate the history of Catholic education in the United States: Archbishop John Carroll of Baltimore, who lived around the time of the founding of the Republic, and whose zeal for Catholic education led to the establishment of Georgetown College and the first seminary at Baltimore; Archbishop John Hughes of New York, in the second period of Catholic education, who is remembered for his vigorous case for using public funds to support religious schools, and when that battle had been lost, for his devotion to parish schools as the alternative; and Bishop John L. Spalding of Peoria, perhaps the greatest educational figure of them all. . . .

Here in the United States, according to the 1961 *Official Catholic Directory,* the Catholic Church is maintaining 13,294 schools (elementary, secondary, colleges, and universities) with a total enrollment of 5,610,704 students.

The Catholic Church exercises her control over the education of her children through the world-wide organizational structure through which she operates on all matters of concern to her. For the American Catholic, therefore, three sources of Church control of education may be distinguished: the universal control of the Pope and his subordinate policy-making agencies, the local control of the bishop, and the national influence resulting from joint actions of the American hierarchy and the voluntary association of Catholic educators.

THE INTERNATIONAL LEVEL OF CONTROL

All control of the Catholic Church resides in the Pope; thus all control of Catholic schools is in the Pope or flows from him, directly or indirectly. This, of course, is not to say that all problems which arise in running Catholic schools have to be referred to the Pope for decision. For the Pope operates through many executives and policy-making commissions in the direction of Catholic schools. All, however, have authority only as their actions are approved, at least by implication, by the Holy Father himself.

At the international level, or the level of the universal Church, basic policies governing Catholic schools may be found in formal letters issued by the Holy Father himself (commonly in the form of encyclicals or letters addressed to the whole Church); they may be found in canon law, a codified set of 2,414 rules and regulations reissued in 1917; and they may be found in the instructions, decrees, and interpretations of canon law issued by the Roman Curia, the Church's headquarters staff or secretariat. . . .

THE LOCAL CONTROL OF THE BISHOP

In general, the local control of Catholic education in the United States, as of all other Church concerns, resides in the archbishops and bishops of the 140 archdioceses and dioceses of the country.

Thus, policies in education set at the international level are carried on, interpreted, and implemented at the local level by the bishops. This relationship between the Pope and the bishops in the government of the Church is carried out principally through the Consistorial Congregation which is responsible for making periodic surveys of the management of every non-Oriental diocese, Bishops must make a report to the Consistorial Congregation every five years in reply to a highly detailed questionnaire; and they must periodically report by a personal visit to the Pope and the Prefect of the Consistorial Congregation. The Apostolic Delegate to the United States, located in Washington, also serves as a two-way avenue of communication between the international and local levels of Church control.

Clearly, however, only the most basic policies on education and the most general guidelines are set at the international level. The bishops, by virtue of their high office as successors to the apostles and spiritual brothers of the Pope, have the responsibility for implementing, interpreting, and expanding these basic policies in their geographical territories. In the United States, this responsibility belongs to each cardinal, archbishop, and bishop in his own territory or diocese. Within the diocese, all parish schools, diocesan high schools, and diocesan colleges or universities are completely subject to the bishop's authority.

Within a diocese, however, there may be other Catholic schools conducted by certain "exempt" religious orders. These orders are under the authority of the bishop only in teaching faith and morals. They are subject to the religious superiors of their orders who in turn are subject to the authority of the Pope. This authority is ordinarily exercised through the Congregation of Religious, which bears a similar relationship to the superiors of religious orders as that of the Consistorial Congregation to bishops.

Just as the Pope himself is unable to handle personally all details of the administration of the universal Church and so needs the assistance of the Curia, so too the bishop of a large diocese needs legislative and administrative assistance in discharging his many responsibilities.

Within the dioceses of the United States, considerable differences exist in organizational patterns for developing school policies and practices. There is, of course, no variation in the source of authority, the bishop. Greatest differences exist in the roles of diocesan synods, school boards, superintendents of schools, pastors of parishes, and principals of schools. . . .

Diocesan synods, the source of much basic legislation concerning education, are consultative bodies which by canon law must be convened by the bishop at least every ten years. Diocesan wide policies and regulations are considered. The bishop presides at the synod, invitations to which must be issued to key diocesan officials. The bishop, however, is the only legislator in the synod, the rest of the members having only an advisory vote. Even though synods are consultative, the real importance of their role in framing educational legislation is shown in the histories of education within dioceses, published and unpublished, which have been submitted as theses for graduate degrees at many universities.

The individual parochial school in the United States is headed by the pastor of the parish who is the agent of his bishop. He is generally responsible for school construction, finance, and staffing. He secures the principal and as many teachers as are available from one of the religious orders of teaching sisters. Ordinarily the principal becomes responsible for administering the instructional program of the schools. Thus it is through the pastor that the educational policies of an individual bishop are implemented in the approximately 10,000 parish elementary schools of the United States. . . .

THE DIOCESE IN CATHOLIC SCHOOL ADMINISTRATION

If the state is to discharge its responsibility as a civil society for the education of its citizens for their common temporal welfare, Catholic education, as well as all private education, must play a role similar to that of the local public school district in maintaining the standards set for education by the state. The roles differ in that in accordance with the decision in the Oregon case, the Catholic schools exist, not on sufferance of the state, but by a right which follows necessarily from the natural right of parents to choose the kind of education which their children shall have.

The diocese, therefore, bears a similar relationship to the state as the local school district in matters of public educational responsibilities, though in a few concerns—notably in child accounting and enforcement of compulsory attendance laws—it is frequently responsible directly to the local public school district.

A Catholic diocese is a geographical area headed by its ordinary (cardinal, archbishop, or bishop), set up by the Holy See for the administration of Church concerns within that area. For convenience, we are using the term bishop throughout this book as though it were synonymous with the term ordinary of a diocese, since most ordinaries carry the title of bishop. In 1961, there were 140 dioceses in the United States, most of them large enough to be sound administrative units for school administration, this figure contrasts, with the nearly 50,000 local units for administering public schools.

The bishop of a diocese, as a successor to the apostles, is the chief teacher of his diocese. As such, he is ultimately responsible for all diocesan schools within his geographical jurisdiction, and within the limits set by canon law, he has varying degrees of control over private Catholic schools operated by religious orders within his diocese. Traditionally, the pastor of an individual parish is the responsible administrator of the parochial school in that parish. This is the basis for our previous comparison of the organization of parish schools in the United States with the district-unit system in public school administration.

In the United States the extensive and increasingly technical aspects of administering Catholic schools—aspects which the bishops, with their complex duties in the whole spectrum of church administration, could not directly handle and aspects with which individual pastors, with similar broad responsibilities, could not be expected to cope without professional assistance—have caused the institution of two intermediate agencies; the diocesan school board and the diocesan superintendent of schools. The resemblance in title, and increasingly in function, between these two institutions and their counterparts in public education is clear. Yet the differences are basic and must not be overlooked.

The most basic difference follows from the fact that the control of public education is fundamentally in the public itself, but control of diocesan education is fundamentally in the bishop by virtue of his divine office as chief teacher. Consequently, boards of education and their relationships to the superintendents of public schools are established by law; but in Catholic schools, boards of education and their relationships to the superintendents of Catholic schools nowhere figure in canon law; they are the creations of individual bishops in response to the needs of schools. As a result, both institutions are what the individual bishops make them. Their functions are precisely what the bishop may delegate to them.

Nevertheless, the influence of both has been increasing in the past thirty years in response to the growing complexity of problems facing Catholic schools. And increasingly, the role and interrelationships of the diocesan school board come closer to the pattern found most successful in public school administration—with always one exception, however; the power of enacting policy for Catholic schools remains with the bishop himself.

The Parish-District Unit

There is a relationship between the idea of the district-unit system, with both its simplicity and its shortcomings, and the organization of Catholic parochial schools. In the Catholic school system each parochial school has been to a great extent an individual entity, a fact which has militated against anything like the present system-wide organization found in public school administration. It is only in recent times that the office of superintendent of parochial schools has become an office of any stature whatsoever. Even today, the size, scope, and responsibilities of the staff of the superintendent of parochial schools do not begin to compare with those of the staff of a superintendent of public schools when a similar number of schools is involved.

Under the parish system it has been possible, for example, to have a surplus of classrooms in one parish, while in the next there is a shortage. With two different pastors operating the schools and two different religious orders teaching in them, little cooperation between the two schools has been likely.

Because of the strictly parish organization, special education in Catholic schools has not developed to the extent that it has in public schools. If there is a need to conduct a class for slow-learning or for severely maladjusted youngsters in the sixth, seventh, and eighth grades — for example, for girls who are more mature socially than academically—an individual parish school would ordinarily have scarcely enough youngsters of this type to conduct a special class for them. If there were enough such girls in three adjoining parishes, moreover, it would be unusual to organize such a class for the three district school units, for they are headed by independent pastors and probably staffed by three different teaching orders of sisters.

HISTORICAL STRUGGLE TO SEPARATE CHURCH AND STATE BY LAWS*

The purpose of the present bulletin is to summarize the legal status of the so-called "sectarian" issue. The problem has exhibited three phases: (a) the elimination of church control over community schools (particularly acute in the early nineteenth century), (b) the introduc-

---

NEA Research Bulletin, IV (December, 1956), 169-170, 213-214 (by permission).

tion of religious doctrine into the educational program (e.g., Bible reading and released time for religious instruction), and (c) the efforts to obtain aid from public sources for sectarian schools (e.g., grants of money, books, health services, and transportation).

DEEP ROOTS OF THE PROBLEM

Religion and education have been closely associated for many centuries, particularly in the home life of tribes and clans. Education in time became a responsibility shared by the home and by the church or religious leaders. Gradually there emerged "the state" or the centralized authority to which the home, the clan, or group of tribes delegated the administration of certain common interests.

Under a relatively simple social organization the home, the church, and the state were so interrelated that little conflict of function existed. As the state grew in power, it continued for many years to be allied with the church, but two factors operated to break this alliance. One was the struggle between state and church for supremacy in governing the lives of men. The second factor, caused in part by the mobility of people, was the growth of many religious sects within each political area or nation. Friction arose from these closely associated but divergent religious views and eventually resulted in the separation of the organized church and political government.

Although the separation of church and state gained wide acceptance in theory, it is not universally practiced even today. Nor has the theory itself been officially accepted by all sects and religious groups. In this long history of dissension lies at least part of the explanation of legislation, court decisions, and other events in the development of public education in the United States.

AMERICAN BACKGROUND

Most of the early settlers in Americal came from nations where the church and the state were not separated. Strangely enough, in seeking religious freedom for themselves, the settlers in several colonies did not wish to extend it to those with differing religious beliefs. There developed, therefore, within these colonies a union of church and state that made for intolerance and provincialism. During the colonial period, Americans repeated many of the religious and political quarrels of the Old World. Sincere men endured persecution or sometimes even gave their lives for freedom of worship. Equally sincere men used political power to restrict religious freedom and even to persecute those with whom they differed.

In various parts of the world as well as in America, the desirability of separation of church and state became ever more apparent. Men came to realize that they could not live together without general recognition of certain basic human rights. By the time of the Constitutional Convention, since most Americans had agreed upon these individual rights, they were embodied in the Constitution and the first 10 Amendments. Among these rights was freedom of religious worship set forth as follows: "Congress shall make no law respecting an establishment of religion, or prohibiting the free exercise thereof." These words were intended to assure the separation of church and state at the federal level.

While America's public schools trace their beginnings to early church-dominated community schools and to the later charity schools, often under church auspices, they began to emerge as separate institutions early in the nineteenth century. In the older states communities took over private and church schools or established new schools of their own. Church control slowly gave way. In the newer states, public-school systems were built up with little or no competition from the organized churches. Most state constitutions provided for the separation of church and political government and most of them forbade any diversion of public funds from all or at least some sources for sectarian purposes.

One must look to these events in American history to understand many of the specific points in state constitutions, statutes, and judicial decisions affecting public education. . . .

On the basis of state constitutional provisions, statutes, and court decisions, certain points can be stated as generally true. For example,

1. All states guarantee religious liberty to a greater or lesser degree.
2. Most states prohibit use of religious tests as qualifications for holding public office; a few states prohibit discrimination on the basis of religion in the employment of teachers.
3. Compulsory support of places of public worship is universally unconstitutional; the prohibition against compulsory support of sectarian education is widespread but not universal except by implication.
4. Differences in language of constitutional and statutory provisions rarely result in differences in application of the language in specific instances.
5. A tax levied for the benefit of a sectarian school is unconstitutional in all states; use of *nonschool* revenue for *direct* aid to sectarian education is unconstitutional also. But courts of the

several states differ with regard to indirect aid—the crux being what is and what is not indirect aid. Indirect aid is usually held valid only when the relationship between the public treasury and the recipients is so distant that the court can say that actually no aid is provided.

6. In a few states use of public-school equipment which in its general terms could be applicable to pupils attending sectarian schools as well as to those attending the public schools, or specific authorization to this effect, has been upheld under the chief-benefit theory or under the police power of the state or as a matter of policy. But the majority of states have not so held.

7. Public and parochial schools cannot be combined legally. However, a public school can be maintained in a parochial-school building if the board of education retains control of the school and no religious tenets are taught therein.

8. Payment of rent to a church for the use of its building as a public school is usually not considered aid to the church if the local school-board acts under permissive legislation empowering it to rent school facilities. However, even in the face of such permissive legislation, such action would be invalid if the public-school authorities do not maintain control of the public school conducted in the church-owned building, even if religious education is eliminated from the curriculum.

9. Most states exclude sectarianism from the public schools at least to the extent that no particular religious tenets may be taught therein. Moral education can exist in the public schools, and to this end many legislatures have required or permitted the reading of the Bible. Most courts have held that the Bible is not a sectarian book. Two minority views, held by courts in several states, are (a) that reading of the Bible in the public schools is a violation of the religious liberty of non-Christians and unconstitutional for that reason; and (b) that reading either the Protestant or the Catholic version of the Bible offends the religious liberty of the other group as well as of those who do not follow either version.

10. Public-school teachers may wear religious dress and insignia unless there is a law or regulation against the practice. The state, however, has power to enact prohibitory legislation, and such enactment is not a denial of religious liberty but merely the control of the state over its public servants.

11. Public-school pupils may be excused from school during school hours to attend religious instruction elsewhere, provided (a)

public funds are not used in carrying out the plan, (b) no pupil is compelled to attend an exercise against his conscience, and (c) the board of education does not exercise control. When such classes are held on public-school premises during school hours, the practice is unconstitutional.

12. Church groups may use public-school buildings and facilities after school hours, in some states even for religious meetings. This situation has been held not to violate the constitutional separation of church and state.

13. General legislation authorizing the state to supply free text-books to pupils attending both public schools and sectarian schools has seldom been attempted by legislatures and rarely tested by the courts. The Supreme Court of the United States has upheld the practice; the books being furnished to children and not to sectarian schools.

14. The Supreme Court of the United States has held that transportation of parochial-school pupils at public expense does not violate the First Amendment to the federal Constitution. However, most state courts have held that this practice violates state constitutional provisions prohibiting use of public or public-school funds for sectarian education.

15. The state, under its police power, may regulate and supervise sectarian schools for the purpose of ensuring each child an education equivalent to the education offered in public schools. State statutes have not attempted to go beyond the state's police power (i.e., the state's power to safeguard the health, morals, and safety of its citizens).

These principles have not been tested judicially in all states. On an issue not previously tested in a particular state, the court would consider the general principles, as well as the majority and minority views of other state courts, but would not be bound by decisions of other states and would render its decision in terms of its own state law and the facts of the particular case.

Several of the Southern states have amended their constitutions and school laws to provide for the operation of a pupil assignment or a private-school plan with the avowed purpose of continuing segregated schools. In all such proposals, no action that has been taken appears to lead to state aid for sectarian schools. However, if these plans are actually put into operation, direct or indirect aid to sectarian education looms on the horizon as a possibility. The current controversy may change from one on segregation under the Fourteenth Amendment to one on separation of church and state under the First Amendment.

THE STATE'S RELATIONSHIPS TO NON-PUBLIC SCHOOLS*

A larger and larger share of American youth are being educated in nonpublic elementary and secondary schools. The Office of Education estimates indicate that, if trends continue, by 1965 the nonpublic schools will enroll 6,840,000, or 14.6 percent of all students in elementary and secondary schools. This will be an enrollment ratio of 1 to 6 as compared with 1 to 11 in 1899-1900 and 1 to 7 in 1953-54.

During the past quarter century, nonpublic colleges and universities have accounted for approximately 1 out of every 2 resident students in institutions of higher learning. These nonpublic enrollments increased from 571,949 in 1931-32 to 1,158,231 in 1953-54.

BASIC RIGHTS

The authors elaborate on two decisions of the Supreme Court of the United States particularly pertinent in defining and upholding the basic rights of nonpublic schools. The Dartmouth case and the Oregon case.

The Dartmouth College case grew out of an act passed in 1816 by the legislature of New Hampshire which would have voided the original charter of the college and created a new corporation of public character. In its decision, the Supreme Court of the United States upheld the right of an educational institution to exist as a private corporation.

The Oregon case grew out of an initiative measure adopted by the people of Oregon, requiring parents and others having control of children subject to compulsory attendance provisions of the law to send such children to public schools. Two corporations owning and conducting schools in Oregon—The Society of Sisters and Hill Military Academy— sought to restrain State officials from enforcing the measure. The Court, deciding in favor of the corporations, held that it was an unreasonable interference with the liberty of parents and guardians. In making the decision, however, the Court pointed out that "No question is raised concerning the power of the State reasonably to regulate all schools, to

---

*Fred F. Beach, and Robert F. Will, "The State and Nonpublic Schools," *School Life*, XL (February, 1958), 13-14.

inspect, supervise and examine them, their teachers and pupils; to require that all children of proper age attend some school, that teachers shall be of good moral character and patriotic disposition, that certain studies plainly essential to good citizenship must be taught, and that nothing be taught which is manifestly inimical to the public welfare."

STATE REGULATION THROUGH GENERAL LEGISLATION

Since the powers not delegated to the United States under the 10th amendment of the Constitution are reserved to the several States, each State has developed a large body of laws to regulate and supervise schools, both public and nonpublic. The authors note that such laws may be general in nature or explicit.

Laws that apply *generally* to non-public schools are those which regulate the activities of individuals and organizations conducting businesses or charitable undertakings within the State. Under the powers and duties delegated by these laws, numerous administrative agencies of the State have direct or indirect regulatory responsibilities for nonpublic schools. For instance, nonpublic schools conducted within buildings are subject to State regulation and supervision through agencies responsible for enforcing building codes, fire regulations, health and sanitation codes, and other codes and regulations pertaining to buildings; nonpublic schools employing workers are subject to regulation as employers of labor; and nonpublic schools that board and care for children are subject to regulation by agencies responsible for the general welfare of children.

STATE REGULATION THROUGH EXPLICIT LEGISLATION

These general laws, however, do not treat nonpublic schools as educational institutions and thus do not serve to accomplish one of the fundamental objectives of the State: insuring an educated citizenry. To achieve this objective, States have established regulations that apply *explicitly* to nonpublic schools as educational institutions. By far the largest number of these laws involve responsibilities of State departments of education.

The authors identify certain common areas of explicit legislation under which nonpublic schools are regulated as educational institutions: (1) Incorporation, (2) State approval of institutions, (3) compulsory education, (4) public support, (5) tax exemptions, and (6) occupational licensing.

Incorporation

The State may require approval or grant approval upon request. through its system of incorporation. The act of incorporation brings the nonpublic school under legislative regulation designed to facilitate self-government. With the powers granted, there are concomitant responsibilities for reporting and for meeting other requirements of the law.

State approval of institutions

The State may require approval or grant approval upon request. Legislation requiring approval, which applies most frequently to private trade and business schools and to private institutions of higher learning conferring degrees does not permit the institution to operate or conduct certain educational activities until it obtains approval. Only a few States have laws that explicitly require approval for schools serving children of compulsory school age.

In many instances, the law provides for granting approval upon request. Institutions that submit voluntarily to State regulation and supervision do so for the advantages official approval affords; for example, private institutions preparing teachers for public schools desire official approval so that their graduates can be licensed or certified under the same conditions as graduates from public teacher-training institutions.

Compulsory education

Legislation for compulsory education is the cornerstone of the State's plan to insure an educated citizenry, for its goal is to provide a basic minimum education for every educable child regardless of the school he attends. Under such legislation States may make express requirements of nonpublic schools: To keep records and make any reports that are needed to establish evidence that children are attending school in compliance with the law; to remain in session for a term that compares favorably with the term prescribed for the public schools; and to provide educational programs that compare favorable with the programs required in public schools.

Public support

Public funds and services are authorized by statute in a number of States to nonpublic schools and/or children and youth attending nonpublic schools. The statutes provide for payments for operation of a school, program, or project: payments for instruction, care, and other services; buildings; scholarships and tuition allowances; textbooks; health and welfare services. When public funds and services are thus authorized, the law generally includes regulatory provisions.

Tax exemption

A state may use tax exemption as a device to regulate educational institutions. The clearest example is found in the laws of Rhode Island, which say that any school receiving aid from the State either by direct grant or by exemption from taxation, is subject to examination by a State educational agency. By refusing to comply with the law a school may be denied exemption from taxation.

Occupational licensing

Persons seeking to practice certain occupations in a State must receive official approval to do so, usually in the form of a license. Authority to approve is usually delegated to boards established by law, and to these boards may be delegated also the responsibilities for certifying or approving the schools or programs that train applicants for licensure. Professional and trade schools voluntarily seek approval so that they may provide suitable candidates.

FINANCING NON-PUBLIC SCHOOLS . . .

FINANCING DIOCESAN SCHOOLS*

With the ever-accelerating growth of Catholic schools in the United States has come an ever-increasing problem of financing these schools. All the developments along the route to an inevitably more complex administration of modern schools take more money. The most significant increase in expenditure for Catholic schools, now and in the years ahead, must be for salaries for lay teachers. As the trend is now established, by 1970 the number of lay teachers in parish schools throughout the United States should exceed the number of sisters; and the cost

*From *American School Administration, Public and Catholic,* by Raymond F. McCoy. Copyright 1961 by McGraw-Hill Book Company. Used by permission of McGraw-Hill Book Company, 316-317.

of one lay teacher at a maximum salary in a public school (the standard of competition) frequently exceeds the cost of an equally qualified sister in a comparable diocese by a ratio of 9 to 1. Even at minimum salaries substantially inferior to those paid in public schools, five sisters (if available) could be supported for the cost of one lay teacher.

As has been pointed out repeatedly in previous chapters, Catholic school administration has been traditionally decentralized. In the financing of the parish school, each parish has been for all practical purposes, a "district unit." The pastor has been responsible for financing the parish school; he generally has depended upon monthly or weekly collections for school support supplemented by other workable means for raising money including income from parish socials, festi als, and paper drives. In some dioceses, a modest tuition has been collected from the parents who could afford to pay it.

With the growth of centralized diocesan high schools in this century, the costs of conducting these schools have generally been shared by the feeder parishes themselves and by the parents through tuitions. Specifically, in one diocese in 1959-1960, tuition of $90 per year for each pupil was charged; $45 was contributed by the parish to which the youth belonged and $45 by the parents of the youth. At the same time the cost per pupil for one youngster in the neighboring public high schools was about $400 per year.

The diocesan office of the superintendent of school has, typically, not been involved with problems of school finance. It has been sufficiently occupied with the problem of securing adequate finances to conduct its own educational services at a minimum level. The superintendent of one diocesan school system in a large metropolitan area, when he was assigned to his position some years ago, was allotted a sum of $500 on which to perform his functions for a year. Currently the beginnings of a diocesan-wide school financing program are to be seen in those dioceses assessing parish schools 25 or 50 cents per pupil for the support of the office of the superintendent.

As diocesan school systems are forced by the complexity of today's problems to greater centralization of school administration, and as the costs of running diocesan schools continue to soar, the unequal distribution of financial resources among parishes will make itself even more apparent. Just as in public school districts the problem of financing adequate education in relatively impoverished districts forced a solution in the form of state-foundation programs, so the problem of financing adequate Catholic education in relatively impoverished parishes is increasingly demanding a solution.

THE ADMINISTRATION AND FINANCING
OF CATHOLIC SCHOOLS*

This nation's 43.8 million Catholics spend approximately $2.3 billion each year to educate 5.7 million students in their 13,686 Catholic schools.

Why do they do it?

How do they do it?

Much has been written about the goals of Catholic education. Stated quite simply, the overall aim is to implant in the young the ideas, attitudes, and habits that will enable them to live Christ-like lives in our American democratic society. But this broad, all-encompassing definition includes many things.

On the nonreligious plane, Catholic education strives to produce physically fit young men and women with a high degree of:

—*economic literacy,* or an understanding of the workings of modern industrial civilization, with a keen awareness of the importance of interdependence and the value of work;

—*social virtue,* which includes a thorough comprehension of American life, the workings of democracy, and the realization that sacrifices of self-interest to achieve peace and unity are an integral part of life in the give and take of society today;

—*cultural development,* accenting the beauty that man has created in his literature, music, and art, and forming a taste for finer things that will banish the vulgar, lewd, and decadent.

If these goals were the end-all of Catholic education, there would be no need for Catholic schools, for certainly they also are the aim of America's public schools. But for Catholics there are other desirables in education too—the religious goals—and these, they feel, are of the utmost importance.

Now, how does the Catholic Church go about its educational task? Since the administration and financing of grade and high schools seems to be the greatest stumbling block to an understanding of the Catholic school system, perhaps it would be best to put the emphasis on these.

Modern school organization is so complex that orderly administra-

---

*Msgr. William E. McManus, "The Administration and Financing of Catholic Schools," by permission of *Phi Delta Kappan,* XLV (December, 1963), 132-135.

tion demands a clear-cut division of responsibility. In the Catholic system, the top officials in the administrative pyramid of each diocese are, in order, the bishop, the diocesan superintendent, the Catholic school board, pastors, and principals.

The bishop is the highest and central authority. However, in most cases the bishop acts in his capacity of leader through the qualified professional educator whom he appoints as diocesan school superintendent.

The superintendent reports directly to the bishop and, where one is organized, to the Catholic school board. This board usually is composed of diocesan priests, men and women of religious communities teaching in the diocese, and, more often in recent years, a diocese's foremost lay leaders in education.

Each pastor functions as the agent for the diocese in managing his own school; for each parish, like the local school district in the public school system, is responsible for building and operating its own school.

The pastor engages the faculty for his parish school (or schools), collects parish funds for operational expenses, supervises maintenance, and plans expansion. Although he is head of the school by reason of his pastoral title, he does not enter directly into day-by-day academic administration. This is the responsibility of the principal.

The bishop has full authority over the teaching communities that are diocesan in origin; he also of necessity has amicable relationships with the nondiocesan communities working in his docese. However, the heads of the varous religious orders teaching in the schools appoint their principals.

Working closely with the bishop, the school superintendent, the board, pastors, and principals jointly consider the professional problems which are the core of school organization and administration.

These problems range from establishing the school calendar, budget, and salary schedules to compliance with state school codes, city ordinances, and regulations of school accrediting associations. The problems are complex and seemingly endless. Proposals for their solution more often than not stem from the planning carried on by the bishop, his superintendent, and the school board.

In any discussion of the financing of the Catholic school system, the current issue of federal aid for nonpublic schools must be kept in mind. There are also four key facts which our government — for the people, all the people — must consider as it adjusts its laws to the educational realities of our days. These facts are:

    1. Catholic schools are here to stay. The Catholic Church is firmly committed to build and operate them. Parents have a right, not a mere privilege, to enroll their children in Catholic schools.

2. Catholic schools perform a public service by preparing young people for their civic responsibilities. It is no less a service or no less public because it is performed under religious auspices.

3. In many localities Catholic schools are an indispensable part of the educational enterprise. This is especially true in our large metropolitan areas; the cities and their suburbs need the Catholic schools. Enrollment figures for 1960 show that 5,253,791 pupils attended Catholic elementary and secondary schools; the total for the public schools was 36,086,771. (Today, of the 2,747,476 youngsters in Illinois grade and high schools, 495,229 — 18 per cent, or almost one out of five — study in Catholic schools.)

4. Catholic schools need and deserve some kind of tax aid to continue the high-quality education which not only their patrons but the whole civic community want and need.

The tremendous growth of the nation's student body in the last twenty-five years is well known. In fact, it brought on the federal school aid controversy. A few figures will underscore the magnitude of the growth and the problems it presented.

From 1940 to 1960, public grade and high school enrollment rose 42 per cent, from 25,434,000 to 36,086,771. In those same twenty years, Catholic school enrollment jumped 219 per cent, from 2,396,000 to 5,253,791. This means that for every ten pupils in public schools in 1940, there were fourteen in 1960. And for every ten pupils in Catholic schools in 1940, there were twenty-two in 1960.

What this expansion has cost — and continues to cost as enrollment keeps rising — can only be reckoned in the millions of dollars. It has meant more schools, additional classrooms for existing schools, new equipment, and more teachers.

The prime sources of funds to maintain a Catholic school are tuition and the Sunday church collection. To fully realize what this means, let's take a look at the budget of a typical Chicago area Catholic parish grade school. We'll call it St. Mary's, where 700 pupils are instructed by ten nuns and six lay teachers, a pupil-teacher ratio of nearly 44:1.

The parishioners of St. Mary's have invested over half a million dollars in their school building and $150,000 in the sisters' convent. During the last three years they also have spent $37,000 for an automatic sprinkler system, fire alarm bells, remodeling of four classrooms, 400 new desks, and a complete paint job. Another $8,000 were spent for new equipment and painting in the convent.

Now, how much will it cost to operate the school for the next year? These are the estimates:

Salaries (lay teachers, $21,600; nuns, $10,000) ....$ 31,600
Utilities (heat, light, gas, phone) 9,000
Maintenance (janitors' salaries, supplies, etc.) 11,000
Convent expenses 4,200
Repairs 4,000
Insurance 1,200
Instructional supplies 1,900
Interest on $400,000 school and convent debt 18,000
Reduction of debt 30,000

Total expenses $110,900

Where is all this money coming from?

Based on past experience, the pastor and people of St. Mary's can figure on about $25,000 from tuition. The balance, about $86,000, will have to be paid from parish revenue, e.g., Sunday collections, special events, etc.

To this educational bill, the parish must add $10,000 for the Archdiocesan High School Expansion fund (inaugurated to provide 22,000 additional high school seats at a cost of $40 million in five years), $4,500 for the archdiocese's seminaries, and $5,000 to help the sisters build an infirmary for their old and infirm nuns.

St. Mary's parishioners also can expect to pay an additional $20 per child for books, supplies, tests, etc. That figure multiplied by 700 adds up to another $14,000 a year for Catholic education.

Add all these figures and the total comes to an astonishing $144,400 which the people of our typical St. Mary's parish will pay in one year to educate their 700 children in the parish grade school. And that total does not even include what some parents will pay in tuition and fees to send their children to Catholic high schools and colleges.

WHY TAXES SHOULD NOT GO TO SECTARIAN SCHOOLS*

The struggle to secure funds for public schools points up clearly what could happen again, should the principle of compulsory taxation for public schools be abandoned. Early ventures show that a tuition system for the support of schools is not sound in a democratic community. It

---

*Donald Ross Green and Warren E. Gauerke, "If the Schools Are Closed," Atlanta: Southern Regional Council, 1959, 34-35.

need but be remembered that the low standards of the public schools in the early period of our history were pointed to as excuses for establishing private schools financed by tuition payment rather than taxes.

Since state abandonment of education is being contemplated in some quarters, the question of use of the taxing right is a basic one. It would seem to be clear that there is no power to tax for an object not within the purposes for which governments have committed themselves. So, it would seem that the principle of tax support for public schools would have to go by the board in some communities should public school doors be shut.

It must be remembered that taxes paid by individuals during the period when their children are in public school seldom, if ever, cover all costs of education. Taxes, however, are collected with regularity throughout one's working life. Over a lifetime, then, most families actually pay the full cost of the education of their children through their tax dollars. The couple with no children and the retired persons have grown accustomed to paying their school taxes as their share of the cost of public education. Just like "breathing out and breathing in," they have learned that it is good business to pay school taxes. Would not the inauguration of a private system of education, not supported by tax payments, get such persons quickly out of this regular and persistent habit?

Lawmaking bodies have been most cautious in implementing the principle of tax support for public schools. Hard-won gains ought not be bargained away. The long uphill fight for public school support seems to demonstrate that the important base is taxation by the state and that sources of state support should be broadened, not curtailed.

STATE AND CHURCH SEPARATION

A fifth principle is this: Public funds and property must be appropriated or used solely for the benefit of public schools, not for the aid or benefit of any private or sectarian school. This principle is consistent and accords with long established constitutional provisions.

The problem of support for private schools without question includes parochial schools. This consideration involves the principle of separation of church from the state. During a part of the nineteenth century it was not uncommon to aid private schools on the same basis as state schools. However, the battle to cease dividing school funds was supposedly won almost a century ago.

In most public schools education is now nonsectarian in nature. In other words, no one religious creed is taught regularly to all pupils as a matter of official policy. There seems to be little assurance from private school enthusiasts, however, that the tendency in a small number of schools to advocate openly a particular brand of Protestantism may not develop into a marked trend.

The argument runs that aid does not breach the wall between church and state. It must be remembered that attendance at a private school is a matter of choice where child and parent abide by the requirements of the curriculum, often including sectarian teachings. The essence of the sectarian position is that religious-oriented private schools are actually public in every sense but two. One exception is that the education offered is not wholly secularized. The second is that the schools are under only partial state supervision. Neither of these two distinguishing characteristics, it is contended, are true disqualifications barring aid in some just and proportional share. Are these protest schools not legitimate expressions of parental rights?

Those fearful of breaching the wall, however, raise different arguments. They insist that Americans have established their own system of public education free from church control. The contentions of opponents — that aid to private church-related schools in other countries has not produced an alliance there between the state and church — are denied. The aversion of these critics to even indirect aid is marked. To protect both church and state, no financial support must be given to those schools which have the avowed purpose of perpetuating one particular dogma and creed.

Questions regarding public tax support for the operation of private schools cannot be discussed without provoking such religious biases. This is surely unwise. State control over education came when state dollars went to schools. Financial aid to private schools would necessitate a complete re-consideration of the thinking about church and state which has crystallized over the past century.

HOW AND WHY TAX MONEY SHOULD GO TO PRIVATE SCHOOLS*

Among obstacles making the task of the public schools in the United States truly herculean are the inexorable leveling and centralizing tendencies so characteristic of our time. Though some observers regard these tendencies as necessary for strong education, I am convinced that

*Winfield S. Fountain, "A Plea for Public Support of Pluralism in America," by permission of *Phi Delta Kappan,* XLIV (June, 1963), 415-418.

they narrow the ability of the public schools to do all they want and need to do.

Involved in this centralization process are such factors as the emergence of well-organized special interest groups that cause the schools to follow a middle course; the accreditation of teacher preparation institutions by national agencies; the rise of national television; the consolidation of textbook publication; the high population mobility; the NDEA and NSF programs; and the straitening of curricula resulting from restrictive state legislation and United States Supreme Court decisions. I believe, therefore, that a sound alternative to public education is needed more than ever before, both for the welfare of the nation and for the integrity of the public school.

Such a conclusion stems from the conviction that the challenges which face us as a nation are closely related to the importance of keeping the United States a strong, responsible, and viable democracy. I believe further that such strength, responsibility, and viability are spawned in an open society, bound together in unity of ultimate national purpose, but nurtured on diversity of view, willingness to try the new, and courage to exceed the norm. It is the thesis of this article that a pluralistic education system is essential to this type of "national liveliness." This system must encompass both the public and independent schools, and the latter should include both denominational and non-denominational schools. In fact, we should have available in the United States adequately organized schools that will teach, live, and experiment with every serious point of view espoused by a significant portion of our people. I hold that such a development would be more than just a manifestation of individual rights or distributive justice; it is in the best interests of the national welfare that a strong, pluralistic system of education be encouraged. If this point of view is valid, then there is a basis for contending that such a system warrants and needs the financial encouragement of our government. . . .

The eight questions posed here are sincere questions honestly asked by people who have devoted their careers to the cause of public education. I hope that my answers will allay some of the usual fears and assuage some of the old irritations.

Is it not true that independent schools operate primarily for private reasons? It is true that independent schools have specialized purposes. It is true that the denominational schools among these feel obligated to develop students who will become adults strongly committed to their individual faiths. On the other hand, all responsible American groups who operate their own independent schools should be devoted to the rights of the individual and should respect lawful authority and the supremacy of the democratic process. Only such responsible groups should be chartered for the operation of a school.

Does not the existence of independent schools create a destructively divisive force in American life? It is true that the existence of a pluralistic system of education will build loyalties to certain institutions and confidences in certain programs of instruction and will create some competitive elements among the various types of schools. As long as such loyalties, confidences, and competitive elements are constructive, as they must be, there is no reason for alarm.

As one ponders the role of loyal opposition fulfilled by our political parties, by labor and management, by our churches, and by our various special interest organizations, it is apparent that constructive divisibility and disagreement are necessary parts of our democracy.

Of course, it is true that in regions of our country where significant numbers of children attend independent schools there has been considerable feeling engendered and opposition manifested by independent school patrons at the time of public school levy elections. Regardless of what the situation was fifty years ago, we are in an era of increasingly more inter-religious understanding, and this periodic "school levy complex" (not universal, by any means) should not be construed as a basic hostility toward public schools but rather as a fear on the part of the independent school patron that the "rich will get richer" and the "poor will get poorer." The suggestions that follow in the context of a later question cited here are aimed at ameliorating this situation.

Finally, some who contemplate the children enrolled in the independent schools become concerned that the differences in dress, schedules, and curricula are in some vague way inimical to the best interests of our country. However, one should search beyond childhood to determine the effect of these schools. As one looks at the constituency of our business and industrial management, at the military establishment in time of war and peace, at our local, state, and national government leadership, and at our communities in general there is little evidence of a destructive, un-American divisiveness emanating from the existence of these independent schools, as some of the critics have warned. However, there is evidence of healthy differences of opinion and loyalties to principle arising from these schools. These differences provide the checks and balances a democracy needs.

Wouldn't public support of denominationally sponsored schools encourage the establishment of a state religion? Denominational schools that have sound, effective programs should be successful in inspiring considerable appreciation and conviction regarding their denominations. In this time of greater religious understanding, we would expect the religiously oriented citizen to be a better American because his faith should teach him greater tolerance for those who believe differently than he does and should imbue him with greater love for his country as well as his God.

As to the part financial assistance would play, one can find the corollary in the charitable deductions allowed the church-going taxpayer and the tax exemptions allowed individual churches. Here is financial assistance in large amounts justifiably made available to our churches because of the key role they occupy in American life. The establishment of a state religion has not resulted, though there is considerable difference in the sizes of our churches and the amount of deductions and exemptions claimed. It is hardly believable that financial support to independent schools even more indirectly rendered and in a smaller amount than is presently allowed our churches, would create a situation contrary to the firm expression of the American people.

Independent schools educated only one in every fourteen elementary and secondary school students at the beginning of this century. Today they educate nearly one in every six. They have realized this growth without public assistance. Why is such assistance necessary now? This growth has been most noticeable at the elementary school level where the cost is least. Growth has been less in the secondary school and a diminishing proportion of our total college population is being prepared by our independent institutions. In nearly every case there are waiting lists of students desiring to attend all levels and all types of independent institutions, for facilities and teachers are not available. It is unfortunate that school costs have increased much more than the growth in enrollment, although such increase is readily understandable.

There are few well-endowed independent schools today of the type patronized only by the wealthy classes mainly interested in an exclusive, finishing-type education for their children. Most of our independent schools are patronized by average Americans who have just as much difficulty in paying taxes as the rest of us. In many of our independent colleges one-third to one-half of the students pay most or all of their individual higher education bills.

Herein, then, lies the dilemma facing all of the independent schools, elementary through college (although my remarks here deal primarily with elementary and secondary schools): Should these schools continue to crowd their already inadequate facilities so as to keep alive the right to free choice in education and thereby do less educationally than they wish to do? Or should they restrict their numbers in an attempt to meet the ever-increasing costs of highly technical and complex education and thereby gradually phase themselves out as a significant factor in national life?

Herein, also, lies the dilemma facing the parent who desires an independent school education for his child (and, incidentally, one real cause of the controversy plaguing federal aid to education legislation): How can he pay the taxes necessary to support improvements in the public schools which are a citizen's obligation and at the same time pay for the constantly increasing costs his independent schools are encountering? He is likely to reason that he has an impossible choice and end up maintaining the status quo, wherein he neither improves nor impoverishes either type of education.

Finally, herein lies a dilemma facing Americans generally: Have we fulfilled our responsibility by merely insuring the independent school's right to exist, if in denying some type of public support we guarantee poorly educated graduates from these institutions? Are these children of less concern to us than the children who emerge from inadequately supported public schools?

Is it not true that all these independent schools wish to do is to get their "foot in the door" so that they can be instrumental in dismembering and downgrading the public school system? Responsible independent school educators and patrons know and respect the contributions public education has made to our nation and realize that there could be no true universality of American education without the existence of a well-organized and well-financed public school system. Those who would weaken the public schools would be guilty of a disservice to the nation.

They recognize that, in addition to its customary school program, the public school must continue to provide most of the special education, adult re-training, adult education, specialized vocational education, and community service programs. Furthermore, most Americans prefer a public school education for their children.

The above question often is prompted by the concern arising from the downgrading of public schools in certain countries of western Europe which have given financial assistance to independent schools. Several basic differences should be noted, however, between the situation in western Europe and the plan I shall suggest for the United States.

First of all, the public education program of these small countries (e.g., The Netherlands) never was as strongly established, fully developed, or universally applied. Countries such as Canada and England, which have well established public school systems, have not seen these schools undermined by the granting of assistance to independent schools, even in a much more direct manner than I recommend.

Secondly, I do not suggest that our government finance either the organization of a school program during the developmental years prior to its reaching stability or the building construction program at any time.

Thirdly, I suggest no direct support to the school.

Finally, the element of personal financial sacrifice inherent in these suggestions would tend to discourage irresponsible spawning of independent schools.

A reasonable estimate, based on the inclusion of children belonging to our religious groups who believe that spiritual and temporal education must be integrated in the school (in contra-distinction to those who believe private study of the Bible is sufficient), plus the doubling of the present non-denominational independent school enrollment, indicate that the public elementary and secondary schools would still have responsibility for educating three out of four American children. This ratio of three to one in our elementary and secondary schools will provide a healthy partnership in American education.

Would not the independent school's freedom to be different, which is the justification claimed for their existence by this article, be hampered by the seeking and utilization of public funds? This is an understandable assumption. Taxpayers have a right to a strict accounting and some expenditure control when they are being asked to provide money for any governmental or quasi-governmental activity. Furthermore, there has been so much feeling aroused recently regarding this type of direct assistance that all types of schools, public and independent, have been hampered in their quest for much-needed funds.

I believe, therefore, that financial support given to the independent schools should be of an indirect nature. Such a plan, to be in the best interests of the citizenry as a whole, should be equitable and should retain an element of sacrifice in return for the privilege of having independent schools. I would suggest that parents who send their children to accredited independent schools be allowed a federal tax credit (which in some cases would become a reimbursement allowance) of 75 per cent of the tuition actually paid to the school. The maximum allowance would be 75 per cent of the average amount being expended for the public schools in the United States for that particular year and for the applicable level of instruction, whether it be elementary, junior high school, or senior high school.

For example, let it be assumed that the average cost of educating an elementary school pupil in the public schools for this year is $400. If a parent is paying $200 tuition to send his child to an independent elementary school, he would be eligible to claim $150. If the parent pays $400 tuition at this school, he could claim a $300 tax credit. On the other hand, if the parent were paying $1,200 tuition, he still could claim only the maximum for this particular year, $300.

In this way each patron of the independent schools would be bearing part of the cost of his own school as well as continuing to assist with the support of the public schools. At the same time, ability to pay large tuition payments would not be rewarded at the expense of the general taxpayer.

Inherent in this plan would be the incentive to increase tuition payments to the independent schools so that these schools would be financed on an approximate parity with the public schools. Also, it will be noted that the patron of the independent school would be more likely to support a necessary increase in the cost of operating the public schools, since such an increase could be reflected eventually in his own credit allowance.

It is primarily upon this point that hope rests for a sound basis of future harmony and understanding among the patrons of the various types of American schools.

Even though no money is being appropriated directly to the independent school, shouldn't there be public concern for any considerable unevenness among independent schools? Since all students, whether educated in public or independent schools, are expected to spend the greater portion of their lives fulfilling the responsibilities of citizenship, there is rightfully a public vested interest in each school.

We hold in our country that every school, regardless of its auspices, must provide those common learnings essential to the furtherance of our democracy. We have legal provisions that relate to the safety and health of the student, the length of the school year, and the adequacy of the preparation of our teachers. We also have established generally recognized standards concerning the size of schools necessary to offer a comprehensive program of studies.

These are necessary standards, laws, and regulations, but they need not be so restrictive that the independent school is precluded from having ample flexibility in determining how these common learnings will be taught, what additional subjects will be offered, what personal values will be imbued, and what experiments will be conducted.

It can be seen that the concept of an accredited independent school recommended here is a well-established, well-organized school which has been approved by appropriate public authority. A tangible evidence of this accreditation would be the according to the approved school of an ample supply of validating tax credit certificates. The school would use these to certify the amount of tuition paid by the parent, who in turn would forward the tax credit certificate to the federal government along with his income tax report form.

Finally, if such an official recognition and encouragement of a pluralistic system of education came to pass, wouldn't there be a lessening of the professional solidarity toward which teachers are striving? It is anticipated that the contrary would be true. Many lingering suspicions and hostilities would be reduced once the traditional opposition revolving around financial support has been relieved. There would be an increased interest in and understanding of the problems and strengths peculiar to each of the various types of schools.

A greater parity of salaries, facilities, class loads, teacher preparation, and teacher improvement could be expected. Discussions regarding parent and student rights and obligations, school responsibilities, professional practices, and ethical conduct should be more fruitful and open than ever before.

There should be no lessening of the numbers of teachers needed, of the competencies required, or of the gains in social and economic status to which teachers aspire. In fact, there probably would be an increased need for teachers. With the new choices of educational system available to aspiring teachers, along with the assurances of proper compensation, it is highly possible that competencies could be recruited and retained that are not presently available to our schools.

The greatest gain to the profession and to our nation, however, would be the emergence of an educational partnership which could produce ideas, methods, action, harmony, and cooperation befitting the true American democratic ideal.

PUBLIC TAXES FOR NON-PUBLIC SCHOOLS — IS IT IN THE INTEREST OF PUBLIC POLICY?*

Some Catholic leaders contend that parochial schools serve a public function in providing for millions of youth an education which meets the required educational standards of the state.

Parochial schools save the taxpayers millions of dollars each year. These schools, therefore, should receive public tax support. In the eyes of many Catholics, to do less is to be guilty of gross religious discrimination.

From the Catholic point of view, the legal right to maintain non-public schools is largely meaningless unless there is the financial means to

---

*Charles C. Chandler, "Public Taxes for Nonpublic Schools Is Not Wise Public Policy," *Education in Ohio*, Release No. 21 (January 24, 1965).

implement this right. Since nonpublic school parents support not only their own schools but must support public schools as well, the financial burden is frequently oppressive.

While many would applaud the contributions of nonpublic schools (90% are Roman Catholic), it does not necessarily follow that such efforts should be supported with public funds. Is it wise public policy to grant extensive financial assistance to nonpublic schools?

A probable outcome of federal aid to private and parochial schools would be the proliferation of these schools. One can foresee various Protestant groups establishing their own school systems.

Schools catering to particular social classes would no doubt rapidly spread. In many sections of the country, publicly supported private schools would be a means of maintaining racial segregation.

There is the very real danger in our cities that the public school would become a pauper school, a school for the indigent and the unwanted of society. Under the circumstances, it is doubtful if the public school could maintain a quality program. Thus, many parents would feel compelled to send their children to nonpublic schools.

Those who believe that the public school is the great unifying force in our society are distressed by the above prospects. Those who believe that the public school serves a unique function in bringing together and educating all of the children of all the people are strongly opposed to any increased public support of nonpublic schools.

Nonpublic schools, it is argued, exist fundamentally to serve their own interests. A sectarian religious point of view, for example, is infused into many parts of a typical parochial school program.

Although all nonpublic schools must meet the minimum educational requirements of the state, such schools are not responsible to any public educational agency at the community level. Their programs and facilities are not part of any overall educational plan developed by the public officials of the community.

It is not clear, therefore, that nonpublic schools serve the broad public interest.

Demands for public subsides suggest a lack of faith in the public school philosophy, in the belief that a strong public school is the foundation of a free society. It is the elevation of the rights of individual parents and religious groups over the rights of the whole people.

While a democratic society properly values diversity, it must not promote divisiveness and religious strife. This, many believe, would be the inevitable outgrowth of a comprehensive program of federal aid to nonpublic schools.

THE CURRICULUM IN NON-PUBLIC SCHOOLS . . .

CURRICULUM OFFERINGS IN
NON-PUBLIC HIGH SCHOOLS*

Social studies. — Almost a quarter of the students attending nonpublic secondary schools are enrolled in United States (or American) history courses and another quarter in world history. This indicates that these two subjects are probably required for graduation from the majority of nonpublic high schools, as they are in the public high schools of most States.

An eighth of the students (139,000) take orientation or guidance. Approximately an equal proportion (141,000) are enrolled in the several subjects included under civics and government, primarily American government. More than 60,000 students are studying sociology. Geography and ancient history engage the attention of over 50,000 nonpublic secondary students each.

Religion. — According to the survey, 89 percent of the students are enrolled in formal courses in religion; this coincides with 89 percent of the secondary students who attend church-related schools. Although a few independent schools allow enrollment in comparative religion or the history of religion, formal religious study seems to be confined to church-affiliated schools.

Mathematics. — Elementary algebra (including UICSM I and SMSG I) has a higher enrollment than any other subject in the mathematics field — 28.4 percent (310,787) of all students in the survey. Plane geometry ranks second, with 20.2 percent of all the students. The third most frequently studied subject is advanced algebra (including intermediate algebra), in which 11.5 percent (almost 127,000) of all the students are enrolled.

Science. — Beginning biology (including BSCS) leads the science field with an enrollment of 250,000 students, or 22.9 percent of all grade 9–12 students.

Ninth-grade general science is being studied by 13 percent of the students. Although for a time it was the most common science subject

---

*Preliminary Report on Offerings and Enrollments in Grades 9-12 of Nonpublic Secondary Schools, 1961-62. Washington, D.C.: United States Office of Education, 1963, 3-4.

studied by high school students, it seems to be undergoing a reevaluation in the light of more extensive science instruction in the elementary grades and an apparent trend toward more intensive science study at the high school level than a generalized survey course.

The next two most frequently studied science subjects in nonpublic secondary schools are beginning chemistry and physics. These subjects show a much smaller number of students enrolled 126,000 and 66,000 (11.5 and 6.1 percent, respectively).

Foreign languages. — The area of foreign languages is far more significant in the program of the nonpublic secondary school than in that of the public high school. The nonpublic school survey indicates that the enrollment in all foreign language subjects in grades 9-12 equals 76 percent of the total enrollment in the schools. The extent to which this represents 76 percent of individual students depends upon an undetermined factor — the extent to which students are registered in more than one foreign language subject. In contrast to this percentage, the latest comparable figure for public school students was 29.3 percent.

The following comparison of foreign language study in nonpublic and public secondary schools points up the differences in the specific foreign languages chosen by students and the extent of student participation in foreign language study.

The greater emphasis on foreign language study in nonpublic schools may be attributed to the requirement of at least 1 year of Latin in the majority of Roman Catholic high schools. Such study is a requirement for graduation from most nonpublic schools, while it is elective in most public schools.

Almost all foreign language study in nonpublic as well as public secondary schools (97.8 and 98.5 percent of foreign language students, respectively) is confined to four languages — Latin, French, Spanish, and German.

THE CATHOLIC SCHOOL CURRICULUM SHOULD BE BROADENED*

One of the weakest links in our Catholic educational system is the failure of present methods to reach about 20 percent of our children in

---

*Sister M. Julian, O.P., "Let's Be Realistic . . . Don't Push Problem Children into the Public Schools!" Taken from *Catholic School Journal,* LXIV (June, 1964), published by the Bruce Publishing Company, 1964, 18-19.

high school. They never learn what they could — even of the three R's. These are the students of the 75 to 90 IQ. The curriculum of the present Catholic high school is geared to average or exceptional pupils. Few attempts have been made to temper the curriculum or method to the student's ability; rather the curriculum and method are held inviolate and the student made to conform — or he quits due to failure or, yes, even shame. Some will go, are even urged by good-intentioned priests, Brothers, and Sisters, to public vocational schools. The public vocational schools seem to be a dumping ground for students who could not make it in the Catholic school. It is not a free choice for them but a second and only choice. Catholic educators have failed to open their eyes to the realism that these students cannot master the shopwork anymore than they could the academic work. One has to be able to read to follow instructions, to reason to operate a machine. What vocational instructor is going to trust his high-priced power tools to youngsters of low mental ability? Shop is not the answer, nor are commercial courses. Automation will soon take over thousands of jobs. Soon machines that type letters from dictation will be on the market. Factory personnel, on letters of inquiry, have stated that they prefer to train young men with no vocational school background.

AWAKEN CATHOLIC SCHOOLS!

The irony of fate is that boys and girls who are literally forced out of Catholic schools, if allowed to continue could live happy, useful Catholic lives appreciating Faith, Church, and school, in relatively unskilled jobs such as dry cleaning, shoe repairing, maintenance, as clerks, waiters, waitresses, home-appliance repair, truck driver, countermen in lunchrooms, diners, or bakeries. More and more of these workers will be needed by the service trades in the coming decade. As graduates of a Catholic school, they would remain an integral part of the parish, retaining Catholic ideals and associations. Will the Catholic schools of this generation finally awaken and fulfill the destiny handed down to them by Christ?

REAL PURPOSE OF EDUCATION

The ability to achieve this goal depends upon the ability to develop a vital educational program that will keep the lost 20 percent within the fold. In order to build such a program, Catholic educators must know exactly and precisely where we are heading and why. We must bear in mind the real purpose of education: "To prepare man for what he must be in life, here and now, in order to attain his sublime destiny."

Does the student of the 70 to 90 I.Q. bracket have a sublime destiny? Catholic schools of today have tended to forget that he has. In the ideal Catholic high school a place will be made for him. He will be accepted where he stands with curriculum and method fitted to him.

FOR FURTHER REFLECTION OR INVESTIGATION

1. If there is a non-public school in your community, make comparisons with your public school system in the following respects:
   a. Curriculum offerings.
   b. Services provided to students and teachers.
   c. Administrative costs on per-pupil basis.
   d. Instructional expenditures on per-pupil basis.
   e. Powers and functions of the governing boards.
2. Interview the head of the local non-public school to determine his attitude toward, and the extent of, a program for public relations.
3. Trace the historical relationships in tax support of non-public schools in the United States, assessing the causes for changing attitudes through the years.
4. What legal authorities does the public have, speaking through either their local, state, or federal governing bodies, over the non-public schools of your community?
5. Distinguish between direct and indirect tax aid to non-public schools.
6. Discuss the morality of conducting a school for personal financial gain for the owners. Is learning a right, obligation, privilege, luxury, or service?

BIBLIOGRAPHY

Ahlschede, Arthur M., "The Protestant Schools: Purposes, Programs, Financing," *Phi Delta Kappan*, XLV, December, 1963.

Beach, Fred F., and Robert F. Will, "The State and Nonpublic Schools," *School Life*, XL, February, 1958.

Chandler, Charles C., Public Taxes for Nonpublic Schools Is Not Wise Public Policy," *Education in Ohio,* No. 21, January 24, 1965.

Fleming, Thomas J., "The Crisis in Catholic Schools," *Saturday Evening Post*, CCXXXVI, October 26, 1963.

Fountain, Winfield S., "A Plea for Public Support of Pluralism in America," *Phi Delta Kappan*, XLIV, June, 1963.

Gertler, Diane B., *Statistics of Nonpublic Secondary Schools,* 1960-61, Washington, D.C.: United States Office of Education, Circular No. 707, 1963.

Green, Donald Rose and Warren E. Gaureke, "If the Schools Are Closed."
    Atlanta: Southern Regional Council, 1959.
Hogan, W. F. "Use of Authority, Subsidiary, and Obedience in Catholic
    School Administration," *Catholic Educational Review,* LXI, December,
    1953.
Julian, Sister M., O.P., "Let's Be Realistic . . . Don't Push Problem Children
    into the Public Schools!" *Catholic School Journal,* LXIV, June, 1964.
McCoy, Raymond F., *American School Administration, Public and Catholic.*
    New York: McGraw-Hill Book Company, Inc., 1961.
McManus, Msgr. William E., "The Administrator and Financing of Catholic
    Schools," *Phi Delta Kappan,* XLV, December, 1963.
National Catholic Educational Association, "Functions of the Diocesan Super-
    intendent," *Catholic School Journal,* LX, June, 1960.
*Preliminary Report on Offerings and Enrollment in Grades 9-12 of Non-
    public Secondary Schools,* 1961-62, Washington, D.C.: United States
    Office of Education, 1963.
Ryan, L. V., "Diocesan Foundation Plan, *"Catholic School Journal,* LXIV,
    May, 1964.
Smiley, S., "Lay School Board for a Grade School," *Catholic School Journal,*
    LXIII, November, 1963.
Walls, D. E., "Centralization of Administration in Diocesan School Systems,"
    Catholic Educational Review, LXI, December, 1964.

Chapter 7

Administration of Colleges and Universities

One of the most rapidly growing opportunities for persons aspiring to administrative careers awaits those with talent and desire to perform executive work in the nation's colleges and universities. The chances are bright not only because of the spectacular expansion of facilities for higher education, especially in the development of new community colleges and off-campus academic centers, but also because there are exiguous organized efforts to ready future college administrators. Only a few institutions have taken any steps toward building a supply of competent administrators.

Indeed, doubt is often expressed about the feasibility of preparing college administrators. The assumption seem to be that there will be someone to administer when the situation demands, or that college administrators aren't really needed to administer. The prevailing attitudes toward college administration are at about the same level as were those toward administration of public school districts a half century ago, that is, the administrator should be chosen from the faculty ranks upon his qualifications of scholarship or seniority. Confusion and disagreement are rampant as to what a college administrator should do, how he should be selected, and how he might be groomed for his work.

Even when a university accepts the challenge to build a preparatory program for college administrators, there can be rabid internal jockeying for the right to oversee the program. In a large university there are likely to be several departments and colleges which have formal programs for executive training. Even those divisions which do not may claim the privilege on the grounds of what their respective disciplines would contribute to the making of a college administrator. College faculties are notoriously defensive about their individual and collegial expertise. They can be as suspicious about the intents of other divisions as the high school chemistry department used to be about the new principal who came from a social studies background, or as elementary school teachers used to be about the new superintendent who had never taught on the lower level.

Meanwhile, the demand for college administrators increases; the opportunities exist and grow brighter.

THE NATURE OF COLLEGE ADMINISTRATION

It is difficult to do more than generalize about the function of college administration. The 2,000 institutions of higher education in United States illustrate great variances in aims, characteristics, and operational procedures. There are large and small institutions, public and private, national, state, municipal, and local district colleges, institutions with several colleges to include a graduate school and those with less than baccalaureate programs, comprehensive and single-purpose institutions, highly endowed and austere schools.

Furthermore, each institution enjoys considerable autonomy. Even those which are part of a state-wide system of colleges and universities under the governance of a state board of regents are permitted much latitude in managing their own affairs.

The discussion of college administration herein must be accepted in light of these variances. The student can, perhaps, grasp the uniqueness of college administration by noting these differences from the administration of elementary and secondary schools, and of local school districts.

Differences in administration start with the differences in the caliber and motivations of students who attend the respective institutions. College students are not only more mature, but they are not compelled by law to participate. College administrators and teachers are, therefore, relieved of much of the onerous disciplinary responsibilities suffered by their counterparts who work in elementary and secondary schools. Disciplining and counseling of college students except for course advising, is largely segregated from teaching and handled by staff specialists.

Centralization of college physical facilities on one site simplifies in some measure the administrative tasks of housekeeping and maintenance of buildings and grounds. On the other hand, universities which provide dormitories must wrestle with different facility, feeding, and discipline problems than those faced by public school administrators.

Differences between the two institutions in the sources of fiscal support introduce differences in the behavior of administrators. While both are forever concerned with extending the money supply, they look in different directions. College administrators pursue the dollar through enrollments, alumni, legislatures, the benevolently inclined, government and private research grants. Only municipal institutions or community colleges which are partially supported by voted taxes, are concerned with winning public enthusiasm as must public schools in order to realize greater investment in their institutions.

Since colleges generally do not need to conduct financial campaigns in communities, they owe no accountability to local citizens and spend considerably less time in rapport-building. They are relieved from the time-consuming activity of creating favorable images through a variety of public relations actions. That is not to say that images and public relations are unimportant to college administrators; on the contrary, many institutions of higher education create public affairs offices. The motivation for creating favorable images on the part of university personnel stems less from financial needs than it does from the drive for prestige.

College administration differs from public school administration most in the performance of the personnel function. American universities have sought to capture the spirit of the European institutions which are largely faculty managed. The "community of scholars" concept has been mellowed in the United States by governing boards which have the legal authority for management. The power of decision making vested by the state and local citizens in the officials of state and municipal colleges modifies the European ideal still further. As a result, the administration of American institutions of higher learning is an unsettled process fraught with a host of notions. One can find on most campuses sharply opposing attitudes toward the administrative function, ranging from the view that college administrators are merely office executives to carry out the wishes of faculty, to the view that college administrators should be executives in the fullest sense, i.e., make decisions upon appropriate consultation with staff members. As a consequence, it can be generalized that college presidents and deans exercise far less authority than do principals and superintendents. It can also be generalized that nearly all college faculty members are quasi-administrators. At least much of the decision-making function is dispersed among a multitude of committees and to the heads of colleges, departments and other areas of operation on the campus. It is not the intent here to argue the merits of either of the two approaches to administering the respective institutions. It would be remiss not to point out for the benefit of the student contemplating a career in college administration that he will find that his relationships there to professional personnel are quite different from those if he chooses a career in public school administration.

The personnel function on a campus differs in ways other than policy making. Recruitment of faculty is nationwide, often international in its search. The faculty has a strong voice in the decisions as to whom will be employed. Prime consideration is given to whatever one understands when he uses the word "scholar," a term which frequently today denotes experience in research and publication rather than teaching success. Advanced degrees are essential; certification is not involved. Previous teaching or practicing experiencing is of little consequence except in the professional colleges. Salary schedules are expressed in brackets for the various ranks and are fuzzy in their administration. Individual bargaining for salary is commonplace, recognizing the law of supply and demand. Salaries are not made public, which partially explains the free use of merit systems. Ambitious faculty members seek to advance in rank, not only for financial reasons but also for status. Rank carries many privileges on a campus, not the least of which is eligibility for the institution's tenure and fringe benefit plans.

Many of the principles of administration recommended herein, and elsewhere, are largely ignored on a college campus. The principle of accountability is a particular case in point. As university administrators seek to conduct their responsibilities in a democratic fashion, approaching that goal perhaps closer than any other organization in American society, accountability is so diffused among levels and personnel as to make understandable the reputation for inefficiency generally won by colleges. It is not so noticeable in small institutions, nor in those where personnel turnover is slight. But in large and growing universities that are adding and changing faculty rapidly, it is difficult for an outsider — be he student or citizen — to pursue channels of authority to obtain consistent or final answers. The looseness of organization violates best understandings of control span, the president typically spreading himself so thinly over many reporting subordinate officers that he cannot possibly execute his myriad functions.

The stranger to university operations will also be dumfounded at financial accountability. In spite of orderly record keeping and audited books, there is such a multiplicity of funds, many of which resemble caches, that the customary principles of financial operations seem to be non-applicable.

Curriculum matters are reserved to colleges, departments, and individual professors. Curriculum is almost a forbidden field of concern for central staff officers. They are not involved except in major changes or in the event additional money, staff, and facilities are affected. Teaching methodology is a matter of individual taste; improvement of teaching is an item annually on the agenda but more imminent matters usually usurp the discussion about it. In fact, it is not too facetiously said that one has to look long to find a full-time teacher on a college faculty and only then among the lesser ranks. So many have reduced loads because of semi-administrative responsibilities, research pursuits, or because of several dozen possible special assignments available on campus. The supervisory and evaluating functions are virtually unknown in colleges; the expert faculty member is "above" administrative help and counsel.

ADMINISTRATIVE ORGANIZATION

Just as there is diversity among institutions, there is a variety of arrangements for the governing bodies of colleges. The membership may be as small as seven or nine and may run as high as forty or fifty. Nearly all members are appointed, either by political offices such as the governor or legislature for state universities, or by the church for sectarian-oriented institutions, or by alumni groups. Occasionally, the board itself appoints other members. The trustees of a state college may be appointed by, and more or less subservient to, a state-wide board of regents in several states.

The powers of the governing body, usually far weaker than those of a local board of education are designated in the institution's charter. A college board is primarily a legalizing body, giving official sanction to actions of the administrative staff and faculty. Many boards convene only a few times each year, perhaps even irregularly.

The president, sometimes entitled chancellor, is the chief executive officer of the institution, but for reasons already cited, he executes much less than the chief executive of a public school district. In some instances the president's office is more of an honorary position, not unlike that of the mayor in a municipality with a city manager, or the king in a constitutional monarchy. Elsewhere, the president has become a dynamic, moving force in the institution, more because of his vibrant leadership qualities than because of legal expectations from the office. There are few prescribed patterns for his behavior, so the chief executive makes out of the position what he wishes, or is able. He may be chosen for his scholarly proclivities, for his religious affiliation in denominational colleges, or for the prestige his prior achievements might bring to the institution, rarely for his administrative understandings or skill. Not unlike the superintendent of schools, a college president is often selected to overcome shortcomings which developed under the preceding administration.

Like a public school district, the size of a college's central administrative staff is dictated mostly by size of the corporation, and by its wealth. In the very small institutions, the president may have not even a dean, only secretarial aides. He performs all the administrative tasks not shared by faculty. Staff assistants are added as the scope of the jurisdiction increases. The business and finance function is usually the first to be delegated to an assistant, now frequently carrying the title of vice-president. The next administrative positions to be created may be assigned responsibilities for academic affairs and student affairs. The demarcations between academic and non-academic affairs are distinct and respected on a college campus. A kind of segregation evolves insofar as the faculty is concerned, most of whom are scarcely aware that non-academic functions go on except when the barriers may disappear on university-wide committees. Indeed, the autonomous ways of individuals and disciplines allow them to pursue their respective specialties without looking to the right or left, causing severe handicaps to administrators responsible for coordinating efforts.

Finding competent specialists for the various central staff positions is complicated by the temptation to appoint from faculty rank, persons who have only a bent or a partial background for the technical phases of the job but not a complete preparation. Hence, the office is often modified to be compatible with the man rather than shaping the man to fit the job requirements. While this practice is superior to leaving the post vacant, it means that several expectations from the office may not be fulfilled, leading to further diffusion of assignments and perhaps more quasi-administrators. This tendency partially explains the perpetuation in colleges of a great number of part-time administrators. Further explanation stems from the common viewpoint that everyone associated with an educational institution should "keep his fingers in" teaching. The attitude has resisted change longer in colleges than in public schools because tradition is prized more at the university level.

Each college of a university is headed by a dean who is accountable directly to the president for some matters, and to other central staff officers for other matters. Faculties are often instrumental in the selection of their deans; the latter's potential for the office being evaluated more by their scholarship and predicted willingness to push the goals of the college than for their administrative ability. Since there is rarely a job description written for the deanship, a dean, like the president, makes of the position what he chooses. Thus, many deans have contributed substantially to the cause of education.

Colleges are subdivided into departments and areas of specialization, each of which is headed by a chairman commonly chosen by members of that speciality. These positions are likely to be compensated for in reduced load rather than by added salary.

If flow of authority were to be charted for a college it would extend from president to collegiate dean to department head to faculty member. However, the diagram would probably indicate flow of communication more accurately than flow of power. As stated earlier, sources and directions of power are confused, often contested. In addition to these apparent channels of authority, a large university will provide several speciality staff positions which seem to fit nowhere in the administrative hierarchy, such as the public affairs officer, the dean of men, a provost, or the dean of the graduate school.

As these remarks suggest—an echoing of the sentiments expressed by many writers in the field of college administration—there is a need for properly trained persons to apply principles of administration to the management of higher learning. Size, complexity, and economic pressures demand a change. The current but rare opportunities for learning about college administration through an internship are promising. However, the benefit of an internship could be minimized by understudying only in the conventional environment. The need for a college executive to understand administrative practices and theory is obvious. The opportunities are favorable for such a person, if he also knows the history and purposes of higher education.

The implications are clear, therefore, that the young person aspiring to an administrative career in higher education should affiliate with college teaching at an early age; this trend to elevate from within will undoubtedly continue. Rarely is an administrator from other social organizations invited for consideration, except for the presidency, and only then after the candidate has achieved some fame. The problem of preparing for college administration is confounded by the lack of deliberate training programs. The specific work of college administration has not even been researched, strange as it may seem in institutions which pride themselves on their talents and facilities for systematic study. Thus, it behooves the serious aspirant to study the art and techniques of administration where it may be found, perhaps in colleges of education or business, qualify to teach in a discipline, and then early seek an instructor's position.

THE AMERICAN UNIVERSITY . . .

A UNIVERSITY'S PURPOSES*

A central focus for intellectual freedom is the university. Only those who have been inducted into the life of a university can fully appreciate the enormous supply of knowledge and talent and cultivated judgment that is lodged in a university faculty. And perhaps only they have gained a full grasp of the immeasurable value that such an institution has for its community.

A university traffics in ideas. And therefore it is an exciting and dangerous place. Those who are afraid of ideas would be well advised to stay away from universities. They are not a compatible environment for any man who is afraid to think, who is offended by a persistent attempt

*Sterling M. McMurrin, "American Education and the Culture," *Teachers College Record*, LXIII (October, 1961), 35-39. By permission of *Teachers College Record* and S. M. McMurrin.

to understand human experience, who prefers dogmatism to evidence and irrationalism to disciplined reason, or who, whatever his pretenses, is really afraid of knowledge or has contempt for learning and is determined to nourish and protect his parochial prejudices.

Universities are made for those who have neither dulled nor prostituted their natural endowment of reason and fine sensitivity, in whom intellectual curiosity is alive and viable, who love knowledge for its own sake as well as for its uses, whose moral capacities invite analysis and perspective in the judgment of value, and who possess that artistic and intellectual irritability that is necessary to genuine creativity. Universities are made for those who have a taste and talent for the life of the mind, who have a determined sense of responsibility to themselves and a commitment to the good of their community, their nation, and the world. Those precious and indescribable resources, which only a university with its vast command of knowledge and creative talent can provide, inspire and facilitate not only a high degree of learning and the skills that attend it, but also that discipline of intellect that is an essential ingredient of genuine morality, of artistic awareness, and of spiritual strength. If the university is properly demanding and exacting, its students may have a rough time. But with the world threatening to collapse around us, a university is no place for pleasure seekers, and even the best intentioned may fail. For those who persist to the end, however, and who fasten their energy and commitment upon the purpose and meaning of education—the achievement of knowledge and the cultivation of the intellect—there should be a strengthening and refinement of those high qualities of the moral and spiritual life that with knowledge are the mark of a man's humanity and the measure of his culture. These are the qualities that must adorn the lives of all those who are committed to the search for truth, the cultivation of disciplined reason, and the achievement of the public as well as the private good.

WHAT IS A JUNIOR COLLEGE?*

Some educators use the terms "community college" and "junior college" interchangeably. Nevertheless, there are clear differences between the terms. While, generally speaking, both community colleges and junior colleges are two-year collegiate institutions, there are many

---

*From *The American Two-Year College,* by Tyrus Hillway, New York: Harper & Row, Publishers, Copyright© 1958 by Tyrus Hillway, 7-8, 257-258.

junior colleges which do not function as community-serving institutions. Both community colleges and junior colleges constitute portions of the same educational movement. As a matter of fact, the modern community college may be thought of as an outgrowth of the junior college movement which began 50 to 75 years ago.

Two-year colleges vary greatly in their purposes, organization, and programs. Many of them simply duplicate the first two years of the standard four-year college course. Others offer vocational subjects only. Some enroll only local students, while others maintain extensive dormitories and enroll students from all over the world. This almost infinite variation has created much difficulty for those who have attempted in the past to supply an accurate definition for the junior college. Walter Crosby Eells, one of the leaders in junior college work and for years executive secretary of the American Association of Junior Colleges, used to remark jokingly that the only sure method of determining whether a given institution could be classified as a junior college was to have it identify itself as one!

It is possible, nevertheless, to formulate a satisfactory description. It is possible also to show a difference between the junior college in general and that special kind of junior college known as the community college.

In 1922, representatives of American two-year colleges meeting in a national convention adopted a resolution officially defining the junior college as "an institution offering two years of instruction of strictly collegiate grade." Three years later this definition was revised and expanded to read as follows:

> The Junior College is an institution offering two years of instruction of strictly collegiate grade. The curriculum may include those courses usually offered in the first two years of the four year college, in which case these courses must be identical, in scope and thoroughness, with corresponding courses of the standard four year college.

> The junior college may, and is likely to, develop a different type of curriculum suited to the larger and ever changing civic, social, religious and vocational needs of the entire community in which the college is located. It is understood that in this case also the work offered shall be on a level appropriate for high school graduates.

It will be seen from the statement just quoted that, as early as 1925, when the term "community college" had not yet come into vogue, service to the community was already recognized as a distinctive characteristic of some two-year colleges.

"Junior college" may be regarded as the generic term to identify an institution of higher learning which offers two years of education beyond the high school. "Community college" is the name applied to an institution which is primarily concerned with providing educational services on the collegiate level to a particular community. The community college draws a student body almost exclusively from among the graduates of the local high schools, while the typical junior college may draw from a wide area. The community college most frequently is under public control and is a part of the local school system, whereas the junior college not primarily interested in community service may be privately or church controlled. . . .

TRENDS TOWARD FUTURE DEVELOPMENT

Three clear trends are apparent in the development of the junior and community college movement. One is the increasing emphasis upon public support and control. Another is the need for more two-year colleges in many areas not now adequately served. A third is the growing attention being given in higher education to purely local needs.

If present indications can be relied on, the time is not far off when every state interested in the welfare of its young people will have a coordinated system of community colleges. Not every state will follow the same pattern in developing such a system. Underlying the whole movement, however, is the swelling pressure for the upward extension of free public education. Instead of stopping at the twelfth grade, public education seems likely to be extended generally into the fourteenth grade, or even higher. Nothing in today's configuration of events argues against our eventual adoption of this major change in our educational policy.

The conviction that more two-year institutions are needed is already widespread in the United States. The studies made by the President's Commission on Higher Education and by the various state commissions all point in this direction. The question has now become not so much whether enlarged facilities are needed but rather of where they shall be located and how they shall be financed. Educators and the American public have pretty much made up their minds that no young person in our nation shall be denied the right to as much education as he can profitably use. The further development of community colleges follows from this as a matter of course.

The one great new idea which has sprung into full flower in American education during the past few years is that of providing an educational program suited to local needs. Educators are sure that a single pattern of collegiate experience will not fit all students equally well. The community college is founded upon the belief that individual differences among our people require variations in the types of training offered.

Some still resist or deny this belief, arguing that education in our schools and colleges should be the same for all. Yet the merest glance at the variety of instruction currently available shows unmistakably which of these two divergent principles has proved more effective in practice, and which is demanded by our American students. If community colleges are successful and popular, the fact serves as an illustration of our continued respect for decisions arrived at through democratic means. On the whole, the American people choose and support the kind of education which they discover to be most beneficial to them.

Having established itself by virtue of its inherent merits as the most rapidly growing movement in American education and as the unique contribution of our system to the entire history of education, the junior and community college movement has now become a permanent characteristic of our national society. To many people, it still remains new and unfamiliar. In another generation, one may venture to predict, it will be as much as part of the accepted educational pattern for Americans as the kindergarten and the junior high school. The junior and community college, in all its various forms, occupies a firm place in our system simply because it effectively supplies a vitally needed educational service.

INCREASE IN COLLEGE ENROLLMENTS IS INEVITABLE*

The demand for college education—the number of potential applicants for college places—is the controlling factor in future enrollments. There is reason to assume that the availability of college places will be accommodated to the demand. The forces that compel and facilitate accommodation of supply to numbers of applicants are many and powerful. Our history from colonial times to the present evidences our nationwide concern with educational opportunities and with broadening these opportunities. Recent events have served to strengthen this concern.

Our national interest clearly lies in a highly educated populace. In this complex world we can maintain leadership only through quality of

*Selma J. Mushkin, ed., *Economics of Higher Education*, Washington, D.C.: United States Office of Education, Bulletin No. 5, 1962, No. 5, 3-4.

Number of faculty and other professional staff in publicly and privately controlled institutions [of higher education], first term 1961-62, with percent changes since 1957-58, by type of position: Aggregate United States*

Type of position	Publicly controlled				Privately controlled			
	Number of positions 1961-62	Percent change			Number of positions 1961-62	Percent change		
		1959-60 to 1961-62	1957-58 to 1959-60	1957-58 to 1961-62		1959-60 to 1961-62	1957-58 to 1959-60	1957-58 to 1961-62
Total number of different persons[1]	(235,851)	12.5	10.4	24.2	(191,982)	11.0	9.0	21.0
Total number of positions	264,193	10.7	9.7	21.4	211,617	9.7	9.8	20.4
Professional staff for general administration	7,603	10.6	17.1	29.5	13,083	7.4	19.9	28.7
Professional staff for student personnel services	7,914	17.1	22.7	43.7	8,808	3.2	16.1	19.8
Faculty for resident instruction in degree-credit courses	164,199	12.6	9.3	23.1	148,488	8.2	8.0	16.8
Instructor or above	136,594	10.4	7.8	19.0	130,030	7.7	8.0	16.4
Full-time	98,107	8.8	5.0	14.2	80,525	9.6	6.9	17.2
Part-time	38,487	14.7	16.2	33.2	49,505	4.8	9.8	15.0
Full-time equivalent of part-time[2]	13,692	25.3	14.6	43.6	15,953	8.5	9.6	18.9
Junior instructional staff	27,605	25.1	18.7	48.6	18,458	11.5	7.7	20.1
Faculty for resident instruction in other than degree-credit courses	9,502	-2.7	21.7	18.4	4,130	-5.4	7.3	1.4
Extension staff	28,132	1.6	-1.8	-0.2	3,277	-12.3	17.4	3.0
Giving courses	12,653	2.3	-0.3	1.9	2,583	-13.1	-5.0	-17.5
Other extension staff	15,479	1.0	-2.9	-1.9	694	-9.0	[3]	[3]
Other faculty, including instructional staff for courses by mail radio or TV, short courses, and in individual lessons	8,514	2.8	30.9	34.6	3,257	-9.4	9.7	-0.6
Professional library staff	5,592	12.8	9.6	23.6	5,433	9.1	8.9	18.8
Professional staff for organized research	27,857	24.5	13.7	41.6	22,201	50.7	14.5	72.6
Instructional staff for elementary or secondary instruction	4,880	-21.4	0.6	-20.9	2,940	-17.9	14.7	-5.8

[1]The sum of the numbers of persons in all types of positions exceeds the number of different persons because some professional staff serve in more than one capacity. "Total number of positions" represents the sum of all types of positions as classified in the survey questionnaire.

[2]Rounded so that fractions of a person are not reported.

[3]Not computed when the figure for either year is 500 or fewer.

*Summary Report, Washington, D.C.: United States Office of Education (November, 1963) (OE-53014-62), 4.

the people, not through sheer numbers. Our democratic society emphasizes higher education as a ladder for social mobility and increased opportunity. For the individual higher education provides economic benefits, social status, and personal development. Both individual and national interest combine with a long historical tradition to form a commitment to education that will not be diverted without a major restructuring of the place of higher education in our society.

The projections of demand for places presented here indicate, however, that the task ahead of providing educational facilities, teaching staffs, and the financial base for adequate plant and staffing is formidable. If we fail in this task, actual enrollment will fall short of the figures projected.

ADMINISTRATIVE PRACTICES IN INSTITUTIONS OF HIGHER LEARNING . . .

HISTORICAL EVOLUTION OF COLLEGE STRUCTURES*

The organization of colleges and universities in the Nation has been influenced and molded by a variety of forces. On the one hand are the patterns and traditions of control and organization which came from western Europe. On the other hand, native American conditions have modified and affected these transplanted administrative designs. The interaction of these two elements with each other and with the American concept of democracy in all areas of living has produced a unique pattern of government for higher institutions in this country.

More Recent Evolution

Down through the years from the Middle Ages, a tradition of self-government existed in European colleges and universities. In most universities, the masters organized and governed themselves in a manner similar to the guilds. The first colleges in America took form along a different line. Harvard, for example, started with a Board of Overseers

---

*Archie R. Ayers and John H. Russel, *Internal Structure: Organization and Administration of Institutions of Higher Education*, Washington, D.C.: United States Office of Education Bulletin No. 9, 1962, 6-8, 71-73, 77-78.

composed largely of clergy, a few magistrates, and the college president. Later, a second group consisting of the president, the treasurer, and five fellows was organized in order to provide a resident group which could be in constant touch with college affairs. Thus, Harvard was the first and leading exponent of a bicameral form of college and university administration. . . .

When Yale came into existence, it set up a unicameral form of organization in preference to the bicameral. Its founders, apparently unimpressed by the European tradition of faculty autonomy, established a single governing board on which they held all the seats, and only years later did they admit the rector (president of the college) to membership in the Yale Corporation. Yale's model of government proved popular in the new Nation. Today, American institutions, with the exception of some of those under church control, are governed by boards of trustees consisting predominantly of business and professional people.

In the early colleges of the Nation, the president was the entire administration; below the board of trustees, as a consequence, no organization for administration was needed. The early president was not only charged with the general oversight of the college, but in addition, he carried a number of specific administrative duties and a heavy teaching load. In the late 19th century and in the 20th century, presidents gradually gave up their teaching duties and, also, began to delegate administrative functions to such lieutenants as registrar, deans, bursar, and librarian. Thus, the American college president gradually became free to concentrate on coordinating functions which he alone should perform.

More Recent Evolution

The number of institutions of higher education in the United States today now exceeds 2,000. During this century, many of these institutions have grown in enrollment to the point that some now enroll more than 20,000 students. The German idea of a university with its graduate and professional schools has been grafted onto the original concept of the liberal arts college. In addition, many formerly independent faculties in such fields as medicine, pharmacy, law, divinity, and business administration have been added to the university structure. The structure of the institutions, into which many new programs resulting from emerging social demands were incorporated, has grown often without plan into the congeries now apparent on campuses in the United States.

Growth in size and complexity of colleges and universities require their reorganization for more effective administration. . .

History is occurring faster than it is being written. Almost frightening acceleration in the growth of higher education has occurred in this century. If prognostications are correct, higher education is on the brink of even greater expansion. Whatever magnitude the problems of higher education has reached in the past, they may indeed be dwarfed by those of the immediate future.

For several years higher education leaders have repeatedly reminded us that the 1960's and 1970's will be a crucial period. Realizing that it is important for colleges and universities to re-examine themselves in preparation for this critical period, many of them are making self-studies. Pressures on regional accrediting agencies are high, and State agencies are asking questions regarding organizational efficiency, economy of operation, and internal organization. No matter is of more far-reaching significance than the development of a concept of the institution as an organic whole, and especially a re-examination of its internal organization in relationship to that concept.

During the 20th century the substance of education has steadily expanded, and colleges and universities have grown in manifold ways. From the simple pattern of internal administrative organization of the 19th century has evolved an ever more complex administrative structure. While various segments of this internal structure (business management, student services etc.) have begun to crystallize their content, and to some extent, their methods of administration, approaches concerned with the whole of administration in higher education have been limited.

A Look at the Administrative Organizations

While considering relationships which characterize internal structure, one should remember that a collegiate institution's organization should be specifically tailored to its peculiarities and needs. On the other hand, as indicated by a look at the organization charts in this study, few colleges foresee the requirements of their expanding enterprise and design the organization for dynamic administration and growth in line with stated objectives in higher education.

In general, the administrative organizations in the institutions have grown up without benefit of critical attention. Once established, they have inclined the institutions toward rigidity rather than toward flexibility adaptable to changing circumstances and special problems. Noteworthy shortcomings include: (a) too many officers reporting to the president, (b) student personnel interests uncoordinated and scattered among a number of officers and faculty members, (c) academic administration not clearly identified, and (d) scant attention given to institutional development as a [discrete] category of general administration.

As a result in many colleges and universities, organization planning is an area of clearly marked weakness in terms of their educational plans. Not only are faculties conservative when internal change is suggested, but trustees are slow to change established institutional statutes which provide the organizational framework. Fortunate indeed is that institution whose trustees understand and accept their responsibilities with respect to the kind of organization required to [marshal] the institution's efforts for the future.

This tendency of institutions to develop and expand their organizations in response to immediate exigencies arising from present problems indicates at least a partial explanation for the kind of relationships found and the way the institutions are organized. Indeed, the present organization structures of a number of collegiate institutions reflect anachronistic patterns of organization developed for particular reasons which existed only in the past.

CONCLUSION

Collegiate institutions must face the practical necessity of improving channels through which the duties of various individuals are related, and through which the measures and policies of those who govern become effective. In spite of the fact that these channels are not the whole of an organization and do not automatically assure distinguished management, they are essential for good administration and must be based on sound internal structure.

In the judgment of the authors, a governing board and president interested in streamlining organization can best begin in cooperation with the executive staff and faculty, by developing a basic plan for the board's consideration and approval. The plan should include (a) a line-staff chart indicating working relationships among the general administrative officers and showing and making explicit their several relationships with operating and subordinate personnel; (b) a clear distinction insofar as it is possible between policy-making and policy-administering machinery; (c) a clarification of the advisory nature of committees; (d) a clarification of the role of the faculty as an organized group; and (e) position descriptions for the various administrative officers containing explicit definitions of responsibility with commensurate authority and procedures designed to help the institution realize its goals.

The structural flow chart should clearly show those members of the staff who work with and report to the general administrators—four suggested in the model of organization—according to the functional areas to which they are assigned. Even in a small college in which the president retains jurisdiction over one of the functions, as he may well do, for example, in the matter of institutional development, that fact does not justify the omission of clear-cut lines of responsibility and authority for performing the particular set of functions in question. Full-time assignment of an individual in each of the four major administrative areas is not essential. Smaller institutions often observe a line-staff arrangement through assignment of personnel on a part-time basis. The important thing, however, in each of the four areas is a clear-cut delegation of responsibility for the administration of a group of functions with an adequate authority for the fulfillment of the assigned tasks.

Job specifications of administrative officers should be published in an institutional guide or manual, along with the flow charts. To assure objective consideration, the qualifications of candidates for vacancies in key positions should be judged in terms of these carefully prepared position descriptions.

RECOMMENDATIONS

Constructive suggestions to boards of control and presidents of colleges and universities can be offered on the basis of outcomes of this study coupled with a general understanding of the problems that commonly confront the administration of higher education. The following, in the judgment of the authors, are sound:

1. Boards of control of colleges and universities should frequently review and revise as necessary the organization for administration of their institutions.

2. A timetable for putting the plan agreed upon into effect should be a first step in its implementation, taking into account obligations affecting the status of individuals now in positions, and the necessity of maintaining morale as high as possible during the time that reorganization is being effected.

3. The span of control of the chief administrative officer should, in general, number four persons; one for each of the four major administrative areas. This number in smaller colleges may be reduced by the extent to which the president himself engages in the direct administration of a given area and by the extent to which administration of two areas may be feasibly combined. The number, on the other hand, may be increased in larger and more complex institutions in those instances (a) in which new programs require direct supervision, (b) in which a geographic dispersion of program requires a separately administered part of the organization, or (c) in which sound personnel considerations preclude reorganization at this time.

4. Job descriptions of administrative posts should indicate their responsibility to recognize and use the standard major instru-

ments of control for effective supervision. These include: preparation and the administration of the budget; procedures of faculty appointment, promotion, and retention; and a variety of reporting procedures. . .

Neither a haphazard organization nor one developed along idealistic lines without regard for the human element can be expected to function effectively. The mold for an organization is essential, but it is the men and women at hand who make the plan work. Good administration not only involves the effective use of individual differences, but establishes methods of correcting imbalances which may exist between the level of competence of an individual on the one hand and the job description and the organization structure on the other. Since no two people can bring the same elements of personality, motivation, and ability to a job, compensating adjustments in the organization should accompany personnel appointments and changes. Most presidents find it more realistic to tailor job patterns to the individual than to tailor human abilities to a particular job pattern. At times, however, such adjustments can go so far that the structure itself can lack an essential cohesiveness; spans of control can grow too large in an effort to adapt structure to competence and personality; and, as a consequence, very real problems can eventually develop when changes in personnel occur.

The wise executive, therefore, will follow the "golden mean" in his emphasis on formalizing the organization pattern. He will try to analyze and understand research on organization behavior. Reliance on recurring reviews of his own organization for light on problems peculiar to his campus will help him anticipate and allay fears of innovations in the administrative structure. As a consequence, his major administrators will not be subjected to the frustrations which can often lead to a devastating power struggle when changes in organization occur. Thus the judicious president will set the stage for developing a sound, streamlined organizational structure for the institution, in which all personnel will be properly assigned and supervised.

Whatever the design of the flow chart found to work best for a specific institution, the chart should have an administrative centralization which tends to create a manageable presidential span of control. As a beginning toward the accomplishment of this objective, the authors recommend keeping in mind the basic 4-man type of control (span) as a workable model with four major categories of administrative activity: academic administration, student services, business management, and institutional development. Of course, in actual practice a specific institution may find many variations and departures necessary in adapting this model to its requirements. Retention of the idea, however, gives direction and consistency to planning and action in administrative reorganization.

The advantages of this 4-man type over some of the other designs include: (1) a unity of control; (2) an opportunity for the president to work with some equality of time and energy with all sectors of the institution; (3) an internal unity of operation for each of the four major segments; (4) a delegation of responsibility with commensurate authority; (5) an excellent overview of operations for the president; and (6) a provision for coordination of the internal organization.

THE INFLUENCE OF A UNIVERSITY'S CHARACTER UPON ADMINISTRATION*

On the basis of the foregoing analysis, this chapter contends that the academic administrator will improve his effectiveness to the degree that he understands and remains conscious of three fundamental facets of his organizational situation.

First, he will serve better to the degree that he recognizes realistically the role of authority in the academic setting. Authority serves as the fuel by which all formal organizations are maintained, of course. But, authority is far more sophisticated than a simple command and obey situation or relationship, and the role of authority in the academic organization is even more [discrete] than it is in other enterprises.

Second, this chapter suggests that effective leadership relates closely to the administrator's ability to draw together those persons affected by a decision into the decision-making councils of his organization. This does not necessarily imply staff decision-making only. Rather, it means collaboration with academic and administrative associates on institutional policy making, whether their opinions establish decisions or not. Such collaborative effort tends to develop logical procedures, what is called herein a rational process for administration. A rational process will encourage decision-making based primarily upon the welfare of the institution and upon the basis of available and pertinent data.

Third, the administrator works within the context of a specific college or university. The character of this college or university sets limits upon what policies can be meaningfully implemented and also identies opportunities for imaginative leadership. The academic administrator works within a distinctive institutional setting; he must understand it well to be effective. . .

---

*E. D. Duryea, "The Influence of a University's Character Upon Administration." From *Administrators in Higher Education, Their Functions and Coordination.* Edited by Gerald P. Burns, Copyright © 1962, by Harper & Row.

The character of each college or university makes its particular contribution to the thinking of its participants. A New England liberal arts college has an atmosphere quite different from that at a midwestern urban university. The tradition of decision-making by deliberate faculty action in one university contrasts with strong executive leadership associated with another. The tendency to rely on departmental heads for educational policy decisions at one differs from the tradition of strong deanships at another. The character-forming elements are numerous and reflect, as we pointed out, both past and present. They include such elements as geographical location; background and general attributes of students who attend; sources of financial support; size; internal organizational arrangements; social prestige, as in the case of certain New England women's colleges; objectives; the local community; personalities of strong leaders; and traditional ways of making and carrying out policies.

This has several implications for administrators. We suggest five.

1. *The character of an institution delimits the area within which administrators can exert effective leadership.* The general postulates held by a society establish the limits within which change is possible—short of revolution. The same holds true for a unit of society such as a college or university. No president, for example, can expect to effect changes which violate too greatly the general character of his campus—unless difficult times make participants receptive to radical alterations.

2. *The character of an institution determines in general the decisions which are made.* The urban university will accept as proper a wide variety of specialized programs of direct value to various professions and occupations; a state university will respond to public pressures for services of value to its constituency; and a rural liberal arts college will hold strongly to a single educational ideal. Certain colleges have established a receptivity to new curricular ideas; others have traditionally resisted any change in their degree program. One university will draw to its ranks primarily scholars who have achieved eminence, another will seek out young teachers with potential and provide opportunity for promotion within its own organization.

3. *Character will affect the manner in which decisions are made.* At one university, educational policy will evolve from various decisions made at the departmental level with only general direction from deans and the president; at another, departments will tend to look to administrative officers for more positive leadership. At one college, a president is bound closely by a tradition of faculty participation in all its affairs, at another, faculties remain relatively indifferent to policies which have no

direct bearing on their particular interests or departments. At one college, student opinion gains respect and holds influence; at another, it rankles faculty members who exclude student participation. In one university, educational policies require a deliberative series of formal actions by faculty committees and councils; at another, such policies emanate from the office of the dean.

4. *An understanding of institutional character makes possible the prediction of the consequences of decision.* One can expect vociferous alumni reaction to the cancellations of intercollegiate football at a large state university. Admissions policies at urban and state public universities which seek to eliminate the less qualified high school graduates may arouse opposition to allocation of public funds. In a more sophisticated situation, the tendency to retain as far as possible the services of all faculty members currently employed cannot help but lead in the future to an "old guard" situation in which the faculty is dominated by numbers more at home in the past than open-minded to the future. The decision to build a new building without consulting faculty members at one college will arouse little comment; at another it will result in a storm of protest and discontent.

5. *The character of an institution affects the kind of faculty members and administrative officers it attracts and employs.* Colleges and universities will tend to draw to their staffs individuals who find the campus congenial. Graduate students whose interests lie in scholarly productivity will look to a major university where this is a basic consideration for advancement. A campus characterized by educational creativeness and intellectual ferment will attract new faculty who find this activity stimulating and satisfying. The smaller liberal arts college will appeal to the scholar who finds satisfaction in teaching and close student relationships. The point here is obvious enough, but its significance for administration frequently fails to receive continuing concern.

THE ORGANIZATION OF COLLEGES AND UNIVERSITIES*

The three elements in the organization of almost every college and university are the governing board, "the administration," and the fac-

*Frances H. Horn, "The Organization of Colleges and Universities," from *Administrators in Higher Education, Their Functions and Coordination.* Edited by Gerald P. Burns. Copyright © 1962 by Harper & Row, 52-66.

ulty. The governing board is generally known as a board of trustees, less frequently as a board of regents, and in the case of a few older universities, Yale and Brown, for example, as the "corporation." The Corporation of Brown, in fact, is composed of two bodies, the Board of Fellows and the Board of Trustees, and they operate in a unique manner, meeting in the same room at the same time, and generally voting separately but in agreement on most matters. Harvard also has two governing bodies, the President and Fellows (referred to as the Corporation), and the Board of Overseers. . . .

More communication and contact between faculty and board members is certainly desirable, but faculty should neither be board members nor regularly attend meetings. Because of their special knowledge and competence, however, more faculty members should serve on the governing boards of institutions other than those in which they teach.

Some colleges and universities have no governing board serving their exclusive interests. This is true of the public institutions in the nine states having coordinating governing boards. Some Catholic institutions do not have governing boards, although they may have a board which holds title to property. Other Catholic institutions have advisory boards, although they do not exercise final authority over educational policy.

Even in colleges and universities with active governing boards, there is a growing tendency to supplement the work of trustees or regents with various kinds of advisory boards, councils, and committees, on the principle that the more individuals involved with an institution of higher education, the more public understanding and support, especially financial support, it is likely to have. Some institutions, limited in the number of its trustees, have established boards of "associates," without the power of trustees, to provide additional persons having one or more of the qualities of "wisdom, work, or wealth" that trustees are expected to bring to a board. Junior colleges in a state system or branch operations of a parent university may have local advisory councils in lieu of their own governing boards. Increasingly, advisory committees are established for component schools and colleges of a university, sometimes even for each department within a college (of engineering, for example) and for special divisions such as museums, research laboratories, and bureaus. They are often set up for new programs at the development stage. Evening colleges and extension divisions tend especially to proliferate advisory committees in accounting, insurance, real estate, office management, personnel administration, and other areas for which organized professional groups exist in the community. Special committees on workers' education are not uncommon, as organized labor wishes a voice in educational programs designed for its benefit. Finally, a few institutions—Harvard among them—provide "visiting committees" for certain traditional academic areas.

In addition to such advisory committees on various phases of the curriculum and the educational program, almost every college or university has an alumni council, and occasionally, several subordinate councils as well; most of those engaged in intercollegiate athletics have an athletic council; and an increasing number have development councils, sometimes concerned with long-range planning, but always concerned with raising money.

The responsibility of these external bodies and their effectiveness varies from institution to institution. In some cases an advisory committee does little more than attend an annual dinner and have its members listed in the catalogue; in others, they do a great deal of work, studying problems and making recommendations, and their contribution to the governance and administration of an institution is substantial.

THE ADMINISTRATION

Historically in this country there was no such thing in our early colleges as the administration. There was the "president and fellows," as Harvard's charter had it. The president taught, raised money, collected fees, managed the physical plant, handled student discipline, and controlled the faculty and the curriculum. He was the "administration," if the term has any meaning at all for those early days. The faculty was not organized. The teachers were few and most of them could teach the whole curriculum. This simple pattern prevailed until well into the nineteenth century. Then increasing specialization of knowledge gradually affected the organization of the faculty, and growing enrollments with consequent enlargement of physical plant and financial management resulted in some specialization of administrative duties. Yet for most colleges there was little change in the pattern of organization until after the turn of the century. The development of universities, however, out of such older colleges as Harvard, Yale, and Columbia, and de novo, with institutions like Johns Hopkins, Chicago, and Stanford, established the conditions which have led to the complex organization of higher institutions today.

After Johns Hopkins was founded, the advancement of knowledge through research became a major objective of universities in addition to the traditional objective of teaching. And following the lead of the Agricultural Extension Service in the land-grant institutions, all kinds of services came to be regarded as legitimate functions of institutions of higher education.

The result of these influences—the specialization and expansion of knowledge, the development of research, the addition of multifarious services, and the increase in size and wealth of institutions—has led, on the one hand, to a multitude of organizational units within one institution and, on the other, to a proliferation of administrative officials to manage these units and other institutional activities.

Large universities, for example, have all kinds of schools and colleges; centers, bureaus, and institutes for this or that; hospitals, museums, and laboratories. But these units are not generally organized, Edward Litchfield points out into "an organic whole."

In American institutions of higher education, the president; or he may be called a chancellor—is the individual who holds together, so far as they are held together, the multifarious units and agencies of the college or university. He is the chief administrative officer, regardless of the size, purpose, or complexity of the institution; and he has been the key figure in the organizational structure since Harvard College was founded. In this respect, the American tradition contrasts noticeably with the practice in European universities, where the official head of the institution, the rector, is elected by the faculty, usually for a short period of time, and possesses little authority, the institution being ultimately responsible to the state minister of education.

Since the president is the chief executive officer of the institution, all other administrative officers are ultimately responsible to him. However, even the smallest colleges today have more subordinate administrative officers than can conveniently report to the president. How best to relate these administrators to the president and to each other is the major problem in establishing an organizational structure for each institution. The resulting administrative organization of the college or university is not an end in itself. The purpose of administration is to facilitate the objectives for which colleges and universities exist: teaching, research, and public service. Since the specifics of these objectives vary greatly, as do the size, complexity, and historical background of institutions, no standard pattern of organization is equally valid for all colleges and universities.

Some institutions have special organizational patterns because they are part of a university system. The University of California constitutes an example, with its seven branches. Geography plays a role in the organizational pattern in another way. Some universities not located in a metropolitan area have their professional schools, especially the medical school, in a city. If more than one such school is located there, a special administrator may head the group. The University of Illinois, for example, has four professional schools in Chicago, headed by a vice-president; in San Francisco, a provost has the same responsibility for the University of California. . .

ORGANIZATION OF ACADEMIC DEPARTMENTS

Traditionally, academic departments have been organized into schools or colleges. If the institution is a liberal arts college not part of a university, there generally are no other academic divisions. Responsible for the academic program and coordinating the work of the departments is a dean, or a dean of the college, who reports to the president, although in some small colleges, the president himself may act as the chief academic officer. A specialized institution, for art, music, or theology, for example, will be similarly organized, with a dean the major academic administrative officer under the president. But if the institution is a university or a college having some professional divisions in addition to the liberal arts college (or "college of arts and sciences"), each unit will generally be under its own dean. Sometimes, however, a new or a small academic division may be under a "director" rather than under a dean. Occasionally, such a division will be called a school; if called a college, its head invariably is called a dean. Occasionally, too, a college within a university may include several subordinate units called schools.

Regardless of whether the institution is one "college" or has a multiplicity of colleges and schools, the basic academic component is the department. With the increasing specialization of knowledge, the faculty member has come more and more to identify himself with his professional discipline, and hence with the academic department in which he is located. With the growth in size of institutions, the number of faculty members has increased so substantially, and department budgets have become so large (especially in departments with heavy research commitments), that enormous power resides in the departments, and, consequently, in the department heads. All too often, this power is used to resist innovation and change. This has resulted in considerable attention to the place of the departments and departmental chairmen in the organization of the institution, especially to the concept of the permanent departmental chairman. . . .

There is another problem stemming from department strength and organization — how to overcome narrow specialization, or at least how to bring about more cross fertilization of academic disciplines, in both teaching and research. The oldest organizational device for accomplishing this is the divisional pattern. Harvard has had divisions since before the turn of the century. The three divisions most frequently operative are the humanities, social sciences, and natural sciences. Although these constitute the standard pattern, a decade ago Johns Hopkins reorganized its faculty and program into four "groups," breaking the natural sciences up into the biological and the physical sciences, and placing engineering with the latter. In some institutions, MIT, for example, the earth sciences have been separated from the physical sciences and located in a division of their own. In the social sciences, the "behavioral sciences" have been brought together administratively in some universities.

Other attempts at crossing department lines occur through inter-disciplinary programs, as in the various area studies dealing with a particular geographical region of the world. In most cases, inter-departmental committees are the organizational medium for such arrange-ments, although increasingly such programs have a "director."

An attempt to meet this problem of overspecialization in another way has been the general education movement. This is primarily a matter of curriculum, but it has had considerable influence in some institutions on the organizational structure of the academic program. Most often, gen-eral education objectives have been achieved, or at least attempted, through special courses or distribution requirements within the standard organization of the schools and colleges in the institution. In such cases, a coordinator, or coordinating committee, may control the program.

Brief comments should be made about several other aspects of the organization of the academic program. In many institutions the general extension program and the evening college program cut across the usual college and professional lines. In a few universities the dean of the particular college — for example, liberal arts, business, or engineering — controls the extension or evening college program in his field. More commonly, extension or evening college is under its own dean or direc-tor, who controls the program and faculty with varying cooperation from the appropriate college deans. . . .

The library is another integral part of the academic program. The librarian in larger institutions usually enjoys a status comparable to that of a dean; in a few cases, he now carries the title "dean of libraries," in others, "director of libraries." He generally reports to the chief aca-demic officer of the institution. . . .

The need to provide some control over the rapidly expanding research activities of universities has resulted in the creation of a new position of coordinator or director of research. This individual, in most cases, is not primarily concerned with the separately organized research operations which characterize some of our largest universities. He is concerned rather with the coordination of research activities in institutions in which most of the faculty do some teaching. Occasionally, the dean of the graduate school has this responsibility. At North Carolina there is a vice-president for graduate studies and research. Increasingly, the work load demands a separate administrator.

The organization of the academic program is quite complex, even in the smaller institutions. Only in the smallest colleges can the president be the chief academic administrator, dealing directly with the faculty and matters of curriculum. In most institutions he must have someone to whom he delegates authority for such relationships. In single-purpose institutions, this is likely to be "the dean" or the "dean of the college." In medium-sized, multipurpose institutions, the authority rests with the deans and directors of the separate schools and colleges, who report direct to the president. But in most large universities, and in an increasing number of medium-sized ones, the president delegates his responsibility for academic matters to an "academic vice-president" or "vice-president for academic affairs." In some institutions the individual carrying this major academic responsibility is entitled "dean of the faculty" or "dean of instruction.". . .

ORGANIZATION OF NON-ACADEMIC SERVICES

It is customary to think of "the administration" as being divided into academic and non-academic areas. Except for the president of the institution, academic administrators are expected to have an academic background and teaching experience; this is not expected of non-academic administrators. This contributes on most campuses to a feeling, held generally by the faculty, but occasionally by the non-academic administrators themselves, that their interests are opposed. Faculty members often think of the budgetary controls of the business office as designed to impede the academic program; consider that those responsible for the operation and maintenance of the physical plant are in a conspiracy to obstruct their teaching and research; look with suspicion upon the goals of the student personnel program; and consciously or unconsciously sabotage the efforts of the public relations program. Conversely, non-academic administrators not infrequently regard faculty members as unreasonable, thoughtless, wasteful, and unconcerned about the institution as a whole.

But there should be no dichotomy between the academic program and the non-academic services which make the academic program possible. The faculty — and the deans who represent them in the administration — and the non-academic administrators are partners in a common enterprise. There needs to be better understanding and articulation of their respective contributions to the welfare of the institution.

There are three major areas of non-academic administration: financial and plant management, student personnel services, and development and public relations. The organization of the subordinate agencies and services within each area varies greatly among institutions of higher education. However, there is increasing recognition that greater standardization will result in more effective operation of these agencies and services. . . .

FINANCIAL AND PLANT MANAGEMENT

There is general recognition that the chief fiscal officer of the institution is, after the president, and after the chief academic officer where one other than the president exists, the top administrator of the college or university. Because budget is a major limiting factor in the growth and development of an institution, the fiscal officer has a close relationship to the academic program and a significant role in the total institutional operation.

Although still most generally termed the "business manager," increasingly the position carries the title of "vice-president for business (or financial) affairs." Occasionally, the individual carries the additional title of "treasurer," although the treasurer is frequently a subordinate officer in the division, whose duties vary from institution to institution. The major responsibilities of the business division concern financial management, the physical plant, purchasing, and non-academic personnel. In the area of financial management, there are likely to be specific positions for a comptroller, a chief accountant, and a bursar. In smaller institutions, of course, a single individual may handle a number of responsibilities. If the institution has substantial endowment funds, management of these investments is handled by one officer, usually by the treasurer.

Plant management is generally assigned to a "director of physical plant." Depending upon the size of the operation, he will have as subordinates, someone in charge of buildings and grounds, of police and fire protection, and of utility services. . . .

Another area of responsibility centered in the business office is the management of auxiliary enterprises. In some institutions, there is a coordinating director for all such services; in others, separate directors for food service, housing, the union, and the bookstore. The athletic association often has comparative fiscal independence. In these areas of auxiliary enterprises, responsibility is sometimes divided between the business office and the officer in charge of student personnel services. Housing, for example, involves a program of dormitory counseling and discipline, with supervision of housemothers, head residents, and counselors, or sponsors, whose activities are part of the student personnel program. In such cases, the director of housing may be responsible to the chief business officer for assignment of rooms and the furnishing and upkeep of the dormitory and to the chief personnel officer for other relations with students. The director of the union may have similarly divided responsibilities.

STUDENT PERSONNEL SERVICES

Such divided responsibility points up the difficulty of staking out clearcut lines of authority in the organizational structure of colleges and universities. This is a problem in such areas as admissions and records. Traditionally, the positions of director of admissions and of registrar have been held by one person. Elwood Kastner in his chapter sets forth arguments for continuing the consolidated position. In large institutions, the arguments are more compelling for separating them, and in more institutions this is being accomplished. These officers are sometimes given the title of "dean of admissions" and "dean of records." Originally they reported to the president. In larger institutions they are being brought under the officer in charge of all student personnel services.

Financial aid, once handled in the admissions office, has become such a large operation, with scholarships and loans amounting in some universities to more than a million dollars annually, that a separate office is now common. Placement, once handled hit or miss by individual professors or deans, is now a highly organized activity which properly belongs in a coordinated student personnel setup. Other activities include the testing and counseling service, sometimes handled by one office, sometimes separated; the office of the foreign student advisor; the health service; extracurricular activities; intercollegiate athletics, generally administered separately from the rest of the activity program; and the student union. Various combinations of these positions occur, depending upon the size, complexity, tradition, and personalities involved in the particular institution. As student personnel work becomes more stabilized, however, it is believed that the standard organization of personnel services as indicated above will become more common. ...

In spite of frequent faculty criticism of the student personnel program, the nature of the educational process today can only result in more, not less, student services. On too many campuses such activities are poorly organized in relation to one another. Coordination under one major administrative officer is essential for an effective program.

DEVELOPMENT AND PUBLIC RELATIONS

The third and final major area of the essentially non-academic administrative organization covers the broad fields of public and alumni relations and "development." In order to provide maximum consideration of these important functions, this volume has chapters on each, but in both theory and practice, there is increasing recognition that coordination of these activities must be effected by one administrative officer at the top level.

NATURE OF THE COLLEGE PRESIDENCY*

The college presidency has an individuality which the person who holds the office must accept and foster if he hopes to meet its responsibilities successfully. Certainly the demands are great. . . .

After accepting the challenge of the office, the incumbent encounters strange paradoxes. He receives recommendations for action from many sources: his administrative associates, the teaching faculty, the students, the alumni, the patrons of the college. It he takes action in contradiction to a recommendation, he is guilty of a liberty which legally is his but morally may not be.

Does the college president have the moral right to deny the recommendation of a committee on a subject of an academic nature? Representatives of the teaching faculty, for example, may insist, "The faculty should have major responsibility for the educational and research policy of the institution." Is the office of president one of passive or dynamic leadership? If the leadership is dynamic, is it in keeping with the academic tradition to veto actions which may have the support of a majority of the students or the faculty? How is the office of president viewed by students, faculty, and alumni? If on the one hand the presidency is to be like the office of rector of the German university, then the president is more passive than dynamic. He is expected to shoot straws into the wind, as it were. If the current of feeling on the campus approaches unanimity and it is evident that academe is vitally interested in an issue, then the president follows the judgment of the majority and the authority of his office is used simply to implement the action.

On the other hand, if the American college presidency has a distinct character of its own and is truly reflected in the activities of Eliot of Harvard, Harper of Chicago, Cotton Mather of Yale, Angell of Mich-

---

*Ralph Prator, *The College President*, Washington, D.C.: by permission of The Center for Applied Research in Education, Inc., 1963, 20-21, 24-25, 30.

igan, Wayland of Brown, and Hall of Clark, then the college president should play a more vigorous role, and his decisions will reflect his own strong moral convictions. . . .

The college presidency has attracted noted men from many fields. It has held out the hope that in this position a goal may be reached, a cause may be nurtured, the truth may finally be brought to light. To Horace Mann the presidency of Antioch College seemed a means of climaxing his dream to do for higher education what he had so successfully done for the lower schools during his distinguished career in many responsible positions in Massachusetts. To William Rainey Harper the presidency of the University of Chicago provided an opportunity to apply unique theories about organizing the college experience for the learner. . . .

In most church-related colleges the president is expected to conform to the tenets of the devout churchgoer. If the college is a technical institution, the president is expected to be conversant with the great skills which are incorporated in the major curricula. If the college is a liberal arts institution, the president is expected to have a broad educational preparation and erudite views on many subjects. In short, the president is expected either to exemplify the ideals of the institution or to be the spokesman for its point of view. This is the role he plays in the minds and eyes of the students.

After the student becomes an alumnus, he views the president differently. The president is no longer a symbol of the college. He may no longer seem so erudite, nor so aloof, nor, in some respects, such a mythical person. He is far more real a person than had been supposed, one with many of the common misgivings and some of the doubts of others. In short, he is human!

Alumni come to regard the president of the college as a resource person. He is the liaison between the alumni association and the college. He is the key figure in alumni development. He is the best drawing card at alumni meetings, for he is the one who speaks with the most commanding voice of the past glories and future ambitions of the college. He is the maker of plans. He is the giver of favors. He is the one who always duns alumni for money. To alumni in the legislature, he is the one who is continuously in need of "your help" in order that alma mater may have her budget favorably considered. The president is also the one who asks the alumni to recruit in their community the finest young people for the college.

Some of the alumni become reasonably well acquainted with the college president when he attends alumni institutes and workshops or performs as the ringmaster on extensive alumni tours. On these occasions the president has a key role in bringing the college to the alumni. Often such tours will take several weeks and may reach a number of important metropolitan areas in the state, if the institution is a state supported college, or may visit the cities of a whole region, if it is a private institution. The theme of such alumni conclaves is generally the same: what is alma mater now doing, what are her needs, and what are the great plans for her future? Many alumni attend these affairs hoping to recapture some of the excitement and thrills they had as students, and some may come to offer service or give advice on the management of the college.

To the faculty the president is the symbol of authority. He *is* the administration. He is the enforcer of the rules, and some say he has the image of management. Generally, the faculty is sensitive to his presence. Restraint normally prevails when the president converses with the faculty. He imposes a certain air of formality and, depending somewhat on his personality, also a feeling of reserve, or on some occasions even arouses a kind of wholesome respect. His approval is most welcome if it comes in response to something that the faculty member regards important. If the affairs of the institution are not going well, the president inevitably is viewed with some irritation. He can console himself that he is usually not the sole source of irritation to the faculty, even though he may be held responsible by the community for everything that takes place on the campus. Too frequently, however, the faculty does credit the president with the authority to correct anything or anyone "if he wants to."

All that has been said about the college president is modified appreciably by the personality of the person in the office. Generally, in the eyes of the students, the alumni, and the faculty, the man and his office are one. If the president is a reserved person, then the reaction to his his office is quite different from what it would be were he an affable fellow. Unavoidably, however, similar pressures produce similar reactions. College presidents tend to act somewhat alike by virtue of the similarity of the problems which confront them from day to day, and these special kinds of problems make the college presidency unlike other leadership posts in American life.

Perhaps it is for these reasons that he especially enjoys the company of his fellow college presidents. The restrictions, the disposition to be on guard, and the shackles of authority fall away. Here a spirit of camaraderie prevails, and the president becomes a very different person in this company from the one he is on campus. . . .

LEGAL STATUS OF THE OFFICE

If any conclusion may be drawn as to a definition of the legal status of the college president, it is that specificity may range from the merest reference to the president's office to a detailed exposition of his responsbilities in the regulations of governing boards.

In order to assess the situation, a questionnaire was addressed to the chief legal officer and the chief education officer of the fifty states in the Union. Their replies revealed that no clear indication as to the legal status of this office is to be found in constitutions, statutes, or administrative regulations. It may, however, be concluded that generally the state college or university president does not enjoy tenure status. In the vast majority of states, he is the appointee of the governing board of the institution and serves at its pleasure, being reappointed year to year or on some other terminal contract basis.

THE NEED FOR RESEARCH IN COLLEGE ADMINISTRATION*

No president or other administrative officer survives long or wields effective control who fails to understand the varied interactions among the units of academic government. Yet, as noted on the pages to follow, little has been done to investigate systematically the formal roles and relationships of administrators in colleges and universities. Nor have extensive systematic analyses been made of the informal roles and relationships described in the following section on the institutional setting.

An experimental view of higher education readily reveals a common pattern of organizational structure for nearly all institutions. Governing boards hold final, legal authority. Presidents tend to serve in a dual relationship as executives for boards and leaders of their faculties. A power flow routes executive authority from presidents through deans and departmental chairmen to faculty members, on the one hand, and legislative initiative moves from individual faculty members to departmental, school, or college faculties to institution-wide senates, councils, or faculty meetings for educational policy, on the other. Because the professionalized personnel of departments are committed to specialized disciplines, departments play a highly autonomous role within the organization. The executive direction of a college accordingly, does not have that "down the line" authority associated with the administration of business and government. Decisions at the departmental, school, or college level —

---

*E. D. Duryea, *Management of Learning*, New Dimensions in Higher Education Series No. 5. Washington, D.C.: United States Office of Education, 1960, 14-15, 31.

especially those which deal with the employment and advancement of personnel — tend to reflect commitments to disciplines and professions rather than to the policies of the institution.

Individual colleges and universities, of course, differ in the authority and responsibility held by various units of academic government. Local traditions, local functions and purposes, geographical location, relations with supporting governments and donors, student clientele, attitudes, values and capabilities of individual participants, and similar elements combine to give each campus a particular pattern of authority and of relationships. In some institutions presidents serve as highly authoritarian executives; in others, they find it difficult to exert educational leadership because their faculties are highly independent and autonomous. That such problems concern administrators is made clear at professional meetings attended by board members, presidents, academic administrators, and faculty members.

Despite this expressed concern, investigation disclosed relatively few studies which focus on the problems involved. Those which do are for the most part inchoate and uncoordinated. From the limited data available, it would appear that two kinds of studies would be very profitable. One would examine the roles, responsibilities, and authorities of individual units of government. The other would study academic organizations as total structures. . . .

Effective administration can be defined in terms of the achievement of creative scholarship and research which is communicated through teaching, publication, and other means to students and to the public. The effective institution, in this sense, is the one which maintains the function of intellectual leadership for society.

Furthermore, colleges and universities present to administrators a set of unique difficulties. The pervading intangibility of many aspects of administration at all levels and the absence of adequate standards and methods of appraisal tend to draw a haze over the making of decisions and to destroy the clarity of issues. The intellectual insularity of the faculty, the increasing demands of their specialties, their lack of training in administrative matters and indoctrination in the purposes of the institution, and their frequent distrust of administration present barriers to effective processes similar to but more sharply outlined than those in other enterprises.

Such characteristics create for universities and colleges a set of relationships which make most difficult the kind of planning, communication, direction, delegation, supervision, and evaluation possible in other enterprises. Yet, the foreseeable demands of the future already press for substantial adjustments in function and, to a degree, purpose if higher education will retain its vigor as the intellectual spearhead of American society.

To date, however, no body of literature addressed to this problem has appeared. The need for systematic study of administration becomes increasingly urgent as the limitations of much of our administrative process and organizational structure show up in the face of demands made on our institutions by our own and other changing cultures.

COLLEGE BUSINESS MANAGERS NEED SPECIAL TRAINING*

Decisions in colleges and universities today are being made more and more by a small group of the top officials. Several developments account for this, including growth of the institution in size and also in complexity of structure, the academic and research pressures on the faculty, and the widespread adoption of a cabinet mode of operation. These officers are likely to meet weekly, confer more frequently, and make decisions that have penetrating and lasting impacts upon the character and program of the institution.

Among these high officials is the vice-president (or other title) in charge of business affairs. Indeed it is not uncommon to find among these key men only one or two officers whose primary concern is with the academic program. This happens when the office of vice-president for academic program is created, with the deans of the colleges reporting to him rather than directly to the president. Thus the top echelon of officers usually consists of the president, whose office is becoming more and more removed fom direct administration of the educational program, and vice-presidents (or other titles) in charge of academic affairs, student personnel, business affairs, public relations, and development.

The effect is to elevate considerably the roles of officers who formerly were regarded as performing functions that were purely service in type, and hence secondary in importance within the institution. This change has special significance for the two offices concerned with the business management and with the promotion ond development of the college.

Not only are these men continuously within the decision-making process at the highest level, but the specific areas of which they have charge

---

*Algo D. Henderson, "How to Educate Business Managers for Their Role as Decision-Makers," by permission of *College and University Business*, XXXVI (May, 1964), 57-59.

have been assuming major importance in the growth and operation of the institution. . . .

Thus the judgments made by the business officer, and to some extent his principal assistants, have impacts that permeate the whole of the college or university.

They affect the long-run planning for growth and change, the adequacy of funds and facilities, the policies and emphases within the operating budget, personnel policies, and, to some extent, the welfare of the students and the scope and nature of the academic program.

This analysis has been made in order to shed light upon the kind of education or preparation the chief business officer should have for his responsibilities. For the position no longer resembles the more familiar type as treasurer, or bursar, or accountant, on controller, all of which have connotations of principal concern with cash receipts and expenditures. The business officer of today is deeply involved in the ongoing educational program, and also in other matters of business and public relations that are a far cry from accounting, purchasing and housekeeping. . . .

Internally the organization and administration are different from business for several reasons: the objectives focus on the growth of young people and on the production of new knowledge, and are therefore highly intangible; in the achievement of the objectives, effectiveness of the program outweighs considerations of efficiency, especially as measured in financial terms; faculty members perceive themselves as peers (and indeed they are experts in their specialized fields) and colleagues of the administrative officers, and not merely as employees; often the rewards of greatest appeal to faculty come from the recognition given individuals by professional societies and associations outside of the institution, thus reducing the impact of the incentives offered by the institution, and sometimes creating a division of loyalties; the problems of communication are complicated both because of faculty insistence that it be two-way communication and because the verbalistic nature of the profession of teaching and writing inhibits the assimilation of routine announcements and directives; faculty demands participation in decision-makng, but the faculty committee is notoriously time-consuming and inefficient, and the so-called democratic idea that everybody should decide everything breaks down seriously in practice. . . .

Administrative officers probably would do a better job in administration if they had some education in administrative theory and practice.

This suggests a second broad area of education for the business officer. I contend that the study of administration, including college administration, is a discipline, and therefore makes an appropriate specialized field for the master's and doctor's degree programs. Not only does it involve organizational theory, but the study of administrative processes and administrative behavior, and of such concepts as authority, power, leadership, persuasion, communication, conflict, consensus and decision-making.

In what respects should the education of the business officer vary from that of other officers?

Probably in the same manner in which it has varied heretofore — in the study of accounting, controllership, investments, nonacademic personnel management, commercial law, and so forth. Subjects such as these would prepare him for the administration of finance, of property, and of personnel, and assist him in solving problems relating to purchasing, insurance, social security, government contracts, and a multitude of other things that are characteristic of any operating enterprise.

Thus we have identified three principal areas of study for the future business manager of a college or university: (1) the history, philosophy and contemporary problems of higher education; (2) the theory and practice of administration, with special consideration of the nature of a college or university, and (3) a section of subjects from the usual curriculum in business administration.

THE AWKWARD POSITION OF DEAN OF GRADUATE STUDIES*

At their meeting two years ago, the presidents and the graduate deans of the AAU universities held a symposium on "The Ambiguous Position of the Graduate School Dean." Most observers, I think, consider it just as ambiguous after that discussion as before, mainly because ambiguity is inherent in the situation as universities are now organized. As a former dean put it, "the graduate school is a residual organization."

Administrative and organizational problems have characterized graduate work so long that most people have become used to them. The subordination of the graduate school to the undergraduate college, the intermingling of graduate and undergraduate students in the same courses, the uneven struggle between the dean's office and the depart-

*From *Graduate Education in the United States* by Bernard Berelson. Copyright 1960, McGraw-Hill Book Company. Used by permission of McGraw-Hill Book Company, 119-121.

ments, the weakness of a dean with no budgetary or appointive authority — these matters have been remarked by generations of commentators on the graduate scene.

Jaques Barzun, when a graduate dean, referred to the graduate faculty as "the amiable anarchy" and Professor Cowley has characterized the graduate school as a collection of small professional schools (i.e., the departments) held together by their devotion to research and the magic of the Ph.D. degree. Someone has said that "you can't build up the graduate dean any more than you can the Vice President of the United States.". . .

In the typical university, even the large graduate university, the undergraduate dean "outranks" the graduate dean partly because of history (he was there first), partly because of size (he has more students and gets more tuition for the institution), and partly because of primacy (he has under him what is usually defined as the major task of the institution). The graduate dean has a voice in academic matters but usually it is only an advisory and consultative one. Compared to the professional deans in medicine and law, he has much less authority. In only a very few institutions is the organization radically different: Chicago is the notable example — in effect, it has a graduate dean for each of the major divisions of knowledge, with a budget and appointive power.

As a matter of administration, the graduate school usually has jurisdiction over the award of the Ph.D. wherever in the university it is given, and less often, over other graduate degrees as well. The major policies and practices in graduate study are "actually determined, regardless of formal regulations," in the following way, according to the graduate deans:

Mainly by the graduate school	*By both*	*Mainly by the department*
Residence requirement	Amount of course	Character of doctoral di-
Foreign language	work	sertation
requirement	Student admission	Type of general examina-
Membership in graduate	Master's degree require-	tion
faculty	ments	

Thus the graduate school is left (1) with determining membership in the graduate faculty, which is *pro forma* in many cases and a matter of departmental recommendation in others; the graduate school can veto, but every such veto costs something in peaceful relations, frequently more than it is worth; (2) with setting the residence requirement, largely a paper requirement that is becoming even less consequential; and (3) with determining the foreign language requirement — small wonder that it is so in contention. As to the joint responsibilities, the department typically makes the decision and the graduate school ratifies or implements it. The graduate school admits students, to be sure, but the departments really select them (what one disapproving university president describes as "something amounting almost to a guild system with restriction of entry at the departmental level"). Even the Master's degree requirement is passing to the departments, reflecting what is happening to the status of that degree.

Indeed, some people seriously propose that under the circumstances the graduate school should abdicate to the departments, thus placing formal responsibility where the actual power is. In any case, how can a dean know enough about the specialized problems and qualifications of English, engineering, economics, mathematics, zoology, history, chemistry, psychology, and all the rest to do more than ask a few questions and ratify the judgment of the departments? (Some departments are so large and diversified that, as one faculty member puts it, "the heads are bumping together there too!")

Under the circumstances one might expect the graduate deans to be discontented and restless, but on the whole they are not. Some deans are appointed as a reward for seniority or earlier distinction, especially when the office is more honorific than substantial. Sometimes top men will not take the post because of its clerical character and lack of real opportunity. But there is no basis for the minor legend in academic circles that the tenure of the graduate dean is extremely short — just long enough for a man of vision to find out how little he can do. The graduate deans are not particularly short-lived: the present group have been in office an average of about seven years. As nearly as I can tell, they do not hold office for a shorter period than the dean of the college or, for that matter, the president himself.

As for their attitudes toward the situation, only one dean in five thinks that "the office of graduate dean at your institution does not have enough authority to do the job properly" although about a third say it "would be better for graduate study if the office were strengthened." By and large, the graduate deans themselves appear to accept the situation as it is. One told me that in view of the absolute requirement for persuasion and consent in a university of strong and independent departments, all he could get was a "paper authority" in any case. Another — who recently put through a basic change at his university — thought that it was desirable to have one important office on the campus without power, as a safety valve for the tensions and conflicts inevitable among other centers of power within the university.

PROFESSORS AS
QUASI-ADMINISTRATORS*

Half a professor's time, then, is devoted to teaching and half to private scholarship or research. A "third half" of his time is devoted to the other tasks which are part of his job.

Legal responsibility for the government of an American college or university rests with its governing board. But boards of trustees, formally or informally, usually delegate matters of educational policy to the faculty. Indeed, trouble results when boards of trustees "interfere" with educational policy. Educational wisdom as well as educational expertness is presumed to reside in the faculty, and the tradition that faculties must be responsible for planning as well as for conducting the education of their students is stronger than the letter of the law.

Colleges and universities differ from one another in administrative organization and in the extent to which responsibility is officially delegated to administrative officers and teaching faculty, but generally the faculty determines what is taught and how it is taught. In some colleges, the faculty as a whole is the designated policy-making body, and everyone who teaches "full time" is considered a member of the faculty. In some larger institutions, a "senate" of senior faculty members (professors, or professors and associate professors, or a body elected from them) has the bylaw responsibility for educational policy.

Characteristically, as in other parliamentary government, the basic work is done in committee. Typical faculty standing committees are the committees on curriculum, on admission, on research, on appointments and promotions, on student affairs, on athletics, and the like. *Ad hoc* committees are formed to study and make recommendations on many other more particular problems. There are departmental committees, divisional committees, senate committees, faculty committees.

Departmental committees meet to select textbooks for multiple-section courses, to discuss changes in the requirements for a major, to recommend inclusion of their subject in the general education requirements for all students, to examine the credentials of nominees for appointment

---

*Van Cleve Morris, et al., *Becoming an Educator,* Boston: Houghton Mifflin Co., 1963. Above extracted from chapter by John S. Diekhoff, "Higher Education." 276-278.

(and to interview them), to recommend promotion of a colleague, to recommend loans and scholarships for students, to award departmental prizes, to schedule classes, to assign elective courses to different colleagues, to formulate requests for government or foundation grants.

Divisional committees meet to consider department recommendations and to forward them to faculty committees or to administrative officers, to plan interdisciplinary courses or programs or majors, to weigh the conflicting claims of component departments, to review departmental course schedules, to plan programs of public lectures, to recommend the formation of new committees.

Faculty committees meet to review divisional and departmental recommendations, to study the academic calendar, to allocate office, laboratory, and classroom space, to plan library policy (perhaps to allocate library funds to divisions and departments), to recommend editors for student publications, to establish policies governing intramural and intercollegiate athletics, to deal with problems of student discipline, to formulate memorial minutes for deceased collegues, and to recommend the establishment of new committees and their membership.

All faculty members serve on committees, and it takes time. College teachers are articulate. They talk a lot. They are enthusiasts for their subjects, and they defend their vested interests and seek to extend their empires as fervently and as persistently as any other enthusiasts. As scholars they are more oriented toward investigation than toward action, and they are likely to delay decisions and recommendations (but not debate) while they seek "more evidence." In educational matters they are conservative, inclined to plan the education of the rising generation in terms of their own education. The education which made them what they are seems to them perfectly satisfactory. Even when the need for change is recognized and when the time is favorable to change, the debate continues. It takes time.

As college professors grow in seniority and influence in their faculties, they are called upon again and again, day after day, week after week, until these deliberative, legislative, and semi-administrative duties do indeed become the third major fraction of the professor's job. The burden is not evenly distributed. Some faculty members avoid committee assignments. Others, somewhat sheepishly, seek them. Colleagues learn who is good at committee activities, who contributes little, who obstructs. And so do administrators, who appoint the committees that are not elected. The same work horses show up again and again, but no one escapes the burden entirely. Few wish to escape entirely, for the committees are the means by which faculties control the educational programs of their institutions, and they guard their prerogative jealously.

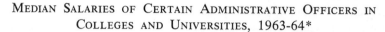

MEDIAN SALARIES OF CERTAIN ADMINISTRATIVE OFFICERS IN
COLLEGES AND UNIVERSITIES, 1963-64*

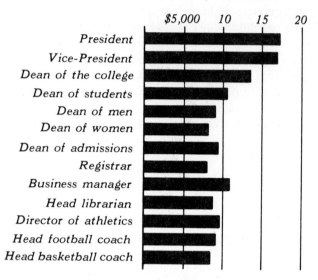

FOR FURTHER REFLECTION OR INVESTIGATION

1. Through a questionnaire or interview, survey the administrative officers of your university to determine career paths to their present positions.

2. Evaluate the administrative practices in your institution in terms of the principles espoused in Chapter II.

3. How can you reconcile the resistance to change which might be encountered on a college campus with the normal expectation that it be on the cutting edge of innovation, ideas, and truth?

4. Justify the absence of supervision and evaluation of teaching effectiveness in college classrooms. Should it be done? If so, how?

5. Interview several faculty members to determine their attitudes toward administration, policy making, and authority on the campus.

6. After studying the history, objectives, and operations of a prominent European university, compare with those at your institution, describing the differences which might have an impact on administrative practices.

7. Obtain permission to observe a meeting of your institution's governing board and compare procedures with those of your board of education.

8. If your university has an administrative organization chart, analyze and compare it with that of a public school system of similar enrollment.

9. If the deans and central staff officers of your institution have written

---

NEA Research Bulletin, XLII (May, 1964), 42, by permission of National Education Association.

job descriptions, evaluate them in terms of those which may have been published in your home school district.

10. In your college or university, tabulate the number of professors with full-time teaching loads, the number with reduced loads and the reasons for the reduction, relating the numbers in each case with professorial rank.

BIBLIOGRAPHY

Ayers, Archie R. and John H. Russel, *Internal Structure: Organization and Administration of Institutions of Higher Education.* Washington, D.C.: United States Office of Education Bulletin No. 9, 1962.

Barzun, Jacques, *The House of Intellect,* New York: Harper & Row, Publishers, 1959.

Berelson, Bernard, *Graduate Education in the United States,* New York: McGraw-Hill Book Company, Inc., 1960.

Blackwell, Thomas Edward, *College Law, a Guide for Administrators.* Washington, D.C.: American Council on Education, 1961.

Boroff, David, *Campus U.S.A.: Portraits of American Colleges in Action,* New York: Harper & Row, Publishers, 1961.

Burns, Gerald P., ed., *Administrators in Higher Education, Their Functions and Coordination,* New York: Harper & Row, Publishers, 1962.

Corson, John J., *Governance of Colleges and Universities,* New York: McGraw-Hill Book Co., Inc., 1960.

Dodds, Harold W., *The Academic President — Educator or Caretaker?* New York: McGraw-Hill Book Co., Inc., 1962.

Dodds, Harold W., "Some Thoughts on the University Presidency," *Public Administration Review,* XX, Winter, 1960.

Duryea, E. D., *Management of Learning,* New Dimensions in Higher Education Series No. 5, Washington, D.C.: United States Office of Education, 1960.

Eells, W. C., and E. V. Hollis, *The College Presidency,* 1900-1960. Washington, D.C.: United States Office of Education, Bulletin No. 9, 1961.

Eliot, Charles W., *University Administration,* Boston: Houghton-Mifflin Co., 1908.

Gibson, Raymond C., *The Challenge of Leadership in Higher Education,* Dubuque, Iowa: Wm. C. Brown Company Publishers, 1964.

Glenny, Lyman A., *Autonomy of Public Colleges,* New York: McGraw-Hill Book Co., 1959.

Goodman, Paul, *The Community of Scholars,* New York: Random House, 1962.

Haas, Eugene and Linda Collen, "Administrative Practices in University Departments," *Administrative Science Quarterly,* VIII, June, 1963.

Henderson, Algo D., "How to Educate Business Managers for Their Role as Decision-Makers," *College and University Business,* XXXVI, May, 1964.

———., *Policies and Practices in Higher Education,* New York: Harper & Row, Publishers, 1960.

Hillway, Tyrus, *The American Two-Year College,* New York: Harper & Row, Publishers, 1958.

How College Presidents Are Chosen, Washington, D.C.: American Council on Education, 1946.

Humphreys, Richard F., "Interdependence of Administration and Faculty," *School and Society,* XCII, February 8, 1964.

Hungate, Thad L., *Management in Higher Education,* New York: Teachers College, Columbia University, 1964.

Johnson, E. L., "Myths of College Administration," *Educational Record,* XLV, Summer, 1964.

Kinane, M., "Evolving Role of Dean of Students," *Catholic Educational Review,* LXI, September, 1963.

Litchfield, Edward H., "Organization in Large Universities," *Journal of Higher Education,* XXX, October, 1959.

Lombardi, John, "Emergent Issues in Administration," *Junior College Journal,* XXXV, November 1964.

Mayer, Frederick, *Creative Universities,* New York: College and University Press, 1961.

McMurrin, Sterling M., "American Education and the Culture," *"Teachers College Record,* LXIII, October, 1961.

Medsker, Leland L., *The Junior College, Progress and Prospect,* New York: McGraw-Hill Book Co., 1960.

Morris, Van Cleve, et al, *Becoming an Educator,* Boston: Houghton Mifflin Co., 1963.

Mushkin, Selma J., ed., *Economics of Higher Education,* Washington, D.C.: United States Office of Education, Bulletin No. 5, 1962.

NEA Research Bulletin, XLII, May, 1964.

Prator, Ralph, *The College President,* Washington, D.C.: The Center for Applied Research in Education, Inc., 1963.

Sanford, Nevitt, ed., *College and Character,* New York: John Wiley & Sons, Inc., 1964.

Scheps, Clarence, "Systematic Financial Analysis and Budgetary Planning as Aids in the Attainment of College and University Purposes," Washington, D.C.: National Education Association, Association for Higher Education, *Current Issues in Higher Education,* Proceedings of the 16th Annual National Conference on Higher Education, 1961.

Snow, C. P., "Higher Education in America" (guest editorial), *NEA Journal,* LII, April, 1964.

Stoke, Harold W., *The American College President,* New York: Harper & Row, Publishers, 1959.

Summary Report (OE-53014-62). Washington, D.C.: United States Office of Education, November, 1963.

Williams, Melvin G., "Does American Higher Education Need to Seek New Directions?" *Journal of Higher Education,* XXXV, March, 1964.

Wriston, Henry M., *Academic Procession, Reflections of a College President,* New York: Columbia University Press, 1959.

Woodburne, Lloyd S., *Principles of College and University Administration,* Stanford: Stanford University Press, 1958.

Part II

Functional Administration in Education

Chapter 8

Communication Responsibilities of the School Administrator

The most needed and the most poorly prepared-for skill of the American school administrator is the ability to communicate effectively. All the talents he may acquire are little more than useful appendages if he cannot maintain successful two-way communication with colleagues, citizens, and students. Most executive failures, by far, may be traced directly or indirectly to the inability to communicate and relate well to others.

Considering the dogmatic weight of this statement one might wonder why administration is not defined as communicating and relating. It could properly be. It is difficult to imagine any aspect of executive work that does not involve communicating or relating to others: planning, decision-making, management, organization, or any of the functional tasks of administration. A high proportion of the administrator's work is accomplished with and through groups of various sizes. Even when he is alone in his office reading correspondence and reports, or professional literature, he is on the receiving end of communication. If he is a silent participant in classroom supervision or merely in attendance at a large community meeting, he is involved in communication and relating. The only times an executive is not so immersed are those few occasions when he is isolated in thought, and even those thoughts will necessitate communications if they are to be activated. Perhaps the only reason communication and relation cannot be used as an acceptable definition of administration is that what has been said about the administrator can also be said about the teacher. The major difference, again, is one of scope, place, and assignment.

Another reason communication skill has not been rendered due emphasis in either the training or the thought about the administrative function arises from the restricted understanding of the term. Tradition-

374

ally, the administrator's responsibility for communication has been considered in terms of his public relations function. It was often assumed that if the administrator-in-training had the standard university course in school public relations he had sufficiently explored the skill. The abundance of literature in the field deals with this single phase of communication. Lately educators have begun to recognize the importance of the organization's internal communication. Not yet is there wide acceptance of the view that the performance of all administrative tasks is predicated upon communicative ability.

This chapter seeks to spotlight the importance of communication, to suggest avenues open to the administrator for its attainment both within the organization and to outside agencies, to provide some techniques in abbreviated form, and to make available pertinent selected readings from authorities.

EXTERNAL COMMUNICATIONS

The premise of local control accounts for the urgency for American public school officials to develop and maintain active communications with citizens, in contrast to the expectations of school executives in foreign countries. A major factor of local control is the system of financing public education which, with few exceptions, depends largely upon local tax support. Since revenue is the crucial element in attaining quality education, the three functions of finance, instructional improvement, and public relations are so intertwined that it is difficult to isolate any one of them. The rationale for the following public relations discussion is explained in its relationship to the other two functions.

What is School Public Relations?

The ultimate aim of efforts toward attaining desirable school-community communications is the same as that for all other efforts exerted by employees of a school system — better education for youth. The immediate aim is to develop understanding and wholesome attitudes between those who work in schools and those who support the schools, for whose benefit the institution is intended. With this understanding of goals, one is ready to examine methods for achieving them.

There are four broad categories of media available to school administrators to promote educational understandings in the community: the medium of students, the medium of employees, the medium of parents, and the medium of citizen groups.

Pupils as a Medium for External Communications

The built-in medium of a school's student body is unquestionably the most fruitful for molding parental attitudes toward the institution. Notwithstanding the other media and the excellent public relations programs which some schools have developed, parents use one criterion above all others in evaluating the success of a school: "How does it affect my child?" All other efforts at rapport-building are secondary. The administrator who desires to win favorable attitudes toward the school will give first attention to the curriculum, and to satisfying the common parental hopes for their children to make progress in school. Satisfied children are the best spokesmen for the schools; dissatisfied children can be the most sabotaging.

In addition to the daily associations of school personnel and students, which have attitudinal implications, the various school-sponsored activities which come before the public's eyes provide another source for public relations. The behavior of students at athletic contests, music and dramatic events, and forensic affairs has an influence upon the thinking of citizens as to how well the school is handling youth. Pupil publications — yearbooks, newspapers, and magazines — reach into many homes. As much as teachers might like to utilize these instruments for youthful self-expression, they cannot permit these publications to circulate in the community without adult supervision. In the reader's mind, the productions represent the school. Wherever school-age youngsters appear before the public — on the school patrol, at social affairs, through club activities, or even walking to and from school — they are shaping the image of the school. School officials have an acres-of-diamonds potential for public relations in their student bodies.

Employees as Medium for External Communications

Teachers and administrators constitute the second most important influence upon community attitudes toward the school, not only through their relationship with the major force of students but through their direct association with citizens. Every employee, certificated and noncertificated, is a satellite for good or poor feelings as he moves among his individual circle of friends in the district. What he says about the school carries considerable weight in formulating judgments. His actions in public are as forceful as his words. Citizens cannot seemingly isolate in their thinking Mr. Jones, the Teacher or Administrator, from Mr. Jones, the Individual. Whatever Mr. Jones does or utters in the community as a citizen is thought of as reflecting the stature and thinking of Mr. Jones, the School Official.

The interrelationships between segments of the school family also have a significant impact upon citizen attitudes. The school system which permits its internal feuds and split-and-divide tactics to spill over into the community must suffer the consequences of citizen confusion, doubt, and sometimes disgust toward the support of that system.

School secretaries serve in a frequently overlooked position for building favorable or unfavorable attitudes toward the school. They are usually the first, often the only, contact which outsiders have with the institution. Their attitudes toward visitors, their helpful tone on the telephone, their sometimes over-protectiveness of their administrators — all these shape attitudes.

Custodians influence citizen attitudes toward the school in their care and cleanliness of the building and grounds, in their personal appearance, and in their manner of accommodating community groups using the school facilities. School bus drivers can create dislikes toward the school by discourteous driving and by the disruption they create in heavy traffic. Cafeteria workers play a part in the attitudes of children toward school, sometimes of adults in dinner affairs at school. School specialists whose work brings them into frequent conversations with citizens: the attendance worker, psychological and medical personnel, the purchasing agent, the business officer charged with allocating school facilities for community use; all are in strategic positions for influencing public attitudes.

The important consideration in this regard is that all members of the school family have a responsibility for building desirable attitudes between the school and home. The chief administrator may have the ultimate accountability for public relations but he cannot achieve the goal alone.

Parents as a Medium of Communication

Parents of school children are both a medium and recipient of communication. Much communicative effort will be aimed toward parents as recipients, but the concern here is with parents as communicating agents. In order that they might become informed and valuable agents, school officials will utilize other media: pupils, teachers, publications, and commercial media in the community.

This approach shifts the emphasis of the school administrators' activities in the conventional school-parent organizations. The standard approach of the administrator in his relationships with the Parent-Teachers Association, Mothers Clubs, at the open house, and in assorted booster clubs for special-interest groups seems to regard parents as the terminal point of public relations. Seemingly, convinced loyal followers would accomplish the school's public relations responsibilities. Actually, the few who normally participate in these parental groups are already convinced. It is important, of course, that they remain loyal and do not degenerate into antagonistic pressure groups. The common complaint of school personnel is that the parents who ought to be reached for understandings don't take part in the approved organizations. The challenge, then, is to reach the casual or disinterested. This goal can be aided by capitalizing upon the availability of the interested believers.

Under this strategem, the administrator takes a more active role in directing the programs of parent groups. Advisedly, it is a role played discreetly in the wings, but nonetheless, definitively. Instead of permitting the groups to become misdirected into entertainment and money-raising sidelines, their meetings can be re-directed into lively studies about youth and students' learning problems, with which parents are already concerned. The alert administrator will seize upon every opportunity which his meetings afford for explaining school problems and achievements, for stimulating awareness of needs, for arming parents with pertinent information, and for sending the believers away as missionaries to the uninformed. The groups can also serve as an abundant fount of parental concerns, if the administrator also provides opportunity for listening.

Some school officials have developed additional organizations for communication purposes. They invite parents in small groups to the school for informal exchanges of information. Furthermore, the manner in which every parental complaint is handled by teachers and administrators has an influence on attitudes. The school official cannot afford the temptation to escape these unpleasantries; he needs to demonstrate not only a congenial willingness to face them, but, preferably, the initiative for solving them.

The system of pupil-progress reporting is another important means of communicating with parents that may become agents for goodwill. No better system for achieving complete communication has been yet devised than the parent-teacher conference which has attained popularity in elementary schools. It is unfortunate that skill in handling these conferences has not gained equal popularity. Recent surveys are revealing that the method sometimes results in poorer rather than improved attitudes. Often neither the parent nor the teacher is sufficiently adept in this sensitive kind of communication. Surveys also reveal that many parents are reluctant to give the time needed for good conferences, and even resent the implication of being called on the carpet by a teacher. The conference reporting technique is recommended, but not without instruction for procedures and continual appraisal.

The Medium of Citizen Groups for Communicating

The approach of regarding citizen groups more as means than the ends of communication also changes the emphasis in an administrator's relationships with those organizations. In utilizing them as means they will become ends, too, but the objective will be to outfit them with information which can be disseminated among their friends and associates. The groups may be deliberately structured by the school: citizen councils, advisory committees, or *ad hoc* groups assembled for a special purpose such as promoting a campaign for a new building, or tax levies. If carefully chosen from the community at large, each member can become a beehive of goodwill. Participants not only carry information to a wider segment of the community but they, too, offer a valuable source for discovering citizen attitudes toward the school if feedback opportunities are provided by the administrator. Some schools are conducting attitudinal surveys within the community to learn citizen feelings toward educational matters. These have proved to be useful when conducted under sound principles of research. If representative citizen groups are used as a source of attitudes, the survey method would probably not be needed.

Meetings of the board of education can also serve as an effective means of communicating with citizens. Not only should their deliberations and decisions be made public, but efforts should be made to interest lay groups in attending the meetings. Attempts made in large communities to cover board meetings through radio and television have not always fulfilled expectations for good public relations. It is extremely difficult to build a routine board meeting into an exciting attraction to woo listeners away from competing programs. A board of education does not intend to put on a show.

School personnel have dozens of opportunities to communicate with community groups, in addition to those units structured by the school. As employees participate in social, civic, church, and fraternal activities, they can communicate and inform. The talent normally found within a school staff can be utilized in planned programs to develop understanding between the school and the community. The frequent use of school facilities by community groups should be encouraged and capitalized upon as another chance for acquainting citizens with school program and problems.

A Communication Specialist for the School

A growing awareness of the importance of communication for the school system and a recognition of the skill necessitated for certain aspects of communication have led many districts to appoint a trained communications specialist. A few universities have developed programs for preparing persons to manage the unique kind of public relations appropriate to an educational institution. The specialist is capable of adapting the skills and knowledge of journalism, advertising, and showmanship to the deliberate plans of school officials in order to communicate with the public. The excellent annual reports and other explanatory publications, the readable press releases, as well as the interesting television and radio programs staged in some cities testify to the usefulness of the specialist.

Administrators who have experienced this value have also learned two necessary precautions in appointing the specialist. They have learned the sensitivity of taxpayers to spending public moneys for "selling" citizens on what they already own. Thus, the title of the communications specialist is often camouflaged with a more acceptable term. Experienced administrators have also discovered that the presence of a specialist, for public relations or for any other function, tends to cause other employees to feel relieved of their responsibility for that function. The role and limitations of a communication specialist must be explained, and perhaps frequently re-explained, to staff members so that they do not neglect their individual efforts for communication.

INTERNAL COMMUNICATIONS

Providing Systems of Communication Between Board of Education and Employees

Important to job satisfaction of employees in any organization, but basic to an institution committed to democratic operating concepts is the maintenance of comprehensive channels for communication within the unit. Communication, especially between teachers and the controlling body, becomes increasingly difficult to sustain with the increasing size of school systems. The problem has become so severe in recent years that teacher organizations have clamored for a means of face-to-face communications with the board of education; the more radical requests take the form of what is described as "negotiations" or "collective bargaining." A few systems have actually voted "contracts" to guarantee communication.

Aside from the dubious legality of such contracts, it seems unfortunate that a positive means of communication has not been developed in large districts before it became necessary to borrow labor union methods in an organization that has historically sought professional status. It is doubtful if the commonly stated objective of contractual communications — increased salaries — will be achieved any better through that process than it has already attained with enlightened and communication-minded boards. A board of education, unlike the governing body of a private corporation, can grant only what the law and the citizens of a district have authorized to be granted. A board of education can allocate only that money which the people — acting through their legislatures and local taxing powers — have authorized for spending.

Furthermore, should the governing body and the teaching force, seek and reach direct agreements, the normal channels of communication and flow of authority essential to an organization would be destroyed. The persistence of this scheme makes administration unnecessary, forcing the operation of schools to revert to the primitive arrangements which existed when schools were tiny and the lay committee could work directly with the teacher or a few teachers. It is doubtful if any citizens could be persuaded to serve on board of education today if they had to spend as much time with school matters as such an approach entails. Nor can lay citizens be expected to be as knowledgeable, and hence, sympathetic, to educational problems needing attention as can the professional administrator who is trained in articulating to them educational concerns.

The positive approach has been used expertly by many school systems for years. In addition to the normal communication channels of teacher to principal to superintendent, forward-looking superintendents have made out-of-channel provisions for exchange of information. Not only are employees of all levels and classifications invited to approach the superintendent directly with important concerns, but consultive bodies are formed to represent all segments of the organization, and meet regularly with the chief administrator. Reciprocally, the superintendent has at his command not only all facts which are pertinent to educational concerns but he also understands the wishes and moods of the board members. These advisory bodies sometimes include representation from the board of education. Thus, the communications, vital to the welfare of all, are handled in an orderly and effective manner, preserving the highly desired professional tenor of the personnel.

Internal Communications Through Printed Documents

With the exception of the very small school districts where employees can satisfy their questions through the daily, casual, direct conflux with the top administrator, the kinds of information which teachers need often must be placed at their convenient disposal, for example, through published handbooks. The basic document is the board of education policy book which sets the direction for action by all employees. If properly conceived, it supplies the overall purposes of the enterprise and provides the guides against which the decisions and actions of all school personnel may be evaluated. A good board policy book does not answer the specifics. The interpretation and implementation of policy should be published in the Administrative Handbook of Regulations, a single document for a small and medium-sized school district to cover all aspects of school operations, but preferably a series of specialized handbooks in large systems. There could properly be individual sets of regulations for such matters as personnel, purchasing procedures, curriculum matters, perhaps details of pupil personnel responsibilities, or any other sizeable segment of school operations about which teachers have frequent questions. Each building may need to publish supplementing handbooks of procedures and regulations applicable only to that attendance unit.

As useful as these published documents are for keeping personnel informed, experience suggests they may not suffice for best communications. There is a tendency to pour such exhaustive effort into their original preparation that the documents are allowed to become obsolescent with time and change. As soon as an employee follows conscientiously the procedures printed in a handbook, only to discover that that procedure has been superseded by a newer regulation, he loses faith in the remaining procedures. Instead of using the still correct procedures elsewhere in the handbook, he is likely to interrupt busy administrators for answers to his problems; and after a rebuff for "not using his handbook," he is prone to abandon the request rather than pursue it.

Under these conditions it is questionable whether handbooks of regulations are a blessing or a detriment to communication. They must be kept up to date through distribution of supplementary changes. Further attention must be given to the matter to assure that employees keep their handbooks current. Teachers don't have time to re-shuffle handbooks. The mechanical arrangement of these documents must be simplified for efficient handling. Likewise, the document cannot be so voluminous as to discourage use. The important point in this discussion is that administrators must give as much thought to the organization, mechanics, and clarity of expression in preparing these handbooks as to content if they are to serve the purpose of the undertaking — internal communications.

Periodic bulletins from the central staff are essential for communicating current information. These, too, demand attention to mechanics and purpose. The common practice of weekly bulletins is desirable until administrators commence worshipping regularity more than communication. Examination of these weekly publications reveals that many are crammed with fillers which meet some arbitrarily determined space prescription and discourage employees from reading any of it. The objective of communication as well as morale and efficiency would be better served if issues would be distributed only when there is matter of importance to disseminate. A single poor bulletin which repels the interest of staff members causes many people to generalize negatively about the entire medium; hence the good brochures may find their way unread to the waste basket. And again, the importance of clear expression must be stressed. Instructions in the techniques of writing pungent reports is a profitable part of an administrative-training program.

Communication with non-certificated personnel should not be overlooked. Since they constitute more than a third of the total working staff in large districts, they are a source of unnecessary morale problems if they, too, are not kept informed.

Oral Internal Communications

Even with the best handbooks of procedures and regulations, considerable supplementing of both policies and regulations will still be essential. Face-to-face communications are the most frequent and vital internal relationships for a successful organization. The voice, the manner, the clarity of understanding, and the extent of opportunities for direct exchange of information—all aid the effectiveness of oral communication. In metropolitan school districts which do not permit easy and natural liaison between teachers and central administration, opportunities must be deliberately designed for as much face-to-face communication as reasonably possible. The previously discussed representative councils which meet with the superintendent and his immediate staff are valuable. Meetings at the building level with central staff officers help. Closed-circuit television offers an aid for direct communication with faculty and non-certificated personnel. As helpful as all of these approaches are, they do not substitute for the direct relationships which are possible in small systems. The urgency of good communications in city districts argues further in favor of decentralizing authority to attendance units. The total administrative organization must be streamlined to facilitate quick communication for action.

The greatest need for skill in oral communication becomes evident in the group approach to managing an organization. The myriad conferences—large and small—necessary for getting work done democratically in all educational organizations require the administrator to master what experience and research have found useful for:

Environmental arrangements for a conference.
Interaction of people in groups.
Leadership that stimulates thought and action.
Psychological motivations.
Use of words for transferring thought.
Techniques (gimmicks) for conducting successful meetings.

It will be noted that three of the six factors cited above for effective communications concern the intangible facets of getting a point across. One of the strengths of face-to-face meetings lies in their potential for communication without sound, referred to by interested researchers as non-verbal communication. It can also be the pitfall of effective communication, if either participant is unskilled in what Halpin (see reading) aptly calls "muted language." The manner in which something is said conditions the listener's receptiveness to the message as much as what is said. Facial expressions, emotions, gestures, tonal quality, timing of punch lines, choice of words—all of these supporting elements powerfully determine whether the message reaches the listener. Important, too, is the physical setting for communicating. The arrangement of participants at a conference has a bearing upon both speaking and listening. An environment uncomfortably hot or cold, austere decor, a room too large or too cramped, distracting noises, interruptions—will hinder the meeting's success.

The choice of location for a conference will be governed by the purpose of the session. The supervisor who wishes to gain the favorable attention of a teacher for correcting a weakness may find that a session held in the teacher's stronghold, the classroom, may permit an instructor to be more receptive to criticism than a conference arranged in the carpeted office of the supervisor. The principal who sits on his desk talking down to a student may succeed at intimidating the youngster but probably fail at eliciting an intelligible response. The administrator who keeps people waiting to commence a conference may have closed the door to receptive ears before he speaks his first words. The initial greeting may determine the success of the conference. And the meeting called at the end of a tense teaching day is unlikely to produce much real communication.

These intangible aspects of communication, some of which can be learned and some of which can be only slightly improved, explain the high regard which boards of education and administrative employers hold for candidates who demonstrate strengths in those qualities which a university does not normally develop in the preparation of administrators. Recognizing the importance of effective communicating and relating to the many publics with which a school administrator deals, an employer can easily be swayed in favor of the prospective officer with favorable appearance, bearing, speech patterns, and personality. It can be argued that a candidate's intellect, degrees, and philosophy should be given primacy, yet employers habitually seek first of all the other qualities in filling leadership positions.

The point underscored often in this volume is that successful administration of a school rests largely upon skill in oral communication. Not enough can be said in support of this talent, but since this text does not essay to become an instructional tool in oral communications, the attempt is made to establish the importance of that instruction in the best preparation program of a school administrator.

Most of the emphasis thus far has been upon downward communication, from the superintendent to the teacher. The implication is hopefully contained in the discussion for providing adequate opportunities for upward communication. The organization should allow for appropriate personal contacts with top administration outside of the established channels. In-service instruction is also advised in most school systems for training subordinate administrators to compose brief but pointed reports to keep the higher echelon informed. Many of the superintendent's decisions must be based upon these second-hand sources of information.

Provisions must be made also for lateral communications at all levels of the school system: teacher to teacher, principal to principal, and assistant to assistant.

EVALUATION OF COMMUNICATIONS

Like all other aspects of the educational program, the effectiveness of plans for communication must undergo periodic appraisal. There are visible signs which indicate the need for testing this effectiveness. Signs of faulty internal communications include the appearance of low morale, movement toward organizations which exclude administrators, excessive complaints about the consistency of administrative decisions or about the inefficiency of services which are offered by the central staff, extensive personnel turnover or requests for transfer, frequent violations of established procedures, or an unreasonable number of solicited conferences with the superintendent.

Indications of poor external communications are more readily visible: failure of voters to support school tax or budget measures, unfavorable publicity, citizen groups for school improvements which are formed outside the system, voluminous critical letters to the newspaper editor, or an unusually large number of uninvited visitors at meetings of the board of education.

School administrators can perform their own evaluations satisfactorily if they seek objectivity and if they use tested survey instruments. An informal but designed survey can be of some appraisal aid if staff members are instructed in the techniques and purpose. Even strategically placed "eyes and ears" of the school is better than no evaluation. However, it is often difficult for those directly responsible for communications to be unbiased in assessing the returns. Moreover, it is not always easy for an "administrator in trouble" to be aware that the trouble may have started from ineffective communications. For these reasons, some schools have found the evaluation conducted by qualified consultants outside the school system to be more valuable.

Considerable help to the school administrator in planning a complete communication system, in the management, and in evaluation of the system, is available from a national organization which functions exclusively for that purpose, the National School Public Relations Association, a division of the National Education Association.

THE NATURE AND IMPORTANCE OF COMMUNICATION . . .

ADMINISTRATIVE OBJECTIVES FOR DEVELOPMENTAL ADMINISTRATION*

COMMUNICATION AND FEEDBACK

An administrative communications system is an attempt to assure at all relevant points in an organization the ability to detect, understand, and respond appropriately to appropriate data. Today, a new technology of decision making greatly facilitates the gathering, storage, recall, and utilization of data and the determination of what data are appropriate. However, major communication problems are still administrative or organizational rather than technological. Put in another way, technology at the present time is far in advance of administration.

A planning activity needs original data out of which to fashion plans and needs, also, feedback data on their effects. It should be concerned

---

*Victor A. Thompson, "Administrative Objectives for Developmental Administration," *Administrative Science Quarterly,* IX (June, 1964), 1-3-106, by permission of A.S.Q and Victor A. Thompson.

both with effects regarding primary goals and also with secondary effects—the effects on other goals, both those of other governmental units and those of nongovernmental units.

Specialized detector roles are required, roles involving various specialized and technical qualifications. If the organization is able to respond to new data, these specialized detector roles become new power roles within the organization, further exaggerating the latent conflict between the general line and the cross-line occupational specialties. Resistance to this new diminution of authority, and hence to communication, will be especially pronounced in the insecure atmosphere of the bureaupathic, hierarchy-emphasized organization. In that atmosphere, particularly, attempts will be made to restrict communication to channels (an exercise of the superior's right to monopolize communication), to the line of command, or to the hierarchy—a channel technically inadequate for specialized communication, increasingly overloaded, and notoriously unreliable because of opportunities and motivations for censorship at each communication station. Development planning, on the other hand, calls for increasing specialization and hence increasing interdependence, the toleration of which depends in part upon the adequacy of communication. Growing pressure for new, nonhierarchical, specialized communication channels is likely to generate further resistance to the diminution of authority, especially in the bureaupathic or insecurity-dominated organization.

To detect and transmit data is only part of the problem. The organization must also be able to respond to it in an appropriate fashion. As was pointed out above, insecurity generates a need to control which greatly restricts innovative responses (innovation or creativity is by definition uncontrolled behavior). Thus, in a bureaupathic, hierarchy-emphasized atmosphere, one of the basic ingredients of development administration—innovative responsiveness—is either absent or very weak.

Furthermore, the authority system (the system of boss-man roles), reinforced by the practice of single subgoal assignment, stresses parochialism, a narrow loyalty to one's program unit, its boss and its personnel, and to one's own program goal to the exclusion of interest in all others. The effects of action on other goals tend to be ignored; in fact, they are usually not even perceived.

All of these phenomena are especially related to an emphasis on the hierarchical institution. They are also related, it is hypothesized, to the extent to which jobs or occupations within the organization are organizationally defined rather than socially defined, or to the extent to which they are skills in operating specific procedures of specific programs of specific organizations rather than social functions relevant to a broad range of human goals and programs. Persons whose skills are purely organizational, who were trained largely on the job, who had no relevant pre-entry training, who started as amateurs, have orientations and attitudes that differ from those of the professional, scientific and technical specialist, the person who did have relevant pre-entry training. The amateurs in organizations have been referred to conveniently as the "desk classes." They have less interunit (or organization) mobility than others. They owe their function and status to the organization and thus tend to become organization men. They are perhaps more responsive to organizational authority, thereby encouraging a hierarchical emphasis. They are apt to be conservative with regard to their program and procedures, since their personal status and function are so tied up with their programs. There may even be a tendency for them to hypostatize their programs and procedures into natural laws and to forget their purely instrumental origin. All of this adds up to a greater loyalty to program goals, units, and authority—in short, to parochialism. Parochialism can make detection of and response to second-order consequences of action, second-order feedback, much less likely to happen, thereby lessening the administrative structure's ability to carry on an integrated development planning activity over a broad spectrum of social and economic life.

Real communication is two way and is a form of mutual influence. Hence, if communication occurs, some decentralization or loss of central power occurs. These facts are equally true with regard to communication with the public, as we shall see below. The interpretation of communication with the public as restricted to "selling the plan" is based on some rather universal myths, such as "the stupidity of the masses" and "the indispensability of leadership." As would be expected, therefore, it results in considerable self-delusion in that actual public hehavior is likely to deviate in unpredictable ways from planned behavior, making the planning illusory. It would seem that no political, let alone administrative, system could operate for long without some devices for articulating and aggregating public needs and interests and communicating the results to government for incorporation in the planning process. If this interest articulation and aggregation is done administratively, it is almost sure to be either highly erroneous or downright spurious, a fact which stands behind the inevitable, periodic, colonial riot. Thus, central control, or the illusion of it is, going to be diluted in some way, either by real communication with the public (or any other group importantly affected by planning), or by peaceful or nonpeaceful nullification—the dilution of the desirable by the possible.

COMMUNITIES MUST BE PREPARED
FOR EDUCATIONAL INNOVATION*

Public acceptance of new ideas and practices in education requires an effective program of community relations. Innovation means change, and this poses an immediate threat to the comfort of the *status quo,* not only for the profession but also for the public. Innovation may mean additional costs for more textbooks and supplies, new equipment, new buildings, and perhaps for more teachers. This is delicate for it prods the community in its individual and collective pocketbooks, which is a most sensitive area. Innovation means a change in the way that parents looks at the schools and what the schools are accomplishing for their children. This is troublesome, for parents may feel that they are becoming too far removed from a direct knowledge of and a secure place in the formal education of their children. It probably is reasonable to infer that they do not want to be so far removed from that is happening to their offspring. This is understandable because parental concern is a fact of life to which the school administrator and his staff need to be sensitive. It is a facet of the power structure of the community which they would be naive to ignore. People tend to resist that which they do not understand or do not even wish to understand. This is likely to prove disastrous because ignorance is fear, and fear obstructs.

UNDERSTANDING INNOVATION IS DIFFICULT

Educational innovation is intangible because it is neither the material and paraphernalia available or proposed, nor is it the use of machines or the organizational changes or varying patterns of staff redeployment. It is rather all of these or, more appropriately, the use of things within the context of new and different insights being brought to bear on the tasks, purposes, and philosophy of education in our society. Truly this is an intellectual concept and, as such, it cannot be measured with ordinary measuring devices. It is an attitude which cannot be felt or tasted. It is a feeling which cannot be weighed. It is an outlook which cannot be carted or crated. Nevertheless, despite the problems involved and the

---

*Clifford V. Jones, "Developing Community Understanding for Educational Innovation," taken from *American School Board Journal,* CXLIX (July, 1964), published by The Bruce Publishing Company, 1964, 29.

resistances often encountered in the profession itself, it is to our credit that schools and school systems throughout our nation are introducing a variety of educational innovations ranging from new patterns of staff utilization to the ungraded classroom, teaching machines, improved curricula, and newer methods of instruction.

CONTINUOUS PROGRESS REPORTS NECESSARY

Poor community understanding might be called the missing ingredient that leads to the abandonment of many well-meant attempts to improve educational practice. Since innovation implies change and cost, planning must be part of a continuous program of assessment and reporting about the schools, their strengths, weaknesses, and needs. In such a setting the public will be afforded the information to enable them to fully understand, and thus be more likely to accept the purposes, designs, and implications for the future of planned innovations.

AVOID THE PITFALLS OF THE OVERSELL

When innovations appear to develop a revolutionary rather than an orderly evolvement of change, there is danger of an anticlimax. Enthusiastic promotional tactics may lead to the kind of emotional involvement that causes people to look for cure-alls or panaceas that do not exist. Furthermore, when innovations are sold to the public in a manner that is inconsistent with a good program of school-community understanding, the unexpected delays and additional costs that frequently appear will generate a kind of public frustration that may lead to curtailment, if not abandonment, of the program.

CREATION OF PROPER CLIMATE FOR INNOVATION

There is no short road to the results to be gained from educational innovation, consequently, favorable atmosphere for innovation must be developed and constantly maintained. The public must be convinced that the allocation of time, money, and personnel involved is worthwhile and that it pays to wait until all the facts are in. Is not the mark of the mature person, and of society, too its willingness to suspend judgment? At the same time, the public must be prepared to accept failure and/or redirection of the project as the price of progress, and to recognize that this, too, is good. They must be prepared to accept the amount of time needed for proper planning of details of the innovation, for administrative decisions to "jell," and for the orientation of teachers and pupils.

Finally, good community relations for innovations must be established in a manner that the climate becomes part of the atmosphere, so that it is not turned off at the whim of an official, the change of a superintendent, or a shift in the board of education. Such an atmosphere for change must become a way of educational life which is a condition of instructional improvement.

THE SUPERINTENDENT MUST LEAD

The chief responsibility for the development of community understanding of the schools, their programs, aims, and needs rests with the superintendent. Only to the degree that favorable community acceptance is achieved can the schools grow strong and move ahead. In this role, the superintendent is the community educational leader. His community-relations practices should provide information that will establish and develop the following concepts:

1. That balance and stability are being maintained in the schools.
2. The public is being given complete and reliable information about their schools on a current basis.
3. That the schools are in the hands of competent people in the board of education, administration, and the teaching staff.
4. That change is an essential ingredient in good education as indeed it is [in] all areas of human effort.

With such a program of educational leadership and an informed public, the necessary setting will be provided for a dynamic educational endeavor where there is balance between the old the new.

THE POWERFUL MUTED LANGUAGE*

1. Verbal communication constitutes only one segment of the total spectrum of human communication.
2. The muted language of non-verbal communication is a rich source of cues in determining the course of interpersonal relations.
3. In addition to whatever information we may intend to communicate in manifest form, we usually also communicate additional information in muted language.

---

*Andrew W. Halpin, "Muted Language. "*The School Review,* LXVIII, spring, 1960, 97. Reprinted by permission of the University of Chicago Press. (Muted language is defined in this article as the language of eyes and hands, of gestures, of time and of status symbols, of unconscious slips which betray the very words we use.)

4. The messages of open language and of muted language may reinforce or contradict each other. In the latter case, the listener must decide which message is the true one.

5. In oral language the muted notes are added through gesture, timbre and inflections of voice, and word choice. In written language the muted messages are transmitted through word choice and writing style. The executive who believes that he transmits only the literal meaning of what he has spoken or written is operating under a pathetic delusion.

6. The confidence that employees place in an administrator's utterances, whether oral or written, is determined by what they have learned about him in face-to-face interactions; under these conditions they can judge whether his open language and his muted language are sending out the same message. Whatever suspicions employees may harbor as a result of direct contact with the administrator are translated into skepticism about the good faith of his formal, written communications.

7. In short, communication is a far more subtle and more complex process than most administrators are wont to admit.

OBSTACLES TO COMMUNICATION*

One of the greatest difficulties in effecting a communication which will change our minds lies in the fact that we all tend to select sources of information which purvey material with which we already agree. This is not at all a deliberate conscious choice to bolster our own prejudices or to avoid seeing the other side of the question. Rather it is because the information from these sources tends to make sense to us, is understood easily, and is couched in the kinds of phrases we understand. All these things at once select the source for us and protect us from having to change our minds. The phenomenon is quite common in industry. When a group assembles to discuss the kinds of problems raised in this book, we find that the personnel men go to personnel meetings, the vice-presidents to vice-president's meetings, and the foremen to foremen's meetings. Each finds himself in a group where the others have the same general kinds of organization of the world that he has. As the meeting goes on, the personnel men say personnel kinds of things to one another, they hear their own points of view presented in different words, and they go away reinforced in their original posi-

*From *Psychology in Management* by Mason Haire. Copyright 1956 by McGraw-Hill Book Company. Used by permission of McGraw-Hill Book Company, 79, 84-85, 87, 89.

tions. Similarly with the others. This example is not meant to belittle personnel men or vice-presidents or foremen in particular. Rather it is a characteristic of all of us, and the tendency to choose sources of information which present facts in agreement with already existing organizations is one of the large barriers to communication designed to change a person's mind. . . .

Still another psychological mechanism which acts to impede communication lies in the fact that people tend, in the interest of simplifying the problem of receiving information from the environment, to evaluate the whole medium of information through which information is received, and to accept or reject the medium and everything it carries, rather than to have to make specific judgments on separate items. Thus, for example, all of us have thrown advertising circulars out of the mail without giving them more than a casual glance. We have a general organization of the sources of communication, and we act on the implicit theory that there is a low probability of getting important information from this one. The medium is seen as one which carries certain sorts of material; since it isn't a kind of material which we particularly want, we reject the whole content without analysis. House organs probably often meet the same fate, and in many cases it seems impossible to make them into good communication media without changing their entire character in the minds of the potential recipients. . . .

The implications of this for the communicator seem to be that he must be very careful of the relation between his statements and the kind of events that are going to occur. If the statement is worth making and has value in its content, it is important to see that it is backed up in practice. Otherwise it may be accepted at first, found to be a liability in action, and discarded with resentment toward the communicator for misleading. If such a thing happens repeatedly, then the communicator, as a medium, may be rejected and ignored because he is stereotyped as an unreliable informant. Often it would be a better policy, from a communications point of view, to refrain from making statements which one hopes were true but which might not hold in practice, rather than to enjoy making the pronouncement with the subsequent risk of other statements being rejected because earlier ones failed to materialize. . . .

Another method that would probably improve communications would be to *transmit information in small units.* A large organized mass of material tends to threaten existing patterns in the listener and so may be rejected. Small units transmitted little by little carry the same message over a period of time without the same likelihood of rejection. Cumulatively they may effect the change where they would be rejected out of hand if they were presented at once.

The importance of finding out what the listener has heard has come up repeatedly. As a check on what was, in fact, communicated, it is essential for the communicator to *provide an opportunity for "feed-back"* from the recipient. Unless one has some way of finding out what was heard, either by observing subsequent behavior or by some kind of restatement, communication must remain pretty much a matter of shooting in the dark, with very uncertain results.

RECENT CHANGES IN THE HOME AND THE SCHOOL REQUIRE INCREASED EFFORTS TO MAINTAIN COMMUNICATION*

In our changing civilization the home has lost some of its influence on the development of children. The mechanization of homes has resulted in (1) the elimination of many character-building work experiences for children and (2) the release of mothers, which, though broadening their opportunities for civic and cultural participation and permitting them to engage in outside work, has also tended to reduce their contacts with and influence on the development of their children.

Changes also have reduced the influence of fathers on the development of children. Fathers, working in specialized occupations, do not have the occasion, in natural occupational situations, to teach their children good character habits and attitudes. The sharing by parents with their children of the creative experiences connected with earning a livelihood has been greatly reduced. Moreover, children now have, in general, fewer intimate experiences with growing things—plants and animals —and with the interdependence of man and nature.

The changes in home responsibilities and experiences have placed on both the home and the school more responsibility for finding desirable substitute situations that provide for pupil experiences by which to develop desirable character traits in children. A greater part of the increased leisure time of parents, resulting from the reduced work week, will need to be devoted to the development of their children.

Recent advances in civilized living have furnished children with broad experiences from reading, travel, social contacts, and television and radio, thus freeing them from the limitations of their immediate environments that were a handicap in the education of former generations. The uses of some of these sources of learning for educational purposes have scarcely been tapped. The schools have taken steps to improve the expe-

*Charles E. Reeves, *Parents and the School*, Washington, D.C.: by permission of Public Affairs Press, 1963, 12-13.

riences provided for children. There has been a merging of curricular and extracurricular experiences to some extent with resulting heightened pupil interest.

Though schools have been improved, they change relatively slowly over long periods of time. It usually requires more than a generation for a majority of schools to adopt the best practices found at any time in the better schools. Teachers, being human, like to continue to use familiar ways of doing their work and to avoid meeting the problems caused by making changes.

Sometimes, also, parents are an influence against progress in the schools. If parents object to changes, they should be very careful not to base their objections solely on blind tradition and prejudice. They should relinquish any opinion that the schools should limit their activities to "old-fashioned" subjects and that creative and character development activities are "fads and frills." They should encourage administrators and teachers to improve the schools.

TAKE THE INITIATIVE — BASIC PRINCIPLE OF COMMUNICATION STRATEGY*

This principle is the action corollary of the communication principle of *primacy,* which is that people tend to maintain their first concept of an event or issue, and that the first message they accept is likely to have the most influence on their opinion. As we have noted, it is easier to shape an opinion than to change it. For example, if you provide facts and ideas which impel citizens to believe that pupils need more up-to-date books (which they do), citizens become emotionally committed to that belief. They are psychologically rewarded by the feeling that they have a satisfactory guide for thinking about that matter and they feel competent to direct their actions with respect to it.

Their opinion, along with the sense of competence it provides, is integrated into their egos. They are inclined to defend the opinion because it has become a part of them. If subsequently someone else attempts to "change their minds" they will tend to interpret what is said in the framework of the opinion you created, and they will resist changing that first opinion because doing so threatens both their ego and their sense of security. They do not want to admit that their first opinion was wrong,

---

*From *Education and Public Understanding* by Gordon McCloskey. Copyright © 1959 by Gordon McCloskey, 103-104.

and they do not want to rethink their way through a problem they feel they have already solved. They may even resent efforts to change their opinion because that implies that their original judgment was faulty, and because they dislike threats to their sense of security.

But if, owing to lack of initiative, you permit someone else to introduce the question of better books with claims that they will be "expensive," that "school costs are rising at an alarming rate," or that "pupils misuse books they already have," citizens will form their first opinion on the basis of that message and their tendency to defend that opinion will be just as strong as in the former case. Then you are confronted with the extremely difficult task of changing opinion, and doing that will require many times as much effort as creating it in the first place.

Unfortunately, many of us, because we are busy with other matters or because we do not understand the strategy of communication, too frequently permit others to seize the initiative. By such default we complicate our communication problem and greatly reduce the effectiveness of our efforts. We cannot always foresee all communication needs. In our free and competitive communication world others will sometimes beat us to the initiative; but with foresight and awareness of strategic need we can greatly improve our performance. Take the initiative. Keep it.

EXTERNAL COMMUNICATIONS . . .

THE SUPERINTENDENT AND SCHOOL PUBLIC RELATIONS*

Since the schools are the people's own work, as Henry Barnard expressed it, the public has a vital concern in them and must be kept informed of achievements and needs. Although the child who is a satisfied customer is probably the most potent avenue for good public relations with adults, the superintendent and his staff should plan the ways and means by which educational matters may best be presented to all of the people. Naturally, press and radio and television loom large in this matter.

Careful consideration should be given to the thin line that exists between informing the public of favorable achievements and explaining realistically the serious defects and urgent needs. The superintendent

---

*Hints to the Beginning Superintendents of Schools, Washington, D.C.: By permission of American Association of School Administrators, 1962, 25-26.

cannot with impunity describe the schools as being superior in all ways and at the same time make an urgent appeal for money to correct glaring defects. A superintendent desiring to contradict criticism or to just "sell" the schools to the public may paint such a rosy picture that the public may fail to listen when he appeals for a bigger budget to improve the program.

Early in his administration the beginning superintendent himself should call on the newspaper editors and reporters and on the program directors of other mass media. He should give them the facts frankly on all educational matters and should encourage them to observe the schools and their products. He should assume that these leaders in mass media are concerned with the welfare of children and will do honest reporting. Until he finds that this is not true, the superintendent should express confidence in them and should be frank on all matters.

Public relations is often a man-to-man affair. The superintendent cannot afford to refuse to talk to clients of the schools, either over the telephone, in his office, or on the street. Above all else the superintendent should fear appearing to be exclusive and difficult to see.

The superintendent himself, however, can do much to relieve the pressure on his time by seeing people but quickly pointing out that there are others in the school system who are better able to give answers and who have more information than he has. Thus the tracks that first come to his door may later lead to a principal's office, to a teacher, or to another staff member. Tracks leading to many members of the staff indicate greater leadership and stronger administration on the part of the superintendent. This process also increases the stature of the superintendent's associates and their willingness to assume responsibility.

THE SCHOOL'S ATTEMPTS TO COMMUNICATE WITH CITIZENS MUST COMPETE WITH MYRIAD OTHER INTERESTS*

In recent years, people's interest in public education has been influenced by major changes in the circumstances under which they work and live. During the past two decades, many traditional ways of working and living have been upset. Social and economic shifts of unprece-

*From *Education and Public Understanding* by Gordon McCloskey, New York: Harper and Row, 1959, 7-8, 23-24. Copyright © 1959 by Gordon McCloskey.

dented magnitude have taken place with unprecedented speed. As a result, people have encountered an unprecedented variety of new problems and new interests.

During the World War II years, most families experienced the emotional disturbances that grew from concern for the lives and safety of men in the armed forces. Millions of war workers and their families moved from one community to another. They were confronted with disturbing housing problems. Inflation complicated family budgets. Millions of businessmen were forced to abandon production and sale of peacetime products and to rearrange their factories or stores to produce military supplies or to sell different types of civilian products. Farmers were asked to expand production.

Those disturbances were accompanied by an increase in government controls and a rise of public expenditures and taxes to unprecedented heights. Under those circumstances, critics of public expenditures found ready listeners.

After the war, military production was cut. Manufacturers and merchants returning to production and sale of civilian goods, faced another round of urgent readjustment tasks. Economic survival depended on immediate attention and action, which required additional amounts of thought and energy. Farmers were urged to return to peacetime production patterns while their incomes declined. Overtime hours of work were reduced and the size of weekly pay checks went down while living costs continued to rise. Millions of war-production workers were laid off and had to seek work in peacetime industries. Again many had to move to another community. Meanwhile "public expenditures" remained high and complaints about heavy taxes increased. . . .

Some communication specialists who are stanch friends of education offer proposals based on honest beliefs that beyond a point efforts to develop thorough public understanding of complex technical details and needs are foredoomed to be ineffective because laymen, busy with many other affairs, cannot be expected to comprehend all of the complicated facts and ideas involved. Those friends remind us that even after years of specialized training, teachers still do not fully comprehend modern educational complexities. They believe it is unrealistic to expect laymen to do so. They also observe that many people who passively "believe in education" do not demonstrate much active interest in it or offer adequate financial support. They point out that there are important differences between professed beliefs and the will to implement them. Therefore, they suggest that public interest in education and support for it can be increased best by more skillful means of "starting where the people are." They recommend more effort to focus public attention on the more easily understood and generally accepted objectives and values of education because they believe that is the best, or only, way to arouse widespread interest. Many educators fear that such means will prove superficial or unethical. Seasoned and successful communication and public-relations practitioners counter with the observation that in the rough and ready competitive world as it is, only such means can capture sufficient attention and interest to make people want to understand education and to support it actively. They present imposing arrays of evidence to indicate that their approach has obtained wider understanding of, and more financial support for, many institutions, enterprises, products, and services.

Other people propose action based on combinations of the above viewpoints. They recognize the long-term importance of creating as much genuine public understanding of as many details as is possible. They are also realistic about the limited amounts of time and energy people are likely to devote to educational matters. They realize that educational values and needs must be presented to citizens in clear, easily understood terms and recognize the immense communication problems involved in doing that. They believe that in the long run only people who genuinely understand education will voluntarily support it adequately and that free people are entitled to such understanding. At the same time they recognize that in a rapidly changing culture in which constantly improved means of communication are used to focus attention on many shifting desires, opportunities, and problems, educational leaders, too, must develop more effective means of stimulating interest in schooling.

At this point let us unequivocally reject all proposals that we adopt practices designed to trick people into thoughtless educational decisions they neither understand nor approve. Such practices are unethical and do more harm than good. In a democracy educators cannot adopt practices that negate the principles of freedom to choose and of intellectual honesty, which are inherent in any acceptable concept of education. Doing so would quickly destroy the public confidence so essential for increased interest and support. *Our aim is the development of the largest possible amount of genuine understanding.*

NOTHING MYSTERIOUS ABOUT GOOD PUBLIC RELATIONS*

A school system has public relations whether it tries to or not. Unavoidably, the public holds certain convictions about the schools,

*Reprinted with permission of The Macmillan Company from *Public Relations for Education,* By Gloria Dapper. © Copyright, Gloria Dapper, 1964, 1-2.

believes certain things to be true, and, when the word "school" is pronounced, conjures up a particular mental picture. These convictions, opinions, and mental images are the product of public relations, planned or otherwise.

However, these convictions, opinions, and mental images may not square with the facts. When that is the case, there has been a break in the lines of communication between the schools and the public.

Some communications avenues operate with very little human manipulation. Take, for instance, that unpredictable medium, the grapevine. Far too often it is the only source of information—generally misinformation—for the public.

Yet public relations is not a science or an art. It is a job for people who know how to employ a variety of techniques in reaching other people. The techniques make use of existing communications media and sometimes create new ones. There is nothing mysterious about public relations but, like newspaper reporting, it involves skills, and not everybody can do it well. Not even every public relations person does it well.

A word should be said about the unskilled public relations people because they have been, in part, responsible for the misleading impression the public has of their craft.

The besetting sin of the poor public relations person is arrogance. He believes that only a certain portion of a story should be told and that he knows better than anyone else what is good for the public. In his withholding of information, which is usually quite transparent, he sows the seeds of mistrust of his client.

If his client happens to be the school system, the results are much more serious than if he represents a client who make deodorants or toothpaste. And, unfortunately, his mistakes are more easily detected with a commercial client because press clippings and sales graphs would give some indication of the mistrust he has created.

Good public relations, on the other hand, operates on an entirely different basis. It begins with the premise that the public has a right to know—and to know everything about such basic social institutions as our schools. A corollary is that, given the facts, the public will act wisely.

This is a dangerous premise if the product is no good. For while an inferior product can be palmed off by surrounding it with a glamorous mist of words, the trick does not last long. Sooner or later, an honest man is going to come along and announce the fact that the emperor is naked.

So having a good product precedes trying to sell it to the public. You don't have to wait until the product is absolutely perfect; but basically the school system should be sound and striving, for there is no point in trying to fool the public.

STUDENTS AS PUBLIC RELATIONS AGENTS*

Whether or not they will admit it, most parents form their impressions of the high school largely on the basis of the reports of their children. The high-school student is old enough to be more reliable as a source of information than the elementary-school child, and what he says about the school carries more weight. The affection of the parent for the child also injects the emotional factor into the situation, and this insures the student a sympathetic audience at home. Every student entertains opinions that are certain to crop out in his conversation about his teachers, the principal, the control of the school, the methods of teaching, the student activities, and other phases or incidents of school life.

It is wise, therefore, to give some attention to the matter of assisting high-school students to understand the school and its procedures and to induce them to take pride in its progress and achievements. It is highly desirable that there be developed in the student body good will and respect for the administration and the staff and pride in the educational side of school life and the educational achievements of the school.

Many principals, aware of the value of creating good will and confidence on the part of students, have employed various types of procedures for the realization of these ends. Among avenues for bringing to the attention of the student body the achievements and good points of the school are assemblies, roll-room meetings, exhibits, bulletin boards, contests, commencement, the school paper, and school news in the local papers.

Through these avenues such items as the following may be made the subject of announcement and congratulation: results of standard tests; victories of individuals and teams in interscholastic contests; achievements and honors of recent graduates of the school at college, in business, or in public life; favorable comment by visitors, inspectors, or other outsiders on the work of the school or the conduct of the students; and honors or special achievements of the faculty.

---

*Harl R. Douglass, *Modern Administration of Secondary Schools,* second edition. Reprinted through the courtesy of Blaisdell Publishing Company, a division of Ginn and Company, 1954, 563-564.

Frequently the students may be taken into the confidence of the administration in regard to proposed or new plans or methods, which may be explained to them and discussed as modern improvements.

In such activities emphasis should be placed upon selling the school, not any given individual, to the student body. It is bad ethics as well as bad psychology to use such activities to promote the individual interests of any particular members of the faculty or the principal or the superintendent.

Though it will have to be conceded that much mention must be made of athletic victories, special effort should be made to arouse pride in achievements in other fields of endeavor, particularly in scholastic achievements and honors.

At all times the value of maintaining good will and a good spirit on the part of the students should be appreciated. It should go without saying that good will should not be cultivated by lowering academic standards, by frequent holidays, by unusual laxity, by fanatical athletic enthusiasm, by special privileges to undeserving leaders, or by other questionable means. Among legitimate and important means may be mentioned a general attitude of dignified friendliness on the part of the administration and faculty toward the students and their activities, reasonable display of confidence in them, abstinence from petty snooping and nagging, and a co-operative attitude in many phases of the management of the school, particularly those in which very often a part in the management is given to the students. It should be taken for granted that the students are interested in the good name of the school and in its honor in all its endeavors, even though this may not always be exactly the fact.

THE FACULTY AND PUBLIC RELATIONS*

The concept that teachers themselves really are the key persons in developing good community or good public relations is a relatively new one. Until recently, "public relations" were thought to be a job for administrators because the task was principally one of furnishing a continuous flow of effective publicity. Teachers, it was assumed, could

---

*Albert J. Huggett and T. M. Stinnett, *Professional Problems of Teachers,* New York: by permission of The Macmillan Company, 1956, 310-311, 329.

have little part in this process. The change from "public relations" to "community relations" has very definitely brought classroom teachers into the picture, as we will indicate later on.

In the preparation program for administrators were usually found courses called by such titles as school publicity, public relations, and social interpretation. Seldom did those who expected to devote their lives to teaching take such courses. Administrators were expected to carry on the publicity efforts.

During the past few years there has been a decided trend in teacher education institutions toward courses in community study. Such courses have stressed the school as an integral part of the social order, the use of community resources, and better correlation between the school and the community. Both administrators and teachers have taken such courses.

There has also been a trend in curriculum courses toward stressing inclusion of community leaders in curriculum building and revision. It has become a common practice to include curriculum courses on graduate programs for all kinds of educational workers.

The emphasis in the community study and curriculum courses, though, has been upon better educational service. There has not been too much stress upon building better understanding between school and community or in acquainting the public with the goals, methods, and activities of the school. It seems to have been assumed that these goals will be accomplished indirectly through better relationships between the school and the community. The authors believe that the direct approach is also needed. This is an age of advertising. The school needs constantly to keep its product before the public if it is to receive its share of the tax dollar, and if it is to render the service that it should.

Teachers, as has been indicated, have not in the past been called upon to do very much with "public relations." They have been expected to maintain good relations with the parents of children in their classes, but that has been the extent of their responsibilities. School officials have done the rest. Now, though, we are entering a new era in which teachers will need to have a part in establishing and maintaining satisfactory "community relations.". . .

Satisfactory community relations are of great importance to the teacher. To secure good relations it is advantageous for the teacher to get to know the child and the parent. Knowledge of the child may be obtained in part by reference to school records, but knowledge concerning the parents must come from actual contacts. Acquaintances with parents may be made through social engagements in the community or they may be made by means of home visits. Home visits should be on a voluntary basis.

The teacher needs to work co-operatively with other teachers and other members of the school staff. The successful teacher takes a normal part in community affairs and makes an effort to become an integral part of the community in which he serves. The parent-teacher association is a valuable means for establishing satisfactory relations between the home and the school.

FACULTY AWARENESS OF PUBLIC RELATIONS SHOULD START IN THEIR PREPARATORY PROGRAMS*

The very nature of teacher education dictates close liaison with elementary and high schools. It is from these schools that teacher education institutions receive students, it is largely there that those students gain experiences in observation and teaching, and ideally it is there that the graduates in teacher education find life-long careers.

On three counts, then, there is need for close relationships between college faculty and officials on the one hand and teachers and school administrators on the other: in the preparation of students for college, in providing those students with meaningful experiences in preparation for teaching, and in the evaluation of the teacher education program through the work of these graduates in the schools.

The hit-or-miss basis for relationships is rapidly disappearing in teacher education, and so is any attitude of superiority that may have been found at times in colleges and universities. Instead, one finds generally a spirit of cooperative endeavor, with all concerned working together for the benefit of the college, of education students, and of the schools.

Many methods and projects for cooperation have proven successful as can be seen in the ideas listed on the following pages of this publication. One very effective way of promoting good relations with the schools is through the use of advisory committees, in which school administrators and teachers sit down with college officials and faculty members for candid appraisal of teacher education programs and of relationships between the college and the schools.

---

*Harold Van Winkle, *Public Relations Ideas for Teacher Education,* Washington, D.C.: by Permission of The American Association of Colleges for Teacher Education, 1961, 11, 42.

FACULTY-STAFF RELATIONS

The maintenance of harmonious, cooperative relationships among faculty, staff, and administration constitutes one of the most difficult of administrative functions. Problems hinge largely on communication, about which we still know comparatively little. Primary responsibility for smooth operation and effective communication rests with administration.

"*I think it can be fairly said,*" stated Dr. Logan Wilson, former president of the University of Texas, "that whenever a serious conflict rends a college or university, the administration is necessarily more at fault than any person or group of persons on the faculty . . . (because) one of the primary obligations of top administration is to prevent conflict . . . not that the administration should yield to the faculty in any dispute over principles or other matters, but merely that it is the duty of administration to keep impasses from developing."

Creating a climate of understanding is not always easy, of course. "There is an abyss between the teacher and the administrator across which neither can communicate his feelings, ideas, and problems," states a report on a recent University of Maryland survey which included interviews with 1,800 professors, former professors, and associates.

SCHOOL CAMPAIGNS FARE BETTER WITH A BIG VOTER TURNOUT*

Some advice is given quite freely that in school finance elections the big vote turnout should be avoided like a plague. Statistics are produced in an effort to show that a small vote means greater chances for success than a large one. A few advisors even contend that the less publicity for a school campaign the better. Some administrators confess recommending that school elections be scheduled on winter days, hopeful that a heavy snow will discourage many voters from going to the polls.

Behind the big idea of the small vote advocates is an unstated assumption — that the voters who do show up will be largely the hard core of strong school supporters. Supposedly the holding of a special election solely for the school issue and the soft pedal on campaigning will not motivate the "anti" voters enough to arouse them.

Trends in School Public Relations (October 15, 1963), Washington, D.C.: by Permission of National School Public Relations Association, 3.

Trouble is that it's just a theory, one which can be upset by many factors. In a small vote election, full responsibility for producing the favorable vote rests largely with the school campaign organization. There is less opportunity to secure "bonus" favorable voters who, although not reached by the campaigners, would support a school issue at a general election.

The small vote election can be a serious threat to success, so much so that school forces may be forced to give high priority attention to methods for bringing more voters to the polls.

In New Jersey this year there was a jump of almost 50 percent in budget election defeats — and the outcome in 1962 had been considered a disastrous year. Failures in capital outlay elections increased by almost two-thirds.

One of the disturbing elements has been that less than 18 percent of the registered voters took part in the New Jersey budget elections in 1963 as compared with 25 percent in 1962. Asst. Supt. John Hagen, South Plainfield, who headed up a study of the budget elections and reported them in the September-October issue of the New Jersey school board association magazine, *School Board Notes,* saw serious trouble in the lagging voter participation in school elections. "A pitifully small minority made judgment and rejected 100 budgets," he reported. "The inference is clear. School election practices have resulted in a small minority of the voters deciding financially the program of public education."

Hagen was greatly concerned because one of the chief reasons given for budget defeats was "silent or unknown sentiments in the community." He strongly urged the stepping up of planned means of two-way communications between school boards and communities. "The problem of getting board and electorate to talk the same language — understand what the other says — must be attacked on many fronts," he said. "A continuous community PR program between board and community appears necessary."

The problem of converting the small vote to a large vote in school elections may be as great as producing sufficient majority votes. At Roslyn, N.Y., this year, the budget was approved by only 93 votes. The system's publication, *Parents' Newsletter,* pointed out that "fewer than 426 of the parents of our 4,388 students voted on the proposed school budget."

At Port Huron, Mich., a large bond issue and operating increase was defeated on the first try by 300 votes and passed the second time by 800 votes, following a huge campaign which involved 500 women telephone campaigners. But the total vote the second time was only 43 percent of the registered voters as compared with 41 percent the first time.

SCHOOL PUBLIC RELATIONS IS STILL IN ITS INFANCY*

The new era in school public relations has not yet arrived. The breakthrough that might eventuate from research in communications is still a dream.

In fact, the current emphasis upon communications as a comparatively new alliance of disciplines has been wreaking havoc with practical professional training in journalism, believes John Tebbel. This journalism chairman at N.Y.U. comments that communications research is a specialty that is far removed from journalism and is the "true child" of sociology. This concerns us because school public relations still enrolls most of its practitioners from the profession of journalism.

Another journalism educator, Warren K. Agee of Texas Christian University, recognizes that the communications school with its interdisciplinary approach is one of the trends having an impact on journalism and public relations, but he warns that journalism must put its own house in order. The specter of obsolescence — in terms of basic knowledge, skills and abilities to adjust to changing conditions — threatens the vital roles that journalism performs in the communication of facts and the interpretation of opinion.

I believe the most thought-provoking address-articles in the school public relations field during the period of this review were contributed by Harry A. Fosdick, public relations executive for the California Teachers Association, and Lee Demeter of the Great Neck, N.Y., public schools.

A real breakthrough in school communications is inhibited by four attitudes, says Fosdick. One of these is the assumption that educators have a monopoly on educational wisdom. We rightfully resent the self-appointed experts who presume to know all there is to know about public education — but that doesn't mean that we can't use contributions of outside experts, self-appointed or enlisted.

The second inhibiting attitude is the "worship of placidity." The so-called public relations programs seek public approval of what already is happening and carefully detour around controversial problems or the need for change. The only problems ever exposed to the public are needs

*Arthur Rice, "School Public Relations: More Inhibited than Effective." Reprinted, with permission, from *The Nation's Schools* (March, 1964), 72. Copyright, 1964, McGraw-Hill, Inc., Chicago, All rights reserved.

for more money. The job of public relations is not to minimize dissension but to keep it focused on important problems.

A third roadblock is the "shortage of experimentation." We talk a lot about the importance of research and experimentation, but we are reluctant to do either.

And the fourth inhibiting factor is the persistent practice of educators of using shibboleths to protect sacred cows. Fosdick counsels that in these times of rapid change, we dare not be satisfied with public acquiescence as a substitute for public understanding.

Demeter says the greatest fault of school public relations is the lack of planning. School public relations programs are conducted on a crisis-to-crisis or hit-and-miss basis.

PROPER USE OF RADIO AND TELEVISION FOR PUBLIC RELATIONS*

To their annoyance, radio and television reporters are frequently treated by many schools as poor relations of the press. Many people think of coverage only in terms of newspapers. But when schools hold a press conference, they should invite radio and television newsrooms as well. When releases are sent to the newspapers, they should be sent to the radio and television stations, too. Even if the stations cannot cover every event, news releases will help keep them regularly informed of the school program and may spark an idea for a special events or feature broadcast.

Television and radio feature sight and sound, and keeping these senses in mind may help to spot a story that is particularly suited to their medium. A visual story usually makes a schoolman think of a picture spread in the newspaper, but it could also be a television program. The newspaper can only describe the new school orchestra; radio can broadcast the orchestra performing. There are sounds and sights in every school that often say more than words in telling the school story. Keep your ears and eyes open for them and tip off the broadcasters when you think you have something out of the ordinary.

Don't neglect using spot announcements. Provide radio and television with very brief — 10-second, 20-second, 30-second, and 1-minute — announcements, each on a separate piece of paper, double-spaced, which

---

*Reprinted with permission of The Macmillan Company from *Public Relations for Education* by Gloria Dapper. © Copyright, Gloria Dapper, 1964, 95-96.

the stations can use in free time. You will be amazed how often you get on the air in this way. Your message will depend on the schools themselves and your public relations needs, but there are many general messages that are true for all school systems. A brief announcement, finally urging listeners to attend the school board meeting Tuesday nights, or to join the P.T.A., or to learn more about the school, or to visit the schools during American Education Week, or to help their children study — these are always timely and always helpful. They will go a long way toward helping you create the image of the schools in the listener's ear and in the viewer's eye.

GENERAL RULES FOR PRODUCING A PUBLICATION*

In producing any publication, there are general rules to keep in mind.

Have a title that attracts attention. If possible, use a strong verb in the title.

Keep the cover uncluttered.

At the beginning, begin. Don't lose your readers with three pages of thank-yous.

Let the story run along without interruptions. Footnotes are distracting. If your explanations are lengthy, maybe you are not stating the point clearly; perhaps explanatory material should be included in the appendix.

Date your publication. Recently, a foundation brought out an excellent report which began, "Eighteen months ago . . ." There was no date on the publication, however, and the reader had no way of knowing when the study was made or what period it referred to.

Include a table of contents. Not everyone is interested in everything, and many like to flip to the section in which they are most interested. Once you get them to begin reading, they may stay with you to the end.

Strive for an over-all impression of clarity and informality. Glance through your publication and see if they look too gray and formidable to bother with.

---

*Reprinted with permission of The Macmillan Company from *Public Relations for Education* by Gloria Dapper. © Copyright, Gloria Dapper, 1964, 111-112.

Select a page size that is usable and economical. Offbeat sizes don't fit regulation envelopes, and special-size mailing envelopes cost extra. Paper also comes in stock sizes, and if a special size is cut, much of the paper you pay for goes to waste. Stock sizes are 8½ × 11 (which fits standard ring binders and file folders), 6 × 9, and 9 × 12 inches. Your printer may have some off-size paper stock he wants to get rid of which you can get at a bargain price. But beware that this doesn't force you to buy expensive envelopes to fit.

If your publication is going to be folded, make sure it is not folded in the middle of a picture.

Include a "masthead" which carries the school address, including the city and state. Your publications are sometimes sent far afield, and there is nothing more annoying than receiving a publication from Portland and wondering whether it's Maine or Oregon or some other state.

COMMUNICATING WITH PARENTS . . .

THE TEACHER'S INDIVIDUAL CONFERENCE WITH A PARENT*

Parent-teacher conferences are teachers' best means of communicating with parents. In this face-to-face relation, information and ideas about the child are exchanged, insight is gained, attitudes are caught, and plans for furthering his best development are evolved. From preschool years through high school, skillfully conducted conferences with parents have been enlightening to parents and teachers and beneficial to children and adolescents. They are part of the modern teacher's responsibility.

The communication process is the core of the parent conference. Communication may be verbal or nonverbal. Words, understood by both parent and teacher, convey thoughts, ideas, and insights. A smile, a nod, a bodily attitude of paying close attention convey interest, concern, and approval. Communication is the basic purpose of parent-teacher conferences.

Underlying the communication process are mutual understanding, respect, and appreciation. The teacher understands some of the parents'

---

problems in bringing up children. The parent realizes the teacher's difficulties in meeting the needs of thirty or more children, each one different in ability and personality. . . .

HAVING FACTS TO COMMUNICATE

Parent-teacher conferences often fail because the teacher does not know enough about the child. Parents want accurate information. As one mother said, "I didn't make the effort to come to the school and hire a baby-sitter just to hear that Jane was a very nice child."

The teacher should have a folder for each child, containing dated samples of his work, anecdotal records that can be periodically summarized, and a well-kept cumulative record. All these enable the teacher to supply and interpret facts about the child that will be helpful to the parent.

NONVERBAL COMMUNICATION

Communication is not necessarily verbal. A teacher may betray a feeling of inferiority by a subdued voice, a sagging posture, downcast eyes, hesitant speech, and many other expressive signs. He may express antagonism toward a parent by a brusque manner, a grim facial expression, and movements that indicate impatience. One shows genuine regard for another person by giving him close attention, smiling in encouragement or approval, and considering his physical comfort. The language of behavior is extensive and subtle. The skilled interviewer is aware of the importance of such nonverbal communication. It is the most effective way of showing a parent that he cares.

VERBAL COMMUNICATION

There are many ways in which verbal communication may affect the success of the parent-teacher conference. It often happens that parents and teachers do not speak the same language; they are separated by seas of misunderstanding. Thus what the teacher says does not evoke the desired response from the parent. Misunderstandings may also arise when the teacher speaks too rapidly, uses long, involved sentences, or fails to cite concrete examples. Sometimes the teacher is too impersonal; the conference degenerates into a lecture on education.

But parent-teacher conferences require two-way communication; what we have said about the teacher's ability to convey facts and feelings applies also to the parent. . . .

"DON'T'S" TO AVOID

During an interview the teacher should keep in mind a few rather important "don't's":

1. Don't put the parent on the defensive about anything.
2. Don't talk about other children or compare this child with other children. It is most unprofessional.
3. Don't talk about other teachers to the parents unless the remarks are of a complimentary nature.
4. Don't belittle the administration or make derogatory remarks about the school district.
5. Don't argue with the parent.
6. Don't try to outtalk a parent.
7. Don't interrupt the parent to make your own point.
8. Don't go too far with a parent who is not ready and able to understand your purpose.
9. Don't ask the parents personal questions which might be embarassing to them. Only information pertinent to the child's welfare is important. Questions asked out of mere curiosity are unforgivable.
10. After the conference don't repeat any confidential information which the parent may volunteer. It is most unprofessional and can be very damaging to the parent or the child.

THE SUCCESS OF PARENT-TEACHER CONFERENCE DEPENDS UPON ATTITUDES*

The attitudes of parents toward the teacher and the conference may have much to do with its success or failure. The teacher who summons parents to come to the school for a conference on their child's behavior or school attendance, in a manner a judge might summon them into court, who uses the sending for parents as a disciplinary threat to the child, who complains to parents about their child's actions, or who visits the home to complain and try to throw responsibility on the parents for

---

*Charles E. Reeves, *Parents and the School,* Washington, D.C.: by permission of Public Affairs Press, 1963, 162.

the child's actions in school, is not in the proper mood for securing the co-operation of parents and will probably cause them to have an unco-operative mood for a conference. Conferences should be initiated in a friendly manner. If the teacher is unfriendly and antagonistic the parents will likely be in a scared, angry, or hostile mood and will not have confidence in the good intentions of the teacher. Parents want support, co-operation, and suggestions from the teacher.

The parent who comes to the conference in an angry or complaining mood, accusing the teacher of bad intentions, favoritism, failure to keep order, and the like, will not be in condition to receive much help from the conference. The parent will be *en rapport* with the teacher if he genuinely feels and expresses appreciation for what the teacher is doing or trying to do for his child and if he recognizes the teacher's difficulty in carrying a heavy teaching load.

During a conference both the parents and the teacher must give individual attention to the matters under consideration. Parents should guard against taking offense at accounts of the child's actions and guard against any feeling of sudden resentment against the teacher and a desire to place blame on him. Instead, they should be thankful if the teacher has been frank. Parents should want accurate accounts even though disappointing to them. A show of displeasure, by parents toward the teacher, will make it difficult for the teacher to be frank with them again. Even if parents should not accept the teacher's analysis, they can better understand their child as a pupil in a roomful of children and his relations with his teacher if they learn the teacher's viewpoint.

COMMUNICATION THROUGH PARENT-TEACHER ASSOCIATIONS*

Local organizations of parents for the promotion or support of schools in this country, extend back to the town schools of Massachusetts, the charity schools of New York, and other types of schools in our early history. There was no connection among such organizations and their purposes varied. In 1897, a meeting of what was designated as the National Congress of Mothers met in Washington, D.C. Interest developed in this organization and in 1908 the name was changed to National Congress of Mothers and Parent-Teacher Associations. Under the new

*Charles E. Reeves, *Parents and the School,* Washington, D.C.: by permission of Public Affairs Press, 1963, 199-201.

name, the local associations extended membership to include fathers and teachers. In 1924, the name of the national organization was changed to the National Congress of Parents and Teachers.

During the period of early development, most public school administrators and teachers supported their local parent-teacher association, if they had one, and they often took the initiative in organizing one if none existed. However, a few superintendents, principals, and teachers opposed the establishment of local associations, or if already established, succeeded in having them discontinued. Some thought they afforded parents opportunities for meddling or interfering in the affairs of the school and for criticizing teachers and the school system. Now, after the passage of years, most superintendents, principals, and teachers have come to realize the importance of local associations and to appreciate the support parents and teachers, when organized, can give the schools, though there is still an occasional school administrator who fears the criticism parent-teacher association members may direct at the schools and who believes the schools can be conducted better without parental interference. In many schools, however, the principals and members of the school staff have been largely responsible for the establishment of parent-teacher associations.

Since 1925 the National Congress of Parents and Teachers has promoted, through its affiliated parent-teacher associations, the "summer round-up" with the aim of inducing parents to have their six-year-old children medically examined, treated if necessary, and vaccinated, as preparation for school. It has accomplished much in promotion of classes in parent education, such as instruction in the functions of the parent in the proper development of the child. An important contribution to the improvement of education has been the practice of nonpartisan endorsement of national legislation affecting schools. State organizations of parents and teachers have made similar contributions to good schools in their respective states; city organizations, within the cities; and local organizations, in the schools for which they, respectively, have been organized. The National Congress of Parents and Teachers helps local associations by furnishing them with study outlines, model by-laws, and other aids.

Parent-Teacher associations have been established in all states and American bases in foreign countries. Both the number and size of parent-teacher associations have greatly increased, especially in recent years. New associations are being formed and others discontinued each year. In each association, membership is flexible. The numbers have been increasing rapidly in recent years. It has been estimated that there are more than fifty thousand parent-teacher associations and more than twelve million members. Some are not affiliated with the National Congress.

Need for Further Development: Even though membership in parent-teacher associations has greatly increased in recent years, it is likely that it will continue to increase further in the future. The problems involved in the maintenance of good schools continue to multiply and, at the same time, society's demands are more and more insistent for an educated citizenry and basic pupil education for many additional highly educated specialists. There are possibilities for further large increases in the number of associations and of members in associations now in operation. Many families have one parent member and many others have none. Then, also, some schools do not have parent-teacher associations or have nonaffiliated parent, or parent-teacher groups.

Some parents believe that parent-teacher associations are needed in high schools even more than in elementary schools. Some of the parent-teacher activities for high schools need to be different. It is at high school ages that pupils develop independence of thought and action, increase their social contacts, begin to think about their future occupations and social relationships, come into contact with many temptations and moral hazards, tend to form exclusive groups and gangs, and need the co-operative guidance of parents and teachers not less, but more, than at earlier ages — guidance that is proffered in a more skillful manner than at earlier years.

Of course distances from home to the high school are greater than to the elementary school for most parents, and the high school community is much larger, The parents want their high school fledglings to learn to fly but they need to observe their trials and errors. The fledglings want to stretch their wings and take off and are, sometimes, sure they can do it without help, but they need guidance that does not interfere with their self pride and independence. At high school ages both home and school still need to be good places for child development, but community problems increase in importance. High school parent-teacher associations need both fathers and mothers in them. To accommodate working parents, the meetings can better be held, as a rule, in the evenings.

Organization of Parent-Teacher Groups. The National Congress of Parents and Teachers provides overhead policy-forming organization for the promotion, guidance, and servicing of the thousands of local parent-teacher associations, but each local unit is largely self-governing, with little control exercised from above but with considerable guidance available from the higher echelons of the organization. The organization, with units arranged in order of geographical extent, but with few control functions exercised, is as follows:

> National Congress of Parents and Teachers (Office: 700 North Rush Street, Chicago, Ill.)
> State Congresses of Parents and Teachers (State branches)
> Parent-Teacher Associations (The parents and teachers of children in each school)

INTERNAL COMMUNICATIONS . . .

TEACHERS SEEK ENFORCED COMMUNICATIONS WITH BOARD OF EDUCATION*

Teachers are proposing, through their various organizations, a more highly formalized system of communication than has existed in the past. They are advocating legislation which would establish their right to carry on formal negotiating procedures. School board members, through their organizations, are opposing mandatory negotiation or bargaining, and legislation which would establish such compulsory practices. . . .

During the past 2 years, numerous articles have been published in professional journals, daily newspapers, and popular periodicals analyzing certain issues which relate to the positions taken by the teacher organizations and the school boards. New terms have evolved for the educator's vocabulary—strikes, sanctions, mediation, professional negotiation, collective bargaining, appeal, and arbitration.

The growing importance of the teacher organization as a vigorous, articulate, and forceful element in the improvement of working conditions for teachers is well recognized. Today's teachers are interested and increasingly active, through their organizations, in such matters as civil rights, academic freedom, manpower needs, and international affairs. Quite recently they have become vitally concerned about their rights and responsibilities in participating in the development of the policies and regulations which determine the conditions under which they work.

---

*James P. Steffensen, *Teachers Negotiate with Their School Boards,* Washington, D.C.: United States Office of Education, Bulletin 1964, No. 40, 1-4, 6-7.

Several significant events have occurred during the past several years which highlight the current activity of local, State, and national teacher organizations. Two of these achieved particular prominence: the threatened strike by the teachers of New York City during the summer of 1963, and the 2-day walkout by the teachers of the State of Utah in the spring of 1964.

A background to this growing activity by the teachers of this Nation can be cited: The history of teaching as a low-salaried occupation, marked by entrance and retention standards sufficiently low to permit a good share of the total group to enter and exit the profession at sporadic intervals; insufficient internal control to restrict the unqualified from filling positions in either real or psuedoemergencies; and a relatively poor image as a career, particularly for males, in the eyes of the American public.

A more positive factor in teacher participation has been the change in the makeup of the public school teacher in the 1960's. Salaries and fringe benefits have improved. Education has received sufficient attention by the American public to elevate at least the degree of importance of teaching and probably its attractiveness as a career. Certainly the proportion of males is increasing so that they are now in the majority in the secondary schools. The public school teacher has also become better educated and more cognizant of the part that public education plays in shaping affairs far beyond the confines of his local school district — at State, national, and international levels. Perhaps it is this combination of greater sophistication plus the awareness of his importance and ability which has contributed most strongly to the increasing vitality of teacher groups at all levels. This, however, would be contributory only if the teachers, as a group, had been denied an appropriate voice in the determination of the policies establishing the conditions under which they work. . . .

One additional possible cause is the action of the teachers, through their organizations, to attain a degree of professionalism considerably beyond that typically associated with the public school teacher in the United States.

There are, however, certain features of teaching which make the professionalism of its membership of continuing difficulty, even though the traditional image may no longer be valid. Perhaps most important, teachers may have failed to make clear whether they regard themselves as salaried professionals or independent professionals, such as the doctor or lawyer.

This effort of teachers to become professional is related to a relatively recent trend in education — the trend toward larger school systems, which entail greater centralization of decision-making, greater distance between the teacher and the chief executive and, like so much of our present society, bureaucratization. The result has been the development of a role conflict in which the teacher as an individual with professional ideologies is operating in a situation where he is confronted increasingly with bureaucratic ideologies. This is a theme which appears rather frequently in the various journals of sociology but has made little impact upon the journals in education. . . .

These causes, then, for the increasing concern of the teachers to obtain a greater voice in the determination of public educational policy as it affects their conditions of work would be several. The depressed economic reward level, paternalism, the bureaucratization of the school organization, recognition of the intellectual and technical resources of the teachers in resolving educational problems, the striving to make education a profession — these have all contributed.

To implement this concern, teacher are requesting, through their organizations, a more formalized procedure for conducting discussions with their boards of education. Much of the attention given to the issue has centered around the need, as teachers see it, to formalize the procedure, perhaps through legislation, and the opportunity for an appeal in the event of an impasse between the board of education and the teacher organization.

These provisions would confront most boards of education and superintendents of schools with a framework of operation dramatically different from the past. Procedures for judicial review of local decisions at the State level have existed for some time. Certainly, many school boards have voluntarily encouraged teacher participation in the development of staff personnel policies, but this practice has not been compulsory except in those relatively few situations where a contractual agreement between the board and the teacher organization existed. In addition, the provision for an appeal from a board-teacher organization impasse to a neutral party presents perhaps an even greater potential modification of both the role of the negotiators as well as the climate in which such negotiations take place. . . .

As a result, national, State, and local teacher organizations are adopting, reviewing, and revising guidelines for conducting board-teacher discussions on matters of mutual concern. These organizations are asking that formal channels for the negotiation of various working conditions be developed and maintained — conditions of work which include salaries but are not limited to them.

For the school boards, the request by the teacher organizations to formalize negotiation procedures has meant another new item to be added to an ever-growing agendum. It has also added to the frequently stated school board concern for safeguarding the policymaking function mandated by State law to local school boards.

For the general public, an increasing amount of information is being presented. Newspaper and journal writings which cover only the larger issue — teacher-school board-superintendent relationships — are numerous. These external publications frequently concentrate upon the central problem of the potential change in the power structure within American public education if either or both of the national teacher organizations succeed in their drive for achieving a larger voice in the determination of their conditions of work. In individual communities, where crisis situations have developed, such as a strike or sanctions, the problem has been particularly acute.

FACE-TO-FACE CONVERSATIONS
DOMINATE INTERNAL
COMMUNICATIONS*

Face-to-face conversation comprises a large percentage of all messages transmitted and received by most people. Practically all communication within family circles is conversational. And research shows that these are high-interest-level communications which receive sympathetic attention and evoke much considerate response. Fortunately most families are interested in schools and, inevitably, schooling is a subject of much family conversation. We can be glad that that is so. No other agency has such constant access to this best of all communication channels. Hunderds of industries and trade associations spend millions of dollars each year to obtain similar consideration in family circles.

Face-to-face conversations also dominate the mass of communication flowing through the workaday world. Just observe in any shop, store, mine, factory, laboratory, office, or school. Most decisions are based on face-to-face discussions. Most instructions and agreements are verbal; chitchat and kidding dominate lunch and coffee hours. The memoranda and bulletins are there and jokes about their volume abound, but most occupational communication is verbal. We also should note that well-trained executives and supervisors are seeking means of increasing face-

---

*From *Education and Public Understanding* by Gordon McCloskey, Copyright © 1959 by Gordon McCloskey, 71-72.

to-face communication and of reducing reliance on relatively impersonal written instructions. This is because they are learning that conversation provides feedback and interplay of personalities, which increase understanding and result in more effective working arrangements. For those same reasons, many school superintendents, principals, and committee chairmen also are relying more on face-to-face, and less on written, communications.

Next let us observe the roles of conversation and discussion in the leisure and social activities which occupy ever larger parts in people's waking hours. Indeed, conversation is one major purpose for which many groups are organized. Civic-organization luncheons, lodge meetings, bridge clubs, cocktail parties, housewives getting together for mid-morning coffee and impromptu back-yard visits, are examples. The fact that much of this social conversation deals with trivialities and that much of it reflects a disturbing lack of interest in, and information about, important public affairs in no way detracts from its dominant place in our communication structure. Our task is to inject into it more well-informed consideration of important events and affairs — especially of schooling.

Many people are also influenced by other more formal person-to-person communications. Executives give pep talks to employees. Ministers preach sermons. Civic-organization members listen to luncheon speakers. Some people go to lectures. These are largely one-way means of communication. Feedback may range from zero to considerable amounts. Depending on circumstances and on speakers' intentions and skills, listeners discuss such messages with speakers or among themselves to varying degrees.

THE SCHOOL ADMINISTRATOR'S NEED TO UNDERSTAND COMMUNICATIONS*

1. All persons who are in an administrative position or who aspire to such a position must acquire a full and comprehensive knowledge of the process of communication and its utilization in a functioning organization. The present research study uncovered evidence that some administrators tend to regard com-

---

*Harold Edwin Wilson, "Communication in Administrative Organizations" (Unpublished PhD Dissertation, Ohio State University, 1964), 184-188 (by permission).

munication as a mechanical process and to disregard the broader personnel implications. . . .

2. The communications system must be planned and not just happen. Again, there was evidence that in some cases the communication was created after the need. In order to be effective, the communication must be planned ahead of the need. Further, every time there is a change in the organizational structure, there must be a re-evaluation of the communication structure and revision to make it adequate to the new needs created by the organizational change. The same would be true every time there is a change in personnel within the organization. A complete briefing as to the communication structure and procedures is an essential part of the indoctrination of the new members joining the organization.

3. Any system of communication developed for the organization must be multi-tracked and involve some system of follow-up to be sure that messages are received and understood. There was ample evidence to suggest that these two factors were key elements of the successful communication situations reported upon by the respondents. The multi-track approach obviously increases the probability that the information will get through to the intended recipient. In almost every instance, one of the channels involves the message in some recorded form thus providing a reference point for the personnel receiving the information. The follow-up insures that the message is not only received but understood. In many cases this can avoid misinterpretations of intent or meaning.

4. Any system of communication must include provisions for keeping all personnel well informed as to the aims, goals, and purposes of the organization as well as the purposes of the various functions and operations of the organization. The results of the present study suggests that this is often imperfectly done, leading to confusion and ineffective communication. This situation can lead to substitution of the individual's own goals or what he believes to be the goals of the organization. Since intent of any communication should be consistent with the goals and objectives of the organization, it is important that all the personnel making up the organization have as nearly the same perceptions of the aims, goals and objectives as it is possible to achieve.

5. The study of the process of communication and its utilization in dynamic organizations must be strengthened and expanded as

a part of pre-service programs of future administrators. In
many cases, the present study of processes such as communication tend to an academic approach involving readings, lectures
and discussions. Programs must be designed which will allow
the pre-service students to develop understandings of the operation of such processes in functioning situations and opportunities to develop skills in dealing with the problems of establishing
and maintaining such processes. Internships, on-the-job prac-
ticums and other procedures of a like nature may be ways of
accomplishing this task.

6. The study of communication within the organization is a necessary part of the organization's in-service program. Some aspects
of this have been discussed elsewhere. This sort of an in-service
program can have excellent benefits to the organization. Such
an in-service program can result in the improvement of the
organization's communication structure and procedures; the
reduction of differences of perceptions of the goals of the
organization as a whole and the perception of the functions by
members of the organization; the emphasis of the role and
responsibility of each individual within the organization; and
other similar outcomes. An in-service program related to the
actual needs and problems of the organization can pay big
dividends in increased effectiveness and efficiency.

7. Administrators who hold the key positions must acquaint themselves with the communication process and must develop skills
which will allow them to evaluate the process and to correct
problems that might occur. Some of the results of the study
indicated that the top administrators tended to take the communication process for granted. They became concerned only
after some breakdown in the process had occurred. One of the
basic tasks of the key administrator is the establishment and
maintenance of a system of communication which will allow the
most effective, efficient accomplishment of the organizational
goals. While he can delegate the actual mechanical aspects of
this establishment, he can never delegate the responsibility
involved. He must be constantly aware of and concerned with
the effective functioning of the communication system.

8. Key administrators must learn more about the functioning of
complex organizations and the implications for action within
the organization of which they are a part. It seems quite evident
that few organizations will ever get simpler; the tendency is
toward larger and more complex organizations. It is also true

that personnel problems, communication problems, and other similar problems increase as a geometric function of the growth in size. Fortunately there is a growing volume of research and literature in the field of complex organization. Much of this information is of real value to the school administrator faced with the problems of a rapidly expanding organization. Information of this sort should become a part of the pre-service preparation of administrators. Administrators on the job will need to make provisions for continuously updating themselves in this area.

9. Processes such as communication must become the basis for a continuous process of evaluation of their effectiveness. As indicated earlier, every change in the nature, function and personnel of the organization brings with such change a need for revision of the process in question to meet new needs. The larger and more complex the organization, the more important it becomes to have some system of constant appraisal of the effectiveness of each of the processes and functions of concern in the organization. The communication structure and process must be made adaptable to the constantly changing needs of the ongoing organization.

THE FUNCTIONAL APPROACH TO GROUP LEADERSHIP*

Group objectives are of two broad types: (1) getting the job or group task done; (2) keeping the group maintained in good working order. Both these types of objectives or group needs are present, for example, in a committee meeting discussing reading problems in the primary grades. To meet these needs, the designated chairman may serve as a leader by *initiating* a creative approach to the problem, a new teacher by *asking for clarification* of the goal of the meeting, and another committee member by *giving friendly support* to a blocking, complaining member. Since these acts aid the group in moving toward effective, personally satisfying accomplishment of goals shared by all group members, they are leadership functions, even if they last only a moment. Thus the importance of

---

*Matthew B. Miles, *Learning to Work in Groups*, New York: by permission of Bureau of Publications, Teachers College, Columbia University, 1959, 17-19.

leadership rather than *the* leader. The essential thing is that functions be supplied when they are needed — not that any particular person supply them.

Note that this functional approach also includes the highly-controlling leader usually labeled "autocratic." The autocrat supplies nearly all the task-relevant functions, but tends to ignore or frustrate the personal needs of group members. Such a leader is followed because not to do so would mean the loss of certain satisfactions — or punishment of some sort. The approach also includes a full range of other styles of leadership:

> *Bargaining,* where a horse-trading approach involving rewards and punishments is central. The focus tends to be on the leader's agreeing to meet members' personal needs if they in turn will work on the official group task.
> *Paternalism,* where the leader supplies nearly all the functions — benevolently — and does not permit members to perform leadership acts.
> *Laissez-faire inaction,* where the leader supplies no functions, and does nothing to help members supply them.
> *Cooperative problem-solving,* where the demands of the problem and the needs of persons are both central, and anyone who sees a missing function is expected to supply it.

As the reader considers these styles of leadership and thinks of group situations he is in, he may well begin judging their relative goodness or badness. Labels are not usually helpful, however. To damn a staff meeting as "paternalistic" is to ignore the fact that paternalism (for some groups, at some times, working on some tasks) may be very effective. Effective in terms of what? Here are some criteria for judging leadership acts:

> *Augmentation:* Does the leadership act *augment* or facilitate group members' positive search for need-satisfaction? Or does it accentuate the negative — threaten people with punishment or loss of present satisfactions if they do not perform as desired by the leader?
> *Effectiveness and efficiency:* Does the leadership act aid the group to do its job rapidly and well (effectiveness), besides improving internal working relationships (efficiency)? Or does it tend to evoke a group product of poor quality and feelings of low morale and antagonism?
> *Learning:* Following the leadership act, have other group members grown — either in knowledge of the subject matter they are working on, or in ability to contribute effectively to working groups? Or do they remain at their previous level of knowledge and skill?

Taking a functional approach, and applying criteria like these, can free us from labeling leadership and leaders as "democratic" or "authoritarian." The focus is on the real consequences of specific leadership acts performed by individuals in a specific situation.

One additional comment is in order: The functional approach does not get bogged down (as other theories tend to) on the issue of the appointed leader versus the emergent leader. Both the official leader and the group member who happens to come up with the right function at the right time are doing the same thing: supplying functions needed by the group. The appointed leader who does not do so will become leader in name only, even though he may retain his authority until he retires twenty years hence. Most groups do have appointed leaders as a kind of "safety net" or guarantee that *someone* will fill needed functions, but the approach taken here assumes that the appointed leader and members alike may exert leadership.

GENERAL QUALIFICATIONS OF THE DISCUSSION LEADER*

Leading a discussion is a difficult task, and frankly not everyone can handle it. But it might help to set down the general qualities needed by such a leader, if only to enable you to check them against your own abilities and know how to be on guard at those points where you may face personal difficulties.

1. *He should know the rules of the game,* should know, for example the Six Steps in Discussion, whether he is directing a Panel Forum or a Symposium Forum, when the audience is to be called on to participate, how to keep on schedule, and how to draw the ends together at the close.

2. *He should be willing to remain in the background.* "A quarterback who always elects himself to carry the ball whenever there is a chance for a touchdown will seldom be popular." A good discussion leader may indeed grow impatient, because a discussion sometimes moves slowly, but the good leader must move patiently with it, and not cut in to tell the group what's what.

---

*From *Speech Communication,* second edition, by William Norwood Brigance. Copyright, 1955, by Appleton-Century-Crofts, Inc. Reprinted by permission of Appleton-Century-Crofts, 147-148.

3. *He should respect the opinion of others.* He may not share those opinions, but he should not let this become known to the audience. Throughout the meeting the leader gives equal opportunity to all members to express ideas. He listens to them, believing that what others think is important. He summarizes the consensus of the meeting without regard to his own personal opinions.

4. *He should be courteous, fairminded, and impartial.* A lively discussion is at times turbulent, and some of the less-controlled participants may clinch in heated arguments and resort to angry words. But the good leader never, even for an instant, loses his courteous manner. He is the moderator who not only restrains the violence of others, but who sets an example of courteous conduct. When the argument gets hot, he breaks in with a smile and gentle hint, such as "I think we all know how Brown and Johnson feel about this. Now who else would like to get in on it?" If a hint of this sort does not break it up, the leader can remind the group that the purpose of the discussion is to reach some solution to the problem, that the argument between the two members is preventing calm discussion, then ask these two persons to cease the argument and to permit the group to continue its discussion. A gentle admonition, courteously given by the leader, will usually quiet even the most violent member.

The good leader, above all, is fairminded and impartial. He never favors one viewpoint or restricts another. He not only permits all viewpoints to be brought out, but tries diligently to have them brought out. To persons of every viewpoint, he conveys assurance that he is a leader who plays no favorites.

THE PROS AND CONS OF COMMITTEES FOR DECISION MAKING*

Some of the principal advantages of using conferences and committees as the medium through which to reach decisions are:

1. Problems are brought out into the open — whether known and held under the surface or actually unknown and identified only through a frank discussion of the symptoms.

*From *The Art of Decision-Making,* by Joseph D. Cooper. Copyright © by Joseph D. Cooper. Reprinted by permission of Doubleday & Company, Inc., 148-150.

2. Varied expert knowledge, opinions and judgments are brought to bear on matters of some complexity or intangibility where group interaction will generate a common understanding and solution.

3. Matters which have been stalemated in the course of handling through ordinary administrative channels may be brought out for re-examination in the hope that a face-to-face approach may help clear the air.

4. Acceptance and enforcement of decisions by the participants is sought through the procedure of enabling them to share in the responsibility for the decision.

5. A "court" of judgment is provided for action on matters affecting people intimately, when executives acting alone would otherwise be subject to pressure or censure.

6. Opportunities for development for higher responsibility are afforded the participants through their exposure to various assignments in the meeting and through the opportunity which they have to observe the solution of problems at close hand.

On the other side of the ledger you can find many notable expressions of dissatisfaction with committee work as opposed to what can be done by well-trained individuals acting through channels. Ralph J. Cordiner, chairman of the General Electric Company, has been quoted as saying, "If you can name for me one great discovery or decision that was made by a committee, I will still find you the one man in that committee who had the lonely insight—while he was shaving, or on his way to work, or maybe while the rest of the committee was chattering away—the lonely insight which solved the problem and was the basis for decision." With this tongue-in-check observation in mind, let's now look at some of the disadvantages of group decision-making:

1. *Most* meetings are risk. Most meetings are run poorly and are a waste of time in spite of years of strenuous effort to improve them.

2. The aggregate return to the participants for the amount of time they spend in meetings in low compared to the aggregate amount of time spent by them in meetings. Thus, if five people are in a meeting, the average time spent in discussion is 20 per cent per person. Even counting listening as a form of participation, the pay-out would still be low. Moreover topics and discussions tend to come up which do not involve all of the people and some times do not interest anyone other than the speaker.

3. Decision-making by committee or conference tends to weaken or bypass administrative responsibility unless the chairman is

in full control and uses the conference as a consultative body. Committees are often used deliberately as burial grounds or as means of passing the buck in order to avoid administrative responsibility.

4. Some people use conference sessions as convenient media for the advancement of their personal aims rather than for the advancement of organizational aims. Committees are sometimes used as public forums, by subordinates, as a means of finessing their superiors.

5. Taken away from their ordinary work places, the participants often find themselves without adequate information on aspects of the problem that could not have been anticipated. To avoid being caught without their facts, they tend to bring along their more qualified subordinates, armed with bulky folders and note-books. The combination of increased participation and mixing of work levels tends to stultify the proceedings. On the other hand, the absence of facts and analyses, not previously antici-pated, may cause postponements, delays and loss of continuity in the decision-making activity.

6. Some people who would not hesitate to express themselves fully from behind their desks, when they have a chance to think through what they are going to say, may freeze in the face of the need for spontaneous give-and-take discussion. The extent to which this occurs may vary with the climate of participation encouraged by management.

7. Meetings often lack an incisive quality because of an excessive preoccupation with feelings, personalities and protocols.

SUITABLE OCCASIONS FOR MEETINGS

The five points which follow should be considered in the light of the pros and cons just described. A positive judgment should be made that the ordinary exercise of administrative responsibility would not be so satisfactory as the calling of a meeting. Also, as a prerequisite to calling a meeting, you should be satisfied that the committee will have the capa-bility and authority necessary to accomplish the mission to be assigned to it.

1. The group has the collective knowledge and experience, through contact with related or similar situations in the past, which would not otherwise be available through ordinary adminis-trative channels.

2. The subject is such that it requires the several contributions of the participants simultaneously, so that they can be interlaced

and brought to bear on a complex or highly intangible topic or one requiring the simultaneous exercise of diverse technical judgments.

3. Time does not permit the referral of a matter in sequence through the ordinary administrative channels. A matter is of sufficiently pressing nature that it will exert its own time-leverage on the proceedings.

4. The participants need to become thoroughly briefed on their respective and mutual roles in a subsequent series of actions so that each will know just when and how his part is to be brought into concert with those of the others.

5. The matter is of a "privileged" nature, requiring referral to a senior group which is privy to the private matters and business secrets of the enterprise.

FOR FURTHER REFLECTION OR INVESTIGATION

1. Develop an instrument for evaluating the effectiveness of a school system's internal communications. After trying it out in at least one large and one small school system, compare the results.

2. Develop an instrument for surveying your school district to determine citizen attitudes toward the school. Plan a sampling system to produce a fair cross-section of community thinking. With the sanction of your superinendent and board of education, try it.

3. Why have teachers traditionally thought of the public relations function as the exclusive responsibility of the superintendent?

4. Develop a plan for a school citizens' council which would permit a fair representation for two-way communication and yet be small enough to become a working, manageable group. How would representatives be selected?

5. If a board of education and its faculty enter into a written agreement to negotiate on welfare matters, what subject would be properly excluded? Will such an arrangement encourage board members to invade decision making in certain educational matters which have been heretofore accepted as the prerogative of professional personnel?

6. What are the differences between an employee's right to be represented in the decision making of his working environment as opposed to his governmental environment?

7. Build a year's program of internal communications for the superintendent in a school system of 10,000 pupils, showing proposed activities and when they should occur.

8. Compose a 100-word announcement which a principal might write for faculty members, trying it out on class members to assure that every thought therein comes through.

9. How can you be certain that people are really hearing what you say?

10. At the next faculty or small group meeting in your building, make a list of the non-verbal factors which influenced favorably and unfavorably the meeting's outcome.

11. Analyze in detail the causes of a meeting you attend which you considered a failure.

12. Do you agree with Dapper that the public has a right to know everything about schools? If not, what items may be considered privileged information by the administrator?

13. Plan a year's step-by-step program of events to conduct a successful bond issue campaign.

14. Reconcile Cooper's attitudes toward group decision making with the principles of democratic administration of a school.

BIBLIOGRAPHY

Bailard, Virginia, and Ruth Strang, *Parent-Teacher Conferences,* New York: McGraw-Hill Book Co., Inc., 1964.

Bereday, George Z.F., and Joseph A. Lauwerys, editors, *Communication Media and the School,* The Yearbook of Education, 1960, Tarrytown-on-Hudson: World Book Co., 1960.

Bortner, Doyle M., *Public Relations for Teachers,* New York: Simmons-Boardman Publishing Corp., 1959.

Brigance, William Norwood, *Speech Communication,* second edition, New York: Appleton-Century-Crofts, Inc., 1955.

Bunker, Douglas R., "Communicating Person to Person, "*The National Elementary Principal,* XLI, May, 1962.

Carter, Richard F., John Sutthoff, Dwight H. Newell, and William G. Savard and Francis M. Trusty, *Communities and Their Schools,* Stanford, Calif.: School of Education, Stanford University, 1960.

Chase, Stuart, *American Credos,* New York: Harper and Row, Publishers, 1962.

Christenson, Reo Millard, and Robert O. McWilliams, *Voice of the People, Readings in Public Opinion and Propaganda,* New York: McGraw-Hill Book Co., Inc., 1962.

Dapper, Gloria, *Public Relations for Education,* New York: The Macmillan Company, 1964.

Davis, William E., and Gordon McCloskey, "What Do People Know About Schools?" *American School Board Journal,* February, 1962.

Douglas, John I., "Communication: A Professional Necessity, "*School and Community,* XLIX, April, 1963.

Finn, David, *Public Relations and Management,* New York: Rheinhold 1960.

Haire, Mason, *Psychology in Management,* New York: McGraw-Hill Book Co., Inc., 1956.

Halpin, Andrew W., "Muted Language." *The School Review,* LXVIII, Spring, 1960.

Hints to the Beginning Superintendent of Schools. Washington, D.C.: American Association of School Administrators, 1962.

Huggett, Albert J., and T. M. Stinnett, *Professional Problems of Teachers,* New York: The Macmillan Company, 1956.

Johnson, Robert H., Jr., and William Hartman, *School Board and Public Relations,* New York: Exposition Press, 1964.

Jones, Clifford V., "Developing Community Understanding for Educational Innovation," *American School Board Journal,* CXLIX, July, 1964.

Jones, James J., and Irving W. Stout, *School Public Relations,* (Issues and Cases), New York: G. P. Putnam's Sons, 1960.

Key, Vladimer O., *Public Opinion and American Democracy,* New York: Knopf, 1961.

Kindred, Leslie W., *How To Tell The School Story,* Englewood Cliffs: Prentice-Hall, Inc. 1960.

Lewis, Anne Chambers, *The Schools and the Press,* Washington, D.C.: National School Public Relations Association, 1964.

McCloskey, Gordon, *Education and Public Understanding,* New York: Harper & Row, Publishers, 1959.

Miles, Matthew B., *Learning to Work in Groups,* New York: Bureau of Publications, Teachers College, Columbia University, 1959.

Reeves, Charles E., *Parents and the School,* Washington D. C.: Public Affairs Press.

School Management. "How to Cope with Attacks from the Fanatic Fringe," May, 1962.

Sherif, Muzafer and Carl I. Hovland, *Social Judgment: Assimilation and Contrast Effects in Communication and Attitude Change,* New Haven, Connecticut: Yale University Press, 1961.

Steffensen, James P., *Teachers Negotiate with Their School Boards,* Washington, D.C.: United States Office of Education, Bulletin 1964.

Steinberg, Charles Side, *The Mass Communicators: Public Relations, Public Opinion, and Mass Media,* New York: Harper & Row, Publishers, 1958.

Stephenson, Howard, ed., *Handbook of Public Relations,* New York: McGraw Hill Book Co., Inc., 1960.

The Schools and the Press, Washington, D.C.: The National School Public Relations Association, 1965.

Trends in School Public Relations, October, 1963, Washington, D.C.: National School Public Relations Association.

Van Winkle, Harold, *Public Relations Ideas for Teacher Education,* Washington, D.C.: The American Association of Colleges for Teacher Education, 1961.

Wilson, Harold E., "Communication in Administrative Organizations." Unpublished Ph.D. Dissertation, The Ohio State University, 1964.

Wendorf, Robert A., "Communicating with Parents," *Clearing House,* January, 1963.

Woodman, D. K., "The Birds and Bees of Public Relations, *"Nation's Schools,* April, 1956.

Chapter 9

Administration of School Personnel

The personnel function in any organization is probably the most difficult task to isolate and identify as a separate administrative activity. Nearly all acts performed by administrators involve personnel directly or indirectly. Even the impersonal function of plant construction, maintenance, and operation performed for and by the school's personnel. All administrators of a school system are concerned with and involved in the personnel task. Only lately, and in larger school systems, is the personnel function compartmentalized.

The complex nature of the school personnel administration function becomes evident from these statements. In the first place, the administrative task deals largely with the organization's human elements. It is concerned with people who work in schools. Secondly, the personnel task is a part of general administration of schools, fused with all other responsibilities of the chief school administrator in a small school system but capable of being labeled and delegated to a subordinate administrator in a large school system. Third, the importance of the function for a school district's success is suggested by the fact that it pervades the work of all administrators; every employee in the district is highly interested in the personnel activity.

The definition is offered, then, that the staff personnel function in schools is concerned with the people and conditions which contribute to the job satisfaction of school employees for the purpose of achieving the institution's objectives.

Since the only reason for a school's being is learning, and since learning is almost totally a "people" activity, it is astounding that the personnel function was neglected for so long in the history of education, both in the professional writings and in the preparation of administrators. Not until the current quarter-century has there been extensive interest expressed in either fount of knowledge. The explanation for today's billowing interest lies in events of the last three decades: the serious shortage of professional personnel, a general re-awakening to the importance of the human factor in the success of any enterprise, increased knowledge about the relation of human behavior to performance, increased legislation governing the working conditions of school employees, and the growing size of individual school districts which greatly increases the number of employees.

PERSONNEL FUNCTION IN SCHOOLS IS UNIQUE

The performance of the personnel task in an educational institution has much in common with its performance in other organizations of society. People are people, regardless of where they work, subject to common stimuli, aspirations, and frailties. Personnel administrators in schools can utilize a considerable portion of the body of knowledge which was accumulated in industrial corporations where the function was pioneered earlier in the twentieth century. However, all of the knowledge is not applicable to the school environment because of certain conditions and practices which are unlike those of any other organization.

In public schools, all personnel are legally state employees but they are hired and administered by local districts. The direction of teachers and non-certificated workers of a school district is influenced largely by state laws, allowing little latitude to local school administrators insofar as the legal status of employees is concerned. Another factor which alters the approach to personnel administration in schools is the preponderance of educated, professional individuals to be directed. Only a few other organizations such as research institutions or hospitals have such a ratio of degreed to non-degreed employees. This is not to say that educated individuals are different from less educated persons *per se,* however an administrator of teachers needs to have a store of motivational techniques different from those for dealing only with "uneducated" people.

Other unique aspects of public school employees include the contractual relationship between employer and employee. Further, professional salaries are administered on an annual basis rather than on a plan of hourly, daily, or monthly wages. And for teachers in most states, the state tenure laws introduce different arrangements. The continuing contract practice in public schools has some similarities to civil service regulations of government employees or seniority rights of union laborers, but with definite differences. Welfare or fringe benefits in public schools often differ from those in industry.

The point becomes clear that the administrator responsible for the personnel function in educational institutions needs some training and background unique from that of the personnel officer in other institutions.

THE PERSONNEL ADMINISTRATOR'S OFFICE

With the rapid growth in the size of school districts during the late 1950's and 1960's, there has been an almost parallel growth in the number of central staff officers, as more superintendency functions are delegated to specialists. The creation of the position for administering the school's personnel duties is largely a development of the past two decades. Donald reported that the first such position was established in the Dallas Public School system in 1919 (although Fawcett claims that Detroit was the first in 1914) but she found little evidence of other cities following the precedent throughout the 1920's, 1930's, or 1940's.* During the five-year period of 1955-60, however, 59 of the larger school districts created the position. If later studies had been made, they would undoubtedly reveal a more rapid growth, and it requires little foresight to predict that the next decade will witness a personnel administrator in most school districts with 200 to 300 professional employees.

It is also safe to forcecast a change in the pattern of selecting persons for this position. It has been customary to promote a principal or another experienced administrator from within the district when the personnel job is created, primarily upon the assumption that performance of this administrative assignment involved little more skill than that acquired through teaching and general administration. An examination of the tasks normally assigned to this officer, however, indicates that some technical training is mandatory for best performance, especially in the tasks of prospect appraisal, the building of salary schedules, formulation of job descriptions, personnel research, administration of the numerous records and fringe benefits, and in the specialized type of adult counselling inherent in this post. In addition to a knowledge of education and general administration, the personnel administrator needs training in law, in the utility of data processing, in interviewing and evaluation techniques; he also needs extensive instruction and practice in psychology. Universities are just beginning to develop graduate curriculums for the preparation of this special phase of school administration and it is expected that superintendents of the future will look outside the school district for professionally trained personnel officers.

---

*See Donald's and Fawcett's readings in this chapter.

There is an increasing trend toward assigning the personnel officer to the second echelon of administrative command in medium size districts, at the level of assistant superintendent. The titles of administrative assistant or director of personnel are also common titles. It is logical that this officer would be found in the third echelon in very large cities, reporting to an assistant superintendent. While most of the personnel officers are men, several districts have already discovered that women are equally talented in the personnel function, and especially skilled in the abstract task of prospect appraisal.

The creation of the office has caused considerable confusion in determining whether the personnel administrator should operate as an authority or advisory officer (line or staff). Fawcett states flatly that he is a staff officer. Responses to Donald's survey reported that some were line officers, others line and staff, and that some superintendents and personnel officers contradicted each other in their responses. It is the same confusion which exists among all central staff administrators in an organization which has a commitment to democratic procedures but also seeks efficiency and control. Actually, the personnel officer, like other assistants, performs both authority and advisory roles. He carries out a few of his tasks without consulting anyone. He must consult with principals and other central administrators before executing most of his duties. He obviously serves in an advisory relationship to the superintendent, sometimes to the board of education, notwithstanding that he executes a superintendency function. As explained in Chapter 7, the way out of this confusion is found in a properly constructed job description which holds the principal accountable for all functions within his building but the assistant superintendent responsible for the performance of a function throughout the system. In dealing with all principals and teachers the personnel officer is an authority officer performing a superintendency function, but he reverts to an advisory status when dealing with a problem in any principal's building.

SPECIFIC TASKS OF PERSONNEL ADMINISTRATION

Recruitment and Employment

The most time-consuming task of the personnel function, and probably the most important, is the selection and employment of new teachers. Since mature superintendents recognize that their individual successes are measured most by the successes achieved by classroom teachers they often are reluctant to delegate this task to anyone. This protective zeal probably accounts most for the fact that other general administrative responsibilities—particularly curriculum, business management, and pupil personnel—are entrusted to a subordinate administrator in the central staff much earlier than the staff personnel function. As school systems grow larger, however, the task grows demanding for the superintendent and in systems employing 300 to 400 persons he appoints a personnel administrator. Fawcett's recommended ratio of one personnel administrator for each 150 employees is translated from custom in business and government.

The character of teacher employment has undergone a major evolution since pre-World War II days when supply exceeded demand. No longer can a school system which wants the best wait for applicants; it must begin seeking prospects in January for the following fall's needs, and must work at it assiduously until school opens. In the current competitive market, the alert employer interviews new teachers on college campuses before they graduate, prepares inviting brochures to lure prospective teachers, raids the staffs of other schools, conducts the *tour-de-grande* for a visiting prospect, and negotiates a contract as soon as possible. In addition to the annual supply which must be employed to replace the customary departures from the system, the employment job goes on the year round in many school districts as the result of a continual parade of resignations through the school year, sometimes for valid reasons, sometimes not.

Schools have been generally lax in adapting modern employment techniques developed in industry. They depend disproportionately upon those measuring devices which have the least predictive value for successful teaching—the credentials and the interview. As school boards, administrators, and college professors increasingly recognize the need for professionally trained personnel officers, the appraisal process of prospective teachers will improve.

Employing officers need training for evaluating the credentials of prospects, especially the portfolio dealing with references. There is a skill in just reading the written statements about applicants, a competence which most administrators are compelled to acquire the expensive way through trial and mistake. Eventually, after they discover that what is not said in a letter of reference is often more important than the words they read, administrators gain useful information through direct conversations with previous employers or college instructors. The number of school classrooms and administrative offices occupied by persons who have never been investigated at previous places of employment testifies to the ineptness, carelessness, or overwork of school officers. Experienced administrators have learned the advisability of seeking evaluation from several individuals in the employing district before deciding to extend a contract. Even when all facts are available about a doubtful candidate, fallible human judgment must decide. Several judgments, therefore, reduce the chances of mistake. The interviewing process is still far from enjoying the status of a science. Each administrator develops his own technique for eliciting the information which presumably gives insight into a candidate's potential. This complacent approach may overlook the possibility that candidates, too, develop their own interviewing techniques and, thereby, create misleading images. The results of an interview can be more fruitful through a quasi-scientific approach to structuring questions. Some administrators are finding that the role playing techniques during an interview will reveal predispositions and likely behavioral characteristics in the classroom.

Some school districts find that interviews with present faculty members are often helpful in determining whether a prospect will "fit into" the prevailing climate. The practice may be too cumbersome to attempt in large districts which must employ many teachers; they cannot afford the time to interview that many candidates. The same problem accrues if building principals are involved in the appraisal process although more and more school systems are using the practice. Even some of the larger metropolitan districts manage to involve principals by having them interview the best prospects after initial screening by central staff officers. The attitude that principals should have a prominent voice in the selection of teachers is growing, since the former are held accountable for teaching effectiveness within the attendance unit. Central staff opinion is still important under these conditions in order to prevent a building from becoming loaded with limited philosophies and instructional approaches. Diversity is prized in an organization which seeks to discover and develop individuality among future citizens. A few boards of education have expressed this desire for their teaching staffs in the statement of personnel policy.

Employment officers for public schools must be especially mindful of observing the legal and ethical prescriptions of the state's fair employment laws. The laws apply to public bodies as well as private corporations, but in addition, an educational institution has an obligation to be in the forefront of implementing the intent of such laws.

School personnel should also accept their responsibility for improving the supply of potential teachers through their guidance resources, future teachers clubs, and by encouraging able young people to consider a career in education. Practicing teachers and administrators can exert considerable positive influence in this direction through their daily contacts with high school students.

Orientation of New Staff Members

The need to facilitate the smooth adjustment of new teachers to their unfamiliar assignments or careers has appealed so much to the logic of school administrators that all but the extremely ordinary systems have made strides in this direction during the past two decades. Dozens of fine programs have been developed and shared with the profession through its professional journals. Even if the program does not exceed the single, staid pre-school conference it is superior to the day when a new teacher's only welcome consisted of the opening day handshake while the other hand extended a room key and grade book. Variations in practice have extended well beyond that type of formal meeting to the week-long extravaganza promoted by the San Diego business firms, churches, government leaders, and teacher organizations which seeks to show its appreciation for good teachers.

Induction programs are not only worthy in motivation but useful to the teacher. However, from evaluation of these programs emerges a caution to personnel administrators, the officers to whom the planning of the activities normally falls: beware of too much at the beginning and too little follow-through. Attempts to cram all the stockpile of knowledge about a school's customs and procedures into the mind of a tense new teacher result in considerable waste of energy. The novice doesn't have to know all that is included in some orientation sessions right away, even if he could absorb them. Pre-school orientation efforts should concentrate largely upon that knowledge which a new teacher needs for a successful opening day and week. Subsequent orientation activities should capitalize upon the principle of readiness for learning. There is a growing recognition that the orientation process should continue in declining dosages not only throughout the first year but for the first three years. Statistics reveal that the biggest turnover of teachers persists during the first two to five years of their experience: many leaving a system because of what is explained away as "incapability of adjusting to the school or community."

There is a further caution that must be observed if teachers are to be effectively assimilated into a building, district, and community, i.e., the willingness of fellow teachers to accept their individual responsibilities for aiding the adjustment. A major influence on any employee's job satisfaction is his daily association with other workers. One, or just a few, unpleasant personalities on a school staff can disturb the joy of a new teacher's day.

Evaluation of Personnel

While the major responsibility for supervision and evaluation of personnel is centered in the instructional division, all administrative personnel share in the task. With increasing frequency, the personnel officer is expected to play a part. In view of his charge for employing new teachers he will want to help them succeed. The success of his employment skill is measured by their success on the job.

The personnel administrator also takes the initiative in assessing performance for purposes of promotion, transfer, granting of permanent tenure, dismissal, and merit awards on the salary schedule where applicable. He will rely mostly upon the opinions of others—principals and supervisors—but he will coordinate the effort and supplement those judgments with his own observations. Perhaps his greatest contribution in this area comes from leading the staff in the development of criteria upon which they wish to be evaluated.

Separation of Personnel from the District

The most disagreeable task of the personnel officer is that of separating employees who have proved to be unsatisfactory in that system. After all the resources of the district have failed to help an ineffective teacher succeed, and assuming that the assessment of failure is the pooled judgment of those who have observed the employee's performance, the personnel administrator must set in motion the ethical and legal steps to dismiss the person. The legal guides are established in state statutes and local board of education regulations. Civil service rules are applicable for non-certificated employees in some communities.

Ethical considerations arise from codes of professionalism, from the fact that educated, mature persons are involved, from respect for human dignity, and from an admission of fallible appraisal. These considerations influence the reasons for dismissal and the procedures followed in effecting the separation. Where the law does not spell out the statutory reasons for dismissal, considerable progress has been made in all but the most backward areas in protecting teachers from arbitrary, personal, and political firing. To be sure, there are still exceptions, but more apprehension is heard from citizens and school officials today that an opposite undesirable condition prevails, i.e., ineffective teachers are too secure in their claims to continued employment. Some tenure laws are so rigid that the dismissing authority must be prepared to prove unsatisfactory performance in court; this is an extremely difficult accusation to substantiate in an occupation which is measured by opinion. Sensitive administrators are reluctant to press public charges with the resultant publicity which may be damaging to the education of youth. The continuance of unsatisfactory teachers in the school system is not only harmful to learning but also discouraging to the morale of good teachers. Therefore, it is incumbent upon personnel officers of the future to learn better methods for handling such delicate situations and to demonstrate the courage for initiating action. Techniques for evaluating performance must be improved, and appropriate steps taken before questionable employees exploit unreasonable legislation. Furthermore, the administrator should show integrity in his subsequent recommendations to other employers, recognizing that a teacher's poor performance in a school system may be the result of the administrator's failure to achieve the basic objectives of personnel work—provision of people and conditions which contribute to job satisfaction.

Salary Schedules

The most sensitive and controversial area of staff personnel administration is the determination of financial rewards for the service. There never has been agreement on the worth of a teacher; there likely never will be. Practically, the worth is reached at that compromise point where the taxpayers and the employees meet. The true worth of a teacher, as measured by his contribution to youth and community progress, is not considered in salary determinations because of the vast range of judgments.

There has been almost universal acceptance of a system of pay for those who work in elementary and secondary schools: the system of salary schedules which recognizes only professional training and years of experience. The system has been so widely adopted in United States school districts that one rarely hears any discussion as to whether or not it is a good system, whether it tends to discourage individuality and to encourage mediocrity, whether it actually amounts more to an administrative device to minimize decision making, or whether the system benefits or hinders the one reason for schools—the best learning of boys and girls. Only recently have members of the profession, as well as some citizens, sought ways to work out of the system, or perhaps around the system, through various proposals which recognize other characteristics of a teacher's worth, particularly his quality of performance, the critical demand for specialized skills, added duties, and even family responsibilities.

With the acceptance of the salary schedule system there have emerged from experience some guides for improved development and administration of schedules.

1. While the board of education has the legal responsibility for adopting a schedule, with some states specifying minimum amounts, the actual development is delegated to the superintendent, who customarily assigns the duty to the personnel officer.

2. Those persons most affected by the schedule should be involved in the deliberations leading to the initial development, subsequent revision, and the designing of regulations for administering the schedule.

3. There is a trend toward the development of schedules for the various categories of employees: teachers, administrators, and the separate groups of non-certificated workers.

4. The schedule should permit a starting point which attracts the quality of employee desired by the board of education as revealed in its policy, and it should provide sufficient incentive for personnel to remain with the district. This objective has implications not only for the number and amount of differentials from one year to another but also for the maximum. There is a viewpoint that the maximum salary of a schedule should be twice the beginning amount, an extravagant goal for most districts. The goal also implies necessary evaluation of employees so that only "desirable" employees will remain in the district and benefit from top salaries.

5. If the schedule system is adopted as a regulation of the district there should be no deviations therefrom without approved and announced procedures for such action. On the other hand, if the schedule is publicized as a guide rather than a regulation, then the administration is free to adopt a plan for rewarding outstanding performance.

6. If the district is committed to the scheduling system which rewards only experience and training, administrative salaries should also be scheduled in some comparable plan. A popular arrangement establishes a ratio between an administrator's pay (except the superintendent's) and that of a teacher with comparable training and experience. The higher amount recognizes the value of the administrator's responsibility, longer work term, risk from lack of tenure, and specialized skill.

7. The schedule should encourage self-improvement through increased professional preparation or that which accrues from

study, travel, or voluntary participation in approved growth experiences designed to enhance competence in the area for which the person was employed.

8. The schedule with its accompanying rules and interpretations should be easy to understand and explain.

9. The schedule should be coexistent with those of other occupations which require similar preparations, responsibilities, and working conditions.

10. A plan of extra pay for teachers who perform approved duties beyond that expected as the regular classroom duties is generally preferred by teachers if they collaborate in assessing the worth of each duty. It is also more economical for the district than a plan of commutation in the form of reduced teaching load.

Record Keeping Task

Though routine and clerical, the maintenance of records for personnel is an exacting and interminable task of the personnel office. In the type of records which should be kept by a personnel office as columnized below, errors cannot be tolerated in light of their importance to each employee's income and professional progress.

Employment history, in the present and previous school systems, both professional and non-professional
College credits and degrees
Certificates
Personal and family data
Recommendations
Evaluations
Tenure status
Salary and pertinent payroll deductions
Health examinations
Absenteeism
Leaves of absence
Retirement
Other pertinent confidential reports

These records must be kept current. Later, they constitute vital statistical information after personnel have left the system, and provide a source for valuable personnel research studies.

Maintenance of these records requires implementing of the controlling laws and regulations pertaining to retirement, leaves of absence, insurance and savings provisions, certification, and tenure. The personnel officer should be the best informed person in the school system on these matters which prompt uncountable questions and conferences.

Improving Working Conditions

In his concern for bettering the working conditions of employees, the personnel officer is observant and sympathetic to physical conditions—rooms, equipment, and materials—and also to the numerous intangible factors which determine one's job satisfaction. The organization's internal human relationships—among peers and between hierarchal levels—undoubtedly constitute the major concern. It is questionable whether an administrator can materially alter personalities, but his behavior toward colleagues and subordinates largely sets the stage for organizational morale. Moreover, the impact of procedures which he sets in motion is a powerful determinant of attitudes toward working in that school.

As essential as regulations and procedures are for the governing of a large system, the greatest fault found in most faculty handbooks is over-prescription. Their wording often suggests rules and methods more likely found in a pupil's handbook. It is difficult, perhaps impossible, to hope that teachers will develop into mature, responsible, self-propelling individuals if they are guided by adolescent directives. One can read into the phraseology of some regulatory statements the administrator's reluctance to deal with unethical behavior directly and the temptation to handle such matters in system-wide rules which humiliate the majority.

Unpleasant working conditions may also be created by over-organization in the large school district. In an effort to attain efficiency and paper accountability, the systems man is capable of building an inefficient machine. A paper-and-form bureaucracy can emerge to actually hamper its purpose—the servicing of teachers' needs. The dignity of educated adults is not served well when they must genuflect to a maze of coded forms for even minor supplies.

Unequal teaching loads are another common source of job dissatisfaction. The profession may have made too much of equalized loads, which are truly a myth. The best formulas, though helpful as guides to defend assignments, and the fairest of intentions cannot allow all teachers the same loads. Neither formulas nor fair intentions can take into full account the differences among students or teachers. It could be argued soundly that assignments should not be equalized. It is fairer to youth that more of them should be exposed to the effective teacher. Furthermore, some teachers are at their best with small groups, others with large groups. The team teaching idea defies equal loads insofar as numbers of students and responsibilities are concerned; it may open the door to a more rational attitude toward equalizing loads. Finally, part-time loads which have been traditionally shunned by school administrators offer a good solution to the still-effective teacher who wishes to taper off during the last few years of service. For the sake of morale, however, efforts should be made to create an appearance of equalized loads while simultaneous attempts are made to explain the impossibility of accomplishing equality.

High on the list of every study of teacher turnover is the factor of excessive non-teaching duties. Although some progress is being made to relieve teachers of non-instructional chores, much more can be done. At the same time, teachers may need to be reminded periodically that teaching means more than holding class. A programmed machine can hold class. Unlike working on a production line, teaching children involves more than six hours of direct interaction.

Motivating teachers toward constantly improving performance, like motivating students, is undoubtedly the most arduous challenge for the administrator. As with students, there is no single technique that works with all staff members; a variety of rewards is called for. Thus promoting to administrative and supervisory posts from within the system is desirable. There are arguments against this as an excluding practice, but it does serve to motivate many of the staff.

As cited often herein, important to job satisfaction in any organization is the opportunity to communicate with higher echelons of the system, to be assured of one's position, to know that one's ideas and efforts are appreciated. Provisions for communication must be built into the school district's structure.

The personnel administrator is constantly on the alert to the sources of friction and discontent, and he tries to remedy them before they erupt into disgruntled, departing employees.

He has a dual responsibility for encouraging professional and ethical behavior and at the same time protecting rights and privileges of professional people. It is in this ethereal area that he can make a vital contribution to morale.

Personal Counseling

The personnel administrator should have skills other than those already named. Much of the time of an officer properly groomed for the assignment will be spent in counseling teachers and other employees in their varied and complex personal problems. Teachers are subject to the same maturational and emotional conflicts which afflict other occupations. But a combination of the nature of the sensitive persons who enter the teaching profession in large numbers and of the classroom and public pressures which bear upon public school employees, there may occur a higher proportion of maladjustment incidences among teachers than among people in other occupations. More than one study has reported a high rate of neurosis appearing within the teaching ranks. Every experienced administrator has learned that his teachers need someone to lean upon for skilled counseling. Much of it will be accomplished by principals and supervisors; the school psychologist will be involved at times; but the personnel officer is the logical person for many staff members to turn to for help. His responsibility for salary, tenure, ratings, leaves, and related personal situations makes him a natural confidant with whom to discuss problems.

Administration of Substitute Teachers

One of the tasks of personnel administration which is often treated as a minor activity but which has a way of becoming a major problem is the management of the substitute teacher program. In addition to the challenge of finding enough qualified teachers to staff the classrooms during periods of heavy regular staff absenteeism, there are concerns about proper assignment of substitutes to satisfy principals and regular teachers, about the precise expectations from substitutes, student management and achievement during the substitute's service, legal implications of substitutes during the regular teachers' absence, the mechanics of arranging for substitutes early in the day, and the accompanying record-keeping for both the substitute and the regular teacher.

Slowly, increased and needed attention is being given to the problem in the literature and even in a few research studies. The supply of substitutes is generally improving with the growing number of former teachers who left the classroom for family responsibilities but who are now willing to assume part-time teaching assignments. Larger school districts find that the practice of employing full-time substitutes for day-to-day assignments simplifies the supply problem. Personnel officers are systematizing the task through written regulations and instructions which aid substitutes, regular classroom teachers, and principals.

Administration of Non-certified Personnel

Except in the metropolitan school districts, the personnel officer is commonly assigned the responsibility for administration of clerks and secretaries, custodial personnel, bus drivers, and food service workers. The daily directing of their activities may be in the hands of other supervisors but the personnel officer may be expected to complete the tasks of employment, evaluation, dismissal, and maintenance of personnel records.

This responsibility adds little difference except in volume to the personnel director's bill of duties. The differences that do appear result from the conventional attitude among professional people that non-certificated employees are interlopers in the educational world. Chronologically, we are not many years past the era when teachers performed the custodial chores, the clerical tasks, and even cooked the hot lunch. Bus drivers and maintenance employees did not exist. Thus, non-teaching personnel have often been rejected by the official family, even by the board of education which does not reward those positions handsomely. Administrators still reap the harvest of neglected non-certificated employees in the form of rapid turnover and less skilled performers without codes of ethics. These workers have often turned to civil service and labor unions under a hope for better treatment.

There is a trend toward bringing non-certificated workers into the official family of the school system. State laws and administrative procedures direct the management of all employees toward similarity. Many districts have salary schedules and advancement opportunities for the non-certificated personnel which are comparable in principle to those for teachers. States and boards of education are extending similar contractual, retirement, absenteeism, and protective benefits. As this trend continues, schools can expect better performance from these employees who have often been regarded as accouterments to educational institutions.

The Personnel Officer as Negotiator

If it should come to pass, as forseen by some, that the future will bring more extensive direct negotiations between teachers and boards of education for salary and welfare conditions, the personnel officer's work will probably become similar to that of his counterpart in private industry. There is concerted effort, both from within and from outside the profession, to force educators from their customary classification as professionals into a labor-management arrangement.

Should this move succeed, as it already has in a few cities, it is illogical that members of the governing body would devote their time to negotiating any more than the board of a private corporation negotiates. Nor can a superintendent properly sacrifice his other responsibilities for this task, any more than a corporation president neglects his total administrative role for labor relations. Therefore, the personnel officer will undoubtedly represent "management" in negotiations. This will forge new dimensions to his preparation and time expenditures. His prime skills would have to be in law and labor relations.

Development of Personnel Policies

The crucial task of personnel which can make the most long-lasting contribution to job satisfaction as well as to ease of administration is that of developing pertinent board policies. It has already been explained that a properly conceived and philosophical policy sets the direction and climate for all employee activity — for administration, teachers, and non-certificated personnel. Once the board of education establishes its beliefs and wants insofar as education and personnel are concerned, the implementation through regulations and decisions becomes less complicated. Thus, the task of developing good personnel policies takes primacy in the order of jobs to be done.

The personnel administrator is the logical person to take the initiative in personnel policy development. He is not only the officer most concerned with implementation but is closest to the feelings of all employees. The process of formulating policy offers the most fruitful opportunity of all administrative tasks for involving staff members. Indeed, if employees have a voice in the development of policies effecting them in this sentient area there will be little demand for subsequent consultation. All segments of the organization should be represented in this process, sometimes in small, special-interest groups and sometimes as part of an overall policy steering committee. Ideally, the board of education and citizens of the district would also participate in these deliberations. The responsibility for finalizing the thoughts of these representative groups will fall upon the personnel administrator, subject to the approval of the committee before submitting it through the superintendent to the board of education. It is essential at this point of policy formulation that the board members have considerable time for reflection, discussion, and eventual approval of the policies.

A complete set of personnel policies would cover all aspects of the personnel function (see list in readings). However, if a board of education should adopt policies dealing with just these four personnel facets, other policies and accompanying regulations will fall into place:

1. Quality of personnel desired in the district.
2. Expected outcomes from teaching efforts.
3. Thoughts of the board of education regarding environmental working conditions.
4. Beliefs of the board pertaining to communication between it and employees.

These four philosophical positions of a board of education give needed direction for all other personnel tasks: employment, salaries, leaves of absence, fringe benefits, teaching load and assignments, and organizational structure for communications and best morale.

THE PERSONNEL FUNCTION . . .

THE PERSONNEL FUNCTION IS A RESPONSE TO THE NEED OF SCHOOLS TO BE COMPETITIVE*

The need for sound personnel programs in any organization is a reflection of the importance of the human element in the success or failure of the organization's purpose. This is particularly true in education, which has no measurable competitive product. But the current interest in personnel programs is also a reaction to the need for the schools to be competitive. First, they must be competitive with each other. It can be assumed that those schools which can offer more attractive working conditions generally will attract the more highly qualified and competent staffs. And, when this is done, the educational program in those schools gains in stature adding another and perhaps most important factor in attractiveness to the professional career teacher.

The second area of competition is with a less tangible goal, frequently referred to in such terms as quality, growth, and national interest. It is evident in the local, State, and national concern about the elementary and secondary curriculums. It is seen in the discussions on the quality of American school teachers and in the preparation programs for those teachers. It is dramatically evident in the annual recruitment rivalry which schools face with other organizations for the most capable college graduates.

The nature of this competition of both types has been to give greater attention to the role of the teacher as part of the total education program and perhaps relatively less attention to him as a personality. The fundamental importance of the teacher to the educational program has long been recognized. But now more concern is with the total conditions under which the most capable staff can be attracted, can teach in a situation which permits them to grow in their chosen profession, and can

---

*James P. Steffenson, "Staff Personnel Administration," Washington, D.C.: United States Office of Education, Bulletin 1963, No. 6, 1963, 1, 2.

assume both the privileges and responsibilities concomitant with their status as teachers of our youth. This attention, it is suggested, is illustrated in the offering of more formal attention to the entire staff personnel program, and of recognizing that the personnel function is too complex, too sensitive, and too important to receive anything but the closest scrutiny.

THE IMPORTANCE OF THE PERSONNEL FUNCTION*

The task of management has never been easy by any reasonable standard of measurement. However, educational management has become more difficult because of greater community expectations and higher levels of job requirements. To meet head-on the numerous and diverse challenges both from within and from without the school system, effective and efficient management techniques must be employed. Of major importance are those concerned with personnel administration.

Today, there are few school district administrators who do not recognize the importance of effective personnel management. Most view personnel administration as a facet of school district operations that contributes significantly to the achievement of educational goals. However, except in the larger school districts where size has dictated the establishment of a personnel office under the leadership of a qualified director, few school systems have given adequate attention to their personnel programs. Boards of Education and Superintendents of Schools, plagued with mounting community pressures and external interferences, increasing pupil enrollments, acute financial considerations, numerous and substantial construction projects, shortages of qualified teachers, significant curricula changes, and the like, have found neither the time nor the motivation to develop areas of personnel administration that "seem" to be running along fairly smoothly.

Neglected in some school districts, forgotten in others, personnel management has been relegated to the status of a part-time function to be carried out as a secondary assignment by some official who usually has neither the training nor the inclination to view this task as one of importance to the total educational undertaking. In general, school districts

---

*Ridgley M. Bogg, From Foreword of "The Administration of Non-Instructional Personnel in Public Schools," by Louis Cohen, Evanston: Association of School Business Officials, International, *Research Bulletin* No. 1, 1964, 7-8.

have failed to benefit from the experience and progress industry has made in developing and fostering sound personnel administration principles and practices.

The day when school districts can afford the luxury of inattention to their employees has long since passed. The changing times have produced formalization of recruitment, promotion, transfer, disciplinary, and retirement procedures; increased enactment of personnel policies by Boards of Education; and a carry-over of management and labor concepts from industry to school district operations. There has been a change in personal relationships — between taxpayer and school administrator, between administrator and staff member, between instructional and non-instructional employees. The net effect of these changes is an employment climate which finds individuals being more articulate, better organized, more knowledgeable about their rights and privileges, more involved in the operating facets of the school district, and a community environment which finds greater emphasis upon efficiency and economy.

It is the direct responsibility of administration to provide for effective and efficient operations with a framework of personnel policies which recognize the dignity of the human being, accept the worth of each individual to the enterprise, acknowledge the importance of each staff member's contribution to the total organizational effort, and insure achievement of predetermined objectives. Therefore, it is imperative that school district officials have an understanding of sound personnel policies and implement such policies in an appropriate manner.

THE PERSONNEL FUNCTION IN EDUCATION*

Personnel management is one phase or aspect of the general field of school administration. School personnel management strives for enthusiastic cooperation of all people — instructional, non-instructional and administrative — toward common goals. Actually, all school administrators are personnel managers whether they realize it or not, for everyone who is called upon to assume administrative responsibility, in however slight degree must at the same time assume responsibility of the personnel involved. In most cases, particularly in small educational systems,

---

*Louis Cohen, "The Administration of Non-Instructional Personnel in Public Schools," Evanston: Association of School Business Officials, International, *Research Bulletin* No. 1, 1964, 9-12.

the same individual must of necessity be charged with the duty of administering educational policies at the same time that he administers personnel procedures. . . .

Non-instructional personnel are those employees of a school district who are not certified to teach, or who do not hold other professional certificates. Generally speaking the non-instructional personnel may be classified in the following groups:

1. The custodial staff
2. The building maintenance and grounds staff
3. The bus drivers
4. The bus maintenance staff
5. The cafeteria staff
6. The clerical staff (Accounting and other office personnel)
7. Health personnel
8. Other non-instructional personnel

It is popularly assumed in business and industry that the various personnel functions will be directed and coordinated by a special personnel division or department. However, a similar setup has yet to be established in most school systems. It may be that school administrators, because of their identification with education as a profession, do not see themselves as personnel managers — a title commonly related to industry. Certainly, it is desirable that management of non-instructional personnel be recognized as a major function and responsibility of school administration.

A more complete understanding of non-instructional personnel problems by all school administrators is important. More specifically, the need is for a general appreciation of such problems and methods of attacking them. . . .

Personnel administration in today's schools is not simply or easily described, for it includes a wide range of functions. In one school system, emphasis is placed on the selection program. In another, the principal activity of personnel management is job analysis and classification as a basis for wage and salary administration. It may be said that personnel management is one phase or aspect of the general field of education. Management involves the active direction or control of men, materials and methods to attain a given objective. In that control, management has its methods, its tools, and its techniques. The methods, tools, and techniques which should be employed to secure the enthusiastic cooperation of non-instructional personnel represent the subject matter of this handbook. The management of non-instructional personnel plays an important part in modern education in every situation where certain individuals entrusted with the responsibilities of supervision, administra-

tion, and management seek to secure and maintain the efficient cooperation of other persons who perform the detailed tasks of the educational
system.

DEFINITION OF PERSONNEL MANAGEMENT
IN RELATION TO EDUCATION

Improvement of the effectiveness of education has been the goal of lay
and professional persons for as long as children have been attending
school. Many of the earlier studies of educational organization centered
upon the non-personal aspects: facilities, budgets, programs, schedules,
policies, and funds. Later experiments led to an increasing emphasis on
the personal aspects, on the idea that individuals are the most important
part of an organization. This handbook assumes that the individual and
the organization are inter-related, and that the total organizational
effectiveness is improved by focusing attention on both the personal and
non-personal dimensions of education. Personnel management is that
phase of education which deals with the efficient control of manpower,
as distinguished from phases which are concerned with all other management tools. It should not be concluded from this definition that personnel management is regarded as a distinct and separate division, set
apart from all others in the field of education. It is recognized that any
such separation is practically impossible. Personnel management, therefore, is of importance not only to those who head personnel departments
but also to those who have or expect to have any administrative
responsibility.

PURPOSES OF PERSONNEL MANAGEMENT
IN OUR SCHOOLS

The purposes of personnel management in schools are inferred from
the purposes of modern education. The basic purpose of all personnel
management and administration is the securing of maximum efficiency
from the manpower involved, in order to better facilitate the education
of children and all of its principles and practices are based upon that
fundamental purpose only.

FUNCTIONS OF PERSONNEL MANAGEMENT
IN SCHOOL SYSTEMS

Each major task of the school administrator is specialized and often is
delegated to a subordinate who can be charged with responsibility for

its performance. The most commonly distinguished personnel *functions* are those of:

1. Analyzing operations
2. Planning
3. Routing
4. Setting standards
5. Inspecting
6. Managing personnel

Each of the six personnel functions above are further sub-divided in terms of their application to the realization of the specific activities of the personnel management program. These sub-divisions are:

1. Securing, selecting, and allocating personnel
2. Controlling working conditions in order to maintain and effectively use personnel after they have been secured
3. Encouraging self-improvement and increased efficiency
4. Maintaining personnel records and personnel research.

APPLICATION FOR NON-INSTRUCTIONAL PERSONNEL

All of the above applies to the specifics of non-instructional personnel management. Therefore, in securing such personnel, the first task is that of job analysis. Job analysis is the determination of the numbers and types of jobs and the development of methods of recruiting for such jobs, after which it is necessary to introduce or perfect devices facilitating selection and placement. After potential employees are located, selected, recruited and placed, the next step is to train them to perform their particular duties efficiently.

WHO DETERMINES PERSONNEL
POLICIES IN SCHOOLS?*

Since the management of an organization involves the operation of a large number of separate activities, the grouping of these activities into related areas is desirable. However, because administration is also a unified process, the establishment of boundaries encompassing related

*B. J. Chandler and Paul V. Petty, *Personnel Management in School Administration,* New York: Harcourt, Brace and World, Inc., 1955, 5, 10-11 (by permission).

areas sometimes becomes quite arbitrary. As an organization becomes successively larger from the standpoint of number of persons employed, it becomes more necessary to divide the administrative processes into these related areas.

Administrative functions involved in the total operation vary greatly among organizations of different types. Even greater than the variation in the functions is the difference in emphasis upon different phases of operation. Certain administrative functions common to most organizations include personnel, materiel, and operations. It is readily seen that an organization using vast quantities of materiel resources would be likely to emphasize that aspect of the total job. On the other hand, an organization in close competition with other organizations in producing for a particular market might find it necessary to give continuous attention to operations. The design and purpose of public school organization seem to demand an emphasis upon the personnel aspect. For purposes of this text *personnel management* may be defined as *that aspect of general administration which is concerned with the operation of the staff personnel. Staff personnel* refers to *all persons assigned to positions in the organization who have a vested interest in the accomplishment of the objectives of the organization.* By this definition the pupils in a public school organization are excluded from the discussion. In a commercial or professional organization, the customers or clients would likewise be excluded. The management of the staff personnel in an organization concerns itself with securing persons and assigning them to duty positions within the organization. In a complete analysis, the component elements of administration are also included in personnel management. These, as previously mentioned, are planning, directing, co-ordinating, controlling, and appraising. . . .

DETERMINANTS OF PERSONNEL MANAGEMENT

The personnel function will always be shaped by certain interacting forces. These forces may or may not permit the function to be conducted completely in accordance with democratic principles. A label of "democratic administration" attached to the personnel function in some cases may not be accurately descriptive. Only a study and an analysis of the motivating forces will give a direct insight into a particular administrative situation. In practice pseudo-democracy can be more vicious than outright autocracy. Hence it is important to have a clear understanding of the exact situation before attempting to pass judgment relative to the type of management exercised in a particular situation.

The first determinant as to the type of administration to be exercised is the attitude of the rank and file of employees within the organization. Some groups are not ready for democracy in their management. Many people have never known anything other than an autocratic type of control. Their reactions are conditioned to decisions being made for them without their consultation. Such employees would find it difficult to conceive of employee participation in management. A transition to a democratic approach, so far as these people are concerned, must follow some study and indoctrination on their part.

A most important factor in determining the type of personnel management is the administrative head or group directing an organization. Although the time may have passed when one individual can effectively make decisions for, and exercise complete control over, a large organization, it is still common for one person to wield a very great influence upon the managerial arrangements. Where employment, dismissal, rating, promotion, and salary scheduling are all subject to the decision of one individual, or a very small group of individuals, a situation bordering upon complete autocracy of administration is still very possible. In the same way an enlightened administration can wield a most potent influence upon the policies of an organization. By the very nature of the managerial function, the influence of high positions in the organization will always be a powerful determinant in personnel administration.

In the case of public agencies or institutions, and to some extent of private institutions, legal enactments may be powerful determinants in personnel administration. A public agency is established within a framework outlined by statutes, regulations, court decisions, and legal interpretations. Changes in organizational plan for these public agencies may be made at the discretion of the legislative body. As a result, in some states, statutes tend to define somewhat in detail the organizational pattern of the state agencies.

It is highly desirable that public law establish a certain framework and possibly place some limitations upon public personnel administration within proper jurisdiction. It is undesirable, however, that such limitations take the form of detailed restrictions and regulations that may hamper the operation of the agency.

The public has always had some voice in determining personnel policy. Sometimes the voice has been indirect and slow in operation. Nevertheless, this voice of public opinion, customs, and mores always prevails over a period of time. This influence has extended alike to private and public personnel management. As an example of these forces in practice, it may be noted that the public has bought or refrained from buying certain products because of known policies of the company producing them. Stockholders have a relationship to private organizations similar to that of taxpayers and voters to public agencies. Each group has the prerogative of exercising its voice in the policy of the organization concerned — and does exercise its voice to a greater extent than is often realized.

THE PERSONNEL OFFICER . . .

THE PUBLIC SCHOOL PERSONNEL ADMINISTRATOR*

The personnel administrator, regardless of title, is usually directly responsible to the superintendent of schools. He usually serves in a staff capacity with the title of director of personnel or assistant superintendent in charge of personnel. Personnel administrators reported experiencing some, but not much, uncertainty among other district personnel about the limits of their responsibility, but this was overcome with cautious initial operation. Personnel administrators are salaried within a wide range of $7,200 to $23,621 and with a median of $12,300. The highest median salary is for assistant superintendents in charge of personnel, with personnel co-ordinators, administrative assistants, and directors following in descending order. Personnel administrators in districts of 30,000 to 99,999 population are paid at a somewhat higher rate than those in districts of 100,000 to 499,999 population. With the exception of written job descriptions, district-wide board policies, and state administrative certification law, personnel administrators are subject to no specific state or local regulation. Personnel administrators report being handicapped by lack of time and staff, and the deliberate pace of the democratic process in accomplishing their work. The personnel budget is typically not separate from that of other central-office administrative costs. The contracted year for personnel administrators is 12 months with three weeks to a month of vacation. They enjoy at least district tenure and in some cases administrative or position tenure. . . .

Superintendents and personnel administrators were asked to report on ways in which the position of personnel administrator had changed since first established and ways in which it was expected to change. Undoubt-

---

*Eleanor Donald, "The Public-School Personnel Administrator," Washington, D.C.: NEA Research Division, Research Monograph, 1962, M1 (February, 1962), 37, 40, 59. (By permission of National Education Association.)

edly the position is still undergoing a process of evolution. More school districts, however, reported past changes than anticipated change. There does not appear to be much foresight or planning on how the position is to develop. Major past and anticipated changes in the position are of two kinds:

1. Increase of administrative status
2. Expanded volume and scope of duties and responsibilities.

Several trends in the position were noted in tabulations of data on origin of the position, administrative status, duties and responsibilities, and personal and professional characteristics of the personnel administrator. These are summarized below.

ORIGIN OF THE POSITION

Study of changes occurring in the position of personnel administrator and of differences between positions of early and more recent origin reveals that

1. The position of public-school personnel administrator is being established more and more frequently in smaller school districts.
2. Personnel administrators whose positions have been established recently are more inclined to be titled director of personnel than assistant superintendent for personnel.
3. The position is increasingly nationwide in incidence but has spread from the large urban centers to surrounding suburban areas.

ADMINISTRATIVE STATUS

1. Because of expanded volume and scope of his responsibilities the personnel administrator can expect to head a personnel office with a professional and classified staff increasing in numbers and specialization of function.
2. Increasingly the personnel administrator will be responsible for both professional and classified (and sometimes pupil), rather than just professional personnel.
3. The personnel administrator originally appointed as director of personnel can expect to be promoted to the rank of assistant superintendent for personnel with two directors under him, one for classified employees.
4. Regardless of title the personnel administrator can expect to become an increasingly important figure in the school district.

DUTIES AND RESPONSIBILITIES

1. The personnel administrator can expect his duties and responsibilities to expand greatly in volume and scope.
2. The personnel administrator can expect to put greater emphasis than ever before on such accustomed activities as recruitment, selection, evaluation, and promotion of personnel, as well as on personnel records.
3. The personnel administrator can also expect to spend more time and effort on such newer areas of the central-office personnel function as provision of employee services and employee negotiations.

Frequency of Mention of Duties and Responsibilities of the Personnel Administrator in Nationwide Survey

Personnel functions	Percent
Personnel records	90%
Recruitment of personnel	73%
Selection of personnel	62%
Assignment of personnel	60%
Compensation	60%
Personnel research	52%
Substitute teachers	49%
Policy formulation	49%
Certification	48%
Transfer	48%
Evaluation	47%
In-service development	44%
Counseling	38%
Communication	38%
Promotion	34%
Orientation and induction	33%
Leaves of absence	30%
Retirement	25%
Formulation of job descriptions	23%
Dismissal	21%
Grievance procedure	19%
Determination of personnel needs for the district	18%
Health examinations	16%
Tenure recommendations	10%
Work load	6%
Working conditions	4%
Supervision	4%

4. The personnel administrator can expect to be assigned additional responsibilities formerly carried out by other administrative personnel as the personnel function is increasingly centralized and co-ordinated on a district-wide basis.

5. The personnel administrator can expect to discover or develop new and more effective ways of carrying out personnel administration on a district-wide basis.

EVOLUTION OF THE POSITION IN EDUCATION*

For some time, a common pattern of organization has been an emphasis, administratively, upon two areas — instruction and business. There is some indication that a third organizational division is now becoming more frequent. This is the department or division of personnel usually headed by an assistant superintendent, a director, or a coordinator. . . .

This reorganization of our administrative structure to accommodate the growing interest in personnel management could be one of the significant changes in educational administration developing in this decade. It may parallel the apparent changing organization for instruction.

This is not, of course, to suggest that the existence of an identifiable personnel office is in itself an indication of the extent or nature of the personnel program. The number of individuals with direct one-to-one relationships involving a guidance and supervisory responsibility attests to the fact that school personnel administration is a highly decentralized affair. However, the existence of and the responsibilities assigned to a personnel department may frequently indicate the degree of recognition of the importance of the problem of the development and coordination of systemwide personnel policy. It may well reflect the importance of location of administrative responsibility for personnel. Despite the relative importance of proper attitudes and climates for good personnel relationships, such an assignment of responsibility must be made. For this reason, much of the examination of the total program of personnel administration is made in terms of the personnel department.

---

*James P. Steffenson, *Staff Personnel Administration*, 6-10.

Within education, the structuring of the personnel responsibility, as evidenced by the increasing number of separate personnel departments, has been influenced by several factors.

1. The growth in the school age population, the demand for additional and specialized educational services, and the general high mobility rate of American society have all added to the teacher recruitment problem. Thus, there has been and will continue to be an increase in the number of personnel departments separately organized within the central administrative staff purely as a result of the quantitative recruitment and selection programs needed to meet the annual staff needs.

2. The total responsibilities assigned to and accepted by the superintendent of schools have forced a continuous evaluation to consider the appropriate areas whose administration can be delegated. The personnel function is one of the most important phases of the chief administrator's total responsibility in education, and the personnel responsibility can never be wholly delegated. However, if the superintendent is to satisfy the ever-increasing number of demands placed upon his time, the delegation of a degree of responsibility for even such important tasks as personnel is necessary.

3. The number of operational units or schools within the total educational organization in any one district is increasing as a result of growth and reorganization as well as through the expansion of the educational program. Attendance centers within a district are becoming larger in number and size. Special programs for exceptional children, for adults, for recreation, and for pupil personnel services are operating across attendance boundaries within the school district. This increase in the number of units, as in their complexity, demands that a large number of individuals — e.g., principals, directors — maintain a large degree of personnel responsibility. But it has also demanded a recognition of a greater problem of centralized co-ordination of personnel policies throughout the total organization.

4. Lastly, there has been developed a broader definition of the term "personnel administration.". . .

The emphasis upon personal relationships (and the subsequential recognition that their most fruitful growth can be realized only through a planned program) constitutes perhaps the most important reason for the trend toward an increasing number of personnel departments within our school systems. . . .

THE EVOLUTIONARY PROCESS

As suggested above, there was observed a considerable range in the scope of the functions performed within the personnel department. This range is not only one which exists between cities on a geographical basis, but is also a temporal one within a school system which can be illustrated by the following brief summary of the growth of a department in one large system. Following a near total absorption in clerical responsibility, the personnel office accepted the administration but not the development of the salary schedule. The next step was to accept responsibility for recruitment, and then it became the final authority for appointments. Development of the salary schedule was then accepted. The personnel office next assumed greater responsibility for the development of staff personnel policy. Placement and transfer functions were next absorbed, and this was followed by the establishment of a districtwide system of appraisal to be administered by the chief personnel administrator. Meanwhile, the departmental head's title changed from director of personnel to assistant superintendent. This process covered a period of about four decades. As to the future, the advisability of assigning ultimate responsibility for staff development to the personnel organization has received some consideration.

Although there was apparently, in this instance, a centralization of certain personnel functions, the emphasis was upon the districtwide planning and coordination of policy as well as the identification of one authority for execution of personnel policy at a high level within the administrative organization. . . .

A large number of specialized skills are associated with personnel administration. An understanding of legal requirements affecting personnel, the maintenance of a comprehensive system of personnel records, the development of personnel policies into a set of regulations — these are among the various responsibilities assigned. Specialization within the total administrative area, such as for personnel, instruction, or business, presents an opportunity for maximum satisfaction in the treatment of specialized problems. It also provides for a strong need to coordinate and integrate the specialized activities. In this way, the school personnel administrator is both a specialist and a general administrator. Such functions as recruitment, selection, and appraisal can be considered as specialized skills; however, the coordination of the total program is a responsibility shared by many individuals. A highly conceptual ability to assess the problems facing the organization is required.

It is perhaps for this reason that there was in several of the districts visited a desire of the superintendent to locate the personnel administrator within the administrative organization so that he could know and reflect the goals and beliefs of the superintendent. In these instances, the personnel administrator was in a position to provide the leadership through which employees could be made aware of existing policies, contemplated changes, and the reasons and procedures for making changes. . . .

The personnel administrator must believe in the importance of good human relations, possess the unique skills associated with their development, and then, as a generalist, be able to describe his beliefs and plan the necessary steps to attain the appropriate districtwide goals.

WHEN DOES A SCHOOL DISTRICT NEED A PERSONNEL OFFICER?*

In planning a personnel administration staff it is incumbent upon the board of education to determine the level of sophistication in terms of the opportunity of a personnel specialist to be used. For the purposes of this discussion of staffing we can assume that the level of sophistication of most school districts in personnel matters is roughly equivalent to the condition existing in industry in 1950. Then, perhaps, we can examine staffing patterns existing in industry at that time to ascertain certain standards for numbers of personnel people.

A survey of the National Foremen's Institute, Inc., reported in the Employee Relations Bulletin of August 5, 1951, gives the relationship of personnel workers to employees in companies of 2,000–2,499 workers as 1–133 on January 1, 1950, and 1–159 on January 1, 1951. The same report gives the ratio among manufacturing plants as 1–120 on January 1, 1950, and 1–118 on January 1, 1951. Among governmental agencies the ratio was 1–300 on January 1, 1950, and 1–204 on January 1, 1951. The ratio of all firms and agencies was 1–115 on January 1, 1950, and 1–133 on January 1, 1951.[1] These figures included clerical assistance as well as professional personnel people.

---

*Reprinted with permission of The Macmillan Company from *School Personnel Administration* by Claude W. Fawcett. © Copyright Claude W. Fawcett, 1964, 143-144.

[1] National Foremen's Institute, Inc., *Employee Relations Bulletin*, Report No. 293, National Foremen's Institute, New York, August 15, 1951, p. 15.

Noting that the ratios are in the order of one personnel worker to 150 employees, and further assuming that a professional personnel worker usually requires at least one clerical employee, we can assume that a school district with 100 employees or fewer will probably accomplish its purposes through the superintendent with the assistance of a personnel clerk. For from 100 to 300 employees, one personnel administrator should probably be hired and the personnel clerk should work with him. When the numbers of personnel, combined certificated and classified, reach to a figure higher than 300, then another clerk should be added until 400 is reached. At that time another personnel administrator should be hired. When 600 employees are in the organization, another clerk should be added until the number reaches 700. At that time another personnel man should be added to the organization. When 900 employees are in the organization another clerk should be added. At 1,000 employees another personnel administrator is needed. Using this system of progression, it is possible to calculate the personnel needs for any size of an organization. At 1,200 employees the personnel department would be composed of four personnel administrators and four clerks. The ratio at that time would be 1–150. In the process of growth the ratio would fluctuate from 1–100 to 1–150, which should certainly be a reasonable range of responsibility for a normal personnel department.

SALARIES AND SALARY SCHEDULES . . .

THE WEAKNESSES OF SALARY SCHEDULES*

The single salary concept was very important to the teaching profession in the second decade of the twentieth century. Many teachers in the secondary schools were college graduates or had completed most of their collegiate education. Most of the teachers in elementary schools were graduates of normal schools only. The principle of equality of salary for equivalent training was really a promise to elementary teachers that they would receive pay equal to secondary teachers if they, like them, sought the collegiate degree. This did much to improve the status of the elementary teacher. As elementary teachers responded to this doctrine and secured collegiate degrees, requirements for secondary teachers were pushed up to the completion of the master's degree. Dif-

*Reprint with permission of The Macmillan Company from *School Personnel Administration* by Claude W. Fawcett. © Copyright Claude W. Fawcett, 1964, 72-74.

ferential salaries were still maintained, but on the basis of graduate work rather than on the basis of the undergraduate program. The door was left open for the elementary teacher to follow suit if he cared to do so. Now the trend is toward requiring elementary teachers to complete the fifth year also. Most salary schedules leave the door open for greater salaries if the doctorate is obtained. As has been noted above, however, this door is left open to a relatively small group of teachers.

There is considerable doubt that, with the coming of the compulsory fifth year before licensing, the single salary schedule concept is still a valid one. The principle of equal treatment for elementary and secondary teachers is hardly ever brought into question. Other differentiations have assumed greater importance. Counselors, department heads, coaches of all kinds, specialists in different aspects of supervision, and other specialists generally receive supplementary salaries that cause them, in effect, to be put on an entirely different salary schedule from other teachers. The single salary schedule, once thought revolutionary, has served its purposes, and needs for other differentiations have been recognized.

The number and size of increments need also to be brought into the evaluation of current salary schedules. There is hardly any need for numerous small increments in our salary policies that are designed either to encourage individuals to keep getting a little more education each year or to prolong the stay of teachers in the school system. Evidence concerning the development of teaching skills, if one already has a baccalaureate or advanced degree, shows that the average time to reach a peak of efficiency in them is about five years. Of course, some never reach a peak of efficiency and some may reach it sooner than five years. A salary policy designed in steps of more than five years must, obviously, be put together for the purpose of keeping individuals in a specific school system, rather than reflecting the advances in skill gained by the teacher. When this fact is recognized, the policy most common today of having 11 steps in the scale serves small purposes of motivation. Many school districts have completely nullified retention motivation by giving unlimited credit for prior experience to teachers employed from other school systems. The large number of steps in the salary scale has, in today's market, proved to be ineffective in meeting today's problems.

The automatic feature of the single salary schedule as we know it was very helpful to boards of education in negotiating salary arrangements. There is some doubt that the conditions which produced the necessity for simplicity still obtain. Salaries are still being negotiated by boards of education although the school districts with a very large proportion of the pupils are urban and large. As a result most attention is being paid, not to the motivational aspects of salary policy, but to the beginning salary for inexperienced teachers and to the maximum salary for the experienced teachers. A highly technical problem involving one of the most difficult aspects of professional administration is being treated as a public debate question. The continuation of this procedure is more a problem of recognizing the nature of the salary policy and its contribution to the organization than it is an emotional issue for public debate. Retention of current salary policies leaves boards of education little other choice.

This problem is further complicated by the tendency of teacher organizations to utilize the debate over salary levels as a device to procure and retain members for their organizations. They use raised salary levels as proof of their services to their members. They define the improved status of the teacher in terms of teacher salaries in relation to the salaries of other government employees. These actions tend to obfuscate the real problem of salary incentives.

Nor is it necessary to treat salary arrangements as a public question to be considered in the most general terms by boards of education. The profession of personnel administration includes a specialty in salary administration. There are relatively few professionally trained wage and salary personnel administrators in public schools, but there are many in the fields of public and business administration. Research in the fields is voluminous and the effectiveness of various policy measures is well known. There is hardly any scientific reason for the denial of current knowledge about the subject by either the teaching profession or boards of education. It is essential that the knowledge in this field be coupled with the utilization of trained individuals to make the payment of teachers more nearly conform to what is known about good salary practice.

SALARY SCHEDULES ARE
UNREALISTIC*

In the course of the inquiry we look at the past and then try to gauge some future developments. At present, the prospects of attracting able,

---

*Joseph A. Kershaw and Roland N. McKean, from *Teacher Shortage and Salary Schedules,* Copyright 1962 by Rand Corporation. Used by permission of McGraw-Hill Book Company and Rand Corporation, 2-4.

well-trained teachers in certain fields, such as mathematics and English, are not encouraging. Things have been happening in the world which present salary schedules do not take into account. We ask the question: What should be done about this situation?

Because several of the issues may be hotly disputed, we examine a considerable amount of new evidence. We conclude, among other things, the following:

1. Shortages in certain teaching fields are likely to become more serious (not shortages of "bodies" to put in front of classrooms but shortages of *good* teachers).
2. Salaries significantly influence the supply of applicants from which school officials can choose and therefore influence the quality of the teaching staff in various assignments.
3. Salary differences of one or two thousand dollars per year have substantial impacts on the ability of schools to attract well-trained teachers.
4. To remedy the shortages in particular fields under the conventional salary schedules would put tax rates at higher levels than most communities will accept.
5. If school districts adhere to present-day schedules, therefore, communities must settle for deteriorating instruction in the fields where there are shortages.
6. School districts should consider the adoption of a new kind of salary schedule, which we call the "3-step schedule."

Like the existing ones, the proposed schedule would have salary steps or supplements according to teaching experience and aggregate college training, but it would also provide steps for course credits in certain subject-matter fields as determined by the local board of education. These additional salary supplements would enable the schools to attract well-trained people in those fields where shortages have become or will become especially severe. As for the practical difficulties of introducing such a change, we believe they are manageable; and we try to show how to overcome them — how to implement this new type of salary schedule.

In the light of the evidence, we feel that communities and school officials should no longer accept unquestioningly the kind of salary schedule that has prevailed for the last twenty years and that now ignores the realities of supply and demand. They should seriously consider the addition to the present schedule of a third set of steps designed to alleviate specific and identifiable shortages and maintain high-quality teaching staffs. Only through the use of such salary structures can the nation utilize its manpower efficiently. Only by having such salary schedules will school districts be able to attract and retain the kinds of teaching staffs they want at acceptable cost. Only in this way, therefore, are they likely to maintain or improve the quality of instruction as the economy changes and develops.

EDUCATIONAL SALARIES SHOULD
RECOGNIZE EFFECTIVENESS*

Beyond the critical issue of the appropriate means through which sufficient funds to support salaries might be established, there is also the issue of the policies through which these funds should be distributed for the compensation of teaching services. Currently, the most common method of administering a teacher compensation program is through the use of a single salary schedule which differentiates salaries only on the bases of years of experience and level of training. Other factors for differentiation which are presently being utilized include sex, dependents, test scores, extra assignments, and promotion to positions involving additional responsibilities.

There are at least three other bases for differentiation which receive some attention. First, there is the suggestion that the salary schedule for teachers should reflect the current imbalance of supply and demand in particular areas of college study. Physics and mathematics teachers, for example, are not available at current salary rates to meet the demand in our secondary schools. Hence, it is argued there should be a salary differential which enables the schools to compete with other employing groups for the most capable college graduates in those fields.

The second proposal is to provide greater differentiation of assignments within the teaching staff. With such a differentiation — e.g., team teachers, teaching aides — there can be provided position specifications which establish different degrees of responsibility and, hence, a differentiated salary on the basis of the level of responsibility. The use of an extended contract to provide compensation for professional activities conducted during the summer, such as teaching or curriculum development, is another example of such additional salary for additional responsibilities.

But over and above these practices and proposals, one of the most publicized issues in salary policy development is that of differentiating

---

*James P. Steffenson, "Merit Salary Programs in Six Selected School Districts," Washington, D.C.: United States Office of Education, Bulletin 1963 No. 5, 1963, 1-2.

salaries on the basis of differentiated levels of teaching effectiveness, with that effectiveness to be defined through an evaluation of the teacher's level of performance with respect to certain locally established criteria. This is the definition of a merit salary program.

TWENTY KEYS TO SUCCESSFUL MERIT RATING*

1. Allow teachers to be admitted to the evaluation phase of the program only through written application.
2. Allow teachers to withdraw from either the evaluation or subsequent salary stipend phase of the program by written notice to the administration.
3. Provide a basic salary schedule that is competitive with neighboring school districts to insure that the merit program does not have "demerit" implications for those who elect not to participate.
4. Provide funds for merit salary stipends from a source beyond the regularly accepted source of revenue for salaries. Stating earmarked funds for merit purposes only, as a part of the total state uniform school fund, will help to fill this need.
5. Establish standards for qualification to receive meritorious service stipends prior to admission of teachers to candidacy for such stipends.
6. Establish an objective system of coded observation of teaching performance with trained observers whose duties are to gather data and not make qualitative judgments.
7. Establish a statistically valid method of relating the results of data gathered by trained observers to the standards of qualification that have been published in advance.

REVIEW OF EVALUATION FILES

8. Provide opportunities for teachers to review their evaluation files frequently by meeting with merit study personnel who are

---

*Terrel H. Bell, "Twenty Keys to Successful Merit Rating," taken from *American School Board Journal,* published by The Bruce Publishing Company, March, 1963, 13-14.

not involved in making salary decisions. The relationship of the teacher to these merit study counselors should be similar to the relationship established between school guidance personnel and students.

9. Make salary decisions only when the teacher candidate has reviewed his file, has determined that he is ready for a decision, and submits in writing a request for a merit salary decision.

10. Appoint one person on the administrative staff to review applicants' files, compare data with previously established standards, and interview the teacher candidate concerning the decision. The discussion at this interview should be confined to the data in the file and its comparison with the standards.

11. Make all merit salary decisions as tentative ones where encouragement is given for the teacher participant to stay in the program if he does not qualify during the first year. The purpose of the entire program must be staff improvement. This is accomplished by a positive approach that points out, in an encouraging way, how some added concentration would possibly improve performance and result in subsequent qualification.

12. Provide an appeal board to which teachers may appeal decisions made by the administrator. This board should have representation of both administrators and teachers on it.

13. Make the role of all principals and supervisors one of objective observation and data recording. Such persons must not be regarded as "merit raters," for this would tend to damage the kind of warm, supportive relationship that must exist between these administrators and the teachers. Only one person, either the superintendent or his designated representative, should actually make salary decisions. His decisions should then be subject to the review of the appeal board.

VOLUNTARY PARTICIPATION

14. Emphasize that teachers are free to participate in the merit program at their own choice and on the basis of their respective philosophies concerning the principle of merit. This implies that not all the competent teachers will be in the merit program since it is an opportunity program for those who elect to participate. Teachers who dislike the merit approach may remain on the salary schedule and not be concerned so long as the basic schedule remains commensurate with neighboring school systems of comparable financial ability.

15. Permit teachers who are in the merit evaluation program to reveal their participation and/or qualification for merit salary stipends at their own discretion. Make no announcements and publish no lists of participants. This will require understanding of the press and, in some states, repeal of laws that require publication of teachers' names and salaries.

16. Use the teacher observation code to evaluate all teachers in the system, but administer more intensive evaluation and data-gathering procedures to merit study participants. The objectivity developed in the merit study program can then be applied to eliminate incompetent teachers and to help those who have promise of becoming more effective instructors. Automatic salary schedule increments could be withheld on a more carefully administered basis through this procedure. Possibly two to four observation visits would suffice for all teaching staff members with from 12 to 16 observations needed for merit salary stipend candidates.

17. Provide for "imposed variables" in the evaluation formula so that teachers in overcrowded classrooms or poor physical facilities will get special consideration. Some teachers merit imposed variable consideration when they are teaching temporarily out of their subject areas at the request of the administration.

18. Include in the teachers' files the nonclass activities that are performed to support the school in such areas as lunchroom supervision, P.T.A. work, hall and playground duty, curriculum work, etc.

19. Recognize the differences in teachers' personalities and in teachers' purposes for being in education work at the present time. Many excellent teachers would prefer to remain on a salary schedule rather than subject themselves to a year of intensive evaluation of their work. Other teachers may see the merit evaluation year as a great challenge and as a tremendous growth opportunity. Some teachers must advance rapidly in a financial way due to family needs in this era of inflation and expanding costs. Others may have relatively few financial pressures and may have little interest of intensity in salary figures. A voluntary merit program where one can either participate or ignore the merit principle will meet the needs of varied groups in the teaching staff who have diverse financial needs. The administrator with a merit program may be able to keep the young man in teaching who has great potential but must leave education or move into administration when he actually loves to teach and

should spend his lifetime teaching for the good of his students and of society.

LIMITATIONS OF MERIT PROGRAM

20. Do not profess to measure teaching competence to the "nth degree" of all its complicated aspects. Tell all merit study participants that there is yet much to be learned about measurement in this area. Assure them that the system of coded observation (there are many very respectable observation codes available) will record the many fine things that teachers do to help boys and girls learn. It will determine the climate in the classroom and ascertain if the conditions for effective learning are present. Hasten to add that mistakes will be made, but they will be honest ones made by an administration that is concerned with the improvement of teaching and with the welfare of teachers. When mistakes are made they can be corrected. The good merit system makes provision for this through a system of checks and balances that helps to guarantee justice and equity.

PERSONNEL POLICIES . . .

DEVELOPMENT OF PERSONNEL POLICIES*

Policy making is a major function of a school board. Policy outlines the plan of action adopted by the board of education. It includes the philosophy of education and the objectives of the local school. It designates responsibility and determines procedure.

In some instances school law may determine policy. Length of school year, teacher tenure and minimum wage laws are examples. However, most policies are made and implemented at the local level. Policy may exist only in the minutes of the local school board meetings or it may be an officially compiled policy statement.

---

*Developing Personnel Policies, Washington, D.C.: National Education Association Commission on Professional Rights and Responsibilities, 1963, 3-6. By permission of National Education Association.

A policy, to be effective, should be a written, agreed-upon statement of directions for action, definite enough to be a guide, yet flexible enough to allow adjustments dictated by good judgment.

Personnal policies are only a portion of the policy structure in a good school system but they are an important part. Administrators, teachers, secretaries, clerks, operation and maintenance employees, health officers, nurses, attendance officers and other non-certificated personnel should be governed by written policy covering requirements for employment, duties, salary, dismissal, absence, resignation, re-employment, workmen's compensation, insurance and other items applicable to a particular group.

Other important areas in school administration that should be governed by written policy are: operating practices of the board of education; use of school buildings and school property; supplies and textbooks; tuition; summer school; adult education program; holidays; the school year; and attendance.

A school policy is based upon written resolutions officially adopted by the board of education. The board should amend those policies that are outdated or conflicting. Minutes of board meetings should show all action on policy matters.

VALUES OF WRITTEN POLICIES

A board of education operating with established written policies, arranged in convenient classification, can function in a systematic, orderly and effective way.

Written policy statements, adopted after careful consideration by all groups, will promote understanding and help maintain wholesome and cooperative relationships within the community. Constant use, revision and evaluation of the stated policies will make them of continued value.

Personnel policies are more favorably accepted and followed if they have been arrived at by the cooperative effort of all groups concerned.

HOW ARE POLICIES DEVELOPED?

1. Who initiates action for local written personnel policies?
   a. The board of education. The advice of lay committees may be sought to obtain the thinking of the community.
   b. The office of the superintendent may initiate action upon request of the board of education, upon his own awareness of need or upon requests received from an employee group.

c. Employee groups may initiate the formulation of personnel policies.

Often policies result from the action of an employee group committee. After careful study of conditions and needs, the committee representing the employee group may submit its policy proposal to its own group for approval. The approved suggestions should be submitted to the superintendent and to the school board for review and suggestion. The committee will review and study the suggestions made by the superintendent and the board, adopting changes acceptable to the group, and submit it to the board again for review. Finally, differences, if any, can be resolved and the board may then adopt the policy.

2. Who adopts policies? *The board of education.*
3. How can board policies be made known?

Copies of policies, and rules and regulations to implement them, should be made available in written form to all concerned. It is the responsibility of each employee to know the policies and rules and to refer questions of interpretation to the administration.

ITEMS GENERALLY COVERED IN A HANDBOOK OF POLICIES, RULES AND REGULATIONS FOR SCHOOL PERSONNEL

A. Statement of Philosophy of Purpose and Function of the School System.
B. Principles and Processes of Selection.
   1. Preparation and certification requirements for teachers
   2. Qualifications for administrative and supervisory personnel
   3. Qualifications for non-teaching personnel
   4. Selection
   5. Re-employment
   6. Eligibility lists
   7. Health Examinations
C. Duties and Responsibilities.
   1. Administrative personnel
   2. Teaching personnel
   3. Building personnel
   4. Food service personnel
   5. Secretarial and clerical personnel

D. Policies Covering Employment Conditions of Certificated Personnel.
   1. Contracts
   2. Salary schedules
   3. Time schedules
   4. Assignments
   5. Transfers
   6. Promotions
   7. Evaluation
   8. Retirement
   9. Substitutes
   10. Tenure
   11. Resignations
   12. Absences:
      a. Sick leave
      b. Maternity leave
      c. Leaves of absence — for study — travel — political activity — military service
      d. Excusing teachers for professional meetings or conferences
E. Policies Covering Teaching Conditions.
   1. School buildings and property
   2. Instructional materials
   3. Teacher load
   4. School contests
   5. Teaching current public problems
   6. Extra-curricular duties
   7. Working routine
   8. Guide line re courses of study

BASIC PRINCIPLES FOR THE DEVELOPMENT AND ADMINISTRATION OF SCHOOL PERSONNEL POLICIES*

The analysis of the literature of the field of personnel administration revealed certain principles basic to the development and administration of any and all personnel policies. Those on which authorities agreed were the following:

---

*Willard S. Elsbree and E. Edmund Reutter, and Associates, *Principles of Staff Personnel Administration in Public Schools,* New York: by permission of Bureau of Publications, Teachers College, Columbia University, 1959, 2-3.

1. Personnel policies should be developed and administered with the fundamental purpose of enabling the best possible staff to operate with maximum effectiveness.
2. Consideration for the worth and dignity of the individual should be foremost.
3. The psychological needs of all individuals should be considered.
4. Long-range considerations as well as immediate concerns should be taken into account.
5. Lines of authority and responsibility should be clearly delineated.
6. Staff members should be encouraged to participate wherever feasible.
7. Interested and capable citizens should be involved where appropriate.
8. Personnel policies should be consistent with pertinent research and experience.
9. Personnel policies should allow that degree of flexibility necessary for dealing with exceptional or unique circumstances that may arise.
10. Personnel policies should be clearly stated in writing.
11. Personnel policies should be communicated and interpreted to the staff and community.
12. Personnel policies should be periodically evaluated and possibly revised in light of changing circumstances.
13. Personnel functions should be executed by a staff adequate both in number and preparation.
14. Adequate budgetary provision should be made to permit the functions of personnel administration to be properly implemented.

THE PURPOSE AND FORMULATION OF PERSONNEL POLICIES*

POLICY AND SERVICE

To establish certain policies of personnel management because such policies are in effect in another similar organization is to overlook a basic principle. This principle holds that policy should grow out of the service

---

*B. J. Chandler and Paul V. Petty, *Personnel Management in School Administration*, New York: Harcourt, Brace & World, Inc., 1955 (by permission).

in which it exists. The only justifiable reason for establishing policies is to facilitate the total operation. It may be false to assume that a policy rendering a service in the operation of one organization will necessarily render the same degree of service in the operation of all similar organizations. Disservice may actually be rendered by a direct transfer.

Reasonable policy may fail to grow out of an operation for any one of several reasons. It may be that the administrative leadership lacks not only vision but an analytical ability in connection with the organization being directed. The administrative organization may be so devised that it lacks the machinery for determining and implementing policy. For example, even though the local school board is recognized as being largely a policy-making body, a local school board may become stale in this regard to the extent that whatever policies are developed come from the concentrated administration rather than the "policy-making" board of education. In effect, the board may have become a "rubber stamp" in matters of policy. In other cases this recommended policy-making body may have attempted to direct more of its attention to administration, which is outside of its normal scope of operation.

AREAS OF POLICY MAKING IN
PERSONNEL MANAGEMENT

Specifically, there are certain areas in which policy making should function in personnel management. Some of the more significant of these areas are as follows:

1. Recruitment, selection, and assignment of staff members.
2. Orientation and in-service education of staff members.
3. Rating and promotion of staff members.
4. Transferring, demoting, and discharging of staff members.
5. Salary administration and policies.
6. Evaluation.
7. Plan for salary payment.
8. Dates and hours of work.
9. Benefits and services.
10. Health and safety of employees.
11. Staff participation in management.

The larger the organization the more necessary are personnel policies, since a large organization obviously cannot deal with each employee on all detailed matters as an individual. Good personnel administration will, however, recognize each employee as an individual with inherent rights, interests, and responsibilities. Where these are being affected differently for one individual than for others, the matter must be handled on an individual basis. Otherwise, the large organization must consider the group first, with each individual being treated exactly the same way.

FORMULATING PERSONNEL POLICIES

If the administrative official responsible for the personnel function had the time to counsel personally with each staff member upon all problems arising from his relationship with the organization, the formulation of detailed personnel policies would be unnecessary. However, such a practice would be impossible in most school systems. Furthermore, it probably would not be desirable in most cases. Although a rule-of-thumb approach may be workable in a small situation, it still lacks consistency and definition as an administrative technique. The formulation of definite policies covering problem areas is the best present answer for this administrative matter.

"Democratic" is the descriptive term used most often to present the current philosophy of administration. In the field of policy making an excellent opportunity is given to practice democratic techniques of administration. A plan should be provided that will permit staffs to contribute ideas to policy formulation. A simple suggestion box used with proper understanding and explanation may be a first step in this direction. Further toward the ultimate goal of maximum participation by staff members is a plan wherein a meaningful representation of all members in the organization has a definite voice in the development of personnel policies. Ideally, in all organizations there should be definite, meaningful, and planned participation by the staff.

MORALE OF STAFF . . .

DETERMINANTS OF FACULTY MORALE*

Important as teacher morale is, many school and college administrators apparently do not give enough attention to the role it plays in achieving excellence in education.

---

*Frederick L. Redefer, "A Teacher Teaches Better . . ." *NEA Journal*, April, 1964, 8, 10 (by permission of National Education Association and F. L. Redefer).

Little is known about what causes good teacher morale, but a beginning has been made by group studies at New York University where fifty graduate students with the cooperation of the administrators of more than fifty school systems and 10,000 teachers tried to find out what factors are involved.

The studies indicate that school systems as a whole may differ strikingly from each other in morale. They indicate also that within a school system there can be schools with high morale and schools with low morale; that within a school there can be teachers with high morale and teachers with low morale.

Almost any teacher can tell you of a colleague whose eyes no longer sparkle and who is content to teach this year as he did ten years ago. Almost any professor can talk about the deadwood in the faculty. But what the teacher or the professor can't describe is what caused the sparkle in the eye to dull or how the deadwooding took place.

The NYU studies suggest that there is no direct causative relation between morale and age, sex, marital status, years of teaching, college degrees, or advanced studies.

Morale is evidently not determined by one factor, but by a constellation of factors, all of which are important, although some are more important than others.

Operationally, the research group at New York University agreed that "morale exists to the degree that teachers freely and consciously released and focused the skills, knowledge, and abilities they possess to achieve known and accepted educational objectives which they have actively participated in formulating."

This seems to be a good definition for a faculty, but what about the meaning of morale for the individual teacher? What do these studies reveal about that?

The morale of teachers as individuals does not always reveal itself in group interpretations of averages and standard deviations. Yet since a faculty is a group of individual teachers, it is possible in the study of schools to obtain insights into teachers as individual personalities. These insights of what is important for many individual teachers need to be reported, because if faculty morale is to be raised or maintained, then these factors are basic considerations of any program.

One important factor is that teachers are human beings and want to be understood nd treated as human beings.

Teachers over and over again report that "the most important task of a principal is to understand me as a person." This awareness is important in large part because it enables the principal to help the individual teacher understand himself better and find self-expression in his work. (The only principals who can provide this help, of course, are those who have self-understanding and the knowledge and capacity to deal intelligently with the varied aspects of human beings.)

Self-understanding, then, is one cornerstone of good morale. This self-understanding requires a knowledge and acceptance of the self in the particular position held and how this is related to other positions.

In the studies of teacher morale, the problem of administrative relations with the faculty stood out sharply. Principals, the studies revealed, occupy a key position in determining whether a teacher has high or low morale.

Two junior high schools, equal in many respects, differed in morale. The one with high morale had a principal who got his internal satisfactions from helping his faculty to grow. The one with low morale had a principal whose satisfactions stemmed from the power of his position and the social status he thought went with it. If teacher morale is to be improved, if relations between teachers and administrators are to be cooperative, educators need to be more aware of the purposes motivating individuals in the positions they occupy.

Studies also brought out that loneliness in one of the occupational hazards of teaching. In the case of teachers of young children, the loneliness may be that of the mature mind associating with the immature mind; in the case of secondary school teachers, the loneliness may be that of the teacher mind associating with the mind of the adolescent in revolt; at the college level, it may be the impersonality of the usual professor-student classroom relationship.

Teachers reveal the need for an "adult community within the faculty" which provides for a real exchange of ideas. Most faculty relations, it appears, are inclined to conceal differences, suppress conflict, and remain on an impersonal basis. Teachers rate faculty meetings as generally unproductive of the exchange of honest opinion that should characterize a community of adults.

Teachers as humans need certain things to keep up their morale, but they also want recognition as professional persons, and this involves something more specific than recognition as teachers. They want to be known as individuals by the board of education, by their superintendent, by their principal, and by the parents. One teacher bitterly reported this comment from the president of the board of education: "You are doing a good job, Miss Brown. By the way, what do you teach?"

A teacher wants his work to be known and appreciated because if it is, he feels he is important; if it is not, he feels he is unimportant. Furthermore, teachers want to be commended in ways they regard as commending.

The teachers who took part in the NYU studies were asked to list in order of frequency how they were commended in their schools. Then they were asked to list the kinds of commendation in order of preference. The lists seldom coincided; in fact, in many cases, they were diametrically opposed. A letter, a word of commendation at the right time, a pat on the back—these came high on the teachers' list of what keeps a sparkle in their eyes.

Other types of recognition are unwelcome. For example, the studies revealed that an entire school faculty resented an annual "Teacher Night" in which each teacher was called to the platform to receive an orchid or a carnation. The teachers regarded it as a patronizing "be kind to teachers" gesture. A similar feeling toward "great teacher" awards is found among college professors, who regard them more as public relations ballyhoo than real recognition for great teaching.

A most important factor of all for individual teacher morale is personal commitment and involvement—belief by the teacher in the importance of what he is doing, in the mission which his acts are directed to achieve. Commitment and involvement result from active participation, and participation requires good communications through the school system. When the low morale teacher feels that "no one tells me anything," it is not because he receives no communications. It is rather that he does not hear them even when they are shouted at him. He does not hear because he cannot hear. There may be many possible reasons for this, but he probably cannot hear because no one hears him and so his mind blocks out most of what these nonlisteners try to tell him.

This problem will not be solved by more communications, simpler communications, or verbal communications. It can only be solved by two-way communication. Unfortunately, many schools have perfected only the downward process of passing on information.

Communication involves more than listening. It involves trying to puzzle out what is being said and what is not being said. One problem of education is that the profession has a long tradition of talking at people. Teachers talk at students. Principals talk at teachers. Superintendents talk at faculties. None of the three groups does enough listening, and seldom do any of them try to discover what people heard them say. The level on which teachers communicate and receive communications has much to do with the morale of the individual teachers.

These are some of the insights that were derived from studies which involved talking with and listening to individual teachers. These are some of the meanings underlying the factors that can change the morale of an entire staff. What they reveal is that morale is a configuration of many component parts, all of which are important. Most important of all, morale is not a thing apart from the life of the group and apart from the life of the individual.

GUIDES FOR BETTER HUMAN RELATIONS IN SCHOOLS*

As clearer answers to the how-to-do-it aspects of human relations in school administration are awaited from research workers, the school administrator does have certain principles which are more reliable than his intuition alone.

1. The objective of administrative activity is generally to effect changed human behavior.
2. Appeal to the intellect through presentation of facts though a *sine qua non,* is in itself usually not enough to change human behavior.
3. Human behavior is generally not changed unless understanding is supplemented by favorable emotional attitudes.
4. Favorable attitudes are frequently developed when groups of people are involved in school decision making.
5. Favorable emotional attitudes may be caught from the school administrator if he is a person who is liked.
6. Administrative decisions will prove most successful if they are made in conformity with cultural attitudes that have already been emotionalized by most people: for example, the cultural concepts of democratic structure, democratic operation, justice, equality of opportunity, and preservation of past values.
7. Representative committees can be useful to administrators since they may reflect cultural reactions to proposals likely to emerge later in the larger group.

*From *American School Administration, Public and Catholic* by Raymond F. McCoy. Copyright 1961 by McGraw-Hill Book Company. Used by permission of McGraw-Hill Book Company, 12.

HOW TO STIMULATE THE
TIRED EMPLOYEE*

One supervisor made it a policy to let his men know when performance slipped. He was proud of his technique and told his men, "Don't worry about how you are making out. If anything goes wrong, you'll hear about it from me!" On the other hand, you may feel it is necessary to tell men who have been around for 15 or 20 years that they are doing a good job. The fact is that practically everyone wants to hear from the boss how he is doing. Sure, we prefer to hear complimentary things and we must have recognition for our efforts on the job.

It is easy to see how a man's productivity can fall off and his attitude change when he is working near his maximum ability and when he is protected by a strong seniority clause. What is the point of putting out with the extra effort? Isn't it easier just to maintain minimum standards which will get by? How can additional effort be generated?

The answer lies in frequent and accurate recognition of each man's accomplishment and in an expression of appreciation for it. The exact manner and frequency of praising vary widely according to each individual's personal needs, but it is safe to say that we should not be niggardly with praise. Be sure to pick the right situation for praising. After hearing an inspirational talk on this subject, a supervisor thought he would stimulate a man toward better performance by telling him he was doing a great job. This really confused the man and embarrassed the group leader who had just been justifiably critical of this man's performance.

This brings up another point which has probably already occurred to you. What about a man whose performance has slipped? If you cannot praise him, what will motivate him? The acknowledgment of performance is in itself an extremely powerful motivator. However, by reminding him of previous accomplishments and the example he sets for others, other stimulation is provided.

At any rate, the performance of all employees, especially those with long service, should not go unrecognized whether it is good or bad. Let them know how things stand.

---

*Curtis J. Potter, "Motivating Long-Service Employees," by permission of *Supervision,* XXVI (August, 1964), 11-12.

THE PURPOSES OF WELFARE PROVISIONS*

An important function of personnel administration is that of meeting the welfare needs of professional workers in school systems. These needs relate to mental and physical health, psychological viewpoints toward employment, social status in the community, and the ability to meet the economic demands of daily life.

The purposes behind welfare provisions in the personnel program are greater efficiency in carrying out the philosophy and objectives of the school system, strengthening staff cooperation, eliminating annoyances and worries which interfere with service performance, helping to bring out each individual's potential for growth and development, attracting high-grade young people into teaching, and increasing the amount of satisfaction derived from employment.

Care must be taken in formulating welfare policies and practices to provide for the non-material as well as the material needs of personnel. Both considerations have an influence on the attitudes, feelings, and efficiency of workers. It has also been discovered that the way in which policies are determined may have even more of an impact on attitudes and actions of workers than the benefits they provide.

The areas in which policies and practices should receive careful attention—aside from salary, tenure, and retirement—are health and recreation, working conditions and environment, leaves of absence, insurance protection, and benefit associations and services. . .

It is generally recognized that teacher performance is influenced by the working conditions and environment of the school system. Districts seeking to develop and maintain maximum staff productivity work to create a satisfying environment for teachers. Environment is regarded as the composite of district contractual provisions, administrative practices, physical surroundings, and community influences; and the districts carefully plan their actions in each of these areas. Many accept teacher par-

---

*Leslie W. Kindred, and Prince B. Woodard, *Staff Welfare Practices in the Public Schools*, Washington, D.C.: by permission of The Center for Applied Research in Education, Inc., 1963, 105-108.

ticipation in the formulation of policies as a valuable practice and use staff advisory committees for this purpose.

Teachers in an increasing number of districts are being informed of their contractual rights and responsibilities through the distribution of district handbooks or policy manuals. These publications include state and local rules, regulations, and procedures concerning tenure and retirement; salary schedules and methods of payment; employment periods and hours of duty; instructional and non-instructional responsibilities; grievance provisions and procedures; professional growth requirements; supplemental employment provisions; and other contractural aspects of their employment.

Greater attention is being directed to the physical characteristics of classrooms and their effect on teachers. Some districts are concerned with classroom furnishings and the environmental influence of color and design, as well as with noise and outside distractions on both teachers and pupils.

A variety of pupil grouping and placement procedures are being utilized to create a manageable task for teachers and thereby to promote pupil learning. A number of districts have policies establishing special programs for atypical children. In contrast, a large number of systems are without any written policy on class size or teacher load.

Although the range is great in the scope of services offered, the evidence seems clear that the majority of school districts recognize a responsibility to provide supervision for teachers. It is the policy of some districts to sponsor in-service growth opportunities for their teachers and to expect their participation. In other systems, teacher in-service growth is considered a personal responsibility. A number of other districts relate professional growth to salary schedules.

It seems important for districts to recognize that community influences may have a substantial effect on the working conditions and environment of teachers. Some districts reflect their concern in their policies on standards of conduct, participation in community life, and the solicitation of teachers for financial support of community activities. In general, these policies support the right of teachers to enjoy the same freedom accorded to other citizens.

TENURE LAWS*

Tenure laws contribute significantly to the security of employment of classroom teachers, principals, and other school personnel.

---

*NEA Research Bulletin, "Teacher Tenure Laws Benefit Teachers in 37 States," XXXVIII (October, 1960), 81-82, by permission of National Education Association.

The basic purpose of tenure legislation is to protect teachers who have successfully completed their probationary period from unjust dismissal for unfounded personal, political, or religious reasons, during competent performance of their duties and good behavior. At the same time, these laws provide for orderly dismissal from the school system of teachers who are clearly incompetent professionally, or whose conduct is proven to be inimical to the best interests of the schools and the pupils they serve.

Contrary to some concepts, tenure laws do not guarantee permanent employment or absolute rights to their positions to those school employees who have acquired tenure status. Rather, these laws require school boards to follow prescribed procedures before removing or dismissing employees, and provide that termination of employment be based on legally sufficient grounds. Moreover, legislatures may amend or even repeal tenure laws.

Except for a 1939 decision of the Supreme Court of the United States which construed the Indiana tenure statute as a contractual type law, the rights which tenure laws confer on teachers have not been considered to be contractual in nature by courts which faced this question. Therefore, subsequent enactments reflecting changes in legislative policies are not regarded as contravening the federal Constitutional prohibition against impairment of contracts.

WHAT IS A TENURE LAW?

Laws containing contract and tenure provisions have been variously denominated in the several states as tenure laws, continuing contract laws, continuing status, civil service, or fair dismissal laws. However, the title given a particular law affords no indication that it is indeed a tenure law.

How is a tenure law to be defined? Measured against the aforementioned objectives underlying tenure legislation, a tenure law may be defined as one which (a) provides for continuing employment of teachers who, under its terms, have acquired permanent, tenure, or continuing contract status; and (b) requires boards to comply with prescribed procedural provisions of notice, statement of charges, and right to a hearing before a tenure teacher can be dismissed, or before nonrenewal of the teacher's contract of employment can be effective.

To be sure, some of the tenure laws are so drafted as to better safeguard teachers against unfair dismissal than others also falling within the definition just given. Those laws which contain specific provisions with respect to dismissal both during and at the end of the school year or the contract term, and which detail as well the causes for discharge, and the step-by-step procedures to be observed when dismissal of a teacher is contemplated, not only make it clear to all concerned what the teacher's rights are, but often avoid the necessity of resorting to the courts for an interpretation of the law.

To be differentiated from the tenure law is another kind of law in force in some states—the continuing contract law of the spring notification type. Such a law lacks the essential provisions of notice, statement of charges, and right of hearing before a teacher's employment can be terminated; it requires only that the teacher be given advance notice of nonrenewal of his employment contract, and ordinarily no reasons need be furnished. Under statutory provisions of this kind, the teaching contract is automatically renewed for the ensuing school year unless notice to the contrary is received by a specified date.

At the start of the 1960-61 school year, tenure laws were in effect in 37 states, either on a state-wide basis, or in certain designated areas only. Teachers in the District of Columbia had tenure rights also. Continuing contract laws of the spring notification type, or annual or long-term contract provisions prevailed in the remaining 13 states. The kind of law in force in each state is given in the table. Here is what a summary of this information shows:

Twenty-five states have tenure laws which cover teachers eligible for the benefits conferred in all areas of the state, without exception. In a number of these state-wide tenure laws, it is not uncommon to find different provisions for school districts of different sizes. And in two of the 25 states, special local tenure laws have been enacted for certain jurisdictions—in Connecticut, for each of its principal cities, and in Florida, for each of four counties.

In addition to the 25 states whose tenure laws must be followed in all areas, six states qualify to some extent the state-wide applicability of their tenure provisions. In this group is Michigan, whose statute books have two different tenure laws, both subject to local adoption, one by the voters, the other by the local school board. In California and Colorado, small school districts may, but need not, use tenure provisions. Conversely, Illinois and New York exclude small districts from the operation of their tenure laws, while Indiana excepts its township schools.

In six states, tenure laws cover teachers in certain places only. As to the nontenure areas in these states, generally simple spring notification provisions or annual contracts may control.

Of the 13 states without tenure laws, five have mandatory state-wide continuing contract laws of the spring notification type. In a sixth state, Virginia, pursuant to state-board regulations, local school boards may, subject to the consent and approval of the state board, enter into contracts with teachers which provide for automatic renewal if neither party gives notice of termination before April 1. Enactments providing for annual or long-term contracts are found in the other seven states.

TEACHER RETIREMENT*

Retiring from service is a difficult transition for most individuals to make. Bridging the gap smoothly from an active to an inactive status requires more than the assurance of financial security, although this is, of course, very important. Full information concerning the many procedural requirements necessary to securing retirement benefits from state and federal sources should be made available to personnel sufficiently ahead of time to preclude any difficulties. The various noneconomic factors related to retirement should also be considered. For example, information regarding climate and living expenses in different parts of the country might be made available. Retiring personnel might be encouraged to cultivate present interests and to take up new ones. Many important psychological hurdles can be overcome by attention to these and other factors. Such policy requires little financial expenditure but aids substantially in readying personnel for leaving active employment.

Once personnel have retired, it is important to aid them in making satisfactory adjustment by keeping them informed on current happenings and involving them, when appropriate, in school activities. Policy of this sort not only contributes substantially to maintaining the morale of retired employees, but enables the school system to benefit in many instances by capitalizing on special talents and resources.

ETHICS, LAWS, AND GUIDES FOR PROFESSIONAL PERSONNEL . . .

THE LAW AND TEACHERS**

1. The schools belong to the state and are subject to state control in any way that the constitution permits and the legislature decides.

---

*Willard S. Elsbree, E. Edmund Reutter, Jr., and Associates, *Principles of Staff Personnel Administration in Public Schools,* by permission of Bureau of Publications, Teachers College, Columbia University, 1959, 55.

**Nolan C. Kearney, *A Teacher's Professional Guide,* © 1958, reprinted by permission of Prentice-Hall, Inc., Englewood Cliffs, New Jersey, 193.

2. Laws provide the formal temporal rules under which we live.

3. Rights conferred by law cannot be surrendered by their recipient. (If the law says you are free, you cannot become a slave even if you wish.)

4. Signed statements by parents relieving teachers of responsibility in certain contingencies may have little or no legal effect.

5. Forced resignations cannot be used to extend the probationary period.

6. In certain cases, teachers, principals, and others are legally liable for damage done to others as the result of written or oral statements regarding them. The time, the place, and the reason are important determiners.

7. It is not a sufficient defense against libel or slander to say that the statements made are true. A person has no exemption from responsibility merely because his damaging statements regarding others are true.

8. Fair employment practices laws in some states regulate the use of references to race and religion in recommendations, application blanks, and other records having to do with the search for employment.

9. Certain records are privileged and need not be made available for public examination, except by court order.

10. Teachers can be sued in most states for legal wrongs, injuries, injustices, or damages to pupils that result from the improper performance of duties. To avoid liability, teachers should exercise prudent care, reasonable foresight, and be careful not to exceed their authority. It is well to avoid the use of corporal punishment even if permitted.

11. Teachers should support "save harmless" legislation for teachers and other legislation designed to save teachers from loss of time and money in litigation.

12. Laws that hold school districts liable do not automatically protect teachers, since school districts may in turn try to recover from teachers the amounts of the awards collected from the school district as a result of their acts. Care should be taken in writing such laws so that teachers receive a maximum amount of protection.

13. Teachers are liable for assault and battery when they use corporal punishment or physical force and when their efforts are not strictly ministerial, or being ministerial, are excessive and extreme. As new methods and insights develop, it will become less and less necessary to use corporal punishment.

14. Teachers' contracts should be as simple and clear as possible. Ordinarily, boards of education are given much discretion concerning the conditions they may write into teachers' contracts. Legal action can be brought by either party to recover damages resulting from failure to observe the terms of the contract. Such actions are seldom advisable or necessary.
15. Tenure laws provide teachers with much more security than many teachers realize.
16. Teachers should examine their liability insurance policies most carefully to see that they have the protection they think they have against things that may occur while teaching or performing duties related to their jobs.
17. Public officials have only such power and authority as is legally conferred upon them.
18. Teachers and others should be slow to sign contracts, agreements, or order forms. Don't let someone "sell" you. Make it a rule to go shopping yourself for what you want to buy.
19. Contracts should be honored. Care should be taken not to become a party to contracts whose terms are not satisfactory.

GUIDES FOR PUBLIC EMPLOYEES' PARTICIPATION IN POLITICAL ACTIVITIES — A MATTER OF ETHICS*

The thesis underlying the following guidelines is this: Restrictions upon the political activity of public employees should vary (1) according to the political stability of the governmental unit, (2) according to the maturity of the career public service in the governmental unit, and (3) according to the position of the employee affected.

But stability and maturity are relative, and each involves subjective judgments. If restrictions on political activity are to vary, criteria for determining political stability and the maturity of the public service are essential.

The following is suggestive of the criteria that might be used in determining the degree of political stability of a governmental unit and the maturity of a career public service:

---

*Donald Hayman and O. Glenn Stahl, "Outdated Political Activity Rules Unfair to Employees," by permission of *Public Management,* XLVII (January, 1965), 10-13.

POLITICAL STABILITY

Governmental unit has history of honest and efficient government for the previous two decades and has been relatively free of bitter political factionalism.

Political campaigns are usually waged on issues and without vicious or slanderous charges, fraud, hoaxes, and other political skulduggery designed to influence the election.

Some continuity of membership on the governing body is maintained by nonpartisan elections, overlapping terms of office, or reelection of members.

The governing body usually rises above political or personal differences to support issues and programs and only occasionally is subject to bitter in-fighting, ruthless opposition, or picayunish harassment.

Majority of legislators exercise discretion and self-restraint in dealings with administrative officers and employees.

Executive and top administrative officers are distinguished for objectivity and discretion.

There is thorough coverage of legislative, executive, and administrative activities by all news media.

MATURITY OF A CAREER PUBLIC SERVICE

There is an active and competent personnel program under the supervision of an executive, manager, or independent civil service commission.

The working merit system publicizes all job opportunities; recruitment and promotions are according to established standards; there is a position classification system and standardized pay plan; and demoted or dismissed employees may have a public hearing before an advisory personnel board or civil service commission.

Legislation prohibiting the political activities listed below under Section III has been enacted.

The three criteria appearing immediately above have received continuous bipartisan legislative and citizen support for two decades.

Majority of employees are stable, dedicated public servants.

POLICY GUIDES

With the above points as background, it is hoped that the following will serve as specific guides to managers considering the appropriateness of existing restrictions on the political activity of career employees—municipal, state, and federal.

I. General Objectives—Seven minimal objectives should govern political activities control for public employees under a career service:[1]

Employees should be encouraged to discharge their obligations as good citizens and should be allowed the maximum political expression consistent with local conditions.

Prohibitions and punishment should be directed primarily at those who misuse, abuse, or coerce public employees in connection with political activity, rather than at confining the employees. In any event, employees should be protected from coercion or reprisal for permitted political activity.

Employees should be prevented from misusing their government positions for political purposes.

Distinctions in limitations on permitted behavior should be made between career employees and noncareer employees.

Distinctions should be made between political activity in the government in which employed and in other governments.

Particular provisions on political activity should vary according to the political stability of the governmental unit and the maturity of its career public service.

Other than to give effect to the foregoing principles, complete model political activity laws, designed to apply to all places at all times, should not necessarily be followed.

II. Activities Generally To Be Permitted—Active public participation, including leadership roles, in connection with state and local referenda on bond issues, constitutional amendments, or charter revisions, except where a conflict of interest would be present or apparent.

Active public participation, including candidacy, in nonpartisan school elections, provided such activity does not interfere with performance as an employee.

Active public participation in other nonpartisan political activity that does not compromise the employee's role of impartiality in his position.

III. Restrictions and Prohibitions—the following should be applicable to all situations:

Penalties should be imposed on any employee, official or person who seeks to require any public employee to contribute to a party or political cause or to require him to support or oppose a candidate in any election.

A career employee *should not* be allowed to: (1) engage in any par-

---

[1] These are not applicable to top officials appointed by the chief executive.

tisan political activity during scheduled working hours or while on duty; (2) neglect his or her assigned duties or responsibilities because of permitted political activity; (3) use office, public position, public property or supplies to secure contributions or to influence an election at any level of government; (4) solicit or receive anything of value as a partisan political contribution or subterfuge for such contribution from any other person; (5) give money, property, or anything of value as a contribution or subterfuge for such contribution for any partisan political purposes to any other public officer or employee, as distinguished from political parties or groups; (6) promise, or use influence, to secure public employment or other benefit financed from public funds as a reward for political activity; (7) discriminate in favor of, or against, an officer, employee, or applicant on account of his or her political contribution or permitted political activity at any level of government; (8) engage in any permitted political activity directed at other public employees while the latter are on duty.

Appointive law enforcement and judicial officers should not be allowed to engage in partisan political activity of any kind or participate in nonpartisan political activity in which officials are elected.

IV. Additional Restrictions—These are desirable in jurisdictions that have politically unstable governments or immature career public services:

Employees *should not* be allowed to: (1) be a partisan candidate for any elective office; (2) manage a political campaign; (3) hold office in a political party, organization, or club; (4) participate in a political convention except as a spectator; (5) organize, conduct, or address a public political meeting; (6) engage in any activity at the polls except voting; (7) initiate or circulate nominating petitions.

Employees *should* be allowed to: (1) vote; (2) campaign for, and hold, any nonpartisan office, except in the jurisdiction that employs them; (3) join a political organization, civic association, or civic betterment group; (4) contribute to campaign funds (but not on public property or to another government employee); (5) attend and participate in discussions at a political meeting; (6) sign petitions; (7) wear badges (but not at work); (8) write a letter to a newspaper on a political subject provided he does not use his public title.

V. Reducing Restrictions—the following restrictions may be reduced from those in *IV* as a governmental unit becomes more stable politically and its career public service becomes more mature:

Restrictions could well be relaxed on a differential basis allowing greater freedom: (1) For manual workers, clerical, and industrial type employees; (2) Professional, managerial, or technical employees not involved in law enforcement or sensitive policy positions.

Maximum freedom may extend to any political activity (including partisan) not prohibited in III above.

Such maximum freedom may be confined to governments other than that in which employed, particularly for professional, managerial, or technical employees.

CONCLUSION

As believers in a republican form of local government, managers should face the facts concerning restrictions on political activity. Are policies and practices guided largely by ideas that are now obsolete or patently harmful for the public, the city, and the employee? Is your city politically stable? Is the career service of your municipality mature? If employees were granted additional freedom, would they use it with self-restraint? What steps can and should be taken in your city, now or in the foreseeable future, to relax the present restrictions on political activity?

ARE TEACHERS' CONTRACTS UNILATERAL?*

Very rarely do employers cancel contracts with teachers, but during late spring and summer every day's mail brings to the desk of school superintendents throughout the country hundreds of letters from teachers presenting resignations or requesting releases from contracts. The increasing number of these incidents involving newly employed teachers is a matter of growing concern to school systems and college placement offices.

Superintendents and school-board members are beginning to wonder whether teaching contracts are "one-way streets." Are they to be honored meticulously by employers and disregarded at the convenience of the employees?

Superintendents report that they may fill a position in March only to have the teacher resign in early April. The next appointee may in turn resign before the end of the month. Even in late summer a number of new teachers may ask to be released from their contracts or simply send in resignations.

---

*H. I. Von Haden, "Is a Teaching Contract a One-Way Street?" *NEA Journal,* LI, February, 1962, 52-53. By permission of National Education Association and H. I. Von Haden. (Words in brackets added by editor.)

A personnel director reports an instance in which a prospective teacher held eight signed contracts, finally selected the one he liked best, and late in the summer sent in seven resignations. Obviously this is an extreme case, but it points up the chaotic condition that can develop if all members of the profession do not recognize the problem and hold candidates to careful observance of their commitments.

A situation involving a beginning teacher differs from that involving one who is already teaching in a school system. It would seem reasonable that the beginner should consider all factors carefully before making a decision, but after having accepted a position, should not consider others. A teacher in service might renew his contract in the spring with the understanding that he could ask to be released if a position of increased opportunity subsequently became available to him. However, after the experienced teacher has accepted a new position for the next year, he should not consider other offers.

Although this policy appears to be reasonable, it must be recognized that personnel practices have changed radically during the past generation. The acute shortage of teachers in the past twenty years has affected the attitudes and procedures of both employers and employees. . .

[Despite the lenient attitudes of both teachers and superintendents (expressed in a sampling survey of superintendents and teachers), the preponderant view seemed to be that of a teacher who said, "Most assuredly a person who cannot himself behave in a responsible and moral manner will never teach children to be moral and responsible people." Ed.]

TEACHER TURNOVER . . .

TEACHER TURNOVER IN PUBLIC ELEMENTARY AND SECONDARY SCHOOLS, 1959-1960*

In the fall of both 1959 and 1960 the number of women teachers in the public schools of this country was more than twice the number of men teachers. More women than men entered and left the public school

---

*Frank Lindenfeld, "Teacher Turnover in Public Elementary and Secondary Schools, 1959-1960," Washington, D.C.: United States Office of Education, Circular No. 675, 1963, 9-10, 14, 18, 20.

systems between these two dates. Of the teachers hired during 1959-60, 163,300 were women and 78,900 were men. Those who left included 139,000 women and 54,200 men.

The rate of separations was higher in 1959-60 among women than among men, but the rate of accessions was higher among the latter. . .

Differences for men and women appear also in losses to the profession and attrition. In each case, the rate for women is higher than the one for men:

	Percent of fall 1959 staff	
	Loss to the profession	Attrition
Both sexes	8.1	4.2
Men	6.3	3.3
Women	8.8	4.6

Some further variations in turnover may be noted among the men and women on the two teaching levels. As mentioned previously, approximately half of all public school teachers in 1959-60 were women teaching on the elementary level. They comprised roughly half of the total separations and almost as many of the total accessions. . .

The separation rates for women were higher than those for men on both the elementary and the secondary level (see table 4). The difference between separation rates of men and women was much less marked,

Table 4. — Accession and separation rates of classroom teachers in public elementary and secondary schools, by sex and teaching level, 50 States and the District of Columbia: Fall 1959 to fall 1960

[Percent]

Sex and teaching level	Accession rate	Separation rate
Both levels	**16.8**	**13.4**
Men	18.3	12.6
Women	16.2	13.8
Elementary	**15.8**	**13.0**
Men	20.1	12.7
Women	15.1	13.1
Secondary	**18.4**	**14.1**
Men	17.8	12.6
Women	19.2	15.7

Source: Computed from table 1 before rounding.

however, on the elementary than on the secondary teaching level. As table 4 shows, the highest rate of separations occurred among women high school and junior high school teachers, 15.7 percent of whom left the school districts in which they had been teaching during the 1959-60 school year.

Also of interest are the distributions of men and women elementary and secondary school teachers into the various types of accessions and separations about which the survey yielded information. In general, the distribution of types of turnover for men is different from what it is for women, but similar for teachers of the same sex on the two different levels. . . .

With regard to types of separation (see table 6) women were more likely to leave the profession by going on leave of absence or retiring, while men were more likely to be dismissed or to change to a nonteaching job in the same district. These findings for types of accessions and types of separations hold for both elementary and secondary school teachers.

The findings noted above reflect firmly established variations in the composition of the teaching staff, as well as differences in the career patterns of men and women teachers. The relatively greater size of the re-entering group among women is linked with the work-to-homemaking-to-work cycle typical of many American women. It is likely that many of the men re-entering teaching had been drafted into military service after a short period of working in the profession.

The greater number of women than of men among those retiring is in part a reflection of the preponderance of women in the teaching force in past years and the concomitant difference in age distribution. . . .

This survey found slight evidence of a direct relationship between teacher turnover and the characteristics of school districts other than their size. There was little relationship, for example, between the proportion of teachers who left their jobs and the average salary paid or the pupil-teacher ratio prevailing in the school system. Growth in enrollment, the relative number of men and women on the staff, and the level of experience of the teaching staff likewise did not appear to be consistently related to the separation rate of teachers.

Table 10 reveals that there was little systematic relationship between the average salaries paid and the separation rate in 1959-60. The accession rate, however, was somewhat higher in school systems that paid an average salary of $3,500 or more than in those that paid less than $3,500. There is a substantially lower accession rate among school systems paying an average salary of less than $3,000. Many of these systems paying lower salaries probably tend to be small and to have stable or declining enrollment. . . .

School district size is the one variable most closely related to school district separation rates. As already noted, lower rates of turnover tend to be found in large school districts and higher rates in small districts. Because of the importance of this variable, further discussion seems warranted.

The size-turnover relationship is much more marked among men than among women. As figure 7 illustrates, the difference between the separation rate in the largest and smallest school systems in 1959-60 was only about 2 percentage points among the women teachers. Among the men teachers, however, this difference was almost 13 percentage points. The separation rate among the latter may be traced in figure 7 from a low of 8.9 percent in school systems with 25,000 or more pupils to a high of 23.4 percent in school systems with 150-299 pupils. It tapers off to 21.6 percent in districts with fewer than 150 pupils. The data for 1957-58 reveal a similar pattern except that the difference between the separation rates of women in the smallest and largest school systems was much larger in that year (almost 13 percentage points) than in 1959-60. Also, the relationship between school-system size and separation of men teachers was more marked (in the same direction) in 1957-58 than in 1959-60.

Both the previous and the present turnover surveys indicate that among men teachers there exists a definite relationship between the size of school district and the rate of teacher separations. For women teachers, on the other hand, school-district size appears to be related to turnover only in systems with fewer than 600 pupils. And even in these districts, it is not nearly as significant a factor for women as it is for men teachers.

Factors which may contribute to the greater holding power of the large school systems include working conditions and administrative considerations. The salary level tends to be higher in the large systems. Many of the small school systems in this survey reported no salary schedules in existence at all. Further, it seems more likely that a teacher could be placed in a job most suited to his capabilities and interests in a large rather than a small school system. Problems in a small school system that could be solved only by a transfer to another school system might, in a large system, be solved by a transfer within the system.

Other factors which may be associated with the relationship between size and turnover are extrinsic to teaching employment. Women teachers are likely to leave their own jobs to follow their husbands if and when the husbands change jobs. But in large metropolitan areas a change in job is less likely to involve a move to another city.

FOR FURTHER REFLECTION OR INVESTIGATION

1. What differences do you see in approaches to administering teachers and factory employees?

2. Survey the teacher departures from your school district for the past three years, classifying the reasons for leaving and noting the years of experience in the district. Were the reasons given real or superficial?

3. How do you identify the grievances heard in the teacher's lounge — as genuine discontent or healthy griping?

4. Interview teachers who joined your staff this year to obtain reactions to the orientation experience. Plan an ideal program to overcome their criticisms.

5. How can the value of teachers be measured in order to determine the proper reward for their services?

6. If your salary schedule is not on the ratio system, convert it to the ratio plan. How would you determine the value of ratio points for different steps of the schedule, for different degrees, for administrators?

7. What would it mean for recruitment, retention, and morale of a faculty if the salary schedule had only five steps with a $1,500 increment between each step?

8. Compare the cost to a board of education between an extra-pay-for-extra-duty plan and a plan of no reimbursement but with teachers released one or two periods a day for handling extra-curricular activities.

9. Argue the case for and against merit pay.

10. Do you believe the fringe benefits in your school system draw teachers there? Into the profession initially?

11. Survey class members or your colleagues to determine when they decide to become teachers. What was their motivation? Who inspired them in that direction? What are the implications of your findings for teacher recruitment?

12. Should a building principal or the personnel officer have the final decision, subject to board approval, in the selection of new teachers?

13. Distinguish between teacher evaluation and teacher rating.

14. What is meant by efficient production for a classroom teacher?

15. Which hurts faculty morale more: rating with the possibility of making errors or no rating at all?

16. Which is more reliable in assessing teacher performance: rating scales or the subjective judgment of experienced administrators?

17. Is it possible to supervise teachers without evaluating performance?

18. Under what conditions is it justifiable for a teacher to break his contract?

19. Is there a conflict between the contractual relationship involving a teacher and a board of education and the contractual right to negotiate with the board for salary and welfare conditions?

20. Distinguish the job protective characteristics of your state's teacher tenure laws, civil service, and industrial labor unions.

21. After an assessment of the *esprit de corps* in buildings represented by members of the class, explain the reasons for differences.

22. Examine your board of education policy manual to distinguish between statements which are policy and those which are rules or regulations.

BIBLIOGRAPHY

Bell, Terrel H., "Twenty Keys to Successful Merit Rating," *American School Board Journal,* March, 1963.

Biddle, Bruce, and William J. Ellena, *Contemporary Research on Teacher Effectiveness,* New York: Holt, Rinehart and Winston, Inc., 1964.

Bogg, Ridgley M., Foreword to "The Administration of Non-Instructional Personnel in Public Schools," Evanston: Association of School Business Officials, Intl., Research Bulletin No. 1, 1964.

Brighton, Stayner F., and Cecil J. Hannan, *Merit Pay Programs for Teachers,* San Francisco: Fearon Publishers, 1962.

Castetter, William B., *Administering the School Personnel Program,* New York: The Macmillan Company, 1962.

Chandler, B. J. and Paul V. Petty, *Personnel Management in School Administration,* Yonkers-on-Hudson, New York: World Book Company, 1955.

Cohen, Louis, "The Administration of Non-Instructional Personnel in Public Schools," Evanston: Association of School Business Officials, Intl., Research Bulletin No. 1, 1964.

Creider, Calvin, "Will Higher Salaries Put Teachers Unrest to Rest?" *Nation's Schools,* March, 1964.

Dennaire, B., "Preparing for the Substitute Teacher," *National Association of Secondary-School Principals* Bulletin, No. 192, February, 1953.

Donald, Eleanor, "The Public-School Personnel Administrator," Washington, D.C.: National Education Association Research Division, Research Monograph 1962-M1, February, 1962.

Elsbree, Willard S., and E. Edmund Reutter, Jr., and Associates, *Principles of Staff Personnel Administration in Public Schools,* New York: Bureau of Publications, Teachers College, Columbia University, 1959.

Fawcett, Claude W., *School Personnel Administration,* New York: The Macmillan Company, 1964.

Garber, Lee, "Should Public Education Mix with Partisan Politics?" *Nation's Schools,* November, 1963.

Gibbons, Neil, "How Superintendents Select Teachers," *Ohio Schools,* XL, April, 1962.

Hayman, Donald and O. Glenn Stahl, "Outdated Political Activity Rules Unfair to Employees," *Public Management,* XLVII, January, 1965.

Hunt, Harold and R. Oliver Gibson, *The School Personnel Administrator,* Boston: Houghton Mifflin Company, 1965.

Kearney, Nolan C., *A Teacher's Professional Guide,* Englewood Cliffs: Prentice-Hall, Inc., 1958.

Kershaw, Joseph A., and Roland N. McKean, *Teacher Shortage and Salary Schedules,* New York: McGraw-Hill Book Company, Inc., 1962.

Kindred, Leslie W., and Prince B. Woodard, *Staff Welfare Practices in the Public Schools,* Washington, D.C.: The Center for Applied Research in Education, Inc., 1963.

Lindenfeld, Frank, "Teacher Turnover in Public Elementary and Secondary Schools, 1959-1960," United States Office of Education, Circular No. 675, 1963.

Mayer, Martin, "How to Get the Best Teachers for Your Schools," *Better Homes and Gardens,* 16, October, 1964.

Morse, G. D., "Are Teacher Associations Playing the Game Squarely?" *American School Board Journal,* CXLVII, October, 1963.

National Education Association, Research Bulletin, "Teacher Tenure Laws Benefit Teachers in 37 States," XXXVIII No. 3, October, 1960.

Nigro, Felix A., *Public Personnel Administration,* New York: Holt, Rinehart, and Winston, Inc., 1959.

Potter, Curtis J., "Motivating Long-Service Employees," *Supervision,* XXVI, August, 1964.

Redefer, Frederick L., "A Teacher Teaches Better . . . " *NEA Journal,* April, 1964.

School Management, "Should You Have a Teacher Orientation Program?" May, 1963.

Shipley, Joseph T., *The Mentally Disturbed Teacher,* Philadelphia: Chilton Company Book Division, 1961.

Steffenson, James P., "Staff Personnel Administration." Washington, D.C.: United States Office of Education, Bulletin 1963, No. 6.

Staehle, John F., "Characteristics of Administrative Handbooks for School Staff Personnel, Bulletin, 1960, No. 13, Washington, D.C.: United States Office of Education.

Van Zwoll, James A., *School Personnel Administration,* New York: Appleton-Century-Crofts, 1964.

Von Haden, H.I., "Is a Teaching Contract a One-Way Street?" *NEA Journal,* LI, No. 2, February, 1962.

Washburne, Carleton, *A Living Philosophy of Education,* New York: The John Day Company, 1940.

Windrow, James, "Why Teacher Recruiting Fails," *School Management.*

Wynn, D. R. and R. W. DeRemer, "Staff Utilization, Development and Evaluation," Review of Educational Research, XXXI, October, 1961.

Chapter 10

Organization and Administration of the Instructional Program

Any work devoted to educational administration could appropriately confine its major attention to learning and teaching. Such is the exclusiveness of school administration as compared with executive activity in other organizations. All administrators of schools are instructional officers, directly or indirectly; all need to be versed in the purposes, techniques, and trends of curriculum. All administrative decisions in schools have at the top of their value scale the learning of boys and girls. Administrators in larger systems differ from each other only in the immediacy with which their decisions and actions relate to classroom instruction. Because of the specialization of administrative tasks in city systems, the job definitions of some administrators may require that their efforts be aimed more at the supplementing forces for classroom instruction; for example, the business manager who is responsible for maintenance of instructional equipment or the accounting for instructional expenses. Nonetheless, the underlying rationale for the task is instruction. Thus, it may be said that some school administrators are merely more instructional officers than others.

Despite the importance of curriculum for all administrators, this book does not purport to be a curriculum treatise; bountiful and excellent volumes on this subject are already available. The educational administrative student will be well immersed in the curriculum of elementary and secondary schools before he completes his preparation, if indeed, he has not already been so bathed. The assumption is made here that the student is knowledgeable of past and prevailing trends in purposes of learning, methodology, and content of one or more subject-matter areas. Curriculum will be treated only from the administrator's point of view: the organization and direction of efforts designed to promote good learning.

ORGANIZATION FOR INSTRUCTION

There are many important decisions to be made about the optimal organization of curriculum content, pupils, teachers, time, and facilities for best learning, most of which are guided by point of view rather than by researched fact. Concepts within the profession vary perhaps even more than they do in that aggressive and sizeable circle of critics of the schools. The influence of conflicting philosophies is so extensive in the schools across the nation that the degree of similarity among graduates is surprising. This variety may be attributed largely to the autonomy of school districts permitted under the pattern of "local control"; hence, the hue and cry from some critics to nationalize the curriculum so that all of the country's children may enjoy the one best learning program. Until that one best program can be found and agreed upon, grounded on something stronger than conjecture, the autonomous and variegated approach remains clearly superior. Here at least, experimentation and innovation are possible.

Educators can agree only that instruction should be good. They disagree even on the definition of the curriculum, the viewpoints ranging by degrees from the extreme "set of isolated facts to be memorized" to the extreme "every experience to which a child is subjected while under the influence of the school." There is no agreement on the essentials for learning. There are violent disagreements as to whether the content or the process of learning is more valuable for a pupil. There are marked differences of opinion as to who should determine the curriculum. There is not even concord about the purposes of the curriculum, or of schools.

Notwithstanding the division in attitude toward all aspects of instruction, the administrator, with the aid of personnel, is expected somehow to organize the school day, the year, the people, the facilities, and the experiences to produce the optimal learning. In an effort to avoid further dilution of viewpoints, this author has no desire to impose his views upon the reader; rather, he will set forth the issues and trends in organizational patterns and the approaches to instructional administration.

The conflicts start with the organization of content. Earliest organizational patterns sought to arrange knowledge in a chronological or "logical" order. No one can dispute the need for orderliness in learning; this would be simple to attain if all children learned in the same way, but what is logical to some minds is illogical to others. Schools have had about equal success in presenting historical materials in successive and regressive chronological order. Under the approach of presenting knowledge according to principles of readiness for learning, schools have pegged packages of facts according to grade levels, only to discover lately that children can learn these facts at earlier ages. Other approaches have sought to identify youthful needs and to build the curriculum around those needs, ignoring the isolated packages and the time for receiving them. Many proponents of this view have wilted lately under the fire of critics who have called such tactics "no organization"; a slight trend returns to "packaging." Until there is better agreement on goals and improved means for evaluating the product, today's administrator has his choice of patterns without going very far wrong, or right.

The issue of grouping youngsters still stimulates great differences in viewpoint. From the beginnings of mass public education, children have been grouped primarily by age: the age for commencing school is determined arbitrarily, and pupils advance annually at the same rate if they accomplish arbitrarily determined standards, producing the "ladder system" of education which is peculiarly American. During the twentieth century of deliberate study of learning, grouping practices have been influenced by other factors: ability, achievement, sex, and vocational interests. These considerations have led to groupings which extend beyond a classroom or a single building on the secondary level to dissuade school officials in city systems from the comprehensiveness of the large high school toward specialized high schools for vocational or ability groupings, or to a few instances of separate buildings for boys and girls.

One of the most rapidly developing organizational groupings of the mid-20th century has resulted from the concern for various types of handicaps which affect learning. Out of this concern for the obstructions to the atypical child's learning caused by a system of education geared to the typical learner has emerged the gigantic field known as "special education" with groupings, especially trained teachers, and special equipment for children with a variety of physical, mental, and emotional disturbances. Even the exceptionally alert or advanced child is handicapped in the "normal" classroom, giving rise lately to the numerous groupings for the "gifted."

Viewpoints are sharply divided over the merits of a heterogeneous or homogeneous grouping of pupils, but the probability is that organizations which recognize the likenesses and differences of children will spread rather than diminish.

Groupings of pupils and teachers have received more attention in recent years through the application of new learning devices, the worth of which is still dubious but improving. The use of television and mechanical teaching equipment could affect grouping dramatically. Likewise, the development of teaching by teams, an idea not totally unlike the nineteenth century Lancastrian or monitorial organization, could substantially change traditional views of organization. If successful, these innovations will probably have the greatest impact on the hallowed notions of class size. The profession has seemed to settle on the contention that thirty pupils per class is a practical compromise between economy and a teacher's capacity to deal with individual differences. Instructional television, programmed learnings, and team teaching are bringing educators to the threshold of a breakthrough which recognizes that class sizes need not be uniform, that some learnings can be accomplished efficiently in groups of a hundred or more and that other learnings must be handled in groups of five to ten.

Educators also debate over the division of the pupil's entire education into units of several years each. The prevailing 8-4 pattern of the previous century resulted merely from stacking four years of the old academy onto eight years of common school. In an effort to discourage youth from leaving school upon the completion of the 8th grade, early twentieth century innovators were led into a 6-3-3 plan with the hope that the junior high school would gradually and successfully ease youngsters into a departmentalized senior high school. The half-century of experience with the junior high, with many efforts to find a special curriculum to meet the developmental and learning needs of the pre-adolescent, has not generated wide satisfaction. A middle school for grades five through eight is currently receiving some attention. Adding two more grades at the top of the ladder in some regions of the country has produced 6-4-4 and 8-4-2 organizations. A variety of other organizations may be found — 6-2-2-2, 7-1-5, 5-4-3, or similar combinations — most of which are motivated by housing conveniences rather than learning philosophies. The greatest perplexity, arising from not knowing what to do with the seventh and eighth grades, is complicated by historical beliefs that those grades should be used for review of the fundamentals and by newer beliefs favoring exploratory experiences on that level. Until better methods and evidence are uncovered, the 6-3-3 plan will undoubtedly continue to be the most popular organization in larger school districts because of the building flexibility which a middle school offers for meeting the changing population demands over the years. An in-between school can be easily and economically converted to either a high school or an elementary school.

A school system's organization is also influenced by other curricular concepts. A commitment to self-contained classrooms in the lower grades necessitates a different organization of subject matter, pupils, staff, materials and facilities than does the departmentalized approach to teaching. Organization is influenced by the staff's beliefs as to the best time to begin learning new subject matter. Reference is made not only to organization for kindergarten and nursery school but also to the trend to commence science, foreign language and complicated mathematics instruction earlier today. The availability of audio-visual materials, libraries, and supplementary instructional tools will influence organization. The effects of a school's marking, promotional practices, and progress reporting on its organization are evident. A faculty's beliefs about the value of related learnings — music, art, physical development, and the host of "extra-curriculars" which are sponsored in modern schools — has an impact on organization. Even the organization of the daily calendar into periods of learning and the over-all length of the day is changed by varying concepts of how children learn.

There are organizational problems stemming from the school district's degree of participation in summer and post-high school programs. At the opposite end of the ladder, educators have generally accepted kindergartens as part of the organizational plan for learning. However, they are not included in many rural and poor districts primarily because of limited financial resources. A few districts add a nursery school to the ladder before the year of kindergarten. Some metropolitan districts have recently developed special pre-school experiences as a compensatory device for overcoming the lack of home motivation in families popularly labeled as "culturally disadvantaged."

Concern for the pre-school youngster is stirring re-examination of another sacred organizational belief of educators — the age for commencing formal schooling. In an effort to maintain order in the handling of thousands of children, school districts have established cut-off points for entering kindergarten or first grade. Some states have adopted a standard age limitation for all elementary schools of the state, following the persuasion of educators to ease delicate admission problems where neighboring districts have different age limits. The uniform admission age denies basic principles of individual differences and readiness for learning. Courageous school districts, therefore, are experimenting with criteria of maturity and ability for starting formalized education rather than the single criterion of chronological age.

ORGANIZATION FOR STIMULATING CURRICULUM AND INSTRUCTIONAL IMPROVEMENT

The aspect of a school's curriculum which has captured the most attention of writers, university professors, researchers, practicing teachers and administrators, and even the critics of education, is that of curriculum change and improvement. The once-upon-a-time view that the ideal curriculum could be developed and "let alone" vanished with changes well beyond the control of teachers, occurring mostly in the nation's economic structure. The term economics is used here in the broad sense to include not only income and working conditions but also family life, moral standards, politics, and international relationships. These changes have altered the needs of youngsters so as to influence the function, hence the curriculum of education. The efforts of educators at all levels have been directed largely to effecting changes in the learning experiences to keep pace with the swiftly moving changes outside the classroom.

Schools have employed a variety of organizational efforts in order to keep curriculum revision moving. The most common approach is at the local level through conferences, workshops, or similar sessions lumped together under the over-worked term — "in-service education." Utilizing the special talent available within the school system, or importing curriculum specialists from the university and state departments of education, time is allocated from the regular school calendar or during the summer months to study ways for modernizing content and methodology. Or schools may send their teachers to county, regional, state, and national conferences of special-interest groups or general educational meetings. School districts also encourage their teachers to return to the campus for up-dating their preparation; the more aggressive districts find ways to reimburse participants for the cost involved. The periodic adoption of new textbooks provides an excellent springboard for re-examining the curriculum.

A movement of the past quarter-century toward the same goal is the employment of curriculum specialists to aid teachers in self-improvement, such as consultants, resource teachers, coordinators, teaching aides, or collaborating teachers. Along with this movement has come the changing role of the supervisor to correspond more to the function of a resource person for ideas, materials, services, and latest developments. He works both with individual teachers and with groups. Expansion of the district's professional library also contributes to the cause of modernization.

One of the most promising recent developments to assist school systems toward solid curriculum improvement is the adaptation of appropriate research techniques in evaluating change. Observers of the educational scene are critically aware of the tendency to effect curriculum change for its own sake, or merely to keep up with the Joneses in neighboring districts. Educators have always suffered from their inability to measure objectively the worth of different curricula. Electronics and research have helped to reverse this trend. Charitable foundations which are funding many of the research projects and the new government moneys for the same purpose should stimulate innovation. The number of experimental projects underway in the public schools scattered across the land and the growing number of educational research technicians in the employ of public schools are bases for pride, enough to justify the trend toward abandoning many of the separate experimental schools of a previous era.

The organizational decision to determine the best way to supervise teacher performance still plagues administrators. Their conflicting opinions are evident as one observes practices in many districts. For most of this century the predominant view called for supervisors working out of the central office, as either subject-matter specialists or general supervisors. This approach came under considerable fire during the 1940's and 1950's as teachers enjoyed deriding these officers under the appellation of "snoopervisors." Though still widely used, doubt grows about the effectiveness of this approach, admitting that most school districts can never afford enough of them to provide the full-time help needed by many teachers. There is even a too-popular notion that central office supervisors constitute the "eyes and ears" of the superintendent, carrying tales to him which result in penalties for the classroom teacher. Furthermore, teachers were often confused as to whose direction they should follow — the principal's or the supervisor's.

During these same two decades professional literature has been calling persistently for building principals to take over the responsibility for supervising and evaluating teaching effectiveness. It is true that the principal is in the best position of any administrator to view a teacher's total performance and render help — if he is competent and not overburdened by office duties. Until lately however, many of the nation's principals have been elevated directly from the classroom, and hesitate to suggest ideas for improvement except to those who teach in the principal's specialty field. Some have not even availed themselves of the professional knowledge which would aid them in supervising classroom general techniques. Moreover, the principal of a large school rarely has a sufficient force of specialized assistants working under his jurisdiction to allow him time to spend in classroom supervision. The trend toward decentralizing autonomy to the individual building is far ahead of the trend toward providing that building with assisting personnel.

Another approach to supervision which is popular in city high schools, then, is the use of department heads. This is probably the most realistic solution to the problem if department heads are released from classroom and administrative tasks long enough to satisfy supervisory demands, trained for the task, and selected on the same criteria of competence for other curriculum leaders.

The proper way to provide supervision has become such a stormy issue in recent years that some observers are questioning its usefulness. Much of the faculty has always resisted it, not so much because of its dubious need but because of the way it is provided. To be sure, the extent of its need may diminish as teachers become better trained. Some educators point to the college and university faculties where, for the most part, supervision does not exist, presumably under the contention that there are no experts available who could assist such highly specialized teachers. Others are quick to explain that the lack of supervision in higher education accounts for the extent of poor teaching at that level. If the contention that highly specialized teachers do not need supervision is valid, the standard approaches to supervision in elementary and secondary schools may be drastically revised as those teachers become experts through increasing preparatory and certification requirements. Since that happy day does not appear imminent, the value of some kind of supervisory aid is likely to be accepted for many years. The troublesome decision is — what kind?

EVALUATION OF TEACHING EFFECTIVENESS

This next area of supervision, evaluating a teacher's effectiveness, poses more refined difficulties. Again, the conceptual disagreements arise more from its use than from its need. Only the most insecure teachers would deny that evaluation of performance is essential; only the most naive would deny that the process occurs in some form. The most able teachers suffer more from lack of evaluation. The greatest objections to evaluation have sprung from its use as a means of introducing salary differentials to develop acceptable merit pay plans. The organizational decisions, then, resolve around who should evaluate teacher performance and under what criteria.

While neither of these decisions has universal agreements among members of the profession, it is generally acknowledged today that the most valid judgments of performance result from pooled efforts. Since evaluation of teaching must rely mostly upon subjective judgments, fairness and justice are likely to be more nearly attained if several persons render those judgments. Certainly the building principal should be represented; other instructional officers should also be involved. Colleagues of the person being judged can contribute some thoughts in the realm of camaraderie on the staff but they are not normally in a position to appraise classroom performance. As much as one might wish that evaluation could be divorced from supervision, it is unsophisticated to expect this. A consultant motivated only by the mission of helping a teacher cannot avoid forming opinions about that teacher's effectiveness. Indeed, the "helping teacher" cannot even commence offering positive suggestions for improvement without detecting faults. Whether or not the supervisor could make a vow of secrecy, or whether teachers could avoid being suspicious of the supervisor's secret knowledge, or whether the knowledge about a teacher's effectiveness which the supervisor obtains ought to be kept silent — all these problems demand a negative answer. It may be concluded that the supervisory assistance will be, and ought to be, part of the team which pools opinions about performance.

The criteria employed for appraising performance should grow out of the accepted aims of the school system. Once these purposes are established, it is not too difficult to select the items which will be used for measuring success. Those persons to be evaluated will be more inclined to accept the measuring elements if they participate in their selection. The determination of evaluative items provides school administrators with one of their best vehicles for democratic administration and group decision-making. If members of the educational profession cannot agree upon aims and the devices for measuring attainment of those aims, one is forced to conclude that there is so much mystery surrounding the teaching-learning process that it ought to be abandoned. Whether the criteria are expressed in lists of objective items, scales of degree, or just in prose is not of major significance. In either case, subjective judgment is required, and the subjective acumen of experienced, fair-minded administrators has been much maligned and under-rated. If such officers cannot render highly accurate assessments about teaching success, then the hoarded knowledge of several generations of teachers and administrators is of small avail.

ORGANIZATION OF THE INSTRUCTIONAL DEPARTMENT

The superintendent and principals are the only officers in small school districts who handle responsibilities for curriculum stimulation and evaluation. As districts grow in size, the instructional task is either the first or second to be delegated to subordinates. Reflection upon the burden of the load which curriculum responsibilities carry, as briefly described in this chapter, explains why a superintendent is prone to transfer them away from his immediate jurisdiction. He cannot possibly give sufficient time to this vital activity without neglecting some of his other duties. Some superintendents consider curriculum development so important that they may delegate other tasks and maintain personal responsibility for instructional affairs.

When a district becomes large enough to justify the creation of a full department of instruction, perhaps in a district with approximately 10,000 pupils, the chief instructional officer is likely to carry the title of

Assistant Superintendent. A district may prefer the title of Director of Instruction, but certainly this officer will rank in the second echelon of command, directly accountable to the superintendent. The number of personnel allocated to the office will depend upon the customary factors of size, district wealth, and assigned duties. A well staffed office will have several supervisors, coordinators of special education, adult education, summer school, and audio-visual materials, and probably those charged with research and duties relating to extra-curricular activities. Any function directly related to instruction is customarily assigned to this department. It is natural that the departmental executive would also coordinate the work of librarians, department heads, and any other personnel who might have special duties pertaining to the curriculum.

The bill of responsibilities written for this officer will hold him accountable for all matters in the school system clearly falling in the realm of learning. He would be charged with the progress of curriculum matters throughout the school system but, as recommended in Chapter 2, he would act in an advisory role when dealing with any one of the principals.

CURRICULAR IMPLICATIONS PERVADE ALL
ADMINISTRATIVE DECISIONS

Despite the conflict and uncertainty about the proper way to organize a school system for learning, an administrator is employed to make the decisions, or at least to see that decisions are made. Nearly all of the major decisions he makes are related to his understandings, or the school-community's understandings, of what good curriculum is, how children learn, or how ideas, people, and things can be organized to achieve the goals. The present text, as well as other administrative books, separates the conduct of a school system into the seemingly divisible tasks of instruction, finance, business management, personnel, pupil personnel, and others. And yet the performance of the "non-instructional" tasks is related to, and performed for, the teacher's work with pupils.

The personnel function is thought of as an isolated administrative responsibility, but it is performed in terms of the administrator's views about the curriculum. The type of teachers sought for the school district is recruited in terms of the administrator's beliefs about how teaching will take place. If the administrator believes in a child-centered, self-contained, problem-solving curriculum in which knowledges are constantly interrelated he will certainly not employ teachers imbued with compartmentalized views about imparting knowledge.

School building construction is regarded as an administrative task, but the type of building erected will be determined by the administrator's understandings about the best setting for learning. Although school finance is an administrative responsibility, the amount of money needed will be determined by the kind of curriculum conducted. It will cost the taxpayers considerably more money to have a laboratory, activity type of program than a lecture-discussion class session. Purchasing is clearly an administrative task, but the supplies and equipment bought will be determined by the understandings of how learning occurs. Supervision — which is not clearly administrative or instructional — must, at least, be performed by persons in addition to the classroom teacher. The type of supervision provided will be determined by its considered purpose and usefulness. The provision of special services to pupils — psychological, medical, guidance, testing, attendance — will be governed by administrators' beliefs about what children need in order to learn.

Even how the principal or superintendent spends his time will be determined by his understandings of instructional matters. If he believes that there is a single curriculum or methodology which will satisfy instructional needs he will set about putting it into practice and then relax with executive chores. His role will become quite different, however, if he perceives the role of an administrator as that of an investigator, innovator, or stimulator of better learning methods.

This is another example of the job centeredness of school administration. It explains why a successful administrator in another kind of corporation may not be equally successful as an educational administrator. It also explains why a school administrator must not only know the specialized tasks of administration but also be deeply grounded in understandings of curriculum, learning, and values.

THE SCHOOL CURRICULUM . . .

CURRICULUM TERMINOLOGY*

The modern concept of curriculum is that it consists of the whole of the interacting forces of the environment provided for pupils by the school and the experiences that pupils have in that environment. It is

---

*Vernon E. Anderson and William T. Gruhn, *Principles and Practices of Secondary Education,* Second Edition, Copyright © 1962, The Ronald Press Company, 105-107.

the school's job to plan and direct worthwhile activities that will help develop the type of behavior outlined in its objectives. The *quality* of the pupil's experience is the important factor. Definitely, the curriculum is not the inert material in the pages of a course of study. It is, instead, the things children do, plan, write, read, construct, talk about, react to, and think about. It includes their field trips, extraclass experiences, student council activities, the study of the community that they make, farm projects in connection with their agriculture courses, and work experience under school supervision. All these are significant learning experiences planned by the school to further the growth of pupils.

The *course of study* is a more limited term than curriculum, since it refers to the outline, bulletin, or written plan that serves as a guide to the activities that the teacher will plan for and with the pupils. It is not difficult to visualize how unlike the experiences might be for two groups of pupils under different teachers, different in temperament and background but following the same course of study. The modern term used frequently for published courses is "curriculum guide."

A *curriculum improvement program* refers to the plan of action adopted by a school, a state, or a committee in order to consider ways of providing better experiences for pupils. A school usually selects some phase of the curriculum for study by the faculty for the year, or over a period of years. "Curriculum revision," "curriculum building," "curriculum development program" are other terms used. In the past, some subject in the curriculum was invariably selected as the topic for study. In recent years, when school people have begun to think of the curriculum in terms of experiences provided for pupils, schools are more frequently attacking any significant problems that deal with the improvement of instruction and content. Generally, such study has yielded good results in actually improving the kinds of experiences that children and adolescents have. Examples of these types of problems studied in secondary schools follow:

1. Selecting instructional materials that promote good human relations and understanding of other pupils
2. Developing a program for the academically talented
3. Planning improved content in junior high school mathematics
4. Studying factors connected with underachievement
5. Making follow-up studies of secondary school drop-outs and graduates
6. Developing means of encouraging creativity in many fields
7. Using the community for pupil experiences
8. Experimenting with a research approach in industrial arts
9. Examining the best means of preparation for college

General education is the basic education needed by all youth in order to become effective, participating citizens who live fruitful lives and who have broad interests and concerns in humanity and the products of man's mind. The learnings essential for a general education are sometimes called "common learnings." These are the learnings considered important for intelligent citizens, competent members of a family, and well-disciplined individuals. Thus, the social studies, humanities, the sciences, and arts are considered vehicles through which activities in general education are planned. For example, in a democracy it is considered essential that people know how to make decisions based on facts and how to carry on discussions and social action as members of a civic group. Activities planned to promote these outcomes are a part of general education.

The *core curriculum* is a specific form or organization of the curriculum that cuts across subject fields and includes a greater block of time in the school day than the usual period. It refers to a way in which some of the important aspects of general education are organized within the secondary school curriculum. The core curriculum is a way of organizing some of the important experiences in the curriculum, centering around the problem-solving approach, using social and personal problems and other content significant to youth, and selecting subject matter from various areas to develop desirable behaviors. Usually English and the social studies are fused in the core, and the guidance function is always a part of the core. But since it consists of basic behavior patterns common to all and is based upon problem situations, it is not a mere fusing of subject matter. . . .

Block time refers to an organization of schedule in which a longer period of time is blocked for the same group of students, usually in English and social studies, permitting correlation or use of aspects of the core. Other terms sometimes used in educational literature as synonymous with core curriculum are "unified studies," "general education," "basic program," "integrated English — social-studies curriculum."

SOURCES OF THE CURRICULUM*

Even though the total environment of the child is his curriculum, there is much that the school can do about influences, such as providing

---

*Reprinted by permission from Jean D. Grambs and L. Morris McClure, *Foundations of Teaching,* Copyright © 1964, by Holt, Rinehart and Winston, Inc., 168-171.

esthetically stimulating classrooms as against ugly or distracting ones, but an important distinction must be made. *The proper and unique function of the school is to convey and make available to learners those knowledges and skills that our society deems important for children and youth to acquire.* Furthermore, this leads inescapably to the conclusion that the orientation of education is intellectual. The school alone is charged with the task of dealing with things of the mind: ideas. The mind cannot be dissociated from nonintellectual influences, such as feelings and emotions and physiological states, and these are factors of which the school must be aware. But this awareness of all the other influences upon the learner and what he will learn takes place, in fact, *after* we have sorted out and identified and put in order the content of learning — the intellectual content.

A look at the history of education shows that most of the actual content of education was inherited. Schools always taught this and that, so they continued to do so. Change was very slow. Non-functional subjects were modified or dropped slowly. Other subjects were added reluctantly, often decades or even centuries after their social need was apparent. Not until the early part of this century, with the development of the scientific study of man, did we begin to make some self-conscious decisions about what ought to be taught. The debate has raged ever since.

The *Seven Cardinal Principles of Education* can be said to mark the new era in education. These principles, published in 1918, state not only the purposes of education, but also clearly state what the curriculum should include. Although these principles applied originally to the curriculum of the secondary school, they also express the general philosophy of the scope of the common school. The school, according to the Committee of Ten, which developed the Seven Cardinal Principles, should strive to educate a youth in health, command of fundamental processes, worthy home membership, vocation, citizenship, worthy use of leisure time, and ethical character. Here, then, was one statement of the scope of education. The principles identify what subject matter should be included — and not very much is excluded.

If *scope* is important, what about sequence, the order in which learnings must occur? Curriculum development moved ahead as educators began to see that what were needed were decisions along two axes of the chart — *what* should be taught, and *when* it should be taught. Under the leadership of Hollis L. Caswell of Teachers College, Columbia University, scope and sequence studies were inaugurated. One of the most famous was that developed for the state of Virginia during the 1930's. Here was spelled out the content appropriate for the school, and the level at which each segment should be taught. The underlying philosophy of this procedure indicated two major bases for curriculum selection: the needs of the individual in society, and the developmental stage of the child. Thus scope included not just the traditional subject matter, but that subject matter as seen in terms of social reality and understanding, and what was to be taught was specified in terms of what was accepted as known about the general level of readiness of children at any given age level.

The Virginia curriculum of the 1930's is the grandfather of much that is done today. We have become more knowledgeable about children and the idea of "developmental tasks" as described elsewhere in this book. We have had to modify our notions about social reality, also, because the world of the child is far different today from what it was in the pre-TV, pre-Sputnik era. . . .

Another significant pressure on the curriculum comes from the social reality around us. In a time of frenetic technological change, such as is occurring in the computer and automation advances of industry today, the schools face educational demands that are unique to this time. Adult education is called upon to retrain workers for entirely new kinds of positions, or doom them to unemployment. The effect of Russian excellence in outer space has placed unprecedented pressure on all levels of schooling to make mathematical and scientific understandings more general, and to raise the level of competence of the most able in these areas as fast as possible. The vastly increased travel of Americans abroad and the extensive programs of aid and information engaged in by the government of the United States have made it necessary for the ordinary citizen to be better informed about the world he lives in and also more able to converse with people in a foreign language. The rapidly expanding programs in foreign language instruction are a response to such drastic new views of society and its needs.

But the curriculum is not infinitely flexible. After a certain point the school day is full. Then anything else added means that something else must be removed or slighted. The struggle of curriculum personnel today — all teachers in the last analysis — is that of achieving balance. To teach well *all* that ought to be taught to *all* children and youth and also to teach what is helpful but not crucial involves everyone in a continual process of judgment and decision making. Would you say it [is] more important to teach understanding of other cultures or Hamlet? Should time be spent on helping youngsters to understand how to budget or to learn the definitions of latitude and longitude? Example after example can be cited to illustrate the kinds of choices curriculum workers face as they struggle with tremendously increasing cultural and factual resources while they view a school day that remains the same size.

BELIEFS ABOUT THE AMERICAN HIGH SCHOOL*

By legislation, the citizens of the United States have made universal education available to all youth through the high school years, and in many states they have made attendance compulsory to eighteen years of age.

The American high school, therefore, must provide youth with experiences which continuously increase the personal, social and vocational competencies needed in our society.

The American high school must provide education for all youth in the community assigned to it through the legal authority of the community.

To maintain individual freedom of choice, each youth must be free to select his vocational goals and to pursue a high school program leading to them.

PROGRAM OF THE HIGH SCHOOL

The secondary school must serve a dual role.

The secondary school should be a comprehensive school.

Certain types of growth must be promoted in all youth who attend the secondary school.

The secondary school must provide a wide range of experience through class and nonclass activities.

The program for each student should be planned on an individual basis.

The program for each individual must contain general education and specialized education.

One-third to one-half of each student's program should be devoted to general education.

One-half to two-thirds of each student's program should be used to develop his talents and to further his personal goals within the framework that the community is willing and able to support.

Any elective course should be available to any qualified student regardless of his grade level.

---

*Kimball Wiles and Franklin Patterson, condensed from "The High School We Need." Copyright © 1959, by the Association for Supervision and Curriculum Development, 2-17.

The testing and guidance program of the school should help each pupil and his parents secure a reliable estimate of this ability and his achievement level.

Choices among the various offerings of the curriculum should be made jointly by the pupil, parents and staff members of the school in terms of the pupil's purpose, aptitude and level of achievement.

The individual's program should be evaluated each year and revised to provide for change in purpose and more accurate estimates of level of ability.

Each student should have one staff member who guides him throughout his high school career.

Each high school student should be a member of at least one home base group with which he has a continuing relationship.

Students should be grouped in various ways in different phases of their high school experience.

The American high school should utilize the new resources for instruction that derive from our culture's rapidly developing technology.

High school schedules should make a wide range of learning experiences possible, rather than forcing activities to conform to a rigid sequence of short periods.

Each high school faculty should develop an organization which guarantees continuous evaluation and planning and coordination of the total program.

The physical organization of a desirable school structure helps make it possible for students to have close relationships with administrators, teachers and other students they know well.

BALANCE IN THE CURRICULUM*

A conception of what "balance" means in the curriculum is a necessity in any time. In these days of upheaval in education, however, such a conception is an urgent necessity. It is possible that the new curriculum patterns, when they have emerged, will prove to be in better balance than anything we have known. However, taken as a whole, it could be that the new curriculum will imply a distorted version of our culture, of our ideals as a people, even of what we want an American to be. This has

*Balance in the Curriculum. Copyright © 1961 by the Association for Supervision and Curriculum Development. From Introduction to the 1961 Yearbook by ASCD President, Arthur W. Foshay, pp. iii and iv.

happened in the past, at those times when it has become apparent that the existing curriculum no longer fitted the times. The changes have not always proved to be improvements; sometimes, despite the best efforts of wise men, the result has been only to substitute one distortion for another.

It seems clear enough that the curriculum as it has been during the past generation does not fit the present time. Whatever its merits are or were, the context is sufficiently changed to require a changed curriculum. It is not yet clear what the changes will be, although some elements appear likely to endure: a new conception of intellectual development, reflected in reconceived subject matter; a re-examination of the teacher's function; a considerable increase in the breadth of educational materials; greater flexibility and variation in school organization and in a student's progress through school; a considerably increased sophistication of testing procedures; more and better school guidance. At the same time, little further attention is being given to the other elements that have been introduced in the schools since World War I: recognition of the implied as well as the overt social learnings the school teaches; the relationship between the various aspects of human development — intellectual, emotional, aesthetic, social, biological, spiritual; social usefulness as a criterion for the selection of subject matter; education as life as well as preparation for life; the place of the school in the array of social institutions that deal with all people.

Generally speaking (and we have to speak generally about these matters, given the present state of knowledge), curriculum designers want the curriculum to respect all of these considerations: the intellectual, the humane, the social. If it does not, the curriculum is out of balance.

SOME QUESTIONS THAT NEED ASKING ABOUT EDUCATION*

What possible grounds are there for believing that education should begin at six or four or three, while before that something different, called child rearing or socialization, takes place? Why is it of value to society to gather children together under outside tutelage that will supplement the home when they are five but not earlier? If this is a statement about children's toleration of group experience or their experience away from

---

*Margaret Mead, "Questions That Need Asking," New York: by permission of *Teachers College Record*, LXIII (November 1961), 89-93.

mothering adults, how do we know that organized stimulating experience, for mother *and* child, should not be provided? It is wholly possible that the fundamental aptitudes for being able to handle mathematics or to play chess, with their accompanying abilities to plan and anticipate, are learned under two.

Similarly, what is the real basis of our present belief that children should be taught how to read *in school*? Originally, reading was taught as an apprenticeship skill by one who could read to one who wanted to learn. It was only when societies wished to change the proportions of literacy within a generation that schools were needed in which the children of non-literate parents could be taught in bunches. But today America's is an almost completely literate society. Why shouldn't mothers, who spend all day with their children, teach them to read, to understand money, to think about numbers, to understand the calendar, the clock, time, space? Now that these are the necessary requirements for a full humanity, just as walking and talking and understanding kinship relations and the local terrain were once the requirements for a full humanity, why can't all such essentials be taught at home? Do we know why not?

What proportions and what parts of the knowledge a child must have today should be taught in school? To brush their teeth? Won't TV and radio and box tops do the job? Geography? Doesn't the weather map for the United States on television every morning and night do a better job than the average school? Small children now learn to divide up the day by TV shows long before they learn about clock time, which can then be slipped in. These are merely passing examples to emphasize that we haven't for a very long time really asked fundamental questions of this sort. Which learning, at which time, by what methods belong in our schools? And how much school work should be done in groups, where error is steadily compounded and children are exposed to each other's determination not to learn French and not to get the examples right? At what ages and for what subjects is group learning appropriate? Which classes should have a wide range of intelligence, or of different kinds of intelligence? Which a narrow range? Which classes should contain chronological agemates, which mental agemates, which physical agemates, which emotional agemates? Our solution to each of these questions has been a blanket answer which has disregarded the others.

Why should learning a minimum be a right, but learning a maximum amount be a privilege? Why isn't the student who works at his studies as much a member of the working group as any boy who gets a job as a bookkeeper or a garage mechanic? Why should we perpetuate the outworn notions that higher education is for the rich who can afford it and the poor with very superior intellects, instead of its being a right and a duty — as a citizen in a country — for everyone to develop his potentialities to the full? Attending an institution of higher learning without either the mentality or the interest to take advantage of the expensive facilities that the generosity and savings of other generations has made possible should be a luxury and should be paid for heavily. But using them as they were meant to be used and for their clear social purposes should be both a right and a duty.

Why should we demand the same prerequisite steps for individuals of different ages with different abilities and motivations? Why can't we have different expectations for the boy with an IQ of 140 who has coasted through poor schools until he is in the 10th grade at 17 but, once enlisted in the Navy, gets his high school certificate in three months, and the girl who graduated from a foreign lycee ten years ago and has become a skilled surgical technician, ready to tackle high level research but who is at present separated from any chance of doing so by seven years of required academic work? Why can't we set up a system in which the emotional, social, and recreational aspects of age-grading are taken care of in other ways than schooling, and we have a variety of routes towards learning a new language or more mathematics or acquiring an academic degree that is prerequisite to a useful career?

But just at the moment when it is urgent that we attain the greatest degree of flexibility in our educational system and use our teachers to teach the new, special skills that will be needed for the future, we are hardening rather than loosening up our bureaucratic requirements.

What would happen if we asked, absolutely freshly, why in the 1960's we should have schools at all, and for what, instead of involving ourselves over and over in pendulum swings between one hoary and unsatisfactory solution and its opposite?

ORGANIZATION FOR INSTRUCTION . . .

THE TERMINOLOGY OF SCHOOL
ORGANIZATION*

Is team teaching more effective than nongrading in providing for individual differences? Is ability grouping superior to grading in fostering

---

*John I. Goodlad, and Kenneth Rehage, "Unscrambling the Vocabulary of School Organization," *NEA Journal,* LI (November, 1962), 34-36. By permission of National Education Association.

academic achievement? Is heterogeneous grouping preferable to depart-
mentalizing?

Such questions frequently are asked about the variety of procedures
available for organizing schools. These questions would be asked less
often if there were general agreement on a common understanding of the
terms describing school organization. Team teaching, for instance, is not
an alternative to non-grading. These terms describe different ways to
fulfill two separate functions of school organization. Ability-grouping can
be used whether or not a school is graded, and a departmentalized school
can have either heterogeneous or homogeneous grouping.

SOURCES OF CONFUSION

Schools are organized to serve specific functions. They must classify
students and move them upward from a point of admission to a point of
departure. *Vertical* organization serves this function. Schools also must
divide the student body among available teachers. *Horizontal* organization serves this second function.

Confusion arises from a failure to differentiate between vertical and
horizontal aspects of school organization. Grading, multigrading, and
nongrading are the vertical organization plans from which to choose. The
horizontal pattern may be determined by grouping children homogeneously or heterogeneously, by organizing the curriculum so as to emphasize
the separateness of subjects or the interrelationships among them, by
having self-contained or departmentalized classrooms, or by using any
one of many possible patterns of interclass grouping.

The remainder of this article will look further into the differences
between vertical and horizontal plans of school organization.

VERTICAL SCHOOL ORGANIZATION

Grading has been the traditional way of organizing schools for the
vertical progression of students. For example, an elementary school
enrolling children aged five to twelve, is divided into seven year-long
steps, starting with kindergarten and going successively through grades
one to six. A rather specific body of subject matter is assigned to each
grade level; textbooks are prepared for the grade; teachers are cate-
gorized as "first-grade" or "fifth-grade" teachers; and children refer to
themselves as being in the "second grade" or going into the "sixth
grade." The pieces fit together in an orderly fashion with a year of work
for a grade of vertical progress through the school as the common
denominator.

The graded system, long the predominant scheme of vertical school organization, is often criticized for ignoring individual differences among learners by demanding that all children cover the same material at approximately the same rate of speed. Those children who fail to keep up with a predetermined rate of progress for their grade are not promoted and are required to repeat the work of that grade.

Periodically, attempts are made to modify or depart from graded structure. In multigrading, for example, each class contains two or more grades simultaneously. Although grade labels are retained, children are permitted to work in several grades at once, depending on their progress in each subject. For example, in a multigraded class containing grades three, four, and five, a child could be in grade three for arithmetic, grade four for social studies, and grade five for reading.

Nongrading is an arrangement in which grade labels are removed from some or all classes. When grade labels are removed from kindergarten and the first three grades, the arrangement is known as a non-graded primary unit. A similar vertical arrangement for the customary grades four, five, and six is a non-graded intermediate unit.

Theoretically, grading and nongrading are the polar opposites among alternatives available for organizing a school vertically. In *pure* grading, the content of the instructional program and its sequential arrangement are determined by assignment of subject matter to various grade levels, by designation of instructional materials suitable for particular grade levels, and by promotion of pupils upon satisfactory completion of the work specified for each grade level. In *pure* nongrading, the sequence of content is determined by the inherent difficulty of the subject matter and the children's demonstrated ability to cope with it; materials are selected to match the spread of individual differences existing within the instructional group; and the children move upward according to their readiness to proceed. Promotion or nonpromotion does not exist as such. An important goal is to provide continuous progress for each child.

Nongrading and virtually all modifications of grading are intended to facilitate curricular and instructional provisions for the individual differences always present in a class group. However, no scheme of vertical school organization automatically makes these provisions. The removal of grade labels, for example, is no guarantee that teachers will take advantage of the opportunities nongrading is supposed to provide. A nongraded school with only grade labels removed remains a graded school, nonetheless.

Exponents of nongraded schools claim benefits with respect to pupil well-being and achievement which have not been proven conclusively. Critics of the nongraded plan claim that what nongrading purports to do can be accomplished as readily in graded schools. To date, research — most of it comparing pupil achievement in graded and nongraded schools — is inadequate and inconclusive. Some studies favor graded schools, some favor nongraded schools, and some show no significant differences between the two.

The crucial inadequacy of most such studies is the failure to identify two sets of characteristics by means of which nongraded and graded schools may be clearly differentiated. Consequently, the researchers often are not making a valid comparison. Several of the studies, for instance, report the use of ability or achievement grouping in the sample of nongraded schools selected but not in graded schools used for comparison. Are differences between pupils in these schools and in the sample of graded schools the product of graded or nongraded practices or of ability grouping?

Nongrading is a vertical plan of school organization. It cannot be compared with ability grouping or any other scheme of horizontal organization. Failure to understand this difference frequently leads to meaningless comparisons of organizational plans and, ultimately, to misleading conclusions.

HORIZONTAL SCHOOL ORGANIZATION

As stated earlier, a pattern of horizontal organization results when an identifiable cluster of students (e.g., all first-graders or all high school juniors) is divided into class groups and assigned to available teachers. Whereas vertical organization allows only two major alternatives — grading and nongrading — horizontal organization permits literally dozens of alternatives. In setting up horizontal class groups, priority considerations may be given to children, to the curriculum, or to teacher qualifications.

If the primary consideration in establishing a pattern of horizontal organization is children, then a choice must be made between homogeneity (likeness) and heterogeneity (difference) in pupils comprising each class group. If the choice is for homogeneity, the criterion of likeness may be age, size, interest, ability, achievement, or a combination of these and other factors. If the primary consideration is the curriculum, a choice may be made between separate subjects and various combinations of subjects as the basis for setting up class groups. If the primary consideration is teacher qualification, one choice is between the self-contained classroom (one teacher for all subjects) and departmentalization (a different teacher for each subject).

Thus simplified, horizontal organization begins to be comprehensible. However, schools often combine the results of several kinds of choices, which complicates understanding of the organization. A high school for instance, might be semidepartmentalized, with a different teacher for each subject except for English and social studies, which are combined in a core curriculum and taught by one teacher. All except core classes might be set up according to pupil homogeneity in achievement. The over-all pattern of school organization might then be further complicated by introducing vertical variety — nongraded classes in the core but graded classes in all other subjects.

Team teaching is one horizontal scheme that combines considerations of children, curriculum, and teacher qualifications in establishing class groups. It is a significant departure from the variety of horizontal plans existing up to the present, just as nongrading in vertical organization represents a significant departure from grading.

Unfortunately, the term *team teaching* is applied to so many different ventures in cooperative teaching that it has come to have many meanings. Communication would be enhanced if the term were used only in referring to ventures embracing all three of the following characteristics: (1) a hierarchy of personnel — team leader, master teacher, auxiliary teacher, teacher aide, intern teacher, clerk, and so forth; (2) a delineation of staff function based on differences in preparation, personal interests, and so on, or on the kinds of learning activities planned; (3) flexibility in grouping embracing all the students under supervision of a team.

Such a definition excludes all those cooperative teaching efforts in which there is no attempt to define a hierarchy of personnel. These efforts might better be called associated teaching.

Schools utilizing team teaching can be graded or nongraded. Since team teaching is a form of horizontal organization, and grading or nongrading is a form of vertical organization, these forms are not interchangeable devices for achieving common organizational functions. A school may practice nongrading and team teaching simultaneously.

TOWARD A COMMON VOCABULARY

Given all this variety and complexity in the organization of American schools, we may expect to find confusion in discourse, practice, and research. Moreover, the mere existence of complexity is a compelling argument for a more precise vocabulary.

Vertically, schools may be graded or nongraded or fall somewhere in between. Horizontally, schools may be organized into any one of many alternative patterns. But all these horizontal patterns are derived from only three essentially different kinds of considerations: considerations of children, of the curriculum, or of teacher qualifications.

Any meaningful description of a school's over-all organizational pattern includes both vertical and horizontal aspects. Such description may be "nongrading (vertical) and ability grouping (horizontal)" or "grading (vertical) and team teaching (horizontal)" or "nongraded (vertical) and departmentalized (horizontal)." To describe a school as nongraded is to describe only half its organization. Likewise, to describe a school as practicing achievement grouping and departmentalization is to be quite descriptive of horizontal organization but to say nothing of vertical.

The use of a common vocabulary for analyzing and describing school organization is long overdue.

A PLEA FOR MODERNIZING THE HIGH SCHOOL CURRICULUM*

When will the comprehensive high school face its responsibilities and talk back to the self-styled authorities in some so-called higher institutions? The purpose of academic studies is not to prepare for college admission; it is to put young people into possession of the discoveries human beings have made throughout the ages as to their collective and individual potentialities. No one should be allowed to graduate from high school who has not achieved dexterity in one or more areas of business and technology as well as awareness of the political and economic institutions which preserve this Republic.

It is time for thoughtful educators to take our case to the people. After Sputnik there was a great flurry over mathematics and science. That was good, since teachers of mathematics and science had sometimes secreted their subjects in erudite language, like flies in amber, so that only students who conformed to their ritual could become informed of their contents. Then the School Mathematics Study Group, as an example, broke out of shackling tradition and showed that youngsters can discover and master mathematical truths at almost any age if only they are presented with simplicity. But let us not forget: no mathematician, chemist, or physician can build an airplane or harness nuclear energy. Only people who handle materials and skillfully use machines can make realities

---

*Frank B. Lindsay, "The Invisible Student in the Comprehensive High School," by permission of *Journal of Secondary Education*, XXXVIII, October, 1963, 7.

out of ideas. Space will be probed and maybe conquered not by armchair speculators but by artisans who take meticulous account of all biological and physical factors and build craft to transport men to the moon or Mars.

If high school is not to become obsolete, it must transform instruction in three principal ways. First, knowledge must be broken out of academic compartments and interconnected, as well as rigorously pruned down to essentials. Items must be drawn as needed from any subject field and organized into intelligible sequence. Second, programmed learning, flexible scheduling, team teaching, and utilization of audio visual materials must be open-mindedly scrutinized and tested and finally substituted for books alone. And third, classroom and shops must lead students out into the whole world of work. Pride of craftsmanship must be extended to spelling and composition, as an illustration, with slovenly thinking and expression not tolerated. Likewise, the same students must be confronted with manual and machine jobs to do and be made proficient in some skills of laboratory, business office, and shop alike. High school students are young adults, inexperienced to be sure, but they deserve to be challenged face to face in adult fashion and held to standards of workmanship. Old ladies of both sexes and varying ages had better get out of American high schools; it is time to blow the whistle for a work-crew to take over. Thus in time we may change high school from an animal farm to a center of all-around learning. Then the invisible students will begin to emerge as competent men and women.

CITY SCHOOLS SHOULD HAVE A MIXED ORGANIZATION*

If one were to put the principal problem of American education in the big city into a single sentence today, one would say that the problem is to bring social integration into the schools. By *social integration* is meant a common sharing of educational experience by children of a wide variety of socio-economic and racial groups.

From social scientists who have studied the relation of schools to society, from judges who have studied the significance of the American

*Robert J. Havighurst, "Education in the Big City: A New Frontier," Kent, Ohio: *Kappa Delta Pi Lectures,* No. 1, November 13, 1963, 25-26. Extracted from lecture before Delta Beta Chapter. By permission of Glenn Maynard, ed.

constitution for the educational system, and from social philosophers and religious leaders has come a common agreement on the importance of the school as a place where boys and girls from all social groups can learn together. It has been affirmed by the courts that schools which are limited by law or by residential segregation to Negroes are not good for Negro youth, and should be changed. It has been found by social scientists that schools attended predominantly by children of lower socio-economic status do not succeed in teaching these children as well as do schools of mixed socio-economic composition.

The call is for the *mixed school* — the school with a mixture of socio-economic groups and a mixture of racial groups where there are such groups in the community. The mixture need not necessarily reflect the exact composition of the city, but it should not be more than perhaps 50 per cent Negro, or 70 per cent working-class, according to the judgment of practical people who have been working with the problem of social integration.

The mixed secondary school is practically a necessity for the success of what is being called *social urban renewal*. In distinction to *physical urban renewal*, social urban renewal consists of the redevelopment of the central city so that all kinds of people — rich and poor, colored and white — will want to live there and raise their children there. This means that there will be large areas of the central city in which middle-class and working-class people will live, and Negroes and [whites] will live, within a few blocks of each other if not in the same block. But those who can afford to move to another area or to a suburb will not stay in a local community if they do not like the schools, and middle class people will not live in an area where they must send their children to a school that is dominated by working-class children. White people will not live in an area where they must send their children to a school which is dominated by Negro children. On the other hand, working-class parents and Negro parents will send their children to school dominated by middle class or by white children, because they think the standards of such schools are better.

Therefore, to serve the process of social urban renewal, the schools must be organized *as far as possible* as mixed schools. The phrase *as far as possible* is important here, because it may be impossible to organize all elementary schools as mixed schools, since they serve such small geographical areas and are likely to continue to serve a neighborhood. It may be impossible, also, to organize all secondary schools as mixed schools, in an area which is predominantly working class or Negro. In such a case, the concept of the regional high school district is useful. This is a district containing several high schools, where students have considerable degree of choice among the schools. There may have to be one school that is predominantly Negro in such a district, or one school that is predominantly working-class through its location; but there should be at least one and preferably more mixed schools in a high school regional district, thus making that region acceptable to all families in the region who insist on their children attending a school with a substantial white middle class college preparatory group.

Skillful school administrators can work with community leaders in a region where a regional high school district is being developed, to secure community support for a set of schools which are realistically organized to meet the needs of the people living in that region, and to hold the middle-class population, white and colored, who are needed as a base for social urban renewal.

PRINCIPLES OF ORGANIZATION FOR INSTRUCTION*

The superintendent of schools sets the pattern and tone of the organization. He should be consistent in decision-making processes and in the procedures which he supports and follows. He should provide an atmosphere where differences are valued and where people are encouraged to initiate change.

The organization of a school system should be delineated in terms of role and function complete with job descriptions, so that each member knows how to relate to the decision-making and decision-implementing processes.

The administrative organization for direction and communication should be as simple as possible, including at most only one intermediary between superintendent and principal and teacher.

Organization for support and service should be by coordinate divisions, each including a cluster of compatible functions and each headed by an administrator directly responsible to the superintendent. The number of these divisions should vary with the size and complexity of the district's administration, but at a minimum it should include separate divisions for business affairs and for curriculum and instruction.

Organizing for Improved Instruction. Joint statement of American Association of School Administrators and Association for Supervision and Curriculum Development. Washington, D.C.: American Association of School Administrators, 1963, 11-14.

Responsibility for maintaining continuity and consistency in the curriculum and objectives from grade to grade and among the schools must be clearly assigned.

Decisions should be made as close to the point of implementation as is consistent with the degree of expertness available at that point, the extent of the effects of the decision, and the optimum economy of staff time and resources.

The individual teacher has a professional responsibility for curriculum and instructional improvement. The organization must focus on the stimulation and support of the teacher in the classroom.

The principal has responsibility for leadership in building-wide curriculum and instructional improvement, and is the agent through whom decisions made beyond the building unit are carried out.

Resource people on the school staff and from outside that school are necessary to supplement the leadership activities of the principal, since the principal's total responsibilities encompass much else, and since some help to teachers is more effective in the absence of the authority relationship.

Resource people have service and supportive rather than directive functions.

Help and stimulation offered by resource people must be coordinated lest it pull teachers in different directions or pile up pressures intolerably at one time on an individual or group.

The organizational structure and the allocation of the district's resources should provide opportunity and encouragement for all professional staff members to participate in curriculum decisions that will affect them and to initiate proposals for new or changed policy.

Long-range planning for curriculum and instructional improvement is essential, as are provisions to keep plans flexible and responsive to unanticipated needs. Plans should provide for systematic review and evaluation of the program, of the organization, and of the plans themselves.

Policies, procedures and organizational patterns are measured primarily by their contribution to the growth objectives for each child. They should be evaluated further for their contribution to the growth and satisfaction realized by all members of the staff.

All resource people in a school system not on the staff of an individual school should be organized in, and their functions be incorporated in, a staff unit we are calling the Division for Curriculum and Instruction, under the leadership of an Assistant Superintendent for Curriculum and Instruction who is the responsible administrative head of the unit.

The Division of Curriculum and Instruction includes the following personnel and functions to the extent that they are provided in a given school system:

Curriculum development and instructional improvement, including curriculum planning, inservice growth programs, and attendant research and evaluation.

Service to pupils, including psychological and child development, guidance and counselling, health, and to the atypical and exceptional.

Instructional materials, media and media services including library, audio-visual devices and materials, television and the like.

Subject and area specialists including specialists in vocational and adult education curriculums.

The Division formulates policy and budget recommendations in these areas and keeps constantly informed of policy, wherever made, which affects curriculum and instruction.

The Assistant Superintendent for Curriculum and Instruction (whatever he may be called in a given system) may well have come to that position from a specialization in one or more of the resource or instructional areas. In his capacity as assistant superintendent, however, he serves as a generalist in curriculum and instruction, as an administrator leading the division itself, and as counsel to the superintendent and board of education in these fields.

The assistant superintendent coordinates the work of all specialists within the division, provides for clear and free communication both within and to and from the division, ensures that decisions, relationships, and activities affecting the curriculum or instruction are in accordance with established policy, and sees to it that recommendations for policy change are formulated and decided or forwarded to the appropriate person or body.

Evaluation and appraisal of instructional effectiveness, of pupil growth and of the curriculum are important elements in the work of the division. The functions, organization, and effectiveness of the division itself and all of its parts must also be subject to continuous and systematic evaluation for which the assistant superintendent may properly be held accountable.

The assistant superintendent must have the full authority of the superintendent as he works in his administrative capacity as head of the division of curriculum and instruction, and the full confidence and support of all those in the administrative structure as he exercises his decision-making, coordinating, and policy development roles.

If conflicts of personality or interpretation arise within the division or between resource people and teachers or administrators they should be settled by the assistant superintendent directly or in consultation with the appropriate administrative authority. His decisions and recommendations are made in the last instance directly to the superintendent.

PATTERNS OF CURRICULUM ORGANIZATION*

The curriculum or course of study can be organized in a number of different ways. The most familiar way of organizing the curriculum is the traditional one, supposedly based on the inherent logic of the subject. In history, one would follow a strict chronological order: the years and centuries and eons march in orderly progression through the student year of study. Or a course of study may be organized [sequentially], as in Euclidian geometry, in which one theorem logically succeeds a preceding theorem. Or in terms of the acquisition of skills, learning the position of the keys of the typewriter before learning how to type words, learning how to sew a seam before learning how to sew a skirt or a blouse. The assumption is that each subject has a logical sequence of learning blocks. The teacher's task is to present each block clearly and explicitly. Then as more blocks are added, the structure of the subject grows and takes on meaning.

Then there is another way of looking at the curriculum. This is to view learning through the psychological structure of the learner. What makes sense to the student? Where is he in term of the subject? Knowing that adolescent boys are interested in mechanics and sports, a history teacher might start his course in world history with a look at the modern version of the Olympic games. After winning the interest of the class, he might raise the question as to the origin of these games. This might lead to a look at the ancient Greeks. He would then suggest other modern activities the roots of which lie far remote in time. Thus he launches a study of world history, though keeping the focus at each point upon some contemporary event. When he wanted to look into the causes of the French Revolution, he would select some contemporary revolutionary movement (with many new nations appearing on the scene he probably would have little trouble) and then raise questions regarding revolutions in general and eventually end with a close look at the French Revolution.

---

*Reprinted by permission from Jean D. Grambs and L. Morris McClure, *Foundations of Teaching,* Copyright © 1964, by Holt, Rinehart and Winston, Inc., 171-173.

Another kind of curriculum pattern having a similar base in the psychological "readiness" of students can be seen in the elementary school classroom where the teacher utilizes the current interests of youngsters in order to teach reading skills. Perhaps there was a great snow storm which closed the schools for a few days. When the children return they are bubbling with stories about what adventures their families went through during this winter crisis. The teacher lets them talk. Then she suggests they write a story about their adventures. In a first grade this might be a group story with the whole class contributing phrases and words. In the third or the fifth grade this might be an individual project in writing so that children gain skill in a basic tool.

Another way of organizing the curriculum is around the predetermined needs of students in our particular culture. This pattern often sounds like the psychologically based approach noted above except that in this case teachers and curriculum experts have studied the age group to be taught and have concluded that certain key skills, ideas, knowledge, and attitudes are essential parts of students' educational needs. The curriculum is then designed to help the youngsters gain such educational increments. One urgent need of the six-year-old is to learn to be a cooperating member of a class group. The curriculum design would include discussion of how hard it sometimes is to sit still in school. The child of ten has a tremendous interest in active play and sports. The curriculum logically includes instruction in team games or study of the American Indians. During the junior high years special instruction would be provided regarding the physiological changes of puberty and the facts of the differential growth rates of individuals. Instead of waiting for student interest to manifest itself, this approach utilizes all that is now known about child growth and development and attempts to peg subject matter appropriately.

Some subjects lend themselves to organizing by major problems or recurring issues or central questions. In social studies, for instance, how man provides for his basic needs can be the unifying problem center for a study of world cultures in the sixth grade. How do people find shelter in the Amazon Valley, at the Arctic Circle, in Switzerland, in India? How man developed means of transporting goods can lead a class to studying the possible source of the first wheel, the first dugout canoe, the dramatic effect of the development of navigational aids on exploration during the fourteenth and fifteenth centuries, the revolution in transportation of steam, of the gasoline engine, of electricity, of atomic power— the possibilities are legion. In literature the central problems might center around the various communication needs: speaking, listening, writing, reading. In science they might center around the key questions relevant to that discipline. What is matter? What is force? What is power? What is light? What is sound?

THE NEED FOR A CURRICULUM COMMITTEE*

In the past, many high schools have left curriculum development to the individual departments. This procedure has resulted in revision of courses, course outlines, and bibliographies within the department, but has not usually led to any major overhaul of the total curriculum. Such a result is to be expected if each department staff has the responsibility of improving only its own program. No one looks at the total high school curriculum.

Each high school should have some group in its faculty organization that has the task of improving the curriculum. Unless some portion of the faculty has this responsibility, the school will probably retain the same curriculum structure that it has.

One of the standing committees of a school faculty should be a curriculum committee. It should be assigned the responsibility of carrying on a continuous evaluation of the results of the present program and then calling to the attention of the total faculty any areas in which the outcomes are not satisfactory.

Some schools have designated all of the department heads as members of a curriculum committee. The practice has two unfavorable results. Each department head feels a responsibility toward the members of his department to maintain the present status of the department or to improve it. As a result, he fights any change that would in any way decrease the size or influence of his department. Secondly, the members of the committee are all status people within the faculty, and their point of view is that of status people. Since these men have usually been on the faculty some time, the result is a tendency to maintain the status quo. Any person who has been in the school long enough to achieve department head status has helped to build the present program and feels a vested interest in retaining it.

---

*Kimball Wiles, *The Changing Curriculum of the American High School.* Copyright 1963. Reprinted by permission of Prentice-Hall, Inc., Englewood Cliffs, New Jersey, 281-283.

A much more effective type of curriculum committee organization is to have a committee elected by the total faculty with no person representing a particular department. As a result of being elected by the total faculty, the member's responsibility is to everyone, not just to his own department. The shift in the faculty member's responsibility gives him greater freedom to consider change that may lead to a reorientation of the power structure within the faculty. Less likelihood exists that members of the committee will be making decisions in light of their effect on a particular department.

The terms of the members of the curriculum committee should be staggered. To insure continuity of work, not all members of the committee should be elected at the same time. For example, if the committee has six members, it is desirable that they be elected for three-year terms, with two members leaving the committee each year and two new members being added. Under this plan, at least four members of the committee, for a given year, have already served one year and two members will have served two years. Problems are carried over from year to year, and the working procedure of the committee can be maintained.

The chairman of the curriculum committee should be elected by the total faculty. If he is elected by the members of the committee, there is a danger that it will become an in-group and the chairmanship rotated on some basis other than the wishes of the majority of the faculty. To insure that the chairman will have a period of training before assuming the responsibilities of his role, it is wise to have him elected a year in advance of the time he is to take office. During his year of training he should serve as vice-chairman and participate in the operation of the committee. In this way the chairman will not only be the choice of the faculty, but will also have experience with the work of the committee before assuming responsibility for coordinating it.

The curriculum committee should serve as a clearing house for problems. When individual members of the faculty feel that some change is needed within a department or within the total school program, they can make their feelings known to the chairman or to a member of the committee. This question or proposal should then be placed on the agenda and a decision made by the total committee as to whether or not an ad hoc work committee should be appointed to investigate the problem. To guarantee even further that the members of the faculty will have a voice in curriculum change, any member of the faculty should be free to present a curriculum problem to the total faculty even though it has been evaluated and deemed unimportant by the committee. If the total faculty agrees with the individual faculty member and decides that something should be done about the problem the curriculum committee then has the responsibility of implementing the investigation of the problem.

It should be understood by everyone in the faculty that the committee does not have the authority to make decisions about curriculum policy. The committee is a faculty organization responsible only for making plans for study and for bringing proposals to the faculty. When the proposals are under consideration by the faculty, the curriculum committee should state its position, but it should be prepared to have its thinking reversed if the total faculty holds a different viewpoint.

In brief, the curriculum committee of the high school is a spadework committee. It has responsibility for helping the faculty identify curriculum problems, for developing the means by which problems are studied, for bringing proposals to the faculty, and for helping the faculty to consider all aspects of the proposals under consideration.

SUMMARY OF 18 RESEARCH STUDIES TO DETERMINE THE RIGHT SIZE FOR A HIGH SCHOOL*

Is there one most desirable enrollment size for high schools? This is a question frequently asked by both laymen and educators who are faced with the necessity of enlarging a school building or establishing a second school elsewhere.

It is fairly obvious that a school of minimum size cannot provide the rich and varied curriculum needed to meet the varying needs and interests of all of its pupils. At the same time the feeling persists that very large schools may have certain psychological disadvantages for pupils. The responsibility of the individual for active participation as a member of the school organization is somewhat lessened in the large school and his opportunity to be "on the team" or in fact a part of any particular activity representing the school in the community is proportionately reduced. Especially is this true for the pupil of average or below average ability.

Even the pupil of greater potential, if he is shy and not self-motivating, may complete the three or four years of high school work with latent abilities undiscovered or underdeveloped. For in spite of the provision of guidance counselors, the very largeness of the school tends to make it an impersonal institution. The quiet conforming individual may be well

*Grace S. Wright, "Enrollment Size and Educational Effectiveness of the High School," Washington, D.C.: United States Office of Education, Circular No. 732, 1964, 1-3.

known to no member of the staff and to but few of his peers, a fact which may reduce to a minimum the conscious worthwhileness of his total school experience.

A few high school principals have circumvented this seeming dilemma by developing the schools-within-a-school organization. . .

These 18 attempts to assess the optimum size of a high school have resulted in widely differing recommendations. Largely responsible, no doubt, are the differing bases of the studies. Most of the researches were conducted within the confines of a single State and drew upon schools whose enrollments place them in diverse groupings. For example, enrollments in the schools in the several California studies had much larger upper ranges than did enrollments in schools in some of the southern or midwestern states where investigations were made. The "small" schools of California were as large as the "large" schools of some other States. Similarly, the grades in the schools studied sometimes included 9 to 12 and sometimes 7 to 12. In two instances they included 7 to 9 only. Three studies used the size of the senior or graduating class as the critical factor, and three others reported upon "secondary schools" without reference to grades.

Although a few studies considered combinations of factors in relation to school size, many of them were concerned with a single variable, viz., *curriculum offerings, extraclass activities, staff qualifications, relationships,* or *pupil achievement.* Because of this fact and because of the variability in grade and size ranges of schools in the several studies, a definitive answer to the question of how large a high school should be is not possible from a survey of these 18 studies. The studies do, however, present some evidence of desirability of size in relation to individual variables, although here too findings differ in some respects.

According to the studies considering *curriculum offerings,* variety is increased with increase in enrollment size, up to a point. This may be 2,000 or something less. Beyond that there is usually a multiplication of courses rather than an increase in variety. An enrollment of at least 1,000 in a 4-year high school appears to be essential to provide the minimum variety in course offerings considered essential.

Also favoring the large high school is the factor of *staff qualifications.* A study of teacher qualifications as the sole variable reported that qualifications in general increased with size of enrollment; schools enrolling fewer than 400 pupils did not usually attract the best qualified teachers. Other studies found that in larger schools there were more experienced teachers, more teachers with graduate training, larger percentages teaching in their major fields, and less teacher turnover.

Some evidence exists that *achievement of pupils* in or from very small schools is not equal to that of students from large schools as measured by standardized achievement tests, college grades, or degrees earned. While three studies found little or no significant difference in pupil achievement relative to school size, three others reported that student achievement in schools having a minimum enrollment of approximately 500 was superior to that of schools of a smaller enrollment size.

In the area of *extraclass activities,* fairly general agreement was found among the studies that smaller schools experience greater pupil participation, although here again two researchers reported no significant differences related to size. A study devoted to learning how life differs for children enrolled in large and small schools reported the most active participants in extraclass activities to be pupils from schools of fewer than 300, adding that while a large school provides a somewhat larger number and wider variety of nonclass activities than a small school, the small school makes the same general kinds of activities available to its students. Other studies found the greatest student participation in extraclass activities in the schools ranging from 150 to approximately 1,000 in enrollment size.

Wide variability among findings appeared in the five researches which considered factors of *relationships,* i.e., school-community, staff, teacher-pupil. Studies concerned with teacher-pupil relationships favored the small school, one suggesting a size of 273 to 490. Studies considering staff relations or school-community relations recommended enrollments of 1,200 to 1,600.

When the findings or recommendations of these 18 studies are compared with the 1956 recommendation . . . one statement seems to be justified: The optimum size of a high school for all-around educational effectiveness appears to be something less than the 2,000 suggested there. Also, optimum size would appear to be equal to or above the minimum of 100 in the graduating class recommended by Dr. Conant.

While this study has purposely considered only the educational factors in relation to school size, in the practical situation facing a school board and the community it serves, other considerations are frequently of equal importance. Availability of a school site, ability of the community to bear a possible increased tax rate, socioeconomic distribution of the population, transportation costs and distance between pupils' home and school, possible anticipated utilization of the building as a community center, architectural design for the type of program planned for the school—all of these will contribute to a determination of the nature of the building and its size.

BASIC PRINCIPLES OF ADMINISTRATIVE ORGANIZATION FOR A SECONDARY SCHOOL*

The administrative organization of a secondary school exists primarily to provide the best possible educational program for the pupils.

The administrative organization of a secondary school should make it possible to offer a broad educational program which meets the needs, interests, and abilities of all pupils in the school.

The administrative organization of a secondary school should make it possible for the principal, counselors, and teachers to know and to work effectively with individual pupils on their educational and personal problems.

The administrative organization of a secondary school should encourage correlation between the learning activities and outcome of different subjects and extraclass activities.

The administrative organization of a secondary school should be sufficiently flexible so that a variety of learning activities may be carried on in classes and elsewhere in the school program.

The administrative organization of a secondary school should make it possible for all pupils to participate in any part of the educational program in which they may be interested and for which they are qualified.

The administrative organization of a secondary school should provide adequate time for teachers to develop the curriculum, to plan learning activities, and in other ways to prepare for their participation in the instructional program.

---

*Summarized from Vernon E. Anderson and William T. Gruhn, *Principles and Practices of Secondary Education,* second edition, Copyright © 1962, The Ronald Press Company, 357-360.

THREE T'S THAT LIMIT TODAY'S SCHOOLS*

Three T's characterize today's schools and stand in the way of the optimum achievement of the goals emphasized in the preceding paragraph. These T's are *togetherness, terminableness,* and *tightness.*

---

*J. Lloyd Trump, "The Principal's Role in Superior Education," reprinted by permission from the *Bulletin of the National Association of Secondary-School Principals,* XLIV, Washington, D.C. (January, 1962) 306-307, 314.

Today's concept of education calls for much group activity in schools —much *togetherness*. Students too seldom are permitted the experience of planned independent study in places designed for that purpose. The setting for instruction is the self-contained classroom. And the classrooms of the secondary school are even more self-contained than those of the elementary school. The self-contained classroom concept says in effect that almost all the learning experiences of individuals must be had in groups of 25-35 within a given room for a specified number of minutes per day, the same time of day, five days a week for a semester or two, with one teacher in charge. That one teacher is responsible for directing all phases of learning for that group of students.

The educational opportunities for students are limited by the talents of the particular teachers which the schedule of classes gives them. Individual differences in talents exist among teachers as they do among students. Opportunities are also limited because usually it is not financially feasible to provide in each schoolroom all the material aids to instruction that modern technology provides. Overhead projectors, sound film projectors, video and audio tape recorders, television receivers, and other instructional aids can not reasonably be furnished in every classroom. And there are scheduling problems and other difficulties which prevent maximum use of these aids when they are placed in special audio-visual rooms and students are expected to go there as groups from their self-contained classrooms.

The educational setting fosters mass instruction—even though the *mass* may be 25-35 students at a time. The creation of sub-groups in the classroom still represents students' working together. Students are assembled sometimes in even larger masses in high-school study halls. Assignments, reports, and evaluation are made largely on a mass basis. Today's school portrays learning as something that happens when students work with a large degree of togetherness.

Terminableness also characterizes today's schools. Students "take" a course during a specified year, pass the examinations, and then in effect are permitted to forget it. The secondary school requires one year, or two, of science and none in other years. The student accumulates a specified number of credits, or reaches a specified age, and his formal education is terminated. In spite of teacher protestations to the contrary, the organization of the curriculum sponsors a terminal point of view on the part of students—and this terminableness is not based on individual differences among students but rather on such mass arrangements as "the fourth grade," "16 units of credit," "attainment of age 16," or whatever the regulations specify.

The *tightness* of the school day also limits the school's attention to individual differences among students and teachers. School bells in the secondary school punctuate the school day into look-alike periods and keep individual students from caring very deeply about anything. So does the notion that a student must sit in class 50 minutes a day, five days a week, for a semester or a year in order to "take" a given subject. Uniformity characterizes administrative arrangements for both students and teachers. Variations are difficult to make because of the tightness in the schedule, in the restricted spaces where learning can take place, and the rules and regulations adopted to insure a "smooth running school."

The plea for recognizing individual needs of students must attack basically these three T's if the school of the future is to be substantially better than that of today. The analysis first needed concerns the individual student.

THE ROLE OF THE PRINCIPAL

The principal exercising the leadership role described in the opening paragraphs of this article has three personal responsibilities: (1) to conceptualize an educational system that will serve individual students better; (2) to develop a public relations program based on experimental approaches to the solution of educational problems; and (3) to produce administrative arrangements that actually reflect the concepts and public relations thus evolved.

ORGANIZING THE ELEMENTARY SCHOOL*

The focal point of the educational program is the child. We need to keep this in mind at all times—whether we are engaged in identifying educational goals, in selecting goal-directed activities, or in setting up an organizational structure to support activities and goals. Obvious as this would seem to be, the failure to keep this fact in mind contributes daily to misunderstanding about the school program, to fuzzy thinking about what it ought to be, to impractical planning, and wasted time.

Sometimes, we seem to remember the child as we set up goals or as we select activities—and then forget child, goals, *and* activities when we set up the organizational structure. The very real and significant fact of

---

Elementary School Organization: Purposes, Patterns, Perspectives. Washington, D.C.: National Education Association, by permission of Department of Elementary School Principals, 1961 Yearbook, 16-17, 19, 125-127.

individual differences, for example, is accepted at some points and forgotten at others. Efforts to meet the individual needs of children are frequently hampered by types of school organization that literally block the use of appropriate and efficient ways of dealing with the child as an individual. It is a discredit to us and a disservice to children to say that we believe in each child's working at the level of his own potential—and at the same time subject him to a common course of study, a comparative marking system, a predetermined structure within which to work, and general goals that may or may not be applicable to him.

We may find, in the attitudes and the behavior of a goodly proportion of children, some evidences of our failure to meet individual needs. We see children who are insecure, disinterested, irritable, lacking in self-discipline. We see children who are aggressively negative in their behavior, and we see the "good little children" who just sit quietly and seemingly listen. True, the schools do not create all of these problems; many of them accompany the children from their homes to the schools. But too often, instead of coping with the individual problems of children, we provide a framework that perpetuates them.

When we think of school organization and its relationship to the education of children, we must see it for what it is—and what it is not. School organization, per se, is void of life. We cannot accomplish, through organization, what can be accomplished only through good programs, an adequate number of competent teachers, and materials and conditions conducive to effective work. But, although school organization cannot in itself achieve the education of children, it is indispensable for facilitating an educational program. And it is effective to the degree that it provides the framework within which accepted educational goals can be achieved —a framework which is geared to children, not to administrative convenience at the expense of children.

Each elementary school staff must determine, within the range of limitations and opportunities in the local situation, how they can best organize their school program. In most instances, this means working within the structure of an ongoing school program—not just suddenly creating something wholly new. This means appraising the current program and determining the nature and extent of changes needed. . . .

Organization should be a direct outgrowth of educational goals and goal activities; it should take shape after the goals and goal activities have assumed form. Organization should not dictate activities; it should be determined by them. Organization cannot set up a school program; it can support a school program. Organization should not be a fixed, static structure; it should be a flexible, dynamic structure. . . .

The elementary school organizational patterns—vertical and horizontal—that are considered in this chapter are different tentative solutions to the problem of how an elementary school organizational structure can better serve the teaching-learning situation.

The major designs and the many variations from them found in practice are important for an elementary school principal to consider when he takes a good, hard look at organization. As all aspects of these structures are studied with respect to how they serve educational goals, the several advantages and disadvantages of each need to be kept in mind. For example, proponents of the self-contained classroom feel that a child's need to identify with a group and to develop close relationships with other children may be met adequately in this organizational plan. This may well be true. But it may be equally true that other patterns of organization also can meet this need.

Few would dispute the fact that there is an interrelatedness of subject-matter fields which can be promoted when instruction in basic learning takes place under the guidance of one teacher as it does in the self-contained classroom. However, spending most of the school day in one room with a single teacher does not necessarily promote better integrated learning in a child, especially if the daily program is a highly fragmented one. Principals need to give thought to this.

Supporters of the nongraded plan feel that stress upon a plan that enables children to progress continuously at their own rates is a strong feature. A principal examining this structure needs to ask himself whether or not the goals being served here can be achieved as well or better in another kind of vertical structure.

Advocates of departmentalization maintain that teachers teach best the subjects they like best. Principals need to examine such a claim carefully and ask whether or not an elementary school teacher, with an adequate background in content areas, can be as interested in how to help children learn as he might be in a "subject." Does teaching, particularly at the elementary level, have to be thought of only in relation to imparting knowledge about a special field? Isn't the total process of education worthy of a person's best efforts?

A principal's study of the dual progress plan can raise important questions. The two broad areas of "cultural imperatives" and "cultural electives" in which this plan divides the curriculum may well be "musts" and "electives" for adults in today's society. By the time children now in elementary school are adults, what will the "musts" and "electives" be?

There are innumerable other implications and questions for the school principal to consider as he examines current patterns of organization and thinks about coming changes. What are the goals toward which an elementary school in a particular community should move? What behavioral characteristics of children are associated with these goals? What learning activities will lead toward the behavior desired? What process or processes will be guiding the changes that may be ahead? Who is to be involved in reaching decisions about organization? What knowledge and information are needed for planning? Should children be organized on the kind of time schedule departmentalization usually provides? Do children grow on schedule? How can organization promote continuity in a child's development? Who is to be responsible for seeing the long view of a child's development over the whole span of his school life?

These questions and many others undoubtedly will arise as decisions are considered. The answers eventually found will determine whether a school improves its organizational structure or simply changes its labels. A school that "adopts" any organizational plan without first carefully examining its own philosophy and goals may find that it has done no more than trade grade levels for reading levels. Or then again it may discover that it has postponed, not solved, the retention problem. The principal and all others involved in the process of deciding about change, must constantly ask what new evidence there may be to support any pattern as a better way to promote goal activities.

It seems abundantly clear that the matter of reorganizing instructional design goes far beyond simply examining current organizational plans and then adopting one that appears to fit the local situation. A principal needs to be aware of and hold back the pressures and arguments that may be advanced in support of adopting a particular plan of organization before goals are identified, clarified, and defined, and before appropriate activities are selected. An elementary school principal also needs to resist the temptation to look upon a "new" plan as a summit to be attained. If he can regard a modification in design, an adaptation in structure, as one of a series of steps in the improvement of education for boys and girls, he will be ready to move ahead as educational goals are modified and as subsequent organizational adaptations evolve.

PROBLEMS AND TRENDS IN ORGANIZING ELEMENTARY SCHOOLS*

Throughout the history of education in this country there has never emerged a clear-cut distinction between elementary and secondary pro-

---

*Stuart E. Dean, *Elementary School Administration and Organization*, Washington, D.C.: United States Office of Education, Bulletin 1960, No. 11, 8, 11, 28-29, 32.

grams. We have had general agreement that 1 through grade 6 comprise an elementary school, and that grades 9, 10, 11, and 12 belong to the secondary school. The uncertainty has lain with grades 7 and 8. In some instances, these grades have been included with grade 9 in a junior high school; in others, they have been added to the basic 6 years of the elementary school, resulting in an elementary program of eight grades; and in still others, prefixed to the 4 final years to form the 6-year secondary program. No single plan has received unanimous acceptance. The decision, always, has remained with the local board of education, in keeping with the American tradition and policy of local autonomy of the individual school district.

As a consequence there has been an acceptance of a set of optional organizational plans for the operation of local school districts. Today, local schools are customarily organized in one of four basic patterns, the so-called 6-3-3, the 6-2-4, the 6-6, or the 8-4. . .

School organization, exclusive of all considerations of publicly supported kindergarten programs, by U.S. totals and percentages and by regional percentages, 1959

Type of school organization	United States		Regional percentages			
	Percent	Total	Northeast	North Central	South	West
1	2	3	4	5	6	7
Total	100.0	4,307	100.0	100.0	100.0	100.0
6-3-3	33.8	1,455	31.0	35.0	36.0	31.0
6-2-4	16.4	706	10.7	21.5	15.2	18.2
6-6	14.6	630	14.6	19.0	10.3	15.0
7-5	3.5	149	5.3	.9	3.7	5.1
8-4	23.9	1,029	32.9	16.7	26.2	18.4
Other	7.8	338	5.5	6.9	8.6	12.3

Throughout the evolutionary period of the elementary school there has been a series of developments and proposals relating to the most effective arrangements for teaching and for learning. Essentially there are two basic and complementary components of the organizational structure of an elementary school. On the one hand, there is organization for strictly administrative purposes, relating to the operational management of large numbers of children and staff, building maintenance, business responsibilities, and ancillary services. On the other hand, there is organization, quite apart from the operational, which relates to the instructional responsibilities and opportunities of the school. Inevitably, these two types of relationships become interwoven, and yet the fact remains that the latter type is of transcending importance and must not suffer by an undue emphasis on operational management. Administration exists as a service responsibility and is not an educational end in itself. It seems apparent that these two types of administrative action and responsibility must be kept clearly apart and that the paramount point of importance is that a school exists solely for the purposes of its instructional program.

Presently there is a recurring wave of experimentation, demonstration, discussion, and agitation with respect to the structural organization of the elementary school. In view of the heightened pace and growing complexity of our cultural patterns in a technological and international world, newer styles and types of organization, plans and programs, and various adaptations are being recommended to make it possible for the elementary school to fulfill its function and to discharge its responsibility. In essence two conflicting points of view emerge: (1) That because of the increasing accumulation and importance of modern knowledge it is no longer possible for the traditionally trained elementary school teacher to be capable of teaching all subjects to all children with equal skill and effectiveness; and (2) that the advancing science of human growth and development indicates that it is more important for a child of elementary school age to have a close contact with a single teacher who will be in a position to understand him and to provide for his individual differences in ability, maturation, and potential.

In terms of specifics, the controversy relates to whether children should be taught on the basis of one-teacher-per-classroom, with additional help from specialists when and where they are needed, or whether they should be taught on the basis of an organizational pattern which provides a series of different teachers in the several subject fields. It is obvious that this difference of opinion is of growing seriousness and importance as it bears upon the future direction of elementary education in the United States. . .

In conclusion, while the type of instructional organization is certainly of considerable importance since it influences the kind of educational program carried on in a school, the fact remains that the administrative organization for instruction cannot, in itself, assure effective and efficient educational accomplishment. What actually goes on in the teaching-learning situation remains of transcendent importance, and it is toward this situation that efforts to improve the quality of education must be directed.

In reviewing the national findings with respect to type of instructional organization these conclusions may be drawn: For the six-grade elementary school there is a heavy preponderance of the one-teacher-per-classroom plan, with small degrees of either partial or complete departmentalization and very limited use of the multigraded plan; on the other hand in grades 7 and 8 of the elementary school organization, there is a preponderance of both partial and full departmentalization, with less than one-fifth of the urban places continuing to use the one-teacher-per-classroom plan and negligible use of the multigraded plan.

ORGANIZATION AND ADMINISTRATION OF THE JUNIOR HIGH*

From its beginning over fifty years ago down to the present time, the junior high school has been characterized by a wide variety of administrative and organizational plans. Among the various combinations used in launching a junior high school are the following grade groupings: 6-3-3, 6-6, 6-2-4, 7-3-2, and 7-5, and, considering the junior or community college as a secondary institution, 6-4-4. At the present time there appears to be a definite trend toward the consideration of the junior high school as a three-year program, usually including grades seven, eight and nine.

The type of junior high school organization in the past has often been determined largely by the rigidity of the school building situation in each locality. However, with the rapid increase in school enrollments throughout the country and the attendant school building program, more and more communities are able to make a value decision concerning the schools for early adolescents. Among other factors which have to be considered locally are financial ability, attendance and state education laws, and the proximity of elementary schools as well as two-and four-year colleges. . . .

---

*Harold F. Cottingham, and William E. Hopke, *Guidance in the Junior High School*, Bloomington, Illinois: by permission of McKnight and McKnight Publishing Co., 1961, 7-9.

Desirable standards of class size and school size may vary somewhat. Assuming an average class size of around thirty pupils, the minimum recommended total enrollment in a three-year school ranges from 250 to 350 pupils with at least three sections per grade. Junior high schools which are smaller in size have difficulty in offering an adequate program and are likely to have financing and staffing problems. Maximum enrollment recommendations vary from 600 to 1000 pupils with an optimum of around 700 pupils and eight sections in each grade. Reasons for restricting the size of the junior high school include the following:

1. Insufficient opportunities for students to participate actively in co-curricular activities.
2. The need for teachers to know each other and to plan the educational program together.
3. The need for a personal relationship between students and teachers.
4. School services tend to become less able to provide effectively for the needs of students as enrollments exceed optimum suggested.

The Southern Association of Colleges and Secondary Schools, in a joint study published in 1958, recommended the personnel listed below as a minimum which should be provided for a junior high school with an enrollment of 720 pupils:

1. A full-time principal.
2. A curriculum or administrative assistant.
3. A full-time materials consultant (skilled not only in library science but also in audio-visual aids and all materials useful and necessary in the junior high school program) with the services of a full-time clerk.
4. A full-time guidance counselor.
5. A sufficient number of teachers (a total of 25 to 35 teachers would be required). Approximately one-half of these teachers should be selected to handle two core groups of from 25 to 30 students each for four- or five-period blocks of time, teach one required subject, and have one free period for individual conferences, record keeping, and planning. Other teachers should be selected to teach required subjects, exploratory subjects, and electives.
6. A secretary and stenographer.
7. A full-time school nurse.
8. Adequate custodial staff (a minimum number of six).
9. A lunchroom manager and workers.

ELEMENTS NEEDED TO PROVIDE AN ADEQUATE MINIMUM EDUCATION FOR EARLY ADOLESCENTS*

1. Be of moderate size.
2. Have a well-stocked library staffed by a professional librarian-teacher.
3. Provide ample guidance services.
4. Offer block-of-time instruction each year for the three years so that one teacher will have a group of children for a substantial period.
5. Maintain flexibility of scheduling.
6. Be staffed with teachers prepared for junior high school teaching and devoted to junior high school age students.
7. Provide help for teachers by principals, by supervisory staff, and by clerical personnel.
8. Provide a modern instructional program in subject areas.
9. Have adequate physical education programs.
10. Have ample laboratory and workshop facilities.
11. Have an established, reasonable teacher load.

---

*The Junior High School We Need, Washington, D.C.: Association for Supervision and Curriculum Development, 1961. 13-19. Prepared by Jean D. Grambs, Clarence G. Noyce, Franklin Patterson, and John Robertson. Copyright © 1961 by the Association for Supervision and Curriculum Development.

WHAT IS THE KINDERGARTEN CURRICULUM?*

The kindergarten curriculum is a design for the education of the five-year-old. It is not a mere course of study where all children must achieve a bare minimum of measurable traits to arrive at a group of itemized goals. Curriculum involves the more subtle and extensive processes of strengthening physical powers, deepening emotions, developing greater

---

*Minnie Perrin Berson, Kindergarten: Your Child's Big Step, New York: by permission of E. P. Dutton & Co., Inc., 1959, 54.

social warmth and sensitivity, and elevating intellectual achievement and competence.

When school authorities give prospective kindergarten parents a handsome welcoming brochure (often produced in a public-relations office) which announces that kindergarten is the place to learn sharing, responsibility, work habits, respect for others, enjoyment of books, expression through music, obedience to authority, sportsmanship, self-control, and numerous other values and skills, they oversimplify a complex, lifelong process. These values and behaviors do not grow by prescription. They advance in the kindergarten year through a good life with other children, the guidance of a teacher, and the child's receptivity, which is tremendously influenced by his experience prior to kindergarten. Broadly, like any other curriculum, the one for kindergarten must be designed to cultivate values and refine behavior while it nurtures intellectual depth and skills.

SUPERVISION AND EVALUATION . . .

WHO'S A GOOD TEACHER*

There appears to be no such single person as the universally effective teacher. Teaching is a complex of professions, each with widely differing requirements and activities. Teaching is as complex as the educational process in the modern world.

No general definition has been worked out to date, and it is doubtful that an all-inclusive definition ever will be worked out before a complete unification of all knowledge is achieved. Teachers differ widely with respect to maturity, intellectual, personal, and other characteristics. The demands of the subjects they teach, and the scope and the structure of the objectives to be achieved — all contribute to diversity. Community expectations also exert great influence on the teaching process. Some communities value intellectual goals; others are more concerned with more "visible" characteristics such as "sociability" and "personality"; some are concerned only with carrying on schooling at the lowest possible cost. In addition, local control exerts its influence toward diversity. For almost any goal one might choose, it is possible to find a continuous

---

*Who's a Good Teacher? Washington, D.C.: by permission of American Association of School Administrators. Edited by William J. Ellena, Margaret Stevenson, and Harold V. Webb. 1961, pp. 36-37.

spectrum of values, opinions, and goals ranging from one polar opposite to another. Teachers in adjoining communities may be rated superior for diametrically opposite reasons. . .

It would be a mistake to assume that teacher effectiveness is only whatever a community wishes it to be. Unfortunately, this position of complete free-wheeling seems to be very appealing to some practitioners and investigators. If teaching is whatever one chooses to make it, then one man's opinion is as good as another's and facts need not clutter the free exercise of fancy. Under this state of affairs teacher competence in the practical situation becomes whatever people, usually figures of power in the community, think it should be. Whenever a school system adopts a device to rate teachers, that device essentially becomes that district's definition of an effective teacher.

THE MEANING OF EVALUATION*

Evaluation has several meanings. An appropriate meaning is determined by a particular experience involving certain circumstances. Evaluation is inherent in every meaningful enterprise in which people engage. As soon as goals or purposes for an activity or enterprise are announced, the question is raised: "To what extent are the purposes or objectives being realized?" The baseball player assesses his batting average and determines whether it is high or low as compared with the other players on his team and the players on the other teams in his league. His predetermined goal is to have a high percentage of hits for the number of times he comes to bat during the baseball season. The salesman makes a daily, weekly, or monthly evaluation of the number of sales he has made. His company has probably given him a quota to reach if he is to be successful as a salesman in that organization. In each of these illustrations a goal or objective is identified, and progress toward that goal is evaluated. Success or failure is measured.

Evaluation is often difficult to define as it relates to education. . . Evaluation is a more inclusive term than measurement because it is more than a testing program: it connotes the making of value judgments.

As used in this book, evaluation means the following things:

---

*Paul J. Misner, Frederick W. Schneider, and Lowell G. Keith, *Elementary School Administration*, Columbus, Ohio: by permission of Charles E. Merrill Books, Inc., 1963, 163-165.

1. Evaluation is the means by which a school, teachers, administrators, and citizens agree upon the purposes or goals to be sought in the education of children. The determination of the goals to be sought is made within the framework of understanding that the school takes its place with the church and the home as important institutions in American society. The church and the home are guaranteed the right to perpetuate the values peculiar to different religions and various patterns of family life. The public school provides for all the children to acquire the understandings, skills, and values that need to be learned if democratic processes and ideals are to be maintained and extended. The values held by society in general become the goals of education.

   It is one thing to state that teachers, administrators, and citizens should agree upon the purposes or goals to be sought in education, and quite another thing to see this objective realized. The process by which these important agreements are to be reached may be long and laborious. This is the place where creative leadership and incisive organization become imperative. Time must be provided for people to sit down and discuss what values they believe are currently held by society, and how these values may be translated into learning experiences for children. A school system will need to perfect an administrative organization that permits these discussions to be held in an orderly, meaningful manner.

2. Evaluation includes the processes a school uses to decide whether the predetermined goals are being realized, and to insure the continued research and experimentation necessary to keep the school program in conformity with the changing needs. Here the school will make use of all the evaluative instruments and data that may be effectively used to measure the outcomes of the teaching-learning process. The measurement will not be limited to written examinations and objective tests. Records of pupil activities, anecdotal records, interviews, reports from parents, behavior checklists, health records, films and transcriptions, sociometric devices, interest inventories, and projective techniques may be used.

   The ultimate purpose of evaluation is to establish, as objectively as possible, a comprehensive picture of each pupil's school achievement in terms of the educational goals the school has accepted. The interpretation of the results of all the findings and experimentation is of prime importance. It is here that decisions are made concerning need for change. The interpretation of the results of evaluation must be made easily accessible to all school personnel and to the citizens of the community. This is the way a school community comes to a rational understanding of the need for change, and when such change is proposed by the school administration the public is usually ready to accept the recommendations.

CAN ADMINISTRATORS ALSO SUPERVISE?*

Although mentioned by few principals in this particular group, there is another question that continues to arise in most discussions of the effects of administrative evaluation: the frequently assumed incompatibility between the role of evaluator and that of supervisor or consultant to teachers. The argument is that a principal cannot at the same time have administrative authority over teachers and also be accepted as their confidant and advisor. It is suggested that individuals withdraw from and avoid those who have some power over them.

This seems to be a very one-sided view. Just as strong an argument—perhaps stronger—is that many individuals are drawn to those they see as having power over them and feel most comfortable in a dependent relationship.

But this approach to the question does not take us very far. We can admit that some principals enjoy wielding administrative authority over teachers and that some teachers enjoy being dependent on a father figure. If we do not wish to have these personality types in the profession, then the problem is one of screening and recruitment.

It would seem to this writer that one of the great potential values of an adequate evaluation program is precisely that it can ameliorate both these aspects of organizational life. If a principal is involved with other principals in a common endeavor to apply criteria and procedures worked out by a larger group, the opportunity for him to act arbitrarily and according to personal biases is reduced. If a teacher's work is being studied by himself and others in the light of these broader based proc-

---

*Gale W. Rose, "The Effects of Administrative Evaluation," by permission of *The National Elementary Principal*, XLIII, November, 1963, 53.

esses, then his point of reference for competent behavior is extended beyond the immediate local school situation. Those who would like to see teaching professionalized—oriented to standards of competence derived from the expertness of the professionals themselves—might note this point.

Aside from the foregoing line of thinking, the fact is that principals differ, just as teachers do. Some principals can readily combine the administrative role and the supervisory role, while others have great difficulty doing so. It would be sensible to find out what a principal can do before requiring both roles of him. We might note in passing that teachers play both roles with pupils all the time, sometimes to their intense discomfort.

There is one requirement that it does seem unnecessary to make of principals in a system of any size. They should not be required to make directly and personally salary, tenure, promotion, dismissal, and other such recommendations concerning teachers. There is no reason why the onus of this responsibility should not begin where it must in any event end—with the superintendent and his staff. If the central office staff is really administering the personnel program, they are accumulating information from several sources, including the principal to be sure, and weighing it as a totality before crucial decisions are made. If the information the principal has supplied to this totality is inaccurate and insufficient, he is doing two disservices to children: discouraging good teaching and encouraging poor teaching.

IS EVALUATION IMPORTANT?

Certainly, the views of the principals surveyed reinforce other experience. Perhaps no point about the whole controversy over teacher evaluation is becoming more clear than that adequate programs are difficult to develop and to operate, demanding the best skills of principals and others. It would seem that such programs are at least as complex and challenging as the construction and operation of a high quality instructional program. If more school administrators and faculties were willing to devote the time and energy and professional competence to this task that they give to curriculum design and revision, we might see some real breakthroughs in this difficult area.

Whether principals and teachers will be willing to undertake this task, of course, depends on their conviction that evaluation is an important, even a vital, element of a quality school operation. Most principals and teachers simply do not have this conviction, and the related but subsidiary issues which have so frequently become involved with evaluation —for example, merit pay—have tended to cloud the basic issues altogether. Whatever the case may be for merit pay or other personnel actions tied to teacher evaluation, these should stand or fall on their own merits and not determine the fate of this serious professional question of teacher evaluation.

RATING IS NOT EVALUATION*

The evaluation of the total supervisory effort must include a determination of the quality of teaching and learning and the quality of supervision itself. These three aspects of evaluation are highly interrelated and, taken together, will give a rather comprehensive picture of the quality of instruction with respect to strengths and weaknesses. Growing out of the evaluation will be the provision for needed changes to cope with the problems revealed by the evaluative procedures.

Problems of evaluation are sometimes difficult to deal with because there is a variety of terminology used, and some of this terminology is inaccurate. For example, there are those who speak of carrying on evaluation, but what they really do is rate. Others talk about evaluation, but what they really do is measure or appraise. Measurement, appraisal, and rating are not evaluations. They furnish the data from which evaluations can be made. Unfortunately rating, measurements, and appraisal often become ends in themselves with the result that evaluative procedures are necessarily incomplete.

Evaluation in the true sense of the word is at the very least a two-step process. The first of these steps involves the collection and collation of information and data about attributes which are relevant and important to teaching. The second step involves value judgments based squarely on the information gathered. Consequently, the quality of evaluation is heavily influenced by the appropriateness of the data collected and by the perceptions, experiences, and skill of those who read meaning into these data. Irrelevant information can yield only irrelevant evaluation. Appropriate information furnishes the raw material for good evaluation, but does not guarantee it.

---

*Reprinted with permission of the Macmillan Company, *Supervision in Today's Elementary Schools* by James Curtin, copyright© James Curtin, 1964, 234.

SCHOOL DISTRICTS ARE UNDERSTAFFED FOR EVALUATION*

In actuality school districts usually employ too few administrative and supervisory people. In most districts the number is so small that they can attend only to the managerial chores. Their time gets spent on problems of the present—on the maintenance, operation, and control of the going concern as it is. Planning problems accumulate until emergencies arise. Evaluation is subjective and unsystematic. The staff has nowhere nearly enough time or resources or qualified personnel to give objective and systematic attention to these problems.

The scarcity of administrative staff is not widely enough deplored. Superintendents hesitate to ask for more staff lest they be accused of empire building. They often recognize the need for more people if time is to be given to collecting and interpreting data that are necessary for adequate planning. But regardless of size, good administration requires that the specific responsibility for evaluation must be assigned directly within whatever central administrative staff is provided. Only then will evaluation be constant and continuous. Provision must be made in every school budget and staffing plan.

Evaluation must not only be continuous but systematic. Provision must be made for the accumulation of specific data that the school board and administration needs for decision making and planning. Data must be accumulated, classified, interpreted, and incorporated into meaningful reports. Staff time must be available within the organization for the continuous appraisal of the information that is available and the determination whether it is adequate as a foundation upon which satisfactory recommendations can be made.

School boards need a plan for their own evaluation of the program. Specific dates should be established when the board will consider evaluative reports on one phase or another. All too often school boards, like their overloaded administrators, operate on the basis of expediency. They deal with a particular problem when it happens to arise or presses most powerfully. They make decisions only when decisions become really critical.

Management Surveys for Schools: Their Uses and Abuses, Washington, D.C. by permission of The American Association of School Administrators, 1964, 27.

A STUDY OF STAFF OPINIONS TOWARD TEACHER EVALUATIONS*

Principals reporting from systems where teachers were given written evaluations and those teachers who had received a written evaluation the preceding year were less distrustful of the plans of evaluation than were the other principals and teachers among the respondents. This was particularly marked among the principals—only 22.5 percent of those using written evaluations expressed doubt or a negative opinion, compared with 35.5 percent of the remaining principals.

DESIRABLE OUTCOMES

The questionnaire also asked all superintendents, principals, and teachers in the survey: "What desirable outcomes from the program of teacher evaluation have you observed in your school system?" This question was to be answered in the respondents' own words; about two-thirds of the superintendents and about three-fifths of the principals replied, but only half of the teachers.

The most frequent response for all three groups was that evaluation stimulated efforts to improve instruction. The school system administrators were forced to examine their criteria of good teaching and what they must know about the teachers in order to evaluate them. The teachers believed that their teaching improved, because if they knew that they were to be evaluated, they were more alert. Also, their weaknesses were pointed out, and they were shown ways in which they could improve.

The second desirable outcome was the development of good rapport between teachers and administrative staff—there was more understanding of what each needed. Good evaluation proceedings can uncover much good teaching that might not be noticed without such a program. This raises the morale of the staff.

Other desirable outcomes noted were better administrative planning and the use of evaluation to rid the school system of really incompetent teachers.

---

*NEA Research Bulletin, "What Teachers and Administrators Think About Evaluation," Washington, D.C.: National Education Association, XLII, December, 1964, 110-111.

ADVERSE COMMENTS

Not all comments concerning evaluation were favorable, however. In fact, one-fourth of all teachers answering the question on desirable outcomes wrote "None." The major criticisms of the evaluation program, as stated by teachers, were (a) that evaluation was not accurate and (b) that the administrative staff was too busy to do an effective job in evaluating.

Some principals also criticized the program. Their main dissatisfaction was that lack of time prevented them from making sound evaluations of every teacher. Some also commented on lack of communication; the program was not completely understood or the teachers never inquired about their evaluation and thus did not know in what areas improvement was expected.

The survey shows that good evaluation programs can be carried on in the public schools, but that to be effective they must be given a high priority on the list of the administrators' duties. This applies to the central-office staff no less than to the principal. Time must be allowed to plan a good program and set up realistic criteria. After this, more time must be allowed to train the evaluators and to explain to each member of the professional staff just what his part in evaluation is. Furthermore, there must be a continuing program of interpretation as new teachers and new administrators are added to the staff. Finally, there is the enormous amount of time that a good evaluation program takes to administer. Yet those persons working under such a program seem to agree that it is worth the effort because of the improvements brought about in teaching.

THE CHANGING CONCEPT OF SUPERVISION*

The early inspectional and dictatorial concept of supervision, one that is still too often held by present-day educators, may be compared to the mechanistic point of view of learning: that one learns one thing at a time most efficiently through passive listening. Since teachers of an

*Paul J. Misner, Frederick W. Schneider, and Lowell G. Keith, *Elementary School Administration*, Columbus, Ohio: by permission of Charles E. Merrill Books, Inc. 1963, 183.

earlier day were largely unprepared and without professional stature, they were expected to listen to the supervisors, and to carry out their directives without question. In contrast to this point of view, the modern concept holds that an individual is unique, dynamic, purposeful, and that he learns and reacts as a "whole" to those things identified with his own purpose. When one applies this organic point of view to supervision, the shift in emphasis moves from subject matter per se to the key factors in the learning process: the teacher and the child. Since improvement of instruction is the primary reason for any supervisory program, and since any such improvement hinges on teacher performance, it follows that the teacher is the key participant in the total program.

In a broad sense, supervision is a school service designed to improve the teaching-learning situation. It is sometimes thought of as an expert service which is provided on a consultation basis. In fact, in some areas of the country the very term "supervision" is being changed to "consultation," and "supervisors" are becoming "consultants," or one of some twenty-five other titles because of the unsavory connotations of the process, which has been identified, variously, as "snoopervision," or "snipervision." In modern supervisory programs, principals and supervisors or consultants serve as skilled resource persons possessing skills which aid administrators, teachers, parents, and children in providing an educational program which will eventually improve the quality of living in the communities in which they live and work.

THE PRINCIPAL'S SUPERVISORY RESPONSIBILITY*

Supervision, concerned with improving the teaching-learning situation, is at the heart of both the instructional program and the productive organization of the elementary school staff. The principal who conscientiously and effectively spends at least 50 per cent of his time in supervisory activities finds that those affected by his activity improve their performance and effectiveness. Success in the principal's supervisory activity depends upon how well he performs his tasks, how well he can develop the cooperative spirit in his team of teachers and other school personnel, and how well he understands them. The principal, as a supervisor, has a right to expect *performance* from the persons on the

---

*Paul J. Misner, Frederick W. Schneider, and Lowell G. Keith, *Elementary School Administration*, Columbus, Ohio: by permission of Charles E. Merrill Books, Inc., 1963, 205.

certificated and non-certificated staffs; he also has a right to expect information from those persons on how the education of children might be accomplished more efficiently and effectively. The teachers and other personnel should expect to perform efficiently and to make suggestions for the more effective implementation of the teaching-learning situation. Since the principal expects to receive the same things that staff members expect to give, the sole remaining objective is to clarify these expectations. This, in essence, is the principal's supervisory responsibility.

The principal expects to acquaint teachers and non-certificated employees with their jobs, to provide them with supplies and materials with which to perform their work, to provide for in-service education so that they may improve their performance, and to give them information about school policies and procedures. The staff members expect these things from their principal and, in addition, have a right to learn from him how well they are performing their work. Staff members can assist the principal in the communication of these things through conferences, questions, and inviting him for visits to their classrooms; the principal helps staff members by encouraging them to raise problems for possible cooperative solution.

Finally, it is the joint responsibility of principal and teachers to continually evaluate the teaching-learning situation, working toward the ultimate goal of improving the education of the students in the school.

THE PURPOSES OF SUPERVISION*

Some writers, for purposes of discussion, prefer to categorize supervision under any one of three headings: autocratic, laissez-faire, and democratic. While such a classification may be convenient, it is far from accurate. No one of these descriptive titles defines today's supervision, for elements of all three are probably present in the supervisory process. When writers berate autocratic and laissez-faire supervision and sing the delights of democratic supervision, they sometimes lose sight of the mark, and democratic supervision becomes an end in itself. It is this concept that undoubtedly gives rise to the rather dangerously and certainly misleading comment that "what you do is less important than how you do it." Supervision of the right sort is less a matter of technique and more a matter of attitude. It is more than "the ability to get along with people." It is the ability to make significant improvements in instruction

---

*Reprinted with permission of The Macmillan Company, *Supervision in Today's Elementary Schools,* by James Curtin, copyright © James Curtin, 1964, 10-11.

through others. Of course, this means that human relationships assume a high priority, but they are not ends in themselves.

Better than the description of supervision in terms of convenient classifications is the definition in terms of purposes. Let it be said as forthrightly as possible that supervision is concerned with instruction. Everything else is subordinate. Thus it would appear that the purposes of supervision subsumed under its ultimate goal are as follows:

1. To set a proper classroom environment for learning.
2. To develop and utilize methods and materials which will insure the steady progress of each child.
3. To work with appropriate personnel to formulate instructional goals for the school or school system that are realistic and achievable.
4. To provide the school or school system with a clearly defined supervisory program that will insure the attainment of instructional goals.
5. To develop evaluative procedures that will appraise the effectiveness of the program.
6. To develop the attitude in the entire professional staff that supervision must be cooperative and that no teacher fulfills his professional obligation unless he works in concert with others to improve instruction.
7. To develop the attitude that instructional improvement is directly related to self-improvement of all members of the professional staff.
8. To provide specific helps to teachers with day-to-day problems.
9. To develop a sound working relationship in which teachers feel secure and confident.

TRENDS IN CONCEPTS AND FUNCTIONING OF SUPERVISORS*

The social-cultural conditions of the times and the expanding body of professional knowledge have made significant changes in supervision. First of all, there has been a vast increase in the number of supervisors employed by school districts.

---

*Reba M. Burnham and Martha L. King, *Supervision in Action*, Washington, D.C.: by permission of the Association for Supervision and Curriculum Development, 1961, copyright © 1961 by the Association for Supervision and Curriculum Development, 31-32, 34-35.

Throughout the 50 states, schools are engaging supervisors, consultants, helping teachers, directors and coordinators. The object is to provide leadership in the studying, planning, organizing, coordinating and evaluating of the school programs and in the handling of the problem areas that materialize in the schools. Paralleling the growth of this supervisory contingent has been a similar rise in the number of administrators, especially elementary and high school principals. Jointly, supervisors and administrators are responsible for furnishing the leadership required in studying, evaluating and implementing changes in the curriculum; interpreting the educational problems and programs to the public; developing in-service programs for staff members; providing orientation sessions for increasing numbers of new teachers; and developing and revising instructional materials to keep abreast of current developments.

The task of supervision is both challenging and frustrating because of the number and variety of problems faced and the suddenness with which they emerge and become critical. However, the developing theory of supervision has furnished guidelines for action, which contribute to the supervisors' feelings of security as they work in complex situations.

CONCEPTS OF SUPERVISION

Some concepts about supervision which may be drawn from the preceding discussion and upon which the remainder of this section of the booklet is based are the following:

1. Instructional supervision is a dynamic, growing process that is occupying an increasingly important role in the schools.
2. The purpose of supervision is to offer leadership in the improvement of educational experiences for children and youth.
3. Leadership is centered in a group, not in an individual.
4. The type and quality of supervision are affected by the situation, the organization, in which the supervision exists.
5. The climate of human relationships within the group and the degree to which members are committed to group goals influence the degree of change in practice.
6. The way in which individuals perceive the problems and the tasks inherent in the situation affects their behavior.
7. The actual role of supervision — and of instructional leaders — is a composite of all the expectations held for the role by the people associated with it.
8. A primary goal of supervisory leaders is to foster leadership in others. . . .

DECENTRALIZATION OF SUPERVISORY SERVICES

Large school districts with complex supervisory organizations are moving in the direction of decentralizing the staffs and simplifying the organization. Many large districts continue to have supervision or consultants in special fields, such as language arts, science, and mathematics. There is, however, a definite movement toward the use of general supervisors who work with teachers in a selected number of schools. In Dade County, Florida, where there are both special area supervisors and general supervisors, the generalists, who are called "zone" supervisors, are assigned certain buildings with which to work. The practice of assigning county office general supervisors to serve local districts is followed in many counties in Ohio. Frequently the districts assigned to one supervisor are in the same geographical location.

The State Department of Education in New Jersey has decentralized the 60 staff members who work in supervision under the direction of the Office of Elementary Education. These instructional leaders in elementary education, who are also members of the state department staff, are assigned to the office of the county superintendent and are titled "helping teachers." In this manner, New Jersey plans to make available to the local school districts the resources of a central office staff, which, because of limited resources, they might not otherwise have.

MODERN SUPERVISORS CONFUSE TEACHERS*

A second group which has contributed to this dilemma consists of those who supervise teachers, in particular administrators turned public relations experts. These professional bluebirds have taken away from the teacher much of the responsibility of making decisions and making education vital. In the process they have not advocated ideals which tell the teacher what he should be but have manufactured images which tell the teacher what he should fit into. The teacher is made out to be a salesman, psychiatrist, and policeman: a smiling, affable, entertaining, intellectual, understanding, persuasive person who can make anything universally intelligible no matter what the limitation of the student and who, at the same time, can keep the student happy and disciplined. When he is not

---

*Richard M. Bossone, "The Teacher's Dilemma," by permission of *The Peabody Journal of Education*, XLI, September, 1963, 92-93.

engaged in this endeavor he is expected to be watchdog of the buildings, grounds, buses and latrines, as well as serve on committees and attend numerous meetings. The teacher confronted with the complexity and proliferation of his role has his thinking pulled in many directions and finds himself in a dilemma: his own thinking tells him he should be emphasizing creative, stimulating teaching of his subject — forces within administration tell him he should be emphasizing public relations and non-teaching duties. Unfortunately these forces usually dominate the teacher and he retreats into the safe realm of prescribed conduct. Is it any wonder that many outstanding teachers quit? Is it any wonder that teachers are confused about their roles? Is it any wonder they are still debating about being called professional?

WHAT TEACHERS LIKE AND DISLIKE IN THEIR ADMINISTRATORS*

Let me give an illustration of how the idea of appraisal, group decision making, and the role of the administrator fit together in coordination of decision making.

Recently I asked our research assistant to interview a number of teachers in our own and neighborhood school districts. I thought they might not tell me the answers as well as they would tell her. She asked seven men and seven women teachers what they liked best and what they liked least about their principals and superintendents.

Here are four things they liked least about us: we hold too many unproductive meetings, we require too much record keeping, we set up arbitrary rules and schedules, and we do not know how to make sound decisions and then follow through.

What did they like best about us? They like it when we create an atmosphere of intellectual freedom, when we let teachers plan their own programs, when we keep the avenues of communication open, and when we encourage teacher participation in curriculum decisions. They also appreciate an administrator who is a leader in curriculum development, who is a resource person, who provides other resource people, and provides an abundance of good teaching materials. I realize that this survey wouldn't qualify as research, but the candid statements of fourteen teachers might give us food for thought.

---

*Robert S. Gilchrist, "The School Administrator as an Instructional Leader." By permission of *North Central Association Quarterly*, XXXVIII, Fall, 1963, 187.

SPECIAL EDUCATION . . .

GROWTH OF THE SCHOOLS' PROVISIONS FOR THE HANDICAPPED*

Today the Nation is providing special education for approximately 1,670,000 children and young people — the largest number our schools have ever served. The number is both a measure of the progress we have made and the distance we must go to provide for the estimated 6 million schoolage children who need special education.

To bring educational opportunity to even 1.7 million children, the American schools have been resourceful and ingenious in developing a variety of special education programs. They have, however, been aided by interested and dedicated laymen, legislative bodies, and many national and State organizations and agencies.

Education programs are available to serve various types of exceptional children, including the blind, partially seeing, deaf, hard of hearing, speech impaired, socially maladjusted, emotionally disturbed, mentally retarded, gifted, crippled, and the ones with special health problems. These children receive instruction in special day schools, special classes in regular schools, residential schools, hospitals and clinics, and when no other plan is available, in their own home. Special school programs are served by numerous persons ranging from itinerant teachers to speech and hearing specialists.

It is in the best interest of some of these children to spend a full day in a special school or class. Some need special education facilities for only part of the day and can attend in the regular elementary or secondary program for the remainder of the day. Some require special education for only a short period — perhaps for a few months; others require it throughout their lives. Still others will need to be transferred from one type of program to another. For example, a physically handicapped child might move from hospital or home instruction to a special class and possibly back to a regular school. Many schools and communities, aware of the advantages of easy and fluid movement of some handicapped children from one type of school program to another, have set up flexible programs for them.

---

*Romaine P. Mackie, "Special Education Reaches Nearly 2 Million Children," *School Life*, XLVII, December, 1964, 8.

In February 1963 the public day schools of the Nation enrolled about 1,559,000 pupils in special schools and classes in all of the 50 States. At the same time, residential schools, public and private, enrolled about 111,000 children. This is an increase of 670,000 pupils in public day schools, and about 23,000 in residential schools in the 5-year period preceding 1963. The public day school figures include all types of exceptional children; the residential school figures include mainly those who are blind, deaf, social maladjusted, emotionally disturbed, and mentally retarded.

Of perhaps even greater significance than the increase in enrollment is the increase in educational opportunities for handicapped children in their own communities. Nearly 5,600 public school systems had at least one such program in 1963. In addition, at least another 5,000 school systems that did not administer a program of their own made arrangements for children in another school system. At the beginning of the century, very few local school systems had any handicapped children in special education programs. Since that time there has been a steady increase in the development of these local programs, and the increase has been accelerated in the past quarter of a century. At least 90 percent of the children receiving special education are now enrolled in programs administered by the local public school system.

Somewhat less than 10 percent of the handicapped children enrolled in special education are in residential schools of one kind or other. They have always served severely handicapped pupils and those who live in sparsely populated areas, but today the character of some of these institutions appears to be changing in such a way as to make them an even more vital part of the total range of school services for the handicapped. For example, more of the residential schools are providing diagnostic services and short-term remedial instruction, which can be especially valuable when there is a close relationship between the institution and the child's home community.

THE MEANING OF SPECIAL EDUCATION
FOR THE EXCEPTIONAL CHILD*

Public schools are concerned with the education of all children, regardless of the degree to which some of their children may differ from

---

*Walter B. Barbe, *The Exceptional Child*, Washington, D.C.: by permission of The Center for Applied Research in Education, Inc., 1963, 1-2, 4-6.

others. It is no longer acceptable as good education to apply the same set of standards to all children on the assumption that in ability, temperament, and physical makeup they are all alike. The standards appropriate to the average child are futile and frustrating to the below-average child. Applying average standards to the above-average is equally frustrating, and wasteful of potential talent.

A basic belief in educational philosophy is that the difference of exceptional children is only one of degree: They are more like other children than unlike them. They must be treated first of all as children who need to express their individuality, and adjustments to their differences made within that framework. The label "exceptional" is only used in order to obtain a better understanding of the child. In times past, in their zeal to provide for exceptional children in need of special help, some educators overemphasized the label and forgot that the "children" part of the label is mcst important.

The manner in which exceptional children think, learn, and behave is not a different kind of behavior from that of other children. Even the degree of difference is not so great that it makes the child radically different from others. But the difference in degree is what makes the child exceptional, whether this difference is in the learning or behaving level of the child.

"Exceptional" refers to children who differ from the average to an extent that their differences warrant some type of special school adjustment, either within the regular classroom or in special classes. It includes both those children whose differences make them unable to perform up to the level of the average, as well as those whose differences allow them to perform above the average. It includes the mentally and physically handicapped and the emotionally and socially disturbed as well as the mentally and physically superior. If exceptional children are different from the average, then the problem becomes one of determining how different a child must be before he can be called exceptional. It is not easily answered for any one of the specific areas of exceptionality, and is certainly unanswerable when applied to all of the diverse areas encompassed by the label "exceptional children.". . .

Special education is that part of education which deals specifically with the exceptional child. The role which special education plays in the education of exceptional children is often confused with the philosophy of special classes. Special education is concerned with the identification of and provision for children who are unlike the average, whether this be in the regular classroom, the special classroom, or in some combination of both. This is a broadened concept from that previously held which limited special education only to the education of those exceptional children who were assigned to special classes.

This broadened concept can be more fully realized when it is noted that "in 1948 one in ten [exceptional] children was enrolled in a special education program; in 1958 one in four was enrolled." Actually, it is neither the goal of special education nor the philosophy of modern education to place children in special classes merely because they can be labeled in some specific way. The purpose of the special class is to make available a learning situation in which children who are unable to benefit to the fullest from regular classroom instruction can be successful. Differentiated instruction within the regular classroom is the necessary first step. When this is impractical or ineffective, consideration should be given to special class assignment.

Special education has developed as an area of study devoted to curriculum development, teaching techniques, identification and diagnosis, materials development, and teacher training for exceptional children. The field is concerned both with the exceptional child in the regular classroom and in the special class. Program development for exceptional children as a part of the total general education program has been stressed.

The program for exceptional children has not been seen as something which separates exceptional children from all others, but something to help the exceptional child to function effectively in an average world. The program for exceptional children is accepted as one part of the public school's total responsibility, not particularly for any specific group but a part of the dedication to the development of all children to the limits of their abilities. The program for exceptional children must not be fostered at the expense of other children; if that happens, it is doomed to failure. A wise program for exceptional children benefits all children. For example, special class programs for mentally retarded children benefits them by establishing more realistic goals, but at the same time it releases the regular classroom teacher from having to move so slowly with these children that she is unable to give adequate time to the remaining children in her room.

SCHOOLS MUST HELP THE UNUSUAL AS WELL AS THE USUAL CHILD*

The rapid changes in our modern world require that the child be able to accept the maximum education which his abilities, as well as his handi-

---

*Joseph S. Roucek, *The Unusual Child*, New York: by permission of Philosophical Library, Inc., 1962, 1-2.

caps, allow him to utilize. America acknowledges that education is a vital necessity for all children, and especially those who are "unusual" children, and that, with the proper approach, understanding, training and placement, even "unusual" children can become fully contributing members of society.

Is there a teacher who, at one time or another, does not have to deal with children who, somehow or other, become a problem because they are not ordinary pupils, and whose difficulties require help in areas with which the teacher's particular professional education has not equipped him (or her) to deal? The difficulty is that society cannot guarantee good parents or environment for every child. But this fact, in turn, imposes the responsibility on all teachers to "know" how to handle practically every problem that comes up in their classrooms. Sometimes, where the home environment is unsatisfactory, the teacher can help to meet the basic needs of all children for affection, for a feeling of belonging, for a sense of achievement and for an opportunity for creative expression. But all too often the overworked teacher must take on the added responsibility, as the laws of many states acknowledge, of serving *in loco parentis* (in place of a parent), since, in recent decades, the American family has been transferring more and more of its share of responsibilities to the school. Whether or not the teachers are expected to know the family of every pupil and discuss the child's progress with the parents, the fact remains that the family, the community and the administration of each school expect the teachers to act as employers of a child-rearing agency, whose influence is carried out even beyond the framework of the influence of the family, and who, therefore, as educated specialists *must* know all about their charges.

This is, indeed, a formidable task and assignment since we live in a very complex society, and each classroom is filled with personalities which have to be handled not only as a group but also as individuals. There are always "deviates," those who are above or below the "average" intelligence, those who are always troublesome, and those who have physical, emotional, and mental difficulties. The realization of such ever-recurring phenomena has produced numerous experiments in handling "exceptionality," floods of specialized studies, and even the training of specialists. But, interestingly enough, most of the available data on the unusual child are of a relatively recent date, resulting mostly from the wide range of studies in child growth and development. In addition, there has been a definite impact from the medical contributions. The same applies to the psychologist and the educator, who have shown how children differ and what factors influence individual differences, and who have indicated programs which would satisfy the needs of each individual child. Furthermore, much has been done by statistical contributions, which show us more about the relationships, the distribution of abilities and the degree of differences, as well as the methods of measuring differences and the reliability and validity of such measurements.

ORGANIZING FOR INSTRUCTING THE GIFTED*

Equal educational opportunity is not synonymous with identical experience. In our efforts to be democratic we sometimes fail to make this distinction. Current critics of efforts to provide for the academically talented often assert that to single out these children for special attention is to be undemocratic. Yet life experience supports the conclusion that identical experience for all is not only unwise — it is impossible.

The physician gives the benefit of his competence to all his patients equally, yet he does not prescribe identical medication for them all. In school programs, those with special interests in creative writing or music do not have identical experiences. The physically handicapped, the mentally retarded, the visually handicapped, those who have hearing disabilities — these children are given the benefit of special attention and special programs geared to their needs. These programs are, for them, equal opportunity.

Then, too, providing for individual differences among children has been a primary concern of educators for many years. The testing movement gave scientific support to the idea more than 40 years ago.

The fact that children are different has become an axiom in educational theory. While application of this axiom has presented problems, efforts to solve them have been continuous. The good instructional program will provide for differences among children in any classroom, yet in some instances the talented are neglected because they seem able to get along on their own. To be consistent with the democratic ideal of providing equal education opportunity, we must make sure that academically talented children are provided with effectively challenging experiences.

However, provision for the academically talented should never be viewed as a crash program, narrow in scope and purpose. It is one aspect

---

*David C. Sanders, *Elementary Education and the Academically Talented Pupil*, Washington, D.C.: National Education Association, 1961, 9-10, 84-85.

of the goal of structuring the learning environment so that each student, in keeping with his interests and abilities, can develop maximally in directions that are mutually beneficial to himself and to society. Provisions for able children should never become a substitute for quality education for all or a device for rescuing those with special talents from a program which is not good for anyone. Provision for the academically talented must grow out of a good program for all children. It is a never-ending process of improved teaching and learning. . . .

The following guidelines may be of help to the principal in making decisions about organization.

First, in developing a program for academically talented children, the focus should not be on organization. Successful and unsuccessful programs may be found within every organizational framework. Second, successful organization is inevitably dependent upon many local factors, such as size, financial condition and socioeconomic status of the community, school facilities, competencies of the staff, educational philosophy and objectives of the school, and tradition. Third, changes in organization should be evolutionary, not revolutionary. The opportunity to help the academically talented child must not be jeopardized for the sake of an organizational innovation.

Many people should participate in the planning process.

Pilot or small-scale changes are often valuable. If this seems somewhat conservative and overly cautious, it is because programs for academically talented children are not to be viewed as temporary. Rather, they should become and remain an integral part of the community's educational program; hence, they should be solidly developed from the beginning.

A thorough study and review of the curricumum both in terms of sequential and horizontal learning will provide the best basis for deciding about organization.

NEW LEARNING APPROACHES . . .

THE NONGRADED SCHOOL*

Are the days of the graded schools numbered? The graded school has been a model ever since 1848, when James Philbrick set up the Quincy Grammar School in Boston, Mass. Philbrick, like all school administra-

---

*Stuart E. Dean, "The Nongraded School; Is There Magic In It?" _School Life,_ XLVII, December, 1964, 19-21.

tors before him and since, was looking for some sort of administrative framework that would provide in an orderly way for large numbers of children and teachers; and the one he finally settled on was based on the persuasive logic of chronological age. He classified his pupils primarily by the number of years in which they had been enrolled in school, and he measured the years by grades — the first grade for the first year, the second for the next, and so on.

Discontent with the graded school began early, as soon as students who couldn't keep up with their classmates began to pile up at the various levels. From time to time during the 116 years since Philbrick set the pattern, waves of disenchantment with the graded school have swept the country; and other forms of organization have been briefly experimented with. The present movement toward a non-graded system, however, is more serious and more widespread than any of the previous efforts to find an organizational structure that would be highly responsive to the needs of individual children.

It is doubtful that Philbrick was aware that he was setting a style. But it is certain that he intended his organizational structure to serve two purposes: To make the administrative operation of his school smooth and efficient and to provide a setting in which the best possible instruction could be given. And it is probably equally certain that he would have been surprised, could be have looked into the future, that his pattern would be used in such a way that it regimented children in lockstep formation and put a premium on conformity and inhibited the individual child from expressing himself.

The fact is that a school needs both system and flexibility — system for handling the mass and flexibility for working with the individual. That is to say, it needs two different kinds of structure — one for administrative operation and one for instruction. But the one must always be subservient to the other. No one needs to be reminded that the schools were created for one purpose — to instruct — and that any operational structure proves its worth only in the degree to which it creates, supports, and encourages an effective instructional program. A school's merit is not to be found in the central administrative office but in the classroom, where teachers teach and pupils learn.

Any school in which operational structure is considered an end in itself is on the wrong course. Here we have the key to the failures laid at the door of the graded school. Conceived as a purely administrative device to aid school operation, it has been trapped into becoming an end in itself and, as such, has limited rather than aided instruction.

What our school people are looking for, obviously, is a form of organization that will be a friendly medium both to [the] administrative system, which imposes limits, and to the development of the human mind, which knows no limits at all. It may be that no such form exists, or that no such form can be ever devised; but surely some way can be found that will permit a school to run efficiently and at the same time have the flexibility it must have if it is to attend to each child as an individual.

Is the nongraded school the answer?

The nongraded school goes by several names — ungraded school, primary unit, continuous-progress program, and multiaged school. But no matter what name it bears, the non-graded school in its simplest form is nothing more than a school that has eliminated grade barriers. It focuses attention on how well a child is doing in terms of his own ability and stage of development, not in reference to a particular grade level.

So far, experimentation with the nongraded system has been limited mostly to the primary school level, and most of the evidence of its efficiency has been gleaned from the "nongraded primary unit". Lately, however, there have been signs that the movement is extending to all school levels: scattered examples can now be found in the intermediate grades and even in a few secondary schools.

Basically, the nongraded school is not a new method of teaching or a different way of running a classroom. It is only an operational type of structure, but it does leave children room to grow in without hitting their heads on artificially imposed ceilings or suffering from unreasonable pressure to advance in prescribed directions. And within its framework teachers are free to deal with the virtually limitless range of abilities that exist in every classroom.

Most of the schools that are trying nongraded systems are doing so in a serious effort to strike a proper balance between operational structure and instructional purpose.

GROWTH OF THE MOVEMENT

Many persons think of the nongraded school as a totally new idea, but it is, as I have said, anything but that. In fact, it has some of the merits of the good one-room rural school, which some persons even today believe was a high-water mark in American education. The teacher who held together the assortment of ages and grades in a one-room school was taking advantage of an excellent opportunity to follow a highly flexible, almost fluid, style of operation.

The first program of nongrading in the primary grades now in existence, is the one in Milwaukee, adopted in 1942. The second is in Appleton, Wis., adopted in 1947. From these beginnings, the adoption of nongraded units has become a movement, which spread slowly at first but which now has become so strong that no one is able to keep a current and reliable count of the total number.

Reports to the Office of Education at the present time show that the movement is reaching into the secondary school, but so far the increase there is slight.

HOW DOES IT WORK?

The "nongraded primary unit" usually combines grades 1, 2, and 3 under one teacher. Some schools combine the kindergarten and grades 1, 2, and 3; a few combine grades 1 and 2 only. Children in a nongraded primary unit are identified by the name of the teacher. No reference is made to "grade." The teacher and group remain together for the length of the program.

In the unbroken setting of the nongraded program the teacher has more time in which to guide, lead, and shape the progress of her pupils. She does not have to worry about attaining fixed levels or keeping every pupil at the same level of growth and progress. She can recognize, adjust to, and respond to the range of individual differences in her pupils. Learning is no longer a prescribed series of exact rules to which she must adhere, and she has a wider range of materials at her disposal.

Of course, even so liberal a structure as that of the nongraded school will not solve the problems of all children. Some may require more time than the 2 or 3 years allotted to the program. But with a more elastic period of time in which to absorb some of the variabilities of the classroom and stabilize the lagging child's rate of learning, there should be fewer cases of children who cannot keep up. On the other hand, some children may be able to move faster than their classmates, but indiscriminate advancing is not always wise. With more information at hand in the nongraded school, the teacher can make a more thoughtful decision as to the child's best rate of progress.

The purpose of the nongraded secondary school is much the same as those of the nongraded elementary school — to educate the individual to his ·full potential. But its administrative problems are larger and more complicated. The secondary school's program is more varied and comprehensive than the elementary school's. Techniques and devices in the two schools differ. . . .

The adoption of a nongraded plan involves endless details of planning, initiation, and execution. To begin with, a system must determine whether such a shift is warranted. The first danger is the temptation to jump into a nongraded program without having worked out all details. A changeover must only follow the most careful investigation and planning. All planning must include school staff members and the community. Without the support of these people, a program's chances for success are poor.

Before moving to a nongraded plan school officials must have firm and sound policies for reporting progress, communication between levels, curriculum changes, pupil mobility, record keeping, and teacher qualification.

Reporting progress

The nongraded school must have a sound policy for reporting pupil progress to parents. Reporting to parents has always been difficult, of course, whatever system a school follows, but the nature of the nongraded school makes reporting even more difficult. Parents used to a graded system are disturbed by so drastic a change.

Coordination between levels

As a school system experiments with nongrading at different levels it faces the problem of internal coordination. Special problems arise when children leave a nongraded unit to go into a traditional school, or vice versa. Some children may have to be reoriented. The school must anticipate such problems and be ready to meet them.

Need for "levels"

Experience so far in the nongraded school points to a continuing need for some definition of "level," based on accomplishment, quantitative expectancy, or both, to replace "grade."

Many nongraded elementary schools continue to rely on a series of reading levels as a measure of pupil attainment. The number of levels varies considerably; one school system has 11 levels for the first 3 years; another has 20; most have about 7 or 8. Many educators are surprised to learn of the use of specific reading levels in a nongraded school. It seems to them as though a new term "reading level" had simply replaced the old term "graded." But this is not necessarily so. Nongrading as practiced by some schools often leaves something to be desired. Very few schools are entirely nongraded. Progress today is only a beginning step in an evolutionary development.

Curriculum changes

One of the lessons to be drawn from the early experience with nongrading and its significance for the future is its effect on the curriculum.

The most evident need is for specifying and defining curriculum structure. Grading has permitted us to evade the issue. But with nongrading, we are coming to realize that the true test of educational merit lies in the responsiveness of education to the range of human variability. We can now assess the value of curriculum in use against the needs of the time. Although nongrading gives some promise of easing administrative restrictions, its greatest potential may be realized in the advancement of curriculum.

Pupil mobility

Can a nongraded system be succesful where there is a high degree of pupil mobility? There appears to be no reason to doubt that it can. Because instruction is individual, a pupil can enter or resume at any time and take up his work at his point of attainment. A pupil transferring from another school is assigned to a group on the basis of the usual factors, such as age and past record. His teacher adjusts his program to an analysis of his skills and accomplishments.

ORGANIZATION FOR TEAM TEACHING*

In good schools teachers have always worked together. Sometimes this has meant two or three teachers sharing their collective skills with each other's classes. Sometimes it has meant something as simple as planning a class trip together to culminate an area of study common to two or more groups. For some schools, it may have meant that staff members with clear understanding of their goals worked hard together to increase their knowledge and understanding of children and to make improvements in the teaching-learning process.

Team teaching in today's schools has come to have a rather specialized meaning. Basically, team teaching is an arrangement that provides for having two or more teachers, with abilities and skills that complement each other, assume joint responsibility for directing the learning activities of a group of students. Together, the members of the team take charge of planning lessons, developing appropriate methods and materials, and teaching and evaluating a program of studies for their student group.

Elementary School Organization: Purposes, Patterns, Perspectives, Washington, D.C.: National Education Association, 1961, 115, 118-119, 124-125. By permission of the Department of Elementary School Principals.

As pointed out earlier, there are many models of team teaching. They range from the simple combining of two classrooms and the efforts of two teachers to complex designs involving many classes, a variety of grouping patterns and a hierarchy of staff. . . .

RATIONALE

Advocates of today's team teaching point to a number of reasons why they believe this organizational plan has special merit. At the elementary school level as well as at other levels, teachers have particular interests and training in a certain area. As a team member, a teacher's strengths can be directed toward tasks which utilize these special skills, and the talents of other team members can be complementary. There are opportunities, too, for well-qualified teachers to assume leadership roles — opportunities not available in the typical school organization plan. These staff members become team leaders and, in some cases, receive additional salary benefits. It is also felt that when a team of teachers works as a group on all phases of the school program, increased involvement in and responsibility for curriculum improvement ensues. Supporters of team teaching maintain further that guidance of students is improved since the teachers of a team know more students and, as a group, can deal with individual and class problems. It is also important and necessary, they point out, to have a method of grouping and regrouping students during the teaching day to provide for individual differences in learning rates. Team teaching, they feel, permits this needed flexibility.

Team organization encourages the use of nonprofessional personnel for noninstructional tasks. It is a common complaint of teachers that clerical duties are too numerous and time consuming during the teaching day. Using teacher aides or clerical help for clerical tasks enables professional personnel to perform the duties for which they were trained.

ORGANIZATIONAL CHARACTERISTICS

The literature describing today's team teaching suggests that it is in a developmental stage. No single pattern of organization or operation has emerged. One organizational plan calls for three teachers and clerical assistance for 75 or more students of similar age and grade level. One of the teachers, designated as the team leader, is usually paid an additional sum for accepting this responsibility. The team leader performs his duties under direct supervision of the principal and works closely with the principal as spokesman for the team. In addition to teaching, responsibilities of the team leader involve making schedules for instruction, grouping students, selecting materials, planning techniques of instruction, and helping to evaluate the program. The remaining professional team members are given the title of cooperating teachers and may or may not receive an additional salary payment. The cooperating teachers work with and assist the team leader in planning, in teaching, and in other activities of the team. . . . If analysis indicates that the team approach requires a greater expenditure of money than does another organizational plan, then it remains for a local community to decide whether or not there is a proportionate increase in the quality of the instructional program. Relative values need to be considered. For example, what would be the effect on the quality of education if the increased amount of money required for the team teaching plan were used in different ways? How would the quality of education be affected, for instance, if these funds were used to employ additional teachers and reduce class load? If it were used to hire additional clerical help? Or to employ one or more specialist-consultants? Or to extend library and audio-visual facilities?

Proponents feel that team teaching presents a needed flexibility in student grouping. Pupils are grouped differently for various purposes. They may be grouped heterogeneously at one time for a particular purpose, and homogeneously at another time for a different purpose. They may be grouped in small or large classes, depending upon the aim, or the whole grade may be together. Supporters point out that instruction, partly departmentalized, does not sacrifice the intimate teacher-student relationship necessary for adequate guidance. The increased opportunities for students to meet and work with a greater number and variety of teachers and students are felt to be advantageous.

ADMINISTRATIVE IMPLICATIONS

Team teaching has important implications with respect to staffing, and the problem of how to use present personnel can be a hard one to solve. Whether all teachers can and want to become involved in teams, what the effects of turnover may be, how recruitment policy is to be modified — these and many other similar questions will need consideration.

The matter of cost will merit exploration in each individual school. After initial outlays for certain kinds of equipment and for special salary increases that may be paid to team leaders, the cost per pupil in average daily attendance may actually show a decline as increasing numbers of teacher aides and clerks are engaged at salaries considerably lower than those paid to certified professional personnel.

Changes in a school program that bring about modifications in the teaching-learning situation will command the interest of parents. This suggests that the usual efforts made by many schools today to keep parents informed need to be maintained as a school moves toward a different organizational plan. Parents need opportunities to become involved in the planning, development and evaluation of changes that are made. The importance of reporting pupil progress to parents will remain undiminished. Other matters having to do with grouping, methods of instruction, departmentalization, changing teacher roles and the like will also need consideration. Schools moving toward team teaching will want to give careful thought to these matters. But most important of all the considerations will be the question of whether or not the proposed new organizational plan improves the quality of the educational program for boys and girls.

TYPES AND POTENTIALS OF TEACHING MACHINES*

There are constructed response machines in which the student writes his answer on a tape and compares it with the correct answer, which is exposed only when the student's answer is covered with a plastic window (so he can't change it after he sees the correct answer). A variation on this allows the student, after he has written his response, to uncover a clue, (at the same time covering his response with a window). At this point he may write a second response if he wishes to amend the first one. The answer may then be unmasked (at the same time covering the second response with the window), and both answers may then be compared with the correct answer.

There are drill devices in which each item comes back again and again; but when the student answers an item correctly a predetermined number of times, it drops out and does not reappear.

There are constructed response machines in which the student does not write the response but rather constructs his answer mechanically by moving sliders.

---

*David Cram, *Explaining Teaching Machines and Programming*, San Francisco: by permission of Fearon Publishers, 1961, 77-78.

There are multiple-choice linear devices which require the student to push buttons, punch holes in paper with a stylus, pull tabs, or type his answer on a keyboard, all of which immediately provide some knowledge of results (i.e., right or wrong).

There is a machine for branching programs which presents the program on a microfilm viewer. The alternatives are selected by a choice of push-buttons.

Finally, there is the computer oriented, self-oriented program for developing motor skills.

What will these machines provide?

First, they all provide an environment in which the learner is, to a greater or lesser degree, in control. *He* decides when "time is up" on a given item, *he* decides when he wants to know the correct answer. The knowledge that his mistakes will be recorded makes the control meaningful and motivates him to attend to the problem. From the teacher's point of view, the recording of responses permits evaluating both the effectiveness of the program and the performance of the individual student. Based on this record, the teacher may provide guidance or assistance as needed.

Second, because the machine is to a greater or lesser degree responsive to the student, it provides an environment in which outside distractions are less noticeable. The student whose mind wanders during a lecture may miss an important point: a machine will not proceed unless the student is ready. The more attractive the learning situation, the more readily will students apply themselves to it. Motivational devices such as visible counters and timers, lights, and even buzzers are available on some machines.

Third, although the initial cost of a branching machine is high, the program is stored on microfilm and thus is less costly and requires far less storage space than the equivalent program in scrambled book form.

Fourth, machines may add a dimension of interaction that could not be achieved in any other way. The self-organizing program represents a constant and highly sensitive interaction between student and machine in the learning of motor skills; designs are feasible that would allow similar treatment of verbal subject matter. A computer with an undistractable brain ready instantly to call forth any information in its memory bank could, on the basis of student response to test items, redirect the student to any number of alternate paths, depending on the background and even the temperament of the student. Because a computer could time responses and compare them with all other responses, it could allow the student to compete with his own past performance, with his aspirations, or with other students. The machine could decide, on the basis of the time taken for each response, whether the student needs simpler steps or harder steps. It could, by constant testing *prevent* the student from stumbling through the program without really paying attention. These designs are still speculative, however, and will require considerable research and improvement in programming techniques and skills before they can be realized.

EXTENDED SCHOOLING VERSUS HIGHER EDUCATION*

American education is enmeshed today in two problems concerning minimal educational experiences for American youth: anguish over the dropout rate and anxiety over the crushing load of applicants seeking higher educational opportunities. An unguided, ill-considered educational structure is emerging, bereft of philosophical roots and scarcely capable of fulfillment without seriously hampering the true role of higher education. Our educational program has been geared toward the inclusion of one huge educated majority.

One of the first to break into the degree-carrying higher educational category was the common school teacher, and many have followed seeking an extended educational experience to qualify for a singular identification and simultaneous admission into a less-selected educated minority. Meanwhile, other countries provide sub-university programs without granting equal privileges with the university degree.

Certainly, few would argue that life in today's and tomorrow's world requires extended education, probably no less for survival than for success. Most assuredly, the great flowering of knowledge and the dire necessity to understand world problems rather than merely those of one's farm or even one's country has enlarged quite suddenly the educational task. Not only is it necessary to learn most effectively and to learn more, but it is vitally essential to master the skills for continued self-instruction in the adult world beyond the classroom.

We seem to have accepted the notion that a college education is to become the goal of every American youngster. The high school is the equivalent of yesterday's elementary education as we worry over the dropout and scheme to keep him through 12 years. It even is said that (somewhere) there is a college for every high school graduate.

*John F. Ohles, "Extended School Versus Higher Education," by permission of *School and Society*, XCII, No. 2242, April 4, 1964, 156-157.

We seem merely to follow the directions of force, as though there is no choice. But there should be numerous choices if we were to bother to seek them. Here, of course, is the black abyss left in the absence of a dynamic educational philosophy. As long as educators continue merely to act, to meet crises only with reapplication of that which is, to forego bothering to think out the consequences or restructure the goals or dream dreams, the American educational nightmare will persist.

We should be engaged in extending our school process rather than simply to settle for the dumping of broader needs upon colleges and universities. A log, a scholar, and a teacher await supplementation with electronic tools and the fruits of that educational research which has been dignified with regulated structuring, careful controls, and honest appraisal. Even in mass education, we are on the threshold of mastering the processes of instructing groups as individuals rather than merely relying on recitation or lecturing with individuals in groups.

Our haphazard, graded progression ought to become a carefully programmed drawing out of scholarly skills leading from truth to truth as thoughtfully as one brick is placed upon another. The efficiency of a teaching tool should be matched with an efficient class hour, both geared to a school year governed by a derived rhythm of learning effectiveness. Extended education within each year should be continued in the 13th or 14th year of *secondary* education. Higher education should be the more complex of the new mountain of knowledge, not last century's infant Paricutin.

Some will say a longer secondary education cannot or will not be assumed by financially strapped school districts. But higher education, by its nature, must cost more than secondary education. Nor is there evidence to show that public schools are careful husbands of public monies. Finally, it is difficult to distinguish dollars going into higher education from those in secondary education, especially since they are pinched successively from the same wallet.

Extended education for all must not mean an extension of mass education from high school diploma to college degree. Consequences must be examined and subjected to a philosophical review. The inevitable lowering of efficiency, growing meaninglessness of a degree, increased random selection of faculty, and pressures to alter graduate study based on the needs of staffing rather than needs for scholarship are some of the consequences to be considered.

Our population needs to be more knowledgeable, more highly skilled. But the gains we seek ought not to be at any price. They should be achieved, instead, through a rational process in which a defensible philosophical position is established and pursued.

ORGANIZATION OF THE SCHOOL YEAR . . .

THE YEAR ROUND SCHOOL*

Recently a number of teachers and administrators who had participated in voluntary summer programs for pupils and an extended year for faculty members were asked to identify the strengths of such programs. Some of the more common responses were:

1. The needs of children, both directly and indirectly, are provided for.
2. The professional growth of teachers is accelerated.
3. Teaching becomes a full-time profession.
4. Teachers begin the regular school year with a greater sense of security.
5. Curriculum revision can take place in a relaxed atmosphere.
6. Greater time can be devoted to the selection of textbooks and other teaching materials.
7. System-wide workshops and committees provide teachers with an opportunity to understand other teachers and their problems.
8. Teachers have an opportunity to become better acquainted with students and parents.
9. Teachers have a greater opportunity to become an integral part of the community.
10. Teachers' salaries more nearly approach a professional level.
11. Opportunity is provided for adequate orientation of new teachers.
12. Opportunity is provided for teachers to learn about the community and to become better acquainted with the philosophy and services of the school system.
13. As teachers participate in workshops, orientation programs, examination and discussion of students' records, and the many other activities of the summer-school program, they become better able to guide and direct children during the regular school year.

---

*Year Round School, Washington, D.C.: by permission of American Association of School Administrators, 1960, 17-18, 21-22.

14. Opportunity is provided for system-wide, vertical curriculum meetings which contribute to an understanding of the total curriculum by all teachers.
15. All resources, human and material, are used to the maximum.

PROCEDURES FOR ARRIVING AT POLICY DECISIONS ON THE LENGTH OF THE SCHOOL YEAR

If the leadership of a community decides to reappraise the length of its school year, a number of approaches might be suggested. The following may prove helpful.

First of all, the leaders should consider thoroughly *who* should be involved in the decision-making process and *when* they should be involved. Clearly, the leaders themselves—the superintendent, the principals, representative teachers, school board members, together with heads of civic, labor, and business groups—must go through a study and discussion experience. They need not all work simultaneously, however. Probably the profession, with the guidance of the superintendent, should be first to examine such questions as:

(a) Is there a need for change in the length of the school year to make the school more efficient, for economical reasons, or to extend pupil services to the end that higher quality education and better learning will result?

(b) Have the educational demands of the time so increased and the curriculum expanded so much that pupils must have more time in school to meet the requirements?

(c) Does the long period of preparation for those who assume complex occupational roles suggest need for acceleration?

Any such review will likely involve serious study of the contemporary social, economic, political, and cultural developments, together with a look at the changing international scene and its implications for education. If such reviews indicate the need for a longer school year, attention should next center on the various plans for operating a year-round program. Faculty meetings devoted to discussions of the plans outlined in this bulletin, along with reports on various publications listed in the bibliography should be helpful. Similar activities and programs could later be undertaken with parent-teacher, civic, and business groups.

Once the leaders from the teaching profession and from other agencies and organizations reach a consensus of opinion on what ought or ought not to be done, then wide publicity and discussion should permeate all strata of the community. Out of this should come general agreement on an appropriate program, together with a plan for securing the additional revenues needed. Only after all this is done is it wise for a board of education to adopt a policy.

FOR FURTHER REFLECTION OR INVESTIGATION

1. Argue the case for and against homogenous groupings of students for best learning. Is there a difference between groupings for best learning and best development of children?

2. What are the complete implications for the administration of schools if team teaching, educational television, teaching machines, and ungraded classrooms should prove to be successful?

3. Is there anything that can be accomplished in the 6-3-3 organizational plan which could not be accomplished in the 8-4 or 6-6 or other arrangement if teachers, administrators, and citizens are committed to making it happen?

4. Interview principals and teachers from a variety of organizational arrangements (6-3-3, 8-4, and others) to determine their reasons for that structure. Then see if any research can be uncovered to establish a factual base for their reasoning.

5. Is the trend to introduce learnings earlier in a child's school experience based on any knowledge of child growth or on fad? Has it ever been determined when a youngster is ready to learn any particular subject matter?

6. Investigate the achievements of 6- or 8-weeks summer kindergartens to determine whether children profit substantially more from a full year of kindergarten.

7. Is the specification of a uniform admission age for first graders based upon educational reasons or expediency to ease administrative decision making? Could school officials "live with" a flexible age specification which recognizes maturity and intellect as well as age?

8. Have workshops, conventions, and similar in-service activities outlived their usefulness insofar as making important changes in curriculum?

9. Discuss in detail the merits of providing supervision by central staff subject-matter specialists, by principals, or by department heads.

10. What may be inferred from the often repeated claims by administrators that they do not need to visit classrooms in order to evaluate teaching effectiveness?

11. With each member of the class listing five important elements which contribute to good teaching, compare the lists and determine whether together the class could agree on ten elements proper for use in evaluating teacher performance.

12. Which is worse for teacher morale: no supervision or excessive supervision?

13. Which is worse for teacher morale: merit pay based upon proper

evaluation of performance, allowing for the occasional misjudgments which may occur, or paying all teachers on the same scale regardless of performance?

14. Should the superintendent (or central staff officer charged with the instructional responsibility) be intensively trained in one subject or extensively trained in several subject fields?

15. Discuss the merits of assigning special education classes to the school system's instructional department or to the pupil personnel department.

16. Prepare a job description for the Director of Instruction in a school system of 10,000 pupils.

BIBLIOGRAPHY

Anderson, Vernon E. and William T. Gruhn, *Principles and Practices of Secondary Education,* 2nd Ed., New York: The Ronald Press Company, 1962.

Bailey, Thomas D., "The School Administrator's Responsibility for Providing an Adequate Program of Adult Education," *School Life,* February 1960.

Balance in the Curriculum, Washington, D.C.: Association for Supervision and Curriculum Development, 1961 Yearbook.

Barbe, Walter B., *The Exceptional Child,* Washington, D.C.: The Center for Applied Research in Education, Inc., 1963.

Berson, Minnie Perrin, *Kindergarten: Your Child's Big Step,* New York: E. P. Dutton & Co., Inc., 1959.

Bossone, Richard M., "The Teacher's Dilemma," *Peabody Journal of Education,* XLI, September, 1963.

Brown, Frank, *The Nongraded High School,* Englewood Cliffs, N. J.: Prentice-Hall, Inc., 1963.

Burnham, Reba M., and Martha L. King, *Supervision in Action,* Washington, D.C.: Association for Supervision and Curriculum Development, 1961.

Costello, Lawrence F., and George N. Gordon, *Teach with Television,* New York: Hastings House, 1961.

Cottingham, Harold F. and William E. Hopke, *Guidance In the Junior High School,* Bloomington, Ill.: McKnight and McKnight Publishing Co., 1961.

Coulson, John E., ed., *Programmed Learning and Computer Based Instruction,* New York: John Wiley and Sons, Inc., 1962.

Cram, David, *Explaining "Teaching Machines" and Programming,* San Francisco: Fearson Publishers, 1961.

Crosby, Muriel, *Curriculum Development for Elementary Schools in a Changing Society,* Boston: D.C. Heath and Company, 1965.

Curtin, James, *Supervision in Today's Elementary Schools,* New York: The Macmillan Co., 1964.

Dean, Stuart E., *Elementary School Administration and Organization,* Washington, D.C.: U.S. Office of Education, Bulletin No. 11, 1960.

————, "The Nongraded School," *School Life,* XLVII, December, 1964.

Elementary School Organization: Purposes, Patterns, Perspectives. Washington, D.C.: National Education Association, 1961.

Ellena, William J., Margaret Stevenson, and Harold Webb, eds., *Who's a Good Teacher?* Washington, D.C.: American Association of School Administrators, 1961.

Eye, Glen G., and Lanore A. Netzer, *Supervision of Instruction, a Phase of Administration,* New York: Harper and Row, Publishers, 1965.

Ford, G. W., and Lawrence Pugno, eds., *Structure of Knowledge and the Curriculum,* Chicago: Rand McNally & Company, 1965.

Franseth, Jane, *Supervision as Leadership,* Evanston, Ill.: Row, Peterson and Company, 1961.

Frazier, Alexander, "New Teacher and a New Kind of Supervision," *Educational Leadership,* XXI, November, 1963.

Gilchrist, Robert S., "The School Administrator as an Instructional Leader." *N.C.A. Quarterly,* XXXVIII, Fall, 1963.

Goodlad, John I., and Kenneth Rehage, "Unscrambling the Vocabulary of School Organization," *NEA Journal,* LI, November, 1962.

Goodlad, John I., and Robert H. Anderson, *The Nongraded Elementary School,* New York: Harcourt, Brace, and World, Inc., 1963.

Grambs, Jean D., and L. Morris McClure, *Foundations of Teaching,* New York: Holt, Rinehart and Winston, Inc. 1964.

Grieder, Calvin, "Let High School Department Heads be Responsible for Supervision of Instruction," *Nation's Schools,* LXXI, April, 1963.

Gwaltney, T. M., "Supervisor's Role," *School and Community,* L May, 1964.

Gwynn, J. Minor, *Theory and Practice of Supervision,* New York: Dodd, Mead, and Company, 1961.

Havighurst, Robert J., "Education in the Big City: A New Frontier," Kent, Ohio: *Kappa Delta Pi Lectures,* No. 1, November 13, 1963.

Hillson, Maurie, *Change and Innovation in Elementary School Organization,* New York: Holt, Rinehart, and Winston, Inc., 1965.

Kowitz, Gerald T., "Examining Educational Innovations," *American School Board Journal,* January, 1964.

Leeper, Robert R., ed., and Evelyn F. Carlson, Chairman, *Role of Supervisor and Curriculum Director in a Climate of Change,* ASCD 1965 Yearbook, Washington, D.C.: Association for Supervision and Curriculum Development, 1965.

Lindsay, Frank B., "The Invisible Student in the Comprehensive High School," *Journal of Secondary Education,* XXXVIII, October, 1963.

Logsdon, James D., "Are Principals Being By-passed in Improvement of Instruction," *National Association of Secondary-School Principals Bulletin,* XLVIII, April, 1964.

Lortie, Dan., "Change and Exchange: Reducing Resistance to Innovation," *Administrator's Notebook,* XII, February, 1964.

Mackie, Romaine P., "Special Education Reaches Nearly 2 Million Children." *School Life,* XLVII No. 3, December, 1964.

McKean, Robert C., *The Supervisor,* Washington, D.C.: The Center for Applied Research in Education, Inc., 1964.

McNeil, John D., *Curriculum Administration,* New York: Macmillan Co., 1965.

Misner, Paul J., Frederick W. Schneider, and Lowell G. Keith, *Elementary School Administration,* Columbus, Ohio: Charles E. Merrill Books, Inc., 1963.

Morese, William C., Richard L. Cutler, and Albert H. Fink, *Public School Classes for the Emotionally Handicapped: A Research Analysis,* Washington, D.C., National Education Association, 1964.

NEA Research Bulletin, "What Teachers and Administrators Think About Evaluation," Washington, D.C.: National Education Association, 110-111, XLII, December, 1964.

Ohles, John F., "Extended Schooling Versus Higher Education," *School and Society,* April 4, 1964.

Riesmann, Frank, *The Culturally Deprived Child,* New York: Harper and Row, publishers, 1962.

Roberts, Jack D., "A Hard Look at Quality in In-service Education," *The National Elementary Principal,* XLIV, September, 1964.

Rose, Gale W., "The Effects of Administrative Evaluation." *The National Elementary Principal,* XLIII, November, 1963.

Roucek, Joseph S., ed., *The Unusual Child,* New York: Philosophical Library, Inc., 1962.

Sanders, David C., *Elementary Education and the Academically Talented Pupil,* Washington, D.C.: National Education Association, 1961.

Saville, Anthony, "Breathe New Life into Faculty Meetings," *Clearing House,* XXXVIII, September, 1964.

————, "Organizational Patterns of the Nation's Secondary Schools," *School Life,* May, 1960.

Shane, Harold G., "What Research Says About Class Size and Human Development," *NEA Journal,* January, 1961.

Siegerl, Laurence, James F. Adams, and F. G. Macomber, "Retention of Subject Matter as a Function of Large Group Instructional Procedures," *Journal of Educational Psychology,* LII, February, 1964.

Smith, Mary Howard, ed., *"Using Television in the Classroom,"* New York: McGraw-Hill Book Company, Inc., 1961.

Stoops, Emery, *Elementary School Supervision,* New York: Allyn and Bacon, Inc., 1965.

"The Junior High School We Need," Washington, D.C.: Association for Supervision and Curriculum Development, 1961. (Prepared by Jean D. Grambs, Clarence G. Noyce, Franklin Patterson, and John Robertson.)

Trump, J. Lloyd, "Problems Faced in Organizing Schools Differently," *American School Board Journal,* CXLVII, November, 1963.

Weber, C. A. and Mary E., *Fundamentals of Educational Leadership,* 2nd Ed., New York: Exposition Press, 1961.

Wellington, C. Burleigh, and Jean Wellington, *The Underachiever: Challenges and Guidelines,* Chicago: Rand McNally & Company, 1965.

Wilcox, John, "Another Look at Supervision," *National Association of Secondary-School Principal Bulletin,* XLVII, February, 1963.

Wiles, Kimball, *Supervision for Better Schools,* 2nd Ed., Englewood Cliffs: Prentice-Hall, Inc., 1955, also

   The Changing Curriculum of the American High School, Englewood Cliffs: Prentice-Hall, Inc., 1963.

_____, and Franklin Patterson, *The High School We Need,* Washington, D.C.: Association for Supervision and Curriculum Development, 1959.

Chapter 11

Administration of Pupil Personnel Services

The collection of professional activities under the title of pupil personnel services is of recent origin. The collective title includes some services which have been provided by schools for many years; others are sufficiently new that they are made available only in those systems which pay more than lip service to meeting the learning needs of all children. Therein lies the generalized meaning of "pupil personnel services" —those professional tasks which aim to assure that no child will be deprived of his best potential learning because of physical, social, or emotional deterrents.

The terminology may be misleading. There is the possibility of inferring that other professional activities—administration and teaching —are not of service to the pupil. Also, it is probably more accurate to say that pupil personnel services are more of a service to classroom teachers than to pupils. While the ultimate goal in providing the services is to aid children's learning, services are offered much of the time through the teacher. Those who perform pupil personnel services may work directly with students to help them adjust to a learning situation, but the immediate motivation is to help the teacher perform his instructional responsibilities more completely.

A school's concern for the physical, emotional, and social well-being of pupils dictates the five broad tasks areas of the pupil personnel division: health services, psychological and counseling services, environmental conditions away from the school building, all of which affect school attendance; the fifth task intertwines the other four but is of such gigantic proportions that it can properly be labeled separately—maintaining pupil records.

The terminology, pupil personnel services, is often misunderstood because it means different things to different communities and because all districts do not provide all of the services named above. The title may not even be used in smaller districts. Moreover, school administrators differ in their understanding of the mission of the individual services, hence, the respective talents may be deployed in various ways.

THE ATTENDANCE SERVICE

The oldest task of the pupil personnel office, concerned with efforts to keep children in regular attendance at school, is based upon the assumption that absenteeism hampers learning. Citizens have through the years steadily lengthened the school term from three or four months per year to the present standard of nine or ten months. Likewise, they have enacted compulsory school attendance laws which require all children of school age to attend for more years. Present state laws envision that all educable youth will have an opportunity to complete a high school education, though the goal is realized about sixty per cent nationwide. Public school systems, charged with the enforcement of these laws, have developed the task and personnel needed for the job.

The child accounting aspect for school operations means just that — accounting for all children who are of school age as defined by each state's laws. The law defines the beginning and ending ages, commonly six to seventeen years of age, although five states go as high as eighteen, and delegate to the board of education the responsibility for seeing that each such child is either in school or otherwise accounted for. The school's first chore then is to conduct an annual census, or enumeration, of all children within the district. School-age children may attend a non-public school, of course, and may not have to enroll in any formalized educational institution if the parents can show that the child is being educated in a manner equivalent to that offered by the public schools.

Since all youth do not see their attendance at school as important, nor do all parents, state laws have provided penalties — fines, imprisonment, or both — for the parents who violate the statutes. Attendance officers are needed to investigate unauthorized absenteeism, to return the child to school, to initiate court action if called for, but more importantly, to assess causes of absenteeism with the hope of removing them. This latter objective has revolutionized its approach during the past quarter-century. The former "police" technique of the truant officer has been supplanted by the visiting teacher or home-and-school officer who is trained to diagnose a child's out-of-school environment as well as his in-school experiences. Though there is still some need to strong-arm truants back into school, officials have long ago learned that this effort may solve nothing more than today's absence. The vital and more efficient long-range solution is to determine what alienates a child from his school situation and try to rectify the shortcoming.

A few schools, mostly urban, have employed qualified school social workers either as visiting teachers or as more advanced experts in case work. They are prepared not only to ease a child's unfavorable home conditions but also to corral the community's welfare agencies in that direction.

All states have made legal provisions, sometimes supplemented by local board regulations, for excepting certain youngsters from the compulsory school attendance laws. They may be judged uncapable of profiting substantially from further schooling, disruptive to other students, so handicapped that the school cannot help them, or perhaps needed more for the family's existence than for further learning. All exceptions must be approved by school officials, hence the need for time and personnel to investigate each case and to process the exceptions. This may mean physical, emotional, and intellectual examinations and, inevitably, considerable paper work.

The cost of tending unwilling learners, as well as the damage they create to faculty morale, is causing some authorities to ponder the advisability of modifying compulsory attendance laws. If citizens knew the disproportionate share of their tax moneys which is concentrated upon those pupils who rebuff teachers' efforts they would probably insist on a modification. Reference is not made to the mental, physical, or emotionally handicapped pupil, rather to those who are able but refuse to profit from education. The per-pupil costs for investigations, counseling, punishments, and making special provisions for the unwilling student are staggering. Moreover, their enforced presence in school is disheartening to teachers who could spend their time more profitably with the majority. After the school has exhausted its resources for reaching this type of student, perhaps it would be wiser to relax the compulsory laws, allow the youngster to discover the merits of education through hard knocks, and then, through a liberalized program of adult education, allow him to complete his education as a self-motivated student.

SERVICE TO PUPILS' HEALTH NEEDS

In order to assure that each child has his best opportunity for learning, most schools have accepted the responsibility for preventing loss of school time resulting from his physical debilities. The school has an obligation to minimize the effects of communicable diseases which it spawns as it assembles great numbers of youngsters in a confined area. The school may also go further to detect physical impairments which would hamper a child's learning; some schools even provide limited corrective measures as a welfare service.

In providing these health services, a city board of education may employ school nurses, physicians, and dentists. In smaller communities, part-time medical personnel may be employed, or the board may contract for the services, or arrange for them on a fee basis. Elsewhere, the county or area public health department may provide the services on a cooperative basis jointly financed. Sometimes the medical personnel also offer classroom instruction in health education although that training is more commonly treated as a separate instructional activity to be conducted by physical education and health teachers.

The preventive role of the medical personnel is accomplished through mass examinations, probably before youngsters first enroll in school, at periodic inspections as students progress through the grades, and at times of emergency when a suspected disease may be prevalent. The school doctor often doubles as the physical examiner and attendant to injuries sustained through the high school's athletic program. In some schools he also examines school employees according to the board's approved plan. Except as a charitable measure, the medical personnel are not expected to treat physical impairments; rather they are expected to refer pupil cases, through their parents, to the family physicians and dentists.

SERVICE TO PUPILS' EMOTIONAL NEEDS

While all teachers and administrators are concerned with children's emotional development they are not prepared to handle more than "normal abnormalities." Teachers need the prompt help of specialized talent in correcting the typical emotional blocks to learning progress. For this reason, boards of education have at last moved rapidly toward employing a school psychologist. This movement has been retarded by the unawareness of board members and professional school personnel of the contribution which a competent school psychologist can make to improved learning. The unavailability of trained specialists in child psychology and in learning has also caused the growth of psychological services to be sluggish. Once the value of these rare experts was recognized, their employment mushroomed. But the supply of trained school psychologists is still far behind demand.

The utility of a school psychologist, in addition to his technical skill, is his ability to help teachers—through helping their pupils—quickly. A teacher loses much learning time if he must await lengthy diagnosis from outside sources. Most of the psychological cases which hamper school progress do not warrant extensive study; those which do can be referred for appropriate clinical treatment. However, larger school systems that can afford it employ enough qualified personnel to conduct their own child-study programs.

As a specialist in child behavior, the school psychologist is also proving himself as a meritorious aid in curriculum development and in improvement of the learning environment. The school situation — either the teacher or the physical restrictions — has often been accused of creating some of the emotional maladjustments suffered by children. Wise school administrators and teachers are utilizing the psychologist's knowledge in planning curriculum, organizational, and facility changes.

The school psychologist also performs most of the individual testing of students, but it is generally acknowledged today to be a misuse of his talents if he is bogged down with group testing. The psychologist works more efficiently with teachers in helping them to understand, interpret, and use the results of mass testing. He can also be useful in detecting emotional problems of employees and in recommending appropriate action.

STUDENT COUNSELING SERVICES

Since gaining popularity in the 1930's, student guidance services have undergone major changes. They were then intended primarily to guide high school youth toward appropriate vocational positions. Though this objective has received renewed impetus in this decade, guidance officers have been emphasizing personal and academic counseling in the intervening years. Even the terminology has changed to reflect the broadened scope of the work. The specialized title of counselor is currently preferred for one who devotes most of his time to individual counseling of students, although the two terms, guidance and counseling, are used interchangeably here. Furthermore, there has been a trend toward extending the function downward in the educational ladder to the junior high level and even to the elementary schools. Counseling in the early school years helps to prevent mistakes in secondary school. The former efforts confined to individual guidance have also been supplemented by techniques of group counseling. Finally, teachers who formerly resented the encroachment of specialized guidance personnel upon their own role in managing the total adjustment of young people, have now generally welcomed the technical advice and have become more guidance-conscious in their relationships with students.

The importance of the counseling service in schools received strong implementation from two sources in very recent years. After his analysis of sampled school systems in America, Dr. James B. Conant lent his influence to the cause by recommending a ratio of one qualified guidance officer to each 200 to 400 pupils in secondary schools; this goal has been accepted as the best standard. Parts of the National Defense Education Act, by providing moneys for the preparation of guidance counselors, encouraged schools to reach this optimum.

While counseling personnel continue to function within school buildings, they are considered part of the pupil personnel services. Their primary aim is to enable classroom teachers to satisfy the total learning needs of all students. The central staff director of pupil personnel services may merely coordinate the counselor's activities. Counselors offer their services to all students, but they inevitably concentrate the bulk of their talents and time upon those pupils whose learning and adjustment blocks preclude the skill and time of teachers.

ORGANIZATION OF PUPIL PERSONNEL OFFICE

Examination of these four broad tasks explains the trend toward consolidating the specialized talents into one office. They are all extra-classroom tasks designed to aid the teacher in achieving his objectives. Forward-looking school systems have been providing these services to their pupils and teachers for several years, but the appointed technicians were often assigned to various divisions of the central staff. The scattered arrangements were found to waste both the teacher's and the specialist's time and talent. It is unreasonable to expect a teacher to pursue a given learning problem through the labyrinth of a large unsystematized central staff. The problem persisted while papers were shuffled and arrangements made for the consultations and investigations. These difficulties caused the recent trend to centralize all of these specialized talents into one division headed by a director of pupil personnel services. In this fashion, a single contact by the teacher or principal to the director can coordinate all of the district's experts to solve a learning problem quickly and efficiently. Immediately, the director can loosen the entire coterie of specialists to determine if a child's progress is being impeded by physical, social or emotional problems, and the department can best recommend to the teacher further steps.

So logical is this trend that some states have moved ahead to authorize special administrative certificates for those who oversee the activities of these specialists. Some far-seeing institutions have already formulated graduate preparatory programs for this unique administrative task. Superintendents are discovering that the temptation to appoint as director one of the department's specialists is often impractical; a highly trained specialist in any of the pupil personnel services may lack the coordinating and administrative skill needed for the departmental head position. Such a specialist is frequently not interested in executive responsibility.

Some school districts have also assigned to this division special education classes and their instructors who handle the separate groups of children with atypical learning problems. In deference to any organizational plan which works best for a school district, it is observed that any educational class, special or otherwise, is instructional. Pupil personnel services are designed as a vital supplement to those who instruct.

Centralization of the personnel who perform these special services encourages another kind of efficiency. Each of the specialists must maintain detailed records of pupils' problems and progress. Much of this information is overlapping and interdependent. Centralization of records in one office eliminates considerable duplication of record keeping and, at the same time, provides each specialist with readily available supporting information for his particular needs. In all but the very largest city school systems, the central office also houses the cumulative records of pupils who have left the system through graduation or other means. The preservation of these records and the dispensing of information about former pupils to the dozens of requests coming to school officials, is normally assigned to the pupil personnel office. It is understandable why the pupil record keeping chore is so vast as to warrant it being considered as a separate task of pupil personnel.

Still another and specialized task often assigned to the pupil personnel department is the district's research efforts. A great amount of the research normally conducted by public schools is of the survey type to aid administrative planning decisions: forecasting building, personnel, budget, and supply needs. Since many of these decisions are governed by future enrollments, and since the personnel often assigned to the pupil personnel department are trained to conduct and handle such research information, it is logical to find research personnel functioning under the director of pupil personnel.

A number of related tasks essential to school operations are frequently assigned to this department: administration of pupil suspensions and exclusions from school, special admissions to the district, issuance of working permits, investigation of tuition and doubtful residence claims, transferring of pupils among attendance units within the district, and the establishment of boundary lines. Department personnel are also likely to be involved in problems relating to class size and grouping procedures, and in plans for grading and promotion.

Opinion on the centralized department differs. It is argued that some of these specialists could work most efficiently if they were assigned directly to individual attendance units. Counselors already are, and large buildings or those with atypical student bodies may have psychologists, medical personnel, social workers, and attendance officers assigned full time. This decision is governed mostly by the size and nature of attendance units. Smaller districts and smaller buildings can scarcely afford such luxury. However, as school districts increase in size and urbanization, the organization of pupil personnel services may be mixed, with more specialists assigned to buildings and the central office providing merely a coordinating function.

PUPIL PERSONNEL SERVICES . . .

MEANING AND PURPOSES OF PUPIL PERSONNEL SERVICES*

The student's ability to learn, most educators would agree, depends on his adjustment to school and society, his readiness to learn, and his general physical and mental well being. If he is to direct himself realistically, he must increasingly understand himself in relation to the opportunities, obligations, and requirements of a democratic society. To provide the student with the best opportunities for learning, the school must give him more than textbooks and teachers, however excellent. It must help him resolve problems, make good educational and vocational choices, and be free of health problems that would obstruct learning. One way in which the school can do this to provide first-rate pupil personnel services.

WHAT THEY ARE

Once the term "pupil personnel services" meant little more than guidance, but today it describes the noninstructional professional school services many elementary and secondary schools provide for their students. These services, as outlined in a policy statement by the Council of Chief State School Officers, are attendance services, social work services, guidance services, health services, and psychological services. Though some school superintendents include still others, such as remedial instruction, speech and hearing correction, and instruction for the

*Hyrum M. Smith, "Pupil Personnel Services—What and How," *School Life,* XLIII (June, 1961), 16-18.

homebound, the five specified by the Council are the ones most often found in pupil personnel departments.

Attendance services have two functions: To conduct pupil accounting, including census taking, and to insure that every educable school-age child has an opportunity to receive an education. The specialists who work with attendance problems are school social workers, visiting teachers, or attendance coordinators (the term "truant officer" with its implication of force is passing from our vocabulary). Habitual nonattendance is often a symptom of such problems as underachievement, lack of confidence, nonacceptance by the peer group, or a physical handicap. It takes professional skill and time to determine the cause and to help the student, and often his parents, to adjust satisfactorily to school. Social work training provides an ideal background for effective attendance work.

Social work services are designed to help children who demonstrate in their attitude or behavior an inability to use school experience positively—an inability which hinders not only their own progress but the progress of others. Casework—helping the students, his parents, and his teacher—requires the skill unique to the professional social worker. The worker must have extensive knowledge of human growth, development, and behavior, and must know how to use community resources and facilities. The professional social worker has had a 2-year graduate program leading to the master's degree in social work.

Guidance services in the past carried the same large meaning as pupil personnel services, but the meaning of guidance has narrowed. The major function of the guidance worker is to counsel students. The counselor works with students on educational and vocational planning and personal problems common to their age group to help them gain insight into problems and to make judicious decisions. The counselor must be trained in the administration and interpretation of standardized tests. He functions as a school staff member and is directly responsible to the principal. He confers regularly with other staff members on student progress, group test interpretation, and curriculum development. Each State sets its own requirements for guidance counselors, and school systems may add still others. Requirements vary from a few graduate courses in guidance to a master's or doctor's degree. In 1960, according to State reports to the Office of Education, the secondary schools alone employed the equivalent of 18,700 full-time counselors and supervisors, but they need an estimated 20,000 more to bring the national ratio of counselors to students in the secondary schools from the present ratio of 1 to 610 to the recommended ratio of 1 to 300.

School health services aim at developing in each child a sense of responsibility for his own health and for the health of others and an understanding of the principles of good health so that he will not be deprived of an effective education because of poor health. Health services are provided by school health nurses, doctors, dentists, correctionists, and therapists. Nurses receive training in child psychology, education, public health, and child growth and development in addition to their nursing training. Correctionists and therapists have at least one year of graduate training in their specialities—working with children who have speech, hearing, sight, or other physical handicaps.

School psychological services supplement the school's reservoir of information about each child's capacities, achievements, interests, potentialities, and needs. The psychologist's function in the school is to work with students who have serious learning or behavior difficulties because of physical, mental, or emotional handicaps. He must be skilled in giving an intensive psychological diagnosis of a problem and interpreting it to the school and home. The school psychologist has at least a master's degree; the American Psychological Association recommends that he have a doctor's degree in psychology.

ORGANIZATION

Each of the five major pupil personnel services has a specific and definite place in the educational process. Each service is dependent on the others for vital information, and all the services work together toward the same goal — helping children to use their school experiences in a positive, constructive way.

Any program of pupil personnel services should be organized in terms of the specific needs of the school system. The charts on the preceding page show the organization of pupil personnel services in three typical school systems: A small system served by an itinerant counselor; a medium-sized system employing at least one counselor for each secondary school (one of the counselors is usually the guidance director and coordinates all pupil personnel services in the school or schools); and a large system providing all its personnel services through one department — an arrangement which gives the student maximum service. Many district and county systems employ itinerant specialists.

Many more secondary schools now employ qualified school counselors for guidance activities than were doing so in 1958; financial aid under title V-A of the National Defense Education Act has encouraged and made possible much of the increase.

It seems evident that in the immediate future our schools' need for employing noninstructional professional personnel will far exceed the number prepared by our colleges and universities. School systems that are fortunate enough to obtain pupil personnel workers to assist their teachers will be able to give more of their pupils the opportunity and satisfaction of reaching their potential.

THE STATUS AND OUTLOOK FOR PUPIL PERSONNEL SERVICES*

In the past few years, superintendents and administrators have become aware of an increasing number of children being referred to school psychologists, speech and hearing specialists, and social case workers, to mention but a few. There has been a resulting growth and expansion of pupil personnel services. These are the services performed in the schools by physicians, psychologists, counselors, nurses, social workers, attendance coordinators, and speech and hearing clinicians.

The basic purpose of the pupil personnel services is to help assure for every child — the gifted, the normal, and the handicapped — the maximum opportunity for a successful school experience. To achieve the goal of educating all or nearly all children effectively, such services are intended to complement the classroom instruction of the schools. Their importance is indicated by a recent survey which shows that from 6 to 14 per cent of the school budget is spent upon pupil personnel services. Estimates place the number of children with reading disabilities, speech and hearing disorders, problems of adjustment and physical handicaps at 25 to 35 per cent of all children. It seems clear then that greater knowledge is needed as to how these funds should be spent so as to secure their maximum return.

The foregoing needs for pupil services constitute a large area to which research activity might be directed. An equally large area concerns itself with the organization of the services. Most of the pupil services had their origin in settings other than the school, in many cases a health or welfare setting. Accordingly, the image of the pupil personnel worker, maintained by both himself and the general public was consistent with the institutional setting and emphasized some form of specialized treatment as a primary objective. When the pupil personnel worker moved into the school, where the primary goal was the facilitation of instruction, the emphasis changed. The need for support-

*Walter B. Waetjen and John K. Fisher, "Pupil Services: Status and Outlook," reprinted by permission from the *Bulletin of National Association of Secondary School Principals*, XLVII (December, 1963), 38-43.

ive service was clear, but too often the service provided was but an extrapolation of those that had proved appropriate in such other settings as the clinic, welfare agency, or medical institution. Consequently, there is at present an urgent need to adapt functions and professional images to the primary objectives of the school.

A second problem arises from the fact that, although persons performing pupil personnel services have unique areas of specialization, they share common areas of knowledge of personality dynamics, diagnosis or measurement, and counseling. Much of the technical vocabulary is the same in the several fields and some differences of function are finely shaded. As a result, the problems of coordination and cooperative planning on the part of those responsible for the total school program have become the more difficult, and there are complications in interpreting the various professional roles to the instructional staff and the general public.

Pupil personnel service programs follow three basic patterns: specialists who are responsible to a full-time director of pupil personnel services; specialists who are responsible and report to an assistant superintendent; and senior specialists who coordinate the work of their associates and report directly to the superintendent of schools. An evaluation of the differently organized pupil services programs for comparable population areas is needed.

At the present time, there is little research to indicate which patterns of organization are more effective. It may be that the most effective pattern of organization of pupil services in large city school districts would not be nearly so effective in smaller districts.

The second large area in which research is needed is that of utilization of pupil services. Over the years, school systems have differentiated the various pupil personnel roles but have given relatively little thought as to how these services might be integrated in such a way as to bring their full force to bear on the learning and adjustment of children. The problems to be researched with respect to utilization are manifold, but we will raise three questions which we believe worthy of both research and demonstration.

We have need to determine what constitutes a model pupil service program in different types of communities and in school systems of various sizes. It seems clear that in relatively large school systems a highly differentiated but coordinated pupil service program is necessary. On the other hand, we have many school systems that are either relatively small in size or are serving a rural community. At the present time we do not know what type of pupil personnel program best serves each of these widely divergent types of schools and communities as well as those school systems in between. In the smaller and less affluent school systems, there may be funds for only one pupil personnel worker. Should this be a guidance counselor, a school psychologist, an attendance worker, or a social worker? Part of the answer depends upon pupil need for services but it may be that we need to research the idea of educating a pupil personnel worker who can cut across the now-existing pupil service lines and supply a variety of services. Promising attempts such as the University of Arizona's program to prepare "duo specialists" are underway. In this program, each specialist will receive one year of training in two of three areas: guidance and counseling, reading, and special education for the mentally retarded and physically handicapped. In this instance, we would not only have to educate such a person but to research his effectiveness in the school setting.

Pupil personnel services have largely been in the nature of direct services to the pupils rather than passing through intermediaries. Perhaps a more effective program would be achieved by the specialist's working with teachers and parents directly, with provision for some direct service to pupils. Such a mode of working would be consultative in nature.

Frequently in initiating or expanding a service we tend to duplicate existing patterns of organization. The wisdom of this should be assessed by an evaluation of the effectiveness of present practices before initiating them in other situations. For example, the movement to provide counseling services in elementary schools tends to take the pattern of existing services in secondary schools with little thought being given to the differing situations and needs.

GUIDANCE AND COUNSELING SERVICES ...

THE RAPID GROWTH OF GUIDANCE SERVICES*

No aspect of the pupil personnel program is growing more rapidly than guidance. Several factors account for this — among them the reports written by James Conant on the American high school and junior high school emphasizing the need for counselors. Unquestionably, the greatest boost to guidance that has ever occured resulted from the

---

*Donald G. Ferguson, *Pupil Personnel Services*, Washington, D.C.: by permission of The Center for Applied Research in Education, Inc., 1963, 46-47.

National Defense Education Act of 1958, which pointed it out as a necessary and vital part of American education. Even more tangible has been the appropriation of millions of dollars by the federal government through the National Defense Education Act to support several aspects of guidance and of counselor training. One section of this Act provides funds to improve guidance, counseling, and testing services in American secondary schools. It authorizes the government to contract with institutions of higher education to conduct institutes for training teachers to become guidance counselors and also for upgrading persons who presently are employed as counselors.

A newsletter of the American Personnel and Guidance Association summarizes some of the effects upon guidance of the National Defense Education Act:

> Fifty states, the District of Columbia and the three territories are participating in the guidance, counseling, and testing program under this phase of the 1958 bill . . . . Specifically, progress is noted in reducing student-counselor ratios. In 1953, for example, the ratio of counselors to students was estimated at 1 to 750. By June 1960, it was estimated that this ratio had decreased to 1 to 600. Much of this reduction is attributed to the fact that approximately 90 per cent of Title V-A funds are being used to pay salaries of counselors.

The same article further discusses the advances that have been made in group testing programs resulting from the Act and points out that substantial growth also has taken place in the number of new state guidance supervisors employed. With respect to state guidance personnel, it comments: "There were 78 directors or supervisors of guidance employed by state educational agencies before 1958. Records in the United States Office of Education presently indicate that there are approximately 183 state personnel carrying out full-time guidance responsibilities."

BASES FOR ORGANIZATION OF GUIDANCE SERVICES*

Mere presence of an organizational pattern is no guarantee of its effectiveness, fluidity, or functionalism. Introduction of such labels as

---

*Franklin R. Zeran and Anthony C. Riccio, *Organization and Administration of Guidance Services*, Chicago: by permission of Rand McNally & Company, 1962, 205-208.

"new designs" or "new dimensions" to describe the organizational pattern, or use of diagrammatic flow charts revealing line and staff relationships will not, of themselves, ensure the operation or the cohesiveness so necessary to execution of the program of guidance services. The foundation of the organization for operation of a program of guidance services must be predicated upon sound bases which include the following:

1. The administration must believe in, understand, and want a program of guidance services.
2. The staff must feel the need for an organized program of guidance services and be willing to participate in the activities.
3. The guidance services are designed for a specific school.
4. The guidance services are for all boys and girls and at all grade levels.
5. The program of guidance services must be predicated upon the competencies possessed by the existent staff and the time available for the performance of these services.
6. The existent guidance services should be evaluated and a program designed to meet local needs as well as to utilize the staff skills.
7. One individual, by virtue of preparation, personal and other characteristics, and acceptance by the staff, should be responsible for the program of guidance services.
8. A program of guidance services will not meet all pupil difficulties.

GROUP COUNSELING*

Group counseling is an exceedingly valuable tool, far too seldom used within the regular school framework. Its advantages are manifold:

1. In dealing with several students simultaneously, it spreads the effect of the counselor and at the same time preserves his effectiveness.
2. It seems to be more readily accepted by students in that, since it occurs within a peer group, it is not as "different" or as threatening to them as individual counseling.

Charles F. Combs, Benjamin Cohn, Edward J. Gibian, and A. Mead Sniffen, "Group Counseling: Applying the Technique," by permission of *The School Counselor,* XI (October, 1963), 13.

3. It makes effective use of the social setting and peer identification.

4. The adult experienced by students in group counseling is unique in that he is accepting of them and facilitating their experiences, rather than imposing an external judgment. He is a resource, a catalyst and, perhaps, a new kind of adult.

5. Often the establishment of counseling groups within the school may facilitate individual counseling and other new opportunities to meet the needs of the students.

The authors would like to emphasize that group counseling is not an art known only to a few practitioners who possess unique skills and talents. Group counseling is a technique that is effective and highly efficient of the counselor's time and energy. Most important, it is a technique which lies well within the capabilities of the perceptive school counselor.

GUIDANCE IN THE JUNIOR HIGH SCHOOL*

On the junior high school level, guidance is at the center of a key transitional period between the general developmental aspects of the elementary school and the more directional, specialized features of the secondary schools. Needs and problems of personal-social adjustment (especially those of early adolescence) are present and pupils are still malleable to guidance and educative influences. But academic preparation for high school now assumes greater urgency, subject matter divisions create channels for the exploration and development of interests; the necessity for making ultimate choices of educational and vocational direction looms.

Because of the intimate interrelation of educational interests, academic motivations, scholastic achievement, and personal adjustment in the junior high school, counselors, teachers, and school authorities must continue to regard the individual as an indivisible person whose educational future, vocational direction, and personal destiny is a unitary thing. Although various groupings and classifications of pupils may be attempted by the administration, each pupil should be appraised and counseled in the light of his unique pattern of characteristics and sit-

*Robert Hendry Matheson, *Guidance Policy and Practice*, 3rd. ed., New York: by permission of Harper and Row, 1962, 236-237.

uational conditions, both current and prospective. Artificially devised classificational approaches may serve to block rather than further individual development and adjustment. The highly important phase of orientation of individuals should be conducted in a cumulative way in the light of the individual's need to understand his own self-situational conditions and relations and to participate as fully as possible in his own plannings, explorations, and choices. If considered solely as an academic unit, a subject-matter unit, or a curricular unit, the pupil will cease to be the unique person-in-course-of educative-development that should be the center and core of the whole educational and guidance process. Even in student populations extremely underprivileged and apparently lacking in motivation, amazing individual progress may sometimes occur at this stage, as the Higher Horizons projects in New York City have demonstrated.

In the light of the preceding considerations, the chief features of junior high school guidance may be perceived as follows:

1. Continuing analysis and evaluation of the broad range of pupil characteristics; interpretation of these to, and with, pupils, teachers, parents, and others.
2. Through classroom procedures, the involvement of pupils in procedures of self-appraisal and situational exploration.
3. Periodic evaluative checks on pupil progress in the key areas of academic achievement, personal-social relations, and educational-vocational direction.
4. Special group work, allied with individual counseling, in the development of attitudes and interests, in the assumption and accomplishment of social responsibilities, in the formation of personal precepts of self-confidence and self-reliance, in the maturation of educational-vocational plans, and in the accomplishment of the developmental tasks of this age level.
5. Advisory interviewing to assist pupils and parents in the formulation of high school plans, election of high school curricula (if locally required at this level), and placement in employment for those leaving school at this level. Identification of potential drop-outs and special forms of preparation among small groups with common characteristics may be undertaken in underprivileged areas.
6. Consultative aid to the administration and to school committees in the preparation of records, reports, and recommendations on pupils to higher levels of education.
7. Articulation of data, records, and activities with the program of the senior high school.

THE NEED FOR GUIDANCE SERVICES IN ELEMENTARY SCHOOLS*

There are many characteristics of the elementary school which make it an ideal beginning place for guidance in the educational framework. Because elementary school children are still young, guidance for these children can be preventative as well as remedial in approach. If the child of elementary school age does have problems, they are usually of fairly recent origin, and can usually be solved much more easily than problems of longer duration. In addition, since he is so young, the elementary pupil is not as fixed in his behavior patterns as an older child, and any unacceptable behavior patterns can be altered more quickly and easily. Because elementary school teachers generally teach children in self-contained situations, they have more opportunity for study of the whole child. They can recognize problems peculiar to individuals, and can work steadily with the child for resolution of these problems.

Frequently, the remedial function of guidance programs receives the greatest emphasis in elementary schools, although it is considered to be the least effective of the functions. It is important for the teacher and others working in a program of guidance to know the developmental patterns of children, and to be able to distinguish short term upheavals in behavior as part of the regular maturation process, or as warning signals that something is really wrong. It is tragic when a child with problems too big to handle alone gets no real or lasting help until he is picked up by the law. Then the pattern of his life is set, and it is often too late for assistance with troubles that are deep-seated. If guidance in the elementary schools could be a continuing, developmental, preventative program, the need for remedial guidance would be greatly alleviated.

Effective programs of guidance are based on the premise that human beings need help—that all persons, regardless of age, have certain basic needs that must, and will, be met. How they will be met depends upon the guidance a person provides for himself, or that which is provided for him by someone else. Children, especially, are often too immature to recognize and isolate their problems, much less solve them, without the aid of adults. How much better it is, for example, when a child, through assistance, learns to channel his energy to learn to read or to solve arithmetical abstractions, rather than to throw rocks on the playground in order to satisfy the universal need of gaining status with peers. Experi-

---

*Paul Misner, Frederick M. Schneider, and Lowell G. Keith, *Elementary School Administration*, Columbus, Ohio: by permission of Charles E. Merrill Books, Inc., 1963, 249-251.

ence has proved that when a child attempts the rock-throwing method of gaining status, the exact reverse of what he wishes occurs—but a second or third grader is unlikely to know this unless some mature adult helps him establish a more socially acceptable and intellectually satisfying pattern of behavior. Situations occur in children's lives, as well as in adults', when it becomes necessary to seek aid in order to make wise decisions. A child may find this aid in the school if an effective guidance program is in operation. A good guidance program is concerned primarily with the outlooks, insights, attitudes, appreciations, and behavior of pupils in their process of growth and development; it seeks to assist individuals or groups in choosing a line of action, a method or procedure, a goal.

The needs and values of our society in general provide the bases for effective school guidance services. Technological advancements have catapulted our culture into an age of specialization and automation. This, along with the rapid tempo of modern, urban life, has tended to increase the number and depth of individual problems, even within the elementary schools. Statistics record the rising incidence of mental illness. Something must be done to help preserve the mental health of coming generations! Part of the answer lies in effective programs of guidance in our schools.

Guidance services rendered to the individual involve counseling which stimulates the child to evaluate himself and his actions, decide upon a course of action, accept responsibility for his choices, and initiate a course of action related to those choices. Guidance services rendered to the instructional staff involve assisting teachers in understanding pupils, providing in-service education activities, and providing a ready referral service. Guidance services rendered to administration include assistance in curriculum development or improvement, provision of pertinent pupil personnel data, and provision of a liaison with the community.

SCHOOL MEDICAL SERVICES . . .

THE ROLES OF PERSONNEL INVOLVED IN SCHOOL HEALTH PROGRAMS*

ADMINISTRATION OF LOCAL SCHOOL HEALTH PROGRAM

As far as the school health program is concerned, administrative patterns vary according to personnel facilities, finances, traditions, and incli-

*Alma Nemir, *The School Health Program*, revised ed., Philadelphia: by permission of W. B. Saunders Company, 1965, 233-235, 240-241.

nations of those in authority. Some phases of the health program are more distinctly the province of the educator; e.g., health instruction. Others involve educator and professional medical personnel. For instance, it would be wise to have the school physician and dentist serve on the committee which passes upon the authenticity of all health textbooks and health curriculum materials.

Basic patterns for administration of a school health program may be outlined as follows:

1. Administration as a joint responsibility of the boards of health and education is a commonly adopted pattern, with the heads acting as co-chairmen and sharing responsibility for coordination. The advantages of having public health officials on a planning committee are:

   (a.) There is a balance between the two interests—health and teaching — and both are concerned with the same child.

   (b.) The health department has supervision over certain areas, such as sanitary regulations and construction codes, which involve health in all schools of the community. Such a provision assures conformity of health standards and practices.

   (c.) The interest of the health department is more comprehensive It is concerned with the health of the individual from prenatal life to old age. Public health people know the gaps in health education as seen in prenatal and pre-school clinics and can offer valid help with curriculum planning and health instruction.

   (d.) The public health nurse is familiar with health problems in the community and family. She can be a valuable consultant.

   (e.) The health department has a close working relationship with hospitals, clinics and health agencies and can expedite services.

   (f.) The health department has the personnel to carry out its part of the program.

   (g.) Small school systems or a single school may not be able to afford a full time physician or nurse. Part-time help may be secured from the local board of health.

   (h.) Duplication of health facilities is avoided.

2. Administration by the board of education. There can be various modifications of the above plan with the administration primarily by the board of education. For instance, a school physician may be hired by the board, while the nurses may be provided by the department of health. Such an administrative

set-up may not prove too satisfactory, however, because the physician has no official authority over the nurses. There may be no board of health in a community or the board may not have the money to furnish medical help. In small towns the county medical society or the one doctor in the area may act as consultant. There are over 400 school health committees of medical societies who are working with principals and teachers on the many health projects of the school and community.

Whatever plan is most feasible and efficient is the one to be implemented. There is no hard and fast rule.

SCHOOL HEALTH COUNCILS

Councils have been organized on a city or district basis which bring together representatives of parents, teachers, school administrators, physicians, dentists, public health officials, civic organizations, community groups, such as labor unions, and the voluntary social and health agencies. One of their objectives is to develop in the community an understanding and appreciation of school health procedures. Another is to evaluate pertinent problems and plan future programs which will improve the health of children and youth. They usually serve in an advisory capacity to departments of education and health. It is possible that in some instances the council may have a budget and function in an administrative capacity, but the fundamental purpose is still to assist the community and schools in maintaining a good health program through cooperative effort. . .

THE NURSE

Large schools may be fortunate enough to have the services of a full-time nurse. More commonly however, one nurse is assigned hours at several schools and reports there daily or several times a week. Public health nurses supported by state, district, county or city may be serving in a generalized program for a community and visit the school occasionally or when summoned on a special case. Since the latter are familiar with the health problems of the community and of many families, their assistance is invaluable. Nurses and school personnel need to work together. A nurse's duties in relation to the school are:

1. To assist in coordinating the nursing service with other phases of the school health program.
2. To assist in planning and carrying out a program in which pub-

lic health nursing procedures will be fully utilized for the benefit of the children.

3. To act as the interpreter of the school health program in individual homes, and to acquaint appropriate school personnel with health problems encountered in homes and with the school and community resources available for solving them.

4. To work cooperatively with school personnel, parents, and community agencies in performing the nursing functions necessary to the successful operation of the school health service.

5. To work with the school staff, the children and the parents to see that safe and hygienic conditions are maintained in school and to give practical help and advice in getting unsafe or unhygienic conditions removed or corrected.

6. To aid the teaching staff in an advisory capacity in curriculum planning, and to aid the teaching staff in using home, community, and school experiences (for example, health examinations) as an integral part of health education.

7. To assist in providing information for the periodic appraisal of the school health program, and in interpreting such information from the public health point of view.

Some nurses have teachers' certificates and serve a dual role (nurse-teachers). More are being encouraged to qualify; their contribution to the school health program will be enriched.

THE DENTIST

The duties of a dentist, whether in private practice or attached to a school system or a state board of health, are comparable to those of a physician. The dental health program is vital, and interpretation of scientific information and needs for dental care should occupy a prominent part of the school health program. The dentist is a specialist and a resource person who may serve as guest speaker at PTA meetings and in the classroom, inspiring action to develop a meaningful program in dental health.

SOCIAL WORKERS

Some school systems employ social workers. One may have a full-time assignment in a single school, or his services may be divided between several schools, depending upon student population and need. This specialist possesses skills in investigating problems, interviewing members in a child's home, and promoting favorable school-family-community relationships. A principal should utilize this particular type of training and achieve a fine working arrangement. The social worker helps the physician, the nurse, the guidance personnel, and the therapist to evaluate the resources of the family in order to help a child. The capacity of the family for adjustment is assayed. A social worker counsels the parents of a handicapped youngster and strives to correct their negative attitudes and motivate them to help the child. Many parents plead for help, and every principal is confronted with needs which can be served by this specialist.

Other specialists are in contact with the schools and make their contributions to the health program. These may be the clinical psychologist, those in charge of special hearing and speech services, architects, engineers, sanitarians, lighting experts and many others.

PUPIL RECORDS . . .

THE INDIVIDUAL INVENTORY*

Individual inventory involves the efforts of the entire school staff and the keeping and analyzing of pupil records, particularly the cumulative records. Its purpose is to collect and make available a variety of information about each pupil which will enable the school staff to plan an optimum educational program for him. Through pupil observation, interview, testing, sociometric analysis, and other techniques, information is collected and made available to teachers, counselors, and others. Information recorded will vary from one school to another but will typically include school marks achieved throughout the school experience, comments concerning general factors of adjustment, facts describing curricular and extracurricular activities, medical history, and social adjustment data. . . .

Some counselors are exploring the feasibility and value of having pupils use cumulative record information. One counselor, for example, has developed a separate cumulative record to which pupils have supervised access. Many kinds of information about the pupil are recorded, such as some standardized test results, past grades, records of interests

---

*Donald G. Ferguson, *Pupil Personnel Services*, Washington, D.C.: by permission of the Center for Applied Research in Education, Inc., 1963, 45-46.

and hobbies, and even teacher evaluation forms. This experiment, the counselor believes, encourages pupils to collect and use information about themselves. After a time, many pupils can be taught to use such records independent of counselor supervision.

PLACEMENT AND FOLLOW-UP

Through placement and follow-up, the school assists pupils to follow through on their choices and decisions in vocational and educational planning. As a result, pupils are often aided in achieving admittance to colleges of their choice, to a business or trade school or in entering the world of work.

Follow-up studies of guidance also provide evaluative information on the basis of which the effectiveness of the total school program can be appraised. This is accomplished through the use of questionnaires, interviews, and other data-collecting devices which record the opinions of employers, college officials, and pupils who have graduated or quit school before graduation. Information thus gained helps school officials to determine whether pupils are being well prepared for requirements they will face in college or on the job. Such information often leads to curriculum revisions or to the development of new instruction methods and programs.

FOR FURTHER INVESTIGATION OR REFLECTION

1. What should be the working relationships between the high school principal, teachers, and guidance personnel for handling student discipline?

2. How far can school medical personnel go in attending the illness of students without invading the controversial realm of socialized medicine?

3. What would be involved in effecting a modification of compulsory attendance laws in order to excuse students who refuse to learn?

4. Calculate the per-pupil costs of a school system's coping with unwilling learners, prorating the appropriate charges of professional personnel who are involved. Compare that cost with the average per-pupil expenditures for your district.

5. Interview one or more school psychologists to determine their annual case loads and solicit their evaluations of the load. Also, obtain the judgments of principals whose buildings the psychologists serve as to the adequacy of service from the psychologists.

6. Interview several superintendents to determine their understandings of the function of guidance personnel, or school psychologists, and of school health officers. What are the implications from your findings?

7. At what age or grade level should students make career choices? What are the implications for the work of school counselors and for the curriculum?

8. Discuss the proper assignment of special education teachers who handle classes for handicapped children — to the director of pupil personnel services, the director of instruction, or to the separate department of special education.

9. Should guidance personnel be required to teach some classes?

10. Explain the friction that often develops between regular classroom teachers and pupil personnel specialists.

BIBLIOGRAPHY

Allinsmith, Wesley, and George W. Goethals, *The Role of Schools in Mental Health,* New York: Basic Books, Inc., Publishers, 1962.

Bushnell, Donald D., *Automation of School Information Systems,* Washington, D.C.: National Education Association, 1964.

Combs, Charles F., Benjamin Cohen, Edward J. Gibian, and A. Mead Sniffen, "Group Counseling: Applying the Technique," *The School Counselor,* XI, October, 1963.

Crow, Lester D., and Alice Crow, *Adolescent Development and Adjustment,* 2nd Ed., New York: McGraw-Hill Book Co., Inc., 1964.

Dukelow, Donald A. and Fred V. Hein, eds., *Health Appraisal of School Children,* 3rd Ed., Washington, D.C.: National Education Association, 1961.

Eiserer, Paul E., *The School Psychologist,* Washington, D.C.: The Center for Applied Research in Education, Inc., 1963.

Evraiff, William, *Helping Counselors Grow Professionally,* Englewood Cliffs, N. J.: Prentice-Hall, Inc., 1963.

Ferguson, Donald G., *Pupil Personnel Services,* Washington, D.C.: The Center for Applied Research in Education, Inc., 1963.

Fusco, Gene C., *Organization and Administration of Pupil Personnel Service Programs in Selected School Systems,* Washington, D.C.: United States Office of Education, Bulletin 1961, No. 22.

Gray, Susan W., *The Psychologist in the Schools,* New York: Holt, Rinehart and Winston, Inc., 1963.

Hill, George E., *Management and Improvement of Guidance,* New York: Appleton-Century-Crofts, 1965.

Kayser, Richard M., "School Attendance," *National Association of Secondary-School Principals Bulletin,* LX, September, 1961.

Litwack, Lawrence, June E. Holmes, and Jane S. O'Hern, *Critical Issues in Student Personnel Work: a Problems Casebook,* Chicago: Rand McNally & Company, 1965.

Matheson, Robert Hendry, *Guidance Policy and Practice,* 3rd Ed., New York: Harper and Row, Publishers, 1962.

Miller, Carroll H., *Guidance Services,* New York: Harper & Row, Publishers, 1961.

Misner, Paul, Frederick W. Schneider, and Lowell G. Keith, *Elementary School Administration*, Columbus, Ohio; Charles E. Merrill Books, Inc., 1963.

Nemir, Alma, *The School Health Program*, Philadelphia: W. B. Saunders Company, 1959.

Obertauffer, Delbert, "Vital Ties Between Health and Education," *NEA Journal*, LII, March, 1964.

Ohlsen, Merle, *Guidance Services in the Modern School*, New York: Harcourt, Brace, and World, Inc., 1964.

Peters, Herman J., Bruce Shertzer, and William VanHoose, *Guidance in Elementary Schools*, Chicago: Rand McNally and Company, 1965.

Sellery, C. Morley, Sara Louise Smith, and C. E. Turner, *School Health and Health Education*, 4th Ed., St. Louis: The C. V. Mosby Co., 1961.

Sinks, T. A., "Data Processing in the Schools," *Clearing House*, 118-20, XXXIX, October, 1964.

Smith, Hyrum M., "Pupil Personnel Services — What and How," *School Life*, XLIII, June, 1961.

Stefflre, Buford, ed., *Theories of Counseling*, New York: McGraw-Hill Book Company, Inc., 1965.

Stewart, Lawrence H., and Charles F. Warnath, *The Counselor and Society*, Boston: Houghton Mifflin Company, 1965.

Valett, Robert E., *The Practice of School Psychology*, New York: John Wiley & Sons, Inc., 1963.

Waetjen, Walter B., and John K. Fisher, "Pupil Services: Status and Outlook," *Bulletin of National Association of Secondary School Principals*, XLVII, December, 1963.

Weitz, Henry, *Behavior Change Through Guidance*, New York: John Wiley & Sons, Inc., 1964.

White, Mary Alice and Myron W. Harris, *The School Psychologist*, New York: Harper and Row, Publishers, 1961.

Willey, Roy DeVerl, *Guidance in Elementary Education*, Rev. Ed., New York: Harper and Row, Publishers, 1960.

Wylie, B. A., "Administrative Support of Key Guidance Dimensions," *National Association of Secondary-School Principals Bulletin*, XLIV, November, 1962.

Zeran, Franklin R., and Anthony C. Riccio, *Organization and Administration of Guidance Services*, Chicago: Rand McNally and Company, 1962.

Chapter 12

Administration of School Finance

The most persistent problem of school administration, by the testimony of those who administer both public and private institutions, is the adequate and prudent financial support of education. It was a perplexing question debated at the launching of a system of free education open to all youngsters—how could it be financed without the aid and control of church bodies? It is crucial today as the demands for more and better education continue. Proper financing is the fulcrum upon which improved education balances. Quality education is purchased in the same fashion as is quality in any other product. It requires money to employ quality teachers, to experiment with and adopt curricular ideas, to provide the necessary facilities and supplies, and to buy the administrative leadership to acquire the other ingredients.

The comprehensive subject of educational finance has two broad elements. One consists of the plans for raising adequate funds; the other is the prudent management and dispensing of those funds. Though the two elements are interdependent, the first can be labeled school finance; the second may be classified as school business management. These are not precise separations, but the subjects will be dealt with in this chapter and the next under these overly simplified definitions.

CRITERIA FOR A SOUND FINANCIAL PLAN

Writers in the field of school finance agree that a sound plan for financing education would meet the following criteria:
1. *Adequacy.* The amount of money raised should be adequate for the needs of good education. Satisfying this criterion is confounded by the variety of understandings of good education. Those who work in education will doubtlessly never concur with those who pay the costs about what is adequate. For prac-

tical purposes, adequacy is determined as these two forces meet in compromise.

2. *Flexibility*. The plan should have enough volubility to adjust to changes in enrollments, program, and other needs. The plan should be flexible as to time and place changes.

3. *Stability*. The plan for producing school income should be sufficiently stable in time so that quality education of youth will continue regardless of economic conditions.

4. *Balance of support* among the beneficiaries from education. The three classes of beneficiaries considered for this purpose are local, state, and federal governments. As logical as this criterion appears, one sees immediately the difficulty of assessing the degree to which each class benefits from education, to determine its share of support.

THE FINANCING PLAN AND ECONOMICS

The relationship between the cost of education and the nation's economic condition has been little understood and little studied in the past. However, when expenditures for all kinds of education in the nation account for approximately six percent of its Gross National Product (the currently popular index of the state of the economy, defined as the total dollar value of all the goods and services produced in a nation during a year), the nation should give attention to the effects of school expenditures on its economic well-being. Undoubtedly, the percentage will increase in future years. Actually, the influence of education on the economy is far more than suggested by the knowledge that 35 billion dollars were spent in 1963 for all educational endeavors, for nursery through graduate school, by public and private institutions.

Most of the operating costs of education go for employees' salaries, and since the earning power of persons has much to do with stimulating a healthy economy, the salaries paid to the two million workers in education are an important economic factor. In many communities, the public school system is the largest employer; thus, the effects on the economy of those communities are significant. Money spent for capital construction of buildings provides more jobs, more spending power, more purchasing, and more production. The interest paid on borrowed money for construction also stimulates the flow of money and affects the investment activities of banks, brokerage houses, and private investors. The millions of dollars spent annually for school supplies has a similar effect on the economy. The bank deposits of a board of education have an influence on that bank's well-being and its relationship to the Federal Reserve System. The various pension plans for school employees affect investment conditions, insurance companies, and the labor supply.

All of these expenditures are paid out of taxes, and taxes extracted from the assets of an individual or of a business reduce the spending power of those groups. From an economic point of view, the process of taxation merely shifts expenditures from private spenders to governmental spenders. Taxation may not change the total expenditures at all. Some economists claim that tax moneys get into the flow of the economy faster than private savings or investments. That is probably true since a government body normally has to spend its alloted income within the fiscal year, or face the possibilities of losing it.

The intangible effects of education upon economics are probably more significant than the measurable ones. Through education, men elevate their chances for better employment which means more spending power and, therefore, a higher economy. The positive relationship between the extent of completed education and personal income has been demonstrated in many studies. Likewise, there is evidence as far back as the 19th century of a positive correlation between educational attainment and reduced crime rate. Also, since one definition of economics denotes a study or process of satisfying human wants, education tends to whet one's appetite for more material gains—greater purchasing power and more money flowing into the economy. The recent emphasis upon regarding school taxes as an investment has much justification. The huge federal appropriation for education in 1965 was justified primarily on economic grounds.

A final intangible influence of education upon the economic system of a country is the strategic position of schools in helping people understand and appreciate our modified capitalistic system. Teachers of America have undoubtedly done more than any other agency to promote faith in our system of reasonably free enterprise. They encourage habits of thrift among children, teach the importance of conserving natural resources, develop respect for the dignity of labor, and promote the spirit of healthy competition.

SCHOOL FINANCE AND TAXATION

All public services are financed through a system of taxation, an activity fraught with emotion ever since civilized society abandoned tribute and plunder as a means of satisfying wants. That ancient practice, like taxation, allowed the governing force to extract material goods from the governed. The only change that has taken place through civilizing and democratizing societies is that the people have become the governing force, acting through their chosen officials. A basic premise for taxation in the United States since the emotion of Boston Harbor, is necessary approval of the people.

Although democratic people accept the process of taxation as a satisfactory method for financing their wants from public services, they are far from agreement upon the means, the source, and the amount of taxes. The extreme views were promulgated by two economists who set opposing schools of economic thought. The Scottish professor of moral philosophy, Adam Smith, advocated that taxes should be assessed in terms of the benefits received by taxpayers. His philosophy was hinged to the protection-of-property concept of taxation: the wealthy man receives more protection from government than the poor man, and hence, should pay more taxes; the more use a man gets from the item purchased by taxes, the more he should pay. Modern taxes levied on this basis are: gasoline taxes, public improvements, licenses, social security taxes, and to a degree, school taxes.

John Stuart Mill, an English philosopher, popularized another theory, namely, that taxes should be paid in relation to one's ability to pay. The wealthy man would miss his tax payments less than the poor man; thus, he should pay not just in proportion to his wealth as compared with the poor man but at an even higher rate. This *progressive* type of taxing procedure is reflected in our federal income tax and in some inheritance taxes. This concept gave rise to a new purpose of taxation—redistributing wealth.

Attitudes toward taxation vary between these two extremes, and both have their complexities in application. Probably most people base their views on how the concepts affect them personally. Nonetheless, both views are evident in the tax structure for supporting public schools. Both possess desirable characteristics for what is generally regarded as a good tax. Other commonly accepted qualities for a good tax, if such a thing exists, are that is is equitable, convenient for the taxpayer to pay, and economical to collect; it minimizes evasion and political manipulation, yields steadily, is innocuous to the economy of the community, and is evident to the taxpayer's view.

SYSTEM OF TAXING FOR PUBLIC SCHOOLS

All three levels of government—local, state, and national—participate in levying taxes for the support of public education in far different proportions and to varying extents from place to place. In general throughout the states, the local community provides about 60 percent of the cost of conducting education, the state level about 35 percent and the federal government about 5 percent. Some authorities maintain that for the sake of stability and flexibility a better ratio would be 50, 30, and 20; this proportion would still leave the local government in control. Others argue that control could be exercised through the threat to withdraw even a minority share, such as 20 percent, once a school district had come to expect that much of its budget from the source.

It should be remembered that the percentages cited are nationwide averages; there are many exceptions. The state government in Delaware collects and distributes to local school districts as much as 90 percent of the total costs of running schools, while in the states of Nebraska and New Hampshire the local community provides more than 90 percent of the total. Within some states which fall into the national averages quoted, a wealthy district might receive only a small share from the state while poor districts will receive most of its money from the state. Some school districts receive no money from the federal government; others may obtain as much as 15 percent or more from that level. The so-called impacted areas which have extensive federal installations obtain substantial federal financing for education. The same will be true under the 1965 Elementary and Secondary School Education Act for districts which have a high proportion of enrollments from low income families. And, of course, the national level has complete financial obligations for schools on federal reservations, overseas schools for children of civilian and military personnel, and for those special schools which that level operates exclusively.

The major source of local district revenue for schools throughout the country is a tax on *real property*—land and buildings. The property tax supplies more than 85 percent of the local tax income; in most states it is the only tax which a board of education is permitted to use. It is one of the oldest forms of taxation, predicated upon the belief that property owners will pay tribute to the government in exchange for the government's promise to protect the owner's investment; the capitalistic practice began in days of ruralism when property represented wealth. While still important, ownership of land and buildings is much less indicative of wealth today than is personal income, most of which is not produced by real estate. Notwithstanding, the tax on real estate continues to be the prime source of school revenue, for both operating and capital expenditures.

This fact presents the severe problem which most school officials have in raising adequate school support. The amount of money any school district can raise depends upon two factors: the extent of real property within its geographic limits (referred to as its *ability*) and the *willingness* of citizens to tax themselves for educational purposes. Willingness is expressed in the tax rate, in some states understood to be *mills* ($0.001) on each dollar of property valuation, in other states, cents on each hundred dollars of valuation, and in still other states, dollars on each thousand dollars of valuation. Citizens show their interest in education (willingness) by voting mills, cents, or dollars of tax rate for school purposes. If they are uninterested in the quality of education their children receive, regardless of their property wealth they may disapprove requests for higher school taxes—consistent with the principle that people decide the amount and the purpose of taxation.

On the other hand, the people residing in a school district of inconsequential property wealth may wish to provide good education for their children, but the lack of a sufficient (ability) base for their willingness may not yield adequate revenue. At least, the tax rate required to yield much income on the *assessed valuation* of poor property is beyond reasonable expectation. For purposes of comparing property wealth or ability among school districts, *per-pupil valuation* is commonly used, i.e., the wealth behind each pupil which is calculated by dividing the total assessed valuation of the district by the number of pupils enrolled.

It is not the real, or market, value of property that entirely determines the tax yield. True value of property remains unknown until it is sold on the open market where there is a willing buyer and willing seller. Therefore, an estimated value is placed on property by an assessor, one designated in law to render a judgment as to the selling value of the property. Since judgment is involved in this process, the estimated value is subject to all the fallibility of opinion: incompetence, partiality, pressures, and lack of integrity. Assessing practices have been so decried as to sway some people away from the property tax as a suitable source of revenue. Progress has been made in improving the techniques through the use of professional appraisers from outside the district and through state laws which require that assessed values be equalized throughout the state. Despite the inequities which may accrue from the process, property values have remained fairly stable throughout history, and generally increase. Therefore, the property tax continues as a steady source of yield for providing public services, including schools. It should be noted that all government-owned property and all other property used for non-profit purposes is exempt from taxation — this makes a difference in the income of a school district which accommodates much of these types of property.

The property tax has been scored at times also on the grounds that it is *regressive* in effect, that is, it fails to recognize the ability-to-pay principle. The small property owner pays at the same rate as does the owner of luxurious property. While the rate does remain the same throughout a taxing district, the tax bills increase with ascending property values. Moreover, this criticism speaks primarily of residence property, which rarely pays the cost of educating children. At prevailing average costs of education, a residence owner would have to pay a school tax of at least $460 annually in order to pay his share of the cost of educating his one child. If he has more than one child in school, someone else pays for the others. If his property does not pay $460 per year in school taxes, he still does not pay the cost of educating his first child. The point being made is that business property, not homes, provides the lion's share of property tax income. A school district which enjoys the location of expansive industrial installations can raise adequate tax money with an insignificant willingness rate. The lower the rate, the more enticing it becomes for other industries to locate there. This vicious circle spotlights the most serious shortcoming of the property tax; it plays favorites within the state.

Because of this type of inequity, some state legislatures have authorized boards of education to seek other sources of income. The *tangible personal property* tax is used in many states, a tax levied against those who own movable property such as automobiles, business equipment, furniture, and inventories of stock and supplies. While providing another source of revenue, the personal property tax is not economical to collect. So much judgment is involved in assessing the value of such property, and it becomes so expensive to engage assessors to verify the extent or value of such property, that many states have discontinued that form of taxation.

In efforts to spread the taxing base, some boards of education are permitted to tax *intangible personal property,* that is, items which have no value in themselves but represent value, items such as stocks, bonds, interest on bank deposits and other types of investment. This has been a lucrative source of revenue in these years of prosperity, but it is not stable from year to year and does not necessarily aid those districts which are poor in property wealth. There is a high correlation between the location of property wealth and the location of interest-producing property.

Other sources of revenue for a school district authorized in a few states are taxes on personal income, amusements, soft drinks, property transfers, and sales of tobacco, and per capita (head) taxes. A board of education can normally expect miscellaneous income from tuition charges for those children who do not reside within the district, from gifts, from re-sales of materials to pupils, from rentals of board-owned property, and from temporary investments of a board's *inactive funds.*

STATE FINANCING OF EDUCATION

The state level of government, having legal responsibility for public education, has always shared in its financial support since the first compulsory education laws were passed in Massachusetts. Originally, state governments used the property tax as a means of raising the state's proportion of costs. For a while state and local governments shared that form of revenue, but gradually most states have abandoned the property tax to local governments.

For many decades the state distributed money to school districts on a per capita basis, allocating a prescribed amount according to the number of children residing within a district, or by the number enrolled, or by the number in average daily attendance (ADA) or according to the average daily membership (ADM). As fair as this approach might seem, it does not satisfy the important need which a state government can supply, i.e., the need to level the inequities of wealth which develop among local communities. Furthermore, the distribution of money according to the number of children aids highly populated areas but does not recognize the higher unit costs of educating children in sparsely settled areas. Thus, nearly all states have assumed the responsibility of equalizing the educational opportunities for all children of the state through some kind of formula which takes into account the inequities.

Early efforts at equalization created nearly as many problems as they solved. Grants were made to local districts according to financial needs. When the state first tapped the same source of revenue being used by local school districts in order to get equalizing money, it nullified the chances of the board of education to raise its own money. More serious was local voter's discovery and acceptance of state aid, and subsequent loss of enthusiasm for local support. Gradually, this condition led to nearly complete state-controlled and state-financed plans, from which a few states have never departed. Since the principle of local control over the education of children has always been basic to the system of education in the United States, and since local interest, pride, and competitive spirit are largely accountable for the successes attained by the American plan of educating all youth, a plan of state-local partnership had to evolve to satisfy the needs of local control with equalized opportunities.

Eventually, the *foundation* concept of equalization emerged. Nearly all states use the foundation idea in some form. The common characteristics of a foundation plan are these:

1. A foundation, or minimum standard, of education is assured for all districts of the state without limiting the heights to which that standard might aspire.
2. There is joint participation in the costs by the state and local government, with major responsibility remaining at the local level.

3. Local support is not only required but is encouraged to continue independently, well beyond the minimum foundation prescribed.
4. The minimum quality of education guaranteed to all youth is defined through certain standards which all school districts must meet, such as size of class, training of teachers, and the like.
5. All major costs of education, including capital outlay and pupil transportation, should be included in determining the base, or foundation minimum.

Each state determines its own plan for funding its share of public services; the most common sources currently used throughout the nation are taxes on retail sales, personal income, corporation licensing or profits, on sales of liquor and tobacco, motor fuel, on inheritance, and legalized wagers.

Some states earmark certain taxes exclusively for school support; others, pooling all state revenue in one general fund, allocate funds according to needs as expressed in budgets submitted to a state authority. Each approach has its merits and its enthusiasts. The practice of earmarking does prevent that revenue from being diverted to other state functions. On the other hand, having only limited sources of revenue for specified purposes denies the flexibility criterion of enabling the state to adjust its income and spending to changes in time, place, and needs.

FEDERAL FINANCING OF EDUCATION

Although the direct support of elementary and secondary education by the Federal Government averages less than five percent of the total cost nationwide, that office makes extensive investments annually in assorted educational enterprises as outlined in Chapter V. The only receipts incumbent for most public school systems prior to the 1965 act are used in aiding lunchroom activities, vocational programs, instructional equipment under the National Defense Education Act, and other special-purpose supports. Therein lies one of the major criticisms of federal supports. States and local boards of education prefer that such funds be received as *general support* without restrictions as to use. It is argued that the central government does not understand local needs as well as those who work locally. Moreover, the argument continues, special grants force a district to distort its expenditures out of relation to needs. Since most federal aids are extended on a matching basis by either the state or local school district, the school system must divert its matching share from other purposes, perhaps needed more urgently there, in order to avail itself of the federal money.

Thus far, Congress has been unwilling, or unable, to win appropriations as general support education. As explained in Chapter V, the legislation of 1965 permits federal moneys to be used in a much broader way than did any previous appropriation. However, there are enough limitations in that act on the means of local allocation spending that it must still be classified as a *special-purpose subsidy*. Efforts to obtain general support have bogged down for three reasons: the concern about local communities losing control of the education of their children, the concern about distributing federal moneys to parochial as well as public schools, and the concern about using federal moneys to support racially segregated schools. These concerns have been of sufficient magnitude to forestall anything but special-purpose aids.

FINANCING SCHOOL BUILDING CONSTRUCTION

The responsibility for financing new building construction and renovation of existing buildings has, for the most part, been reserved to local school districts. The rationale for this decision seems to be only custom. Some states regard costs of capital outlay in the same vein as costs of operation, and they participate in financing both. But since a local district generally must stand capital expenditures alone, the board of education is forced to use the only source of revenue which the state has authorized, namely, the property tax. This situation has been aggravated further in recent years by state limitations on a board of education's power to incur long-term debt. These *debt limitations* may be expressed in the state constitution which makes change difficult. Changing to a higher limitation is much easier to attain if it is found only in legislation. Many states have had to raise their debt limitations in recent years so that rapidly growing districts can keep up with classroom needs.

The costs of an occasional new building in a small district or that of many buildings in a mushrooming district are too exhorbitant to expect citizens to vote enough increased property taxes at one time to permit paying for the buildings out of current operating money. Since the tax levy approach, then, is often insufficient for capital construction, the district is compelled to borrow money which must be paid back over a period of as much as twenty to thirty years. A school district borrows money through the process of issuing bonds. A *bond* is simply one of several kinds of negotiable instruments approved by the business society for borrowing money. Here, a lender, usually a bank or some large investment company, provides the money for construction, and the school district signs a promise to repay the loan with interest at regular intervals. Most states permit governmental bodies to use only *general obligation bonds* instead of *mortgage bonds* in borrowing money. There is no tangible security for the lender, only a general obligation of the citizens of a school district to make payment of premium and interest. Most schools also use *serial bonds,* that is, the promises to pay (bonds) are numbered serially when issued and they are retired in order of lowest numbers first.

The hardship of capital construction through borrowed money results from the interest costs. Should the money be borrowed at a time of high interest rates, citizens will have to pay half again as much for a building as its actual construction costs. Even a reasonable rate of three or four percent paid over a period of twenty years means, for example, that a million dollar building will cost the taxpayers about a million and a quarter dollars. In order to eliminate this major cost of a new building, many districts go to the *pay-as-you-go* plan for financing new construction as soon as they possibly can. Under this plan they do not borrow money but pay for the construction costs out of a voter-approved tax levy. A slightly higher tax rate for a few years permits extensive savings for taxpayers which are denied under a bonding plan with a lower tax rate for a long period of time. Some districts have managed continuously to maintain a steady and modest tax levy for construction and, barring a sudden, abnormal growth, can keep up with needs for new and renovated buildings.

A few states have authorized another means for overcoming high interest costs for districts which may have become poor risks or for districts which are restricted by debt limitations. Under this method, the state creates a state *building authority,* an agency which is approved for issuing bonds, constructing buildings, and leasing the facilities to a school district for an annual rental, which eventually retires the debt. Because of the state's wider taxing power, lenders can more safely borrow at a lower interest rate. Pennsylvania exemplifies a state which also permits the creation of a local building authority to perform in the same manner as a state authority, although the interest rates there are often less favorable than if the board of education had borrowed the money itself. Nonetheless, it permits a school district to move ahead its building plans without a vote of the taxpayers. The bonds so issued by an authority are classified as *revenue bonds, viz.,* the principal and interest are paid from the revenue derived from the use of the object constructed; in this case, the revenue is the rental paid by the board of education.

THE SCHOOL BUDGET

Public schools are required to conduct their fiscal affairs according to budgetary procedures adopted in each state. From a monetary point of view, a budget is merely an estimate of the income and expenditure for the fiscal year which may run from January to December or from June to July, depending upon state regulations. From an educational point of view, it represents much more. The budget actually determines the nature of the learning activities, for it specifies the amount of money which will be allocated to each type of expenditure: salaries, supplies, administration, maintenance, plant operations, construction, and any other purpose for which the district proposes to spend money. Its relationship to the quality of education is so significant because state laws prevent a board of education from spending for any other purpose than that stipulated in its approved budget.

For this reason, the planning of the budget by the superintendent and his staff has received considerable study. A commonly accepted guide for good budgeting is known as the *equilateral triangle concept,* with the three sides labeled the income element, the expenditure element, and the educational goals element. The concept becomes relevant for planning when the educational side is used as the base for the other two sides. The base is studied and decided upon first. The staff decides what is needed for good education of youth within that district. These needs are then translated into costs which become the second side of the triangle, then income—the third side—is sought to cover the costs. The concept is important also since the length of the base line—the educational program—automatically determines the length of the other two sides of an equilateral triangle. Thus, the staff will ask for no more money than it needs to carry out its plan; neither will it spend any more. This concept becomes only an ideal in districts which have no control over increasing the amount of money they can receive during a year. Under such conditions, the income might as well be the base, for the expenditures and educational program must be fitted to available money.

Another accepted concept of good budget planning is that of long term budgeting for five or more years. Wise administration looks far ahead of the present year in planning educational improvements and divining methods to attain them. A job well done in looking to the future makes the short-term budget — the annual budget — a fairly simple process.

Good budget planning also involves the entire staff. All divisions of the school system should be solicited for ideas of improvment and should have a voice in determining allocated amounts. This is more than democratic administration; it is a way of obtaining wider, and perhaps wiser, decisions regarding educational programming. Used tactfully, it is a vehicle for curriculum improvement. It can inspire teachers to dream about innovation and better teaching. It can also lead them subtly into becoming cost conscious. Moreover, budget planning by the entire staff offers a medium of employee-superintendent communication which can make "negotiations" seem superfluous. Most authorities also agree that citizens should be brought into the planning stages as a means of bettering community understanding of school operations, needs, and costs.

The formalizing steps of budgeting are prescribed in state law. In general, a board of education must conduct a public hearing on the budget before it is approved; in some states the budget must be publicized prior to the hearing. In New Jersey the citizens actually vote on the budget annually. In New England areas the budget is approved at a town meeting. In fiscally dependent districts the budget must be approved by the city council or some other local governmental body. In all cases, the state government has power of review over the board of education budget.

Another indicator of the maturation which is taking place in the management of a school's fiscal affairs is the trend of more school districts to employ what is known as *performance, or functional, budgeting.* The principal advantage of performance budgeting is the extent of information, usually in narrative form, which it avails the reader. Instead of mere figures and account titles, the performance budget describes in some detail the purpose for which money is being spent. It focuses the reader's attention on ideas, practices, and goals instead of dollars. Other government agencies, particularly the federal level and some municipalities, which have been using performance budgeting for many years, have discovered the merits arising from legislative understanding of why money is being requested. Certainly a board of education is entitled to complete understanding of what it approves for spending. More importantly, taxpayers would undoubtedly be more sympathetic to requests for educational expenditures if they knew precisely what their dollars were buying.

ISSUES IN FUTURE FINANCING

In addition to the question of further participation by the central government in future financing of education, there are other questions to be resolved by school administration if the plan is to measure up to the established criteria of adequacy, flexibility, stability, and balance. It is clear that educational costs will continue to increase with population growth and with the continuing upward trend of the economic cycle which boosts the costs of everything schools buy. Yet many solutions today brighten this outlook.

Arrangements for equitable sharing of the costs by the state and local communities must be sought; some states need to participate more extensively in order to satisfy the four criteria of sound financing, while elsewhere the communities need to exert greater efforts. The trend toward centralizing the responsibility for school financing to the state or national level must not be allowed to destroy local enthusiasm. History has already given us that lesson. Expanding the base beyond the property tax upon which local boards of education can raise money is one solution. Some states can reduce the costs of collecting taxes through centralizing the process in county, regional, or state offices. Other states need to work toward fairer and more objective methods for assessing the value of property.

School administrators have a major role to play in this challenge by stretching the available tax dollars still further. The appropriate actions fall into the other half of the school finance jurisdiction—school business management as detailed in the next chapter. Suffice it to point out here that officials need to be informed in business-like methods of purchasing, insurance management, transportation and food service, plant maintenance, construction, and operations, and investments of inactive board funds. The march toward larger and more efficient school districting must be sustained. Educators and parents must re-appraise the functions of education, determining what is proper for public schools to do for the upbringing of children and what is proper for other agencies. Improved communications between school personnel and citizens are essential to finding agreement upon purposes and means of finance. There is positive evidence that many citizens do not yet appreciate the personal and economic potential returns from their investment in education.

INVESTMENT IN EDUCATION AS AN ECONOMIC ACT . . .

THE CONTRIBUTION OF EDUCATION TO THE NATION'S ECONOMY*

Increased education is not only one of the largest sources of past and prospective economic growth [,it] also is among the elements most subject to conscious social decision. The laws governing school attendance and child labor have a pervasive effect, and schools are largely publicly operated and financed.

---

*Edward F. Denison, *The Sources of Economic Growth in the United States and the Alternative Before Us,* New York: by permission of Committee for Economic Development, 1961, 74-78.

However, the influence of education on output is dispersed over a very long period. The changes in the educational background of the labor force reflect mainly improvements in schooling that were achieved many years earlier.

The median age of all persons in the labor force is 40 years. Only improvements in education achieved by about 1925 affected as many as half of the members of the 1960 labor force throughout their schooling. The education provided before World War I was still of importance. Even radical extensions of schooling for children now in school would change the average educational background of the labor force only moderately from that already in sight in the next decade or two.

This observation is in no sense intended to discount the importance to growth of decisions affecting education. We should take the long view. But it is only realistic to stress that for the near-term the educational background of the labor force has already been largely determined.

The following crude calculations illustrate the point. Suppose that, starting with those who would otherwise complete school in 1962 and continuing indefinitely, some action were taken that resulted in everyone remaining in school one year longer than he otherwise would. Suppose further that the additional year raised the ability of these individuals to contribute to production by 7.5 per cent.

By 1970 only about 15 per cent of the labor force would have benefited by extra education, and the average quality of the entire labor force would therefore be raised by 1.1 per cent. But loss of those in school instead of at work in 1970 would cost us about 2.6 per cent of the labor force. If these young workers are counted as of half the quality of the *average* worker, this would mean an offsetting loss of 1.3 per cent of labor input. On balance, total labor input, adjusted for quality, would be reduced 0.2 per cent.

By 1980 we would be ahead. Almost 40 per cent of the labor force would have received the extra education, so average quality would be 3.0 per cent higher than otherwise. The cost would still be 1.3 per cent, so that total labor input, adjusted for quality, would be increased 1.7 per cent and national product 1.4 per cent. This would raise the growth rate of the national product, computed from 1960 to 1980, by 0.07 percentage points.

Ultimately, sometime around the year 2010, the quality of the entire labor force would be raised by 7.5 per cent, while the cost in labor lost that year would still be around 1.3 per cent. Labor input would be larger by 6.2 per cent and national product by 5.2 per cent. Over the entire 50-year period from 1960 to 2010 we should have raised the average annual growth rate of national product by 0.10 percentage points.

Provision of an additional year's education would require the continuing use of 0.3 or 0.4 per cent of the national product, leaving that much less for other uses. So far as output available for noneducational purposes is concerned, this would deduct the equivalent of .02 percentage points from the growth rate over a 20-year period but less than .01 over 50 years.

Aside from its noneconomic benefits, the net effect of the additional year's education would thus be to add 0.09 percentage points to the growth rate of output available for uses other than education over the next 50 years.

To add a full year's schooling, over and above the considerable increase in education already in prospect, would be a large step, and the addition of [0.1] percentage points to the growth rate for 50 years would be a large result. However, it may surprise the reader that the effect would not be even larger in view of the importance of education to past growth. The reconciliation lies in the huge amount by which education has been extended in the past.

To consider growth over the long-run future, we must ask what changes in education are likely or possible. In practice, the amount of education received by young people cannot increase in the future at the rate that it has in the past.

The past great increase in schooling has been stimulated by the geographic expansion of 12-year public school facilities to cover the nation, the prohibition of child labor, and compulsory school attendance laws, as well as the decline in agriculture and such continuing influences as rising income. Though still exerting a strong delayed impact upon the educational level of the labor force, the effect of these great reforms on school attendance is running out. The remaining possibilities for increasing education through the high school years, though important in absolute terms and especially so in the South, are slight compared with past achievements. The average number of *days* a year that students spend in elementary and secondary schools is twice that of 1870. But in recent years it has been almost stationary. Indeed, except for some possible further reduction in absenteeism, to double it again would require the schools to remain open for all students 365 days a year. There is discussion of lengthening the school day, but little agreement as to the benefits this may be expected to bring.

A large further expansion in the proportion of young people attending college may be confidently anticipated. Moreover, an additional year of education at the upper grades (and especially if college is completed) adds more to earnings than an additional year in the lower grades.

But what is required to maintain the contribution of more education to the growth *rate* is maintenance of the *percentage* increase in the amount of education received, adjusted for the greater importance of the upper grades. For the long pull, this seems simply unattainable.

This prospect makes it all the more important to seek improvement in the quality of education, so as to offset the slackening of the increase in its quantity. But we should not be overly sanguine about this. Such objective evidence as is available suggests that the quality of a day's schooling has been improving for many years, even though my estimates cannot measure it. What is needed to prevent the contribution of education to growth from falling very sharply before the end of this century is a great *acceleration in* the rate of increase in quality.

This chapter has focused on education of the young, which comprises the great bulk of all formal education. Adult education, formal or informal, also affects the quality of the labor force, and more quickly. Its expansion could also help to maintain the contribution of education to growth.

The calculations in this chapter do not cover on-the-job training (unless provided by schools and colleges). This is undoubtedly a very important form of training but I do not know whether or not it has increased or decreased in amount per worker. Its omission involves the implicit assumption, so far as the past is concerned, that it has not changed in importance. In considering possibilities of stimulating future growth, more or better on-the-job training, as well as other forms of adult education, should not be overlooked.

"INVESTMENT" IN EDUCATION VS INVESTMENT IN CAPITAL GOODS

In the measurement of national income or product, expenditures for education, like those for food, housing, health and other commodities necessary to sustain an effective labor force, are considered outlays for final products, not intermediate products like the consumption of capital goods. Hence, in assigning a share of the growth of the observed national income to education no deduction was made for the costs of education. Moreover, and more basic, I think that the national income treatment is correct. Education directly benefits individual welfare and improves the individual's ability to participate wisely in social decisions, and these are probably even more important than its effect in raising income, large though this may be.

However, in considering the costs of stimulating education in order to accelerate growth, we must remember that individuals attending schools are ordinarily lost (or largely lost) to the labor force. As education is pushed to more advanced grades, the value of a year of this lost labor increases. The costs of providing schools must also be considered. The preceding section examined these costs. From this examination, I conclude that there can be no real doubt that, within the context in which actual decisions will be made, additional provisions for education will make a significant net contribution to long-term economic growth.

This conclusion must still deal with the contention that to devote more resources to education may not make a net contribution to growth because use of the same resources for capital investment might contribute as much or more. This argument can be dismissed rather easily, given the way decisions governing educational and investment expenditures are actually made in the United States. . . .

Insofar as the costs of higher education are publicly financed through taxation, this supposition requires that one believe additional taxes do not reduce consumption at all, but come entirely out of private saving. Insofar as the costs (including foregone earnings) are borne by the student and his family, it requires that over their lifetimes they spend no more for consumption, other than college expenses, than they would spend if they received the additional earnings that the student has foregone by attending college and if they did not incur expenditures for attending college.

I think it reasonable to suppose that the great bulk of the full cost of attending college replaces other consumption rather than saving, so that additional college enrollments would make a net contribution to growth even if the rate of return on a college education were only a small fraction of that on capital investment in "things."

All this is not to deny, of course, that there may be *some* immediate offset in a lower rate of capital formation. But in the long run the indirect effect of more education on the growth of the capital stock is more likely to be favorable than adverse, simply because the larger national income it will create will add to investment opportunities and to saving.

What is true of college education applies with even greater force to education in the lower grades, where both the earnings foregone and per pupil costs are much smaller.

RETURNS FROM INVESTMENT IN EDUCATION*

Investment in education brings returns which are essential in our kind of society. It yields economic dividends in the form of higher standard of

*John K. Norton, *What Everyone Should Know About Financing Our Schools,* Washington, D.C.: by permission of National Education Association, Committee on Educational Finance, 1960, 57.

living and greater national security. Investment in education increases the productive and earning power of individuals. It provides the growing number of leaders and trained workers which we must have. Basic research and its indispensable product — new knowledge — are another outcome from expenditure for education. Better-informed citizens, to deal with domestic and foreign problems which ever grow in number and complexity, are a principal product of education. The schools are a chief instrument in keeping the door of opportunity open for all. Education is a primary means whereby we may learn to use the increasing amount of time free from work for purposes which elevate our conduct as citizens and as individuals.

QUALITY SCHOOLS ARE HIGH-EXPENDITURE SCHOOLS*

Substantial increases in expenditures for public schools will be required if economic and other returns from investment in human capital are to be maximized. While money is not everything in providing quality schooling, it is something. Quality schools almost universally are high-expenditure schools.

The problem is one of making additional funds count most in buying the quality of schooling demanded by the type of society and economy to which we aspire.

Currently wide variations in the quality of schools in the United States are in considerable degree a result of enormous and indefensible differences in the financial support of schools in different regions and localities. States and communities with low levels of financial support for schools are the sources of millions of disadvantaged citizens.

There has been inadequate response in school expenditures to the mounting demands made upon the schools. Between 1900 and 1958, the purchasing power of the money available to pay for each day of schooling provided in public schools declined. Taking account of all factors, boards of education in the United States generally had less ability to buy first-rate schooling for each child, for each day he was in school, in 1958 than in 1900.

A recent Congressional study concluded that this low elasticity in the support of public schools should be of deep concern to those convinced

*John K. Norton, *Changing Demands on Education and Their Fiscal Implication,* Washington, D.C.: National Committee for Support of Public Schools, 1963, 108-109.

that improvements in education are essential if the United States is to remain a leading world power.

A number of citizens committees have estimated what it would cost to finance quality schools in all communities in the United States. They agree that there must be a substantial increase in school expenditures to achieve this end. Their estimates are that approximately a doubling of present expenditures for public schools will be needed during the 1960's.

Adequate support for public schools will require decisive action on the part of many citizens. There must be recognition that investment in public education pays handsome dividends. The fiscal obstacles that now block the road to adequate financial support for public education must be removed.

The rewards of decisive and intelligent action in providing excellent schools everywhere in the United States would be substantial. The penalties of failure in this regard would be severe. Leaders throughout the nation should ponder these alternatives with great care.

LOCAL SUPPORT OF SCHOOLS . . .

A PROPOSAL TO GIVE MORE FLEXIBILITY IN LOCAL TAXES*

In the traditional division of tax sources between State and local governments, the property tax has been more or less reserved to local governments; and nonproperty taxes, notably those on sales and income, have generally been the province of the State. As a consequence, a single decision answers two questions:

> How much money should come from the local district and how much from the State?
> How much should come from property taxes and how much from nonproperty?

In other words, to vote yes on a proposal to increase the local government's contribution to the State-local partnership in support of the schools is virtually tantamount to voting yes on a proposal to increase the property tax.

---

*Eugene P. McLoone, "Flexibility in Local Support of the Schools: A Proposal," *School Life*, XLIV (May, 1962), 5-6.

I propose that these decisions be separate — one for the type of tax, one for the level of government. But before I undertake to outline a method of separating them, let me try to give some perspective on the *need* for separation, by reviewing, first, the changes that have taken place in the last decade in the sources of support for local government and, second, the relation between the State-local partnership — that is, the foundation program — and the reliance on the property tax.

Even to persons familiar with State and local financing, a review of recent changes in the sources of support for local governments may bring some surprises. During the past decade local governments financed from their own sources an increasing percentage of their total expenditures and would have had to spend more had they not received Federal funds for public assistance and for highways. State aid dropped off in relative importance. Although nonproperty taxes were introduced on the local scene, at least in some places, the property tax maintained its relative importance in the State and local system of taxation.

Today the property tax is the source of more than 85 percent of local government's tax dollars and, since State law limits school districts almost entirely to this source of local funds, it supplies more than half of the school's. Its continued importance has resulted from increases not only in the tax base but in the tax rate. True, the percentage of school revenue provided by this source has declined, but school revenue from local sources has increased both in dollars and in the percentage it represents of property tax collections — generally, that is, for States vary in their reliance on the property tax for the schools. As for the States, in 1961 they collected, on the average, only 3.3 percent of their revenue from the property tax, and only 3 States — Nebraska, Wyoming, and Arizona — collected more than 10 percent.

The relation between the foundation program and increases in the amount of revenue collected through the property tax can be traced to the lack of flexibility in the two variables in the program that are subject to control by government — the level of support and the uniform local tax rate. Although no direct evidence is at hand, two facts offer a reasonable explanation:

First, a fixed foundation level becomes almost at once out of date; it is scarcely established before it is left behind by the rising prices. In the past decade almost every revision of State aid has been upward, to make up for the lag.

Second, whenever a local community has wanted more money for its schools, either to offset price increases, to improve the quality of education, or merely to keep up with the increasing school population, it has had nowhere to turn except to the property tax. As a result, school revenue from the property tax in the past 10 years has kept pace in dollars with State aid.

The fact that inflexibility extends in two directions — to the foundation level and to the local property tax rate — makes the problem of school support doubly complicated. Fortunately a number of States already are attempting to correct the inflexibility in the former. Wisconsin, Rhode Island, and New York, for instance, all have adopted plans by which to make the foundation level respond to local effort; their foundation programs will provide a range of dollar amounts rather than a fixed amount. Almost no attention at all, however, has been given to mitigating the effect of inflexibility in the local rate chargeable to the district in the foundation program; and it is this side of the problem that I wish to consider here.

Whenever the value of property rises in a community, either because new buildings are constructed, prices rise, or property is revaluated, the local property tax base increases; and even without any change in the levy the revenue chargeable to the local district increases. The effect on the State-local support program is to increase the contribution by the local district and to reduce the amount from the State. This effect is not lessened even in those States where the foundation level varies with local effort, for the local effort does not increase unless the community increases the property tax rate.

From the property taxpayer's point of view, therefore, the State-local foundation program makes things no easier, at least not for him: the level of support specified in the foundation program generally operates to push property taxes higher. And he is not likely to be consoled by the fact that the total amount raised throughout the State for the schools by means of the uniform local rate in the foundation program is less than the amount that could be raised if the same rate was applied on a statewide basis. Almost every State has its industrial enclaves, its wealthy residential communities, and its small contracting districts which do not participate in the equalization part of the foundation program; these usually can have an adequate school program without levying a rate as high as the uniform rate required by the foundation program, and they usually levy a lower rate.

This inequity among the State's property taxpayers in support of the foundation program could be corrected by a statewide property tax at the level of the uniform rate in the foundation program. Through such a tax all property, not only property in the participating districts, would contribute to the foundation support. Making it statewide would not make it higher but would merely shift part of the property tax levy from the localities to the State.

Nor would it curtail the freedom to tax at the local level if the tax sources now generally reserved to the State were available also to local governments. Under this condition, local communities with the capacity and the desire to spend more on their schools could, instead of increasing their property taxes — as they still could if they wished — levy local nonproperty taxes over and above those levied by the State. These would be supplemental levies riding atop the State tax base, and the revenue would be collected by the State for the community. Already this is being done in several States; in California, Illinois, and Mississippi, local governments are using supplemental, or "piggyback," rates on the State-administered sales tax. Adding nonproperty taxes to the realm of the local government in this fashion not only increases the number of choices available to citizens when they go to vote for more taxes for their schools but also spares the local government the difficulties attendant on administering a nonproperty tax. Anyone who doubts the propriety of such an arrangement should remind himself that, after all, it is commonplace in education to declare that the area of fiscal responsibility for collecting taxes for schools does not need to be the operating area; this is a principle repeatedly demonstrated in State-local foundation programs.

One problem — that school districts organized for efficient operation of the educational program may be too small to permit piggyback levies on sales taxes — finds a solution in many Western States, where the county, situated halfway between the State and local districts, is a third partner in the school support program. Most of these counties already levy a countywide tax for the schools, the proceeds of which are added to the State and local contribution to equalize educational opportunities in the local districts within the county. With its large area, the county government would no doubt be more effective than the local government in adding a supplement to the State sales tax. In fact, the State-county-local partnership seems made to order as an aid to separating the question of tax source from the question of government level.

At least one argument for combining, for public school purposes, a State property tax with local supplements to State nonproperty taxes is that it will help to disabuse many people of a popular misconception — that State aid exists to reduce or replace the property tax. True, State aid was established for this purpose in many States, but it cannot serve that purpose now. We live in a time that calls not for replacements of existing tax sources but for supplements to those sources: for additional taxes at increased rates, not fewer taxes and lower rates. The choices now available to local communities hard pressed for more school funds — higher local property taxes, new local nonproperty taxes, or additional State aid financed by State nonproperty taxes — must somehow be made broader.

GUIDELINES FOR THE ADMINISTRATION OF LOCAL PROPERTY TAXES*

1. Assessors should be qualified and licensed by the state in order to serve. Only licensed property appraisers should be employed as assessors.
2. Assessors should be appointed or elected from a list of qualified applicants. Appointment should be either by state board, by a civil service commission, or by a county board.
3. The state should conduct a school to train and re-train assessors.
4. A state manual for the guidance of assessors should be published. It should be kept up-to-date.
5. There should be state-directed property assessment equalization, both inter-county and intra-county. This should be based on adequate sampling of property values and assessments in each county.
6. Exemptions should be limited to such property as that owned and used directly by government, churches, hospitals, private schools and colleges, and other nonprofit organizations.
7. Prompt assessment and reassessment is essential and may be facilitated by constant checking of building permits and utility installations.
8. Unless assessments are fully equalized, the property assessment equalization program should include an assessment ratio plan which requires a higher levy for districts which are under-assessed or a mandatory increase in assessed valuation of property in such districts.
9. The public should be helped to understand the assessment procedures and the equalization program through continuous publicity.
10. The appraisal of utilities and large industries calls for appraisers specially trained in this area.
11. Inventories of equipment and stock on hand should be included in appraisals and the laws and regulations should permit inspection of such inventories by the assessor. The law should authorize assessment at any time during the year.

---

*George D. Strayer, Jr., *Guidelines for Public School Finance*, Bloomington, Indiana: by permission of *Phi Delta Kappan*, National Advisory Committee on School Finance, 1963, 6-7.

GUIDELINES FOR STATE AND LOCAL TAXATION*

1. The benefits of citizenship require financial support from those sharing such benefits. One measure of tax support ability is the individual's net income. Income tax rates should be graduated.
2. All tangible property is protected by and benefits from government and should be taxed to support continued protection and benefits. This local tax should be levied according to the value of the property.
3. All business and industry conducted for profit receives many benefits from government, and its profits should be taxed for the support of the government and the continuation of these benefits.
4. When the personal income tax, the property tax, and the tax on business conducted for profit are levied, "reasonable" tax rates used, and the tax revenue is still insufficient to support adequately the governmental services desired, various supplementary taxes, i.e., sales taxes, amusement, tobacco, and other luxury taxes, are defensible.
5. Exemptions for dependents in assessing the personal income tax are defensible, but these should not exceed a similar exemption in the federal personal income tax. Exemptions under a retail sales tax should be limited to the essentials of life and health.
6. The federal, state, and local tax systems should be viewed in terms of the individual taxes which belong to a defensible system of taxation and in terms of their proper coordination into a balanced tax program within the state. The rate of each tax should be determined according to governmental needs for tax money, equity among the various taxes in the total tax system, and the possible consequences of present or anticipated taxes upon the total economy and "business climate" of the state.
7. The life-blood and vigor of our cherished popular control over education should be safeguarded by scrupulously avoiding any and all regulations, through taxation or other means, which handicap the control of education by local boards of education.

*George D. Strayer, Jr., *Guidelines for Public School Finance,* Bloomington, Indiana: by permission of *Phi Delta Kappan,* National Advisory Committee on School Finance, 1963, 4-5.

8. Taxation, beyond the general power to levy taxes, is a legislative matter which usually should be reserved for the state legislature. Constitutional provisions which limit or restrain the state legislature in the exercise of this responsibility should usually be eliminated.

9. Since financial support of the schools currently rests heavily on the efficient use of the local property tax, the schools have an inherent interest in the best possible administration of that tax.

10. While the earmarking of certain taxes for school support has been and presently is used widely in programs of state support for education, the welfare of a service so basic to all aspects of democratic life makes it desirable for at least a significant part of state support for the schools to be derived from the total state tax system and hence appropriated from the state general fund.

GUIDELINES REGARDING THE RELATIONSHIP OF FINANCE AND SCHOOL DISTRICT REORGANIZATION*

1. Progress in school district reorganization is generally good in states which encourage reorganization through features of their state support program.

2. Provisions in school finance programs aimed at encouraging school district reorganization should promote better educational opportunities for pupils.

3. State support programs facilitate reorganization when they include a number of special features such as financial assistance for transportation and capital outlay support for larger units.

4. Loss of state support by reorganization is undesirable.

5. The foundation program should include adequate support for all *necessary* small schools.

6. A foundation program of educational offerings and services

---

*George D. Strayer, Jr., *Guidelines for Public School Finance,* Bloomington, Indiana: by permission of *Phi Delta Kappan,* National Advisory Committee on School Finance, 1963, 14.

which cannot easily be provided by small districts should be required in order to encourage reorganization.

LOCAL NONPROPERTY TAXES FOR SCHOOLS*

Local nonproperty taxation for schools has not been widely adopted even though it has been widely discussed. There are several explanations for this limited use. The property tax has until fairly recently provided adequate local revenue in most cases where there was sufficient wealth to meet local needs. Where this wealth did not exist, it was necessary to look to other levels of government which could draw on a broader tax base. In the case of schools this has been predominately at the State level.

The States have withdrawn from the property tax field and this withdrawal has provided more leeway at the local level, at least until governmental service demands increased sharply. It is generally assumed that the larger units of government can best administer nonproperty taxes and the States have moved extensively into the fields of income, general sales, and selective sales taxation. The Federal Government has long dominated the income tax field and is also heavily involved in selective sales and excise taxation.

At the local level the major adoptions of nonproperty taxes have been made by the municipalities with the net result that the school districts are left in the residual position of being the major users of the property tax and, in turn, dependent almost entirely upon the property tax for their local sources of revenue.

So long as abandonments by other units of government have provided additional potential revenue from this source, or so long as the States have provided additional sums of money from State sources, the fiscal needs of the schools could be met. In more and more cases today, however, the property tax has reached its limit, either constitutional, legal, practical, or emotional. Additional State appropriations have not been forthcoming, and the local district is faced with the direct problem of seeking additional sources of revenue.

---

*Albert L. Alford, *Nonproperty Taxation for Schools,* Washington, D.C.: United States Office of Education, Bulletin 1964, No. 4, 1963, 135-136.

This study has attempted to analyze some of the alternatives available in the nonproperty tax field to see how they might be adapted to local school district use. Many nonproperty taxes are administratively feasible for use by local school districts, though they may not always be suitable for other reasons. The property tax is no better suited to efficient local administration than are most of the nonproperty taxes and not as well suited as several. The main advantage that the property tax holds is that it is in existence and being administered at the local level in spite of many inefficiencies. Resistance to change and fear of the unknown are always strong factors.

While an attempt has been made to dispel some of the misconceptions and fears of nonproperty tax use at the local school district level, this study does not necessarily recommend the use of nonproperty taxes, as such. From the point of view of adequate educational financing, there may be several alternatives which are more desirable. There are certain economies in the administration of taxes by a larger unit of government as well as the tapping of a broader base of wealth. Increased State aid, therefore, is held out by many as a most desirable alternative. Some support Federal aid on similar grounds.

Improvement of property tax administration is offered by others as a way to obtain larger revenues on a fairer basis at the local level. This is a hope, however, which has been held out for generations, and does not appear much closer to fruition today than 50 years ago.

Reorganization of school districts into larger and more efficient units has had strong support in recent years with substantial results.

All of these methods are useful and desirable. When, however, these alternatives are not being utilized and when the school district is being handicapped in its function of providing adequate education for its children, those responsible for the district's operation have a right and duty to examine other possibilities. If resistance to the property tax has reached the point where school budgets are endangered and if for political reasons the school district must rely on its own resources, then it may well turn to one or more of the nonproperty sources discussed herein.

The broadest based taxes should be used where possible, specifically the income and general sales tax, but conditions may not always allow this. The discussion of a broad range of nonproperty taxes is designed to provide information to those school districts which are seeking some guidance. Nonproperty taxation for school districts cannot solve the major problems of educational finance, but it may alleviate the particular problems faced by many school districts in the never ending struggle for adequate revenue.

THE NATURE OF BONDS*

A bond is one of several approved devices developed in business society for borrowing money. Other common devices are notes, stocks, or simply a person's oral promise to pay back the money borrowed. A bond has certain characteristics that distinguish it from other forms of borrowing.

In the first place, only certain organizations are permitted by law to borrow money through the use of bonds. These are organizations, private or public, which are incorporated under the laws of the state. "Public bodies" include school districts among the various forms of governmental units eligible for borrowing with bonds. As will be seen, the laws even distinguish between public and private corporations as to the kind of bonds each may use for borrowing.

The corporation which uses a bond for borrowing agrees not only to repay the sum (or principal) of the amount borrowed over a definite period of years, but also to pay an additional amount in the form of *interest* to the lender for the use of his money. The primary difference between a bond and other forms of borrowing in this respect is the length of time allowed for repayment — bonds involving perhaps ten to thirty years, whereas notes are repaid usually in a matter of days or months.

Bonds may differ in the manner by which they are to be repaid. If the total principal is to be repaid at the end, or *maturity* date, of the borrowing period they are known as *term, straight-term,* or *sinking fund* bonds. In the latter type the borrower builds up the amount needed for repayment by making regular deposits to a sinking fund for that purpose. This procedure is not recommended for school boards. [It] is prohibited in some states, because of occasional mismanagement of the savings and because of the turnover of board of education personnel which has sometimes diverted the savings to some other purpose. The common, and much preferred, method of repayment of a bonded loan is by *retiring* a certain amount, usually in equal installments for each year over the life of the loan. Bonds retired in this method are classified as *serial* bonds. Such bonds are numbered before issuing, and they are paid back *in series* annually, or more frequently, semi-annually.

---

*Robert E. Wilson, *Accounting and Record Keeping for Schools,* © 1959, Kent, Ohio, Kent State University, 98-99.

A bond differs from a share of stock as a means of borrowing money in that the latter represents a portion of ownership in the issuing corporation. Persons who buy a corporation's bonds do not have any claim on the assets of the organization unless those assets are pledged in the written agreement as collateral for repayment. If collateral is put up by the corporation as security to borrow money, such bond is classified as a *mortgage* bond. Public bodies are legally forbidden to issue mortgage bonds. Bonds also differ from stocks in that the borrower does not promise to repay any stated amount of money. The stock buyer assumes the entire risk as to how much return he might get for "lending" the borrower money. The buyer of *common* stocks, in contrast to bonds, is not even assured of receiving interest payments for the use of his money. This reduction of risk for the lender who buys bonds explains, of course, why the bond is considered a more conservative method of borrowing money with its generally lower accompanying rate of interest.

Since the bond is a written promise to repay the lender a stated amount of money, and since the original lender frequently has the right to trade, sell, or otherwise transfer this written promise to another party, the paper becomes a *negotiable instrument*. This characteristic makes it incumbent upon the borrower to be concerned with its mechanical preparation — wording, engraving, quality of paper — in order to prevent fraudulent duplication and misuse. The mechanical quality of the bond even influences the rate of interest. Here is one of the areas of bonding activities in which the school finance officer needs the competent and reliable counsel of specialists. It is common practice to attach coupons to a bond, each coupon being detachable and serving as the claim for interest payment at stated intervals. These, too, are negotiable and demand care in preparation in order to protect the borrower's interests. Some protection may be obtained by issuing *registered* bonds, meaning that the name and other identifying information of each buyer is registered with the borrower and only the registered owner can redeem the coupon or bond, assuming that both are registered. Registering bonds, while providing protection, detracts slightly from the bond's marketability

OTHER TYPES OF BONDS

Since schools cannot issue mortgage bonds, they normally use what is known as *general obligation* bonds. Residents of a school district, operating through their duly elected or appointed officials, the board of education, obligate themselves to repay the loan. The only collateral which the lender has is his faith in the ability of the residents to make good the loan. The relative strength of that faith is a determining factor of the interest rate he will "charge" for the use of his money. His faith is measured by the past history of the district in repaying its loans, the extent to which the district is already in debt, and the business-like procedures and reputation of the borrower's management.

In a few instances, school boards may utilize *revenue* bonds, so designated because the moneys to repay the loan are raised from income derived through use of the construction financed by the loan. Revenue bonds are used more commonly by other types of public bodies, such as turnpike commissions, or municipalities when building sewers or water plants, and the loan is paid off from fees charged to the beneficiaries of those facilities. Boards of education may use revenue bonds, however, when borrowing to finance the construction of athletic stadia or field houses, or perhaps an auditorium or library from which an income may be expected through public use. Two states, Pennsylvania and Maine, permit a type of revenue bond through the creation of another public corporation known as a state or local district *authority* to issue bonds for the construction of school buildings, which, in turn, rents these buildings to the school district. The rental fee constitutes a revenue for retiring the bonds over a period of usually twenty to forty years.

STATE FINANCING OF EDUCATION . . .

GUIDELINES FOR STATE DISTRIBUTION OF SCHOOL FUNDS*

1. A foundation program plan incorporating the local-state partnership of financing a defensible program of education for every child should be adopted.
2. The foundation program should be broadly defined by law in terms of educational standards interpreted in terms of cost.
3. The extent of the foundation program should be determined by means of an objective and easily comprehended formula for measuring educational need.
4. The cost of the foundation program should embrace all educational services (special education, pupil transportation, etc.) for

---

*George D. Strayer, Jr., *Guidelines for Public School Finance,* Bloomington, Indiana: by permission of *Phi Delta Kappan,* National Advisory Committee on School Finance, 1963, 11.

children from kindergarten through the twelfth grade, and where need is evident, through the fourteenth grade. The cost should include support for capital expenditures as well as current operational expenditures.

5. A satisfactory basis for measuring local financial ability is essential to the successful development of a foundation program where a local contribution to the foundation program is required.
6. The state's share in financing the program should be the difference between the cost of the program and the available local resources after application of the mandatory local tax rate.
7. The mandatory local tax rate should be low enough to give all or nearly all districts a share of the equalization aid.
8. The mandatory tax rate should be low enough so that all districts will have some tax "leeway" to pay for new and experimental programs without levying taxes at excessive rates.
9. Certain special purpose state funds may be needed to promote experimentation and the development of special projects on a temporary basis.
10. A small state contingency fund should be available for allocation under controlled conditions in case of emergencies.
11. The foundation program should be based on attendance for the current year rather than the prior year.

QUALITIES OF A GOOD STATE FOUNDATION PROGRAM*

No state has yet developed a perfect plan of state support. All plans are in evolution. No state has yet provided a really adequate foundation program of education for all children which actually meets the needs of the times. . . . Since all foundation programs are inadequate, the important thing to consider in appraising each foundation program is whether the plan provides a sound basis upon which to build an adequate program. . . . Authorities on school finance agree that the foundation program should include financial provision for all necessary elements of school costs. . . . Expenditures for capital outlay and debt service are continuing expenditures. All districts, even districts not growing in population, have capital outlay needs. School buildings depreciate at the rate

*R. L. Johns, *Problems and Opportunities in Financing Education,* Washington, D.C.: by permission of National Education Association, Committee on Tax Education and School Finance, 1959, 59-61.

of 2 to 2½ per cent per year, and must eventually be replaced. Districts with a growing population need not only to meet replacement costs, but also to provide for plant expansion.

The foundation program should include long-range provision for the capital outlay needs for all districts. For example, the foundation program might include $600 per classroom unit to meet the depreciation costs of all districts. This is based on the assumption that a building costs $30,000 per classroom unit and that $600 per unit per year for 50 years would provide $30,000. Actually, buildings may cost more than $30,000 per classroom unit in many states. The long-range plan should also include an additional allotment for districts experiencing a growth in attendance.

METHOD OF CALCULATING NEED

It is generally preferable that the appropriation for the foundation program be expressed in a lump sum per weighted classroom unit or per weighted pupil. Such a plan has the advantage of simplicity and avoids unnecessary earmarking of state appropriations. When state appropriations are made in great detail for many separate items of school expenditure, local control of the school budget is undermined. Therefore, authorities on school finance are unanimous in their opposition to detailed earmarking of state appropriations.

However, many state legislatures are reluctant to make lump-sum appropriations. They insist that they need assurance that better educational opportunities will be provided when additional funds are appropriated. To argue that it is not good public policy simply to pay more money for the same type and quality of education is rational and should be recognized by school leaders who seek additional funds from state legislatures.

Intelligent local-school budgeting starts with a study of educational needs. An educational plan providing the educational services needed is developed before the budget request is made. It is not good local policy to start with a lump sum of money and then try to defend it. It seems reasonable to request support for educational services needed rather than a lump sum at the state level as well as at the local level. Stress on educational services needed has a distinct psychological advantage and may result in obtaining more state funds than can be obtained by requesting a lump sum.

The problem is to use the educational-services-needed approach without incurring an unnecessary earmarking of school appropriations. Some states have solved this problem by making the foundation program appropriation in broad budget categories without unnecessarily restricting boards of education in the use of the funds provided.

The cost of all elements in the foundation program, except transportation, can be calculated rationally in terms of weighted classroom units or weighted pupil units. . . . Every foundation-program formula should include a sparsity correction for necessary small schools. No extra allowance should be made, however, for unnecessary small schools which can readily be consolidated. Several techniques are available for determining whether a small school is necessary. A very simple technique is to prescribe the minimum number of miles by a traveled road which a small school must be distant from another school of the same grade level before a sparsity correction is made for that school. . . .

The transportation costs included in the foundation program should be based on (a) the number of children transported who need transportation as defined by law and regulations of the state board of education, and (b) variations in the per-pupil cost of transportation due to factors beyond the control of local boards of education.

CURRENT EXPENDITURE PER PUPIL IN AVERAGE DAILY ATTENDANCE AND SCHOOL REVENUES FROM STATE AND LOCAL GOVERNMENTS*

State	Current expenditure per pupil				Percent of school revenue from state and local sources				
	1953-54	1963-64	Change, 1953-54 to 1963-64		1953-54		1963-64		Gain or loss in state percentage points
			Amt.	Ann'l rate	State	Local	State	Local	
United States	$265	$455	$190	5.6%	39.2%	60.8%	41.6%	58.4%	......
Alabama	151	280	129	6.4	76.4	23.6	68.8	31.2	−7.6
Alaska	411	634	223	4.4	79.2	20.8	64.0	36.0	−15.2
Arizona	282	455	173	4.9	31.6	68.4	37.2	62.8	5.6
Arkansas	139	302	163	8.1	53.1	46.9	51.4	48.6	−1.7
California	345	530	180	4.4	44.4	55.6	41.2	58.8	−3.2
Colorado	280	460	185	5.1	19.1	80.9	25.4	74.6	6.3
Connecticut	297	552	255	6.4	18.4	81.6	36.3	63.7	17.9
Delaware	325	498	173	4.4	89.6	10.4	81.4	18.6	−8.2
District of Columbia	302	517	215	5.5	......	100.0	......	100.0	......
Florida	229	388	159	5.4	53.4	46.6	57.6	42.4	4.2
Georgia	177	306	129	5.6	73.3	26.7	69.5	30.5	−3.8
Hawaii	226	402	176	5.9	88.3	11.7	76.0	24.0	−12.3
Idaho	238	316	78	2.9	23.7	76.3	33.9	66.1	10.2
Illinois	319	479	160	4.1	17.8	82.2	25.3	74.7	7.5
Indiana	280	467	187	5.3	33.5	66.5	34.9	65.1	1.4
Iowa	274	456	182	5.2	12.6	87.4	11.2	88.8	−1.4
Kansas	264	448	184	5.4	24.7	75.3	21.6	78.4	−3.1

*"Financial Report on the Public Schools," *NEA Research Bulletin*, XLII (December, 1964), Washington, D.C.: National Education Association, 125.

CURRENT EXPENDITURE PER PUPIL
Cont'd.

State	Current expenditure per pupil				Percent of school revenue from state and local sources				Gain or loss in state percentage points
	1953-54	1963-64	Change, 1953-54 to 1963-64		1953-54		1963-64		
			Amt.	Ann'l rate	State	Local	State	Local	
Kentucky	153	300	147	7.0	40.8	59.2	57.0	43.0	16.2
Louisiana	247	399	152	4.9	63.7	36.3	68.8	31.2	5.1
Maine	199	378	179	6.6	23.9	76.1	32.7	67.3	8.8
Maryland	268	489	221	6.2	33.2	66.8	35.8	64.2	2.6
Massachusetts	298	475	177	4.8	16.9	83.1	25.1	74.9	8.2
Michigan	283	452	169	4.8	52.5	47.5	44.0	56.0	−8.5
Minnesota	287	509	222	5.9	41.4	58.6	39.8	60.2	−1.6
Mississippi	123	241	118	7.0	51.9	48.1	60.6	39.4	8.7
Missouri	233	419	186	6.1	32.3	67.7	35.8	64.2	3.5
Montana	328	493	165	4.2	33.4	66.6	27.8	72.2	−5.6
Nebraska	262	385	123	3.9	6.4	93.6	6.6	93.4	.2
Nevada	294	464	170	4.7	40.8	59.2	68.2	31.8	27.4
New Hampshire	256	427	171	5.2	6.0	94.0	7.7	92.3	1.7
New Jersey	333	568	235	5.5	11.8	88.2	23.3	76.7	11.5
New Mexico	265	440	175	5.2	85.2	14.8	88.1	11.9	2.9
New York	362	705	343	6.9	36.1	63.9	44.8	55.2	8.7
North Carolina	177	320	143	6.1	72.8	27.2	74.7	25.3	1.9
North Dakota	262	420	158	4.8	28.6	71.4	25.0	75.0	−3.6
Ohio	254	446	192	5.8	26.3	73.7	24.3	75.7	−2.0
Oklahoma	224	351	127	4.6	48.4	51.6	31.1	68.9	−17.3
Oregon	337	549	212	5.0	31.4	68.6	33.9	66.1	2.5
Pennsylvania	299	485	186	5.0	41.1	58.9	45.0	55.0	3.9
Rhode Island	268	500	232	6.4	14.8	85.2	32.9	67.1	18.1
South Carolina	176	265	89	4.2	69.4	30.6	72.1	27.9	2.7
South Dakota	275	403	128	3.9	11.1	88.9	12.7	87.3	1.6
Tennessee	166	291	125	5.8	61.4	38.6	58.9	41.1	−2.5
Texas	249	387	138	4.5	52.6	47.4	54.2	45.8	1.6
Utah	208	394	186	6.6	44.1	55.9	53.8	46.2	9.7
Vermont	245	387	142	4.7	21.8	78.2	24.9	75.1	3.1
Virginia	193	350	157	6.1	47.0	53.0	45.3	54.7	−1.7
Washington	305	515	210	5.4	59.8	40.2	64.9	35.1	5.1
West Virginia	186	300	114	4.9	63.2	36.8	53.8	46.2	−9.4
Wisconsin	293	498	205	5.4	15.8	84.2	26.2	73.8	10.4
Wyoming	330	540	210	5.0	38.9	61.1	42.8	57.2	3.9

STATE-IMPOSED TAXING LIMITATIONS ON BOARDS OF EDUCATION*

A large part of local public-school support comes from taxes on real property, but state constitutional and statutory provisions limit the

---

*"Tax Limitations on School Revenue," *NEA Research Bulletin,* XLIII (May, 1965), Washington, D.C.: National Education Association, 51-55.

amount of school revenue collectible from property taxation. Under-assessment of property and tax overlapping are also limitations on school revenue.

ASSESSMENT BASES

If property is assessed at less than its full value, a higher rate of taxation obviously is required to collect an amount equal to the revenue collectible from a lower rate on property assessed at full value. Comparison of tax rates, therefore, without consideration of the assessment policies is meaningless.

Most states require, by constitution or by statute, that property be assessed at full or true value. Several provide that the assessment base shall be "actual" value; others, "just" value; and still others, "fair" value. The assessment bases reported by Commerce Clearing House and Moody's Investors Service, however, show that regardless of constitutional or statutory requirements property in most states is assessed below current selling prices. Differences exist among states, but there seems to be little connection between the constitutional or statutory requirements and the actual assessments. The differences in language have had little bearing upon the assessment base in practice. . .

TAX LIMITS FOR CURRENT EXPENSES OF SCHOOLS

Tax limitations in use in the 50 states defy classification into mutually exclusive groups. Some fix only upper limits, a few fix only lower limits, some provide differing limits for various sizes and types of school systems, and many of the limitations laws also state conditions under which the limitations may be raised or lowered.

Most states have a maximum millage which legally can be levied on real estate for school purposes, although many provide that these limits can be changed by the local voters. A tabulation of these millage limits has little real meaning for comparative purposes unless a number of other facts are known; first, because of differences in assessment bases, and second, because the limits in many states vary in their application to the different kinds of taxing units. Furthermore, tax limits in a number of states depend upon the school organization, the class of school district, or the population of the district. Also, school taxes are sometimes earmarked for specific purposes or programs.

In most states, a specific number of mills or cents or a percent applied to assessed valuation is the way the limitation is expressed. Several states do not have any tax limits for current expenditures. In these states the amount of tax is decided largely by the voters or by the governing body of each municipality.

Several other states do not set a maximum rate, but specify that the rate shall be sufficient to produce a stated amount per pupil in average daily attendance. This amount is the maximum which may be collected by the school tax in Iowa, the minimum in Arizona and Oregon. The amount that is to be raised in Illinois is to be a percent of the assessed valuation.

Several New England states, without maximum limits on school tax rates, have minimums which must be raised for the support of local schools. In addition, in several states, school districts are required to raise a minimum amount in order to qualify for partial or complete participation in the state aid program.

In about a dozen states, in some districts if not in all, the voters must approve the tax rates for school purposes.

In addition to or including some of these states are those in which a separate tax is authorized for high schools, especially county high schools and high schools of consolidated districts. In at least four states provisions for school taxes depend upon the level of education offered. . . .

The states without limits on tax rates for current expenses do have limits on the amount of indebtedness that may be incurred for school buildings. Every state has some sort of limit for capital outlay. In almost every state this restraint is in the form of a limitation on the amount of indebtedness that may be incurred, usually a percent of the assessed valuation. The limit may be in the form of a specified tax rate that may be levied for building purposes; in several states the limit is stated in terms of an amount of money.

Debt limitations usually pertain to all outstanding indebtedness, current and funded. The limits may differ for different rates of interest, for different maturity dates, for buildings of different kinds, for different classes of districts, or according to other bases. The tax provisions are most often "sufficient to pay interest and principal" on the bonds outstanding. Occasionally, there is a law, especially applicable in the case of emergency, as when a school building is destroyed by fire.

In recent years several states have enacted special state aid for school construction. Georgia, Maine, Maryland, Michigan, Pennsylvania, and South Carolina have differing provisions of this sort.

Many of the differentiations mentioned in connection with school taxes for current expenses exist in the same states for the school building fund. These differences, however, seem more justifiable for school buildings than for current expenses. Even for school buildings, nevertheless, there is considerable legislation with narrow applicability which should be replaced by general provisions applicable for each state as a whole.

FEDERAL SUPPORT OF EDUCATION . . .

EQUALIZING EDUCATIONAL OPPORTUNITIES ON A NATIONAL LEVEL*

Americans have always held schools dear to their hearts. Public opinion has brought many improvements to education over the years: The time of formal education has been extended from a few years to almost two decades, reaching from kindergarten to the graduate school; standards for teacher preparation have been raised; and educational opportunities have been so increased in character and depth that the gifted, the average, and the less capable all have better chances than ever before of living effectively in society.

WASTE OF TALENTS

But despite the trend toward improving educational opportunities for all children, the quality of education children are receiving today ranges from poor to excellent. Despite the principle of equalization of educational opportunity for all children,[1] the waste of human talents and abilities in many schools continues.

The public schools have long been castigated on this score. But criticizing the public schools is not new: ever since they were first established they have been under attack. Almost every major study on the status of American education, no matter when it was made, reports neglect and lack of educational opportunity. Study after study tells the same familiar story of crises in education, of teachers poorly paid and poorly trained, of teachers inadequate in number and lacking instructional materials, of

---

*Orlando F. Furno, "Equalizing Educational Opportunities: The Next Step," *School Life,* XLII (December, 1959), 17-19.

[1] The term "equalization of educational opportunity" is used here in the specialized sense of *raising* opportunities — and not in the dictionary sense of "evening up" opportunities by "raising some and lowering others."

poor communities struggling to pay mounting school expenses, of class-room shortages, and of limited opportunities for learning.

Even a brief look at a few recent studies gives evidence of today's criticism of the schools.

The "Rockefeller Report" on Education, *The Pursuit of Excellence,* says that many of our schools are "overcrowded, understaffed, and ill-equipped."

The Educational Policies Commission, in its booklet *The Contemporary Challenge to American Education,* emphasizes that ways must be found to improve the educational program in schools where educational deficiencies exist because of lack of support, lack of public understanding, lack of proper school district organization, or lack of professional leadership.

Norton and Lawler, in a study entitled *Unfinished Business in American Education,* state that public schools are not providing equal opportunities for all children. Having found great variations in the quality of educational programs, they consider equal educational opportunities for all children to be a myth.

Mort and his students in *Administration for Adaptability,* report that great differences in educational opportunities exist even among schools with the highest costs in the country.

These are only a few of the studies that vividly point out the continuing waste of human talents through lack of educational opportunities.

REASON FOR FAILURE

There never has been equality of educational opportunity in the United States; and under the present financial support plans for education, there apparently never will be.

To begin with, when States were divided into school taxing districts, some districts found themselves with less wealth than others. The ability to support schools became an accident of the distribution of children and wealth. Some school districts, left to their own resources, found it impossible to even hope to equalize educational opportunities for all children.

Moreover, the providing of education on a local school district basis necessarily limited local communities by the tax system available to them.

It was only logical that the States should assist the local communities in supporting education. The reward-for-effort and the doles-to-the-needy approach epitomized by Cubberley in the early 1900's magnified rather than equalized educational opportunities for all children. So did the Strayer and Haig proposal in the early 1920's, despite the fact that it specifically called for the equalization of educational opportunities and the equalization of tax burden. Both these approaches increased educational opportunities but did not equalize them.

In the Cubberley approach we have an emphasis on reward-for-effort, which was a boon to pioneer lighthouse schools; in the Strayer and Haig approach, we have an emphasis on raising educational opportunities but from the bottom up to a certain minimum level.

The minimum level, or foundation program, as it is generally alluded to, is different in each State. These differences in level themselves result in tremendous variation in the quality of educational programs. The financing of education under the present decentralized systems can never accomplish the equalization of educational opportunities for all children. Clearly the inability to do so can be attributed to the financial support plans that focus on equalizing educational opportunities within each State up to a minimum level rather than within the whole Nation.

But even if each State could equalize educational opportunities up to the same minimum, tremendous inequalities would still exist. The very fact that only a minimum program of education is equalized leaves communities with adequate revenue sources free to give their children educational opportunities far beyond those of less fortunate communities. Also, present financial support programs equalize only units of expenditures (and, in some instances, unit of tax burden) and not educational programs. It's true of course that educational opportunities bear a strong relationship to cost, but no serious researcher of the cost-quality relationship has found it to be perfect. Forces other than cost affect school quality, too; in fact expenditures alone determine only about 40 percent of it. Besides, a school dollar in one State or local unit does not purchase the equivalent amount of education it does in another State or unit—a fact that underscores another shortcoming in the attempts to equalize educational opportunity by equalizing units of expenditures.

THE NATION'S NEEDS

Because explosive changes in scientific technology have resulted in an increasingly complex world social organization, the waste of human talents and abilities is a luxury the United States can no longer afford. The tasks that society must perform to continue functioning are not only growing ever more intricate and demanding, but constantly changing in character and scope. To perform these tasks requires more highly trained, competent people than the Nation has ever needed before. The implications of this demand for manpower for the Nation's survival are becoming self-evident; and the strategic importance of education as the one means of satisfying this demand is becoming apparent to all.

Another reason we can no longer afford the luxury of wasting human talents and abilities is that now the national demands on education run deeper than ever before. Since we are engaged in a technological race for survival, our educational system must do more than discover and educate the relatively few people who are creative. The need for providing excellent education for the gifted will always be with us, but modern society cannot be sustained by the gifted alone. Our educational system must train the large numbers of persons capable of operating the great economic mechanism that is one of the frameworks of the American way of life. Seeking out a few highly gifted individuals will not supply the mounting needs of the American economy for skilled and professional workers, which now constitute about half of all workers, and the almost as large number of semiskilled workers. America cannot long survive unless it provides advanced high-quality education for more and more persons in the middle range of intellectual ability.

A CHANGE IN PHILOSOPHY

When the Soviet Union hurled the earth's first manmade satellite into outer space, the American people were startled into a great interest in education. Out of this interest, the Congress enacted the National Defense Education Act of 1958. This Act provides for loans and fellowships to students and for financial aid to States to improve instruction, especially in mathematics and the sciences.

The deepened national interest in education has caused many persons and organizations to reexamine the financial underpinnings of education. They have found them sadly wanting for the job that lies ahead. From these financial assessments has emerged what seems to be a change in philosophy about achieving equality of educational opportunities.

Despite this change in philosophy, the equalization of educational opportunities for all has remained a goal. In fact, it has assumed even greater importance, because now the needs not only of the individual but of all society impinge on this goal. What the change has brought is the realization that increasing educational opportunities through a foundation program established at a relatively low level is not the answer; that the answer lies in a much bolder approach — *providing each child in the Nation educational opportunities of such depth and scope that he can develop his potential to the fullest.* Viewed in this light, the goal of equal educational opportunities for all—an ideal America has long held —emerges as an economic and political necessity.

This shift in philosophy has far-reaching meaning for the financial support of education. What remains to be solved is a number of great questions: How should a program of education assuring each child equality of educational opportunity be designed to maximize each child's potential? How should it be financed? How can national concern and interest be assured and yet State and local control of education retained?

Too many schools are trying to equalize educational opportunities by popular but essentially ineffective measures. Some schools put children of low ability in one group and children of high ability in another, and leave all the rest, perhaps 80 to 90 percent of their pupils, to mass production procedures. Yet this middle group possesses the very abilities and talents whose development is vital to American survival and prosperity.

Equal opportunity in the new sense will come closer to realization if our efforts succeed in meeting these educational needs: (1) Enough people to do the job, (2) professional staff with the training and competence needed for educating all children, (3) sufficient teaching materials, in far greater variety than is required by mass production schools, and (4) maximum, not minimum, educational programs, in which no child anywhere is deprived of educational opportunities afforded to any other child. This does not mean a uniform program for each child, but an equal chance for each child to develop to the fullest.

Since the national demands on education are felt throughout the Nation, citizens of one State have a justifiable concern for equalizing educational opportunities for all children in all States. Today very few persons remain in the same State all their lives, much less in the same school district. In 1958 approximately 31 million Americans changed residence, and over 5 million moved from one State to another. The mobility of our population shows us how long overdue is the equalization of educational opportunities in terms of units of educational program rather than in terms of units of expenditures.

It all adds up to this: the approach we have tried has not succeeded. The approach through a minimum educational program rather than a maximum, through units of expenditure level rather than units of program capacity—all this has hit wide of the mark in making equality of educational opportunity a reality.

But we cannot afford to miss again. If our next effort to equalize educational opportunities for all children is to succeed, we must reexamine with care the roles of the Federal Government, the States, and the local school districts in financing education.

EDUCATION AND THE NATIONAL ECONOMY*

The purpose of the economy of a modern nation is to encourage the greatest possible production and consumption of goods and services which satisfy human wants. This, in effect, is how we define a high standard of living, especially when we compare it with other nations.

Production depends upon many factors but of great importance are the number of workers and the efficiency with which they can do their work. (The number of workers engaged in production reaches its full potential when there is full employment of the available labor force). Efficiency of production per man hour increases as education and training of workers are increased and as power and technological processes available to him are increased. Production of goods and services is also affected by the natural resources available, the quality of management, the level of consumption, the distribution mechanism, and other factors.

Consumption of goods and services is principally affected by quantity of goods available, wants of consumers and their purchasing power, and the distribution mechanism.

Production and consumption of goods and services are so closely interrelated that they should be studied together. These generalizations are so basic that they are applicable to all types of economic systems— private enterprise, state socialist, communist, or a combination of these. . . .

A major increase in the investment in education will provide job opportunities for the unemployed in the private economy, will provide markets for the private economy, and will provide investment opportunities for idle capital. But most of all it will increase the production and consumption potential of young citizens as they become adults. This is absolutely essential to an expanding economy.

An investment in education is good for the economy, whether in good times or in bad. Education expenditures have advantages as anti-recession measures, but it should be kept in mind that there is a need for these expenditures regardless of their economic impact. They will have beneficial effects because they stimulate increased consumer demand and contribute to a rising standard of living.

---

*R. L. Johns, *Education and the National Economy,* Washington, D.C.: NEA Legislative Commission, 1958, 2, 10-11.

Despite overwhelming evidence to the contrary, there may be some who are so ignorant of the factors influencing the national economy that they believe that taxes for education should be reduced in order to stimulate the economy. Actually there is a greater economic need to expand the investment in education in times of economic recession than normal times.

POOR EFFECTS OF TAX CUT

Let us assume for example that taxes for the public schools over the nation are reduced by one billion dollars in the hope that it would have a favorable effect on the economy. What would be the actual effect? Expenditures for education would have to be reduced by that amount because boards of education are not permitted by law to operate schools by deficit financing. It would be unsound fiscal policy for boards of education to incur operating deficits even if permitted by law. Reduced budgets would result in reduced purchases of goods, a reduction in the number of persons employed, a reduction of salaries and wages, resulting in a reduction of their purchasing power. It would mean one billion dollars subtracted from the private economy.

However, theoretically, one billion dollars would be added to the purchasing power of the private economy and the net effect on the economy should be zero. Actually it is not quite that simple. A considerable number of persons and corporations receiving the reduction in taxes would not spend it but save it as surplus. This would reduce employment and market opportunities needed by the private economy and further increase unemployed capital. Therefore the short-range effect of a reduction of taxes for education would be to depress the private economy. The long-range effect would be the same. A reduction in educational expenditures would reduce the quality and quantity of educational services which in turn would reduce the production and consumption potential of the nation.

NEED FOR FEDERAL ACTION

It is not the purpose of this booklet to present arguments for federal financial support for the public schools. But the implications of the evidence presented herein for federal fiscal policy relating to education are so significant that they cannot be ignored. Public education is essential to the national economy. It is essential to national security. It is necessary to supply human wants.

The taxing mechanism of the federal government is more efficient and equitable than the taxing mechanisms of state and local governments. The welfare of the nation and of the people require that we discard the ancient legend that education is exclusively a state and local responsibility. That legend is economic and political nonsense. The world is no longer safe for a nation which leaves its human wants and needs for education unsatisfied.

FEDERAL SUPPORT NEEDED

Experience over a long period of years has shown that present financing policies have not satisfied those needs in thousands of communities and even in whole regions of the nation. If we wish our economy to continue to grow and if we wish to maximize our chances of survival as a nation, the federal government must assume at once its rightful share of the responsibility for financing education.

PERSONAL INCOME, CURRENT EXPENDITURE PER PUPIL IN ADA, AND HIGH-SCHOOL GRADUATES*

	Per-capita personal income 1963		Personal income per child of school age (5-17), 1963		Estimated current expenditure for public schools per pupil in ADA 1964-65		Percent of increase in estimated current expenditure per pupil in ADA, 1954-55 to 1964-65		Public high-school graduates in 1964-65 as percent of ninth-graders in 1961-62	
	Amt.	Rank of state	Amt.	Rank of state	Amt.	Rank of state	Per-cent	Rank of state[a]	Per-cent	Rank of state[a]
50 States and D. C. ..	$2,449	....	$ 9,616	....	$483	....	....	....	73.9%	....
Alabama	1,655	47	5,904	48	288	49	91.4%	11	64.3	38
Alaska[b]	2,839[b]	9	10,507[b]	9	643[b]	2	44.6	49	63.5	40
Arizona	2,142	29	7,990	32	451	26	56.5	42	64.5	37
Arkansas	1,607	48	5,996	47	317	45	161.6	1	62.8	41
California	2,974	5	12,088	6	570	5	80.1	16	88.9	1
Colorado	2,464	18	9,585	16	470	21	62.2	38	67.4	27
Connecticut	3,185	3	12,922	3	593	4	92.2	10	77.1	19
Delaware	3,298	2	12,661	4	536	9	67.5	32	64.4	30
Florida	2,111	32	8,979	25	403	36	79.3	19	67.1	28
Georgia	1,864	42	6,732	42	330	42	83.3	13	62.3	42
Hawaii	2,462	19	8,914	26	422	30	80.0	17	83.7	6

a Computation carried a sufficient number of decimal places to give an exact ranking.
b The purchasing power of $1 in four large Alaska cities averages about 76¢ as compared with the average purchasing power of $1 in areas covered by the Consumer Price Index of the U.S. Bureau of Labor Statistics. Therefore, all dollar amounts shown for Alaska should be reduced by about one-fourth.

*NEA Research Bulletin, XLIII (February, 1965), Washington, D.C.: National Education Association, 26.

PERSONAL INCOME, CURRENT EXPENDITURE PER PUPIL IN ADA, Cont'd.

	Per-capita personal income 1963		Personal income per child of school age (5-17), 1963		Estimated current expenditure for public schools per pupil in ADA, 1964-65		Percent of increase in estimated current expenditure per pupil in ADA, 1954-55 to 1964-65		Public high-school graduates in 1964-65 as percent of ninth-graders in 1961-62	
	Amt.	Rank of state	Amt.	Rank of state	Amt.	Rank of state	Per-cent	Rank of state[a]	Per-cent	Rank of state[a]
Idaho	1,916	39	7,078	39	332	41	41.3	50	81.6	10
Illinois	2,948	6	11,870	7	551	8	64.0	35	71.0	24
Indiana	2,481	15	9,348	19	490	19	81.5	15	76.6	20
Iowa	2,302	26	9,051	23	465	24	69.7	30	63.6	39
Kansas	2,255	27	8,911	27	462	25	73.0	26	67.6	26
Kentucky	1,792	44	6,673	43	323	43	108.3	3	61.5	43
Louisiana	1,776	46	6,286	46	418	32	67.2	33	66.9	29
Maine	2,007	36	7,853	34	371	39	75.5	23	60.0	45
Maryland	2,786	10	10,484	10	503	17	107.0	4	77.2	18
Massachusetts	2,853	8	11,854	8	502	18	56.9	41	81.8	9
Michigan	2,541	11	9,513	18	510	15	73.5	25	77.3	16
Minnesota	2,329	23	8,766	28	528	12	67.1	34	85.6	3
Mississippi	1,390	50	4,801	50	273	50	101.6	5	58.4	48
Missouri	2,518	12	10,293	11	437	29	79.1	20	66.4	31
Montana	2,197	28	8,131	29	516	13	50.9	46	77.2	17
Nebraska	2,312	25	9,149	20	407	34	54.8	43	81.5	11
Nevada	3,386	1	13,116	2	505	16	71.9	27	85.0	5
New Hampshire	2,313	24	9,119	21	448	27	54.5	45	NA	....
New Jersey	2,915	7	12,106	5	607	3	82.8	14	75.6	21
New Mexico	1,918	36	6,643	44	470	22	54.6	44	57.0	49
New York	3,013	4	13,218	1	790	1	110.7	2	79.3	13
North Carolina	1,807	43	6,591	45	322	44	94.0	9	66.0	33
North Dakota	2,050	35	7,303	36	422	31	58.6	40	78.6	14
Ohio	2,474	17	9,649	15	469	23	75.0	24	86.2	2
Oklahoma	1,953	37	8,017	30	366	40	62.7	37	73.0	23
Oregon	2,502	13	9,577	17	569	6	63.5	36	82.6	7
Pennsylvania	2,452	20	10,114	13	479	20	69.9	29	80.5	12
Rhode Island	2,433	21	10,204	12	514	14	80.0	18	85.2	4
South Carolina	1,588	49	5,410	49	289	48	71.0	28	65.4	35
South Dakota	1,886	40	7,202	38	416	33	47.3	47	73.9	22
Tennessee	1,783	45	6,743	41	300	47	97.4	7	66.0	32
Texas	2,068	33	7,801	35	396	37	60.7	39	68.6	25
Utah	2,119	31	7,208	37	407	35	68.9	31	64.9	36
Vermont	2,121	30	7,876	33	438	28	95.2	8	77.9	15
Virginia	2,057	34	7,996	31	380	38	100.0	6	58.6	47
Washington	2,484	14	9,902	14	534	10	77.5	22	81.9	8
West Virginia	1,883	41	6,833	40	315	46	79.0	21	60.1	44
Wisconsin	2,368	22	9,047	24	532	11	88.0	12	65.8	34
Wyoming	2,475	16	9,065	22	554	7	45.8	48	58.6	46

FOR FURTHER REFLECTION OR INVESTIGATION

1. What is a fair and adequate proportion of the GNP that should be allocated for education in the United States today?

2. Calculate the spending power in your community created by the system of public education.

3. What benefits accrue to the taxpayer with no children in school from his expenditures for school taxes?

4. What is meant by the statement, "The unlimited power to vote taxes could spell the end of the free enterprise system"?

5. Debate the merits of levying taxes on the benefits received basis vs. the ability-to-pay principle.

6. Evaluate each of the major taxes in your community and state in terms of the criteria for a good tax.

7. Should the property tax be abandoned?

8. Formulate an ideal taxing plan, by type and by governmental level for collection, to assure steady progress in education and palatability to taxpayers.

9. Why do people expect so much from their schools but seem reluctant to spend in relation to their expectations?

10. Discuss the feasibility of asking parents to donate in addition to the existing tax structure, let us say $100 per child annually, to support public education as a deductible contribution on the federal income tax.

11. Is there any need today to collect property and personal property taxes on a township or county basis?

12. Should the state and federal allocation of funds for schools be raised through earmarked taxes?

13. Is there any justification for the state to impose debt limitations upon local governments today in view of the requirement that citizens vote on additional taxes?

14. What actual dangers are there in unrestricted borrowing by school districts for capital construction such as might occur under the powers of a building authority?

15. How much of the total cost of the latest school construction project in your district went for interest on borrowed money?

16. Translate portions of your school budget into a performance budget.

BIBLIOGRAPHY

Alford, Albert L., *Nonproperty Taxation for Schools,* Washington, D.C.: United States Office of Education, Bulletin 1964, No. 4, 1963.

Benson, Charles S., *The Economics of Public Education,* Boston: Houghton Mifflin Company, 1961.

————, *The Cheerful Prospect,* Boston: Houghton Mifflin Company, 1965.

Bracken, Charles and A. S. Hurlburt, "A Checklist of Public School Budget Message Content," *American School Board Journal,* CXLIV, March, 1963.

Corbally, John E., Jr., *School Finance,* Boston: Allyn and Bacon, Inc., 1962.

Denison, Edward F., *The Sources of Economic Growth in the United States and the Alternative Before Us,* New York: Committee for Economic Development, 1962.

Extron, E., "New Studies of School Finance Can Make or Break the Case for Federal Aid," *American School Board Journal,* CXLIII, November, 1962.

Financing the Public Schools, 1960-1970, Washington, D.C.: National Education Association, 1962.

Fluckiger, W. Lynn, "The Art and Science of Money," *Overview,* October, 1962.

Furno, Orlando F., "Equalizing Educational Opportunities: The Next Step," *School Life,* XLII, December, 1959.

Innes, Jon, Paul B. Jacobson and Roland J. Pellegrin, *The Economic Returns to Education,* Eugene, Ore.: Center for the Advanced Study of Educational Administration, 1964.

Johns, R. L., *Education and the National Economy,* Washington, D.C.: NEA Legislative Commission, 1958.

Johns, R. L., *Problems and Opportunities in Financing Education.* Washington, D.C.: National Education Association, Committee on Tax Education and School Finance, 1959.

McLoone, Eugene P., "Flexibility in Local Support of the Schools: A Proposal," *School Life,* XLIV, May, 1962.

NEA Research Bulletin, "Financial Report on the Public Schools," Washington, D.C.: National Education Association, XLII, December, 1964.

―――――――, XLIII, February, 1965.

Norton, John K., *What Everyone Should Know About Financing Our Schools,* Washington, D.C.: National Education Association, Committee on Educational Finance, 1960.

Ovsiew, Leon and William B. Castetter, *Budgeting for Better Schools,* Englewood Cliffs, New Jersey: Prentice-Hall, Inc., 1960.

School Management, "How to Avoid Pitfalls in Issuing School Bonds," VII, December, 1963.

Strayer, George D., Jr., *Guidelines for Public School Finance,* Bloomington, Ind., *Phi Delta Kappan,* National Advisory Committee on School Finance, 1963.

Vaizey, John, *The Economics of Education,* New York: The Free Press of Glenco, Inc., 1962.

Chapter 13

Administration of School Business Affairs

The scope of school business affairs is broader than the suggestion in the previous chapter that they concern only overseeing expenditures of school funds. In addition to the fiscal aspects of the school business management function, this extensive field of administration includes two other broad areas: the management of physical facilities and of related non-instructional administrative activities. This arbitrary division into three general task areas and their overlapping will become evident as each is discussed separately.

While most of the business tasks of school management have existed since the beginning of formalized educational institutions, their importance has increased rapidly since the Second World War. Evidence for the rise in importance may be found in the number of new positions created for the work, in the studies showing the amount of time administrators devote to it, in the growth of the professional organization for school business officials, and in the appearance of bountiful publications pertaining to the work.

There are reasons for this sudden attention. The immensity of the monetary transactions of schools has caused concern on the part of patrons as well as school officials. Only small districts handle less than a million dollars annually in these days of rising costs and expanding school districts. Management of that much money spurs citizens into demanding that prudent business techniques be applied to school operations. A school district's investment in plant and equipment is a still more staggering figure. Expansion of non-instructional services, particularly pupil transportation and lunchrooms, has thrust new management responsibilities upon school administrators. Growing enrollments and costs, squeezed by dwindling per-pupil revenues, have forced administrators to seek ways of getting the most mileage out of existing dollars. This, in essence, is the mission of school business management — to assure that school tax moneys are being used in the most efficient and effective manner.

The increasing time required to accomplish this mission explains the trend toward organizing a separate division in the central office and assigning the job to a qualified business officer. In a school district of as many as 1,500 pupils with an annual budget approaching a million dollars, the superintendent cannot give direct supervision to business affairs without serious neglect of his other obligations. The school business manager, who may serve under other titles such as director of business affairs, supervisor of buildings and grounds, or assistant superintendent for business management, becomes a vital force in the second echelon of a school system's central administration. To avoid duality of control, he must be accountable to the chief executive, not directly to the board of education. In the interest of assuring unit control, his functions are not to be combined or confused with that of the board's secretarial officer.

Until very recently, it has been extremely difficult to recruit a person with knowledge and experience in the three broad categories of school business management. About half of the appointments to the position have come from industrial or financial backgrounds with no experience in educational operations. A person grounded in financial disciplines would have to learn the other two functions on the job, the same being true if he is employed from either of the other backgrounds. The other half of the appointments have come from within the school system, capitalizing upon teachers who are knowledgeable in either the commercial subjects of the high school or in the engineering fields of industrial arts or vocational shop. Again, the appointee must learn many of his responsibilities through expensive trial and error while on the job. The educator with the best preparation for the work of school business management is often the chief executive of a small district who has had to learn how to administer all the tasks involved. He has frequently been willing to "step down" from the pressures of the superintendency to the lesser salary of business manager in a larger district.

Lately, universities have begun to develop preparatory programs on the graduate level for the unique position of school business manager. The programs have been tardy in coming, but their appearance recognizes an unavoidable trend resulting from consolidation of small districts—the need for many specialists in the subordinate administrative roles of large central staffs. Some training in the area of school business management is also becoming popular for all school administrators. Each administrator, regardless of specialized assignment, is expected to perform certain of the business management functions. The principal of every attendance unit is normally charged with protection of the physical property under his jurisdiction, a responsibility which is facilitated by his knowledge of building construction, maintenance and operation of mechanical equipment, safety precautions, insurance matters, mass feeding, and mass transportation affairs. He needs some familiarity with accounting and record-keeping principles in order to discharge his responsibility for internal school funds. More and more the principal is becoming involved in budgeting and purchasing procedures. Administrative specialists from the central staff are also assigned decision-making powers for purchasing, fiscal management and related record keeping. Thus, under the prevailing trend of decentralizing authority close to the task, only the superintendent is deeply involved in matters which have traditionally been found in the course known as School Finance. While he, too, must have some knowledge of the business management aspects of school administration, he is the sole district authority for the development of school revenue.

It may be expected, then, to see all future school administrators participating in at least some of the new university programs which offer instruction in each of the specific tasks delineated below:

> Accounting for receipts and expenditures of all board of education
>> moneys, including the appropriate auditing and fiscal reporting
> Bonding, payroll, investment of inactive funds, taxation and some-
>> times the management of internal funds
> Insuring school property
> Purchasing
> Management of school district real estate
> Maintenance of plant and equipment
> Operation of plant and equipment
> Construction and renovation of physical facilities
> Pupil transportation
> General supervision of food service
> General administration of non-instructional personnel

A careful study of the above general tasks which constitute the school business management activity will explain why this volume could not aspire to be a detailed how-to-do-it manual. The remaining portions of this chapter seek only to clarify for the student the nature and scope of the administrative responsibility in this connection. The content has been chosen merely to satisfy this objective, allowing the selected readings to specify some detail; complete references are cited in the bibliography.

FISCAL MANAGEMENT

After the annual budget has been approved, its administration becomes a part of school business management. The business manager properly serves as a watchdog over expenditures, overseeing the enforcement of state laws and board of education directives pertaining to budgeting and spending. He accomplishes this assignment less through the decision-making process than through a system of records and accounting. One of his most important assignments is that of installing an efficient, thorough, but not too burdensome accounting system.

Accounting for school funds has similarities to that of governmental and industrial accounting, but it is not identical with either. Since state laws and administrative directives prescribe the system of records to be used, the regulations for reporting and auditing, for purchasing and investing, and for payment procedures, not all of the principles of general accounting are applicable to a public school. The major shortcoming of most school record keeping, however, is that it does not utilize enough of those principles which have been accepted by the accounting profession. Even auditors and experts in the fiscal accounting field often have difficulty understanding the unique system of records and reports which have become common in schools. Obviously, citizens, board members, and teachers cannot easily interpret such data. Therefore, the peculiar and archaic accounting systems of public schools deny the communication goal of modern school administration.

Considerable improvement is on the way, largely through the efforts of the Association of School Business Officials, the U. S. Office of Education, state departments of education, and professional writers who are turning their attention to accounting materials aimed exclusively at helping those responsible for keeping school fiscal records.

In 1959 the U. S. Office took the leadership in publishing the document popularly known as Handbook II, *Financial Accounting for Local and State School Systems, Standard Receipt and Expenditure Accounts.* The publication offered the first acceptable plan for standardizing the several dozen kinds of transactions which schools customarily make. It defined and classified both income and expenditure accounts so that school fiscal officers everywhere would have common meanings for the way they handle transactions. Most of the states have adopted the ideas promulgated in the document, so that now school business managers throughout the country can profit from comparisons of record-keeping processes. Currently, the Office is readying a companion booklet intended to be a self-teaching system of accounting adaptable to school systems. That publication will take a giant step toward making school accounting respectable through sanctioning the *double-entry* system. Several states are already requiring that school bookkeeping use the double-entry plan.

Proper accounting for school moneys involves more than complying with legal prescriptions. Accounting is a valuable tool for decision making by management. Facilitating the use of school fiscal records for improved administrative decisions, *cost accounting* is also making a breakthrough in school fiscal management. Cost accounting is essentially general accounting of a finer degree, enabling managers to know precise costs of operations and to discover wastes. Recognizing that teaching and learning to not lend themselves completely to finite dollar costs in evaluating their worth, the cost factor cannot be ignored in making intelligent educational decisions. Failure to do so in the past has lost schools much of the goodwill necessary for community support of educational improvements.

How does a superintendent typically answer a board member or citizen when queried about the cost of establishing a new course in, let us say, foreign languages? He usually includes only the cost of a teacher's salary and perhaps some additional supplies and equipment. A cost accountant would investigate and report all the overhead costs, too. He would include pro-rated costs of supervision and administration, utility, maintenance, and custodial operations, the costs of providing space and insurance, and any other "hidden" charges which may be properly allocated to the new class. This figure may substantially alter the estimate provided by the normal cursory report of costs. The same would be true for any of the curricular or non-educational changes contemplated by a board of education: the change-over to mechanical record-keeping systems, a proposal to purchase and operate the district's own buses, the decision for constructing a new building or renovating an old one, the conversion to team teaching in lieu of a conventional approach, the addition of a special class for gifted children.

Of course, the anticipated value from the change may outweigh the cost factor. However, few decisions about innovations can be made today without considering fiscal implications. A more intelligent decision can be made with all readily attainable facts at hand. The purpose of cost accounting in educational institutions is to provide some crucial facts for administrative decision making.

The bulk of the accounting activity in schools deals with the *general fund* of the board of education. The general fund accommodates the income and expenditures of the board of education for one year—its annual operating costs. The current operating fund includes expenditures for administration, instruction, plant operation, plant maintenance, fixed charges, and auxiliary services.

All expenditures not handled through the general fund are processed through *special funds*. The special funds commonly used by a board of education are these:

Bond, or capital, fund: all transactions pertaining to the retirement of bonds and to the interest charges.

Cafeteria Fund: Transactions applicable to the school's lunchroom program.

Internal Fund: Those normally small accounts for athletics and student activities. These transactions may be managed by a school treasurer instead of the central office, although the trend is toward cenralizing these under the direction of the board's fiscal officer.

Payroll accounting is a part of the general fund operations but has become a task of such magnitude in large districts as to deserve separate categorization. The record keeping pertaining to payroll, including the typical parade of deductions, is enormous. *Property accounting,* that is, maintaining records of physical equipment for inventory and insurance purposes, is still another part of the total accounting function in schools. Arranging for the auditing of all the fiscal records, and preparing reports for the myriad requests from outside groups for information about the school's fiscal position, constitute further aspects of the school accounting activity.

Another fiscal task of the school business management office is the supervision of investments of a district's inactive funds. Two typical financial transactions, and one not so typical, allow a board to accumulate moneys not needed immediately. In the first instance, the board normally receives its operating tax moneys in large quantities two to four times a year, each to cover the district's costs for the next few months. The amounts not needed for payment of immediate bills can be invested as interest-bearing bank deposits or in short-term government securities, the exact type specified in state law. In a second common transaction, the sale of bonds in connection with the construction of a new building will produce another large amount of money, all of which is not needed presently. This, too, can be invested. Occasionally a district will accumulate surpluses in the bank for some future project—a third kind of transaction. These surpluses, too, might more lucratively be invested than remain as non-interest-yielding bank deposits. The returns from these investments increase the total revenue of the school system. Failure to take advantage of these opportunities, proceeding according to law, amounts to negligence.

Insuring School Property

Managing the board of education's insurance program not only has fiscal implications but also cuts across the other two broad categories of school business management. The major purpose of insuring school property is to protect the taxpayers' investment in physical facilities: buildings, equipment in those buildings, and vehicles. Many boards also carry liability insurance to protect employees who drive school vehicles, and some districts manage or pay for teachers' personal liability insurance policies. Medical and hospitalization plans are commonly a part of the district's total insurance program insofar as record keeping is concerned. All districts are involved in workmen's compensation laws. And the school business office may become involved in injury insurance plans for pupils. *Security,* or *fidelity,* bonds are also required by state law to cover employees who handle school moneys. Then, there are *bid bonds* to insure the good intentions of vendors who submit bids on school purchases, and *performance bonds* to insure that work which has been contracted for will be finished according to specifications.

The major portion of a board's insurance costs has to do with protection against loss through fire and related perils. Much progress has been made during recent years in securing more efficient coverages for school property. Schools often paid and still pay excessive premiums because no one affiliated with the system was tutored in ways to economize. New insurance plans specifically designed for schools with their typically low risk have appeared lately; especially popular is the *public institutional property* plan described in the selected reading. Some states and large cities have chosen *self-insurance* plans. Many districts purchase insurance through competitive bids based upon standard specifications. A *co-insurance* provision—by which the insuring company and the board of education share the risk and losses sustained and which forces the school administrator's attention upon insurance matters — has become common in school districts which have not adopted one of the other plans to effect economy.

Probably the most difficult decision school officials must make regarding the protection of their public facilities relates to the question of how much insurance should be carried. What is the SIV—*sound insurable value*—of a school building? Should the value be based upon the community's original investment in the facility, the cost of replacing it on today's market, or something else? The answer is not as obvious as a passing glance would suggest. The tendency is to insure enough to convince the citizens that they could quickly replace a destroyed facility at no additional cost. In a period of rising construction costs, premium charges will, of course, rise correspondingly. Insuring at replacement cost may not allow for depreciation and the fact that with each passing year of building usage, taxpayers have received more value from their original investment. The complete loss of a building after seventy-five years of use would mean, technically, no dollar loss to the community. And yet a board of education could scarcely explain satisfactorily to taxpayers the absence of any insurance coverage upon sustaining a serious loss. This decision is more difficult for a board of education than for a private property owner.

Over-insuring school property results in wastage of tax money; the owner will not collect more than "true value" of the loss sustaine' Under-insuring may also mean loss to taxpayers if they cannot recover adequately following damage to school property. The problem suggests the need for a knowledgeable person in the employ of a board of education, the possible use of outside professional appraisers, and the maintenance of *insurance registers* which avail complete information about school property and its policy coverage.

School administrators must also reduce risk factors, hence insurance costs. This may be accomplished through knowledge of building construction, protective devices, appropriate safety measures, inspectional procedures, and of how insurance rates are established in the state.

Still another serious concern stems from the placing of insurance business with proper carriers. Community agents have been known to pressure the board of education into parcelling the business out to all local carriers in a desperate effort to please everyone; this practice may result in inefficiencies, inadequate or duplicating coverages, and delay in obtaining equitable adjustments after a loss.

These are time-consuming but important headaches for school business managers who are unlearned in the complex insurance area. Fortunately, much help is available now from the studies and publications of the Association of School Business Officials and of the United States Office of Education. Several useful privately produced books and pamphlets have also appeared recently.

ADMINISTRATION OF PHYSICAL FACILITIES

Plant operations include those activities essential to keeping the buildings and grounds in suitable condition for teaching. They have to do with the lighting, heating, and plumbing operations. They are concerned with the daily cleanliness and safety of facilities and with taking proper precautions to protect buildings and equipment from damage. In achieving this latter objective, the business officer is usually charged with the responsibility for administering regulations associated with use of buildings and grounds by community groups during out-of-school hours.

The major work load for personnel assigned to this division is carried by the custodial force, headed by a supervisor in the larger and wealthier districts. His duties include employing men and women for the custodial staff, training them in the modern methods for performing their jobs, and evaluating their performance. Progress is seen in upgrading the caliber of persons hired for custodial work and in preparing them to utilize efficient techniques. The new materials and equipment which schools are using demand continual in-service programs for custodial personnel.

Plant Maintenance

The mission of *plant maintenance* personnel is to perform the repair and upkeep of buildings and equipment in order to prevent loss of learning time. The extent of this charge, like other educational administrative chores, has swelled with the addition of many new facilities and a variety of technical teaching equipment: television, teaching machines, language laboratories, electronic installations, and vocational educational equipment. These are in addition to the maintenance tasks which school districts have assumed for many years; the magnitude of these may be appreciated by this listing of common facilities and equipment demanding the attention of maintenance skill:

> *Building:* Roof, chimney, flashing, walls, foundation, windows, several types of flooring.
> *Grounds:* Walks and driveways, parking lots, playgrounds and athletic facilities, and landscaping.
> *Equipment:* Furniture, plumbing, heating, ventilating, and electrical fixtures, chalkboards, clocks and bells, office equipment, musical instruments, science, home economics, and physical education, laboratories, audio-visual and special education equipment, lockers, cafeteria and refrigerating items, and perhaps air conditioning, swimming pool and elevator installations, school buses and other mobile pieces owned by the board of education.

For the most part, the upkeep of these items necessitates skilled tradesmen, although a school system may employ some general repairmen. The extent to which the district will employ its own maintenance crew will depend upon the size of the unit and the amount of technical repairs needed. A small district will have to contract with outside trades for its repair work. As districts grow larger, officials find it more economical to employ full-time painters, carpenters, plumbers, machinists, automobile mechanics, and other skilled tradesmen who they think are needed on a salaried basis. Moreover, a district's own maintenance crew can generally give more prompt attention to breakdowns which threaten loss of school time, and the plan enables a district to have better control over the quality of workmanship.

Construction and Renovation of Buildings

The only phase of new building construction which is not normally considered a responsibility of the school business management division is the educational planning of the facility. That is a task for the professional educator, aided by counsel from the business manager and the architect. A business manager blessed with engineering knowledge can be of special help in the planning stage through his recommendations for mechanical installations, site selection and development, and in assessing the judgments of architects and contractors.

The remaining activities associated with construction of a new building may be regarded as business management tasks. The business manager's office will process all the contracts, advertise for bids, negotiate sale of bonds, purchase equipment, and arrange payment for all costs connected therewith. He often serves as clerk-of-the-works during the construction process, representing the board of education in assuring that specifications called for in the building contract are fulfilled.

The construction and renovation of physical facilities has been a major preoccupation of school administrators during the past two decades as they desperately tried to reverse the neglect of physical facilities during the 1930's and World War II and also to keep abreast of the population growth and shifting. The movement out of cities has presented building problems to both city and suburban school officials. The total amount being spent for capital construction and debt service is nearly half that of the total annual budget. As of 1966, school districts are still behind in providing sufficient classrooms, and predictions are that the 1970's will see another splurge of additional buildings.

This experience has allowed experimentation with new ideas in building to effect both economy and better learning facilities. School administrators have learned the importance of long-range planning of classroom needs, often soliciting the consultancy help of university specialists and private experts in this kind of study. A few architects have elected to concentrate upon institutional construction in order to bring together the best of imaginative design, new materials, and new construction techniques for effecting a better building. The spectacular display of award-winning designs at the conventions of the American Association of School Administrators is a yearly testimonial to the progress being made in abandoning conventional notions of box-like classrooms. Campus-style or educational-park arrangements may be the answer to rural transportation problems as well as to city racial segregation problems. Where land values permit, the trend is toward expansive single-story buildings; where they do not permit, the trend is upward, even to office-type buildings in metropolitan areas. Windowless buildings, air conditioning, and flexibility of arrangement and of room sizes are being tried. Elsewhere, school officials save both money and construction time in utilizing standard plans, or modifications thereof, in recognition that it is not the building which determines most the quality of learning.

The Boles reading at the end of the chapter lists many other money-saving approaches to school construction. None of these, however, are as significant in the stretching of taxpayers' dollars as is the pay-as-you-go plan which eliminates interest costs on borrowed money.

Perhaps the biggest challenge to today's administrators and architects is to design buildings which will accommodate the rapidly changing curricular ideas. The trends toward ungraded classrooms, team teaching, educational television, mechanical teaching devices, middle schools, longer use of school facilities, more adult education and vocational preparation — all these are affecting the type of buildings to be constructed. The most perplexing aspect of the problem for those who make decisions about new buildings is the uncertain future of curricular ideas which presently engage attention. Will the building constructed to handle present trends be adequate for those of fifty years hence? Among the other lessons which school administrators have learned from the past two decades of construction experience is the importance of providing flexibility in a new structure which will facilitate subsequent change at reasonable costs.

Administration of Non-instructional Personnel

School districts disagree about the assignment of the personnel function for non-instructional employees. In many districts the personnel responsibilities for clerks and secretaries, custodians and maintenance employees, bus drivers, and food service workers are decentralized to their immediate supervisors. Larger districts are discovering, however, that the number of non-teaching personnel required to keep the system operating is approaching half the number of certified personnel. The increasing scope of the responsibility argues for centralizing the personnel tasks of employment, record keeping, evaluation, promotion, and dismissal. Therefore, the trend is to assign the personnel phase of the work to either the staff personnel officer or the business officer.

Moreover, as implied at an earlier point, the difference between administering certificated and non-certificated personnel is diminishing. Salary schedules, fringe benefits, records, policies, need for communications, employee organizations, and administrative practices are similar for both. The primary remaining difference in the administration of the two categories of personnel arises from the difference in the nature of their work and in the extent of formal preparation prior to employment.

THE PURCHASING FUNCTION

The enormous purchasing function of a school district has been traditionally afflicted with difficult decisions, dissensions, pressures, and temptations. Long regarded as an unpleasant appendage of school administration, the procurement task has been allowed to lumber along to spawn its headaches. Dissensions between the business officer and faculty often erupt over the authority to make selections among competing educational materials and equipment. The purchasing officer may be subjected to the pressures which arise from competition between local and out-of-town merchants, between ethical and unethical vendors, between price and quality, between accountability and service to colleagues, between legal specifications for purchasing by a public body and efficiency, and between conscience and the lure of self-gain.

Growth in the size of school districts and in the amounts of money administered opens the door to modernization of the procurement function. Citizens are expecting responsible management of their dollars, and the process of buying provides a fruitful source for achieving economies in school finance. An educational agency certainly cannot justify using less skill in performing this task than industrial organizations have used effectively for years. Thus, many of the burdens which have accompanied the purchasing function are beginning to be lifted.

The first step taken by a growing district is to appoint a qualified pur-chasing officer who can give the deserved attention to the function. A qualified person can systematize the procedures to permit accountability and still provide quick service for teachers' needs. He can develop variance in the overall plan to provide for the procurement of annual supplies, the emergency purchases which cannot be completely avoided, and the occasional large expenditure for vehicles and expensive equipment. He can introduce a plan of quality control which permits verification of items received to assure that they comply with specifications. A good plan prevents internal collusion by separating the ordering from the paying tasks. A sophisticated purchasing officer initiates board policies that guide him in purchasing decisions. And the qualified purchasing officer makes possible many economies which might not occur to the generalist in the field of business management.

Other steps are being taken toward improved purchasing practices for schools. Already sufficient evidence supports the contention that cooperative purchasing by neighboring districts will yield a greater return from the tax dollar. Joint purchasing plans, on a county or regional basis, bring the savings of quantity purchasing within reach of small school districts. Centralized warehousing in large districts also affords the savings which accrue from mass buying. The additional costs of building and operating a district's own warehouse may be offset by the improved availability of supplies and better inventory control. Another beneficial trend is the development of standards and tests for evaluating competing products which schools normally buy. Standardization of supplies, equipment, and specifications conserves tax dollars. Further improvements are coming from the codes of ethics developed by state and national organizations of school business officials.

ADMINISTRATION OF PUPIL TRANSPORTATION

The transportation of pupils to and from school is still another responsibility customarily assigned to the business management division. The responsibility has expanded dramatically from the early part of this century when school buses were intended merely to facilitate the development of the centralized high school in rural America. The abandonment of the one-room elementary schoolhouses gave the transportation program another boost. More expansion resulted from further consolidation of school districts, and from the post-World War II suburbia boom. Lately the large city has been compelled to enter the pupil transportation business in order to use to capacity its building facilities as populations shift within the city and in efforts to achieve racial balances among attendance areas. At present writing, the task is being complicated further by the possibilities of public schools' transporting more pupils to private and parochial schools. Today over one-third of the nation's elementary and secondary school students ride to school.

Additionally, school districts are using their transportation facilities in order to enrich learning through field trips. While the cost of transportation varies among districts according to the extent of service, five cents of each school tax dollar is consumed on the average nationwide for this purpose. The amount will probably increase. School district reorganization plans will undoubtedly mean that more children will live even farther from their attendance schools than they do now. Improvements in roads and vehicles will facilitate greater transportation services by the school. Further bisecting of school districts by major expressways also augurs expanded pupil transportation. And the continued increase in vehicular traffic, aggravating safety conditions for children who customarily walk to school, will likely lead to parental demands for more pupil transportation.

The spread of this new administrative chore has produced an abundance of professional literature to aid school officials in the management of pupil transportation. Extensive guides are available for the administrative elements of routing, purchasing and maintenance of vehicles, selection and training of drivers, control of discipline while driving school buses, related insurance matters, and safety precautions. The technical complexities of the pupil transportation task advise the employment of a transportation supervisor when a district operates as many as fifteen to twenty vehicles. The need for better records and cost accounting is self-evident.

ADMINISTRATION OF FOOD SERVICE

The general overseeing of the school lunch program rounds out the kaleidoscopic responsibilities of the business management function. The scope of the food service task is, of course, dictated by the policies of the board of education according to the extent to which it supports a lunch program at school. The business officer is customarily limited to matters pertaining to purchasing, records, fiscal and property accounting, cafeteria construction and maintenance, and sometimes the employment of food service workers. The food service manager, where the position exists, is ordinarily assigned administratively to the business officer. The manager actually operates the lunch rooms but many decisions and operations still remain for the chief of the business management department.

The increasing involvement of schools in this non-educational task is a product of school consolidation, the encouragement given through federal allocations of money and surplus foods, the changing employment picture which leaves fewer mothers in the home at lunch time, and the desire to improve children's nutritional intake. The monumental size of the school lunch program is reflected in the recent report from the Department of Agriculture which revealed that the three billion meals served annually in schools today provide a one billion dollar market for the nation's food industry.

The responsibility adds many new burdens to the work of school personnel, teachers and administrators, as described in a reading accompanying this chapter. It also adds cost to the operating and capital outlay budgets of the district. Despite the cost and the burden, the numerous special interests in the school lunch program will likely induce further expansion.

Again, the professionals in the school lunch program are rising to meet the challenge of increasing programs. Considerable specialized literature is now available in the form of books, pamphlets, and articles in the standard school journals. The trends of central kitchens, catered lunches, frozen foods, and dispensing machines are modernizing and simplifying this responsibility.

THE SCHOOL BUSINESS MANAGER . . .

HISTORY, STATUS, AND FUTURE OF THE SCHOOL BUSINESS MANAGER*

School business administration has existed since the beginning of the public school system, although originally it may not have been considered as important as it is today. Always, there were taxes or fees to collect for the support of the early schools, teachers to be paid, financial records to be kept, rents to be paid, and fuel to be supplied. At first, these duties usually were performed by local town or city officials, and later by members or committees of local school boards as they were established. Even today, in some communities, some of the business aspects of public education are handled by local municipal officials other than those directly associated with the schools, or by members or committees of local school boards.

Historically, it appears that the necessity for the appointment of a full-time school business administrator was first recognized more than a century ago — in 1841 — when the city council in Cleveland, Ohio, passed an ordinance providing for the appointment of an "Acting Manager" of schools whose duties would be "to keep a set of books, in which he shall open an account for each teacher in the employ of the city, and to make an accurate entry of all moneys paid out, . . . to keep [an] accurate account of each school district, whether for teaching, or rent, or for other pur-

---

*Fred W. Hill (Chairman of the Committee), *The School Business Administrator,* Chicago: by permission of Association of School Business Officials, International, 1960, 10-13, 30-31.

poses, . . . to provide fuel, take charge of the buildings and fixtures, and certify to the council the correctness of all accounts against the city for teaching, or for rents, fuel, repairs or fixtures on or about the school houses." It is also interesting to note that Cleveland did not appoint a superintendent of schools until twelve years later. Likewise, Chicago and Philadelphia also appointed full-time school business managers several years before appointing their first superintendents of schools.

It appears clear that the men who were first appointed to serve as school business administrators were not primarily interested in the instructional program, but were appointed because of their knowledge of business.

In the 1880's, according to the published proceedings of the National Education Association, some professional educators of that period were emphasizing the importance of school business administration, and urged the creation of a business division in city school districts.

During the late nineteenth and early twentieth centuries, many school trustees and school superintendents recognized the importance of good business administration of the school system. They felt that the way to accomplish this was to employ a well prepared business administrator to whom important business management responsibilities could be assigned. Accordingly, some school trustees employed a professionally-trained educator to be the superintendent of schools and a businessman was appointed to be the business administrator. Both individuals had equal status in the administrative hierarchy; each was directly responsible to the board of education for his own area. This concept of management commonly referred to today as "dual control" received favorable reception in some areas, among which New Jersey, Pennsylvania, and Canada are examples.

In most other areas, school trustees have adopted the "unit control" plan, which places all administrative responsibility under the superintendent of schools. The school trustees in those areas have delegated to the superintendent of schools complete responsibility for the administration of the school district, while they concentrate on policy development and determination. . .

By the turn of the century, the administration of school business affairs began to have the "tone" of professionalization; that is, the leading school business administrators commenced to realize the importance of their duties, the effect their services would have on education, and the need for obtaining further information regarding the specifics of their various duties and responsibilities. In 1910, a significant step was taken by these leading business officials in the formation of the National Association of Public School Business Officials, which later became the Association of School Business Officials of the United States and Canada.

In the early part of the current century, some literature began to appear dealing with aspects of school business administration, chiefly in the areas of school finance and accounting. Literature dealing with the broad topic of school business appeared in the 1920's sparked by the writings and stimulation of Professor N. L. Engelhardt, Sr., of Teachers College, Columbia University. He was the first instructor of a specialized course in school business administration which was offered in the summer school session of 1926. The first book devoted entirely to school business administration, written by the brothers, N. L. Engelhardt and Fred Engelhardt, appeared in 1927. Since that time, numerous volumes and articles have been published dealing with various aspects of school business administration, and it now may be said with full confidence that school business administration has arrived as a potent and positive force in American education.

At present, there is no single pattern of school business administration, no single pattern of administrative organization, and no one title applicable to the chief business official. It is of interest to note that since 1940, the presidents of the Association of School Business Officials have held the various titles of: Secretary-Business Manager; Assistant Superintendent — Business; Business Manager; School Architect; Business Administrator; Director of Vocational Education; and Director of Administrative Services.

Of greater significance is the fact that, over the years, the position of school business administrator has become increasingly important. The position more often calls for a person trained and experienced in the field of education, with emphasis on school business administration, or trained and experienced in various phases of business together with a knowledge of educational practices. In the unit control plan, this person is considered an associate of or assistant to the superintendent of schools and an important member of his cabinet. In both dual control and unit control plans, he is a powerful force supporting the improvement of educational opportunity rather than serving chiefly as a watchdog of the treasury, which too often was considered his chief role decades ago. He has the special responsibility to make business and financial operations accomplish most in operation and improvement of the schools. To him the Superintendent looks for leadership in making business affairs add to educational efficiency and progress.

Within the context of this publication, and in answer to the question, "Who is the School Business Administrator?", persons dealing with specific phases of school business administration will be referred to as *school business officials*. Persons dealing with the total area of school business, and with subordinate school business officials, will be designated as *school business administrators*.

Within the historic framework previously suggested, the school business administrator may therefore be defined as follows:

> The school business administrator shall be that employee member of the school staff who has been designated by the Board of Education and/or the Superintendent to have general responsibility for the administration of the business affairs of a school district. In any type of administrative organization, he shall be responsible for carrying out the general business administration of the district and such other duties as may be assigned to him. Unless otherwise provided by local law or custom (as in dual control areas), he shall report to the Board of Education through the Superintendent of Schools . . .

While it may be said that no fixed set of qualifications or training requirements will guarantee competency or adequately fit a school business administrator for the needs of every school district, it should be added that a professional program of preparation will provide the greatest assurance of success.

It is very clear, however, that the position of school business administrator is becoming more professional as time passes, and that the large majority of future appointees in such positions will be college-trained and, in many cases, will have had previous professional teaching experience. In certain subordinate positions, such as those of school business officials having specialized responsibilities in such areas as plant operation, financial accounting, auditing, transportation, purchasing, etc., educational experience may be overweighed by experience and training in the practical area involved. However, in most cases, preference may still be given to those persons having broad training as well as specialized competencies in a particular field. . .

In the preparation of future school business administrators, having chief responsibility for all school business functions, it is probable that a minimum of a B.S. or B.A. degree, with appropriate systematic study in school business administration, general administration, school law, finance and accounting, school plant operation, planning and construction, school curriculum, management techniques, and personnel work, as well as broad general education, will be required. In many communities no administrative posts will be assigned to persons having less than a Master's degree. Additional specialized preparation in certain areas may be suggested as prerequisites for *particular* responsibilities. Preference will probably be given to those whose training and experience include some aspect of education or teaching. In this connection, it should also be noted that boards of education, in selecting superintendents or chief school administrators, frequently recognize the special worth of those candidates who have knowledge and appreciation of school business affairs. Many of today's outstanding school superintendents have had previous experience as school business administrators. Likewise, many school systems recognize the special worth of school business administrators who have an appreciation of the importance of the educational program and its needs.

IMPORTANCE OF SCHOOL BUSINESS MANAGEMENT*

School personnel have been tardy in their recognition of the importance of the financial and business aspects of school operations, frequently to the regret and amazement of citizens. Many taxpayers are more concerned, and more comprehending, of this phase of education than any other. Even when school administrators have been especially skilled in managing school moneys to the point of developing a highly efficient system for handling business operations, laymen are ofttimes critical. They can feel the effects of financial operations directly more than other educational endeavors. Moreover, poor management of public funds by other governmental bodies has often stimulated a mental association with managers of public school funds. Too, there obtains a point of view in society, perhaps justified, that an ability to handle mundane business affairs and an ability in educational philosophy are not to be found in one person. This attitude has prevailed since the early custom of appointing the outstanding teacher as head of the school system, and predates the professional training of the modern superintendent.

Educational hierarchy itself does not always regard the business aspects of schools with significance. Teachers, and trainers of teachers, are sometimes inclined to believe that if all effort is devoted to the one purpose for having schools, namely, the education of children, somehow the financial and business function will take care of itself. Some educators have been heard to opine that nothing should be sacrificed for the education of a child, that efficiency and financial accountability are inconsequential since it's all for a good purpose.

---

*Robert E. Wilson, *Accounting and Record Keeping for Schools,* Kent, Ohio: Kent State University, copyright 1959, 2-5.

As lofty as this joint of view may be, it ignores one basic premise for the success of any educational enterprise, public or private. Quality of education is directly related to money. There are no shortcuts. The availability of money for educational purposes depends upon two processes — obtaining it and using it wisely. Wise use of money for any group or person involves planning, budgeting, and maintaining records of past uses. Furthermore, the process of obtaining money for educational purposes is usually dependent upon satisfying the "givers" that what has already been subscribed is being used wisely.

It could be reasonably argued, therefore, that the management of school funds, equipment, supplies, and buildings becomes the most important aspect of school operations. This attitude cannot be properly weighted, however, without consideration of the one reason for managing school funds and property, viz., the education of children. Accepting the first point of view in isolation from the latter causes most of the friction that develops frequently between the business and educational forces of a school system. Some business officers, overly conscious of their strategic position in the control of the disbursement of moneys, have maneuvered educational personnel into a "begging" posture or have exceeded authority and ability in deciding how educational moneys are to be spent. . . .

The chicken-and-egg argument as to whether financial or educational interests should take precedence contributes little other than sparkling conversation. It is vital for school business personnel to develop a proper perspective as to their relationship to the total enterprise. Their responsibility is one of providing a valuable service to the school system, the chief administrator, the board of education, and to the public. Although their function must be subservient to the fundamental purpose of the enterprise, it is a service without which the organization could not function successfully for long. . . .

WHEN IS A SCHOOL SYSTEM LARGE ENOUGH TO "AFFORD" A BUSINESS MANAGER?

There is no clear criteria for answering this question, and there are conflicting points of view prevailing. *Any* school system is large enough to require good business management from its officers. In fact, it cannot "afford" to be without that, and the trustees who do not demand it of their executive officers are not keeping faith with the stockholders. It is unrealistic, however, to expect in the forseeable future small schools to employ a qualified business manager with this sole responsibility.

Smaller schools, therefore, must rely on the chief executive to manage fiscal affairs as his time permits, while he is also overseeing all other functions of the school and, in some cases, teaching classes also. As school districts grow in enrollment, however, every administrative detail requires more of the chief's time. Eventually, there comes a point beyond which a superintendent cannot give adequate attention to business affairs if he is also responsible for general administrative duties. He has only one of two alternatives. Either he must have specialized assistance to look after the business affairs or neglect the educational aspects of the schools. Since financial and building matters normally cannot wait, these receive priority in the allocation of his time and educational matters suffer. It is at this point that many superintendents have earned, perhaps unjustifiably but inescapably, the allegation from teachers and parents that he is a "brick and mortar" manager but not an educator.

Exactly where this point occurs in the ascending enrollments of school districts is uncertain. . . .

In an effort to reconcile an ideal situation with the hard facts of economy and public willingness to spend money for administrative "overhead," it is recommended here that a school system of approximately 1,500 pupils avail itself of the services of a qualified full-time business manager. To require a superintendent in larger systems to perform all the business functions while he neglects his educational leadership role constitutes a short-sighted false economy. The salary cost of a trained business manager will actually save money for the district.

STEPS RECOMMENDED FOR IMPROVING THE SERVICE OF THE SCHOOL BUSINESS MANAGER*

The findings and conclusions of this study suggest the following recommendations which should assist in the improvement of relationships

---

*Murrell M. Miller, "A Critical Evaluation of the Superintendent-School Business Official Relationships in School Districts of California," Ed. D. Dissertation, University of Southern California. Reprinted by permission of *School Business Affairs*, XXX (April, 1964), 15.

between the chief school business official and his superintendent: (1) School business officials should be made more aware of the necessity to work with and through people in accomplishing purposes within the school business management field. (2) Superintendents should encourage the study and development by school business officials of actions and procedures designed to improve human relations. (3) School business officials should be made more aware of the fact that although efficiency and effectiveness within the business management field depend on the perfection and technical expertness of business procedures the ultimate success of the school business official is more dependent on the concern and respect for persons, their abilities, and morale. (4) Schools and colleges offering specialized courses in educational administration, including business management, should provide more emphasis and training in the area of human relations. (5) Provision should be made in school districts for periodic evaluation and review of the personnel interrelationships among staff members and departments. (6) The key role played by the chief school business official in assisting the superintendent to achieve the educational goals of the district should be emphasized to business officials, board members, staff members and to the superintendents. This can be done by the development of policies within districts which outline clearly the duties, responsibilities, and interrelationships to be performed by the business official. These policies should be developed in terms of the contribution to be made to the total educational program. (7) The chief school business official should strive constantly to encourage and maintain a harmonious working relationship within the area of business services. This involves personal actions of the business official as well as policies and procedures designed to create and sustain wholesome and positive working conditions. (8) The chief school business official should strive to establish and maintain relationships with other departments and areas within the district which demonstrate that the role of business services is to assist, facilitate, and support the educational functions of the district. (9) The chief school business official should work continuously for increased understanding of the extent and limitation of business services support. (10) The chief business official should be concerned with the essential understanding which should accompany all communications to and from the business services field. This involves understanding by the person sending the information and by the person receiving it. Full recognition should be given to the necessity of proper timing, adequate orientation, and review by all concerned in relation to any action or change which is contemplated or accomplished.

SCHOOL ACCOUNTING . . .

THE NEED TO IMPROVE SCHOOL ACCOUNTING PRACTICES*

Financial accounting procedures are basic to good educational administration. They form the basis for setting up sound administrative procedures; for informing the public mind, which must understand before it will support; for enabling business management to service the educational program; and for providing controls and safeguards for public money and property. Although we generally admit the vital importance of financial accounting for public school funds, we do not know the status of that accounting. We do know, however, that financial accounting and reporting have not kept pace with changes in education; both educators and accountants agree that there is a lag between the adoption of new practices in education and the adoption of new procedures in accounting.

In the last few years emphasis on the various phases of education has shifted: new methods have been developed and widely adopted; the value of using cost accounting principles has been increasingly recognized; and research on the cost-quality relationship in education has created a demand for accurate data. Despite these developments and the increased interest in financial accounting for public schools, we do not know the extent of improvements needed, the impediments to improvement, nor the best procedures for making necessary changes. . . .

PROBLEMS OF PRINCIPLES AND PROCEDURES

There are differences of opinion on accounting for public school funds. Some persons maintain that the accounting system of a school district, as a unit of local government, should conform to recognized governmental accounting standards. In contrast, others maintain that certain principles and procedures apply specifically to public school accounting.

---

*James W. Whitlock, "Financial Accounting and Reporting: Where to Improve?" *School Life,* XLIII (June, 1961), 18-21.

Between these two opinions there are various others. All, however, revolve around the degree to which business and governmental accounting principles should apply to public school accounting. On questions of depreciation, for example, the argument is made that accounts related to depreciation are necessary only for working capital funds, that is, for funds used to cover the operations of self-supporting service units such as a central storehouse or central garage. Those who make this argument believe that the school district would be enforcing double taxation if, in setting tax rates, it considered depreciation as well as acquisition cost.

Persons holding opposing views believe that since tangible assets depreciate regardless of the status of the owner, financial statements ignoring depreciation are neither correct nor informative. The source of the income which may or may not replace depreciating assets has no effect, they say, on the fact of depreciation.

The extent to which public school accounting is adaptable to full-accrual double-entry accounting and the principles and procedures that should apply are not yet agreed on. We need a statement of the principles and procedures of financial accounting and reporting that apply to public schools and that educators and accountants can accept. . . .

Assignment of responsibility for financial accounting varies with the size of the local school district: in small districts the superintendent of schools may be responsible; in large districts, the school business administrator. Financial accounting is usually separated from other school business early in the growth of the school district and the position of bookkeeper or accountant created; as the system grows, subsidiary positions — budget control officers or auditors — may be created. Generally speaking, the larger the system, the more likely school business functions are to be divided among several persons, each charged with specific responsibility. . . .

EFFECT OF LEGAL PROVISIONS

A public school district's accounting system must show that officials have complied with State laws and regulations. State legal provisions and restrictions, some of them stringent, may make it difficult or even impossible for an accounting system to follow sound principles and procedures.

Public school accounting must conform to all statutes governing the control of revenues, funds, trusts, borrowing, property assessment, collection of taxes, selection of depositories, fidelity bonding, and similar financial matters. Here, too, sound principles and procedures of accounting may conflict with those required by legal provisions.

Generally speaking, school revenues and expenditures are segregated into special funds to insure their use in accordance with legal provisions. Some States prescribe an excessive number of such funds; such a prescription needlessly complicates a financial system and tends to make it inflexible.

When legal provisions and sound principles and procedures conflict, legal provisions must of course prevail. When that happens, both educators and accountants should, as a professional responsibility, encourage authorities to revise legal requirements to make them compatible with the principles of sound accounting.

We do not know the extent of such conflict in the States and local districts. We do know, however, that the legal framework governing accounting for public school funds is important in considering the status of financial accounting.

SCHOOLS NEED A COMMON ACCOUNTING SYSTEM*

Most school administrators work under severe handicaps in trying to give their school systems sound financial accounting systems. They work without adequate manuals or handbooks on school financial principles and procedures and without trained employees. They are under great pressure to spend the school's money on certain things — and school financial accounting systems is not one of them. In some States laws covering school financial accounting work against sound business practices.

There are no adequate manuals or handbooks on the *fundamental* principles and procedures of financial accounting written specifically for school officials. The Association of School Business Officials and the American Institute of Certified Public Accountants have recommended that public schools adapt municipal accounting principles and procedures to school use. Adapting these principles may help employees already trained in the fundamentals of accounting, but it will not help those with little training, and therefore will not get to the root of the problem. . . .

Many school people believe that *Handbook II, Financial Accounting for Local and State School Systems, Standard Receipt and Expenditure Accounts,* is just such a handbook. It is not. *Handbook II* was prepared

---

*Bert K. Adams and Joseph A. Perkins, Jr., "Needed — Better School Financial Accounting," *School Life,* XLV, May, 1963, 11-13.

by the Office of Education in cooperation with five professional associations and published by the Office in 1957, as a financial accounting manual. Rather than being a manual of fundamental accounting principles and practices, it is a guide to receipt and expenditure accounting for local and State school systems, designed to improve comparability of data collected. It contains standard receipt and expenditure accounts, classified and defined, and definitions of other terms necessary to the effective use of the system. Its introduction points out the need for handbooks on such subjects as the general ledger, fund accounting, and financial statements. Since it was issued 5 years ago, 43 States have put *Handbook II* into effect or are in the process of adopting it. Some States have achieved 100 percent comparability for applicable minimum items; others only 20 percent. The average comparability for these 43 States is 60 percent.

We find from a study of many curriculums for the training of school business officials that colleges and universities have made only spotty and slow progress toward the inclusion of accounting for school finance in their programs. Graduates of many schools of education at all levels are going into administration ill equipped for financial management, although it will be one of their prime responsibilities. In many instances, institutions of higher education are still "fence-sitting" on whether to include courses in financial accounting in their programs. Doing nothing does a great disservice to our public school systems.

Many State laws play havoc with or ignore sound accounting principles. Too often these laws, written expressly to govern State aid, make it difficult or even impossible for an accounting system to follow sound principles and procedures. In some States the laws place the responsibility for accounting for local school system funds under a local official who is not an employee of the school system. Too often, since he also has the responsibility for accounting for all branches of general government, he has neither the inclination nor the time to give special financial services to the various departments of government. . . .

There are a number of reasons why our schools do not have adequate financial accounting. The most powerful force against improvement is the ignorance of the public and of many school administrators themselves on the importance of good school financial accounting. Too few people know that school financial accounting is not just a simple bookkeeping job. One State accounting manual, for example, in explaining the accounting system it establishes, says that the system "can be maintained by anyone having successfully completed a high school course in bookkeeping or having equivalent training." Even if the mechanics of accounting could be accomplished effectively by a high school graduate, such an attitude ignores the need for intelligent use of data developed from a system.

At the same time, accounting should not be allowed to be "the tail which wags the dog;" rather it should be stressed that accounting is one of the tools of good administration.

THE ACCOUNTANT

To understand the size of the task of improving school accounting competency, we must know what a "school accountant" should be and what he actually is. As defined in the *Handbook for Staff Accounting for Local and State School Systems,* the school accountant is a staff member performing assigned technical duties such as planning and directing the keeping of financial, staff, pupil, or property records; summarizing, analyzing, or verifying such records; or controlling and certifying expenditures. Ideally, this person should have at least a bachelor's degree in business administration and a major in accounting. Ideally, the accountant will have taken some courses in educational philosophy and administration. As a minimum he must be sensitive to and supportive of the objectives of public education.

In practice, the public school "accountant" may be a young high school graduate with no education in business subjects. He may be a former elementary school teacher, a former high school principal, a former local businessman, or he may be the school board member who drew the short straw.

In a great many school districts the superintendent is also the accountant, since he is all things administrative. He is superintendent, director of instruction, business manager, accountant, board secretary, principal, part-time teacher, and officer in charge of whatever other duties arise. His secretary may be a part-time accountant in addition to her other duties.

Larger school districts may have both a business manager and an accountant, but too often neither is professionally trained in business administration or accounting. Usually, only those districts with full-time accounting staff members are likely to have trained and experienced accountants. These districts in terms of the number of districts are the exceptions. Although most school districts do not have these staff members trained, it must be said that the comparatively untrained people employed by thousands of districts perform fairly satisfactorily in controlling cash but provide little or no management information.

GLOSSARY OF TERMS PERTINENT TO
SCHOOL FISCAL ACCOUNTING*

ACCRUE—To record revenues when earned or when levies are made, and to record expenditures as soon as they result in liabilities, regardless of when the revenue is actually received or the payment is actually made. Sometimes, the term is used in a restricted sense to denote the recording of revenues earned but not yet due, such as accrued interest on investments and the recording of expenditures which result in liabilities that are payable in another accounting period, such as accrued interest on bonds.

APPROPRIATION—An authorization granted by a legislative body to make expenditures and to incur obligations for specific purposes.

AVERAGE DAILY ATTENDANCE, ADA—In a given school year, the average daily attendance for a given school is the aggregate days attendance of the school divided by the number of days school was actually in session. Only days on which the pupils were under the guidance and direction of teachers in the teaching process should be considered as days in session. The average daily attendance for groups of schools having varying lengths of terms is the sum of the average daily attendances obtained for the individual schools.

AVERAGE DAILY MEMBERSHIP, ADM—In a given school year, the average daily membership for a given school is the aggregate days membership of the school divided by the number of days school was actually in session. Only days on which pupils were under the guidance and direction of teachers in the teaching process should be considered as days in session. The average daily membership for groups of schools having varying lengths of terms is the sum of the average daily memberships obtained for the individual schools.

BOND—A written promise, generally under seal, to pay a specified sum of money called the face value, at a fixed time in the future, called the date of maturity, and carrying interest at a fixed rate, usually payable periodically. The difference between a note and a bond is that the latter usually runs for a longer period of time and requires greater legal formality.

---

*Financial Accounting for Local and State School Systems, Standard Receipt and Expenditure Accounts, Washington, D.C.: United States Office of Education, Handbook II, Bulletin 1957, No. 4, 214-35.

CAPITAL OUTLAY—An expenditure which results in the acquisition of fixed assets or additions to fixed assets. It is an expenditure for land or existing buildings, improvement of grounds, construction of buildings, additions to buildings, remodeling of buildings, or initial or additional equipment. Includes installment or lease payments on property (except interest) which have a terminal date and result in the acquisition of property.

CONTINGENT FUND—Assets or other resources set aside to provide for unforeseen expenditures, or for anticipated expenditures of uncertain amount.

CURRENT EXPENSE—Any expenditure except for capital outlay and debt service. If any accounts are kept on the accrual basis, current expense includes total charges incurred, whether paid or unpaid. If accounts are kept on the cash basis, it includes only actual disbursement.

DEBT SERVICE—Expenditures for the retirement of debt and expenditures for interest on debt, except principal and interest of current loans.

DEPRECIATION—Loss in value or service life of fixed assets because of wear and tear through use, elapse of time, inadequacy, or obsolescence.

DOUBLE ENTRY—A system of bookkeeping which requires for every entry made to the debit side of an account or accounts an entry for the corresponding amount or amounts to the credit side of another account or accounts.

ENCUMBRANCES—Purchase orders, contracts, and salary or other commitments which are chargeable to an appropriation and for which a part of the appropriation is reserved. They cease to be encumbrances when paid or when actual liability is set up.

ESTIMATED REVENUE—If the accounts are kept on an accrual basis, this term designates the amount of revenue estimated to accrue during a given period regardless of whether or not it is all to be collected during the period; if the accounts are kept on a cash basis, the term designates the amount of revenues estimated to be collected during a given period.

FISCAL PERIOD—Any period at the end of which a school district determines its financial condition and the results of its operations and closes its books. It is usually a year, though not necessarily a calendar year. The most common fiscal period for school districts is July 1 through June 30.

FIXED CHARGES—Charges of a generally recurrent nature which are not readily allocable to other expenditure categories. They consist of such charges as: school board contributions to employee retirement, insurance and judgments, rental of land and buildings, and interest on current loans. They do not include payments to public school housing authorities or similar agencies.

FUND—A sum of money or other resources set aside for specific activities of a school district. The fund accounts constitute a complete entity and all of the financial transactions for the particular fund are recorded in them.

FUND, GENERAL—The fund used to finance the ordinary operations of the school district. It is available for any legally authorized purpose and consists of all school money not specifically designated for some particular purpose.

FUND, SINKING—Money which has been set aside or invested for the definite purpose of meeting payments on debt at some future time. It is usually a fund set up for the purpose of accumulating money over a period of years in order to have money available for the redemption of long-term obligations at the date of maturity.

INTERNAL CONTROL—A plan of organization under which employees' duties are so arranged and records and procedures so designed as to make it possible to exercise effective accounting control over assets, liabilities, revenues, and expenditures. For example, under such a system, the employees' work is subdivided so that no one employee performs a complete cycle of operations. Again, under such a system, the procedures to be followed are definitely laid down and such procedures call for proper authorizations by designated officials for all actions to be taken.

LIABILITIES—Debt or other legal obligations arising out of transactions in the past which are payable but not necessarily due. Encumbrances are not liabilities; they become liabilities when the services or materials for which the encumbrance was established have been rendered or received.

OPERATION OF PLANT—Those activities which are concerned with keeping the physical plant open and ready for use. It includes cleaning, disinfecting, heating, moving furniture, caring for grounds, operating telephone switchboards, and other such housekeeping activities as are repeated somewhat regularly: daily, weekly, monthly, or seasonally. It does not include repairing.

PRORATING—The allocation of parts of a single expenditure to two or more different accounts in proportion to the benefits which the expenditure provides for the purpose or program area for which the accounts were established.

SERIAL BONDS—Issues redeemable by installments, each of which is to be paid in full ordinarily out of revenues of the fiscal year in which it matures, or revenues of the preceding year.

TAXES—Compulsory charges levied by a governmental unit for the purpose of financing services performed for the common benefit. The term includes licenses and permits. It does not include special assessments.

SCHOOLS SHOULD INVEST THEIR IDLE FUNDS*

By investing its temporarily idle funds, one small school district in a Midwestern State earned $50,000 in interest in fiscal year 1961 — enough to pay the salaries of its school business official, estimated at $7,750, and of 8 teachers at the 1959–60 United States average of $5,135. (I use the term "temporarily idle funds" here because it is, I believe, more precise than the frequently used "surplus funds," which may give the mistaken impression that a district has a large unencumbered balance.) If in 1959 all districts had invested as prudently, the public schools would have been richer by $124 million.

These data incidentally support the theory, fairly widely held, that a business official should save his district an amount of money equal to his salary. That, however, is neither the reason for employing a business official nor the reason for investing funds. Whether the district employs a business official or the chief administrator handles school funds, the primary consideration is the efficient and economical use of funds to attain the goals of the educational program of the district.

We do not know how much interest school districts earn by investing idle funds, as no agency collects this information. The Bureau of the Census, however, collects data on the interest cities earn by investing municipal funds, and these data show us the value of managing public funds efficiently. During the fiscal periods that ended in calendar year 1960, cities spent $15.3 billion and earned $154 million in interest (excluding income from investment of retirement and insurance reserves

---

*Forrest Harrison, "Investment of Idle School Funds," *School Life,* XLIV (January-February, 1962), 9-10.

and similar funds). Since their earnings represent approximately 1 percent of their total expenditures and since some administrative officers and controlling boards prohibit the investment of public funds, many cities must have aggressive investment policies.

We do know that many districts recognize investment as a fruitful source of income, as more effective than reducing the unit cost of supplies. Although these districts are taking advantage of their opportunities to earn additional income, they might earn even more if their business officials planned carefully.

Business officials know that in transacting school business there is seldom a steady flow of cash, that peak periods of expenditures and income seldom coincide. They know, too, that they can control the timing of expenditures to some extent, but not the timing of income. They can, however, generally predict the timing of income, and they should use their knowledge in scheduling the investment of temporarily idle funds. When bonds are sold, school administrators can predict with reasonable accuracy the need for expenditures from the proceeds. Right then, they should invest a part of the proceeds. They should also work out a program for investing idle current funds in such securities as U.S. Treasury bills, bank certificates of deposit, bank time deposits, or other safe, interest-bearing obligations. The interest earned on school funds rightly belongs to the district and not to the depository. Since banks are entitled to remuneration for their services, business officials should protect their accounts by maintaining a balance large enough to avoid payment of service charges. . . .

In addition to their restriction on investments, States have other requirements that sometimes unnecessarily complicate the management of school funds and, indirectly, the investment of them. For example, some State statutes require districts to keep various school funds in separate bank accounts. This type of stewardship is no longer needed, if it ever was, since present accounting methods make it easy to keep separate records for various funds and to maintain all money in one bank account. This is not to say that fund accounting is not important: it is and it should be continued. Fund accounting for debt service and teachers' salaries is particularly important so that lenders and teachers may be assured of payment.

If local districts are to make efficient use of their funds, they need the cooperation of all concerned. State legislatures should consider removing legal bars that make investment of idle funds difficult or impossible. State departments of education and other State agencies should give technical assistance to local units. It is possible that the U. S. Treasury would help by making available special securities to meet the needs of school districts. Local school administrators should make the changes necessary to facilitate investments; they should consider interfund transfers to investment and use this device where necessary. In all of their financial dealings, business officials and other school administrators should maintain safeguards to protect the credit standing of their districts.

THE FUTURE OF DATA PROCESSING IN SCHOOLS*

If the question were asked whether or not education could afford the medium- or large-capacity computer, the answer today would have to be "No." But multi-processing, miniaturized, large-capacity computers are on the horizon, and it is felt that the tools will become economically feasible in the next two or three years even for the small school district. The following developments are seen in future hardware trends:

1. The distinction between the "computer," or the central data processor and its associated peripheral devices will become "blurred." That is, storage, printers, etc., will become more of an integral part of the computer itself.
2. Vast magnetic tape files will be extensively used for all types of records.
3. The capacity of computer memory will be limitless for all practical purposes. Magnetic drums, disks and cards will probably become the main computer storage media for information retrieval systems during the next five to ten years. However, these techniques may be displaced in the interim by thin film or woven screen memories. This improvement would mean storage of from 10 to 100 billion bits — a capacity more than adequate for most educational systems.
4. Magnetics will increase in popularity.
5. Computer access time will commonly be measured in billionths of a second.
6. Communication between geographically separated computers will become as commonplace as voice communication between

---

*Don D. Bushnell, "Educational Data Processing and Public Education, Chicago: by permission of Association of School Business Officials, International, *49th Annual Volume of Proceedings,* 1963, 277-278.

humans today. The communication will take place via land-lines and micro-wave facilities.

These predictions serve to underscore the fact that computer hardware has reduced in cost by one-fifth over the last three years and there is every reason that this reduction in cost will continue.

If computer-aided instructional systems are to be applied on any vast scale, they must be economically competitive with other systems performing similar functions. Some increase in equipment costs can be justified by improved teaching efficiency and subsequent reduction in training time and operational waste. It seems clear that computer-based systems must approach the over-all cost of more conventional equipment if they are to be used for more than specialized military or industrial applications. This development seems to be the trend, however, in miniaturized, large-capacity systems.

There appear to be other avenues by which the cost of computer-base instruction might be reduced. The first is through development of special purpose computers and associated equipment designed for specific educational applications. Such computers could be of highly simplified design since they would need to incorporate only the storage capacity and the operating speed and flexibility necessary for one specific job.

The special-purpose computer offers the advantage of greater efficiency in a particular task. On the other hand, the inflexibility of a special-purpose-computer may prevent it from serving as a basis for expanding electronic techniques to other areas of the operations. Since these computers do only a specific job, they contribute to a compartmentalized view of school operations.

As we have seen [, progress] must be made not only in data-processing technology, but in our knowledge of educational requirements. Automation requires a clear, operational statement of objectives to be accomplished by the system being automated. The desired student behaviors must be more precisely defined, and research must be directed toward discovering optimal combinations of instructional techniques to produce these behaviors. We must learn much more about the kinds of information needed by students, teachers, counselors, and administrators. More standardized methods must be developed for coding and recording this information, so that high-speed processing techniques can be used efficiently.

A multitude of such practical problems must be solved if computers are to have widespread utility in education. If these problems can be solved, and if the full potentials of high-speed data processing can be realized throughout the educational system, we may expect some of the greatest changes seen in education for hundreds of years.

INSURING SCHOOL PROPERTY . . .

PIP — A PLAN FOR SAVING ON SCHOOL INSURANCE*

A new, far-reaching, and money-saving fire insurance program which few municipalities know about has been developed recently. Called the Public and Institutional Property Plan, it is designed for a specific class of fire insurance risk: institutions that serve the public such as churches, colleges, hospitals, schools, and of course governmental units.

Ohio was the first state to adopt the Institutional Plan on May 2, 1960, and the Cook County (Illinois) Inspection Bureau followed on May 16, 1960. Forty-three states now have adopted the plan.

REASONS FOR PIP

This form of fire insurance has been developed in response to competitive factors in the fire insurance business and the much greater desire of institutional property owners to cut insurance costs. The major factors are the following:

1. This is a preferred class of business. Values in most cases are substantial, producing large premiums. Loss experience generally has been good.
2. Classes of risks with a public interest most readily go in for fire safety self-inspection programs. This is especially true in schools and churches because recent spectacular fires have made these public institutions unusually fire conscious.
3. Institutions are more interested than ever in premium saving and are concerned with catastrophe possibilities.
4. There has been a trend in the growth of self-insurance programs, or even no insurance programs, especially in these institutional classes.

---

*Frank R. Spence, "A New Plan for Instructional Fire Insurance," *American School Book Journal,* CXLIV (February, 1962), 23 (published by the Bruce Publishing Company).

ADVANTAGES OF PIP

The most important advantages of the Public and Institutional Property plan are the following:

1. The plan is designed specifically for the institutional-type property—traditionally in the preferred-risk category.
2. The plan is flexible. The rating structure takes into account that some institutions may have unusually high building values, while others have substantially higher contents values. Building and contents can be insured together, or separately, or specific insurance can be obtained on items of greatest risk, all within the framework of one policy.
3. Complete replacement cost coverage is provided.
4. The plan provides broad protection for buildings. Single structures or units at multiple locations within one state can be covered in a single policy.
5. It covers contents of nearly every description.
6. It eliminates the coinsurance clause by use of an Agreed Amount of Insurance Provision—the institution annually providing a sworn statement of values.
7. It provides for inspection service.
8. The plan is adjusted annually to new values. This acts as a check against the possibility that the institution is overinsured or underinsured.
9. It provides insurance on newly acquired property. If additional property is acquired in the same state during the term of the policy, insurance is automatically provided up to 180 days in the amount of five per cent of the total amount of insurance carried by the institution, or $100,000, whichever is the lesser amount.
10. It provides coverage on property away from the premises. Institutional property temporarily located elsewhere in the state is covered up to $5,000.
11. It provides coverage of employees' personal property, not covered by other insurance, while it is in insured buildings against insured perils up to $500 per employee.
12. The plan permits administrative savings to be passed on to the insured institutions, such as lower processing costs, less loss frequency and severity due to the inspection programs, and reduced loss adjustment expense.

SCHOOL CONSTRUCTION . . .

HOW SCHOOL OFFICIALS CAN EFFECT ECONOMIES IN SCHOOL CONSTRUCTION*

The following 25 items have been credited with (1) actually saving money in schools which were recognized as "low cost" or (2) providing potential dollar savings which could have been used to advantage in those same schools. Items which any who are planning new plant developments would do well to consider are listed in the order of importance attributed to them by those who planned the school-plant developments in which the items were or could have been savings factors; comments are those of the writer.

1. *Be sure competitive bids are taken on all projects.* Apparently there is no substitute for competitive free enterprise! Those who have observed the bidding process many times marvel anew each time at the great range of bids on each branch of the work—and at the number of contractors who manage to stay solvent and operating despite that range! There is no accounting for the discrepancies other than to believe that what a man "loses on the bananas, he makes up on the potatoes," and perhaps vice versa on the next bid.

2. *Make sure there are several bidders on each project.* Some competition is not enough. Other things being equal, the more numerous the bidders on a branch of the work, the greater the "spread" of the bids. If only a limited number of bidders is to be found locally, it may pay to solicit bids from some distance away—both to increase the likelihood of a "spread" and to decrease the likelihood of collusion or price-fixing.

3. *Purchase all equipment on competitive bids or comparative prices.* Free enterprise works to the buyer's advantage here, also, care must be exercised to make certain that bids or prices

---

*Harold Boles, "25 Significant Economies in New School Buildings," *American School Board Journal,* CXLVII (January, 1964), 19-20 (published by the Bruce Publishing Company).

are *on comparable items* of equipment. More discussion about this will follow.

4. *Be sure that drawings and specifications are complete, concise, and free of ambiguity.* Just remember that any time a contractor is in doubt, he will add a sum to his bid sufficient to cover the more costly of the possibilities. It is only when he is in no doubt about what is intended that he is able to slice every penny of "fat" from his bid.

5. *Take special care to eliminate waste area.* This admonition relates to floor areas. Don't allow the architect to show "unassigned" areas just in order that he may round out some plan to fit a predetermined exterior design. Take care that corridors, lobbies, storage rooms, etc., are no larger than actually needed.

6. *Hold down cubage by eliminating lofts, attics, basements, and other nonusuable areas.* While cubic-foot costs have been generally discredited and discarded as a basis for calculating construction costs, it *does* cost something to add even 1 in. of unnecessary height to an area. In addition to initial cost, the heating, lighting, and ventilating of unnecessary space increase operational costs.

7. *Be sure the architect thoroughly understands the building budget from the start.* Remember, when school people talk about the cost of a building, they usually are thinking of *all* costs—site, site development, construction fees, equipment, incidentals—while "cost of a building" usually means cost of construction only to an architect. If the architect draws more building than you can buy, he must be paid for his total work—and perhaps for redrawing. More than one building project has foundered after site development or equipment funds were diverted to construction because there was no clear-cut budget of proposed expenditures.

8. *Specify as much of the equipment as possible yourselves, thus saving the architect's fee on it.* While this item was rated high as a potential dollar-saver, it may be over-rated. There are a few school administrators who (1) could not spend their time to greater profit for pupils than in listening to equipment salesmen and writing specifications, (2) know enough about both the educational and the technical aspects of equipment to write proper specifications, and perhaps to draw some items, (3) can analyze bids to determine which is "lowest and best." Architects often are as ill-qualified for this chore as are school administrators or board members. Undoubtedly, significant savings

can be achieved by having *those who will use the equipment* (generally not administrators) indicate the quantities, types, sizes, etc., but someone then must be found to do the three things indicated above, and he will invariably charge a fee. "Aye, there's the rub. . . ." Perhaps the greatest weakness in the entire process of school-plant development is lack of knowledgeable people to specify and purchase equipment. A penny saved is not a penny earned if it leads to inferior equipment.

9. *Keep most equipment separate from construction contracts.* Even if equipment is specified and drawn by the architect (and any item which must be fitted, built in, or attached should be), bids should be taken at a different time than the bids for construction contracts. For example, if the general contract includes bleachers or cabinets, the manufacturer quotes the same price to the general contractor that he would to the school board. The difference lies in the fact that the general contractor then adds on his 15 or 20 percent margin for doing absolutely nothing, since such items are customarily priced by the manufacturer to include installation by his men.

10. *Make sure hardware is simple and functional.* Most persons are staggered when they learn the cost of hardware in a modern school building, and the ornate is likely to cost twice as much as the plainer, but equally serviceable, style. One further possibility for savings is to check carefully and put locks only where needed. Many new buildings contain dozens or hundreds of locks (even the simplest of which are expensive) which are seldom or never used.

11. *Use exterior ornamentation* (such as cut stone, columns or cupolas) *only if it serves a useful purpose.* This will be determined to a large extent when the architect is chosen. However, board members are inclined to disregard elevation and perspective sketches which may be the only places where expensive "gingerbread" shows. One can never rely completely on past practices of the architect.

12. *Do not purchase excess equipment which will be unused.* Even with classroom furniture, there is sometimes overbuying. If most classrooms will contain only 28 pupils, it is wasteful to buy 35 units for each room. Better practice would indicate purchase of 28 units for each room with a dozen or so spares which could be shifted about.

13. *Allow bidders at least one full month to prepare their proposals.* They have to "take off" quantities and get subbids on hundreds

of materials and dozens of trades, sometimes with as many as five or six suppliers pricing each material. If the time is inadequate to secure, total, and check all prices, contractors will "pad" to protect themselves—and who can blame them?

14. *Hold numerous "give-and-take" conferences between architect and school personnel in translating educational specifications into building plans.* In no other way can the architect learn what the school personnel really need. He and they can act as checks on each other, to make certain that waste is not being introduced by either.

15. *Have the architect's contract clear and definite in regard to services to be performed and fees to be paid.* As in any business transaction, understandings should be crystal clear. It is a bitter and costly experience to find that one must pay extra for something he thought was included. In fairness to architects, it must be said that they often render services which are not required of them by their contracts, and that boards of education frequently expect services which the architect is in no way obliged to render.

16. *Use stock items of equipment when possible.* There may be exceptions, but the custom-made or built-on-the job item generally costs more than its mass-produced counterpart.

17. *Do not make many changes, even minor ones, after bids are received.* Architects are often blamed for change orders which they issued, even though they did so at the client's request. Any change order is a temptation to the contractor making the change to make a few bucks of easy profit by overcharging. After all, he has no competition at that point!

18. *Keep noninstructional spaces to a minimum.* This is perhaps the most controversial item in this list, as we in Education cannot agree on the meanings of "noninstructional" or "minimum." However, it seems unlikely that there will be much criticism if walls, circulation space, etc., meet but do not exceed code requirements.

19. *Give careful attention to ascertaining that contractors are competent before awarding contracts.* While this is primarily the responsibility of the architect, neither he nor the board should overlook the fact that the state laws generally require acceptance of the lowest *and best* bid. A low bid is not economical if the bidder cannot complete his work.

20. *Plan one or more areas for multiuse.* While many people have misgivings about some of the combinations which have been

tried (such as auditorium-gymnasium and cafeteria-gymnasium), there are some low-utilization but sorely needed large areas for which secondary uses may be found. Examples are auditoriums or dining rooms used as study halls and music studios used for large group instruction. In one new high school, the auditorium and gymnasium share a common lobby (not at all unusual) which is also used as a wrestling room (and this *is* unusual!).

21. *Keep roof lines straight.* Each change in height costs money, and this is especially true of curves, folded plates, and other exotic roof forms. These latter forms more often than not introduce waste cubage, and may introduce unnecessary maintenance hazards.

22. *Allow the architect ample time to complete his drawings and specifications.* It has been noted previously that anything which confuses a bidder or leaves him in doubt is likely to cause him to "pad" his bid to cover himself. Too often, boards of education panic with remorse for having delayed their decisions years too long and attempt to compensate by shaving days from the time allowed their architects.

23. *Select your architect through careful screening of several architects.* The man whose work establishes him as an expert designer with an eye for economy usually charges the same rate of fee as the profligate wastrel. There are many economies which are the sole province of the architect, and the time to learn how cognizant of economics a particular architect may be is before he is employed.

24. *Keep ceiling heights constant except in special areas.* What was said in Item 21 about the "top" of the roof applies equally well to the "bottom." However, the fact that roof lines are straight is not an automatic guarantee that ceiling heights are the same. Both should be scrupulously checked.

25. *Be sure your building specifications allow the use of competitive materials.* An example may serve here: A few years ago, a new roof-deck material was introduced at low cost, and was vastly superior to competing products. As architects specified the material, with no provision for substitution, costs rose spectacularly and ominously. When the architects realized what was happening, they started specifying either of two types of deck materials and costs fell to their former levels almost immediately.

Board members, school administrators, and citizens have for years bruited about the charge that only the architect can control the costs of school buildings. Careful rereading of the foregoing suggestions for economy will indicate that the charge is an obvious canard.

Of these 25 suggestions which, let us remind you have been agreed upon as the most important of all possible economies by a number of architects and administrators, *all except nine* (Numbers 4, 5, 6, 10, 11, 19, 21, 24 and 25) *may be completely effected by boards of education and their administrators regardless of architectural practices! All of the remaining nine economies may be effected by boards of education and their administrators through supervision and criticism of their architects' work.* All of the listed economies and more may be achieved by careful educational planning in which staff personnel participate.

Any board of education members who say that the board has no control over building economies are either ignorant of the facts or unwilling to accept their responsibilities.

URBAN CENTERS PRESENT
UNIQUE PROBLEMS
IN SCHOOL CONSTRUCTION*

There is a great shift of the middle class to the suburbs, while the central cities are becoming increasingly the place of residence for the impoverished. This movement is destructive of the heterogeneity of function, of purpose, and of people on which the viability of the modern urban community is dependent. Nearly every one of the school officials responding indicated that this was one of his major problems. The solid occupation of many neighborhoods by the economically and culturally disadvantaged gradually leads to economic disaster — inefficient land use, traffic congestion, deterioration of businesses, low tax revenues, and high municipal costs. These changes affect the quality of the school district attendance centers and subsequently the educational program planning and school-facilities needs.

Closely related to this is the matter of seasonal migration within the school year, which results in over and under utilization of school buildings. During the winter many of the school buildings become seriously overcrowded because of the influx of migrant workers' children. During the spring, when the migrant workers take their children out of school so

---

*William W. Chase, *Problems in Planning Urban School Facilities,* Washington, D.C.: United States Office of Education, Bulletin 1964, No. 23, 46-47.

that the entire family can follow crop planting, cultivating, and harvesting, many classrooms are left unused. In terms of planning educational programs and buildings, this creates serious problems, as nearly one-half of the school officials interviewed indicated.

Three-fourths of the officials said that they encountered problems in trying to identify the effects of population replacement in the redeveloped areas and the areas adjacent to them. As large numbers of people are uprooted and relocated, existing school facilities are crowded in numbers and ways that are hard to predict.

Moreover, the attitudes of the people in these areas, although understandable, add to the existing problems. These attitudes seem to be reflected in a weakening of the idea of the neighborhood as a distinct community, with the school as its core. Approximately one-half of the school officials indicated that this type of loyal support has broken down.

These factors have caused serious problems in establishing and accomplishing community goals; this problem was mentioned by nearly three-fourths of the respondents.

The actual physical problems caused by these socioeconomic problems were closely related. A large majority of the school officials indicated that the population movements not only created problems regarding the use of individual school buildings, but that they often created problems regarding entire school attendance or service center boundaries. The necessity to constantly revise attendance boundary lines and shift pupils from one building to another because of overcrowding affected transportation, program planning, and staff relationships.

PLANT OPERATIONS . . .

DUTIES AND POSITIONAL RELATIONSHIP OF THE CUSTODIAL STAFF*

School plant management, an area of major responsibility in educational administration, involves all services, activities, and procedures concerned with keeping existing school facilities open and in usable condition. Operation, one phase of plant management, includes, among other

---

*R. N. Finchum, *School Plant Management: Administering the Custodial Program,* Washington, D.C.: United States Office of Education, Bulletin 1961, No. 4, 1-2, 23.

things, those day-to-day services which are essential to the safety, comfort, and well-being of those who occupy and use school facilities. These services, for the purpose of this bulletin, are restricted to those performed by school-plant custodial personnel, and are regarded here as elements of the total program of school plant services.

PURPOSES OF CUSTODIAL SERVICES

In former years, custodial services for schools were primarily concerned with sweeping floors, dusting furniture, tending furnaces, and similar chores. To a large degree, the methods were haphazard and unproductive. Those who performed them, usually referred to as "janitors" and generally regarded as handy men, were often given the job without regard to their individual abilities to achieve high performance standards. These attitudes and administrative practices generally resulted in the payment of low wages, the purchase of cheap supplies, the neglect of minor repairs, and the consequent deterioration of buildings and equipment.

Fortunately, these practices are not so prevalent today as they once were. The recent increasing emphasis on adequate school facilities, coupled with newer concepts of property preservation, learning environment, safety, and a greater utilization of school facilities by the public, has led boards of education and school administrators to recognize the value of adequate custodial services and the importance of providing trained people to do the work.

This recognition, together with careful evaluation of school-plant operational needs, has contributed to the development of certain well-defined purposes of custodial services. Among these purposes are (1) preserving property values, (2) protecting health and safety, (3) providing a climate for learning, (4) developing good will, (5) maintaining cleanliness and neatness, and (6) effecting operating economies. . . .

LINES OF AUTHORITY

Lines of authority for supervisory control of school personnel should be so clearly defined and well established that each employee understands his relationship to all other employees. This is particularly true for school custodians because their services may be demanded, supervised, and praised — or condemned — by all who have any interest, real or imagined, in the operation of school plants. For example, pupils, teachers, lunchroom workers, and even parents may exploit the generosity of some custodians to such an extent that the latter are unable to perform their regular duties in an efficient manner. A reasonable adherence to sound policies governing supervisory control should protect both the custodian and the school district against unjustified demands for custodial time.

Good administrative practice dictates that the executive officer of the board, the superintendent, be responsible to the board, and that all other school employees, regardless of rank, be responsible to him or to his designated assistant. In the case of the school custodian the line of authority should begin with the superintendent and extend through designated administrative heads to the school principal. There seems to be general agreement that, while the actual supervision of adequate performance and checking the work standards of custodians is the responsibility of either the superintendent or his designated assistant, all directions, procedures, and orders from the central office should be transmitted through the principal. Furthermore, it is essential that the principal of each school have immediate supervision over all custodial employees in his building.

THE MAINTENANCE FUNCTION . . .

THE IMPORTANCE OF AND ORGANIZATION FOR SCHOOL MAINTENANCE*

School plant operation and maintenance, two closely related areas of school plant management, constitute one of a number of complex problems which confronts public school boards. An essential factor in efficient school administration is a well organized and properly functioning service for the operation and maintenance of the school plant. Operation includes those day-to-day services and activities which are necessary to keep the physical plant open and in a usable condition. Maintenance consists of those services, activities, and procedures which are concerned with preserving, protecting, and keeping buildings, grounds, and equipment in a satisfactory state of repair. It covers a wide range of activities including some repairs, replacements, renovations, and adjustments.

*R. N. Finchum, *Organizing the Maintenance Program,* Washington, D.C.: United States Office of Education, Bulletin 1960, No. 15, 1-3, 61, 80.

THE PROBLEM

The problem of school plant maintenance begins on the day the school board accepts a building from the contractor and continues throughout the entire life of the building. Experience indicates that in far too many instances school officials fail to recognize this fact. They seem to assume that a new building requires little or no maintenance until it has been in use for several years. It is a mistake, sometimes a costly mistake, for school officials to permit maintenance needs to accumulate before they attempt to develop a planned maintenance program. An adequate school plant maintenance service is vitally important to the pupils, to the educational program, and to the community, because the well-kept school building not only serves as a shelter and a school home for the pupils, but also as a tool of education and frequently, the center of community life. It is essential that school plants be so operated and maintained that they provide optimum service. Adequately planned, well-built school buildings may be so operated and maintained that they fail to provide this service. On the other hand, average or sometimes mediocre buildings may provide satisfactory service if they are properly operated and maintained.

The public school plant, usually planned and often financed through cooperative community efforts, frequently represents the most substantial as well as the most important community investment. Dedicated to school and community uses and representing a major community interest, the school plant should be so maintained that it merits continued community appreciation and adequate financial support. Good school plant management programs do not "just happen." They must be well planned, manned by competent personnel, given a fair share of the school district revenues, operated to serve the best interests of the pupils, and managed efficiently. When a program is carried on in this manner, it will not be difficult for school officials to justify maintenance costs.

Importance of Maintenance

It has been estimated that the present value of all public elementary and secondary school property in this country was between $28 and $30 billion in 1958–59. Present trends in school construction indicate that approximately $3 billion will be spent for capital outlay in 1959-60. Future classroom requirements will be influenced by such factors as the present backlog of needs, increasing birth rates, normal school plant obsolescence, and population mobility.

Both the existing facilities and those that are to be added from year to year will require adequate maintenance if they are to function satisfactorily as tools of education. The importance of maintaining these facilities lies not only in the necessity for obtaining optimum service from them but also for protecting the district's financial investment in them. It seems axiomatic that expenditures for maintenance accomplish both purposes. Such expenditures make possible a cleaner, healthier, safer school environment, and purchase additional years of usefulness, thus prolonging the interval between replacement dates.

Another significant point is that maintenance, if adequately financed, consumes an important segment of the school dollar. This is demonstrated by the fact that if a planned maintenance program has been followed by the school district, it is generally believed that not less than 5 percent of the district's current operating budget, a figure which seems to have national acceptance, will be required to support an adequate maintenance program. For a new school building it has been suggested that from one-half to 1 percent of the total plant cost should be allocated annually for its maintenance. For older buildings which have been properly maintained from year to year, some authorities suggest that from 1 to 2 percent of the current replacement cost of a school plant should be budgeted for each year of its maintenance.

Although the recommended minimum expenditure for school plant maintenance is 5 percent of the total annual operating budget for the district, reported data indicate that the school systems of the country spend slightly less for this purpose. A review of the biennial reports on expenditures for all full-time public elementary and secondary day schools in continental United States from 1947–48 through 1955–56 reveals that in only one geographical section of the country — the North Central — have expenditures for maintenance equalled or exceeded recommended amounts, and in this case, for only 2 of the 5 years. . . .

Good maintenance practices contribute to economy by improving efficiency and preventing waste. They may include: (1) Planning preventive maintenance; (2) following a schedule; (3) utilizing staff specialization; (4) establishing work sequence; (5) installing two-way communication; (6) negotiating service contracts; and (7) using central maintenance shops. . . .

THE MAINTENANCE BUDGET

In preparing the maintenance budget, school officials should be careful to distinguish between physical improvements which can be charged to capital outlay, and repairs and upkeep chargeable to maintenance. It is generally agreed that expenditures for extensive remodeling of buildings, major replacements of buildings and equipment, additions to buildings, and improvements to grounds are capital outlay expenditures, and may or may not be placed on a pay-as-you-go basis, depending on local policy, tax limitations and other factors. On the other hand, all maintenance expenditures should be placed on a current basis, using funds from local tax levies, from State allocations, or a combination of local and State funds.

Uniformity of maintenance expenditures is another important point to consider in developing annual maintenance budgets. Maintenance should be planned so that expenditures can be apportioned as uniformly as possible every year to prevent excessive costs [one] year and meager costs the next. This uniformity will contribute to the development of a systematic plan of work for maintenance personnel, will create a favorable impression on taxpayers, and may play an important part in determining whether or not boards and fiscal authorities accept and approve maintenance budgets. . . .

Utilizing Staff Specialization

In recent years, school administrators have come to realize that the jack-of-all-trades maintenance worker is not as efficient as he was once thought to be. They now recognize that maximum individual skills can be developed if workmen are organized by conventional trades, such as carpenters, electricians, plumbers, painters, pipefitters, mechanics, and the like; and that performance standards are improved if workers are assigned to their respective areas of specialization. However, if emergencies arise, all workers, regardless of areas of specialization, should be expected to assist in making repairs.

THE MAINTENANCE SURVEY*

Top management in our school systems must have complete information about facilities and their upkeep requirements if orderly, efficient, economical maintenance programs are to be planned and conducted. These programs depend on adequate budgets; hence pertinent data must be received early enough to allow thorough study and analysis of prospective programs in relation to money available. Some responsible person in each school district should collect and keep adequate records on each school building. On the basis of information thus assembled, offi-

---

*R. N. Finchum, *School Building Maintenance Procedures,* Washington, D.C.: United States Office of Education, Bulletin 1964, No. 17, 6-9.

cials can plan the program, assign priorities, and schedule the work. Three methods commonly used in keeping track of maintenance needs are (1) maintenance surveys, (2) routine inspections and periodic checks, and (3) reports submitted by building personnel.

THE MAINTENANCE SURVEY

The first step in planning sound, long-range maintenance programs is to collect data on all district-owned school buildings, grounds, and equipment. This can be accomplished by the maintenance survey, conducted by the district's director of buildings and grounds, the maintenance supervisor, or some other official responsible for the maintenance program.

The survey director and perhaps an assistant, both with wide practical knowledge of school construction, should visit and thoroughly inspect every school building in the district. Other members of the survey team may change from school to school, but for each school the team should include the principal, head custodian, one or more teachers, and one or more lay citizens representing the community in which the school is located. Lay citizens who have some knowledge of building construction can contribute more significantly to the team's efforts than those lacking such knowledge. Board members, at their discretion, may wish to join the team from time to time.

Survey techniques may vary from district to district, but experience has shown that satisfactory results can be achieved only if the team uses a carefully planned checklist. This document should list items to be checked and should provide space for writing in comments, observations, and estimated costs of each needed repair. School officials may wish to develop a checklist of their own. For convenience, the list may be divided into three parts — one for buildings, one for grounds, and one for equipment. The building checklist may start with the roof and end with the footing. . . .

Although the building maintenance survey can be conducted at any time, the summer months, when school is not in session, may be most practical, both from the standpoint of administration and of unhampered working conditions for the survey team.

When the survey document for a given building is completed, it should be transmitted to the official responsible for keeping maintenance records. When all school buildings of the district have been checked, necessary data on maintenance needs can be tabulated, analyzed, and reported to the superintendent and through him to the board of education.

ROUTINE INSPECTION AND PERIODIC CHECKS

Once a complete maintenance survey has been made and the needs of the district's school buildings have been tabulated, analyzed, and evaluated, priorities can be assigned and the work programed over a period of time according to a reasonably well-defined schedule. This programing, however, does not assure that a record of maintenance needs will be kept current. For example, a roof judged sound and in good condition at the time of the survey may be damaged by extremes of summer heat and winter cold; extremes of temperature might also have caused stone and masonry walls to move and joints to open. If not detected and corrected at the proper time, these failures can result in heavy damage to building structure, interior walls, ceilings, floors, finish, furniture, and equipment.

Routine inspections should be made by the school principal and the building custodians, the principal being particularly alert to conditions affecting the health and safety of students, teachers, and other school employees; custodians, to conditions of roofs, gutters, downspouts, walls, doors, hardware, and mechanical systems — points where defects or failures can cause serious damages if not repaired. All needs of an emergency nature should have immediate attention by the maintenance department; those that can be deferred should be reported to the department where they can be given a place in the maintenance schedule.

Periodic checks, preferably twice annually, should be made by maintenance personnel who should inspect such items as electric motors, starter controls, heating and ventilating systems, water heaters, pumps, valves, fuel lines and connections, warning devices, safety equipment, and fire control apparatus. The services of other technically trained people may be required when special inspectors are considered necessary — architects and structural engineers if structural safety is to be checked; boiler inspectors if boiler problems are involved; and safety engineers, often assisted by fire chiefs and insurance officials, if fire safety is to be determined.

REPORTS BY BUILDING PERSONNEL

Close surveillance of the school plant by the principal may require the help of all school employees in a position to detect maintenance problems in their earliest stages. Custodians may discover and either correct or report malfunctioning safety controls for boilers, and thus prevent possible explosions causing property damage, plant shutdown, and injury to building occupants. Teachers may discover and report damaging moisture infiltration during seasons of heavy precipitation. Lunchroom workers, in daily contact with food preparation and service equipment, may report conditions which they consider hazardous. Similarly, other building personnel (and pupils) can and should inform the principal about maintenance problems that appear to need attention.

Every reported instance of maintenance need should be investigated by the principal, or should be referred by him to the head custodian for checking. Some complaints, reports, and observations by building personnel may be of little significance; others, of great importance. In school districts where board policy permits or directs custodians to perform maintenance functions, they should make simple repairs; more complicated jobs should be referred to the maintenance department, with emergency items assigned first priority. In districts where board policy prohibits custodians from performing maintenance functions, the principal should refer all established needs to the maintenance department, assigning a priority to each need. These procedures, if followed, will be helpful in preventing additional or prolonged property damage, will save money, will spread maintenance expenditures evenly over the years, and may prevent injury or death.

THE PURCHASING FUNCTION . . .

COOPERATIVE PURCHASING BY SCHOOLS*

1. There is evidence that cooperative purchasing is of considerable value. In cooperative purchasing agreements, several school districts together submit a simple large purchase requirement rather than several small individual purchases of the same items.
2. Cooperative buying with discretion [of] selection can be easily achieved through the intermediate administration unit which is rapidly becoming a service unit to local school districts.

---

*Aldan F. O'Hearn, "Cooperative Purchasing Pros and Cons," Chicago: by permission of Association of School Business Officials, International, *48th Annual Volume of Proceedings,* 1962, 207.

3. Cooperative purchasing agreements clearly indicate their usefulness. Savings can result through buying in carload lots and case lots rather than small units.

4. Where cooperative buying has taken place, it has proved to be both practical and economical. Savings from cooperative programs were reported to be from 17 to 43.5 percent. Many schools have discovered the advantages of cooperative buying with city or county governments.

5. An orderly calendar of purchasing requirements during slack manufacturer season can be determined to provide an additional cost reduction and contribute to production volume during these periods.

6. More often than not, the same supplier offers services to the same locality rather than quote to representative bids with a diversity of crash deadlines. A smaller number of bids in volume can be attended to more efficiently in cost analysis utilizing carload lots in many instances from their respective factory suppliers. Service and delivery schedules can be formulated and projected.

7. Schools generally tend to be understaffed administratively. This is especially true of suburban school systems which have grown so fast during recent years. Cooperative purchasing, then, can serve as a partial answer to the problems created by this phenomenon.

8. Cooperative purchasing does enable several small and medium sized schools to realize the purchasing power of the nation's major cities. Utilizing the additional time that is saved, the respective talents of each school business administrator can be directed to other important facets of his performance assignment. In addition to this, it provides a natural liaison for business managers to become better acquainted with their neighboring associates and the sharing of other pertinent ideas contributory to the effectiveness of their responsibility role.

9. In the last analysis, more time and resource of talent can be extended in gaining an understanding of materials available as well as a more favorable process for the testing and evaluation of products.

10. Stereotyped standardized specification lists do not have to be evolved, but rather those general supplies of standard use can be considered and revised, still leaving a major degree of autonomy to the participating districts to bid individually their custom curriculum and operational requirement needs.

CONS OR DISADVANTAGES TO COOPERATIVE PURCHASING

1. One possible danger of cooperative buying is that the bureaucracy and red tape involved might become too cumbersome as to limit flexibility and local adaptations. However, in an attempt to overcome this danger, many vendors offer such arrangements as joint and open-end contracts, dispersed deliveries and special packaging.
2. If a school district does not have central warehousing for one trip deliveries, the home front distribution may be more costly than direct deliveries to several locations by the jobber.
3. The adage, "You never get something for nothing" is often stated. "Where there is a difference in price there must also be a difference in quality, utility, and/or service. In a cooperative purchasing situation, the individual school district gives up many things, and the person or district heading up the cooperative assumes certain burdens and responsibilities."
4. Schools do not have the same opportunity of having many regular salesmen call on them with the ensuing service they can render.
5. Schools are prone not to have as many new materials brought before them for demonstration.
6. Schools may not have the same degree of adjustment satisfaction.
7. If leadership changes are not strong in the cooperative purchasing venture, the effectiveness of the program may be affected.
8. Large one-a-year purchases curtail the opportunity for custom attention to curriculum supply requirements.
9. Purchasing of low bid items may be the rule rather than the exception, sacrificing quality for price.
10. Local autonomy is jeopardized.

Summary

It is significant for public school administrators to acknowledge that cooperative purchasing does exist and its trend is gaining impetus. Volume buying is no longer a cost cutting technique to be used only by the giants of business, industry or large institutions. The concern for fair profit or even for survival has caused all types of institutions, from hospitals to schools to motor hotels to abrogate their mores of the past and pool their purchasing potential in an effort to acquire not only better prices on items, but better quality.

One continually hears the phrase, "That you never get something for nothing." This, in strict context, is true. However, as it relates to cooperative purchasing, if one extends effort in the planning of technique, of selection of items and volume purchasing for price and service, then he does accrue in the last analysis, more. On the other hand, he has not, as some folks would say, received something for nothing, but something in return for the district's professional effort to stretch dollars. Difference in price does not mean difference in quality. Often the same brand item is purchased for a different price because of volume and prompt payment discount.

Public schools across America have the responsibility of educating boys and girls. To do this, they must use public funds. Since budget expenditures are generally diversified in their adequacy to do the job, school administrators are constantly endeavoring to effectively use funds and stretch dollars. Cooperative purchasing may have some merit and use in this direction. It now becomes the professional responsibility of school administrators to determine and appraise if or to what extent cooperative purchasing might serve their school needs.

SCHOOL SERVICES . . .

SCHOOL LUNCHROOMS ARE A HEADACHE, BUT INESCAPABLE*

A school lunch program, from one point of view, is a *service* a school system provides its pupils. It is one of the nonessential services for conducting an educational program, one of several extracurricular activities generally accepted as a necessity. It has been around long enough that few people any longer debate its value. A school just isn't a school in this area without a lunch program. Occasionally we are reminded, however, especially in times of economic stress, that the school lunch program — like many other activities that have gained a foothold onto the educational system — is only a *service* that has little relationship to the fundamental purposes for which schools were originally established.

---

*Robert E. Wilson, "Eleven Headaches and Four Tranquilizers," reprinted, with permission, from *The Nation's Schools,* (December, 1957, 66-72.). Copyright 1957, The Modern Hospital Publishing Co., Inc., Chicago. All rights reserved. (Portions paraphrased.)

CONVENIENCE FOR MOTHERS

From another point of view, the school lunch program is a *convenience for working mothers,* or for mothers who play bridge, who take part in community social and welfare activities, or who just don't want their kids at home. The impetus to this baby-sitting function of school lunches was given during World War II when great numbers of women assisted in the defense efforts of the nation. The need for lunches served at school for this reason is no longer as severe as it was during the crisis. Once the habit is started, however, there is no backtracking! Today a school lunch program is unquestionably still a convenience to many parents.

From another standpoint, the school lunch program merely means an extra duty for teachers, and is at least partially responsible for their accusations that they are overworked, that they have jangled nerves, and that they don't even get time to go to the restroom. It gives them an opportunity to introduce the issue of extra pay for extra duty.

A school lunch program is a risk, an additional hazard with which school officials must cope: a risk from food poisoning, scaldings, cuts or falling on slippery floors.

From another point of view, the school lunch program is a charitable gesture for indigent children. This objective was stimulated during the depression years, when it was true that the only balanced, hot meals some children received each day were at the school lunch counter. Although the need for free lunches to indigent children has decreased substantially since World War II, and even though we are in the highest peak of prosperity and family income of the nation's history, most schools continue to provide many free lunches.

The school lunch department is a source of headaches so numerous as to be exceeded only by the number of headaches generated by the athletic department.

There are headaches arising from purchasing, management of personnel and wages, public relations, discipline during the lunch hour, from creating an inducement to school break-ins, from trying to perform mass feeding while complying with health and sanitation department requirements, from an additional set of records, and headaches from handling another set of complaints. . . .

FOUR ESSENTIALS FOR A GOOD PROGRAM

The two most important elements for developing an outstanding lunch program are the same as they are for any other enterprise; that is good management and good personnel.

The qualities essential for a good manager, again, are similar to those required for any other executive capacity. However, a good manager of a school cafeteria has the same problem as the manager of any other *public school* department, but differing from most business executives, namely, the school executive must be an expert in many fields.

The lunchroom manager must be an expert in human relations. She must possess good organizing and planning ability. She must be a dietitian. She must know purchasing and accounting, and she must have the freedom to plan and operate as her particular skills and abilities dictate.

More than any other factor, except for good management, I think the key to a good school lunch program is having good personnel. Again, I would list as the primary qualification for a successful cafeteria worker the ability to get along amicably with other people. The person must be able to adjust smoothly and quickly to a variety of changing situations and emergencies. These qualities are more important than skill. . . .

The third necessity for developing an excellent lunch program, of course, is *good equipment and utensils* — equipment that is economical and efficient, and easily maintained.

The fourth obvious ingredient needed for a good cafeteria program is *good food*. I am not sure whether this should be classified as an ingredient or as an outcome. No lunch program can be very successful if the food is not of acceptable quality in meeting the desires of the majority of the pupils, recognizing full well that we cannot please every child everyday. I would only suggest here that we need to exert greater effort toward achieving *quality* more than *economy* in our school lunches. We are so accustomed in school operations to trying to get by with as little money as possible that we have a tendency to serve a substandard meal rather than to charge what we ought to charge to serve good quality.

PRINCIPLES OF ORGANIZATION AND RESPONSIBILITIES FOR ADMINISTRATION OF SCHOOL FOOD SERVICE*

Each function in the central administration should contribute to the operation and improvement of the educational program for its ultimate goals. These functions include:

---

*Lewis R. Crum, "Responsibilities of the Superintendent and School Business Administrator in Working with the School Lunch Supervisor," Chicago: by permission of Association of School Business Officials, International, *47th Annual Volume of Proceedings,* 1961, 172-3.

1. A concern for all system-wide aspects of the educational program.
2. A determination of the results to be accomplished, plans of how those results are to be accomplished, the building of an organization to secure those results, direction and supervision of this organization, and control over the plans, organization and the results.
3. A concern of the problems of policy, organization, personnel, facilities and methods.
4. The supplying of leadership.

Every level of management is concerned with these same functions. Responsibilities are assigned by use of "job descriptions" and "assignments of responsibility." The levels at which one is to operate determine the specifics of his particular role and relationships he has with other people.

BASIC PRINCIPALS OF ORGANIZATION

There are certain principles of organization that should serve as guides to all who have responsibility to build an organization. Some of these are listed below.

1. Careful definition of duties, relationships and delegation of authority must be made thereby making it easier for persons to work together.
2. Provisions should be made so that people have an opportunity for growth and exercise initiative.
3. Those tasks that are most closely related should be grouped together.
4. Clear channels of communication should be maintained.
5. Opportuuity should be provided for all to participate in planning, policy making, and evaluating their own fields.
6. Provisions should be made for coordination and reinforcement of administrative positions.
7. The span of control should be within the limits of the people involved in the organization.
8. While the organization is built on functions and responsibilities and not the unique characteristics of individuals, flexibility should be provided that will permit adaptations necessary for operation.

RESPONSIBILITIES OF THE SUPERINTENDENT WITH REGARD TO THE SCHOOL LUNCH PROGRAM

The differences in the responsibilities of the Superintendent, Business Administrator and the Director of the School Lunch Program vary according to the levels of operation set up in the school organization. The size of the school district, its needs, its community and many other factors influence these differences.

However, some responsibilities can be listed that might be general enough to apply to the majority of school districts.

1. He should understand the aims and objectives of the school lunch program, as well as its requirements and regulations.
2. He should organize the central administration to maintain a lunch program.
3. He should establish district policies relative to the program.
4. He should interpret the school lunch program to the school and community.
5. He should help school lunch personnel become aware of their responsibilities for safety.

RESPONSIBILITIES OF THE SCHOOL BUSINESS ADMINISTRATOR IN WORKING WITH THE SCHOOL LUNCH SUPERVISOR

The School Business Administrator might have the same responsibilities as those of the Superintendent, except he is working at a different level and has a more direct responsibility to see that the goals are accomplished. Depending on the policy of decentralization of authority, he may be completely responsible or he may have a shared responsibility only.

Some of the responsibilities assigned to this position are:

1. He should plan and recommend for
   a. Food purchasing, storage, and distribution.
   b. Planning, equipping, and maintaining physical facilities.
   c. Personnel policies.
   d. Financial management.
2. He should periodically appraise and evaluate the program.

GENERAL VIEWS

The school lunch program must function in its proper perspective as a part of the total program.

Administrators expect all lunch personnel to respect all regulations that are necessary to govern the students. A negative attitude toward policies is detrimental.

Problems should be brought to the school business administrator so that he might work toward the solution of these problems. There should be in existence an open two-way system of communication allowing for free and open discussion of existing problems.

Personnel of the lunch program should have full authority to expedite the operation of their program. With this authority must come wisdom and understanding. If authority is used under these conditions, the program can deserve full support of the administration.

The execution of any plan of organization usually involves many other complex aspects, human relations, staff-line patterns, etc. To this end, I believe all job assignments should contain flexible provisions so as to permit smooth operation and quick adjustment to meet the needs of the situation.

QUALIFICATIONS FOR PUPIL TRANSPORTATION PERSONNEL*

The first member of the pupil transportation team is the school bus driver. In the beginning he was virtually the entire team. His qualifications—he had to know how to drive the bus. In the small, largely rural districts of that day, most anyone knew all the roads and where the children lived. It was simple to send the driver out with instructions to bring the children to school and take them home again.

Today, the entire picture has changed. Instead of transporting a few dozen children daily, individual drivers in large urban areas may transport several hundred children daily; the school discipline and public relations have become a part of the school bus driver's job. The qualifications for a school bus driver have obviously changed over the years. Yet in many places, school bus drivers are still employed on the basis of driving ability alone.

While he is at the wheel the school bus driver is the most important person in the school system. The lives of all the children on the bus are in his hands. It is our job as school administrators to see that they are capable, well-trained hands.

Today's school bus driver must not only be trained in the mechanics of driving the school bus; he must be proficient in the ways of handling students safely in and out of traffic, of teaching them safety, both on

*Lester C. Winder, "Qualifications for Pupil Transportation Personnel," Chicago: by permission of Association of School Business Officials, International, 47th Annual Volume of Proceedings, 1961, 191-193.

and off the bus, and of maintaining order and discipline on the bus. He must also be adept in public relations and have enough mechanical aptitude and training to be able to check his bus and make sure it is always in safe operating condition.

MECHANICS AND SHOP PERSONNEL

It is obvious that when the school bus driver checks his bus and finds something wrong, he will, in all probability, not have the time, tools or aptitude to make the necessary repairs. This brings us to another, and a relatively new, member of the pupil transportation team—the school bus mechanic.

With greater numbers of larger more complex school buses, many school boards and school administrators are realizing the advantages of school operated shops for the maintenance and servicing of equipment. A school bus mechanic, particularly one with factory training on the type of equipment he is working with, who works day after day with the same equipment and knows all its components, can maintain and service the equipment more efficiently and economically than an attendant at a neighborhood service station.

DIRECTOR OF TRANSPORTATION AND SUPERVISORS

Today there are 155,000 school buses in operation, transporting 11½ million pupils daily. More and more school buses are school owned. In the past 25 years, the trend has changed from 80% contracted buses to today, over 70% school owned.

Pupil transportation has become an integral part of the educational process. Unfortunately, many school boards have not accepted this fact. They look on transportation as a necessary evil which has been forced on them by reorganization and consolidation.

The merits of the enlarged school plant are accepted and the necessary expenditures are made to properly manage the academic program. But this is not so with the transportation management. All too often, it is pushed on an already overloaded school official who may have no experience or training in this field. He in turn delegates many of the responsibilities to the maintenance department or a junior who may also serve as a school bus driver. The program starts off on a haphazard basis and continues that way. Then the administrators go to national meetings such as this one and ask: "What can be done about our transportation problems?" The answer, in many cases, is: "Start with proper management."

The size of the transportation program should to a large degree, determine the management program. In a small operation, it can well be a part-time position, but it should be filled by a person "qualified" in pupil transportation management. In proportion to the size of the program, a full time director of transportation may be required, and in some cases, a director with one or a number of supervisors working under him.

A well-managed program is a well-coordinated program. The director of transportation, or the person in charge of the transportation management, should be proficient in all phases of the operation.

DIRECTOR OF TRANSPORTATION QUALIFICATIONS

1. Write specifications for the proper type of equipment to do the job most efficiently and economically for his particular type of operation. There are many types of equipment on the market, and varying conditions, such as terrain, climate and density of population must be considered.
2. Establish bus routes and schedule them so as to fully utilize the equipment. For example, in many cases, by properly staggering school hours, the same fleet can serve several schools.
3. Set up a preventive maintenance program and see that it is properly implemented so that the equipment is kept in first class condition. If the equipment is not properly maintained, it will be reflected in all other phases of the operation.
4. Provide a driver training program and train school bus drivers in all areas of driver responsibility.
5. Establish a "safety program" for school bus riders to acquaint pupil and parents with the "safety rules" and why they are necessary for the pupil's well being.
6. Handle student discipline pertaining to school bus riding.
7. Keep or cause to be kept all office records, including student, driver equipment, and financial; and submit all required state reports, etc.
8. Provide a program for special services, such as educational field trips, athletic trips, etc.

In addition, he should have all the necessary moral and character qualifications and be very adept in public relations.

FOR REFLECTION OR INVESTIGATION

1. Rationalize the hesitancy on the part of universities to develop programs for the preparation of school business managers.

2. How would an undergraduate program for training school business managers be superior to a graduate program?

3. Should school business managers be prepared by the College of Education or the College of Business[?]

4. Survey your state to determine the growth in the creation of the position of school business manager. Show the trends according to enrollment, per-pupil valuation of district, and amount of annual budgets.

5. What are the arguments for and against certification for school business managers?

6. Are there any school districts of your region which assign the school business manager in authority directly to the board for education?

Interview the business manager, superintendent, and board members to uncover the reasons for this arrangement.

7. Compare the costs of fire insurance premiums paid by your school district during the past ten years with the amount of money recovered through fire losses sustained by the district for the same period of time. This is referred to as the *loss-cost ratio*. Compare the ratio with those of other districts represented by members of your class. How can the ratio between costs and recoveries be maintained at a reasonable proportion?

8. Distinguish between plant operations and plant maintenance. Compare the percents of the total budget in your district spent for the two items this past fiscal year with that of other districts represented by members of the class. Explain the discrepancies.

9. Conduct a complete cost analysis of a repair job recently performed by the maintenance crew of your district to include overhead costs. Would the district have saved money through having the work performed by an outside contractor?

10. What are the different factors entailed in maintaining high morale for certificated and non-certificated personnel?

11. For the purchases made by your district during the past year, assign the authority to appropriate officers for making the decisions as to what to buy.

12. Select several common items which schools buy and compare what your district paid for those purchases last year with what was paid by other districts represented by members of your class. Find explanations for the differences in price.

13. Argue the case for and against transporting pupils to parochial schools on buses owned by a public school district. What are the merits and disadvantages in turning over all pupil transportation to a separate governmental agency?

14. Compare the costs among districts represented by members of your class for transporting pupils on board-owned buses as opposed to contract method.

15. Evaluate costs and other claimed advantages for central kitchens, catered lunches, frozen food lunches, and food dispensing machines.

16. Determine the actual subsidy of your school food service by the board of education during the past year.

BIBLIOGRAPHY

Adams, Bert K., and Joseph A. Perkins, Jr., "Needed — Better School Financial Accounting," *School Life,* XLV, May, 1963.

Baker, Joseph J., and Jon S. Peters, *School Maintenance and Operation,* Danville, Illinois: Interstate Printers and Publishers, 1964.

Boles, Harold W., *Step by Step to Better School Facilities,* New York: Holt, Rinehart and Winston, Inc., 1965.

————, "25 Significant Economies in New School Buildings," *American School Board Journal,* CXLVIII, January, 1964.

Bushnell, Don D., "Educational Data Processing and Public Education." Chicago: Association of School Business Officials, Intl., *49th Annual Volume of Proceedings,* 1963.

Casey, Leo M., *School Business Administration,* Washington, D.C.: The Center for Applied Research in Education, Inc., 1964.

Chaffee, Arthur and Joseph MacAllister, "Can Small Districts Afford a Business Manager?" *School Management,* VII, February 1964.

Chase, William W., *Problems in Planning Urban School Facilities.* Washington, D.C.: United States Office of Education, Bulletin No. 23, 1964.

Cronan, Marion L., *The School Lunch,* Peoria: Chas. A. Bennett Company, Inc., 1962.

Crum, Lewis R., "Responsibilities of the Superintendent and School Business Administrator in Working with the School Lunch Supervisor." Chicago: Association of School Business Officials, Intl., *47th Annual Volume of Proceedings,* 1961.

Feathertone, Glen and D. P. Culp, *Pupil Transportation: State and Local Programs,* New York: Harper & Row, Publishers, 1965.

Financial Accounting for Local and State School Systems, Standard Receipt and Expenditure Accounts, Washington, D.C.: United States Office of Education, Handbook II, Bulletin No. 4, 1957.

Finchum, R. N., and Glenn C. Boerrigter, "Improving the Fire Loss Record," *School Life,* XLIV, 8, June, 1962.

————, *Organizing the Maintenance Program,* Washington, D.C.: United States Office of Education, Bulletin No. 15, 1960.

————, *Organizing the Maintenance Procedures,* Washington, D.C.: United States Office of Education, Bulletin No. 17, 1964.

————, *School Plant Management: Administering the Custodial Program.* Washington, D.C.: United States Office of Education, Bulletin No. 4, 1961.

Foster, Charles, "How to Organize for Effective School Business Operation," *Nation's Schools,* LXVI, October, 1961.

Gross, Mason, "Modern School Buildings," *Nation's Schools,* LXVII, November, 1963.

Harrison, Forrest, "Investment of Idle School Funds," *School Life,* XLIV, January-February, 1962.

Hill, Fred W. (Chairman) *The School Business Administrator,* Chicago: Association of School Business Officials, International, 1960.

Hunt, R. L., "Why Bus Transportation," *Phi Delta Kappan,* XLII, May, 1961.

Knezevich, S. J., and J. G. Fowlkes, *Business Management of Local School Systems,* New York: Harper and Row, Publishers, 1960.

Miller, Murrell M., "A Critical Evaluation of the Superintendent-School Business Official Relationships in School Districts of California." Unpublished Ed.D. Dissertation, University of Southern California, 1963.

Mitchell, Herbert S., *School Budget Policies for Financial Control,* Danville, Illinois: Interstate Printers & Publishers, Inc., 1964.

O'Hearn, Aldan F., "Cooperative Purchasing Pros and Cons," Chicago: Association of School Business Officials, Intl., *48th Annual Volume of Proceedings,* 1962.

Olsen, L. C., "School Architecture and the Learning Process," *American School Board Journal,* 28-31, LXVI, October, 1961.

Roe, William, *School Business Management,* New York: McGraw-Hill Book Company, 1961.

Sack, Thomas F., *A Complete Guide to Building and Plant Maintenance,* Englewood Cliffs: Prentice-Hall, Inc., 1965.

School Management, "How to Take the Battle Out of Budget Adoption," IX, March, 1965.

Singer, H. Halleck, and Charles M. Micken, *The Law of Purchasing,* Danville, Illinois: Interstate Printers & Publishers, 1964.

Spence, Frank R., "A New Plan for Institutional Fire Insurance," *American School Board Journal,* CXLVI, February, 1962.

Whitlock, James W., "Financial Accounting and Reporting: Where to Improve," *School Life,* XLIII, June, 1961.

Wilson, Robert E., *Accounting and Record Keeping for Schools,* Kent, Ohio, Kent State University, 1959.

————, "Eleven Headaches and Four Tranquilizers," *Nation's Schools,* LX, December, 1957.

Whitlock, James W., *Automatic Data Processing in Education,* New York: The Macmillan Company, 1964.

Winder, Lester C., "Qualifications for Pupil Transportation Personnel." Chicago: Association of School Business Officials, Intl., *47th Annual Volume of Proceedings,* 1961.

Yankow, Harry, "Schools May be Using Obsolete Business Procedures," *Nation's Schools,* LXXV, March, 1965.

Chapter 14

Administration of an Attendance Unit — The Principal

The first position to be created for administering schools was that of principalship, a title succeeding that of headmaster. Creation of the office was the earliest administrative reaction to the phenomenon of large size in educational institutions. The teacher and the lay committee could share administrative chores as long as there were no more than two or three teachers per building. After the administrative tasks became too burdensome for either teachers or citizens to look after, a headmaster or principal was appointed from among the teaching corps to assume these duties.

This mode of emergence for the principal's position explains why it has taken nearly a century and a half for acceptance of the contemporary concept of stature and leadership which is advocated for that officer. At the beginning, the post was viewed merely as an office-type activity, a chore-performance, an appointment which relieves one of teaching responsibilities in order to do those executive jobs which teachers had not the time to do. Further, it was assumed that a more experienced teacher in the building was entitled to relief from the classroom, especially if it meant a reward of more money. The position, primarily an honor, entailed no special training or talent. This attitude lingers today in the minds of some citizen board members, indeed some teachers, despite the urging of students of school administration through most of the 20th century to think of the position as something more.

CHARACTERISTICS OF THE MODERN PRINCIPALSHIP

The major characteristic of the principalship today is its changing nature. Of the many definitions of the position offered in the past quarter-century, nearly all stress its leadership potentialities. Writers accent different segments of his jurisdiction which they want the leader-principal to lead — community, pupils, or staff — but the common denominator of leadership responsibilities refers to curriculum improvement. The final recognition of the principal as an instructional leader comes from the almost universal accounting practice today of classifying his salary as an instructional expense rather than an administrative expense.

This emphasis on educational leadership has forged new dimensions to his preparatory program and to the type of person who should be appointed to the post. Not only must he be knowledgeable about all those formal learning experiences which constitute the curriculum but he must be filled with learning theories and an understanding of child development. Beyond the process and content of learning, he needs the ability to relate classroom learning to the broader aspirations of the community, state, and nation, a talent sharpened by a study of philosophy, history, sociology, economics, political science, and the arts. Even these two enormous areas of skill are useless to a leader of curriculum improvement who lacks the crucial knowledge of how the objectives are to be accomplished through other people. The task implies expertness in supervision and evaluation, but more than that, the always important skill essential to leaders of social organizations—the ability to stimulate others—is necessary for the principal.

Another major change taking place in the task of principalship results from the trend toward decentralizing authority from the system's central office to the local attendance unit; this trend is unavoidable as school districts grow larger. The releasing of greater responsibility to the building means increased autonomy for the principal and his staff in decision-making, to the point that we find almost a complex of "local superintendents" within the large school system. Thus, today the principal is expected to be not only a curriculum leader but also the administrator of physical facilities, of school-home relationships, of personnel, and of limited financial affairs. He is assisted in these responsibilities by specialized personnel from the central office, but he is the accountable officer within his attendance unit. This change has also brought more extensive preparation for the position to include partial knowledge of nearly all the tasks normally associated with the superintendent's job.

This changing posture of the principal's post has also fostered one of the most difficult operational relationships within the entire school system. As an autonomous administrative unit, the principal is clearly in an authority or line position, accountable for everything within his jurisdiction and accountable directly to the superintendent. Accompanying the expansion of administrative organization within the total system has been the addition of one or more echelons of central staff officers. In large city districts the second echelon consists of assistant or associate superintendents with a third echelon of directors, coordinators, supervisors and perhaps another layer of specialized officers normally functioning under such titles of psychologist, therapist, public relations officer, and health personnel.

Conflict marks the relationships of these central staff officers with principals. It must be remembered that the superintendent's assistants are performing a part of the superintendency function and, therefore, carry authority. At the same time, they perform an advisory, or consultive, role in their relationships to the superintendent and to fellow administrators, including the principals. Since channels for flow of authority must be preserved for the sake of efficient and amicable operations in any organization, and in deference to the basic principle of accountability, it has been found that central staff personnel must be assigned to an advisory status when working in any single building; the principal's authority prevails should disagreements erupt. The staff officer is accountable for the achievement of a function throughout the system and, as such, operates "over" all principals. Within a building, he operates "under" the principal.

The decentralizing trend has made the principal's position more like that of the superintendent's position. The principalship has become more of a coordinating activity and less of a "doing" activity. The extent of this likeness is one of degree, however, and depends primarily upon the size of the building. The principal of a small building has no one to whom he may delegate administrative tasks, often not even an office secretary, and therefore, his job is still that of personal "doing." Only the larger buildings, which for the most part include junior and senior high schools, are fortunate enough to have assistant principals, department heads, guidance personnel, supervisors attached to the building, and other specialized personnel who can absorb some of the administrative load. It is in these larger units, or small ones located in spectacularly wealthy school districts, that the similarity between the principal's and superintendent's *modus operandi* may be seen clearly.

This point does not argue that the two positions are identical and require the same preparatory programs. There are still differences in the day-by-day functioning, which should be recognized in the training programs and in the selection of officers. The principal is much closer to teachers and students than is the superintendent. Each day the principal of even a large high school is likely to be involved in counseling and discipling of students, in lunch room or transportation incidents, teacher assignments, classroom schedules, curricular and extra-curricular events, direct supervision, grading systems, and probably parental anxieties. Without attempting to depreciate the importance of these activities, the building principal's daily calendar is innundated with [minutiae] which have a way of crowding out " big thinking" unless he is fortified with a broad philosophy, organizational talent, a proper concept of his role, and adequate staff to relieve him of task doing.

Probably the major handicap to achieving the stature and expectations of his position as urged by administration experts is the failure of boards of education to overcome their traditional attitudes toward the office. Still thinking of the principal as an upgraded teacher, too many boards continue to assign him a part-time teaching load. Other boards, motivated by economic pressures, believe they are saving money by having the principal teach classes, unaware that they are getting neither a principal nor a teacher from the expenditure for his salary. Elsewhere, board members acting upon the advice of the superintendent, cling to the belief that a principal ought to teach at least one class in order to understand the teacher's point of view. There is no research to establish how long it takes for a person to gain an understanding of teachers' problems and viewpoints, but if he has not learned them by the time he is appointed to the principalship it is doubtful that he ever will. One shouldn't have to pump a well for a lifetime to discover the water.

Some principals are deprived the chance of becoming what is expected from the office by lack of adequate clerical assistance. The duties involved in the administration of any office divide themselves into postponable and non-postponable chores. Reports with deadlines, accounting, telephone calls, attendance problems, and assorted emergencies cannot be postponed. Most of these do not demand the attention of a highly trained executive. But unless they may be delegated to an appropriate clerk, the postponable instructional and leadership tasks will wait while the taxpayers reap the false economy of paying a $15,000 administrator for doing the work of a $4,000 secretary.

When a building is adequately staffed in the office, classrooms, and special services as called for in the modern concept of education, the principal's daily schedule changes substantially from the conventional one. After he has organized personnel into an efficient team, he devotes most of his day to acts of coordinating, consulting, advising, stimulating, communicating, planning and evaluating. One of the major changes in his approach may be seen in the conduct of faculty meetings. A total staff meeting will rarely occur, except when essential for achieving commonality within the building. Rather there will be numerous small work groups, gathered because of common interests by grade, subject matter, or special project, led by department heads or grade chairmen, or *ad hoc* appointments.

TRENDS IN OPPORTUNITIES AND PREPARATION
FOR THE PRINCIPALSHIP

The opportunities for an entree into an administrative career will continue to be most numerous in the principalship for several years in the future. There are approximately 92,000 public elementary schools in the United States today and 26,000 secondary schools. Nonpublic schools number about 20,000. Allowing for the number of schools without principals, and for those which have assistant principals, it can be interpolated that there are about 137,000 principalship positions in the country. It is predictable that this number of opportunities will remain static for the remainder of the 1960's, probably increasing in the following two decades if population estimates for succeeding years prove to be accurate. The normal growth in the number of buildings which will result from slightly increased enrollments will be offset by school district consolidations which gradually eliminate old and small buildings. While the number of principals' positions is not expected to increase sharply, the principalship provides the best vehicle for an administrative aspirant seeking his first appointment. Further openings are being created by the expansion of vocational schools, adult educational programs, and special summer schools.

The avenues to the appointment are being altered, however, by the upgraded status of the position. It is expected that there will be far fewer elevations directly from the classroom without some intervening readiness attempts. State certification and board of education specifications for the position are insisting that the appointee hold at least a Master's degree with training in school administration.

Spreading throughout the country, especially on the elementary school level, is the most fruitful device yet developed for preparing an applicant to assume the heavy responsibilities for the work—the on-the-job programs of one or two years which appear under labels of cadet principal, apprenticeship, or internship. Under the sponsorship and financial underwriting by a local board of education, these programs entail a critical screening and an assortment of understudy experiences. However, as valuable as apprenticeship programs are, experience is already pointing to some unnecessary weaknesses. In some districts cadets, undergoing an otherwise rich practical training [,] must perform tasks poor in training value just to get the jobs done. Elsewhere a fledgling trainee is assigned to a well-structured program but allowed to fend for himself without a progress evaluation. A third possible weakness arising from on-the-job training programs is the threat of inbreeding. A school district needs to promote from within to the principalship for various reasons, but it should never shut the door to recruiting new talent from without. To this date the fine apprenticeship programs have not been evaluated widely, but are merely assumed to be good. All of these alleged shortcomings can be overcome. One of the most promising solutions appears in the few systems which coordinate their on-the-job experiences with a university's faculty and research resources.

While the practice still exists, another avenue to the principalship is gradually disappearing. The thought of natural ascension from elementary school to junior high to senior high school is being replaced by the recognition of the differences in the curriculum and pupil problems at the various levels. As the expected prime mover for curriculum improvement, the principal must be a resource person for ideas and know-how. He must not only recognize faulty teaching methodology and weaknesses in subject content but he should also suggest panaceas. Further, he must recognize when it is time for outside help. The "promotion ladder" system ignores the uniqueness of each level of school organization and is especially demoralizing to the elementary school principal who is regarded as the bottom rung.

Training programs for an elementary principal reflect the need for being an expert in primary and intermediate curriculum problems; the requirement for curricular understandings may be seen in preparatory programs for the secondary school principal. The major void in principalship preparatory programs continues to exist for the person who wishes to administer a junior high school. The trend toward reorganizing school systems to develop a middle school only complicates his preparation. As educators seek answers to the unsettled question of how to provide appropriate learning experiences for the pre-adoléscent, and as universities build teacher-training curriculums for that level, perhaps a path will be cleared toward an ideal readiness program for this principal.

State certification laws which require that an applicant for an elementary principal's certificate must have had teaching experience in the elementary school, and secondary school teaching experience for obtaining a high school principal's certificate, are also testing the "natural ascension" practice of elevating principals.

The changes being effected in the building principal's position are stimulating serious discussion as to whether prevailing preparatory programs will produce the caliber of administrator demanded by these changes. There is reason for doubt that the prototype undergraduate program in teacher-professional education augmented by a master's degree which stresses more educational and "how-to" administrative courses will yield a man or woman ready for the authority handed him. While he is an authority delegated from the superintendent and board of education, and although there may [be] carefully delineated job descriptions for his action, the principal is having thrust upon him a position of unlimited potential. This responsibility calls for an individual who not only knows curriculum, principles of administration, communications, and business management, but also for a visionary who can fit the school's program into the needs and wants of society. As the "superintendent" of his attendance unit, his skill should be only slightly different and perhaps slightly less than that of the chief school administrator. It is understandable, then, that there is considerable discussion among professional educators, and within the principals' professional organizations, about upgrading the preparation to the sixth year, two full years beyond the bachelor's degree. Although a few states already have these certification requirements, the National Elementary Principals Association and the National Association of Secondary School Principals have under consideration the proposal to specify for membership in those organizations a preparation attainment equivalent to that of the American Association of School Administrators. It is reasonable to forecast extensive in-service activity for experienced principals in the next few years. In addition, more research and recommendations for screening future principals in training will occur through such devices as the simulated materials of the University Council of Educational Administration.

As these preparation and job expectations increase, one can predict a decreasing differential between the salaries of principals and superintendents. Notwithstanding the many exceptions, the average high school principal's salary tends to be about two-thirds that of the average superintendent's; salaries for junior high and elementary principals trail behind those of the senior high principals.

A bold look at the future suggests the possibility of a major reorganization of administrative hierarchy in school districts. One envisions all principals becoming assistant superintendents with the typical specialized services functioning within the building. The central staff accountable to the superintendent would include only administrative specialists for such matters as finance, public relations, and business affairs. There might be associate superintendents in large cities for coordinating the activity of assistant superintendents — the principals. An abbreviated sketch of this dream appears below.

It will be noted that this proposal takes central staff specialists out of the channel of authority between the superintendent and his "assistant

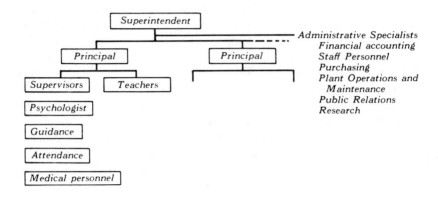

superintendents" of attendance units. Central staff service officials, those not assigned directly to buildings or perhaps a cluster of smaller elementary buildings under the administration of a regional assistant superintendent, would be regarded strictly as service or advisory personnel for the overall administration of the school system. They would have no authority over principals or other personnel in buildings.

The plan would solve the persistently disturbing relationships concerning accountability. Only the superintendent and principals would be accountable officers; all others would be service specialists accountable to either the superintendent or principal. The idea would be especially suitable to the organizational plan, becoming increasingly popular, in both large and medium-sized school districts, of the *Educational Park* concept. In essence, this concept calls for a return to the older K-12 plan, still operative in tiny school districts, with its many advantages for control and for casual personal interrelationships. A large school district could become a series of K-12 plans scattered throughout the community. Each plan would be a semi-autonomous subdistrict with a senior high school as the hub of an area which includes the feeder elementary and middle schools.

The idea is closer than it seems. Several large districts are already trying to operate administratively with central staff officers serving in advisory roles to principals. They find it difficult to arrange, however, under the conventional line-and-staff concepts. The next problem-solving step may be the final move as suggested here.

THE BUILDING PRINCIPALSHIP ...

HISTORY OF THE PRINCIPALSHIP POSITION*

The high school principalship is the oldest administrative position in American education. It antedates both the superintendency and the elementary school principalship. That the early high school principalship was not a professional position as it is conceived in progressive school systems today is illustrated by the duties the early principal was called upon to perform.

The duties of master or principal of the early colonial secondary school were extremely varied. In addition to teaching and administering his school, he often served as town clerk, church chorister, official visitor of the sick, bell ringer of the church, grave digger, and court messenger and performed other occasional duties. . . .

Development of the principalship in city schools. While the elementary school principalship does not extend backward in point of time so far as does the high school principalship, it began to emerge a century ago. Cities developed rapidly in the United States after 1830, and school enrollments, especially in the elementary schools, increased at a very rapid rate. In the fast-growing cities the number of schools and their increasing enrollments made it physically impossible for the superintendent to administer and supervise the work of the individual schools in person. It was evident that someone must be responsible for the organization of the school. This individual must see that there was continuity of teaching materials and that pupils progressed through the grades in an orderly manner. Consequently the superintendent turned to the head teacher in these local schools as the person best qualified to carry out his policies.

In an earlier day it had been a frequent practice to have reading and writing schools housed in the same building. The grammer master presided over the reading school and the writing master over the other. Children usually spent a half-day with each master. The divided authority

---

*Paul B. Jacobson, William C. Reavis, and James D. Logsdon, *The Effective School Principal,* second edition, Englewood Cliffs, N.J.: reprinted by permission of Prentice-Hall, Inc., 1963, 491-498.

quite naturally hindered the development of local school administration. The Lancastrian, or monitorial, system also hindered the grading of the schools, since under this system one person was responsible for the instruction, although he was assisted by a number of monitors. At first the person in charge of the schools was known as the "principal teacher" or "headmaster," the latter term being one in common use today to designate the administrative head of a private school. The former, shortened to "principal," is the common term used to designate the person responsible for a public school.

As might well be expected, the relations between the principal teacher and the other teachers were not clearly defined and could easily become a source of friction. The early records of Cincinnati show how the school committee differentiated between the respective duties of principal teachers and teachers in 1839.

The principal teacher was: (1) to function as the head of the school charged to his care; (2) to regulate the classes and course of instruction of all the pupils, whether they occupied his room or the rooms of other teachers; (3) to discover any defects in school and apply remedies; (4) to make defects known to the visitor or trustee of ward, or district, if he were unable to remedy conditions; (5) to give necessary instruction to his assistants; (6) to classify pupils; (7) to safeguard school houses and furniture; (8) to keep the school clean; (9) to instruct assistants, (10) to refrain from impairing the standing of assistants, especially in the eyes of their pupils; (11) to require the cooperation of his assistants.

The assistant teachers, on the other hand, were: (1) to regard the principal teacher as the head of the school; (2) to observe his directions; (3) to guard his reputation; (4) to make themselves thoroughly acquainted with the rules and regulations adopted for the government of the schools.

The committee further pointed out that principal teachers were selected on account of their knowledge of teaching methods, characteristics of children, and common problems of schools. Lack of firmness in the performance of duties by the principal teacher was at times felt by the trustees. Many assistant teachers were so well versed in their work as to require little or no working relations. Mutual cooperation between principal and assistant teachers was especially important, the committee felt, because of frequent changes in the teaching personnel, and because, without it, good order and teaching efforts would suffer.

It is claimed that one of the first elementary schools to have all departments united under an administrative principal was the Quincy School in Boston in 1847. John Philbrick, the principal of the school, who later became the Superintendent of Schools in Boston, is generally credited with this achievement. . . .

The cities of the Middle West had less trouble in eliminating the "double-headed," or reading and writing, schools than in the East, where these schools had become more firmly entrenched. Philbrick was able to eradicate them in Boston in 1855. In New York, however, there were a dozen or more such schools at the end of the nineteenth century.

By the middle of the nineteenth century, the status of the principalship in large cities was as follows: (1) a teaching male principal was the controlling head of the school; (2) female and primary departments had women principals under the direction of the male principal; and (3) the principal had prescribed duties which were limited largely to discipline, routine administrative acts, and grading of pupils in the various rooms.

Release of principals from teaching. In order to carry out their duties efficiently, the principals were frequently released from teaching part of the time. As early as 1857 the principals in some of the schools in Boston were relieved of their teaching duties for part of each day, and in other schools one or two half-days a week were set aside for inspection and examination of classes other than their own. A teacher known as the head assistant took charge of the principal's class during these periods. Other cities employed similar plans to free the principal for the performance of administrative and supervisory duties which were beginning to emerge.

During the period from the middle of the nineteenth century to 1900, a shift occurred in the administrative duties prescribed for principals. New duties, such as responsibility for organization and general management, and control of pupils and buildings and grounds, were required. School authorities were beginning to realize that the principalship offered professional opportunities. The individual who merely met emergencies as they arose in the local school was no longer entirely satisfactory.

During the last half of the nineteenth century, the prestige of the principalship was greatly enhanced. In the large cities the principal gained the right to decide which pupils should be promoted. Orders to teachers from the central office were sent through his hands. He gained the right to have a part in the transfer and assignment of teachers. The last responsibility was important to the local school, since the supply of trained teachers in cities was not always equal to the demand. However, if a principal wished to keep a teacher who desired to teach in a better part of the city, particularly if it was nearer her home, his wishes were likely to be ignored. The principal also was expected to enforce standards which would safeguard the health and morals of the pupils, to rate and supervise the janitors, and to requisition both educational and maintenance supplies and equipment. By the year 1900 the principal in city systems was clearly recognized as the administrative head of his school.

Changes in duties in recent years. By 1900 it was customary for principals in large cities to select their administrative assistants. They had also gained the right to choose cadets to assume full teaching status in the schools, and to assign or transfer teachers to their duties within the building except when salary increments were involved.

Clerical help had to be provided if the principal was to be relieved of routine tasks to give attention to important professional duties. In large cities the first and second decades of the present century saw the principal's office staffed with clerical assistants roughly in proportion to his needs. It was usually not an easy task to secure adequate clerical help in a public school office. The first relief for the principal from clerical routine was secured by using substitute teachers on a part-time basis. It is now generally conceded that a clerk should be provided in a school on the basis of approximately one for each 20 teachers in the elementary school or for each 500 pupils enrolled in the high school.

As the schools were increased in size, the problems of heating, ventilating, and caring for buildings by the custodial staff increased enormously.

In most moderate-sized and large cities, the principal was generally relieved of direct responsibility for the condition of the school plant, except for those duties of a general supervisory character. The development tended to free the principal for educational leadership instead of burdening him with details. However, not all principals have taken this view. Some seem to think that the developing responsibilities of the head engineer or custodian infringe on administrative prerogatives. Occasionaly unfortunate situations have arisen between the principal and the head engineer, although, happily, such cases have been relatively infrequent.

During the early years of the twentieth century, many principals experimented with various ways to break the "lockstep" of the graded .system. Whereas their efforts had been focused on inaugurating the graded system for 50 or 75 years preceding, they were now trying to remedy the defects which had become apparent in use. Various plans were tried, often with success, to individualize instruction or to care for individual differences.

The organization and supervision of the extracurricular duties in both elementary and high schools have become increasingly important since 1920. How such duties are cared for constitutes a challenge to the principal's competence as a school administrator.

THE RISE OF SUPERVISION BY PRINCIPALS

The administrative duties of the principal developed before his supervisory function was fully realized; and, as a result, the former have often tended to monopolize the major portion of the principal's time. Quite generally the superintendent intended to improve the instruction in the schools, as was expected of him. In many of the smaller school systems, supervision is still his function and is performed by him if it is done at all.

CHANGING CONCEPTS OF THE PRINCIPALSHIP . . .

CUBBERLEY'S CONCEPT OF THE PRINCIPALSHIP IN THE EARLY 20TH CENTURY*

The principal must remember that he holds a particularly responsible position as a model in his community, somewhat corresponding to that of the priest in the parish under the old régime of the church. He must, in his dress, his manner, his speech, and his bearing so conduct himself that he will easily win and hold the respect of those teachers and pupils who have grown up under the best home influences, and who know the best social usages and practices of the world.

To this end he must remember to carry himself at all times as a gentleman of the world should and would. He must be clean, both in his person and in his speech and acts. His clothing, his cuffs and collar, and his shoes should be kept in good condition. His hair should be trimmed frequently and kept clean and neatly combed. He must be careful to shave every morning. There must be nothing offensive about his breath or his person. On the streets and about his school, at least, he must not smoke. He must not frequent places where gentlemen do not go. In his dealings with his teachers he must be impartial, considerate, and just, and must show no special attentions and play no favorites in the group. His statements must be absolutely reliable; he must not shilly-shally to and fro; and his loyalty and support of both teacher and superintendent should be unquestioned.

---

*Ellwood P. Cubberley, *The Principal and His School,* Boston: by permission of Houghton-Mifflin Company, 1923, 26-27, 40-41, 45, 269-270.

Every executive, too, needs a good saving sense of humor. Many a situation is partly solved by laughing over it, or at least seeing its humorus side. In all his contacts with teachers, pupils, and parents he must seem both genuine and human. Pompous dignity will count for nothing, nor will a too familiar manner inspire respect. Freakish clothes, a singular manner, obsequiousness, or roughness and lack of consideration for others must all be equally avoided.

Given good personal qualities, good training, good executive sense, energy, industry, the ability to concentrate his efforts, studious habits, and the willingness to postpone present pleasures for the sake of a larger future, a young man or woman, entering the principalship in a city school system to-day, should be able to succeed in a large way. The service is important, and the scope of one's influence larger than most principals realize. . . .

A principal's work calls for good practical business sense, a good time sense and sense of proportion, punctuality in all official relationships, some genuine political skill in handling difficult people, frankness combined with courtesy when frankness is called for, and at times courage and conviction. Occasionally he will find it necessary to assume control and command the situation; at other times he will offer good advice; again he must be a petitioner and take what he can get; and at still other times he must execute orders and not question why. It will call for much good judgment to know which rôle to assume as different situations present themselves. He must know his rights and also his duties; know when to stand firm and when to go slowly; have a genius for quickly getting close to the heart of every situation and deciding what ought to be done; know the meaning of loyalty to the decisions of those in authority; be able to establish fixed places of authority in his school and to have that authority met; and know how to handle difficult situations with both firmness and tact. To have a good grasp of the fundamental principles involved in proper school administration, and to settle problems arising in the light of these principles, is one of the surest means of handling difficult situations correctly.

It should be the aim of every principal to settle wisely and satisfactorily as many difficult situations as possible; to refer as few cases as possible to the central office for decision; and to have the smallest possible number of appeals from his decisions go to the central office. Few surer means than just this ability could be thought out for winning the approval of those above for his administrative skill. . . .

Saving time for work. Most principals who find themselves swamped with routine administrative duties could emancipate themselves if they desired to do so. A first step would be to make a careful analysis of what they actually do. One good means is to make an accurate record by minutes of what one does during each school day, for a week or two at a time, and analyze this record into percentages of a day. Then, with such a table before one, raise the question for each item as to whether the time spent on it was time well spent. . . .

FIGHTING AMONG PUPILS

Fighting is another common cause of trouble in every school. Among boys from the ages of ten to twelve fighting is more common than among either the older or the younger children. At this age the instinct for fighting seems to be at its height. Boys appear to fight from the love of the game. Girls seldom fight, and when they do it is usually more distressing than serious. Boys on the whole fight fairly, and frequently a fight between two boys clears the atmosphere and makes friends of the combatants as nothing else could do. If the mothers of the boys can be kept from taking too active a part in the affair it usually has no bad results.

When two boys, fairly evenly matched, between whom trouble has long been brewing finally "get at it," it is a good plan for the principal not to be in any great hurry to arrive and stop the fight. Sometimes it is a good plan to let hostilities proceed until there are signs of slackening, and then step up and tell boys they would better stop now and go in and wash up. The case can be investigated afterward. If the case was one where a mutual settlement was inevitable, and would have taken place outside if it had not happened on the school ground, and if it seems that a satisfactory settlement has now been arrived at, it is usually best not to inflict punishment at all.

A CONTEMPORARY VIEW OF
PRINCIPALSHIP*

Within the system the recognized administrative unit is the individual school, whether it be elementary, junior high school, senior high school,

---

*Herold C. Hunt, "Educational Administration and Finance," a chapter from *Becoming an Educator, Van Cleve Morris and others,* Boston: by permission of Houghton-Mifflin Company, 1963, 299.

technical, vocational, or "special," i.e., serving special educational interests and needs. For each school there is a principal, a position evolving from the expanding one-room school to today's larger and more complex instructional unit.

The duties assigned to the principalship are usually classified under large divisions. These generally include program organization, supervision of instruction, relationships with directors, supervisors and other central-office personnel, community leadership, personnel management, clerical routines, and the professional leadership of the school staff. In many small schools, some teaching is also expected. The duties are both large and small, significant and trivial, permanent and fleeting, the kind that consume time and energy — frequently preventing the principal from giving appropriate attention to the educational program and yet so essential to operating the school smoothly that they cannot be delayed or disregarded.

THE PRINCIPAL MUST ORGANIZE AND DELEGATE*

Some principals never differentiate between jobs that can be performed by others and those that belong strictly to the school head. As a result those principals themselves try to meet all the demands made upon them. In order to do so they are usually compelled to neglect certain important matters that are not immediate in their demands and can usually be postponed. The urgency of immediate demands is allowed to usurp attention to the exclusion of ultimate school objectives. The principal who yields to this tendency becomes an administrator of emergencies. He seldom leaves his office during the school day because of requests from inside the school which are directed to his office or because of outside demands made over the telephone.

Everything in the way of demands or requests is encouraged to converge on the principal's office, with the result that the principal becomes engrossed in administrative details.

---

*Paul B. Jacobson, William C. Reavis, James D. Logsdon, *The Effective School Principal,* 2nd. ed., Englewood Cliffs, N.J.; reprinted by permission of Prentice-Hall, Inc., 1963, 21-22.

ORGANIZATION OF FUNCTIONS NECESSARY

Other principals study the character of the demands made upon them as a means of avoiding enslavement to details. They also study the personal qualifications of their teachers and students with a view to delegating responsibilities in the interest of personal development and effective administration. Instead of trying to do everything, this type of principal organizes his work functionally and delegates to clerks, teachers, and students the duties which can and should be performed by persons other than the school head. In this way the time and energy of the principal are conserved for the consideration of demands which he alone can meet. He is thus able to plan an organization of duties for his school based on functional differentiation, cooperation, and participation. The organization is potentially as effective as the total abilities of the persons who share in its functioning.

The absence of such an organization in a school can be quickly detected by the confusion which prevails when the head is absent. Without the principal to assume responsibility for everything, there can be little driving ahead for definite results. Activities will be aimless, for there is no one to call the signals for the school team. Everyone waits for orders which do not come because of the leader's absence.

In schools with an effective administrative organization, the presence of the leader is not essential to continued functioning. Everyone knows his duties and assumes his customary responsibility without waiting for orders. Distractions were largely eliminated when the organization was formed. Each member of the organization performs his particular duties. In brief, the team knows its plays and can carry on effectively in the absence of its leader.

EMPHASIS IN ORGANIZATION

The emphasis given by many principals to duties of the managerial and clerical types may be accounted for partly by the prominence given to such duties by boards of education in their published rules and regulations. Since approximately 85 per cent of the published rules of boards of education made for the benefit of principals are concerned with managerial and clerical activities, it is little wonder that principals tend to engage in such activities to the neglect of professional duties, as is often charged. The implication is that board rules for principals, as well as the conception by the principals of the best way for professional officers to utilize their school time, should be improved.

THE DECENTRALIZING TREND
IN SCHOOL ADMINISTRATION*

Before specific programs currently in use are described, it is appropriate to take a brief interpretative view of the problem: Should administration of the school district be centralized or decentralized? This problem will, ultimately, have an effect on the organizational plan for instruction which will be most effective in an individual school. Admittedly, the pattern of organization is secondary to program, but it is also true that an appropriate organization will facilitate the formulation and practice of a good program of instruction.

Line-and-staff organization, district-wise, has been the traditional scheme in America's schools. Under this design, in which planning and performance are almost completely separated, administrators in the central office make the plans and send their instructions down the line of authority to teachers and pupils. Such a plan is probably most effective in the small community with only one school. Centralized control under this plan is considered to be highly efficient in the prevention of friction and avoidance of waste which results from duplication of effort, since all schools in the district are usually controlled from one central point.

As a community grows and school units become a part of the larger district, the exclusive use of the line-and-staff organization becomes ineffective. The principal at the local level tends to view it as a far-away power with preconceived and unchangeable ideas. To counteract this feeling, some districts have placed a large degree of ultimate power in the hands of the local school principal, have set up official lay, or lay-teacher, bodies, and have given them responsibility for outlining policy for local schools. Such decentralizing procedure tends to provide local checks and balances of such strength that control by the immediate community becomes more feasible and important.

A striking example of a large city organizational structure involving a decentralized line-and-staff distribution is that of Chicago, Illinois. Each of the twenty district superintendents is responsible for the educational program in the elementary and high schools within a specific geographic area. The district superintendent is the instructional leader within the district. The district superintendents in turn are responsible

---

*Paul J. Misner, Frederick W. Schneider, and Lowell G. Keith, *Elementary School Administration,* Columbus, Ohio: by permission of Charles E. Merrill Books, Inc., 1963, 66-68.

to the Associate Superintendent in Charge of Instruction for the north or south section of the city, and the Associate Superintendent in Charge of Administration. The district superintendent works with Parent-Teacher Association representatives as well as representatives of community organizations within his area of responsibility. According to General Superintendent Benjamin C. Willis, each of the districts includes an enrollment of approximately 25,000 children.

There seems to be a trend at present toward decentralizing school administration. Houston examined the problem of decision-making in industry and related his findings to the problem of decision-making in centralized and decentralized school units. He found that decentralized administration is identified with democratic administration and that professional people need the freedom and autonomy that accompanies decentralized administration. He concluded that decentralized administration within a school unit leads to the improvement of teachers, pupils, and administration, just as it leads to improvement of industrial decision-making, and subsequently to the improvement of the operation; that decentralized administration brings a decision closer to an actual need, and thereby betters the organization; and that the greater the individual differences influencing teacher professionalism among staff members, the greater the need for increased democratic administration.

The outstanding schools in this country and abroad, whether public or private, are those possessing a considerable degree of autonomy. Principals and teachers in these schools seem to experience an increased sense of unity in meeting needs and interests of boys and girls in the community. Some authorities are recommending that no decentralized unit exceed a maximum of fifty teachers.

1959 SURVEY REVEALS THAT SCHOOL SYSTEMS ARE SLOW IN DECENTRALIZING ADMINISTRATION TO ELEMENTARY SCHOOL*

In recent years a new trend in the administration of elementary schools has been emerging. Increasingly there have been indications that the growing complexity of the program and purpose of the public elementary school has brought with it a realization that the individual

---

*Stuart E. Dean, *Elementary School Administration and Organization,* Washington, D.C.; U.S. Office of Education, Bulletin 1960, No. 11, 89-91, 94.

school must have wider administrative latitude. If education is truly a process which reflects its environment, then the manner in which it meets this responsibility must vary from place to place. If education is to be related to a dynamic society, then it must be sensitive in responding to changing conditions. If the schools are sincere in their desire for effective community relations, then they must be in a position to assimilate and to act upon the beneficial results. . . .

It is, therefore, from the point of view of exploring this new concept and trend that the subject was included in this national survey of public

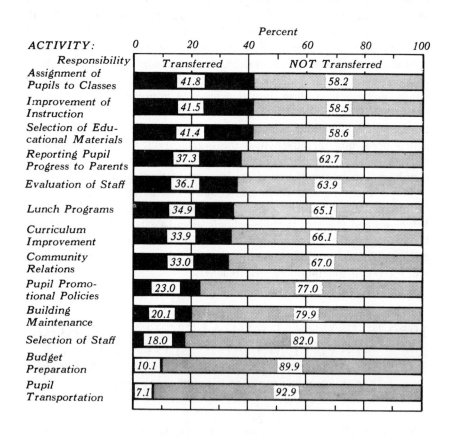

EXTENT OF TRANSFER OF ADMINISTRATIVE RESPONSIBILITIES FROM THE CENTRAL OFFICE TO THE INDIVIDUAL LOCAL ELEMENTARY SCHOOL, IN URBAN PLACES WITH POPULATIONS ABOVE 2,500, BY U.S. PERCENTAGES.

elementary school organization and administration. This pursuit has had two applications: First, to ascertain to what extent this development is actually taking place; and, second, to see if a followup study on implications for principals of elementary schools is necessary. . . .

In summarizing these findings, several conclusions are reached. In the first place, despite a certain amount of transfer of responsibility from the central office to the local individual elementary school, the movement, as a whole, is not yet being carried on to any major extent. Actually, in no case has this type of transfer been made by more than 50 percent of the urban places of the United States. Second, the greatest amount of this type of change has taken place with pupil accounting policies and with instructional policies, i.e., the assignment of pupils to classes, the improvement of instruction, and the selection of educational materials. Conversely, the least amount of change has taken place with business policies and staff personnel policies, i.e., pupil transportation, budget preparation, and the selection of staff. Third, about one-third of the urban places report this type of activity in lunch programs, curriculum improvement, and community relations. Finally, as based upon this evidence, for the present time, at least, it is clear that there is no concerted drive to transfer responsibility for administrative policy from the central administration to individual schools.

From an analysis of the population group practices in this connection, some additional observations are pertinent. In general, there is a pattern which suggests that the largest city group has undergone the least amount of change in this development, and the pattern varies inversely with the size of the urban places. In other words, there is a greater incidence of local, elementary school autonomy with respect to administrative policy and responsibility among the group IV urban places than among the group I urban places. Again, the greatest amount of change is with respect to instructional procedures and the least change is in the realm of business management functions. This leads to the supposition that elementary school principals in the smaller urban places are more likely to find themselves carrying a higher degree of policy responsibility for administrative activities. Similarly, the lesser degree of this type of responsibility carried by principals in the largest urban places undoubtedly reflects the existence of larger central office administrative staffs, with an attendant standardization of operational and administrative procedures.

Regionally, no apparent deviations or trends stand out. The findings rather closely parallel the national situation. However, there is some slight indication that the West, in general, shows less of this transfer of administrative responsibility, and the Northeast slightly more.

Therefore, with reference to the theory that the individual school should have a higher degree of administrative policy autonomy, present indications are that this plan is not being put into practice. Less than one-half of the urban places in the United States report that this has actually occurred for 13 selected administrative activities. The greatest change has taken place in reference to pupil and instructional policies and the least amount of change in reference to business management policies.

A MODERN CONCEPT OF THE PRINCIPAL'S OFFICE AS A SERVICE CENTER*

The final stage in the development of the principal's office is that of a service center for the school. This conception calls for a functional office suite and a type of school principal who visualizes the potential services to be rendered through the office to the school and its supporting community. Ten such services are discussed by the authors cited.

Briefly stated, the office should serve as (1) the communication center of the school, (2) a clearing house for the transaction of school business, (3) a counseling center for teachers and students, (4) a counseling center for school patrons, (5) a research division of the school for the collection, analysis, and evaluation of information regarding activities and results, (6) the repository of school records, (7) the planning center for solving school problems and for initiating school improvements, (8) a resource center for encouraging creative work, (9) a coordinating agency in cultivating wholesome school and community relations, and (10) the coordinating center of the school enterprise.

Before this conception of the school office is brought to fruition, many principals will no doubt have to undergo considerable preparation for democratic leadership. Many will have to realize that office organization and administration are not an end but only a means in the operation of an efficient school. The efficiency of the school depends on the quality of the learning in the individual classroom. To the extent that the principal, through his office and office practices, facilitates and promotes superior instruction and sound learning, he will justify the office layout discussed in this chapter and the expenses of office operation.

---

*Stuart E. Dean, *Elementary School Administration and Organization*, Washington, D.C.: U.S. Office of Education, Bulletin 1960, No. 11, 376.

THE ELEMENTARY SCHOOL PRINCIPAL ...

PROFESSIONALIZATION OF THE ELEMENTARY SCHOOL PRINCIPAL*

The principalship, one of the three essentials of an effective elementary school program, is the oldest school administrative and supervisory position. Despite its long history, it has been slow in developing into a position of major educational significance. The various steps of development include the one teacher stage — chief duty teaching, the head teacher stage — chief duty teaching, the teaching principal stage — chief duty administration, and the supervising principal stage — chief duty supervision and educational leadership. Three fourths of the principals in urban cities are now classified as supervising principals, but most of that progress has been made within the past decade. The development of the full-time supervising principal has lagged in the nonurban schools, especially in those states with many school districts. There is general recognition of the importance and desirability of having every elementary teacher working with a full-time supervising principal, but that goal has not yet been attained.

The professional status of the elementary school principal has greatly improved as the principalship progressed through its various stages of development. A major role in this professionalization has been carried by the Department of Elementary School Principals of the National Education Association. Through its publications, it has worked for greater collegiate preparation and higher standards. The growth in the duties of the supervising principal has made the master's degree a minimum educational qualification in many school systems. This improvement in the professional status is also evidenced in higher certification standards. All states now require an elementary principal's certificate. Although specific requirements vary by states, the general tendency is to become more selective. A master's degree with a major in administration and supervision plus successful teaching experience are common requirements for state certification.

---

*Roscoe V. Cramer and Otto E. Domian, *Administration and Supervision in the Elementary School,* New York: by permission of Harper and Row, 1960, 401-402.

The major role of the elementary principal today centers on his multiple human relationships. He holds a unique position in the school. The central administrative and supervisory staff are at his call. He must know fully the strengths and weaknesses of each member of his school staff. He is close to pupils and parents. He is strategically located to make contact with all the groups, agencies, and organizations of the neighborhood. The professional organizations, state departments of education, and colleges have their entry to the school through his office. He has the task of coördinating and directing all these forces to achieve the greatest possible development of the children and the community. He must truly be an educational leader and a master in human relations.

THE LEGAL POSITION OF THE ELEMENTARY PRINCIPAL*

It would be unrealistic in appraising the functions of the principal in the modern elementary school to ignore the plain fact that the principal does not operate on his own. Of course, it would be equally erroneous to suggest that the principal is merely another specialized clerk or manager in an authoritarian chain of command and that all he has to do is carry out the orders of higher authorities. A balanced view of the relationship of the principal to his superiors would be that the principal exists in a dual capacity, neither aspect of which is more important than the other.

On the one hand, he is legally and actually an agent of the board of education and its administration. He is appointed by the board, upon the recommendation of the chief administrative office or superintendent of the local schools, to carry out certain established policies. In that capacity he is also, by virtue of his appointment, supposed to initiate new policies and to act with some independence in the interpretation of existing policies. His second function is that of a representative of his teaching and noninstructional staff. He speaks for his staff and his school to the administration and represents them in official and unofficial deliberations on school policy and practice. . . .

---

*From *Elementary School Administration* by Peter Palmer Michelson and Kenneth H. Hansen. Copyright 1957 by McGraw-Hill Book Company. Used by permission of McGraw-Hill Book Company, 31, 44-46.

Much has been written about the specific legal responsibilities and duties of the elementary school principal. Certainly, it is important that the principal undertake his job of school organization and management with a clear knowledge of the limitations, responsibilities, and privileges imposed upon him by legal authority. However, there is such great variation among the several states and in the actual practices found in different districts with respect to the legal responsibilities and duties of the elementary school principal that any detailed discussion here would constitute a digression from our main question: within what general legal framework does the elementary principal operate? Basically, the answer is embodied in two major statements.

First, the principal is a *delegated agent* of the school board to carry out policies established by law and by school-board action. Some specialists in the field of school administration have argued cogently and convincingly that the principal should be regarded not merely as a delegated agent but also as an educational leader. We agree with this viewpoint, because the function of the elementary principal *is* primarily one of educational leadership. The more independence, initiative, and imagination that the principal can exercise in his job of educational leadership, the more effective his work will be. Nevertheless, it is unrealistic to deny that the elementary principalship, as it now exists, is primarily a job of delegated authority in a legal sense. There is virtually no limit to the range of educational leadership and independence of thought in educational matters that may characterize the work of an elementary school principal — *provided he does not do anything specifically prohibited by law or anything for which he has no legal authority.*

Second, the legal responsibility of the principal has been determined to be very close to that of the elementary teacher himself. It is a well-established point of law that the teacher acts *in loco parentis,* that is, the teacher is legally entitled to act in the place of the parent of the school child both while he is at school and on his way to and from school. In that capacity the principal has the same right as any teacher to exercise parental authority and guidance over the children under his jurisdiction.

Consider, for example, the matter of corporal punishment. It is generally agreed by educators and laymen alike that corporal punishment, even when specifically permitted by the school laws of the state, is usually unwise. However, if permitted by the school laws, corporal punishment should be exercised in the same manner as it would be by the parents of the child — with due regard to the child's welfare and to his total development, with no cruelty or sadism allowed. Regardless of how the individual teacher or administrator may regard corporal punishment, however, the point here is this: that whatever right the teacher has to administer corporal punishment is likewise vested in the principal. Thus, too, in other matters of control and guidance of the child, the principal has the same right as a teacher in the same school system.

These two factors, then — that the principal operates under delegated legal authority, and that his legal position is almost identical with that of any teacher in the same school system — are well established, but further specific responsibilities and duties of a legal nature must concern him. For example, the principal is often legally responsible for rendering certain official reports required by school law. He is legally responsible for the protection of the health, safety, and welfare of the school children under his jurisdiction. He is legally accountable for proper receipting and disbursement of such school or "activities" funds as come into his hands. Therefore, the principal does have certain *legal* responsibilities and duties which are established by law or by specific judicial decision. His concomitant *administrative* responsibilities are to know thoroughly the school laws under which he operates and to discharge with careful attention to detail the responsibilities vested in him by law.

MOST SEVERE PROBLEMS OF ELEMENTARY SCHOOL PRINCIPALS LIE IN INSTRUCTIONAL RESPONSIBILITIES*

In relation to the performance of his duties as the leader of an elementary school what are the most persistent problems facing the principal? Along with determining policies, practices, and trends with respect to the administration of an elementary school, it is important to know what impact recent developments have had on the requirements and demands being made upon the principal. Therefore, this survey has undertaken to explore on-the-job problems of principals.

Respondents were asked to indicate which administrative responsibilities, in their judgment, are presenting the most difficulty for the elemen-

---

*Stuart E. Dean, *Elementary School Administration and Organization*. Washington, D.C.: United States Office of Education, Bulletin 1960, No. 11, 97, 100-101.

tary school principals in their school system. This was done through the medium of a check list of 17 administrative categories:

Assignment of pupils to classes	Reporting pupil progress to parents
Custodial Staff	Scheduling
Obtaining adequate physical facilities	School-community relations
	School libararies
Obtaining sufficient instructional materials	School lunch programs
	Selection of instructional materials
Programs of special education	Staff relationships
Provision for the exceptional child	Supervision of instruction
Pupil promotional policies	Transportation of pupils . . . .
Recruitment of teachers	

What conclusions and inferences can be drawn from these reports? First of all, it becomes apparent that the type of responsibility which is causing the greatest difficulty lies in the field of instructional activity. The general improvement of instruction, programs of education for meeting the needs of children, and programs of special education, all cause concern, with emphasis on the qualitative aspects of the educational offerings of the school. That the educational administrators are expressing and reflecting this type of sensitivity is most reassuring. Second, these findings suggest a drive and dedication toward encouraging the principals of elementary schools to apply their efforts to the instructional phases of administration of an elementary school. Third, the fact that many of the so-called purely administrative routine responsibilities received relatively lower mention in these rankings, would, perhaps, imply that items of this operational nature are being adequately handled. Fourth, the items which consistently appear at the lower limits of each ranking may have a two-fold implication: That they are being competently dealt with, and that they are not of relative major administrative importance and priority. Finally, the message is clear that the administrators of the public schools of this country are very definitely oriented to the necessity for improvement of the quality of instruction in our schools.

When analyzed by population groups, exactly these same results appear. Without exception, each population group reflects the same priority of concern with the problems related to the improvement of instruction, provisions for the exceptional child, and programs of special education. There is a similar pattern of least amount of difficulty for the areas of school libraries, pupil transportation, custodial staff, scheduling, and selection of instructional materials. These trends parallel the national findings in all listings, total weighted responses, and listing by first, second, and third choices. Therefore, it is concluded that the problems which present the most difficulty for principals of elementary schools are common to all population groups and that the size of the urban place is not a signficant influence.

On a regional basis, again, the same basic pattern appears. Major concern is with the problems of the instructional program; minor concern is with the administrative responsibilities of a general routine type. The only departure from the national pattern is a higher expression of difficulty with school lunch programs in both the North Central and the South. Once again, the conclusion follows that the problems of most frequent mention, nationally and by population groups, are also regional problems. The location of the school has no bearing upon the kinds of problems which are causing the most difficulty to the principals.

In conclusion, the greatest difficulty which elementary school principals are experiencing lies in the field of instructional programs — how to improve their quality and how to provide programs for meeting the special and varied needs of children. Principals evidently are doing more effective work in routine and operational procedures. The implication for [pre-service] and [in-service] training programs for principals is that more assistance should be provided to help them to improve instruction and develop special programs of education for children of divergent needs and abilities. The prominence given to the needs and problems of an instructional nature reflects credit upon the school administrators of this Nation.

DEMOCRATIC ADMINISTRATION ADDS BURDENS TO THE PRINCIPAL*

The growing emphasis on democracy in school administration puts a premium on good educational leadership. Democracy does not, in any sense, mean anarchy. Efficient operation of a democratic school requires more, not less, professional leadership. If democracy is erroneously conceived to be the practice of letting everyone do as he pleases, then the

---

*From *Elementary School Administration* by Peter Palmer Michelson and Kenneth H. Hansen. Copyright 1957 by McGraw-Hill Book Company. Used by permission of McGraw-Hill Book Company. 296-297.

elementary school principal has little place in the educational enterprise. If democracy really means working more effectively as a group toward goals determined and accepted by the group itself, then the democratic school system needs more, and more effective, leadership at the professional level.

This emphasis on the necessity for democratic leadership has led some persons to think of the principalship as entirely a job of stimulating good human relationships. According to this viewpoint, the principal becomes a person skilled in group dynamics, a clever and able psychologist, and a person especially endowed with skill in working with people of varying backgrounds and interests, different personal and professional outlooks, and a variety of levels of age and maturation.

All of this is true; the principal does need a great deal of finesse in interpersonal relationships. Coupled with this, however, must be a substantial degree of technical skill. An aura of good feeling within the elementary school is necessary, but that alone is not enough. The principal must be competent to develop this desirable spirit or climate within the elementary school, not only through his skill in interpersonal relations, but through his possession and use of some very technical knowledge about elementary education.

At the risk of sounding professionally shortsighted, we must reiterate that the tendency in the past twenty years or so to say loudly and frequently that the schools belong to the people, and that whatever the people want is what the school should provide, has led us into a morass of self-deprecation in the profession of education. Perhaps this is simply a part of the national "do it yourself" movement; the theory today seems to be that anybody can do anything if he really tries. In a commendable eagerness to achieve and maintain good relations with the community, gain common consent before moving ahead on educational frontiers, and make the schools public in the sense not only that they are supported and open to the public but are controlled by the public as well, leaders in elementary education have sometimes deprecated far too much the value of technical knowledge and technical skill. If the principal does not know more about the technical aspects of the instructional methods, selection of instructional materials, curriculum construction, administration of the school service programs, and the like — if he does not actually know more about these things than the typical layman, then he has no business being a principal.

Developing good democratic feeling in the school is important; equally important is having and utilizing the special skills of the profession of public education. The principal who exercises true professional leadership must have both skills.

TRENDS IN PREPARATORY
PROGRAMS FOR PRINCIPALS*

Educational programs for the preparation of elementary school principals have assumed new and promising directions as the job has grown from a "head teacher" situation into a recognized school-community leadership position. Recognition of the importance of the principalship as a position of educational statesmanship has prompted a change in emphasis in preparatory programs from job-related knowledge to job-related behavior, since a large part of the principal's work is in the area of human relations. Great stress by colleges and public schools is currently and properly being placed on selection of likely candidates for administrative positions; the key to having good administrators in our schools lies in the proper selection of prospects. Once a dedicated aspirant is selected, the administrative education which is provided by the colleges and school district working cooperatively will more likely be effective.

A promising trend in the pre-education of elementary school principals and other administrators is the use, in professional courses, of "life-like" techniques such as case studies, "in-basket" cases, role-playing, individual and group research techniques, and situations of all kinds in which scientific problem-solving methods are used. It seems a natural thing, then, for administrative candidates to move from these "life-like" situations in the classroom to *life* situations in the actual school community in such relatively new practices as field work and internship. In the latter two areas, the prospective principals and other administrative candidates have an opportunity to work, under close college and school district supervision, in real school administration situations and have an opportunity to engage in decision-making activities to implement the theory previously learned in the classroom.

In the light of an ever-changing culture and an ever-changing profession of school administration, the school principal's education does not — can not — end when he receives his license or degree. The research and experimentation currently [underway] have indicated new concepts and more effective techniques in elementary school administra-

---

*Paul J. Misner, Frederick W. Schneider, and Lowell G. Keith, *Elementary School Administration,* Columbus, Ohio: by permission of Charles E. Merrill Books, Inc., 1963, 33-34.

tion. There are indications that as additional research and experimentation continue, still newer concepts and more effective techniques will emerge that will make the principalship a vastly more effective position for leadership in providing the best possible education for each child in America.

Principals need to be aware of the changing programs provided for the preparation of elementary school administrators. They need to keep abreast of all emerging practices which affect their profession. They must be particularly aware of the educational programs in which they themselves may be serving as teachers of future elementary school administrators. In order, too, for principals to be aware of the educational backgrounds of teachers who will be joining their staffs in the future, and to be able to provide valid in-service education for them, the administrators must know of the current and emerging programs for the education of teachers.

ADMINISTRATION OF THE JUNIOR HIGH SCHOOL . . .

TENANTS FOR THE ADMINISTRATION OF A JUNIOR HIGH SCHOOL*

To provide an administrative pattern based upon our knowledge and understanding of the learning process as well as the nature of the learner, we believe:

— that the principal is the key to the continuous success and improvement of the junior high school;

— that administrative acts must be in harmony with the purposes of the total school program;

— that the size of the school should be large enough to provide for efficient staffing and effective educational offering and services, suggesting a minimum administrative unit of 300 to 450 pupils;

— that large schools should be divided into internal units so that the individual identity of pupils and staff will be retained;

*By permission of *Clearing House,* "Ten Tenets of Junior High School Administration" (Prepared by Council on Junior High School of New York City Principals), XXXVIII (February, 1964), 331.

— that every pupil, at some time during his daily program, should be placed in at least one class — for example, language arts or social studies — that is composed of pupils fairly representative of his entire grade level;

— that instruction will be most effective when the scheduling of pupils has been in accord with the pupils' goals of learning, thus providing a compatible learning situation for all in the group;

— that where groups are formed to reduce the spread of differences within a class section, the purpose of the group should be well defined, and the criteria of selection should be consistent with the goals of the group and in harmony with the purposes of the total school program;

— that there should be one full-time administrator or supervisor to each 15 to 20 professional staff members, exclusive of the building principal;

— that balance in the program should be maintained through a supervisory organization that is general in nature rather than departmental;

—that the several subject areas and activities may require different time allotments and may be scheduled accordingly.

GUIDELINES FOR JUNIOR HIGH SCHOOL EDUCATION*

There are certain points of view which for many years have been basic to the program of junior high-school education. Through the years our interpretations of these points of view have been refined; our understanding of the nature of the early adolescent has been extended; and in some ways our approach to the implementation of the philosophy of the junior high school has changed. But the basic points of view underlying junior high-school education today are essentially those which were developed and accepted early in the history of this school. These points of view should continue to give direction to the educational program of the junior high school. They should serve as guidelines for

---

*William T. Gruhn, above guidelines summarized from "Guidelines for Junior High School Education," reprinted by permission from the *Bulletin of the National Association of Secondary-School Principals,* XLVI (February, 1962). 3-13.

developing the administrative organization, the curriculum, the [extra-class] activities, the guidance services, the professional staff, and all other aspects of the junior high-school program.

THE GUIDELINES

1. The junior high school should provide an educational program which is designed to meet the needs, the interests, and the abilities of a particular age group — the early adolescents.

2. The junior high school is primarily a transitional school, taking the pupil from the elementary school with its relatively simple organization and instructional program and sending him on to the senior high school with its broad objectives, its multiple curricula and courses, and its complex administrative organization and control.

3. The junior high school should challenge the increasingly mature abilities and interests of early adolescents by introducing them to new studies and by offering greater depth in studies which they have previously begun in the elementary school.

4. The junior high school should be concerned with all aspects of child growth and development — the intellectual, physical, emotional, character, citizenship, personality, and cultural.

5. The junior high school should prepare early adolescents for more independence, self-responsibility, and leadership as they participate increasingly in larger and more complex social groups and in the life of a wider community.

6. The junior high school should provide opportunities for pupils to explore present interests and abilities and encourage them to develop new interests which may be related to further education, vocational careers, and various cultural, intellectual, and avocational pursuits.

7. The junior high school should provide increasingly for the guidance and counseling of early adolescents in their success in school, their plans for further education, their vocational plans, and their growth toward adulthood.

8. The junior high school should provide an educational program which will meet the many different backgrounds, interests, aptitudes, abilities, and needs of individual pupils.

9. The junior high school should provide a program which is primarily one of general education rather than specialized learnings for specific educational and vocational goals.

BEGINNINGS OF THE JUNIOR HIGH SCHOOL*

The history of college-high school articulation is long and interesting, and careful scrutiny of it must await a discussion of purposes. However, it should be noted that college and university personnel played a greater role than did secondary school educators in the creation of the junior high school. The National Education Association's Committee of Ten (1893), the Committee of Fifteen (1895), the Committee on College Entrance Requirements (1895), and the Committee on Economy of Time in Education (1912) were all composed predominately of college presidents, deans, and professors; and all recommended the downward extension of secondary school education into the seventh and eighth grades to facilitate increased preparation for college.

In the early 1900's various communities began to experiment with the development of a senior and a junior high school division. Junior high schools in Columbus, Ohio, and in Berkeley, California, claim to be the first in the nation. Many communities were content to departmentalize the seventh and eighth grades and retain the typical 8-4 organization, but even in these early years one could find 6-6, 6-2-4, 6-4-4, and 6-3-5 plans as well as the more typical 6-3-3 arrangement.

Although the idea of better, or at least more, preparation for college gave impetus to the junior high school movement, psychological and sociological bases soon gave added support. Psychological studies indicated that children of the age to be in the seventh, eighth, and ninth grades were undergoing great psychological changes that required special recognition. Problems faced by students in the transition from elementary to secondary schools also gave support to a transitional school.

Finally, expediency played an important role in the rapid growth of junior high schools during the 1920's and 1930's. School enrollments rapidly outgrew school facilities and many communities chose to build junior high schools rather than construct more expensive high schools. By eliminating the ninth grade from the senior high school, high school facilities were often made to meet enrollment growth without constructing new high schools. This led to many high school programs that were little more than upper elementary school program transferred to a separate building.

---

*John Corbally, Jr., Theodore Jensen, and Frederick Staub, *Educational Administration: The Secondary School,* Boston: by permission of Allyn and Bacon, Inc., 1961, 24-25.

ADMINISTRATION OF THE SENIOR HIGH SCHOOL...

THE THREE MAJOR DIMENSIONS OF THE HIGH SCHOOL PRINCIPALSHIP*

High-school administration has three major dimensions: technical, managerial, and conceptual. The technical dimension is typically represented by specialized skills related to such activities as testing, measuring, interviewing, disciplining, coaching, scheduling, recording, accounting, spending, operating, and maintenance. The duties of assistant principals, deans, counselors, teachers, teacher aides, secretaries, clerks, and custodians all call for technical skills.

The managerial dimension involves the co-ordination of technical skills and the management of the physical features of the enterprise. In this dimension there is concern for the effectiveness of people for the adequacy of plans, for conformity to rules, for economical use of space, time, and funds. Decisions must be made on scheduling of content, staff, and students; on accounting for students; on budgets, purchasing, and accounting; on plans for school-building, maintenance, and operation. Most studies on the activities of the principal indicate that the major portion of his time and energy is spent on managerial duties.

The conceptual dimension provides stimulus and direction for the other two dimensions as the total educational enterprise strives to achieve perfection. In the conceputual dimension the administrator's concerns are directed to the entire school program, to the community setting, to learning and the individual. In this phase of his role the administrator seeks out, and capitalizes on, the teachers' interests and goals. He meets, encourages, and helps teachers as they strive for quality in educational practice. The excitement and the adventure of unusual ideas inject novelty into the program and invigorate growth. . . .

How can the principalship encompass these three dimensions? What kind of personnel and what kind of administrative structure are needed to accommodate functions associated with these dimensions? Can a principal be both theoretician and practitioner, both creator and manager? Should the principalship consist of a single position in which are vested the responsibilities and the authority necessary to all three dimensions?

---

*Conrad Briner, "Unhinging the High-School Principalship," reprinted from *The School Review*, LXVIII (Summer, 1960), by permission of the University of Chicago Press, 318-328.

Or should responsibility and authority be shared among several members? Should the school administrative structure change to permit increased opportunity for delegation of responsibility and authority beyond the typical organization of line positions existing in most high schools?

Answers to these questions are not readily available, but certainly we know what the staffing patterns should not be. One person cannot fill this position adequately. Ordinarily the principal lacks the time, the know-how, and the energy to satisfy the demands of all three dimensions. The traditional pattern typically represents a compromise, usually at the expense of the conceptual dimension and in favor of the managerial. As a manager, the principal may be concerned chiefly with the planning and the construction of new facilities, with keeping costs at a minimum, with discipline, and with communication between school and community. In the traditional pattern, the principalship typically does not display the dynamic administrative leadership focused on the conceptual dimension.

Unquestionably, some one individual in the school must bear the major responsibility for leadership and authority. Probably this individual should also be the key person in the agitation for improvement in educational performance. He should be a font of challenging ideas. But more than challenging ideas are needed. Without appropriate management decisions and technical skills, creative ideas may be made ineffectual by a decision, or power, vacuum. Implementation of ideas must be planned to involve people, time, space, and materials, and plans must be put into action by appropriate decision-making. Management and technical resources must be mobilized if practice is to have a chance to succeed; inventiveness and ingenuity must have opportunities to be expressed if ideas are to be put to work in the educative process.

To accommodate these dimensions may require an administrative organization that provides for three interdependent administrative functions. The following diagram depicts one possibility in organization:

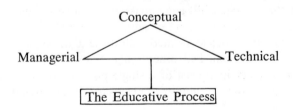

The diagram suggests a shared or overlapping leadership that has the knowledge and skills essential for effective decision-making. The responsibilities of the principalship are carried out not by a single individual but by several individuals who perform various functions by virtue of special training, experience, and interest as well as assignment. The actual number of staff members needed for the principalship may vary with the size of the high school.

CHARACTERISTICS OF HIGH SCHOOL PRINCIPALS AS REVEALED BY PROJECT TALENT SURVEY*

Information was also gathered about the characteristics of the principal of each school. No outstanding differences were found regarding the principals of the different groups of schools except that there were virtually no women principals except in the large cities and non-public high schools. Almost 13% of large city high schools have female principals, and 56% of the non-public high schools. The principals of the non-public high schools had not had as many years' experience as principal as had those for the other four groups. A tendency was found for the principals to be considerably older in the larger city high schools, and vocational high schools. A very high proportion of all the school principals have Master's degrees or better. In the large city high schools, 14% of the principals have a Doctor's degree, and over 99% have a Master's degree or better. Less than 20% of the Southeast, other regions, and non-public high school principals have less than a Master's degree, but 48% of vocational high school principals have less than a Master's degree. It can be seen that outside of the vocational high schools very few of the principals have had less than 20 hours in education courses. In the non-public high schools the average principal has had over 35 hours in education courses.

---

*John C. Flanagan, John T. Dailey, Marion F. Shaycroft, David B. Orr, and Isadore Goldberg, *Project Talent, Cooperative Research Project No. 226,* "Studies of the American High School," Pittsburgh: University of Pittsburgh, by permission of the Project Talent Office, 1962, 2-27.

THE HIGH SCHOOL PRINCIPAL AS AN ADMINISTRATOR*

The degree to which the secondary school principal is actually a school administrator cannot be determined apart from considering the size of the school and the extent of the program the community has been willing to support. The vast majority of the more than 23,000 public high schools in America are small schools. In many of these schools, the principal is only nominally an administrator, being in practice a teaching principal and little more than a head teacher. In many medium-sized schools and in most large ones the principal has functions of management and leadership in his own school paralleling those of the superintendent of the whole system. Between these two extremes, the administrative functions of the principal vary greatly from community to community and from school to school. Here we would expect to find theory and practice combining into an almost infinite set of patterns and we do. We also find the theory of administration in conflict with prevailing practice. The two need not be antagonistic and each suffers a loss when divorced from the other. The assumptions largely ignored in the theory of school administration are scarcely more open to criticism than the lack of clarity of purpose in much of our administrative practice.

With such exceptions as the Illinois Township High School and the California Union High School, where the school leader is a superintendent, the principal is a subordinate line officer, working under the superintendent of schools. In such schools, the success of the principal revolves on his recognizing the complementary relation of his duties to those of the superintendent. Conversely, our most successful superintendents are the first to acknowledge that the success of their program is largely dependent on the administrative ability, vision, tact, and frankness of their principals. Loyalty to, and cooperation with the superintendent are primary obligations of the principal. This loyalty may be a highly personalized one and often is, though there appears to be a trend toward emphasizing the teamwork qualities of the principal with less stress on personalities. In any case, where administrative authority and

*Ivan H. Linder and Henry M. Gunn, *Secondary School Administration: Problems and Practices,* Columbus, Ohio: by permission of Charles E. Merrill Books, Inc., 1963, 19-20, 29-30, 42-43.

responsibility are shared by the superintendent and the principal, these must be balanced and they must be kept together.

In the better organized school systems, more authority is being extended the secondary school principal for operating his own school in order to define and sharpen his sense of responsibility for the whole program. Even with such a trend, there is increased need for a working definition of the functions of the secondary school principal. Such a definition should clearly distinguish those duties for which the principal is completely responsible, from those he should share with his superiors on the one hand, and with his staff and the school patrons, on the other. This would go a long way toward resolving the not uncommon conflict between individual principals and superintendents on their sharing authority. . . .

In recent decades one of the most significant developments in school administration has been the increase in the administrative status of the school principal. In the chain of administrative command in the school system as a whole the principal remains a subordinate line officer, but within his own school his position is primary. So strongly do some superintendents believe that the principal must be responsible for the total program of his school, that the superintendent himself does not enter the school on official business without first contacting the principal. It should be obvious that he has no legal obligation to respect the principal's position in this way. Nor does he do it only to elevate the status of the principal, but also to provide for unified administration of the secondary school program and to extend to the principal, along with the obligation of implied leadership, every inducement to exercise it. In this manner the superintendent, in organization and practice, acknowledges that each secondary school should have a single administrative head with lines of authority between his office and the principal kept as direct as possible. He recognizes also that "keeping within channels" should not be permitted to obstruct progress or to confuse the principal's responsibility for his school's total program.

This is more than a mere operative principle of administration, more than a gesture of recognition extended the principal; it is a very significant mandate to exercise his leadership in the fullest cooperation with the line and staff officers of the central administration. If this does not make his leadership easier, it holds out the promise of making it more effective. That effectiveness depends not only on the ability of the principal but also on his attitude toward his job and his associates in and out of the high school. He must learn to rely on others for advice, because regardless of how competent he may be, he must remain amateurish in many things about his school; but he must never surrender his authority.

He must of course analyze his problems, but he will absorb more than he analyzes and remain sensitive to the constructive suggestions of those with whom he works. . . .

THE MYRIAD EXPECTATIONS OF THE HIGH SCHOOL PRINCIPAL*

The principal's position within the district is undefined, too. In some, he is second only to the superintendent. In others, there are assistant superintendents, business managers and assistant assistants, all of whom claim authority over the principal and his job. In still others, the principal co-exists happily with these officers, exerting leadership over the high school with the aid of the superintendent's staff.

This point can be best illustrated perhaps, by two neighboring districts in New York. Each has the same administrative setup—a superintendent, assistant superintendent, business manager and high school principal.

In one district, the assistant superintendent is himself a former high school principal. When the superintendent is out of the district, or when leadership is needed in instructional areas, the job falls to the assistant superintendent. If he, too, should be out of the district, the business manager—also an educator—handles many of these responsibilities. The job of the high school principal is simply to run his school.

Right next door, the business manager is *not* an educator and the assistant superintendent's main areas of responsibility and knowledge are in administration and building. In that school system, the high school principal assumes the leadership of the district whenever the superintendent is out of the area or when special emphasis is needed in instruction. His job is not just running a school — it is really that of *the top instructional leader* in the district. (It should be noted, of course, that this principal has the assistance of a very able assistant principal.)

WHAT IS HIS JOB?

The principal of a secondary school is too important a man to have his job so ill-defined that it can range from being a clerk and custodian to responsibility for a large segment of a district's program. Real clarification is needed concerning his responsibilities, how large a staff he

*School Management, "What Should You Demand of a High School Principal?" Vol. IV (September, 1960), 24. (By permission.)

needs, how much he should be paid and how large a school he should administer.

To get answers to some of these questions, *School Management* editors went to Washington, D.C., to interview Ellsworth Tompkins, executive secretary of the National Association of Secondary-School Principals. The following questions and answers are taken from the tape-recorded interview. . . .

Q. Let's move on a slightly larger school, somewhere around 1,000 or 1,200 students. How much administrative staff should we properly add at this point to make our principal an effective leader?

Tompkins: Ideally there should be a full-time principal and a full-time assistant principal—who, perhaps, has some responsibility for instruction, too. In addition, there should be three guidance counselors. There should be a minimum of four, and possibly five, on the secretarial-clerical staff. This would depend somewhat on the number of students going on to colleges. The size of the clerical staff can also be affected by the legal structure under which the district works. Some states require a great amount of legal reporting, attendance checking and that type of thing which other states do not. These obviously are time-consuming. . . .

Q. Does this complete the administrative setup in a large high school?

Tompkins: There is another group of people who can be of great value to the principal in a school this size: the department heads. With 1,000 students, you might not have a chairman for each department, but you might have four "area chairmen." For example, there would be a chairman of the department of language arts, a chairman of the department of precise sciences, a chairman of the department of practical arts, and a chairman of the department of business education. In larger schools, each department should have a chairman. I think this is an important point. The department head can be an important factor in the division of work and supervision in the schools.

Q. Then the department heads, in some instances, may almost work as assistant principals? Would they be expected to exercise some supervisory control over the other teachers in their departments?

Tompkins: That's what they should be doing. Too often our department heads do administration and the details of administration and are not particularly concerned with their role as instructional leaders. Perhaps because they are teaching a large share of the program, it is most difficult to release them for that kind of duty which I think is most important as a service of a department head. Of course, this goes back to the principal and ultimately to the superintendent. . . .

Q. How about appointments with parents? Is this a job for the principal or should they properly be assigned to someone else?

Tompkins: "What do you want?" This is the first question asked when a parent calls up. "Whom do you wish to see? What can we do for you? What is it about?" In most cases, the principal probably could not help the parents if he saw them. They really [want] to speak to a particular teacher, or the registrar, or guidance counselor . . . .

Q. When you say "overall design" does this mean working with students or simply planning the general approach the guidance counselors should take?

Tompkins: As a general rule, the principal would not get involved with individual student counseling. Now, obviously, there may be cases where it's good to have the student and the principal get together in a full and frank discussion. But under a proper guidance program, this should not be necessary too often.

Q. How about meetings with the faculty? Do you favor regular staff meetings where problems can be discussed?

Tompkins: I take a dim view of faculty meetings to discuss the behavior of one or two individuals. Some staff meetings are undoubtedly important but they should be concerned with general problems facing all teachers. Many schools spend a lot of time calling the faculty together so that the principal can hold forth on the need for improvement, with veiled comments that pertain to one or two people. I think individual problems should be dealt with on a face-to-face basis with the people involved. That's a basis for exerting real leadership.

Q. Many principals get involved in such duties as appearances at football games, basketball games, dances and the like. Is this something that should be considered a part of their job?

Tompkins: In smaller towns it probably should be. For the principal of the large high school this is a personal matter. It is not essential that he attend all these events, but I would think that he should have representation at them.

THE FUTURE OF THE SECONDARY SCHOOL PRINCIPALSHIP

The above sketch of the working attitudes of the principal may appear forbiddingly involved and discouraging to one looking toward high school leadership as a career. But the principal in training should remember, too, that the American people have great faith in the high school in spite of its many weaknesses. They look to this institution to provide both opportunity and security for youth, and they expect the high school program to develop and release youth's energies and creative potential into the service of the nation. Even when this expectancy is accompanied by a naive faith in what formal education can do, it extends a challenge to all persons connected with the school, and especially to the leader.

A young man with some successful teaching experience may look forward to a small principalship and to moving from this to a larger school. Or he may first secure a minor administrative position in a larger school and go from this to a principalship. In either case he will find his remuneration increasing and the intangible rewards of satisfaction mounting as he grows in competence. In spite of the many difficulties surrounding the high school principalship, it affords an opportunity to work more closely with teachers and pupils than is ordinarily true of the superintendency. At the same time, successful experience here is often considered good evidence of preparation for the position of superintendent should the individual look forward to a wider area of school leadership.

There is a rewarding future in the principalship for any young man who has an abiding sense of the importance of the high school's service to youth and to the nation. Along with this, he needs to have a realistic grasp of the factors which contribute most of the school's success. Having these primary qualifications, he can devote himself to the school's improvement with the full assurance that he is performing a public service second in importance to no other. He must learn, however, to keep to the main channel of service to his school and must not be washed ashore by some inconsequential cross current. He must not allow himself to become bogged down in despondency at the imbalance between his accomplishments and his purposes. It is characteristic of democratic institutions that bringing about improvements is a slow process; for this reason school administration can be very trying for the impatient. The principal must learn to face discouragement without indulging despair, to list toward the hopeful without becoming visionary, and to keep his expectations of others well within reasonable boundaries. All of this demands a steadiness of purpose, an innate sense of when to get excited and when to relax. He needs to work at his job in something of the spirit of adventure, and the literature of adventure carries the age old message of life that the absolute essentials of survival are few and that courage is one of them.

To develop the competence to perform effectively the array of tasks surrounding the principalship, and to do this in a manner to sustain a growing confidence in his leadership, is a challenge worthy of the devotion of a young man of the highest leadership potential. And still, no one should enter upon the task of high school leadership and at the same time expect an upholstered seat in the general scheme of things. Public opinion is presently engaged in sharpening its concept of the role of the high schools in the future of the nation. Such an effort will make conflicts more pointed rather than ease them.

SELF-ASSESSMENT FOR ONE CONTEMPLATING A CAREER IN SECONDARY-SCHOOL ADMINISTRATION*

Those who anticipate a career in secondary school administration might well begin by asking themselves two questions: Do I like, and enjoy working with, people? Am I challenged to action when confronted by problems? Stop reading here if your answer is "No" to either of these questions, for to be an administrator of a secondary school under these circumstances would be frustrating to you and dispiriting to those with whom you might work. The corridors and classrooms of modern secondary schools are humming with activity, and the sound is not pleasant to the introverted, the cynical, or the misanthropic. The mix that results from playing the best possible organized learning experiences for the teen-age pupil against the moving backdrop of his now volatile, now grimly earnest nature is shot through with problems. Not to be stimulated by these problems is never to know the challenge of secondary school administration.

At almost any given point in time it might appear that a secondary school principal's life is compounded of seemingly disconnected problem situations. A telephone rings and a parent reports that her son's shirt has been torn during an initiation skirmish, the office door opens and a student requests permission to change his schedule, it is 3:30, and the principal heads for the faculty meeting. The problems of the moment seem always to be there, springing from the interactions of the day. Lest solutions to these problems be thumbs hastily applied to a leaking dike, however, the administrator needs to think, by himself and with others,

---

*John Corbally, Jr., Theodore Jensen, and Frederick Staub, *Educational Administration: The Secondary School,* Boston: by permission of Allyn and Bacon, Inc., 1961, 3-4, 332-333.

about plans that might forestall certain kinds of problems. But by this process other broad-based problems are created. To solve both kinds, a disposition to do so and a systematic approach are required. . . .

Those who write speculatively about the science of administration often express the opinion that a person might be an excellent administrator in public education and yet never had had a day's classroom teaching experience. Further, it is also seemingly true that some excellent teachers, either rewarded for their good teaching or seeking additional rewards, usually of money or status, go into administration with miserable results both for themselves and for the schools they serve. Whatever the long-range implications of these factors may be, the current picture is that secondary school administrators pass first through the teaching ranks. For the professional rapport vital to the success of administration, as well as for some other reasons, it is probably well that this route exists.

Every teaching position has its administrative aspects. There is constant planning, delegating, coordinating, and appraising activity. With these component aspects of teaching, there is ample effort for the teacher to assess his own skills and satisfaction pattern in reference to these processes. If teaching brings satisfaction because it is a one-man effort, primarily, then this should be a clue that an administrative future would likely not be advisable. If, however, considerable satisfaction exists in having set the stage so that others can see relationship, comprehend problems, work individually and cooperatively toward their solution, then the evidence augurs well.

Further signs for the individual teacher to note are the following: Am I comfortable in positions of responsibility? Can I make needed decisions with dispatch, when they need to be made that way? Am I inclined to look for best evidence before deciding on a course of action? Do I enjoy working with adults at least as much as I like working with teenage youngsters? Do my interests in education go beyond my own subject-matter fields? Do I have a tolerance for frustration and ambiguity? Answers to these questions are vital to an individual considering a future in secondary school administration.

Given favorable responses to these and like questions, there is much that a teacher can do to gain administrative experience. Dozens of tasks that need leadership exist in every secondary school. Classes need advisors, dances need chaperones, extracurriculum activities need guidance and coordination, committees need volunteer members and often volunteer chairmen, to mention but a few. The energetic teacher, interested in testing his administrative potential, often finds ample opportunity to do so by expressing interests in one or more of these activities to the principal. Many find opportunities in out-of-school functions as well, in church work, in service club activities, in civic ventures. Initiative and energy can supply the opportunities, a personal satisfaction pattern can supply the evidence.

THE HIGH SCHOOL PRINCIPAL'S RELATIONSHIPS TO CENTRAL STAFF ADMINISTRATORS*

The problem of cooperation between the principal and the central administrative staff, quite obviously, varies greatly with the size of the school systems and with the number of administrative assistants, supervisors, and special service agents involved. Ordinarily only assistant superintendents share the general administrative authority of the superintendent; the others are expected to provide expert assistance in their respective fields without general administrative authority. Sometimes cooperation between the principal and individual staff members becomes difficult to achieve. This may develop from the principal becoming oversensitized to the prerogatives of his position, or may grow out of confusion in the minds of teachers on the respective responsibilities of the principal and the central staff member and the teachers' working relations with them. Even when overt personality clashes are avoided, routine and formal working relationships may be substituted for more genuine and helpful operation. Potential difficulties exist too in the fact that some central staff members feel obliged to make their own position, and an occasional one may become an aggressive empire builder in promoting his own specialty.

The principal has a primary obligation to make proper use of the central staff specialist without permitting the specialist to push him into indefensible over-emphasis on one aspect of the school program. There is always the possibility that when influences multiply and the resources of assistance are extended, instead of strengthening the leadership of the principal, they will merely submerge it. To avoid the latter, the principal must know his own school program, its operative strengths and weaknesses, and must be able to properly evaluate the assistance he

*Ivan H. Linder and Henry M. Gunn, *Secondary School Administration: Problems and Practices,* Columbus, Ohio: by permission of Charles E. Merrill Books, Inc., 1963, 35-37.

receives, including that of central staff members. When he displays such a grasp and communicates freely with central staff specialists, and at the same time thinks for himself, he will have laid the proper foundation for an effective cooperation with them. Here, as elsewhere, there is no substitute for the principal's displaying a type of competence that is increasingly recognized and so becomes inherently persuasive.

The young principal, in particular, needs to be reminded that there is a sort of aristocracy of competence in a leader that attracts its own following because it is readily acknowledged and welcomed by his associates. Developing a natural following has been recognized throughout history as the very substance of leadership. This normally develops with experience, though always within the limits of one's native endowment. Such competence carries its own self-assurance, lifting the principal's performance above the distractions of petty rivalry, or self-centered suspicion of others, whatever their administrative status.

THE PRINCIPAL AND THE CENTRAL OFFICE SUPERVISORS

Any school system large enough to have a central administration usually has several supervisors of instruction representing the major subject fields or combinations of such fields. Unless the school system is unusually large these supervisors have vertical responsibility, that is, in their respective fields, their services cover the elementary as well as the secondary schools. Theoretically at least, they do not rely on authority so much as on the prestige growing out of their competence as persons of superior training and resourcefulness in assisting teachers to improve instruction. Conventionally, general supervisors devoted their time largely to classroom visitation and conference, whereas in more recent years they have become general resource persons, with less emphasis on classroom visitation, particularly of the traditional authoritative and inspectional type.

As a resource person, the general supervisor conducts conferences and workshops for teachers, assists in organizing and advising vertical and horizontal curriculum committees and seeks to improve the subject articulation between schools of different levels. In addition to these activities, the supervisor may conduct general surveys of the status of instruction in the special field, assist teachers in planning instruction and keep them informed of new instructional methods and improved learning materials. And perhaps most important of all, the supervisor stands ready to assist individual teachers to improve their instruction, either on call from the teacher or at the suggestion of the principal.

As with other representatives of the superintendent's staff, the supervisor is supposed to work with teachers in the secondary school with the consent of the principal if not under a more immediate direction. This relationship assumes a degree of unity of purpose between the principal and the supervisor which cannot be taken for granted and which is at best difficult to achieve. Effective co-operation demands basic agreement on the general goals of instructional improvement, out of which mutual respect may develop and in which responsibility for improving instruction can be shared without any significant degree of suspicion by either. Overt personality conflicts are less a threat to smooth working relations than a tendency of each person to operate without reference to the other until conflicting purposes are disclosed by developments. If we assume that the principal is in direct charge of his school program, this means that he has an obligation to take the initiative in using the services of the general supervisor. On the other hand, the supervisor ought to consult with the principal before calling meetings which may conflict with similar engagements of teachers within the school. And, of course, developments and innovations in the school program which may grow out of the supervisory meetings with teachers must be cleared with the principal before they are officially adopted.

THE BEGINNING PRINCIPAL SHOULD NOT IMITATE HIS PRINCIPAL*

The man just entering upon his first high-school principalship should realize that, if he wishes to render the highest type of service to his school and to advance in his profession, he cannot afford to model his school administration after the administration of the school which he attended or even after that of a school in which he has taught. Such great progress has been made in the theory and practice of high-school administration that many principals lag ingloriously in the rear of the leadership of the much smaller group of men and women who have studied carefully, diligently, and systematically the objectives, principles and techniques of the organization, administration, and supervision of secondary schools and who have been blessed with ambition, energy, and courage in such quantities as to cause them to lead in the development of new practices.

---

*Harl R. Douglass, *Modern Administration of Secondary Schools,* 2nd ed., reprinted through the courtesy of Blaisdell Publishing Company, a division of Ginn and Company, 1954, 21.

The beginning principal cannot hope to solve a great many of his problems *de novo* through plain common sense, even though common sense is a very valuable asset. Many principals of the passing generation were men and women who were certified with a minimum of professional preparation and who succeeded to high-school principalships through the quality of their personalities, their success as teachers, and their popularity in their communities. Because of superior qualities of personality, a number of them have enjoyed more than average success. Their admirable personal qualities, not their principles and practices in school administration, are the things worth imitating.

THE PRINCIPAL SHOULD ALLOW
TIME FOR STUDENT COUNSELING*

In the small school an elaborate organization for guidance is often not possible and to a certain extent not necessary. In schools in which it is possible for every student to have immediate personal conferences with the principal and in which the principal may find time to give careful study to all the pertinent data and to call into his office students apparently most in need of guidance, much valuable guidance service may be rendered. In some ways he is in the best position to render it, being most likely to come naturally into contact with all the various types of data desirable for guidance—through records of various sorts, knowledge of attendance and misdemeanors, and contacts with parents. On the other hand, it is difficult for him to assume the double role of "terror" to evildoers and "friend" of the sinners. If the principal will, as far as possible, handle disciplinary cases more as guidance opportunities and endeavor to solve problems on the basis of good mental hygiene, he may go a long way toward dissolving the duality of the role of one who must punish in some cases but also act as a counselor. In a situation where the student must be punished by the principal, the principal should transfer the student to some other counselor and not attempt to carry on the dual role. The principal of the small school, however, will miss golden opportunities and will labor under a distorted perspective if he becomes so busy maintaining discipline and carrying on routine and subject-matter supervision that he does not find the time and the occasion to come into

*Harl R. Douglass, *Modern Administration of Secondary Schools,* 2nd ed., reprinted through the courtesy of Blaisdell Publishing Company, a division of Ginn and Company, 1954, 306.

the lives of many boys and girls at critical moments with sympathy and advice, encouragement and caution, and assistance in arriving at right decisions.

FOR FURTHER REFLECTION OR INVESTIGATION

1. Justify the differences in salary for elementary, junior high, and senior high school principals.

2. Observe a principal on the job for a day in order to classify the tasks he performs into postponable and non-postponable activities.

3. What is behind the statement, "My principal doesn't understand the teachers' point of view"?

4. Write job descriptions for the principal and two assistant principals in a comprehensive high school of 1,500 students.

5. Debate the merits of a comprehensive high school vs. special vocational high schools.

6. What are the obstacles to a good elementary principal becoming an equally good secondary school principal?

7. Discuss the advantages and disadvantages of promoting to the principalship from within the school system.

8. Is it reasonable to expect a principal who was formerly a science teacher to supervise and perhaps evaluate the effectiveness of teachers of English or social studies?

9. Discuss (impassionately) the merits of male or female principals.

10. What are valid justifications for a principal to call a meeting of the full faculty? How often?

11. Should principals be rotated periodically among the buildings within the system?

12. What should be different about the preparation of a principal for a middle school as opposed to principals for other buildings?

13. What are the implications of the organization proposed in this chapter for principals becoming "assistant superintendents" in the following respects: salaries of principals and central staff administrative personnel? titles and stature of each? preparatory programs for each?

BIBLIOGRAPHY

Burr, James, William Coffield, T. J. Jensen, and Ross Neagley, *Elementary School Administration,* New York: Allyn and Bacon, Inc., 1963.

Anderson, Lester and Lauren A. Van Dyke, *Secondary School Administration,* Boston: Houghton Mifflin Co., 1963.

Anderson, Vernon E., and William T. Gruhn, *Principles and Practices of Secondary Education,* 2nd ed., New York: The Ronald Press Company, 1962.

Briner, Conrad, "Unhinging the High-school Principalship," *The School Review,* LXVIII, Summer, 1960, 318-328.

Burrup, Percy E., *Modern High School Administration,* New York: Harper & Row, Publishers, 1962.

Clearing House, "Ten Tenets of Junior High School Administration," (Prepared by Council on Junior High School of New York City Principals,) XXXVLLL, February, 1964.

Corbally, John E., Jr., T. J. Jensen, and W. Frederick Staub, *Educational Administration: the Secondary School,* Boston: Allyn and Bacon, 1961.

Cramer, Roscoe V., and Otto E. Domian, *Administration and Supervision in the Elementary School,* New York: Harper and Row, Publishers, 1960.

Cubberly, Ellwood P., *The Principal and His School,* Boston: Houghton Mifflin Company, 1923.

Dean, Stuart E., *Elementary School Administration and Organization,* Washington, D.C.: United States Office of Education, Bulletin 1960, No. 11.

Douglass, Harl R., *Modern Administration of Secondary Schools,* 2nd ed., Boston: Ginn and Company, 1954.

Elicker, Paul E., *Administration of Junior and Senior High Schools,* New York: Parker Publishing Company, 1965.

Ellsbree, Willard S., and Harold J. McNally, *Elementary School Administration and Supervision,* 2nd ed., New York: American Book Company, 1959.

Erickson, Donald A., "Changes in the Principalship," *The National Elementary Principal,* XLIV, April, 1965.

Flanagan, John C., John T. Dailey, Marion F. Shaycroft, David B. Orr, and Isadore Goldberg, *Project Talent, Cooperative Research Project* No. 226, "Studies of the American High School," Pittsburgh: University of Pittsburgh, Project Talent Office, 1962.

Fox, Willard, and Alfred Schwartz, *Managerial Guide for School Principals,* Columbus, Ohio: Charles E. Merrill Books, Inc., 1965.

Gross, Neal and Robert E. Herriott, *Staff Leadership in Public Schools,* New York: John Wiley & Sons, Inc., 1965.

Gruhn, William T., "Guidlines for Junior High School Education." *Bulletin of the National Association of Secondary-School Principals,* XLVI, February, 1962.

Hamburg, Morris, *Case Studies in Elementary School Administration,* New York: Teachers College, Bureau of Publications, 1957.

Hansford, Byron W., *Guidebook for School Principals,* New York: Ronald Press Company, 1961.

Hemphill, J. K., "Progress Report: A Study of the Secondary School Principalship," *Bulletin of the National Association of Secondary-School Principals,* XLVIII, April, 1964.

Herbert, M., "Principles for the Principal," *The Instructor,* June, 1964.

Hunt, Herold C., "Educational Administration and Finance," a chapter from *Becoming an Educator,* Van Cleve Morris and others, Boston: Houghton-Mifflin Company, 1963.

Jacobson, Paul B., William C. Reavis, and James D. Logsdon, *The Effective School Principal,* Englewood Cliffs: Prentice-Hall, Inc., 1963.

Linder, Ivan H., and Henry M. Gunn, *Secondary School Administration: Problems and Practices,* Columbus, Ohio: Charles E. Merrill Books, Inc., 1963.

Lipham, James M., "The Role of the Principal: Search and Research." *The National Elementary Principal,* XLIV, April, 1965.

McCleary, Lloyd E., and Stephen P. Hencley, *Secondary School Administration,* New York: Dodd, Mead & Company, Inc., 1965.

McIntyre, Kenneth E., *Selection and On-the-job Training of School Principals,* Austin: University of Texas, 1960.

McNally, Harold, "Theory and Practice in Administration," *National Elementary Principal,* XLI, January, 1962.

Michelson, Peter Palmer, and Kenneth H. Hansen, *Elementary School Administration,* New York: McGraw-Hill Book Co., Inc., 1957.

Misner, Paul J., Frederick W. Schneider, and Lowell G. Keith, *Elementary School Administration,* Columbus, Ohio: Charles E. Merrill Books, Inc., 1963.

School Management, "What Should You Demand of a High School Principal?" September, 1960.

Trump, J. Lloyd, "The Principal's Role in Superior Education," National *Association of Secondary-School Principals Bulletin,* XLIV, January, 1962.

Williams, Stanley W., *Educational Administration in Secondary Schools,* New York: Holt, Rinehart and Winston, Inc., 1964.

Wright, Grace S., "Enrollment Size and Educational Effectiveness of the High School," Washington, D.C.: United States Office of Education, Circular No. 732, 1964.

Chapter 15

Administering a School System
---the Superintendent

Much of this volume has dealt, either directly or by innuendo, with the work of the chief school system administrator, entitled according to local preferences as the superintendent, executive head, general superintendent, or supervising principal. This chapter will undertake the impossible: to define the role of the public school superintendent. The probability of failure in this undertaking stems from the fact that it is rarely defined by those who should do it—the appointing board of education. The literature of educational administration is deluged with definitions by those who are expressing sincere belief about what it ought to be. Teachers, citizens, and occasionally students are magnanimous in offering their job definitions. Nonetheless, it remains as the most poorly defined administrative job within the entire school system, and from that void appears the major roadblock to successful performance. Lacking precise directions as to what this singular officer in the system should do, each superintendent makes of the post what he thinks it should be. Judging from the turnover in office, the consensus of opinion is that his interpretation is inaccurate.

Complete returns are unavailable for the year of this writing, 1965, but advance tabulations indicate that a new high has been reached in departures from the superintendent's position, either at the request of the board of education or by themselves as they seek professional positions which are better defined. From the nation's largest cities, from tiny rural outpost districts they are leaving. The untenability of this important position at a time when educational institutions need and deserve society's strongest leaders warrants more than a one-day headline. There should be concern about the supply of qualified persons to fill the vacancies if so many are unable to discover what the superintendent is supposed to do. And yet each vacancy, especially if there is one with an attractive price tag, finds dozens of applicants, perhaps naively unaware of the expectations or perhaps hoping to be the Messiah who leads the district forward. Moreover, some school communities are jealously holding to their chief school administrators, indicating that some superintendents are finding the correct interpretation of the role, at least for the time and the place.

The position has been plagued with ambiguity since its beginning. Rarely does one uncover evidence of the employing school committee spelling out in any detail what it expected the appointee to do. Apparently the directions are verbal, as most of them unfortunately still are. Similarly, state laws equivocally delineate his assignment. The most that can be found in many statutes is the mere authorization for a board of education to appoint a superintendent. Even when a fairly clear understanding does develop between a board and its superintendent, new board members may seek the elective office intending to revise the previous arrangement. It is true that the highest officer of an institution which ought to be dedicated to change as conditions warrant, should not be hamstrung by rigid job specifications. Job definitions should be broad enough to allow latitude in adjusting to fluctuating conditions, and discretion in the interpretation of expectations. Nonetheless, the vagueness which has characterized the position of public school superintendent lies at the root of the instability, which is another of its characteristics.

As the head of a social organization which is subject to human fickleness and bias, the superintendent stands in the vulnerable position of representing whatever humans dislike about the organization. He is the symbol of the school system which touches people in two sensitive spots —their children and their pocketbooks. It is natural, then, that when citizens become dissatisfied with any facet of the gigantic operation they anticipate satisfaction through a change in the responsible officer. Since the role is not fixed, and naturally subject to alteration, and since the superintendent does not have tenure for the position, his enforced departure is easy to effect.

After a century and a half, there has been no studied decision, widely accepted, as to the precise function the superintendent should perform. Statutes and custom have clarified that public education is a public function to be managed by the representatives of the public, the board of education. State laws allow the community's representatives to, among other things, engage necessary personnel to perform the public function. But exactly how a superintendent fits into this public but technical arrangement is left to the fumbling of the governing body and the initiative of the superintendent. The arrangement allows every mother's child to apply his personal predispositions to what can be expected from the office; thus, thoughtful persons frequently conclude that it is an impossible position under prevailing conditions.

In addition to the avalanche of wants to be satisfied by all those who are touched by the school system, recent major events beyond his control have been aggravating the impossible nature of the superintendent's situation. Sudden changes in the employment market have thrown many breadwinners out of work, unprepared for new demands, with the blame eventually coming to rest on the head of the institution which is supposed to prepare individuals for self-support. Many people are looking to the schools to correct the social injustice which the schools did not make, which segregates attendance by race. A widespread philosophical disagreement, dormant for many years, between those who favor either public or parochial schools, has been resurrected in the search for sufficient money to conduct educational systems. The persistent problem faced most directly by school superintendents has grown worse with spiraling costs and enrollments confronted by an increasing reticence on the part of taxpayers to provide more money. This reticence has stirred a restlessness within the organization which, in some instances, seeks to ignore whatever common understandings have developed about the superintendent's role between the governing body and the staff. The in-between characteristic of the superintendent's position has always given it a precarious status; now it is an impossible one, they say.

THE SUPERINTENDENT'S TWO COMMON TASKS

It is impossible to produce a single taxonomy of duties which superintendents perform. No two superintendents pursue their objectives in precisely the same way, nor identical objectives. No two working days in a superintendent's life are the same. One can only talk about the common duties which most superintendents perform. Even under this limited approach, there can be found only two tasks which enjoy unanimity in thought about his work; after that the listing varies according to viewpoint.

The most common assignment given the superintendent is that of executive officer of the board of education, who carries out the policies and directions of the governing body. This capacity accounts for the frequent assumption that he is the board's officer, not the staff's, and a sort of errand boy from the board carrying messages to the troops. The role gives employees the impression that the superintendent is aligned with management. In practice, however, the opposite is generally true.

In the first place, a superintendent is a professional educator, schooled as a teacher. He understands the processes and products of teaching more than he does those of the board of education. He is not placed in the office as representative of the community, except in those few districts in which he is elected to office. Therefore, if he carries messages at all they are mostly from the troops to the board of education. After consulting with the various segments of his unit, harmonizing conflicting aspirations as much as possible, he presents their views to the board for action. Further, he is the chief adviser to the board in the performance of its most important task, the formulation of policies. In best practices, the agenda of matters to be considered by the governing body is his agenda, not theirs. Board members are not close enough to operations to know what ought to be considered. As the professional technician for the school system, he advises the board not only of items for decisions but helps them with the decision. This method of operation will continue to be true in the future as districts grow larger, taking board members farther away from the day-to-day activities of schools and as education becomes increasingly technical. That is not to say that the community, acting through its representatives on the board, will become a rubber stamp for the chief executive. The statutory powers of a board of education to act for the district remain, and are unlikely to be altered materially. Larger school districts, however, move the board of education farther away from a true representation of community thinking. Except as the community chooses its representatives, people have less direct and continual voice in the operation of their public schools. This fact explains why out-of-channel means — citizens councils, a number of special-interest *ad hoc* committees, and frequent use of mass media — must be devised if there is to be desirable communication between citizens and their schools.

In actuality, then, the superintendent has the difficult role of liaison between the board of education and the staff. This two-way function gives rise to the question often discussed, "Whose man is the superintendent?" While he must represent both elements, he has and will continue to be more so in years ahead, the executive officer of the staff.

The second commonly acknowledged job of the superintendent is that of accountable officer for the entire school system. Although legally accountable to the board of education, school personnel hold him answerable, as do most citizens. This expectation introduces the risk factor to his office as well as the reputation of its being an "impossible" post. It means that as much as he delegates tasks and decision making, he must be held accountable for the results. It means that the probability of his success depends upon the caliber of persons he finds, or inherits, to carry out the workings of the organization. It means that he has to be a generalist insofar as the kaleidoscopic activities of the organization are concerned. He has to know something about every phase of the operation, even though he will personally do none of them in larger districts. It means that his only "doing" speciality needs to be in the one area as cited in the original definition of educational administration — the coordination of forces. It means that the running of a large school system is no longer a one-man operation; rather, it is a team approach under the direction and accountability of a person called a superintendent. The divisible tasks which were once pooled into a taxonomy to describe the work of a superintendent are becoming more divisible, each being assigned to a specialist as a subordinate officer. The combined efforts of these administrators produce what is more accurately described as the "superintendency function" to denote a joint rather than a one-man operation. *The* superintendent coordinates the work of several specialists and is accountable for their actions.

Efforts to define the superintendent's role beyond these two broad assignments lead into either subordinate elements of the two tasks or to opinion, and the reader is invited to pursue those interpretations in the selected readings.

SKILLS NEEDED FOR THE SUPERINTENDENT'S ROLE

Authorities dealing with the work and the preparation of the school superintendent part company according to the conceptualizations of what he does or ought to do. Each would prescribe the needed skills to conform to the roles he would assign the officer. And, as already pointed out in this chapter, the prescriber would receive little help from the widely divergent understandings of what the superintendent does or should do. The student will recognize, therefore, that the skills suggested here are predicated upon the author's understandings of what is and ought to be the chief administrator's work. The reader must accept the two broad tasks as being the most important before he can accept the four recommended skills hereinafter noted as basic to successful performance. No priority of importance is assigned to these four skills. Each is regarded as crucial, and others of lesser importance could be cited.

Essential to the superintendent for assuming the post and for withstanding the numerous pressures which will inevitably accompany such an ill-defined but responsible office is good health, both physical and emotional. To be everything to everybody and totally accountable calls for a vigor well beyond that expected for most occupations. The author is not ready to advocate that school "superintending," like coaching a sport, is a young man's game, despite the temptation to do so. There are too many older men who manage the situation admirably. Experience as a superintendent provides an equanimity and stoic perspective which enables a mature person to classify pressures into those which deserve worry and those which do not. Nonetheless, the myriad demands for his presence necessitate an extremely healthy body and mind.

A second essential skill in order to perform the two common tasks — liaison between staff and governing body and coordinator of all school operations — is the ability to communicate and relate well to others. Liaison is accomplished only through communication: verbal, written, and the non-verbal muted language. Coordination is accomplished only through communication with and through people; hence, one sees the inevitable return to all that is meant by the words, "human relations skills."

The superintendent must be whatever is meant by the term "administrator." Here, it is intended to mean the skill for getting things done. Though disagreements will continue as to what should be done, each advocate of a mission involving education of elementary and secondary school students turns to the superintendent for getting it done. Administrative skill, the subject of this volume, stems from a knowledge of organization, processes, human behavior, and objectives. A job gets done only by moving from thought to action; thus, the superintendent as an administrator, unlike most who earn a living, must be action-oriented.

The fourth crucial skill for the superintendent is the capacity to envision. Envisioning as used here means more than predicting the results of a decision. It is more than the ability to "see the parts in relation to the whole picture," as is often named the most important talent of a superintendent. It is more than planning. It is intended to mean a skill, needed by the superintendent more than anyone else associated with education, to divine what the resources of education should be doing. It is goal setting. Envisioning for a superintendent means that he is not the victim of power pressures; he is the power that is moving pressures in a direction. As a realist, he recognizes the existing powers, works with them, perhaps temporarily compromises with them, but moves each day toward a vision.

Since envisioning is a mental activity, one needs for it at least above average intellectual powers. Pure intellectualism may not suffice, nor will a talent for merely storing knowledge. The kind of mentality needed to envision is creative, imaginative, and uninhibited. Further, the exercise of that native talent in developing goals for education must be guided by knowledge of what instructional efforts can do, of what other social forces can or should do, and of what mankind wants or should be wanting.

The implications for an ideal superintendent preparatory program may be extracted from these skills, if one accepts their accuracy. The program must be selective in admissions, providing breadth of knowledge as well as depth in technical knowledge for the unique elements of school administration, philosophically and historically grounded, and challenging to the mind.

THE SUPERINTENDENT'S ROLE IN CENTRAL ADMINISTRATION . . .

WHAT DOES A SUPERINTENDENT REALLY DO?*

Generally speaking, there are a number of basic functions of the superintendency. These functions are an integral part of the work of every superintendent of schools, regardless of type or size of school system. *Planning and evaluation* underlie the entire complex. *Organization* establishes a framework. *Personnel, business, buildings,* and *auxiliary services* establish the necessary operating conditions for the educative process. *Information* and *advice* provide a two-way sharing of knowledge and ideas with the public and the school staff. *Coordination* binds all together so that the manpower and the materials of the entire school system may be focused on the larger function of *instruction*. A good superintendent of schools must be competent in each of these areas.

A great many research studies have been completed on the qualifications necessary for success in the superintendency. Generally speaking, the following factors seem to be among the most important:

Ability to see the whole picture
Unusual understanding of people
Unusual ability to live with a high-pressure job
Administrative experience — usually as a high school principal
Ability to handle the multitude of technical aspects of the job
High intelligence.

On Selecting a Superintendent of Schools, Washington, D.C.: by permission of the American Association of School Administrators, 1962.

THE SUPERINTENDENT AS
A LEADER*

The superintendent is in a key position to influence the development of the school. His professional competence and his way of approaching problems set the tone of how people work together. The superintendents of these adaptable schools show more likenesses than differences as administrators and as people. It is significant that in these schools so many different men show such striking similarities. These superintendents think of the whole staff, including themselves and business and custodial workers, as a team, a functioning unit working on a common problem. They tend to view lay people as team members or potential members. They are not jealous of power. They delegate responsibility and authority freely to those who can or will try to do the job at hand. Their attitude induces the feeling among their co-workers that personal prestige of the team members comes best from the accomplishment of the whole group. They are willing to learn from co-workers. They rely on the give-and-take of democratic discussion because they believe that the best solutions to problems come from this method. This personal demonstration of their belief in the effectiveness of the democratic process has a far-reaching influence among the staff and the community. The peculiar abilities of co-workers are freely recognized and every opportunity possible is utilized for each to have his place in the sun. Personally they are vigorous, highly trained, and self-critical men. They give others an impression of personal integrity and professional competence.

---

*Alfred H. Skogsberg, *Administrative Operational Patterns,* New York: Teachers College, Columbia University (Metropolitan School Study Council), 1950, 18. (By permission.)

SCHOOL ADMINISTRATION —
A PROFESSIONAL SPECIALTY*

Just as school systems are unique among organizations, so their administration naturally enough has a history and characteristics that set it

---

Management Surveys for Schools; Their Uses and Abuses, Wash., D.C.; by permission of the American Association of School Administrators, 1964, 15-17.

apart. Many school districts were being administered by a "manager" responsible to a "board of directors" who represented a large number of "owners" long before this became the typical pattern in corporations. . . .

The earliest management of the public schools in America was directly by lay citizens, either as sole trustees or as committees who split up tasks among themselves. With few exceptions the early districts were small rural or neighborhood enterprises. Managing them was a simple thing at best. The farmer and storekeeper had businesses of their own which were more complex and bigger than the school's. As people who were accustomed to call their own preachers and run their own churches, they had few qualms about managing their neighborhood schools. Hiring a teacher, arranging to board him, buying the fuel and few supplies, and keeping some [kind] of records were chores that any solid citizen could do in his spare time.

In some states and in the larger cities school systems soon became more complex. Their management quickly became a burden on trustees who could give only their spare time to it. In a few cases one of the trustees took on the job full time. More typically the board hired a promising educator to take over, usually without any clear specifications as to his job. The title *superintendent* came into early usage, designating at first someone who was little more than a head teacher. In the beginning he was not often in full charge of all the affairs of the schools.

By 1865 the position of superintendent had become widely enough established so that men who had a few years earlier led in the establishment of a National Teachers Association felt the need for a special organization of their own. In that year they formed an association of school superintendents which devoted itself to the improvement of public education generally, which enabled these strong leaders to make their collective voice heard, and through which they could work together on common problems in school administration.

Even then it was only in the larger systems — mostly in the cities — that the superintendent had much help in administration from professional assistants or specialists. In smaller systems he often did only part of the total job while individual board members did the rest. Even in the larger systems, the board members frequently hired specialists for accounting, purchasing, and other administration chores, who reported directly to the board or even to a committee of the board.

Most early superintendents had to work out for themselves the full shape and scope of their jobs. Naturally enough they tended to find roles that conformed in part to their own particular interests and capacities and in part to the traditions and dispositions of the particular school board. In business affairs board members were apt to feel more confidence in their own abilities and less confidence in a school man. As a consequence they tended to center responsibility in someone else who was directly under their control.

Here and there one can still find a multiple-executive school administration in which the management of the business affairs is formally independent of the educational leadership. In small districts there are still boards who don't trust school men with full executive responsibilities, particularly in business affairs. But these are exceptions. Generally speaking, most school superintendents today administer all of the internal affairs of the local school system. Most boards of education consciously and conscientiously fix their attention on policy.

THE SUPERINTENDENT — HIS ROLE AND PROFESSIONAL STATUS*

All these circumstances suggest that the major role of most superintendents must be that of arranging the environment so that the educational enterprise may remain vital. This means, we think, that most superintendents cannot be the instructional experts in their schools. To be sure, superintendents need to have a very clear notion of what schools are for and what kinds of people and physical facilities are needed if the objectives are to be attained. But it is chiefly at the level of goals and policy that the superintendent can give leadership to the staff and to the community. While subordinates to the superintendent may extend and implement his leadership with the staff, frequently only the superintendent can make the case with key groups and individuals in the community.

Obviously, we are ascribing a political role to the superintendent, but a political role with educational underpinning. As long as education remains as decentralized as it is in the United States, we see no alternative. If the superintendent of schools does not make the case for public education and wage the fight for community support, there will be a serious void in most communities. This does not suggest that the superintendent is without allies. Actually, much of his job may be the cultivation of lay leadership for education in the community. His board

*Roald Campbell, "The Superintendent — His Role and Professional Status," *Teachers College Record,* LXV, (May, 1964), 676-678. (By permission of Teachers College Record and Roald Campbell.)

members and other lay citizens may become the community spokesmen for education, but behind them a catalytic agent is needed, and for that role the spotlight is directly on the superintendent.

PROFESSIONAL STATUS

If we accept the superintendent as an educational politician, the man who mobilizes the support of his board and his community for defensible programs of teaching and learning, we may begin to examine his professional status. The professional, as we have noted, possesses a unique body of knowledge, performs an essential social service, is carefully selected, undergoes rigorous training, is altruistic with clients, and enjoys considerable work autonomy.

With such criteria in mind, approximate though they may be, we can usefully examine the current status of the superintendency as a profession. We have already indicated that the role of the superintendent is somewhat confused. In part, this is due to many small scale operations and in part to the unrealistic expectations in many quarters that he must be an instructional expert. With the role of the superintendent not clear, it becomes difficult to define the body of knowledge thought to be pertinent to his practice. Since there is no general agreement on such a body of knowledge, there tends to be variety in the content and method of training programs with perhaps more reliance on experience *per se* than on understandings and skills. Some shift in this balance may now be taking place as exemplified by the recent action of AASA in requiring, as a prerequisite for membership, an approved two-year training program at the graduate level.

There appears to be little question about the importance of schools to society, but there is still a question in the minds of some as to just how the administrator contributes to the improved operation of those schools. With respect to altruism, superintendents probably rank as high as most occupational groups. While many superintendents are not without personal ambition, they give, by and large, devoted service to the people of their school districts. As to professional autonomy, superintendents have relatively little. Education is a public function and the people insist on having a hand in it. Moreover, with the role of the superintendent not generally understood, boundaries surrounding the domain of the superintendent appear to shift and at times to collapse. . . .

If the superintendency is emerging as a profession, what can be done to improve its professional status? A number of possible courses of action, some of which have already been implied, are worth considering.

COURSES OF ACTION

First, the heterogeneity of the position should be reduced. This action is tied closely to school-district reorganization and the elimination of school districts with very small enrollments. . . .

As a second course of action, it seems necessary to define more clearly the role of the superintendent. If he is the educational politician, as contended here, he has a unique function to perform. This function includes the capacity to help professional school people and lay citizens understand more clearly the role of education in society — particularly in our society — the capacity to visualize the components of an educational program appropriate to the school district and in keeping with the larger purposes of education, the capacity to build and direct an organization to implement such an educational program through its planned content and its personnel, the capacity to manage needed physical resources, and the capacity to secure community understanding and support. . . .

The place of the university is even more strategic in the third course of action — the definition and development of a body of knowledge thought to have particular relevance to the superintendency. While this cannot be done without consultation with the practitioner, the major responsibility remains with the training institution. If the fundamental capacities of the superintendent are to be developed, then the relevant body of knowledge must include educational history and educational philosophy, the psychology of learning and alternative strategies for instructing and guiding students, the nature of organizations and of administration, community decision-making as affected by social, political, and economic forces, and an opportunity to relate concepts and theory to practice by means of case studies and actual field experience under adequate supervision.

SELECTION, TRAINING, SKILL

More careful selection of students for administrative training is a fourth course of action. If teaching experience is retained as a prerequisite, I suggest that no more than two years be required so that candidates can get on with their administrative training while still young and without heavy family responsibilities. I think it highly desirable that some programs of training in which no prior teaching experience is required also be established in the hope of tapping a new population for administrative work. . . .

As a fifth course of action, training programs themselves need substantial improvement. Much less reliance on experience *per se* and much more on acquiring understandings, attitudes, and skills under the direction of a university with the necessary opportunity to practice in the field seems urgently called for. This training would appear to require no less than two years of graduate study in full-time residence at a university, followed by a full-time internship in the field. Obviously, most candidates would require fellowship assistance for the first two years and a stipend from the receiving district during the internship year.

Finally, it seems to me that the superintendency will become still more professional when the superintendent practices more skillfully. When he demonstrates greater insight regarding the role of education in society, when he conceives more adequately the needed components of the school program in his community, when he builds a more effective organization to implement such a program, and when he increases understanding and support for the program with which he is charged, his professionhood will be manifest. Professional status is extended by society only when society is convinced that an occupational group has relevant and effective procedures for selecting, training, and disciplining its members. . . .

ADVICE TO A SUPERINTENDENT FIFTY YEARS AGO*

He must learn to lead by reason of his larger knowledge and his contagious enthusiasm, rather than to drive by reason of his superior power. The powers and prerogatives which are guaranteed him by law he must know how to use wisely, and he should be able to win new powers and prerogatives from the board largely by reason of his ability to use them well. He must constantly remember that he represents the whole community and not any part or fraction of it, and he must deal equal justice to all. As the representative of the whole community he will be wise not to ally himself at all closely with any faction, or division, or party in it.

He must, out of his larger knowledge, see clearly what are the attainable goals of the school system, and how best and how fast to attempt to reach them. From his larger knowledge, too, he must frequently reach up out of the routine of school supervision and executive duties into the higher levels of educational statesmanship. As a statesman, too, he must know how to take advantage of time and opportunity to carry his educational policy into effect. . . .

---

*E. P. Cubberley, *Public School Administration,* Boston: by permission of Houghton Mifflin Company, 1916, 138-139.

THE IMPORTANCE OF A THOROUGH KNOWLEDGE OF THE POWER SYSTEM*

The most successful school superintendents are probably persons who understand the critical elements of the power structure and have used this knowledge to advantage in school politics. A successful school superintendent in a city with a population of over 300,000 related:

> About 30 years ago, when I was a young school principal, I decided to find out who the eight families were that run this city. I found out who they were and I have watched these families pass this influence right on down to the younger generation. They have all the banks and insurance companies. They operate the local industries of any size and own all the downtown property.

One might question the scientific accuracy of the superintendent's contention that eight families monopolized city politics. Perhaps he has oversimplified and overgeneralized. However, his theory of politics has served him and the school system well. His theory helped to enlist the power of the city in educational improvement. This school system at the time his statement was made had the highest expenditure per pupil of any school system in the state and was recognized as a good school system. A theory that results in improvement is worth more than a dozen academic suppositions.

Some educators have expressed concern about the insistence that the school leader should understand the power structure, calling this attitude undemocratic. Yet, to possess a knowledge of the decision-making process is not undemocratic. A colleague of the author, commenting upon the contention that the use of such knowledge was not democratic, stated the issue succinctly as follows: "In other words, a person who does not know what he is doing is democratic — a person who knows what he is doing is autocratic." In reality, it is probably the lack of knowledge of the decision-making process which has resulted in very undemocratic decisions. Unless the school leader knows the political process, he may err through misinformation about the extent to which democratic procedure is involved in the decision-making process.

---

*Ralph Kimbrough, *Political Power and Educational Decision-Making,* Chicago: by permission of Rand McNally & Company, 1964, 274-275.

The practicing school administrator must begin to look beyond the immediate membership of the official decision-making system. Who are the strongest power-wielders in the school district? What is the form of the power structure (monopolistic, competitive, pluralistic), and what groups (formal and informal) constitute the critical elements of power over big policy decisions? What resources do the men of power control in the district, and how are these used to affect policy? What are the operational beliefs that give direction to groups in the power structure? What patterns of interaction characterize the dynamics of the power structure in the resolution of issues? What are some possible latent power resources which are not often used? How solidary are the educational forces in political issues?

Students of educational administration should be given considerable preparation in educational politics with a behavioral bent. In the past there has been a tendency to send students "out" for catalogue courses in political science, sociology, and economics with the expectation that this will assure some form of social and political literacy. The behavioral disciplines can help greatly if they are coordinated and selected. However, there are different schools of thought in political science just as there are several brands of educational philosophies. If we happen to select the wrong school of thought in course selection, the prospective educational leader will be uninformed about the behavioral politics of education.

THE ADMINISTRATOR IN POLITICS ...

THE SUPERINTENDENT AS A POLITICIAN*

Two factors limit a superintendent's objective judgment on politics in education: (1) the nature of his community; and (2) his own personality and techniques of administration. Viewed from the perspective of individual experience, the observations of scholars and researchers often appear generalized, superficial and even droll.

As I write these lines, the influence of state and national legislatures, politicians and educational theorists seem pitifully obscure in relation to a matter that recently came to my desk and is likely to haunt me for

*Charles H. Wilson, "The Politics of Education," *Educational Administration Quarterly*, I (Spring, 1965), 70-76. (By permission of University Council for Educational Administration and Charles H. Wilson.)

months. Our secondary principals decided to abolish inter-scholastic football! No number of scholarly books, no amount of educational research, no state or national legislatures can offer the slightest assistance in weathering the storm that undoubtedly lies ahead. . . .

My life is a constant political search for the power structure and votes to inch the schools of my community toward a more constructive educational role in the lives of boys and girls.

As a politician, I am continuously compromising. The compromise is the essence of my existence. If it were solely up to me, I should abandon all interscholastic competition, eliminate grades and report cards, make schools voluntary in attendance, extend the school year to eleven or twelve months, maintain a twelve-hour staggered school day, triple the size of some classes, cut to a third the size of others, double teachers' salaries, reduce Board meetings to one a year, cut the administrative staff in half, prohibit parents from stepping foot in a schoolhouse, and otherwise improve the educational system. It is plain to see that I am a first-rate compromiser, a wheeler-dealer in the art of the possible.

I shall endorse, however, a conclusion reached by Burkhead in *Public School Finance* that "There is an apparent need for better scientific theory about human conduct." To put it in my own words, it would be useful if every superintendent were endowed with a supernatural gift of clairvoyance which would tell him in advance how many "yes" votes he could expect on the upcoming bond referendum. He could then be like the man who sought to learn the exact time and place of his death so that he could conveniently fail to show up.

It is not my intention to disparage the careful study and effort that went into the preparation of these books under consideration. They are well researched and all offer broad constructive suggestions to the student anticipating a career in school administration. My only concern is that the gap between the scholar and practitioner may be widening with the growing interest in educational research. Where it would seem that educational research should center more and more upon children and how they learn, we see too many broad surveys and theoretical speculations that have little or no value to the teacher or administrator working with boys and girls. . . .

Indeed, it often seems that an invisible but impenetrable curtain separates the research scholar from the practical administrator. We meet occasionally at state and national conventions like emissaries from the United States and Red China and return to our bailiwicks to pursue separate courses, totally ignoring the pleas and propaganda from the other's camp.

I know this is an old lament, and perhaps there is no remedy for the isolation of scholar and practitioner short of total reorganization of graduate schools along the lines of medical colleges. (I am reluctant to state this problem lest some research grant be designed to study it.) But the superintendent needs to spend at least a third of his time away from the pressures of Mrs. Busty and Monday Morning Quarterbacks in the calm, literate environment of the college classroom; and there is no scholar of my acquaintance who could not profit immeasurably from periodic responsibility for a budget, a Board and a bond referendum.

For it is an indisputable fact of life that the most important consideration in the superintendent's existence is winning the next tax referendum. No matter how the scholar purses his lips and wryly asks if a good educational program will not gain the public's support, the painful fact is that there would be no program to speak of without the successful passage of the next tax levy. The graveyard of superintendents is loaded with brave young idealists who were taught, or who imagined, that communities were breathlessly waiting for bold innovations, theoretical reflections, or far-seeing educational planning.

Nor does it matter that there are almost as many political techniques as there are practicing superintendents. Even within the same communities, superintendents may succeed using different techniques with different power structures. One man may appeal to the athletic crowd and still manage calm among the intellectuals, while the second may be the darling of the intelligentsia and fend off the Booster's Club. In either event, the problem still remains one of somehow delivering a majority of favorable votes on election day.

Thus, in the most literal terms, a superintendent is a politician, relieved only of the necessity of finding immediate employment in event he fails to garner a majority of the votes. But it is only temporary relief. His two- or three-year contract is often brief by comparison with a governor's four-year term or a judge's six years without intervening elections and a substantial advantage for [re-election].

There is a strong temptation on the part of a superintendent who has been successful (that is, who has never been directly or indirectly urged to seek another assignment) to indulge in the questionable vice of offering counsel. It is a vice to which I am as addicted as most men beyond the stage of "smooth, round belly" passing into the "lean and slipper'd pantaloon." But I am sensitively conscious that what has worked for me may not work for the next fellow. I preface all advice of mine with the warning that I am basically a lazy, gregarious, emotional ham who has learned more of life from the theatre and novel than the classroom and textbook. To the energetic, intellectual, well-balanced student, any political suggestions of mine might well be an invitation to professional suicide.

But having given the warning, I shall restate that the superintendent is a politician, that his continued existence as a superintendent depends upon his ability to deliver the votes. He may, or may not, also be an educator. He may well be dedicated to maintaining the status quo, indifferent and unfeeling toward children, totally disinterested in scholarship and learning; but if he is able to balance the budget, pay teachers' salaries, and somehow accommodate all the children under rain-proofed roofs in reasonably balanced temperatures, he can survive and possibly even thrive in superintendency.

Until one recognizes and accepts this basic political fact about local control and operation of American public schools, he is unprepared to dip his toes into the icy waters of school administration. But having thoroughly digested this knowledge, and then by endowment or study equipped to live with realities, he may proceed cautiously toward the end of actually improving the educational program in the schools for which he is responsible. I repeat, it is not essential he be an educator or bent upon school improvement. But most of us attracted to the profession have a mild, or at least cathartic desire, to do good. Having accepted and mastered the political realities, we are prepared, so to speak, to carry water on both shoulders. We can become educators as well as politicians.

It is beyond the scope of this short polemic to dwell at length upon what I might have in mind when I use the word *educator*. I have previously indicated some of the revolutionary changes I would make in schools if I were an educator freed of political considerations. I might also wish to establish completely ungraded schools, abolish textbooks, inaugurate grand-scale team teaching, in short, to shake hell out of our traditional, stereotyped, ox-cart system of educating the young. Moreover, much of what I might do as an educator could well prove to be hair-brained and need to be abandoned.

But we are here concerned, according to my assignment, with considering the political role of the superintendent. Wilfred E. Binkley once defined politics as the art of shifting an unpleasant burden from one set of shoulders to another. In school administration, one is daily confronted with an unending success of "shoulder shifting." The high school football coach laments the woeful instruction at the junior high level, while the junior high coach agonizes over the appalling failure of the high school coach to *develop* the material sent to him. The English teachers scream about their intolerable load, while the music teachers decry the emphasis upon traditional academics. The Tax Savers' League howls at waste as the P.T.A. demands smaller classes.

In the midst of this threatening and gross confustion, the superintendent-educator keeps one wary eye on the demands and the other on the ballot box. To the tax saving interests, he perhaps threatens the need of an additional three mills, hoping that an additional *one* mill will soften their sting; to the English teachers he promises relief with three mills and careful consideration of their problem with anything less. With victory at the polls, he is confronted by the coaches, the music and English teachers, and the P.T.A., all of whom read into the results approval for their special demands. Whose interests does the superintendent-educator heed?

He heeds his own, of course, according to his orientation and political acumen. Analyzing the election as best he can, he determines to improve the English department. Or, however odd it may seem, he may add to the coaching staff with the conviction that he needs to strengthen the support of this segment within the community, so that next year he may strengthen the English department. And on and on. Intuitively, or by careful analysis, he estimates the political strengths within his community, inching one way and then the other toward those goals which he deems desirable.

Do I give the impression that the superintendent determines the direction in which a school district moves? The answer is, of course that he does, if he is an educator in addition to being a politician. Remember, he need not be an educator. But if he is, he is in a more advantageous position to move a school district in any given direction than any other individual or group within the community, whether he moves an inch or a mile. Often, the man who moves an inch may be more of an educator than the man who moves a mile when he could and should have moved two.

In effect then, a community or its Board of Education is helplessly at the mercy of the conscience, the intelligence, the integrity, the courage of the superintendent it employs. If my thesis is accepted that the superintendent must inevitably be a politician to survive, then we are dependent upon other factors to hope for real educational leadership. And it is in this area that the scholar, the researcher, the professor of education must look if he is to have an impact upon American education.

If I am correct in my assertion that the gap between the administrative theorists and practitioner is widening, I suppose it is only fair to ask how the gap could be closed. I am not sure that I know. But I am reasonably confident that a dialogue among scholars, passing over the heads or the attention of the practicing administrator, is scarcely a productive enterprise. . . .

It seems to me that a more purposeful dialogue between scholar and practitioner might result from more extensive exchanges in assignment. I should like to see a fraction of what seems to be vast amounts of money devoted to esoteric research funneled into a system of scholarships which would bring the superintendent back to the college campus; similarly, I should like to see a system of endowed "sabbaticals" that would bring distinguished scholars into school districts — if they did nothing else but to conduct badly needed research projects or simply serve as question-asking gadflies. I suspect, however, such practical and useful gestures as these might be regarded with a jaundiced eye by the great money-granting foundations, which seem to prefer voluminous mimeographed and printed reports for safe filing.

SUGGESTIONS FOR IMPROVING THE SUPERINTENDENT*

1. *Educational administration is a dynamic profession which does not remain fixed but constantly is shifting, changing, and growing.* Educational administrative practice is not of such a nature that it can depend upon fixed associations, specific and unchanging skills, and static knowledge. Each new day and each new year presents novel situations for the superintendent of schools. He either must be equipped to deal effectively with such situations or be willing to accept the consequences of ineffective performance.

2. *Regardless of the amount or the quality of education a superindent of schools receives prior to assuming his position, his education is never completed.* So much is expected of the superintendent of schools in terms of leadership, technical knowledges, human relationships, and related job skills that it is becoming increasingly difficult for him to prepare fully for his position through preservice preparation programs. The very nature of growth and acquisition of knowledge is such that specific educational achievement at any particular time is merely a road marker on the highway of life. Growth and education are continuous throughout the life-span.

3. *The recent rapid advance of science and technology has placed new societal demands upon the schools and, in turn upon superintendents of schools.* The accelerating rate of change in

---

*W. H. Seawell and George W. Holmes, III, "Improving Administrative Leadership," *The American School Board Journal,* CXLVIII (February, 1962), 9-10 (published by the Bruce Publishing Company).

recent years staggers the highest levels of the imagination of man. The way of life, customs, culture, institutions, and more of the American people constantly are being altered. The political world changes so rapidly that obsolescence is apparent before maps can be drawn and geographies can be written. Scientific and technological innovations have appeared so rapidly that the theory and practice of the art of science of education have failed to keep pace with societal demands. Superintendents of schools constantly must be alert to develop fresh mental outlooks if they are to keep abreast of change and meet the demands placed upon them by those whom they serve.

4. *Some superintendents of schools have not engaged in adequate programs of professional preparation prior to assuming their positions.* Certification regulations of most states require minimal professional preparation in order to qualify for the position of superintendent of schools. Such minimal requirements, as a rule, do not give assurance that adequate professional programs have been completed before individuals become eligible for the position. Occasionally, local school boards select as superintendents of schools able young men who have demonstrated potential leadership and administrative ability and who have not completed adequate professional preparation for their positions. In such instances, it should be remembered that good men can become better men through continued professional preparation.

5. *Superintendents of schools are less transient than once commonly was believed; therefore, they should be assisted in their efforts to avoid the danger of "becoming stale" or "getting into a rut" after a long tenure in their positions.* Recent research reveals that superintendents of schools throughout the nation have remained in their present positions, on an average, for a nine-year period. Dangers of becoming enmeshed in the detailed work of helping to run the civic affairs of the community, becoming involved in business interests on the side, and becoming buried in the administrative minutiae of the job must be avoided. Superintendents of schools are subject to the same temptations to "become stale," or "get in a rut," as are men and women engaged in other professions. There is the ever present possibility that a superintendent of schools can become a 20-year veteran who has had one year's experience 19 additional times! Job efficiency rarely remains constant. In most cases, it either improves or deteriorates.

6. *The superintendent of schools, as an educational leader, must exhibit professional growth if those, whom he professes to lead, are to grow.* The most influential aspect of the leadership of a superintendent of schools is the example he sets. Professional growth is contagious. The superintendent of schools cannot expect his staff and his teaching personnel to grow [in service] unless there are evidences of continuous professional growth on his part.

7. *The superintendent of schools must keep abreast of newer educational practices in order to lessen the time lag between the discovery and application of new knowledge.* The problems related to the improvement of education in America are too crucial to permit any great time lag between the discovery and application of new knowledge. The superintendent of schools must involve himself in activities which will keep him conversant with what is happening in the professional field of education. Only through such involvement may school systems be assured of enlightened administrative leadership.

SUGGESTIONS TO SCHOOL BOARDS

Local school boards that are interested in maintaining the efficiency and effectiveness of their able and dedicated superintendents of schools often ask: What can be done by a policy-making body, such as a local school board, to provide opportunities for in-service professional growth for superintendents of schools? No one answer is a panacea for solving this problem. There are, however, some suggestions which might be helpful to those local school boards that are interested in the problem:

1. Administrative assistance should be provided for the superintendent of schools so that he may be relieved of routine administrative tasks and thereby be able to spend more of his time with underlying problems of leadership than otherwise would be possible.

2. Budget provisions, however small, should be made in every school system to support educational experimentation whereby new ideas and procedures may be tested.

3. Adequate travel allowances should be provided for the superintendent of schools so that he may attend state and national conferences pertaining to educational problems.

4. Leaves of absence for the superintendent of schools should be granted for educational travel.

5. Budget allowances should be provided so that the superintend-

ent of schools, from time to time, might employ consultative help in management practices and educational planning.

6. Leaves of absence should be granted for formal study.
7. Means should be provided whereby it would be possible for the superintendent of schools to visit other school systems in order to gain new ideas and insights.
8. Provisions should be made whereby a local school system and nearby colleges and universities may engage in a cooperative program of educational improvement within the local school system.
9. Provisions should be made whereby the local school system might affiliate with a cooperative school study council.
10. Adequate vacation time should be provided so that the superintendent of schools may have time for reflective thinking and recreational activities, thereby renewing his mental and physical vigor which is so essential to the rigorous demands of his position.

Many local school boards already have made provisions for effecting many of the suggestions offered. Others will improve opportunities for their superintendents to grow [in service] as time passes on.

Worthwhile outcomes of any enterprise are dependent upon the effective orientation of human effort and efficient utilization of material resources through the processes of administration. Whatever opportunities are provided for improving executive leadership within local school systems will be reflected in improved educational programs for the children and youth of America.

ADMINISTRATIVE STAFF OPERATION
AND MANAGEMENT . . .

THE ADMINISTRATOR'S JOB IS
PEOPLE, NOT PRODUCTION*

The superior is in a superior position because he is responsible for more work than one man can do. That is why he has subordinates. The fact that he has subordinates is the mark by which we know he is in a

*From *Psychology in Management* by Mason Haire. Copyright 1956 McGraw-Hill Book Company, 47-48. Used by permission of McGraw-Hill Book Company.

superior position. The principal defining characteristic of his job is as simple as that. He is responsible for more work than he can do alone; therefore, he has subordinates to help him get it done. The successful accomplishment of the superior's job depends primarily on his ability to get help from his subordinates in getting the job done.

This means that the superior's job — at any level of the management hierarchy — is people, not production. He may be responsible for production, but the medium through which he accomplishes it is people, and his success or lack of it depends chiefly on his ability to work through people. Only at the level of the hourly paid worker, at the bottom of the organization chart, do we find people whose job is production. At any step of management above this — from the first level of supervision up to the top — the job is to accomplish production through the intervening medium of the subordinates who are there because the superior is responsible for more production than he can accomplish by himself. To be sure, at various levels of management the superior may have to worry about production schedules, distribution of products, the flow of materials, and the like, but he cannot *do* the production. He must create a situation such that his subordinates will help him accomplish his objective by actually achieving the production. If he gets this help from his subordinates he is a successful superior; if he does not get this help he is failing, in some degree, in his job.

THE ROLE OF AN ORGANIZATION'S TOP-LEVEL STAFF*

Before discussing the major contributions that can be made by staff work, let me first reaffirm the fact that the job of establishing policies and making major decisions — in government as in business — belongs to the line organization, which for top-level matters means, of course, the chief executive. And the executive must assume full responsibility ·for these decisions.

There are six principal functions to be performed by the immediate staff assistants to top management:

1. to relieve the executive from routine matters which do not require his attention by making decisions on these matters in accordance with policies established by the chief executive;

---

*From *Executive Decision Making* by Marion B. Folsom. Copyright 1962 by McGraw-Hill Book Company, 10-11, 21-26. Used by permission of McGraw-Hill Book Company.

2. to collect and analyze data, both from within and outside the organization, and make carefully considered recommendations regarding new ideas, plans, and the formation of policy;

3. to review and follow up major policy decisions by acting as liaison and helping the principal department heads to interpret these decisions;

4. to help coordinate the work of the various divisions and departments;

5. to follow certain aspects of the business, such as product development or pricing policies, throughout the entire organization; and

6. to undertake special assignments. . . .

ROLE OF THE STAFF AS A "CHECK AND BALANCE"

The use of staff by management can be an effective tool not only in coordinating the activities of the various divisions, in liaison work, and in the follow-up of decisions, but also in the development of new programs and products.

Staff people, such as a budget officer, chief statistician, and other assistants to top management, can often keep a more objective viewpoint of the company's over-all situation than can the head of a division. It is their responsibility to see that the chief executives are given the full picture, with arguments pro and con. In this way, they serve as something of a "check and balance" for management. With adequate staff work, there is no reason for top management to make decisions that are not based on proper consideration of the pertinent facts.

One of the principal differences between management in business and in government is that business management, if it chose, could make quick and perhaps arbitrary decisions. The principal executive reports to the directors, who are concerned only with general, over-all policy matters.

In government few, if any, major policy decisions can be made by the top executives — even the President — without full discussion by many individuals with widely different viewpoints. The ability to persuade is a most important trait. Even if the top official has the authority to make the decision, he can be called and questioned about it before and after by Congressional committees. As a result, most important matters are thoroughly discussed by people representing various interests and groups before a decision is reached. The resulting decision is presumably based on what is considered best for the country as a whole. The process is slow, but it is democratic and provides many safeguards against hasty and undue action.

Through a staff that has the respect and confidence of line executives, business management can obtain this same protection. The process, of course, does not have to be as long and drawn-out as in government, as management is dealing with a closely knit group of people, all of whom have the same basic objective.

Many executives find that as important matters are fully discussed with their immediate staff and department heads — and assistant department heads who are probably closer to certain matters — not only will new facts be developed but the process itself will have an important effect upon the morale of the organization. Similarly, when differences of opinion exist, executives are finding it more effective to establish their point of view through persuasion rather than peremptory decisions. The ability to persuade can be as important in business as it is in government. The more people who feel they are participating in major decisions, the more effective will be the follow-through, and the easier it is to build *esprit de corps.*

Businessmen can also learn from government that while many incentives — such as salary, bonus, and stock options — are important, they are not the only incentives which are necessary to build up a good organization. For example, many top Civil Service career men who have reached the limit of their salary range perform just as capably for the government as many men doing similar work in business for much higher salaries. These people are dedicated to public service, and recognition and appreciation of their services help to spur them on. These less tangible incentives are equally as important to people in industry. This leads to a question as to whether, in addition to financial incentives, business should not give more attention to other types of motivation in general — particularly the need to demonstrate thoroughly to organization members the useful function they are performing for society.

STAFF ORGANIZATION HAZARDS

There are several serious hazards which must be guarded against in the growth of management staff and staff departments.

One is over-staffing. It is difficult, of course, to establish effective rules of thumb regarding the optimum number of staff people for any given situation. Generally, small groups of highly qualified staff people seem to work out best.

Over-staffing can be suspected when non-pertinent information is frequently brought up, when issues often become confused, and when decisions are too often delayed — and particularly when all three symptoms exist at once. A further aspect of over-staffing is that too many opinions, once the facts are assembled, can often lead to indecisiveness on the part of the executive.

One factor leading to over-staffing may be the attempt to fit people to an organization chart rather than fit the chart to the persons concerned. When an executive position changes hands, the new executive may need more or less staff people than his predecessor. It is foolish to fill a staff position without first questioning whether the position is still necessary or whether the position will be used in the same manner as it was previously. There are times when staff positions should be eliminated, as well as times when new ones should be created.

Another hazard arises when the executive depends too much on his staff for getting his information. When this occurs, the executive's contacts with the line departments will probably suffer, and by getting his information second-hand he will lose the opportunity to discuss matters with the department heads, who are meeting the problems every day. Furthermore, the morale of the organization is likely to suffer. On the other hand, if he listens to the discussion of all viewpoints, he will better sense the feel of the problem and be able to learn of different approaches. Without such complete background he will not be in a position to exercise sound judgment.

Still another danger is that the staff man, to save his boss time, will begin making policy decisions for him, especially if the staff man is of high rank. For the best relations between the staff and line organizations, it is particularly important that the staff man not make major decisions except in extreme cases where the executive is unavailable, and at all such times he should make it clear that he is acting *for* his boss. The executive will have to watch this situation as, without his knowledge, some staff men are apt to assume these policy-making functions.

(These remarks do not apply, of course, in those instances when an individual serves both a staff and line function, where the chief executive delegates authority to him in certain areas.)

A corollary to this situation is when staff people fail to call important issues to the attention of management because they believe the solution will cost too much to justify its acceptance, or because they think they know in advance that management would turn down their recommendation. When they do this, they are making the decisions themselves and are not giving management the opportunity to decide.

For example, suppose a company's wage administration staff people believe that the current wage incentive plan includes some provisions that run counter to the company's general wage policy. If they do not call the problem and the preferred solution to the attention of management because they believe it would cost too much to rectify past mistakes, they are in fact making the decision that no correction is possible. This, however, should be management's decision.

There is also a tendency by some staff men to shield their bosses from unpleasant news and contacts. Such protection can often go too far and prevent the executive from gaining pertinent information or learning of alternative points of view. As I pointed out earlier, the chief executive must be sure that all lines of communication are open to him.

A further hazard is that top staff people may refer matters to their boss which should first have been referred to a principal department head — who actually may have been able to make the decision.

These organizational hazards can be corrected without much difficulty, but they can creep in without top management becoming aware of them. It is unfortunate when they do creep in, because a *properly utilized* staff can be so helpful to management in arming it with the pertinent facts upon which to base sound decisions. In fact, effective staff work is one of the chief reasons why business management has become, as President Eliot suggested, a *profession* as well as an art.

WEAKNESSES OF THE ASSISTANT-TO POSITION*

Where the assistant to the chief executive does not fulfill his primary purpose — relieving the burden of the chief — or where he actually disrupts the smooth functioning of the organization, the causes are fairly clear-cut.

A few years ago the American Management Association investigated (by means of workshop seminars and private interviews, conducted by the authors, with assistants-to and their chiefs) the way in which assistants to high executives in some 140 organizations were functioning. In the cases where the assistant-to was not working out well, lack of success could be traced to one or more of the following causes:

1. *The duties of the assistant-to had not been defined.* "Just come into my office and see where you can be of help to me," the president had told him.

---

*From *Staff in Organization* by Ernest Dale and Lyndall F. Urwick. Copyright 1960 by McGraw-Hill Book Company, 166-168. Used by permission of McGraw-Hill Book Company.

2. *Relations with other executives had not been made clear.* "You may find Mr. Smith a little difficult, but you'll know how to handle him."

3. *Not enough attention had been paid to the selection of the assistants.* They lacked training or adequate experience in line jobs. In a number of cases, the authors found that young men were imported as presidential "brain trusters" immediately after taking their degrees. Those who have studied for six or seven years sometimes aim high and hope to get into top management by starting as assistants-to. In some cases, the character of the assistant left much to be desired.

4. *Executives failed to distinguish between general staff and specialist functions.* In consequence the assistants themselves had too much to do and so were unable to relieve their chief of many burdens.

5. *Executives failed to distinguish between personal and general staff functions.* Private secretaries and personal assistants tend to be apprehensive when an assistant-to is appointed. This is in part fear of the unknown, of the difficulties of adjusting to a new person. In part, it may be jealousy of the attention the chief gives the assistant. Also, the personal assistant or secretary may have been acting partly in a general staff capacity — handling the paperwork, acting as an interpreter, and communicating the chief's intentions to his immediate subordinates. Hence, when the assistant's job is defined, the private secretary's job and the relationship between the two functions should also be defined.

6. *Assistants-to were used almost exclusively on new or special projects.* Thus they had no time to relieve their chief of routine.

7. *Executives attached too much importance to paperwork and refused to allow the assistants to handle it for them.*

8. *The assistants were allowed, or even directed, to report (sometimes overtly, sometimes covertly) on the work of their chiefs' subordinates whose status was higher than their own.* As a result, the subordinates joined forces against them.

9. *Executives who had worked out a reasonable relationship between their assistants and their principal subordinates then went away for long periods without nominating any senior officer of the organization to "answer" for them in their absence.* This placed the assistants-to in an embarrassing position. They had either to act for their chiefs—and so arouse opposition—or do nothing, leaving all the problems to accumulate.

10. *Assistants-to were left in the position too long and felt that their prospects were uncertain.* The authors found a sense of frustration among a number of assistants because of this. There was a widespread feeling among them that an assistant should be a picked man with an assured future in the organization, and that he should be moved back into the line as soon as the training value of the position had been realized. After four or five years, at the most, they believed, the assistant-to should be moved into the line at an executive level just below that of the chief's immediate subordinates.

11. *Assistant-to positions were a dumping ground for the "organization's problem children,"* and so lost status in the eyes of the rest of the organization — with the result that able young executives avoided the job.

THE NEW BRAND OF SCHOOL SUPERINTENDENT*

A new brand of school superintendency is emerging upon the American educational scene. Its advent may not be widely heralded; nevertheless, it is quietly, at times sporadically, and certainly unequivocally, becoming apparent to the seasoned spectator. It is with the basic nature of this new superintendency, the requirements it makes of those entering the profession, the opportunities it offers, and its techniques of operation, that this book is concerned.

Until recent years it has been almost impossible to delineate either the characteristics of the superintendent's job or the personal and professional attributes of the man holding the post. As a result, no clearcut profile of the composite superintendency has been available to guide the individual who is contemplating the profession as a career. It is still difficult to accomplish such an analysis with a high degree of accuracy. Responsibilities of the office have crystallized to a considerable extent. Job descriptions can be written which specify its general functions. Yet today one finds superintendents whose endowments, approach, and methods of operation differ, but whose performances are appraised as creditable. It is still true that no single pattern of administration

*Robert E. Wilson, *The Modern School Superintendent,* New York: by permission of Harper & Row, Publishers, 1960, xi-xiii.

guarantees success in the superintendency. At the same time, it is possible for the experienced observer to identify certain emerging patterns of operation which are likely to be the most successful.

It is also becoming evident which characteristics of the successful superintendent entitle him to be labeled as the "new brand."

In the first place, the new school superintendent is professionally prepared for his work. Most boards of education have abandoned the traditional practice of elevating the best teacher in the system to the superintendency. They have come to realize that good teaching service alone does not assure good administration any more than a good courtship guarantees a successful marriage. The new species of superintendent has acquired successful experience in the classroom and in subordinate administrative posts, but has gone ahead to specialize in public school administration on a graduate level, possibly to include internship experience. Frequently, he holds a Doctor's degree.

Secondly, he is a dynamic fellow, personable, healthy, tactfully aggressive, and a leader. He has discarded the blue serge, severe demeanor, and professional reserve in favor of contemporary raiment, friendly helpfulness, and congeniality. He is intently curious about people as well as ideas. He has adapted to his peculiar needs the tools of the salesman, the diplomat, the trial lawyer, and the gracious receptionist.

Third, the new superintendent is a utilitarian psychologist. He is a student of human nature and a deft manager of people. He has acquired a practical discernment of motives, of individual and group differences, and of emotions. Although he may have protected himself with a tough armor to resist critical barbs, he is capable of both sympathy and empathy.

Fourth, he is an all-round able person. He not only knows sound educational theory and practice, but he is comfortable with the banker, the welfare agent, the sports enthusiast, the plumber, at the ladies' afternoon tea, or at the Great Books discussion. He possesses the necessary qualities for success in several occupations, and unless he has been approached by at least one industry for a much more lucrative position, he doesn't qualify for the category of the new brand. The only reason he remains in the superintendency profession is that he is still motivated by the same humanitarian philosophy that led him into teaching originally.

Finally, he is advancing to better posts rapidly, perhaps with greater speed than is good for him or the school systems he serves. He has arrived early in a good position, and the opportunities for the best superintendencies in the country are ahead of him.

IMPORTANCE OF THE
SUPERINTENDENCY*

A professor of education, noted for his interest in curriculum, was asked why he regularly attended the annual American Association of School Administrators' Convention, not noted for its concern with curriculum. His reply was flattering and challenging to practicing superintendents. "I have become convinced that if there is to be any progress in curriculum improvement, it must come through the superintendents of the nation. I want to get to know them personally. I'm discouraged with working through teachers' committees and college students. The superintendent is in a position to block change or to promote it."

Notwithstanding legal limitations placed upon the powers of the school superintendent, public restrictions that temper his decisions, and boards of education that want to run the show, the superintendent possesses enormous influence. Today most boards won't take action without the recommendation of the superintendent. From a practical operating point of view, therefore, he has authority over:

1. Who may teach.
2. Salaries of those who teach.
3. What is to be taught.
4. How it is to be taught.
5. Equipment and supplies that will be used to implement teaching.
6. Textbooks to be used.
7. What facilities will be built.
8. Where facilities will be located.
9. What school buildings children will attend within the district.
10. Hours and days of attendance.
11. Safety and sanitary conditions for school children.
12. Regulations governing the conduct of students from the time they leave home in the morning until they return.

Should one reflect seriously upon the significance of each one of these powers, multiply it by the 14,000 superintendents in the land, and consider that the powers extend to 1,000,000 teachers and 35,000,000 young people each year, one can begin to conceive the gigantic strength of this body of men. The importance of proper selection and training of every superintendent becomes obvious.

---

*Robert E. Wilson, *The Modern School Superintendent,* New York: by permission of Harper & Row, Publishers, 1960, 20-21.

FOR FURTHER REFLECTION OR INVESTIGATION

1. The idea is sometimes advanced that in our largest cities the superintendent of schools should be chosen from industry, or perhaps the military, successful administrators who are accustomed to the "rough and tumble" of public life. Discuss the feasibility of the idea.

2. Obtain through an interview with the following persons their views of what the job of public school superintendent should be: a practicing superintendent, a board of education member, a college professor, a teacher, and a community citizen. How do you explain the discrepancies in their expectations?

3. Write model job descriptions for the superintendents of school systems with 1,000 pupils, 10,000 pupils, and 75,000 pupils.

4. What differences may be extracted from the phrases: the "superintendent as a politician" or the "superintendent as a statesman."

5. A superintendent must be held accountable for all actions and decisions within the school system. Today he is also expected to delegate decision making to subordinates as much as possible. Is there a dichotomy in these two objectives? Can both be attained?

6. There are many demands upon the public school superintendent's first loyalty: teachers, students, board of education, citizens, his family, his conscience. Rank these six elements in order of priority as he makes educational decisions and defend your evaluation.

7. What emotional, physical, and intellectual differences are there involved between the study of superintendency, the internship in superintendency, and the performance of a superintendent on the job?

BIBLIOGRAPHY

Anderson, G. E., "Those E.D.P. Words Belong in a Superintendent's Vocabulary," *Nation's Schools,* LXXV, October, 1964.

Bell, H., "Role of the Superintendent in the Small School District," *Phi Delta Kappan,* XLVI, December, 1965.

Burbank, N.B., "How to Superintend the Board," *Nation's Schools,* LXXII, August, 1963.

Campbell, Roald, "The Superintendent — His Role and Professional Status," *Teachers College Record,* LXV, May, 1964.

Cubberley, E. P., *Public School Administration,* Boston: Houghton Mifflin Company, 1916.

Dale, Ernest and Lyndall F. Urwick, *Staff in Organization,* New York: McGraw-Hill Book Company, Inc., 1960.

Education of a Superintendent, Washington, D.C.: American Association of School Administrators, 1963.

Engleman, Finis, "Board-Superintendent Relations," *Overview,* January, 1962.

Fensch, E. A., and Robert E. Wilson, *The Superintendency Team,* Columbus, Ohio: Charles E. Merrill Books, Inc., 1965.

Folsom, Marion B., *Executive Decision Making,* New York: McGraw-Hill Book Company, Inc., 1962.

Haire, Mason, *Psychology in Management,* New York: McGraw-Hill Book Company, Inc., 1956.

Kenney, James, "Consider the Mirror Effect on the Administrative Staff of a School System," *American School Board Journal,* CL, February, 1965.

Kimbrough, Ralph, *Political Power and Educational Decision-Making.* Chicago: Rand McNally and Company, 1964.

Lock, J.C., "Superintendent: The Coordinator," *Texas Outlook,* XLVIII, July, 1964.

Management Surveys for Schools: Their Uses and Abuses, Washington, D.C.: American Association of School Superintendents, 1964.

Misner, Paul, "The Superintendent's Job Can Be Well Defined," *Nation's Schools,* May, 1963.

On Selecting a Superintendent of Schools, Washington, D.C.: American Association of School Administrators, 1962.

Professional Administrators for America's Schools, 38th Yearbook, Washington, D.C.: American Association of School Administrators, 1960.

Seawall, W. H., and George W. Holmes, III, "Improving Administrative Leadership," *American School Board Journal,* CXLVIII, February, 1964.

Skogsberg, Alfred H., *Administrative Operational Patterns,* New York: Teachers College, Columbia University (Metropolitan School Study Council,) 1950.

Smith, Sampson G., "Superintendent of Schools," *Teachers College Journal,* XXXIV, March, 1963.

Spears, Harold, "Superintendent and Leadership," *American School and University,* XXXVII, October, 1964.

Stimbert, E. C., and A. R. Dykes, "Decentralization of Administration," *Phi Delta Kappan,* XLVI, December, 1964.

The Unique Role of the Superintendent of Schools, Washington, D.C.: Educational Policies Commission, 1965.

Wilson, Charles H., "The Politics of Education," *Educational Administrative Quarterly,* I, Spring, 1965.

Wilson, Robert E., *The Modern School Superintendent,* New York: Harper & Row, Publishers, 1960.

Chapter 16

To Point the Direction for Educational Administrators

It has become trite, though still true, in the writings of professional education to cite the impact of social changes upon the lives of teachers and administrators. Such is the inescapable fortune of persons engaged in a social enterprise in a free society. The dramatic changes in the mid-twentieth century are undoubtedly more forceful in their impact upon the quality, training, and expected performance of public school administrators than for any comparable previous period. Anyone contemplating a career in educational administration should assess his own nature and ambitions in light of these changes before he squanders much time and money in pursuing the objective.

The most essential skill which the dynamic character of contemporary society thrusts upon all school administrators is, as suggested in the previous chapter, not the talent to adjust to change, but to evaluate and guide it. Not all changes are beneficial. At the same time, our public institutions are traditionally tardy in accepting desirable innovation. Because of the power inherent to the authority positions of school administrators, they, of all people, must be able to assay changes affecting the good man in a Good Society, to determine what their institution can do about it, and then throw the full weight of their power into augmenting or resisting the change. This responsibility calls for the caliber of person not often found at the school administrator's desk in the past.

What do the current change forces mean for the role of the school and its administrator? It is known, for example, that the trend toward large school districts as the result of both population growth and school district consolidation will continue. But what are the implications of this trend for the daily *modus operandi* of the administrator? What do the trends toward urbanization and suburbanization mean for school organization and the curriculum? What can be inferred for the schools from the accelerating transformation of the labor market as the result of technological changes? Does this mean a mere alteration of curriculum offerings, or something more? Do school people remain as awed observers of the fact that more and more mothers are employed, women already constituting a third of the nation's working force? What do the emerging young nations, world tensions, and shrinking distances between points upon and beyond this planet mean for education? Do those who influence the minds and values of youth need to do anything about the statistics of crime, divorce, disease, and mental disturbances, and if so, what? Are there implications even for the elementary school principal in the knowledge that over thirty million adults are voluntarily enrolling in some form of post-high school educational classes each year?

These are obviously not simple questions to be answered by men and women of mediocre talent. Nor are their solutions to be activated by people of mediocre emotional and physical stamina. It is hoped that these chapters have pointed some directions for educational administrators who desire to know what to do and how to do it when confronted with the implications of these questions. If the questions do not intrigue him, he is already too tired, intellectually and emotionally, to give any more thought to educational administration.

If he is intrigued, over two hundred thousand opportunities await the young man or woman to express his moving-and-shaking talents in the schools of America. He can expect to face at least two years of graduate work, necessitating sacrifice of money, time, and family. Whether or not the ideal preparatory program is ready for him, there are many good ones struggling, like the profession of administration itself, to become better. He can expect learning experiences in the emerging programs which emphasize multidisciplinary knowledges, research, theoretical and practical principles, curricular understandings, guides to human behavior, administrative techniques, and internship.

If this scope seems too wide, the aspirant would have wasted his effort anyhow.

THE FUTURE OF EDUCATIONAL ADMINISTRATION AND PREPARATION OF ADMINISTRATORS . . .

PREDICTIONS FOR THE YEARS AHEAD*

The forces which in the 1950's gave impetus to inquiries into what is to be taught in the schools and how it should be taught will grow

---

*Gene C. Fusco, ed., "Educational Administration in the Decade Ahead," *School Life,* XLIII, No. 5 (January, 1961) 5-11. (Material contributed by staff members of United States Office of Education.

stronger in the 1960's; and there will be an intensive examination of curriculum, organization, instructional technology, and use of staff. Many communities may well lengthen the school day to 8 hours for intermediate and secondary grades, and the school year to 200 days for all. Summer sessions will become increasingly common as a means of expanding and improving programs. Education will be extended both upward and downward: there will be more kindergartens and nursery schools, more community colleges (most communities of 50,000 and more will have their own), and more publicly supported junior colleges and technical schools.

Above all, the people of the United States will increasingly recognize that no nation can be stronger than the sum total of the capabilities of its citizens and that education is the key to the development of those capabilities. The Congress will be more and more concerned about the manpower needs of the Nation as a whole — needs that no State or group of States can meet alone. And the idea will gain ground that education, like military defense, social security, and highways, is a matter of national interest and should be financed by the entire national economy.

Because knowledge is part of readiness, this article offers educators and lay citizens some measure of the revolutionary changes that will take place in educational administration in the decade ahead.

ADMINISTRATIVE ORGANIZATION

Almost everywhere the adequacy and efficiency of the school administrative organization will be severely tested. Massive population shifts will continue to reduce pupil enrollment in open-country areas and to press heavily on urban and suburban localities. In densely populated areas the task of maintaining quality programs in the face of increasing enrollments and rising costs will require widespread organizational changes and adaptations. Rural areas will have to adjust to pupil loss. All levels of administration — State, intermediate, and local — will be affected.

Over three-fourths of the increase in public school enrollment will be concentrated in fewer than 200 metropolitan areas. The great increase in the size of metropolitan school systems will create problems of organization, facilities, finance, staff administration, and problems of adapting programs to meet new needs.

Metropolitan areas will be the new frontier in educational administration. A broad array of socioeconomic problems will call urgently for solution in metropolitan areas. We can look forward to numerous governmental improvement programs, most of which will influence school administrative organization, either directly or indirectly.

Decentralization of administration will become increasingly common in very large school systems. More and more large school systems will be subdivided for certain administrative services. There will be other changes, too, to counteract the undesirable effects of bigness and to keep the schools closer to the people.

Greater emphasis will be given to school redistricting in suburban localities. In the past, district reorganization was considered almost wholly a rural problem; but in the 1960's it will come to the suburbs also, in a particularly complex form. New programs will be specifically designed to deal with it.

The number of school districts will go below 20,000. Reduction in the number of school districts, now estimated at 42,000, will continue. Almost all nonoperating districts will be eliminated. Most new districts will be 12-grade units and will be larger, on the average, than those established in the past. An increasing number of reorganized districts, particularly in sparsely settled areas, will be of the county-unit type.

The internal administrative organization of medium to large school systems will undergo marked change. More pupil personnel services, more supervisory services and efforts to improve instruction, more emphasis on instructional materials, more attention to school business management—such changes will modify internal organization. Such changes will become increasingly common in large-area systems of the county-unit type and in recently reorganized districts.

Many small high schools that unnecessarily operate as separate units will be consolidated. As large administrative districts are created, many small high schools will be eliminated. Much of this kind of consolidation is likely to take place in States having the county-unit type of organization. In this process sharper distinctions will be drawn between necessary and unnecessary small high schools.

As the traditional idea of the intermediate administrative unit is reexamined, its organization structure will be altered. In a number of States, regional intermediate units of 2, 3, 4, or more counties will be established to provide many kinds of services to supplement and support educational programs of local districts. In a few States where no efforts have been made to strengthen an already existing intermediate structure, intermediate units may be abandoned.

The school principal will assume more responsibility for the instructional program. Concomitantly the central staff will assume responsibility for purchasing, transportation, food services, and maintenance. The trend toward decentralization of instructional responsibilities will lead to an increase in the number of professional assistants to the principal and to the practice of employing them for 12 months.

In State systems the trend toward board-appointed chief State school officers will continue. At present 22 States have their chief school officer appointed by the State board of education; 14 of these have adopted this method of selection since 1945. The trend toward this practice accents the policymaking functions of the State board of education as it provides control and direction for the State system of education and makes the chief State school officer the head of the board and the chief technical administrator of the State department of education.

The role of the State department of education will be broadened. As State governments expand their educational activities, it will become more and more necessary to provide for positive administrative coordination and direction of activities at the State level. It logically follows that greater administrative responsibility will be given chief State school officers and State departments of education.

The duties and powers of these departments will be broadened and their staffs increased. Consequently, State departments of education will be confronted by such problems as these: (1) Recruitment of specialists and technicians to conduct growing programs and to provide professional leadership to the field; (2) organization of staffs for efficient performance; (3) establishment and maintenance of cooperative relations with other administrative agencies; and (4) provision of adequate working and housing facilities for staff.

PLANNING

The challenges to public education in the decade ahead demand sound educational planning at all levels of government. Population mobility and the increasing interdependence of all units of government require that local planning be coordinated with statewide and nationwide planning. Long-range planning will supersede much of the haphazard planning that now responds to each new crisis. Planning will be increasingly based on reliable and comparable information and will be supported by quality research; it will require recruitment of people of the highest integrity— people whose zeal for truth is surpassed only by their dedication to the educational welfare of young people.

Educational program objectives will increasingly become the focus of the budget process. Budgets and accounting systems will be set up in such a way that it will be possible to measure the effort expended on specific educational objectives. The financial plan will develop from the educational program plan, not dictate it.

Complete, accurate, and timely information will be increasingly recognized as essential to sound educational planning. Since educational statistics must be used for both comparison and synthesis, data drawn from many sources must be comparable. Standardization, therefore, will be the keynote of recording and reporting—standardization of definitions, terms, and measures; and a continuing evaluation of terminology will lead to new terms and measures as conditions change. In addition, educational accounting will be expanded to take in all the elements of management—not just dollars but pupils, staff, property, and programs. Accurate accounting and prompt reporting will contribute much to sound educational planning.

Greater emphasis will be placed on systematic research as a basis for solving problems. Research will come to be considered the key to dynamic progress in education. Schoolmen will be more and more eager to accept and apply the results of research, to close the gap between the possession and the utilization of knowledge.

More modern machines and systems will be used in accounting and in recording and reporting information. Automatic processing of educational data will be standard practice. As local districts decrease in number and increase in size, a greater percentage of them will install machines. Machine techniques will be applied to data on pupils, staff, facilities, and school programs. As a result, teachers will be able to devote to the instructional program much of the time they now spend in record keeping.

State departments of education, equipped with a technical staff and the machines for automatic data processing, will become educational data centers. Much basic information will be recorded at its source in machine-usable form, and therefore can be quickly transmitted to local, State, and national agencies, to become part of a true intercommunicating system.

LEGAL STRUCTURE

To handle the educational problems that will continue to grow in complexity at all levels, officials will give increased attention to the legal structure for education.

School board members will need to understand not only immediate community problems, but also State and national problems. Board members will make greater efforts to be well informed and to be continually alert to changing needs. School board associations and related organizations will provide new and varied types of services to board members.

School board members will spend more time and effort in formulating policies to strengthen and improve the educational program. As a consequence, the administrative staff will be challenged to put forth its best effort to give board members timely and accurate information on developments in the school program and to call attention to forces influencing developments.

More local school systems will have the advantage of carefully organized and well-written school board policies, supplemented by administrative rules and regulations. This development will help school superintendents and the school board to differentiate between policy-making and administration, and will strengthen the relation between superintendent and board.

Many States will do more codifying and recodifying of their school laws. They will give attention to the substantive content of the school law and to the structure, form, and indexing of the school code. They will recognize the pressing need for codification of the rules and regulations of State administrative bodies that have regulatory powers over local districts. In addition, the sheer volume of statutes and administrative rules and regulations will result in an increasing demand for court interpretation and clarification, particularly on sensitive questions of public policy.

There will be increasingly urgent problems of coordination between school systems and other government agencies directly influencing educational planning. Such problems will be most prevalent in rapidly growing suburbs, which typically have many local government agencies. In some communities the overlapping jurisdiction of agencies will add complexity to school planning.

STAFF

Both size and quality of the staff in educational institutions will be affected by society's demands in the 1960's. Standards will be raised for training and selection, for performance and growth, not only because society demands these improvements but because the educational profession itself will take on more responsibility for seeing that improvements are made. This increased acceptance by the profession of responsibility for its own excellence may be the most significant contribution of the decade to development and utilization of staff.

The quality of the candidates for instructional staff positions will be substantially higher. A greater proportion of college graduates will be attracted to education as a result of improved professional standards and conditions, including a better reward system.

Major changes will be made in the reward system, including salary, fringe benefits, and other compensations which influence the achievement of personal and professional goals. As the several professional duties in the teaching situation become more clearly differentiated and the number of specialized positions is increased, professional and nonprofessional responsibilities of the instructional staff will be more clearly defined. Opportunities for growth and advancement within the profession will rise sharply.

Greater reliance will be placed on objective measures in recruitment and selection of staff. Such measures will materialize from current research into prediction of success. Use of these measures will be stimulated by the larger number of specialized positions for which requirements can be carefully delineated.

The teacher-class as the basic unit of the instructional program will be severely scrutinized. Advances in curriculum development and instructional materials and methods will necessitate the use of specialists and more flexible schedules from grades 1 through 12.

The total program of personnel administration, including the responsibilities of principals, personnel directors, and superintendents will be more highly organized. Although many personnel functions will be decentralized, the development and coordination of systemwide policies, paralleling a carefully planned program of personnel administration, will be centralized.

The current emphasis on the improvement of professional preparation programs for school administrators will be intensified. The characteristics of sound programs will be more clearly defined. If single discipline programs fail to meet the demands, interdisciplinary programs will become increasingly common. The early identification and recruitment of potentially successful administrators will be more highly organized.

Fewer members of the professional staff will be trained in public teachers colleges. The change of teachers colleges to State colleges will be accelerated, and by 1970 there will be few public teachers colleges left. Educators will be trained in institutions that prepare people for other professions too.

Organized and systematic inservice education programs for professional staff will be developed. Because of the rapid additions to knowledge in all fields and the scrutiny being given to teaching methods, educators will not long find their preservice training adequate. To maintain their professional status, educators will regularly participate in many types of inservice education programs.

FACILITIES

Predictions of population and school enrollment indicate that the United States will need more than 600,000 additional classrooms and related facilities in the 1960's. Design and use of these facilities will be influenced by —

1. An acceleration of and an improvement in State services by responsible agencies to local school districts, particularly in the interest of long-range educational planning and the coordination of Federal, State, and local efforts to provide the needed schools.
2. Technological developments in construction methods, engineering, building materials, and the manufacture of school equipment.
3. Research and experimentation in building design.
4. Socioeconomic influences on the size and number of school districts, the organization and size of each school, the methods of financing school construction programs and educational services, and the degree to which facilities are used by school and community groups.
5. Instructional innovations, including various teacher-student ratios, team teaching, educational television, machine teaching, and other technological developments in instruction.

School buildings will have more flexibility. Instructional and other spaces in buildings will be adaptable to changing teaching methods and varying scheduling patterns. For example, walls will be easily movable, permitting two or more rooms to become one large room or one room to be divided into two or more small rooms. They will make it possible to subdivide auditoriums into instructional areas of various sizes for both small and large groups, and thereby increase the use of auditorium space by as much as 90 percent.

School facilities will be more extensively used for both school and community activities. Trends toward a longer school year, a longer school day, more adult education programs—all these will increase the use of school facilities. Junior and senior high school facilities will be used for evening programs of community colleges and for college and university extension courses. Groups in many communities will use school facilities more and more for such purposes as recreation, meetings, and projects.

School planners and architects will make significant changes in school building design. In large cities, where land costs are high, there are likely to be schools with underground gymnasiums, auditoriums, civil defense shelters, and automobile parking and with towers for instruction, utilities, and general service facilities. There will be other innovations, such as—

1. The windowless school, artificially lighted and mechanically ventilated.
2. The "school in the round," which requires less building material, less corridor space, and gives each classroom more outside glass than conventional buildings.

3. Movable rooms made up of modular sections. These are easily assembled and taken apart; can be set up singly or in a cluster; are comfortable, functional, and architecturally pleasing.

4. Small neighborhood schools for young children (in some combination of kindergarten through grade 3) in heavily populated areas. These will not have to provide pupil transportation services and, since they do not need large gymnasiums, auditoriums, and cafeterias, will not need large sites.

School buildings will be planned and constructed so that they can be adapted to nonschool use. Urban schools that are abandoned as a result of outmigration or changes in land use will be convertible to office, factory, warehouse, or other business and industrial use at minimum cost.

Buildings for joint occupancy will be constructed in heavily populated urban and suburban areas. These buildings will include dwelling units and school, or business offices and school. A tall apartment building, for example, will have families living on the upper levels and their small children (perhaps kindergarten through grade 3) attending school on the lower levels. As the need for space in the primary grades decreases, space freed can be converted into dwelling units. If more school space is required, the process can be reversed. This plan will eliminate idle or waste space and will prevent overcrowded classrooms. In a similar manner, schools located in or near business districts can share buildings with store offices, and other type of business not incompatible with the operation of a school.

The school environment for both teachers and students will be more pleasant and comfortable. Year-round air conditioning will become more common, lighting will be improved, furnishings will be more attractive, and instructional equipment and furniture will be practical, functional, and easy to use.

School plant operating costs will increase. Factors in rising costs will be the maintenance of complicated equipment and the increased consumption of electricity for improved lighting and for electrically operated devices and equipment, such as air-conditioning systems.

School buildings will be more economically and efficiently constructed. Modular design, repetitive use of component parts, new and faster construction techniques, and improved building materials—all these will be part of the new efficiency. Improved building materials will make maintenance easy and long-range maintenance costs low.

Pupil transportation will grow more complex. As suburban areas continue their remarkable growth, they will increase their demands for more and better pupil transportation services, will require more rigid standards in the selection and training of schoolbus drivers. There will be greater uniformity among States in bus operating practices and· improved management and supervision. . . .

FINANCE

Federal support for public education will increase. If the past is an index to the future, the Congress will continue to discuss two kinds of Federal aid to public elementary and secondary education—general support and support for special programs. Federal revenues for public education will very likely continue to increase, and the relation of the Federal Government to State and local school systems will be more carefully delineated.

State surveys for financing education will be widespread. In view of the economic developments, shifting financial abilities within the State, and changing tax structure, many States will authorize comprehensive surveys of educational financing. Findings in these surveys will be useful to those who plan and adopt new laws affecting educational finance.

State support for public education will change. Most States have distributed flat-grant funds and equalizing funds to local school districts to support foundation programs, and funds for special purposes. During the 1960's, extensive interest in high quality educational programs, coupled with increasing public recognition that each person must be developed to his highest potential, will cause States to change their plans of support. The percentage of funds from State sources is likely to increase, particularly in States where this percentage now is low.

Local school spending patterns will change. Increased emphasis on quality education and on programs for identifying and developing talent will cause local schools to change expenditure patterns to meet new requirements.

Property taxes will yield more but will contribute a smaller proportion of school revenues. Although the public schools will receive larger amounts from the property tax, the proportion of total school revenue derived from this tax will decrease in most States as revenue from other sources increases.

Competition for the tax dollar will become acute. Revenue demands for higher education will necessitate substantial increases in State funds. Other public services such as health, highways, and welfare also are likely to compete for the tax dollar.

School bonds will be issued for shorter terms. As more boards of education realize that interest rates on long-term school bonds are higher than those on short-term and that the total amount of interest is much greater, more of them will issue bonds for shorter terms and thereby permit faster recuperation for the bonding capacity. It is estimated that by 1970 boards will be issuing school bonds for an average term of 15 years, rather than for the present average of 20 years.

School business management will become increasingly important. As school districts decrease in number and increase in size, and as educational expenditures mount, more attention will be given to all aspects of school business management. More school districts will employ professionally qualified management officials.

SCHOOL AND COMMUNITY RELATIONS

During the 1960's public schools and community junior colleges will increasingly become integral parts of the community. Community schools will be deeply involved in improving the quality of community living, and measures will be devised to determine how well they meet this objective. The high school and, especially, the community college will serve as intellectual and cultural centers for adults and for the near-adult student body. As the community depends more and more on its educational institutions for programs and services, the community in turn will become a vital part of the classroom and the laboratory.

Our traditional ideas of isolation and parochialism will have been severely shaken by 1970. Local, State, and regional groups will intensify their efforts to coordinate their educational planning and to take account of national and international interest. The schools will play a leading role in shaping community attitudes.

Organized programs for school-community relations will be tied closely to advance research techniques. Measurement scales will be developed which school administrators can use in analyzing and describing community characteristics. Opinion polling and other means of testing community attitudes will be more widely used.

The role of local citizen advisory committees will be refined and developed. By making continuing studies and engaging in long-range planning, these committees will serve as key agencies in strengthening public understanding of and support for education. They will be increasingly helpful to the superintendent and school board members in developing school policy.

More and more school systems will employ staff with special competence in the techniques of communication. These staff members will work closely with all staff members and school building representatives in interpreting educational information and communicating on a regular and systematic basis with the community.

Schools will conduct regularly scheduled and special television programs to increase public understanding of the educational program. The superintendent, his staff, and lay citizens will make the presentations; and, as a means of evaluating the influence of these programs, the school will provide the community with opportunities to respond.

Quality education will be major news in newspapers, magazines, and other mass media. As public concern centers on what is happening in the classroom, other school activities will receive less attention. Sponsors of television programs will become increasingly alert to the commercial value of programs that show developments in education, and networks will give more and more prime evening time to such programs.

IF I WERE AN ADMINISTRATOR TODAY*

My thoughts turn frequently to the times when I was a practicing school administrator. I look back on my work as a principal, a superintendent of schools, a member of the administrative staff of two large school systems, a State Commissioner of Education, a dean of a college of education. If I were in any of those positions today, I wonder where I would place the major emphases, to what I would give intensive effort.

I believe I have learned to trust those who work with me more fully than I formerly did. I know that my associates are equally concerned with the success of whatever tasks are undertaken. As a result, I would with confidence delegate more responsibility and authority to the members of the team.

I would put much greater emphasis on cooperative planning. Good planning results in better execution, it begets better results. It requires time, and that has to be found and scheduled. It has to be carried on continuously. It requires study, lots of it. It involves many people, and hence the need for constructive leadership.

Planning helps to sift the wheat from the chaff. It helps to resolve what is important and what is unimportant. It builds teamwork and group responsibility. It saves time, for planning seeks to discover what should be done, and how, and why. Planning gives better returns for the efforts expended, for there is understanding on the part of those who are involved in the undertaking.

I would put greater emphasis also on people, and probably less on techniques, methods, procedures. Not that these things are unimportant,

---

*Walter D. Cocking, *As I See It* (A collection of Essays on People and Their Schools), reprinted by permission of *The School Executive, American School and University*, 1955, 75-78.

but rather because emphasis on them tends to detract from the emphasis on people. Schools first, last, and always are concerned with people, how they can be helped, what can be done to lift their vision and assist them in their march to the stars. I would trade a thousand good techniques, no matter how perfect, for the satisfaction which comes in helping just one person to love, and live, and perform a little better. Yes, the business of the schools is people.

I would work more closely with the people of my community. I would spend less time in my office in the schoolhouse, and more out in the streets, the places of business, and the homes — where the people are. I more fully realize that the schools belong to the people, and that I am simply one of their servants whose job it is to help them get the most from their schools. My aim today would be to further and develop a real and continuing interest by the people in their schools. I would strive to help them discover what their schools could mean to them, and how they could work to achieve these ends. I would spend less time "selling" schools, and more time in helping people to know what good schools can do and working with them toward these goals.

I would spend more time and energy on the program of the schools. Teaching knowledge and skills, however well done, is not enough. Schools must help to improve the communities of which they are a part. Programs for community improvement must be based on an understanding of the resources of communities: people, social organizations, natural and physical resources. If I were an administrator today, I would devote myself in large measure to helping to formulate and operate a program which could improve these resources.

I would devote great energy to improving my associates and myself for the jobs we have to perform. I would not argue the need for expertness in the original selection of personnel for schools. All of us need to do a better job than we have done. However, regardless of the wisdom used in original selection and regardless of the competencies which staff members bring to their jobs, they must continue to grow.

There is no such thing as a constant level of competency. A person becomes either better or worse. One of the most important responsibilities of the school administrator is the continuing improvement of the staff. There can be no one formula which is guaranteed to give results. Constant analysis of needs, abilities, capacities must be made. Experimentation must be carried on. There must be courage to try new things. Time has to be found for study, visitation, travel, research. To improve oneself and to help others to improve are all essential to successful accomplishment.

Major Changes in Preparation Programs During the Past Five Years*

Major changes	Frequency	Rank
1. Increased emphasis upon interdisciplinary approach.	42	1
2. Establishment or strengthening of internship program.	39	2
3. Revision and up-grading of admissions, selection, and screening procedures.	38	3
4. Initiation of a two-year program.	35	4
5. Major revisions of courses — content, scope, etc.	30	5
6. Strengthening of staff — quantity and quality.	29	6
7. Addition of new courses.	25	7
8. Use of simulated materials, case studies, etc.	19	8
9. Raising of minimum preparation level for superintendents to above master's degree level.	15	9.5
10. Initiation of doctoral program.	15	9.5
11. Establishment or expansion of field experience programs.	13	11
12. Development or improvement in core and block course programs.	12	12
13. Revision of entire program or establishment of new program (type not specified).	11	14
14. More emphasis upon use of practicing school administrators in advisory capacity on program, in selection of candidates, etc.	11	14
15. Establishment of, or increase in, residence requirements.	11	14
16. Introduction or strengthening of seminars.	10	16.5
17. More emphasis upon research.	10	16.5
18. More emphasis upon field experience and involvement of students in area studies, surveys, etc.	7	18
19. Orientation of program to needs of practicing school administrators.	5	20
20. Development of cooperative programs with other institutions.	5	20
21. Establishment of central research and/or service centers.	5	20
22. Increased emphasis upon theory.	4	23
23. Expansion of library facilities, audiovisual materials, etc.	4	23
24. Increase in number of workshops, conferences, etc., provided.	4	23
25. Improvement in cooperative relationship with practicing school administrators.	3	25

*The Professional Preparation of Superintendents of Schools, Washington, D.C.: by permission of American Association of School Administrators, 1964, 28.

827

THE INTERNSHIP FOR PREPARING
SCHOOL ADMINISTRATORS*

WHAT THE INTERNSHIP IS

In order to constitute a bona fide internship in educational administration, the following conditions must be satisfied:

1. The student's field experience which is labeled "internship" is an integral part of his professional education which comes after or near the completion of his formal program of professional preparation.
2. His internship involves a considerable block of time — at least one semester on a full-time basis or the equivalent.
3. The student must be expected to carry real and continuous responsibilities in his field situation under the competent supervision of a practicing administrator.
4. The board of education or board of trustees of the institution in which he is interning supports the program at the policy level.
5. The professional school in which he is enrolled is joint sponsor of his program along with the school system or institution. The professional school also assists in his supervision.

Two additional conditions are highly desirable:

1. The state department of education recognizes and endorses the internship program for the state as a whole.
2. The national and state associations of educational administrators are on record as endorsing — and even requiring — the internship as part of each practitioner's preparation and as part of his requirement for membership in the respective associations.

Thus an internship in educational administration is a phase of professional preparation in which a student who is nearing the completion of his formal study works in the field under the competent supervision of a practicing administrator and of a professional school representative for a considerable block of time for the purpose of developing competence in carrying administrative responsibilities. The program, in addition, is soundly based upon the state's legal structure through the state education department and upon the approved standards of the profession through its associations.

---

*Daniel R. Davies, *The Internship in Educational Administration*, Washington, D.C.: by permission of The Center for Applied Research in Education, 1962, 1-3.

WHAT THE INTERNSHIP IS NOT

The internship is not an apprenticeship. There are a number of similarities which make it easy to confuse the two. Both involve direct, on-the-job experience. The difference is largely one of timing and degree of difficulty. Unfortunately, the two terms tend to be used interchangeably in practice. It is important, therefore, to clarify their differences.

Apprenticeship is the term applied to an on-the-job experience program, usually in the candidate's own school system or institution. There may be or may not be a working relationship with a professional school to assist in the process. The initiative lies with the school or institution, which selects promising candidates, gives them direct practice under the supervision of its own administrators, and even helps each candidate decide whether or not he should seek formal training required for the license.

GETTING STARTED . . .

HOW TO START AND ADVANCE IN EDUCATIONAL ADMINISTRATION*

How does a man or woman get a start in local school administration? With few exceptions the start will be made as a classroom teacher. The exceptions may be in fields of specialization where students prepare themselves specifically in school finance and business management, in accounting, in school housing, in school transportation, in school cafeteria operation, or in statistics and research. These kinds of special preparation will be almost entirely functions related to central office services. With such preparation—especially now that internships and administrative assistantships are becoming more common as an initial starting point — the individual may get a start in a school system large enough to justify such specialization.

The more traditional route may be described as follows: The individual prepares for a teaching position in elementary education, teaches and carries additional graduate work in preparing to supervise elementary education or to accept a position as an elementary school building principal. In such a position he carries additional work or gains a variety of

---

*Van Miller, *The Public Administration of American School Systems,* reprinted with permission of The Macmillan Company. © Copyright Van Miller, 1965, 538.

experiences in special assignments as he seeks a desirable elementary school principalship that will serve as a challenging and satisfying career post for him. Or he may seek a central staff position appropriate to his interests and training and may eventually seek appointment as a school superintendent. He may well find any of several central staff positions to his liking as career posts. Or an individual prepares for a secondary school teaching position, teaches and takes additional course work, including courses preparatory to serving in administrative positions, seeks a high school principalship, and then takes additional course work and gains additional experience in seeking a principalship that is challenging and satisfying. Or again, he may seek a central office position and eventually seek consideration for a superintendency.

If the grade classification and the year-by-year promotion of the present gives way to ungradedness and to programs of continuous progress, the distinction between elementary and secondary levels may not be as sharp a division of career routes as has been the case in the past.

Positions in state departments of education offer one of the best areas for specialization in administrative service to schools. The areas of specialization possible may be represented in the kinds of divisions found in state departments of education. Such areas most commonly found are vocational education, vocational rehabilitation, instruction, school lunch, administration, secondary education, elementary education, special education, certification, finance, transportation, health education, school buildings and grounds.

GUIDES FOR SCREENING APPLICANTS TO ADMINISTRATIVE PREPARATORY PROGRAMS*

Five years of experience with Foundations in Educational Administration lead to certain cautious and highly tentative inferences concerning the selection of persons for educational leadership:

　　1.　There is no one measure of any kind that will adequately provide the information needed for selection. Until, if ever, such an omnibus device is developed, we must utilize several of the best known techniques, and use our best judgment in weighting the various factors.　◆

---

*Kenneth E. McIntyre, *Recruiting and Selecting Leaders for Education,* Austin, Texas: by permission Southwest School Administration Center, 1956, 36-38.

2. The typical letter of recommendation is practically worthless. Certainly the selection of educational leaders is important enough to justify spending more than three cents to find out what people *really* think.

3. The usual brief interview seems to be almost as useless in the selection process as are letters of recommendation. We are assured that interviews can be conducted in such a way as to yield valid results, by such means as multiple ratings, well planned and closely controlled situations, and conscientious training on the part of the interviewers. Our experiences have taught us that we are often in disagreement with each other or with our criteria even after three days of careful observation, but that our ratings tend to converge and to approach our criteria after several weeks of observation. We are convinced that after ten weeks of close association with prospective administrators, in a leadership-stimulating environment, our ratings are quite valid.

4. Although there is not enough evidence to justify their use in screening out those individuals with scores deviating a certain distance from some point, there is justification for considering such measures as the *Guilford-Martin Inventories* and the *Minnesota Teacher Attitude Inventory*. The results of such consideration could be expressed in a staff rating factor in the selection program.

5. Assuming that intellectual power, even as imperfectly measured by existing tests, is a factor not to be deplored in school administrators, we would suggest the use of the combined results of two or three reputable tests in a screening process. This we would suggest on general principles, even if our studies did not show a rather significant relationship between our three-test index of intellectual ability and our own judgments of professional promise after ten or twelve weeks of contact. Since some of our promising people have scored fairly low on the tests that were employed, we would set the cut-off point fairly low.

6. On an experimental basis, we would suggest a multiple-factor selection process, tailored to individual institutional conditions. In order to provide an "out" for the promising student who happens to fail unaccountably on one factor, it might be well to permit one such deficiency. One might suggest, for example, that candidates be rejected who fail to measure up on *more than one* of the following:

   (a) Score above 55 on the combined percentile scores on the

Miller Analogies, the *Cooperative English C2,* and the *Watson-Glaser Critical Thinking Appraisal.*

(b) Place above the 25th percentile of the group on a device such as the Peer Acceptance Inventory (provided the group is similar in size, composition, and procedure to the F.E.A. groups discussed in this report).

(c) Place above the 25th percentile of the group on staff ratings at the end of the term (conditions being as stated above). These ratings would take into account *all* relevant information concerning the candidate, including scores on tests and inventories that are not included more specifically in other parts of the screening process.

(d) Place above the 25th percentile on a sociometric device designed to get student choices of "best principals" in the group (conditions being as stated above).

If such a procedure seems arbitrary, it could well be. It would be pointless to argue for specifics. A program of this type, however, would have many strengths, and would be a step in the direction of introducing a quality factor into preparation programs. In the case of the F.E.A. groups of 1953 through 1956, 30 of the 80 people in those four groups would have been rejected by the process outlined above. In no case would it have eliminated a person who, in the opinion of the staff members, would make a strong school administrator. Since staff ratings, peer ratings, and test scores are all involved, no one deficiency would be enough to rule a person out of the preparation program.

If the procedure seems ruthless, it could perhaps be defended on the grounds that educational administration is too important a profession to be left to the self-selected. On the other hand, every safeguard should be placed in the selection machinery to eliminate the possibility that a worthy candidate could be rejected through caprice, spite, or favoritism. Every effort should be made to involve the candidate himself in the selection process through a guidance program in which the student either participates in, or fully understands, decisions that affect him.

In the complex matter of selecting leaders for education, there is doubtless an element of luck, but there is no place for the fourleaf clover or the rabbit's foot. There is a need for faith and spiritual guidance, but no place for superstition, mummery, or prayer wheels. There is probably such a thing as better-than-chance ability to pick a winner, but there is no place for the "quack with a knack" — the charlatan with a gimmick or a "system," whose mental divining rod can supposedly reveal the presence of administrative ability from across a desk in a half-hour interview. The selection of outstanding leaders is a tough, exacting science, but its problems can be made to yield to, or at least retreat from, scientific methods.

PROFESSIONALIZATION OF EDUCATIONAL ADMINISTRATION*

It is extremely doubtful whether any organized educational program designed exclusively for the preparation of school administrators was offered in any recognized college or university in the United States prior to 1900. Few colleges offered courses at the graduate level that could by any stretch of the imagination be termed appropriate formal educational experiences for school superintendents or their administrative aides. Columbia University, in its catalog for 1899-1901, listed only four courses in educational administration: School administration, seminar — administration of public education in the United States, national educational systems, and practicum — the professional training of teachers. The program purported to prepare school administrators was an extension of teacher education identified in the catalog as "A graduate course leading to the Higher Diploma for research and investigation in any field of education, and for the highest professional training of teachers in colleges and normal schools, and of superintendents, principals and supervisors of public schools."

When we consider that Columbia University was one of the recognized pioneers in the subsequent development of professional education for school administrators, it is readily apparent that educational administration in the United States is relatively new.

The question may arise then regarding the way in which school administrators were prepared for their work prior to the development of formal education programs suitable for professional preparation. An honest reply would be that most school administrators — school superintendents, principals, and their administrative aides — had no formal training for the specialized services they were called upon to perform. They were mustered primarily from the ranks of successful teachers, but often experience, and, at times, formal education were not considered important enough prerequisites to disqualify those seeking administrative posts.

Once appointed, the school administrator performed the duties required of him by law and the school board that employed him; the more

---

*Fred F. Beach, "Professionalization of Educational Administration," *School Life*, XLII, No. 2, October, 1959, 5-8.

enterprising practitioners worked to improve the schools. Successful experience was the most significant indicator of competence in educational administration; thus the astute practitioner worked his way up acquiring administrative know-how in the smaller districts and trading on this experience to get better paying positions in larger districts. If any damage resulted from this practice, it was borne largely by the smaller districts.

The professionalization of an occupation or related occupations is in many respects a social and a political process. Professional status must be earned over a long period of time at both the individual and the organizational levels. In the development of any profession, individuals achieve status first. The respect dearly won by dedicated practitioners provides the foundation for professionalization at the organizational level. A full-fledged profession is one that has reached the advanced stages of organization under which a pattern of self-government is adopted and enforced.

STEPS ALREADY TAKEN

Any occupation that requires a long period of specialized study or training ultimately gains some recognition as a profession. This is particularly true when the practitioners must complete specified periods of preparation and earn advanced degrees to satisfy the educational requirements set by a recognized institution of higher education for an occupation or related occupations. There are at present at least a hundred institutions of higher education offering programs leading to advanced professional degrees or professional diplomas in educational administration. Obviously, there is a firm educational foundation for the profession of educational administration.

In the development of any profession, strong associations are formed to promote the general welfare of individual members. These associations usually originate as friendly gatherings of persons engaged in a particular occupation or related occupations and eventually evolve into organizations that regulate membership by establishing and enforcing standards that must be met by members. The American Association of School Administrators (AASA) is the overall national association for school administrators. There are a number of other associations of educational administrators functioning at national and State levels, and most of them have working relationships with the AASA. The foundations of association have therefore been firmly laid for the profession of educational administration.

To complete the professionalization of an occupation or related occupations, however, the practitioners must collectively provide for and conform to a recognizable pattern of self-government. There must be a regulatory force within the profession — a moral force capable of disciplining members who violate the trust placed in them by the public they serve, a moral force that insures quality service, and a moral force that protects those who have need of the services provided by practitioners of the profession.

The Cooperative Program in Educational Administration initiated in 1950 and supported by the W. K. Kellogg Foundation has been particularly instrumental in awakening school administrators to the problems confronting them in the professionalization of educational administration.

Significant developments in recent years give heartening evidence that educational administration is rapidly becoming a full-fledged profession. The AASA has embarked upon an action program dedicated to the professionalization of educational administration. It has created a special Committee for the Advancement of School Administration with a full-time executive secretary. A milestone in its program was passed at the 1959 Atlantic City Convention of the AASA, at which the membership voted to amend the association's constitution as follows:

> Beginning on January 1, 1964, all new members of the American Association for School Administrators shall submit evidence of successful completion of 2 years of graduate study in university programs designed to prepare school administrators and approved by an accreditation body endorsed by the Executive Committee of AASA.

New organizations principally concerned with the professionalization of educational administration have been formed to improve the educational preparation of school administration. The National Conference of Professors of Educational Administration has been established to bring together the teachers of the profession. The University Council for Educational Administration has been established to bring together the universities offering a doctor's degree program in educational administration. The National Council for Accreditation of Teacher Education has formed a unit particularly concerned with the formal approval of programs for the professional preparation of school administrators.

Tangible evidence of the development of the profession is further provided by the emphasis now being placed on graduate degrees as a requirement to qualify for certificates for school superintendents and other administrative posts in the several States.

School administrators are much concerned about the new profession that they are forming. The formation of a professional government has presented obstacles, but none have thus far been insurmountable and the progress in the last decade has been very gratifying.

STEPS YET TO BE TAKEN

While the profession of educational administration has advanced well into the organizational stage, for a number of reasons it has not yet achieved recognition as a full-fledged profession. Foremost, undoubtedly, is the uncertainty on what occupations should be included in the profession of educational administration. Many past efforts to improve school administration have centered on the school superintendency. The first official proposal to the W. K. Kellogg Foundation submitted by the AASA, for example, called for a project on the superintendency of schools. The Cooperative Project on Educational Administration, which was subsequently approved by the Kellogg Foundation, included school superintendents, principals, supervisors, and other administrators.

Obviously, prior to the establishment of an effective professional organization for educational administration, there must be a reasonably sound basis for identifying the occupation or related occupations that are represented. Who should be classified as school administrators? Should the profession be limited to superintendents of schools. State and local? Should the profession be open to administrative aides of superintendents, for example, deputy or assistant superintendents, directors, and supervisors or consultants; to principals and their administrative aides, for example, assistant principals, guidance officers, supervisors, and consultants; to presidents of colleges and universities and their administrative aides, for example, deans, business managers, directors of admissions, and registrars; to teachers of educational administration in our colleges and universities; to educational specialists in State departments of education and the Office of Education or for that matter in other Federal and State agencies of government?

What are the occupations or related occupations in educational administration? Until this question is decisively answered, no defensible educational program for the profession as a whole can be advanced.

Once the occupations to be included in the profession of educational administration are agreed on by leaders in the field, it will be necessary to determine what shall constitute the basic or fundamental program of education for the profession. Acknowledging that areas of specializing do exist in any profession, particularly when a number of related occupations are represented, it will be necessary to make adequate provision for extending the basic program to meet the most pressing educational needs.

Much of the research conducted to determine the work of the superintendent of schools should be very helpful in program development. The Southern States Region of the Cooperative Program in Educational Administration for example, found the superintendent's "job" covered eight critical task areas: Instruction and curriculum development, pupil personnel, community school leadership, school plant, school transportation, organization and structure, staff personnel, and school finance and business management.

When we realize that the superintendents of schools in large districts must delegate much of their responsibility in these so-called "critical task areas," it may be that the "superintendent's job" as defined by SSRCPEA is representative of the profession of educational administration.

In any event, it is of paramount importance that firm agreement be reached on the educational foundation program for the profession and on the extensions to this basic program that are essential to permit the flexibility required for specialization.

We do know that, in addition to the graduate schools, some 300 institutions of higher education purport to prepare school administrators. Some of these institutions offer programs that are undoubtedly excellent, some offer programs that are undoubtedly very poor, but there is no basic education program for the profession from which any reasonably objective judgment on quality may be made.

Professional integrity should dictate that every institution that claims to prepare school administrators should provide at least the basic educational program for educational administration. Since no educational foundation program for educational administration now exists, each institution is free to chart its own course, which in effect means that any institution desiring to go into the business of preparing school administrators may do so by declaring such intent in its catalog and by offering a few subject-matter courses each year of the kind commonly offered by other institutions purporting to prepare school administrators.

Once a basic foundation program is established, it will be possible to ascertain under objective criteria what institutions have the capacity to prepare school administrators. The recently organized University Council for Educational Administration is much concerned with the problems of establishing standards for institutions that offer graduate programs in educational administration. The Council in setting criteria for institutional membership has provided a rallying point from which the profession can work toward the development of solid enforceable educational standards. The Council could well become the agency recommending the standards for the profession on matters concerning the educational preparation of school administrators.

The University Council for Educational Administration — or any similar agency — will need the support of everyone concerned with the improvement of educational administration before it can be called on to exercise essential leadership for the profession. Somewhere along the line it will be necessary to name the institutions of higher education providing programs for the preparation of school administrators that are acceptable to the profession. This cannot be accomplished until the members of the profession develop the organization that is necessary to take authoritative action. The experience of other professions should give ample guidance. The medical profession was prodded into exercising a more forceful regulation of its graduate schools by the facts turned up in a study sponsored by the Carnegie Foundation for the Advancement of Teachers. The story told by the Flexner report alerted the medical profession to the condition of many institutions purporting to offer programs of medical education. The medical profession, once cognizant of the state of medical education, acted promptly to correct the shortcomings.

Since any full-fledged profession is made up of individuals, it is imperative that decisions be made on their demeanor, particularly in professional matters. Members of a profession should live by a written code of ethics that explicitly regulates their conduct. This code should be rigidly enforced. Minor violations should bring censure, major violations discrediting the profession should result in disbarment.

Currently, membership in many associations for school administrators may be gained by any practitioner on the payment of fixed dues. This by no means elevates the profession in the eyes of the general public. The associations of school administrators must serve as authoritative forces representing the profession. They must present a common front at all levels — national, State, and local. One of the most pressing problems of the profession is that of combating the practice, common in some parts of the country, of selecting school administrators without regard to professional preparation or experience. In fact, some States require no professional qualifications for superintendent of schools and other important posts in educational administration. Where this practice may be followed, the profession is obviously not recognized; in fact, the implication arises that any reasonably intelligent person can do the work required, and the need for university training is seriously questioned.

When associations of school administrators accept these persons as members, they grant approval to the practice. This practice must cease. The "good fellow approach" in associations must give way to the professional approach.

Efforts must be made within the profession to gain some voice in formulating State certification requirements for school administrators. In many respects the degree to which State occupational licensing requirements parallel the nationwide standards set by a profession is a positive indicator of the effectiveness of the professional organization. It reflects the ability of practitioners in a profession to regulate their activities so as to provide the maximum benefits for the common good and general welfare of all members of the society they serve. One thing is certain, where there are no nationwide professional standards, practitioners of the occupations subjected to regulation under the law are at a decided disadvantage in making their common views known.

THE KEY, PROFESSIONAL SELF-REGULATION

Full professional status is reached only when practitioners of the profession are organized so that they can effectively present a common front. Organization and the power to make and enforce professional standards are the two essential elements of professional unity.

Anarchy in professional pursuits provides the atmosphere in which unqualified practitioners may operate without censure. There are many people who now believe that no special preparation or training is necessary to do the work of educational administration. At least part of this belief arises from the fact that school administrators have not yet promulgated standards for the profession that would indicate otherwise. School administrators must convey to the general public the complex nature of their work; they cannot do so effectively as individuals.

The promising developments that are now taking place are encouraging signs of what may be termed the crystallization of the profession. School administrators, as a group, are alert to the problems facing them. They realize now that their house must be put in order before the profession of educational administration may command the respect it should rightly be accorded. If educational administration is to best serve society, it must take its place along with medicine among the top professions. This is the real challenge to those who administer the Nation's schools and colleges. The future looks bright.

Scheduled Salaries for Administrative and Supervisory Personnel, 1964-65*

Position	Median minimum and maximum scheduled salary by enrollment stratum:[a]					
	1— 100,000 or more	2— 50,000- 99,999	3— 25,000- 49,999	Total— 1, 2, and 3	4— 12,000- 24,999	5— 6,000- 11,999
	Median minimum scheduled salary					
Central-office personnel:						
Assistant superintendent	$15,220	$15,000	$13,350	$14,251	$12,663	$11,827
Director	10,716	10,161	9,860	10,164	9,792	9,250
Co-ordinator	9,500	8,750	8,600	8,833	8,280	9,390
Consultant	7,950	9,243	7,697	8,535	8,357	9,042
Supervisor	8,381	9,080	8,011	8,296	7,728	7,154
Personnel assigned to individual buildings:						
Supervising principal						
Elementary	8,725	7,770	7,683	7,800	8,040	7,988
Junior high	9,600	8,976	8,150	8,718	8,836	8,439
Senior high	10,032	9,543	9,175	9,569	9,480	9,305
Assistant principal						
Elementary	7,100	8,074	7,324	7,637	7,400	7,776
Junior high	8,003	7,940	7,552	7,885	7,740	8,000
Senior high	7,842	8,657	8,138	8,138	8,225	8,200
Counselor	7,326	5,389	5,609	5,675	5,973	6,090
Dean	b	7,123	7,505	7,445	7,440	6,464
Head of department	b	5,632	6,000	6,000	6,068	5,800
	Median maximum scheduled salary					
Central-office personnel:						
Superintendent[c]	$27,500	$23,000	$21,925	$23,000	$18,725	$17,500
Associate or deputy						
superintendent	25,675	17,400	20,592	20,950	17,835	15,870
Assistant superintendent	19,188	16,576	17,690	17,465	15,750	15,700
Director	14,956	13,793	13,874	13,880	13,333	12,785
Co-ordinator	12,660	11,309	12,424	11,500	11,660	12,230
Consultant	11,663	11,757	12,340	12,129	10,775	11,485
Supervisor	12,688	11,250	11,558	11,790	10,996	10,144
Personnel assigned to individual buildings:						
Supervising principal						
Elementary	12,500	11,250	11,550	11,638	11,186	11,190
Junior high	13,045	11,940	11,900	12,014	12,153	12,156
Senior high	13,930	12,790	13,280	13,163	13,140	13,018
Assistant principal						
Elementary	10,725	10,289	11,527	10,688	10,880	10,570
Junior high	10,890	10,492	11,092	10,700	10,910	11,169
Senior high	11,621	10,863	11,657	11,200	11,278	11,600
Counselor	10,181	8,800	9,690	9,185	10,036	9,968
Dean	b	8,985	11,660	10,295	10,189	10,125
Head of department	10,576	9,220	10,366	10,425	10,000	10,060

[a]Minimum salaries are based on the master's degree preparation level if indicated: otherwise, they are based on the lowest salary indicated for the position shown or for lowest class of the position if different levels are given for an occupational title. Maximum salaries shown are the highest salary scheduled based on the highest preparation level recognized or the highest salary scheduled for an occupational title, exclusive of long-service increments.

b Not computed; too few cases.

c Based on contract salary for 1964-65.

*NEA Research Bulletin, "Scheduled Salaries for Administrators and Supervisors, 1964-65." XLIII (May, 1965), 41. By permission of National Education Association.

BIBLIOGRAPHY

Beach, Fred F., "Professionalization of Educational Administration," *School Life*, XLII, October, 1959.

Bryant, B., "Academic and Professional Education Requirements for Elementary Administrative Credentials," *Journal of Teacher Education*, XVI, March, 1965.

Cocking, Walter D., *As I See It*, New York: The Macmillan Company, 1955.

Davies, Daniel R., *The Internship in Educational Administration*, Washington, D.C.: The Center for Applied Research in Education, 1962.

Fisher, R., "Personnel Policies Still Neglect to Develop Administrators," *Nation's Schools*, LXXV, March, 1965.

Fisher, William H., "School Administration — A Profession," *Education*, 100-01, LXXXIV, October, 1963.

Foster, R. L., J. D. McNeil and C. J. B. Macmillan, "Climate for Self-improvement," *Educational Leadership*, XXI, May, 1964.

Frasure, Kenneth, "Early Identification of Educational Leaders," *New York State Education*, LI, April, 1964.

Fusco, Gene C., and others "Educational Administration in the Decade Ahead," *School Life*, XLIII, January, 1961.

"How Schoolmen Get Their Jobs," *Nation's Schools*, LXXIV, September, 1964.

McIntyre, Kenneth E., *Recruiting and Selecting Leaders for Education*, Austin, Texas: Southwest School Administration Center, 1956.

Miller, Van, *The Public Administration of American Schools*, New York: The Macmillan Company, 1964.

NEA Research Bulletin, XLII, No. 1, February, 1964.

Pitt, Gavin, "Conducting the Executive Search," *American School and University*, XXXVI, April, 1964, 30-31.

The Professional Preparation of Superintendents of Schools, Washington, D.C.: American Association of School Administrators, 1964.

Rice, Arthur, "Administration was Just as Rough 100 Years Ago," *Nation's Schools*, LXXII, December, 1963.

——————, "The Next 20 Years in School Administration," *Nation's Schools*, LXXI, April, 1963.

Schilson, D. L., "Elementary Principal: Selection and Training," *American School Board Journal*, CL, April, 1965.

Taylor, H. A., "Women in Administration," *American School and University*, XXXVI, December, 1963.

INDEXES

Author Index

Subject Index

849